West
of
the
West

By Robert Kirsch

Do Not Go Gentle, a novella
In the Wrong Rain, a novel
Madeleine Austrian, a novel
The Wars of Pardon, a novel

By William S. Murphy

A Pictorial History of California
Los Angeles: Wonder City of the West
The Dolphin Guide to Los Angeles and Southern California
Burn, Baby, Burn! —The Los Angeles Race Riot, August, 1965
  (with Jerry Cohen)

WITNESSES TO THE
CALIFORNIA EXPERIENCE, 1542-1906

West of the West

*The Story of California from the Conquistadores to the Great
Earthquake, as Described by the Men and Women Who Were There*

BY ROBERT KIRSCH
AND WILLIAM S. MURPHY

NEW YORK ¶ E. P. DUTTON & CO., INC.
1967

FIRST EDITION

23092

Grateful acknowledgment for permission to reprint the following material is given to:

The Huntington Library and Art Gallery, San Marino, California, for permission to reproduce excerpts from rare books and manuscripts.

The Ronald Press Company for material from *Chapters on the History of the Southern Pacific*, by Stuart Daggett. (New York: The Ronald Press Company, 1922).

The University of California Press for material from *Cortés: The Life of a Conqueror by His Secretary*, by Francisco López de Gómora, translated and edited by Lesley Byrd Simpson (Berkeley: University of California Press, 1964). From the *Istoria de la Conquista de Mexico*, printed in Zaragoza in 1552.

Donnan Jeffers for excerpt from "Epilogue," from *Flagons and Apples*, by Robinson Jeffers, published by Grafton Publishing Company, 1912.

Albert & Charles Boni, Inc., for material from *Ambrose Bierce, a Biography*, by Carey McWilliams (New York: Albert & Charles Boni, Inc., 1929).

The Meredith Publishing Company for material from *Frémont, Pathmarker of the West*, by Allan Nevins (New York: D. Appleton-Century Company, 1939). Copyright, 1939, by Allan Nevins.

The Macmillan Company for material from *The King's Peace*, by C. V. Wedgwood (New York: The Macmillan Company, 1955).

Alfred A. Knopf, Inc., for material from *From Wilderness to Empire, A History of California*, by Robert Glass Cleland (New York: Alfred A. Knopf, Inc., 1959).

CONTENTS

ILLUSTRATIONS

Halftones

Drawings   PAGE

Maps

PREFACE

The literature of California is vast, and constantly increasing. One of the many ways the California experience contradicts the expected is precisely in the amount of writing that was done at a time when her men and women were thoroughly engaged in action. It is as though some awareness of history, of the need to observe and record, was present from the earliest European settlement. This is true not only of the historians. (Bancroft was busy in his history factory almost before there seemed to be any history worth recording.) And it is true not only of the poets and novelists, the journalists and essayists (Twain and Harte, Helen Hunt Jackson and Mary Austin, Joaquin Miller and Edwin Markham, Robinson Jeffers and Lawrence Lipton, Ambrose Bierce and Jack London, William Saroyan and John Steinbeck, to name a sampling), of whom, again, such response was the very nature of the talent and calling. Most important from the point of view of this anthology, it is true of those who lived and experienced and often made that history: explorers and soldiers, merchants and lawyers, mountain men and priests, housewives and miners, lawmen and out-laws; virtually every sort of person.

"A writer approaching a controversial and lively subject," the noted English historian C. V. Wedgwood wrote, "on which much has been written, owes it to the reader to make his own position at least as clear as it is to himself." [1] This obligation we accept. We are observers of a period in California; this role we hold in common with many if not most of the writers represented here. We are not writing a history of California. There are a number of fine histories by such scholars as John Caughey, Robert Glass Cleland, Andrew Rolle, and others. This is not a collection of the best writing about California. Such antholo-gies are available, and indeed somewhat repetitious in their selections.

The criteria are these. First, to select a representative group of wit-nesses to each recorded period of the California experience from the earliest discovery to the beginning of the twentieth century. Second, to allow, insofar as it is possible, the words of these men and women to carry the burden of the narrative. Third, to include such writing as is not easily available to those interested in the subject. The emphasis, therefore, is on witness, direct, proximate, and frequently unadorned.

Our function, apart from searching out and assessing this vast store of writing, is to provide a larger historical framework, a linkage of explanation and introduction, a setting, in time, place, and circum-stance. We have tried to avoid the two perils of writing about Califor-nia: the exaggeration of boosterism, the equal distortion of deprecation. But, as it shall become clear to most readers, this does not mean we are without a point of view. We believe California is of importance to America and to the world. We think it an exciting place in which to live, and a beautiful one despite some of its disadvantages, natural and man-made. Beyond this, we believe that in the uniquenesss of the California experience lie lessons and illumination for man in general.

Again we turn to Miss Wedgwood. The historian is a product of his time and background. "No historian has ever been," she says, "or ever will be, omniscient in his knowledge, or infallible in his deductions. None can see the whole or undivided truth.

"The contemporary could not do so either. Puzzled by the variety of events which came so confusingly upon him from day to day, and ig-

[1] *The King's Peace* (New York: The Macmillan Company, 1955).

norant of much that time alone would bring to light, he steered his way through his own world—as we do now—by the imperfect judgement of an ill-informed mind. But the contemporary knew one thing that the historian can only imagine: he knew what it felt like to be alive at that time, to experience those religious doubts, political fears, and economic pressures as a part of his life. He may not have known or suspected influences which have later been revealed; but he knew what he experienced in his mind or suffered in his flesh, and he knew what beliefs and what interests he admitted to be the motives of his action. 'Here we are subject to error and misjudging one another,' said Strafford on the scaffold. The day-to-day events of history arise at least in part from error and misjudgement. On this level falsehood itself is a part of truth."

By adopting this point of view, we do not seek to diminish the role or the importance of the historian, any more than does Miss Wedgwood. "It is legitimate," she goes on, "for the historian to pierce the surface and bring to light motives and influences not known at the time; but it is equally legitimate to accept the motives and explanations which satisfied contemporaries. The two methods produce different results, but each result may be a fair answer to a particular question that has been asked. They become misleading only if either is accepted as the whole truth."

This volume, then, is not the whole truth. Not because we are opposed to the whole truth, but because we believe that there is something to be gained from the restoration of the immediate experience. Thus, the words of the witnesses are reproduced as close to their original writing as it is possible to get without sacrificing clarity for the modern reader. In notes and introductory passages (indeed, perhaps in the very process of selection), we have taken certain positions. These are made amply clear in the appropriate places. But insofar as we are able, we seek to present to the reader this raw material of history to be read as a direct transaction between him and the contemporary who lived through and recorded these events.

The absence of fiction (conscious fiction would be more exact a term) does not imply a lack of belief in the value of the creative or imaginative forms. Indeed, these often come closer to the spirit of the experience than the journal or the diary or the letter. Much of the fiction is readily accessible, and has been anthologized many times.

Given the choice between Helen Hunt Jackson's transmutation of the Indian experience in *Ramona* and her report on the Indians, we have chosen selections from the latter in terms of the criteria cited above.

This anthology ends at a point in time that may appear to cut off much recent history. Indeed, it does. The direction of this period is indicated in the Epilogue. But the decision was motivated by certain considerations, of which the prime one is space. To cover adequately the crowded and complex years of the twentieth century in California would require a volume at least the size of this one. Perhaps such a book will be forthcoming from us or from others. There are problems of perspective and problems of documents. Some of the latter are available. Most are not. Preparing an anthology of twentieth-century witness to the California experience must await the passage of time. The private papers of public figures, not to mention the writings of the relatively obscure or specialized individuals, await future editors.

Yet there is something different about the twentieth century in California that should be mentioned. It is perhaps not merely the perspective of time that leads us to believe that the four centuries or so with which this book deals were simpler in historic terms, although not necessarily in contemporary terms. The terminus of this anthology is the point at which the greatest of all migrations into California began. This tide of people, while it is California's greatest resource, is also in itself the source of complication. In the areas of industry, science, politics, religion, in every sort of human endeavor and experience that constitutes culture in its broadest sense, change is palpable. And of this myriad of personal and social experience, only the surface has been touched. There is a literature of Hollywood, a literature of post-earthquake San Francisco, a literature of politics and social protest. But there are areas that have barely been touched. Of the experience of minority groups, written by those who have lived through crucial years, there is indeed very little. For contemporary witnesses of the adventure of science in California, the development of the aircraft industry, the problems of water or of sectarian development, there must or should be sources as yet unexplored.

"The West is a country in the mind, and so eternal," the poet Archibald MacLeish wrote. And, of this country in the mind, California is an important region. It is so as much for what it represents in the dreams of men as for what it represents in reality. In the pages that follow we shall trace the beginnings and the development of that region of the mind, that region of men and women, that region of the past. There is evidence, and this book may be taken as a small part of that evidence, that a freshening, a resurgence of interest in the California experience is taking place. When men in the press and flurry of daily affairs pause to question the past of the land, the identity and motives and works of those who came before, there is hope for the present. There have been periods in which this interest has been mocked or diminished. There have been times when it has been romanticized in a kind of golden glow, times when the past seemed insupportable in its cruelty and its errors (Gertrude Atherton in her *California: An Intimate History* could write of the "paradox" of that history: ". . . How many good men we have produced in California and what bad history they have succeeded in making."). Good history or bad, we owe a debt to the men and women, the institutions and societies, the universities and libraries, who have attempted to cultivate, store, and assess the records of this past. Whether we recognize it or not, we are products of this past; we have dreamed these dreams. The land and its people are constant reminders that both the present and the future are rooted in that past. Our curiosity and concern are not the result of simple nostalgia or sterile antiquarianism. A vigorous, confident, and aggressive technology is changing the face of California. But are we not given pause by the way that the land answers us? Our bulldozers level hills, but the land replies with flash floods, mud slides, and fires. We pour into a golden land, a young and open land; our factories and our automobiles poison the air and kill the vegetation. We live in seeming security and prosperity, but the land, still in the process of growth and change, reminds us of its terrible power in earthquake and volcanic activity.

Below us beyond the border is Baja California, geologically and geographically a living museum of what this land was a century or two ago. Around us are the artifacts and the records of those who preceded us, borne by their own visions of a golden shore. To learn of them, to learn of the land, to witness the drama of their lives, to share their dreams, are the varied purposes of this volume.

All who read and work in libraries can appreciate the extent of our obligation to those librarians and scholars who helped. This book would not have been possible without the rich and varied collection of the Henry E. Huntington Library and Art Gallery at San Marino, California. The authors wish to express their deep appreciation to the Library for granting permission to publish materials from its archives. Individual members of the staff of the library who have generously given valuable assistance and encouragement include: Dr. John E. Pomfret, director; Robert O. Dougan, Librarian; Anne Hyder, Mary Isabel Fry, Carey S. Bliss, Edwin H. Carpenter, Leonard Gregory, Janet Hawkins, Erwin Morkisch, Phyllis Rigney, Graydon Spalding, Lyle H. Wright, and Dorothy Bowen.

There were many others: Dorothy Martin, Librarian, and Betty Begun, Assistant Librarian of the Los Angeles County Museum Library; Mary Helen Peterson, director, and Irwin Stein of the Los Angeles Public Library History Department; Richard West, collector of rare books on California; Romeo Carrero, Librarian of the Los Angeles *Times*. We seek some words to express our appreciation. The simplest and most accurate are thanks.

West of the West

For our country here at the west of things
Is pregnant of dreams; and west of the west
I have lived; where the last low land outflings
Its yellow-white sand to the edge of the bay;
And the west wind over us every day
Blows, and throws with the landward spray
Dreams on our minds, and a dreamy unrest.

—ROBINSON JEFFERS, *Flagons and Apples,* "Epilogue"

INTRODUCTION:
THE INDIANS
AND THE LAND

For European man, California began in the imagination. His eyes, when the dreams began, had not yet seen its long, bold coastland, its Valley of Death, its great mountain ranges, its pastoral valleys. The land was to be given its very name out of a romance, *Las Sergas de Esplandin,* one of those epics of fictional knights on unreal quests. In 1510, a decade before Cortés conquered Mexico, decades before Cabrillo, there was described in this widely read Spanish work of fiction by García Rodríguez Ordóñez de Montalvo, an island, said to be the home of the powerful Queen Calafia:

¶ Know ye that on the right hand of the Indies there is an island called California, very near the terrestrial paradise and inhabited by black women without a single man among them and living in the manner of Amazons. They are robust of body, strong and passionate in heart, and of great valor. Their island is one of the most rugged in the world, with bold

rocks and crags. Their arms are all of gold, as is the harness of the wild
beasts, which, after taming, they ride.

. . . Over this island of California rules a queen, Calafia, statuesque in
proportions, more beautiful than all the rest, in the flower of her woman-
hood, eager to perform great deeds, valiant and spirited, and ambitious to
excel all those who have ruled before her.

That it was no island, that the Indies were across a vast and perilous
sea, that griffins did not fly over it, that gold was still held in the beds
of mountain creeks and in the grip of quartz, made little difference.
The dreams of wealth, of adventure, of courageous deeds, of beautiful
women were fashioned by the aggressive and the ambitious long miles
away. Ultimately, the land was to be called California.

Yet, was that the beginning? There were many beginnings. The
long weary journeys of Alarcón and Melchior Díaz which may have
brought them to what is now California, the voyage of Juan Rodríguez Cabrillo, beating northward against the prevailing winds, certainly brought his party to what is now the bay of San Diego.

In another sense, California began hundreds of thousands of years
before in a succession of thrustings of rock from the bottom of a sea,
the emergence of a long new terrain between the fortress of the Sierra
Nevada and the new line of surf on the Pacific, a young region of the
earth in contrast with the older, more stable land masses.

Does the chronicle start with the first primitive men who struggled
to survive? Or the first men of those tribes wandering into these hills
and valleys from the north, trekking slowly or sailing in skin boats
down from Alaska? Or was it uncovered, as some think, by Chinese
explorers who made landfalls along its coast at the time Hannibal was
ravaging the peninsula of Italy?

Always the beginnings are "pregnant with dreams." Long before
the arrival of the Spaniards in the sixteenth century, the land was
populated by Indians, tribes as varied in their language and cultures as
the land itself. Tribes related by blood and speech to five of the six
great linguistic superfamilies of the North American Indians, yet in
many ways different. Later, this myriad cluster of peoples would be
lumped together in the pejorative term "Digger Indians." We know
now that there was never such a tribe as the Diggers. It was, like

another deprecating noun with which it rhymes, a creation of the minds of those who came later.

One characteristic of the California experience, which we shall see repeated over the centuries, is the tendency of successive waves of settlement to blot out culturally, intellectually, and sometimes physically the heritage of those supplanted. But it is equally true that beneath the surface obliteration, the supplanted culture retains an identity often sought out by men and women whose own people have participated in the destruction. Thus, it is only in fairly recent times, and owing to the work of such scholars as A. L. Kroeber and his wife, Theodora, C., Hart Merriam, T. T. Waterman, John Caughey, that we are able to learn of the people who lived once on this land. To hear their voices, to know of their ways, we must rely on those who at a crucial moment in time worked to retain some record of their existence. Later, we shall come more explicitly to the fate of the California Indians, the bloody violence, the unremitting pressures of "civilization," which was their fate from the time of the earliest European settlement. There is no way to mitigate or understate the crime against the California Indians. Hubert Howe Bancroft, that exceptional bookseller turned historian, who shared some but not all of the prejudices against the Indians, wrote:

¶ That part of the early intercourse between aboriginal Americans and Europeans which properly belongs to history may be briefly given. For short work was made of it in California. The savages were in the way; the miners and settlers were arrogant and impatient; there were no missionaries or others present with even a poor pretense of soul-saving or civilizing. It was one of the last human hunts of civilization, and the basest and most brutal of all.

The story of the human hunt that belongs to the nineteenth century in California will be told in due course. Here we must reconstruct the Indian experience before Spanish, Mexican, and American settlement. And that story can be told only indirectly. For the Indians left no written records. Theirs was an oral tradition, and apparently a rich one, of which we have retained only a small part. What we now know of them is obscured by time, filtered through the conditions of a variety of observers, of research at a much later period, or a critical reconstruction of the statements of the priests and ranchers, the teachers and soldiers, the miners and government officials who met the Indians when many of them had already been corrupted and corroded by contact with the so-called civilized people who used and ultimately destroyed them.

Though the Spanish, the Mexican, and the American periods carried in them the seeds of Indian extinction, there was the curious paradox that in each of the eras there were those who, through compassion, understanding, curiosity, and simple human decency, reached out to understand these people who had known the land and lived on it for centuries. From them, from priests like Father Boscana, from pioneer ranchers and Indian agents such as Benjamin Wilson, from diarists such as Judge Benjamin Hayes, from journalists such as Charles Lummis, bits and pieces of the Indian experience were gathered.

As history goes, the doom of the California Indians was an accelerated process. One writer has observed: "It was quite possible for an aged Indian to have encompassed the whole story, from the coming of the Spanish colonizers to the destruction of the Fifties, in a single lifetime." Yet, the collapse of this world did not occur at once. And to understand the story, one must understand the way of life of the California Indians. For in penetrating the world of the Indians, we begin to discern something of the collision between the dream and reality that foreshadows the California of today. That we must deal with it in fragments is due to the way in which that world disappeared. If whole tribelets are now wiped out, there were a few survivors left to tell of that life. To them we are indebted: to Ishi of the Yahi, who stumbled out of the wilderness, starved and near death, the last man of his tribe, who was to live out a few years in the twentieth century, surrounded by friends from among the enemy who had destroyed his people; to Usee George of the Modoc, son of a shaman, who lived long enough to bear witness to the ways of his nation; to Robert Spott of the Yurok, to blind Sam Osborn of the Wuksache Yokuts, and to scores of others of the Mohave, the Wintu, the Yana and the Maidu, the Yokuts and the Mohave, the Pomo, the Costonoan, the Salinan, the Chumash and the Yuma, the Shoshone and the Miwok.

Out of their memories, out of the earliest reports of the explorers and the settlers, out of the work of scholars, we can now reconstruct the Indian experience prior to the first European settlement. For thousands of years they lived on this land. For them it was both literally and figuratively a land of dreams. On the level of reality, of the tangible, by the criteria of societies that value the imposing accomplishments—great buildings, the amassing of measurable wealth, levels of technology, might in war—they were a backward people. They lived in huts and caves; they wore little more than aprons round their middles; they wove baskets. Through the great and varied land, there were hundreds of tribelets and nations. These communities, bound by language and customs, remained largely within their own boundaries.

The first Europeans saw only a few of the tribes, along the coast. But in the hills, in the great central valley, along the lower reaches of the great mountains, there were others. The early reports were accurate, as far as they went. They described a people who appeared friendly, healthy, happy, who lived simply. "The women are very beautiful and virtuous, the children are fair and blonde and merry," we are told by an observer with Vizcaíno, describing the Indians on Santa Catalina Island. At Monterey, he speaks of their affability and generosity, their excess of affection. A member of Drake's crew is impressed by the frankness and the physical strength of the Indians.

These first observers saw what their eyes told them. Earth-covered houses or brush-thatched huts, hunters pursuing game, or fishermen taking fish from the sea, and simple rituals of some mysterious kind, sweathouses where the Indians sat and spoke in languages incomprehensible to the explorers, small villages that offered little sign of the measure of prosperity in the land. What they could not see and in the end what they destroyed was the dream. For these were the people of the dream.

Out of dreams came their religion, their literature, their values, their rootedness to the earth. Only now do we begin to realize the richness of their cultures, the variety of them. In such works as *Primitive Pragmatists: The Modoc Indians of Northern California* by Verne F. Ray, or Theodora Kroeber's magnificent collection of California Indian tales, *The Inland Whale,* or Jeremiah Curtin's *Creation Myths*

of Primitive America, we are given access to this world of the imagination. Is there something about the land of California that makes it
even today so fertile a ground for these dreams?

Perhaps. One thing is certain. The vastness of the land, the relative
ease with which the physical needs of man were met, the overpowering terrain with its natural beauty, gave the California Indians an
existence stabilized in material ways. But it did nothing to limit these
dreams.

For thousands of years before the arrival of the Europeans, that life
went on with little outward change. The great disaster and destruction myths of other primitive peoples are scarcely present in the literature of the California Indians. Creation myths in each of the tribelets
and nations are framed within the borders of the particular region in
which the group dwelt. "After the waters which covered the world
went down . . . ," he was in the center of his world: the place its
nation had always known. For some it was the desert, for others the
coast, or the hills overlooking the sea. For still others it was the river
or lake or mountain on which the tribe had lived forever.

For they lived in virtually every part of what is now California, and
each subculture was conditioned by the region in which it lived.
There were not many: the best population estimate is between 150,000
and a quarter of a million, in twenty-one known or identifiable
nations, further divided by distinctions in language, setting, and mode
of life into perhaps two hundred and fifty subtribes. We may never
know all of them, the attrition of some was so complete.

It is easy to fall into the trap of romanticizing the Indian experience. Nostalgia is a by-product of irksome reality and old dreams, and
California is rich in it. Every one of its periods has been painted in the
golden glow. But of the realities of the Indian experience, there is
objective evidence. In this land, the nations lived for centuries with a
minimum of the senseless and periodic destruction of war.

For one thing the land was large enough to make retreat possible
before extinction (that is, before the white man came). The Wintun
could invade and force the Yana higher up into the hills, but in the
end both survived side by side to face the catastrophe of the "human
hunt."

If we must go into the material culture, which was, after all, the criterion imposed by those who came later, the Indians do not come off badly either. The early generalizations about them were made by individuals who had known of the great wealth and the great temple cities of the Aztecs. The California Indians could not approach this level. Their tangible and overt life was that of the Stone Age. The term itself evokes ideas of crudity and barbarism. But the facts do not support these notions. The wheel was unknown to them; they had no written language. On the other hand, in various ways, depending on the region in which they lived, they came to terms with the land. Indeed, the challenge of the land as a provider was the challenge they met. What was the point, for them, in going beyond this, at least in a technological sense? That they went beyond it in the realm of the imagination becomes increasingly evident. Food and shelter, clothing and artifacts depended on where they lived and what was available to them. Water, of course, was the first consideration, then, as now, in California. It was the very source of existence. Where there were rivers, lakes, and springs they built their villages. But where the land was arid, they dug deep wells. The desert tribes not only found the subsurface water; they dug deeply to make those waters accessible.

The California Indians were a rooted people. Movement and travel was within the range of their well-defined tribal lands. And again, the movement was purposeful. Where food and water remained available, the tribe stayed. Where seasonal migration was necessary to hunt game or to fish or to gather the seeds and plants for food or for ceremony, they moved. Life was richer, generally, in the north.

Because the first penetrations of the European explorers in the sixteenth and seventeenth centuries were in the coastal and desert regions, and because they did not remain long enough to distinguish the variety of the different tribes, certain generalizations about the material culture of the Indians have persisted even to the present. These have always to do with the obvious: what the Indians wore, the kind of dwellings they lived in, what they appeared to eat at some given time and place. We know now that these generalizations are misleading. It is regarded as a truism that the acorn, leached out and pounded into a mush or made into a jelly, was the staple item in the diet of California Indians. In some cases it was. And certainly, the use of the acorn made edible through a fairly complicated procedure was fairly common. Yet, even this turns out to be an exaggeration. The California Indians, says A. L. Kroeber, "are perhaps the most omnivorous group of tribes on the continent." The variety of their diet, not only in the individual tribes and tribelets but across the entire land, was remarkable. And this variety is interesting from two points of view. First, in the readiness with which the Indians could shift from one supply to another, from acorns to other seeds or even snails, grasshoppers, maggots, turtles, shellfish. The Indian woman's digging stick that was regarded with such contempt was in fact a tool that could secure a whole menu of foods. This was true of other artifacts as well: "Again, it is only a step to the taking of minnows," Kroeber writes, "in brooks, of gophers, of lizards or small birds: the simplest of snares, a long stick, a thrown stone even, suffice with patience, and a boy can help out his grandmother. The fish pot is not very different from the acorn receptacle, and weirs, traps, stiff nets, and other devices for capturing fish are made in the same techniques of basketry as the beaters, carriers and winnowers for seeds. Even hunting was but occasionally the open, outright affair we are likely to think. Ducks were snared and netted, rabbits driven into nets, even deer caught in nooses and with similar devices."

Here we see the other point. Survival required ingenuity, an ingenuity that was not obvious to those blinded by their own biases.

You will note that earlier we had described "the relative ease" with which food was obtained. California was not then and is not now, despite all the persistent myth, a land of the lotus-eaters. Now, another important point emerges, a point about California, no less important in the present than in the past. It is a land that lends itself to illusion, to the projection of dreams and visions. The two Californias again: the California of the obvious and the California of the subtle. The obvious we know. It is the California of large and hypnotic statistics, the California of the great mission ranchos, self-sufficient and fertile, the California of the Gold Rush. But beneath it there is something else. The Indians knew this as few of the later Californians were to know it. We shall see this over and over again. But let us take this simple matter of food, the bounty of the land. It was not obvious to the first explorers. They saw a vast and arid, nearly empty land. Their dreams of wealth were not borne out; they saw no artifacts of gold. A few pieces of turquoise mined by the Indians, some clever basketry, even planked boats built by some of the tribes (the only ones of their kind on the Northern continent). It is intriguing to conjecture why, after the initial penetration of the Spanish and English explorers, no settlement was made for nearly one hundred and fifty years. For the Indians, of course, this was a reprieve, though they could not have realized it. For all the political and economic reasons given, the first explorers saw that California was only a vast, empty land. It would hold; it would wait until they could digest the great empire of the South. Indeed, the press to settle and defend California did not come except as an answer to the threat of Russian exploration and colonization in the north much later.

The bounty, then, of the land as the Indians knew it from their intimate and mystical attention to what the land said to them was this: The land is generous and hospitable to those who love it and are willing to respect it. And it was rather a different sort of bounty than Indians elsewhere had known. There was no single source of food in overwhelming abundance. No herds of buffalo, no great runs of salmon in the river, no single crop such as corn. The bounty was variety. And the tribes utilized that variety. Even the acorn, that favorite and facile staple, was in truth a limited source. The oak did not grow everywhere, and its supply was seasonal and occasionally sparse. If the acorn failed, there were a score of other supplies that could be taken, by tools that were easily modified, by a people willing to live in harmony with what the land offered. Behind the façade of timelessness was an adaptability. In return for this, the hospitality of the land, the California Indians were spared the catastrophic periodic famines that are part of the lore of most other Indian groups. Their oral literature reflects little of this, as it reflects little of the migratory lore.

Virtually every aspect, then, of Indian life blended with and reflected the environment. We may take for a moment a journey through this landscape, for it is crucial to any understanding of the California experience. Lawrence Clark Powell, that eloquent observer of California landscape and literature, suggests that one cannot understand the lure of California without understanding the face of the land, the sea, and the sky. Most obvious are the extremes: the highest mountain within the United States, Mount Whitney, affords from its summit a view of Death Valley, 282 feet below sea level, the lowest point in America. Vegetation varies from the cactus of the south to the giant Redwoods of the north; deserts are within comparative proximity to the sea. Along the great central valley are flat and fertile lands, in contrast to the alkali soils of the desert and the rock-strewn slopes of the great mountains. Water is generously available in the north with its lakes and streams, hidden and uncertain in the south. Yet within this spectrum of contrasts and extremes another curious element emerges. One historian has said quite accurately that America, for the Europeans, was part invention and part discovery. This was true for California as well. The imagination had invented a California; voyage, exploration, and settlement discovered another California. For the European and the transplanted European we call American, the invention had to give some ground to the discovery. Though he saw a land that was in certain ways more fantastic than his imagination could produce, there were parts of that land that reminded him of the places from which he had come. In the landscape of California, virtually every other place in the world was reproduced. It is no accident that the film makers, the manufacturers of illusion, could use locations suggesting Spain or the Holy Land, Devon or Cornwall, France or Australia.

The difference between the primitive Indian and the European was in the simple reversal of these elements. For the Indian, discovery came first and then invention. He started from the reality of the land and then penetrated its mysteries with visions and illusions. It might seem a minor point, but tied to it is the vast difference between the California of the Indian experience and the California of today's experience. For better or for worse, the Indian accepted what he was given, tied his fate and life and hope to the land as it was. Those who came afterward, increasingly, shaped the land to *their* dream, changed its face, filled it with cities and roads, factories and housing tracts, recarved its contours, polluted its clean air, changed the flow of its water.

This is not to argue against progress but to point up the contrasts between values. The one people was wedded to the land; the other, not without arrogance and confidence, attempted to make the land do its bidding. And the land resisted in its secret ways: with earthquake and flood and forest fire and smog.

Who were the people of the land and how did they live before the first Europeans came?

Like the land itself, as we have suggested, they were varied. Varied in their physical appearance, their community organization, their religion, their language, their material way of life. For every generalization, there are exceptions. Only in central California was the native culture unique, and central California was surrounded by the natural fortresses of two great mountain ranges. The Indians of the north were influenced by the mode of life of tribes living in the Pacific Northwest; the Indians of the south had a culture similar to the Indians of Arizona and New Mexico. Yet, each of the groups was distinguishable from its neighbors, in terms of culture, mode of life, and values.

The California Indians were pale brown in complexion. They ranged in stature from the six-foot-tall Mohave of the Colorado River region of the southeast to the shortest, something over five feet tall, the Yuki of Mendocino on the northern coast. The shape of the head and face was varied as well: narrow-headed, broad-nosed Wailaki of Tehama and Trinity counties; the high-faced, broad-headed, narrow-nosed Hupa of Humboldt and Del Norte counties; the western Mono, high-faced, relatively narrow-headed, medium-nosed, in almost contrast to the eastern Mono, both residing on the Nevada border. E. W. Gifford, writing on the physical types of the California Indians, made an ironic point when he said in 1926: "In the living Indian population of today (totaling about 16,000 souls) five types and subtypes are distinguishable. . . . As the Indians in the more thickly settled parts of California became extinct before anthropologists had opportunity to gather data from them, *it is necessary to rely upon skeletal material to determine the physical type of the aborigines in these parts.*" (Italics added.)

Depending on the climate and topography, the Indians clothed and shod themselves. Where the weather was mild, generally in the south, the men wore breechclouts, the women a narrow apron or skirt;

sandals rather than moccasins were worn. As a protection against rain and wind, both sexes wore a skin of deer or sea otter as a cape or toga.

The dwelling places reflected this variety. The Yurok and the Hupa constructed frame houses, sometimes using hewn planks. Southward, where the weather grew milder, bark or brush cover was utilized. In the Valley of the Sacramento, the homes were partially dug out of the earth. The Chumash preferred the plank house; the Modoc, Achomawi, Yuki, and Miwok built earth houses.

If there was one structure common to most of the California peoples it was the sweathouse. Yet the Mohave and the Yuma, whose relationship to the southwestern tribes has been noted, did not use the sweathouse as the Pueblo Indians used their Kiva or Estufa. Gathering in the sweathouse was a daily affair, not the ritual purification or medication it was in other cultures. Women were forbidden. Men sat in the warmth of the fire and in the redolence of the herbs. The experience was that of a clubhouse.

Life was a relatively simple affair. Some of the northern tribes and some of the extreme southern tribes made wealth a matter of importance; for most it was a matter of indifference. Hunting and fishing, seed and plant gathering provided food; the methods were varied, ranging from the harpooning of the Modoc to the nets and weirs elsewhere. The tribes of the Colorado region did not use the harpoon in those murky, muddy waters. Fish poison made of buckeyes and soaproot were used in small streams and pools by the Pomo, the Yokut, and Luiseno.

Beyond the gathering of food and supplies, the material culture was sparse. Basket weaving was fairly well developed; some of the southern tribes were skilled potters, particularly in the farming areas. Rattles and flutes were made for ritual purposes. Shell money was a medium of exchange. A species of native tobacco was smoked. Certain plants were used in connection with religious rituals and shamanism.

It is in the area of institutions, religion, and a primitive form of law that the substantial distinctions between the California Indians and others must be made.

The great student of the California Indians, the anthropologist A. L. Kroeber, points out that the traditional tribal organization as it was known elsewhere was present in only a few cases in California: "Tribes did not exist in California in the sense in which the word is properly applicable to the greater part of the North American continent. When the term is used it must therefore be understood as synonymous with 'ethnic group' rather than as denoting political unity."

With the exception of the Mohave and the Yuma, who were interestingly the most warlike of the California Indians, and who could be described as "tribes," the remaining groups represented a loose political organization, ranging from the individual family and slightly larger kin-group units of the Yurok, Karok, and Hupa, to the rudimentary tribelets of the Pomo, Yuki, and Maidu of northern central California, and the fuller tribal systems of the Yokut, the Modoc, and the Shoshone.

For most of the Indians, says Kroeber, gave "the impression of being attached first of all to a spot, or at most a few miles of stream or valley, and to . . . blood kindred or a small group of lifelong associates and intimates." Chieftainship in many tribes was a civil office, for the most part hereditary. The leader in battle or war was an individual who earned the respect of his fellows as a warrior, and only occasionally was the civil and war chief the same man.

Warfare was with rare exceptions (in the north a few tribelets had the institution of slavery, and raided neighboring tribes to assure a supply of slaves) the result of a need, real or imagined, to avenge; plunder or the need to prove manhood were ruled out as causes of war. But war itself, as we have seen, was the exception rather than the rule.

It is the inner life of the California Indian that is the most intriguing part of his story; yet this was precisely the aspect least accessible to the earliest observers. For the California Indians did not ritualize and totemize their imaginative culture in artifacts and ceremonies to the extent that was done elsewhere. To the ordinary observer, then, this life appeared impoverished of myth and dream, of vision and wisdom. But we know now that the reverse is true. If little appeared on the surface, there was much beneath. Some scholars, such as Theodora Kroeber, have described their system of legends and myths as being as rich and moving as those of Greece. And what is more, the tales of

The Inland Whale, among other books, seem to support this view.

For one thing, the transcendentalism of the California Indian experience stands out. Through the dream, man could approach the spirits and the supernatural. Shamans derived their power from repeated dreams, from trances or visions. The power of curing disease, the power to call rain down, the power to prophesy was derived from these mystic experiences. Dreams are another sort of wisdom; from them come the myths and the insights of a people. Curiously, little was done to embody the dreams in concretely expressed symbolism. Perhaps, in the end, this comported well with the land itself, which was symbol enough.

Such an observer as Pedro Font, describing the Colorado Yumas in 1775, could write: "In religion they recognize no special idolatrous cult, though it appears there are some wizards, or humbugs, and doctors among them who exercise their offices by yelling, blowing and gestures. They say that there is a god, and that they know this because the Pimas have told them so. . . ."

True so far as it goes, but neither Font nor the other early writers could see beyond the surface. It disturbed them that "these people as a rule are gentle, gay and happy." They could not tell why. They had no access to that world of dreams.

But they brought, the Spaniards, the Mexicans, the Americans, other dreams, and a world of artifacts that added up to another civilization. The California Indian was unequipped, as we shall see, to compete with this.

Yet, as we read the later witnesses, let us keep in mind the world they supplanted. For if genocide is a tragedy, it is made even worse by the slander of its victims. Ironically, even as recently as 1950, a well-known educator discussing the educational methods of the Franciscans in Spanish California repeats the old gossip that California Indians were a "heterogeneous lot of culturally destitute, peripheral peoples, among the most backward and abject of American red men."

Yet, of their intelligence and capacity there is no serious question, as recent studies indicate. The Mission experience demonstrated, on the level of vocational training alone, a competence. On the spiritual level, many of the Indians wanted to believe the dreams of the friars who taught them. But impatient history was not to give the Missions a chance. Secularized before their self-imposed task was completed, the Indians who had been the "masons, carpenters, plasterers, soapmakers, tanners, shoemakers, agriculturists, horticulturists, vineros, vaqueros" —in the words of Indian Agent Benjamin Wilson in 1852, were thrown upon the mercy of men who had no use for them. They were the castoffs of the land; they were taught how to drink; they were exposed to exploitation, torn from their lands, and the very men who destroyed them had to be reminded by Hayes that "these same Indians built all the houses in the country, and planted all the vineyards."

But that which perhaps they imagined in nightmare visions was still to come. The gay, gentle, affable, happy, peaceful people perhaps knew they were to die. In the *monte* and in the canyons, in the visions of the *toloache,* in the smoke of the jimsonweed, perhaps they foresaw what awaited them. One thing is certain: between the early explorers and the later observers, the Indians had changed. The great past was gone; the land was taken by others. Among the Chumash, women practiced abortion to prevent children from being born into a world from which the dreams of peace had fled.

Other dreams were being dreamed. In Spain, in Mexico, in far-off England, in places remote from their isolated lands, the forces that were to result in cataclysm for the Indians were gathering, and would one day be realized along the coasts and in the deserts of California.

Gold is most excellent; of gold there is formed treasure and with it whoever has it may do what he wishes in this world and come to bring souls into Paradise.

—COLUMBUS, 1503

1

THE FIRST EXPLORERS

While the land and the Indians waited, there was another beginning. In Spain under Ferdinand and Isabella, the Moors were finally driven from Granada. On October 12, 1492, a squadron of three ships under Christopher Columbus, a Genoese who had sold his dream of finding a route to the Indies to the Spanish monarchs, made a landfall on what is now believed to be a tiny island in the Bahamas. He went on to discover Haiti and Cuba. In three subsequent voyages, between 1493 and 1504, a necklace of islands, including Jamaica and Puerto Rico, came under the Spanish flag. The first Spanish settlement in the New World was founded on Haiti (Hispaniola), and the great surge of exploration and conquest that marked the sixteenth-century Spanish expansion began.

What is now California was discovered in one of the minor thrusts of that enterprise. The first Europeans known to have set foot on this land, and whom we can identify, were under the command of Juan Rodríguez Cabrillo, a seasoned professional, one of that band of original conquistadores who served with Hernando Cortés in the campaign that conquered Aztec Mexico between 1519 and 1521. Probably a native of Portugal, Cabrillo's fame as the discoverer of Alta California came long after his death. By that time much of the specific detail about him had been lost. California was considered marginal; its wealth was not obvious to the land-sated Spanish. Later it would become a way station for the treasure ships sailing from the Philippines to Mexico. That alone ensured the land and its Indian inhabitants a relatively undisturbed period of more than two hundred years.

By 1542, when Cabrillo sailed with his two crude ships from the Port of Natividad on the west coast of Mexico, the great spasm of exploration and conquest had lost its major thrust. Obscure men were being sent to test out the dreams of El Dorado and the theories of a Northwest Passage, which the Spaniards called the Strait of Anian. The peninsula of Baja California was then, and for decades thereafter, believed to be an island off the fabled Indies.

Against prevailing northwesterlies, Cabrillo's two ships took three months to beat up to what is now San Diego Bay. The first recorded sight of California comes from the report of that voyage. The document bears the name of Bartolomeo Ferrelo, Cabrillo's pilot, a Levantine sailor who succeeded to the command of the ships after the death of Cabrillo. It was written in the third person, and describes the events of September 27 and 28, 1542:

¶ On this day they saw on the mainland some great smokes. The country appears to be good, with large valleys. Inside, there are some high sierras.

On Thursday they sailed about six leagues along a north-north-west coast and discovered a very good closed port in 34° 20', which they named San Miguel. After anchoring they went ashore where there were some people three of whom awaited them, while the rest fled. To these some presents were given, and they explained by signs that inland people like the Spaniards had passed, and they displayed much fear. That night some went ashore from the ships to fish with a net, and it seems that there were some Indians who commenced to shoot arrows at them and wounded three men. The following day in the morning they went with the ship's boat farther up into the port, which is large, and brought back two boys who understood nothing by signs; they gave them some shirts and shortly sent them away. The following day in the morning three large Indians came to the ships and explained by signs that some people like us, that is bearded, dressed and armed like those aboard the vessels, were going about inland. They showed by signs that these carried cross-bows, and swords; they made gestures with the right arm as if using lances, and went running about as if they were going on horseback, and further showed that these were killing many of the native Indians, and for this reason they were afraid. The people were well-built and large and go about covered with the skins of animals. While in this port a great tempest passed over, but nothing of it was felt as the port is so good. It was from the west-southwest and the southwest and violent. They were in this port until the following Tuesday; here they call the Christians *Guacamal*.

On Tuesday following, October 3, they left San Miguel . . . [1]

San Miguel did not take hold as a place name. Years afterward it would be known by its later christening, San Diego. The tone of the report and its lack of excitement indicate something about Cabrillo and the nature of his voyage. There was nothing about the captain that suggested the ambition or prominence of his late commander, Hernando Cortés, or the hero Pedro de Alvarado, who was to have commanded the 1542 expedition originally. Cabrillo was reliable, responsible, and judging from the sentiments expressed by his crew after his death, a good captain. Personally, his share of the conquest had brought him and his family comparatively little. Twenty years after his death, Cabrillo's widow and children sought a return of certain *encomiendas* (estates) which had been taken from him by Francisco de la Cueva, the governor of Guatemala.

From this litigation in 1561, we learn something about Cabrillo. Another veteran of the Conquest, Bernal Díaz del Castillo, who wrote *The True History of the Conquest of Mexico,* testified in behalf of his old comrade-in-arms:

¶ I knew [Cabrillo] in New Spain and I declare that he came with Narváez and served in the conquest and capture of the city of Mexico and vicinity. I saw him serve always with the diligence such conquests demand. It seems to me that he served as *quadrillero* of crossbowmen, as

[1] Henry R. Wagner, *Juan Rodríguez Cabrillo, Discoverer of the Coast of California* (San Francisco: California Historical Society, 1941).

he was a very capable man. Since then I have seen him in this city [Guatamala] as a captain of the provincial governor Pedro de Lavrado, [who] sent him with certain ships to Antonio de Mendoza, who sent him on a voyage of discovery.[2]

If Cabrillo is credited with the discovery and the first exploration of what is now California, his effort was linked to a chain of circumstances going back to Cortés, a strange, complex man, who energized the original enterprise. Between 1519 and 1521, he had led the campaigns that conquered Aztec Mexico. This was the most dramatic episode of his life, but perhaps not the most important. Energetic, imaginative, ambitious, and except for those two years, unlucky, his very accomplishments opened the way for personal disaster.

The Western Sea fascinated Cortés; there is reason to believe that the fantasy of wealth that was realized in the City of Mexico could itself be eclipsed by the yet undreamed-of treasure in the legendary island of the Amazon queen, the tales of El Dorado, the discovery of the Northwest Passage, which would open up a way to the Indies.

Díaz wrote later, echoing Columbus' words on the potency of gold:

¶ Curious readers will be desirous to know how it happened that the conquerors of Mexico who had gone through such dangers to obtain possession of that city should now quit it to search for new settlements. To this I reply, that the books which contained the accounts of Montezuma's revenues were examined to find from whence the gold and other valuable articles of tribute, such as cacao and cotton manufactures were sent; and it was to these productive districts that we wished to go.

If Cabrillo's life is obscure, that of Cortés is well documented. His secretary, the secular priest, Francisco López de Gómara, who was the first chronicler of the Conquest, describes him as:

¶ . . . of a good stature, broad shouldered and deep-chested; his color, pale; his beard, fair; his hair, long. He was very strong, courageous, and skillful at arms. As a youth he was mischievous; as a man, serene. . . . He

---

[2] Capt. Bernal Díaz del Castillo, *The True History of the Conquest of Mexico Written in the Year 1568,* translated by Maurice Keatinge (London: printed by J. Wright, Piccadilly, by John Dean, High Street, Congleton, 1800).

was much given to consorting with women, and always gave himself to them. The same was true with his gaming, and he played at dice marvelously well and merrily. He loved eating, but was temperate in drink, although he did not stint himself. When necessity demanded, he could suffer hunger, as he proved on the Honduras expedition, and on the sea that he named for himself. He was a very stubborn man, as a result of which he had more lawsuits than was proper for his station. He spent liberally on war, women, friends and fancies, although in other things he was close, which got him the name of new-rich. . . . Over his doors and on his coat-of-arms he caused to be inscribed: *Judicium Domini apprehendit eos, et fortitudo ejus corroboravit bracchium meum.* (The judgement of the Lord overtook them; His might strengthened my arm.) [3]

Díaz, who wrote his book as an antidote to the idealized Gómara chronicle, said he would "give to historians sufficient whereby to celebrate our general, Cortés, and the brave conquerors by whose hands this holy and great undertaking succeeded, for this is no history of distant nations, nor vain reveries [a thrust at Gómara, who was not personally present at the Conquest]; I relate that of which I was an eye witness, and not idle reports and hearsay."

Díaz, like Cabrillo, was one of the unsung men. They shared with Cortés a dislike for the ones who came later, royal favorites and grandees, who would reap what Cortés and his small army sowed in the Conquest. Díaz wrote in near-poverty and with a sense of neglect. He wanted to give Cortés his due, but he also wanted to show that the great conqueror was human and that his victories were purchased with the blood and effort of the men who followed him. Compare his Cortés with the portrait drawn by Gómara:

¶ His features were, if faulty, rather too small; his eyes mild and grave. His beard was black, thin and scanty; his hair in the same manner. His chest and shoulders were broad, his body very thin. . . . He also possessed the heart and mind, which is the principal part of the business [of arms]. I have heard that when he was a lad in Hispaniola, he was very wild about

[3] Francisco López de Gómora, *Cortés, The Life of the Conqueror by his Secretary,* translated and edited by Lesley Byrd Simpson from the *Istoria de la Conquista de Mexico,* printed in Zaragoza, 1552 (Berkeley and Los Angeles: University of California Press, 1964).

women, and that he had several duels with able swordsmen, in which he always came off with victory. . . . He was very affable with all his captains and soldiers, especially those who accompanied him in his first expedition from Cuba. . . . When he was very angry, the veins in his throat and forehead used to swell, and when in great wrath, he would not utter a syllable to any one. He was very patient under insults or injuries; for some of the soldiers were at times very rude and abusive with him; but he never resented their conduct, although he often had great reason to do so. . . . He was very determined and headstrong in all business of war, not attending to any remonstrances on account of danger. . . . Where we had to erect a fortress, Cortés was the hardest laborer in the trenches; when we were going into battle, he was as forward as any. . . . In his early life he was very liberal, but grew close, later; some of his servants complaining that he did not pay them as he ought, and I have observed that in his latter undertakings he never succeeded. Perhaps such was the will of Heaven, his reward being reserved for another place for he was a good cavalier. . . . God pardon him his sins, and me mine; and give me a good end which is better than all conquests and victories over Indians.

It was one of the later unsuccessful undertakings that culminated in Cabrillo's discovery of California: unsuccessful by the standards of the time because no tangible wealth emerged.

Cortés had organized and sponsored a number of expeditions in the Western Sea. He had built ships on the West Coast of Mexico, a prodigious accomplishment, since all hardware and rigging had to be sent overland from Vera Cruz to Zacatecas. In 1527, three ships under the command of Cortés' cousin, Alvaro de Saavedra, reached the Moluccas in an attempt to open up trade. Two were lost to storms; the third was captured by the Portuguese. From 1532 on, he turned his attention northward, spending his funds lavishly to outfit expeditions, to build new ships. One expedition failed; another, ravaged by mutiny, was all but wiped out in a fight with the Indians near the present La Paz. Two surviving seamen reported "good evidence of pearls." Cortés took command of an expedition in 1535, but his luck was little better; he took possession of what we now know as Baja California, named the present Gulf of California the Sea of Cortés, but hastened back without the wealth he sought. For he had learned that a viceroy had been appointed, his future adversary, Don Antonio de Mendoza. His bad luck was compounded by troubles with the court and the new officials. Once more in 1539, just before returning to Spain, Cortés, seeking to realize his "hopes of mighty treasures to be found and the vast city of Cibola," sent Francisco de Ulloa from Acapulco north along the coast to find the strait to the open sea. Ulloa failed to do so, and may not even have survived the voyage. He managed to work his way north to the mouth of the Colorado River, and the expedition's journal concedes the possibility of "a great error in not searching out the secret whether that were a strait or a river which we had left behind us unsearched at the bottom of this great sea or gulf." Ulloa's three small ships sailed back down the western gulf coast to the point of Lower California, San Lucas, rounded it, discovered Cedros Island, sailed against contrary winds to Punta Baja, which they named Cape Disappointment, a fitting term for the last expedition under Cortés' sponsorship. Gómara says, of Ulloa's voyage, "The game was not worth the candle."

For Cortés, this was certainly true. Yet all the voyages were part of a pattern that informed those who came later. Mendoza had no intention of allowing his feud with Cortés to interfere with using the information the expeditions uncovered. He too was aggressive and hopeful of fulfilling the dreams of treasure. He had the report of Fray Marcos de Niza who had walked north to the Pueblo Indian lands and whose reports were transmuted and adjusted to the legend of the Seven Cities of Cibola.

Cortés was still alive (he was to die in Spain five years after Cabrillo's voyage), but Mendoza had effectively replaced him in the enterprise. The viceroy sent a two-pronged expedition northward: Francisco Vásquez de Coronado set forth in 1540 to search for the Seven Cities (he ended in what is now Kansas); and Hernando de Alarcón was to sail north along the coast of Sinaloa and Sonora to the mouth of the Colorado River, to pick up what Ulloa had missed. The two expeditions were to attempt to maintain contact. Their routes diverged, and it is Alarcón's that is more relevant to the discovery of California. For it is possible that he rather than Cabrillo was the first European to see what is now the State of California, and he may actually have set foot on its soil. Ascending the river in late August, 1540, in a boat dragged by Indians, Alarcón went upriver for fifteen and a half days. (The voyage back took only two and a half days.) If we accept Alarcón's report at face value, he went up the river 85 leagues (approximately 225 miles), in which case he saw a portion of present-day California. He mentions landing in several places, though he does not specify whether it was on the left or right bank. If he landed on the left, Alarcón rather than Cabrillo was the first identified European in California.

The point is of minor consequence. Even Cabrillo's landing at San Diego was not considered notable at the time. In 1540, the year of Alarcón's expedition, the project involving Cabrillo had started. Pedro de Alvarado, one of the heroes of the Conquest, had a concession to explore the South Seas. Mendoza had a third interest in the expedition. Alvarado began building ships at Istapa, just east of San José de Guatemala. Juan Rodríguez Cabrillo was placed in charge of construction of three galleons, seven 100-ton ships, and three smaller vessels. When the fleet was completed, Mendoza used his authority to increase his interest to one-half. By the time the fleet reached Santiago, there were complications, a rising of the Indians in Jalisco. The fleet went to Natividad, but Alvarado was dispatched to lead troops against the rebel Indians. In an attack on Nochistlán, Alvarado's troops suffered a sharp defeat. Alvarado himself was killed during the retreat when another soldier's horse crushed him. It could not have failed to affect Cabrillo, and there is, in general, a somber tone to the reports. The fleet by this time had shrunk considerably. Alarcón had used some of the ships. Another expedition under Francisco de Bolanos sailed with three of the ships in 1541, was considerably roughed up in storms. There is some belief that Bolanos first used the term California to describe the southernmost tip of the peninsula of Baja California. True or not, this is virtually all he did. Things were in very bad shape. Alvarado had died in debt. Only two ships, the *Victoria* and the *San Salvador,* remained. Mendoza decided to go ahead, and ordered Cabrillo to take command. We do not know the specific instructions, although it seems likely that the same general purposes that were given for earlier expeditions remained in force: Find the Strait of Anian, locate good harbors, Christianize the Indians, and, as always, stated or unstated, find treasure.

They left Natividad on June 27, 1542. It was the worst season for such a voyage and it took the two ships three months to reach what is now San Diego. The ships were primitive, the crews poorly trained, and there were no charts or maps. Yet Cabrillo seems to have kept the morale of his men high; certainly they respected his ability and courage.

Something of the man emerges in the pages of Ferrelo's journals. Three men were wounded by Indians at the "very good closed port of San Miguel," yet Cabrillo did not order his crews to return fire. This bespeaks good discipline. More than that, he seems to understand the cause of the "much fear" of the Indians, stemming from the "people like the Spaniards" who had been seen inland. Who were these Spaniards? Considering the difficulty of communicating time and place in sign language, they might have been Ulloa's men or even Coronado's. Cabrillo had evidently seen enough of bloodshed and violence. His treatment of the Indians is in sharp contrast to that of many of his contemporaries, though not, if Cortés' policies are carefully scrutinized, completely at odds with others'. It should be remembered that Cortés' conquest of Mexico was made possible because of his diplomatic treatment of the enemies of the Aztecs who, in turn, offered substantial assistance in the campaign of the Conquest.

In any case, Cabrillo's peaceful methods worked. They sailed from San Miguel on October 3, landed on one of the Channel Islands (probably Catalina) on the 7th. Ferrelo reports (remember that the journal is written in the third person):

¶ As the boat was nearing land a great number of Indians came out of the bushes and grass, shouting, dancing, making signs to come ashore. As from the boats they saw the women fleeing, they made signs to them not to fear; so shortly they became assured and put their bows and arrows on the ground. Launching into the water a fine canoe containing eight or ten Indians, they came out to the ships. These were given some beads and presents with which they were well pleased. . . . The Spaniards afterwards went ashore and both the Indian men and women and everybody felt very secure.[4]

On the 8th of October, "they came to the mainland in a large bay, which they named Baia de los Fumos on account of the many smokes

[4] Wagner, *Juan Rodríguez Cabrillo, Discoverer of the Coast of California.*

they saw there." This has been said to be the Bay of present-day Santa Monica, although there is a possibility that it was present-day San Pedro. They followed the coast, describing it with substantial accuracy. On October 10, they anchored off present-day Ventura, "saw on land an Indian town close to the sea with large houses like that of New Spain." Again the Indians reported the presence of Spaniards inland. Cabrillo sent two men inland. They saw a large town that they called Pueblo de las Canoas, and a "very beautiful valley" where there "was much maize and food."

At least twenty-five Indian towns are given by name. "They are in a good country with fine plains and many trees." The Indians are friendly in this "well-settled" area. "They go dressed in skins and have very long hair tied up with some long cords. Inserted between the hair and these cords are many daggers made of flint, bone and wood."

Unfavorable winds just past Point Concepción forced them out to sea and they took refuge in a port on the Channel Island of San Miguel. They called it La Posesión. It was here Cabrillo broke his arm. The injury would lead to his death, on this very island some months later. They left the island on October 25, and the sailing difficulties continued. One day there was no wind, the next, an onshore wind drove them toward the coast. It was depressing. "During this month they found the weather on this coast from 34° up, like that in Spain, very cold in the mornings and afternoons and with great storms of rain, heavy clouds, great darkness and heavy air."

If they praised the land, wrote favorably of the Indians, disappointment creeps through. Is there an ironic echo of the Amazon queen of an island of treasure in the following?

¶ This town at the Puerto de las Sardinas is called *Cicacut,* and the others from there to the Cabo de Galera are: Ciacut, Anacot, Maquinanoa, Palatre, Anocoac, Olesino, Caacac, Paltocac, Tocane, Opia, Opistopia, Nocos, Yutum, Quiman, Micoma, and Garomisopona. The chief of these towns is an old Indian woman who came on board the ships and slept two nights in the *capitana.* . . .

There are maize and fish, acorns and pelts. But there are no gold, silver, or precious stones. And the storms are ferocious. ". . . Such a rainstorm came up that they could not carry an inch of sail." The ships became separated. "The sea was so high it was frightful to see. . . ." When they found each other, it was along a coast where "there are mountains which seem to reach the heavens, and the sea beats on them; sailing along close to land, it appears as though they would fall on the ships."

The pair of ships under Cabrillo reached Cape San Martin. Exhausted, Cabrillo decided to go back to La Posesión to restore himself and his men. But it was the end for him:

> ¶ While wintering at the Isla de Posesión, there passed from this present life, January 3, 1543, Juan Rodríguez Cabrillo, the captain of the ships, from a fall which he had in this island the previous time they were there, in which he broke an arm, close to the shoulder. He left as captain the chief pilot, who was one Bartolome Ferrelo, a native of the Levant, and strongly charged him at the time of his death not to fail to discover as much as possible of all that coast.

His crew renamed the island for him: Isla de Juan Rodríguez. But like all the place names given on this expedition, it did not remain.

Ferrelo followed orders and sailed north, some believe as far as the coast of Oregon, but the exact point is not known beyond doubt. With Cabrillo gone, the expedition began to lose its driving force. Supplies were running out. There is even a change in the tone of the journal; more emotional, less understated than it was when Cabrillo commanded:

> ¶ . . . The wind came from the southwest with great fury, the seas coming from many sides, which molested them very much or broke over the ships. As these had no covered decks, if the Lord had not aided them, they could not have escaped. . . . Considering themselves lost they commended themselves to our Señora de Guadalupe and made their vows. . . . At this hour the Mother of Our Lord succored them with the grace of Her Son, and a very strong rainstorm came up from the north which made them run before it towards the South with lower foresails all night and all the following day until sunset.

Ferrelo brought the ships back to Natividad, on April 14, 1543, after half a dozen close calls, including one over some reefs at the Isla de

Juan Rodríguez, where "the sailors made a vow to go to their church stark naked and Our Lady saved them."

In retrospect, Cabrillo's voyage has been magnified as a great success. It was nothing of the sort, just a brave probe to the north, which found neither the passage to the Indies nor the fabled treasures of Cibola or the island of the Amazon queen. The real riches of the land remained hidden. And if there was anything New Spain did not need when it was still digesting the vast Conquest of Mexico, it was more land. California was marginal, and as such it was given a low order of priority. Thus the land and its Indian inhabitants were not at this time seriously disturbed. There would be other explorations, and an English privateer named Drake would land briefly on its coast. But the Spanish settlement of California would have to wait nearly 120 years.

The Philippines first deflected the thrust of exploration in California, and later provided the incentive for another penetration. These islands, discovered by Magellan, ultimately became a base for a profitable trade with the Orient. Cortés, as we have seen, sensing the possibility, sent the unsuccessful Saavedra expedition in 1527. Antonio de Mendoza's brother-in-law, Ruiz López de Villalobos, took six ships to the Philippines in 1542, but died there in 1546. The barrier was the very trade winds that made it relatively simple to sail from Mexico to the Islands. One of Villalobos' ships made a desperate voyage to the northeast, trying to get back to Mexico, but could not.

By 1564, an expedition commanded by Miguel López de Legazpe was sent from Mexico with Andrés de Urdaneta, Spain's foremost navigator, nominally as chaplain, actually as chief pilot. Legazpe subjugated the Philippines, set up the basis for the lucrative trade that was to endure for 250 years: Mexican silver for the silks and spices and artifacts of the Orient, brought from Manila to Acapulco. Antonio de Morga describes the merchandise of that trade:

¶ Usually there come from Great China to Manila a large number of *somas* and junks, which are great ships laden with merchandise. . . . The goods which they usually bring, and sell to the Spaniards are raw silk in bundles of the thickness of only two strands, and other silk of inferior quality, soft, untwisted silk, white and of other colors in small skeins, much smooth velvet, and velvet embroidered in all sorts of colors and patterns; and other with the ground of gold and embroidered by hand with the same material; stuffs and brocades of gold and silver upon silk of various colors and designs, many other brocades . . . tablecovers, cushions, carpets, caparisons of horse of the same stuff, and with bugles or seed pearls; some pearls and rubies, sapphires, stones of crystal . . . large assortments of nails of all sorts, sheet iron, tin, lead, saltpetre and powder, wheat flour, preserves of oranges, peaches, viper-root, pears, nutmeg, ginger . . . much fine thread of all kinds, needles, knick-knacks, little boxes, and writing boxes; beds, tables, chairs, gilt seats . . . and a thousand other gewgaws and ornaments . . . peppers and other spice; and curiosities, to recount all which would be never to come to an end, nor would much paper be sufficient for it.[5]

These were the cargoes of those floating treasure houses, the big-bellied, awkward Manila galleons. Yet, before these riches could be brought back to Mexico, a route had to be found. Urdaneta is credited with this accomplishment. He took command of the *San Pedro* in the spring of 1565, sailed far to the north to catch the prevailing westerlies, a great-circle route that brought his ship across the Pacific, thence down the California coast back to Mexico. It became the major route, though each voyage was an ordeal. Urdaneta had lost a total of twenty-four men on his voyage, and this became part of the pattern: food ran out, water turned brackish. Often on making the California landfall, the crews were so weak that they did not dare drop an anchor for fear that they might not have the strength to raise it again.

The Philippine trade had a dual effect on the exploration of California. It convinced colonial administrators of the need to find a safe, protected harbor, with adequate supplies of water and food, to restore galleon crews for the last leg of the voyage to Mexico. And it brought privateers to prey on the galleons. Here too was another reason for a California port. Convoy vessels could be based in it to escort the vulnerable galleons to Acapulco.

Sir Francis Drake was one of those drawn by the prospect of plunder. Much has been made of his connection with California, but this is the result of a general paucity of significant events in this

---

[5] Antonio de Morga, *The Philippine Islands at the Close of the Sixteenth Century,* translated by the Hon. Henry E. J. Stanley (London, 1868).

region in the sixteenth century. Drake sailed from Plymouth Harbor on November 15, 1577, holding a commission from Queen Elizabeth to "annoy the King of Spain in his Indies." Spanish agents were probably not deceived by his carefully leaked false plan that gave Alexandria as the destination of his fleet of five ships. They expected some sort of incursion in the Caribbean. Drake had more ambitious intentions. Gradually his fleet was reduced to his flagship, the *Pelican,* which he renamed the *Golden Hind.* Through the Strait of Magellan, he entered the Pacific, where in a series of raids and captures he filled his vessel with an extravagant collection of loot. He took wine and gold from a Spanish ship off Valparaiso, overhauled and captured the Panama-bound treasure galleon *Nuestra Señora de la Concepción,* which furnished him with "a store of fruits, concerves, sugars, meal . . . besides a quantity of jewels and precious stones: 13 chests of plate; 8 pound weight of gold; 26 tuns of uncoined silver, two large silver and gilt bowls, valued in all to 360 thousand pezoes, which was the cause of her slow sailing." [6] With characteristic wit, the account continues: "For these commodities they gave the master a little linnen, and such other things, and so dismissed him to go on his voyage with more speed."

Drake's men ransacked the Mexican port of Guatulco. When they left, the *Golden Hind* was as fully loaded as any galleon. The Spaniards were on the hunt for him to the south; the winds were unfavorable for a run to the Moluccas. Drake headed north as far as a 48° latitude, the report of Francis Fletcher, his chaplain, tells us. But "such alteration of heate, into extreame and nipping cold . . . the pinching and biting aire . . . the very roapes of our ship . . . stiffe, . . . commanded us to the southward whether we would or no."

At 38 degrees, 30 minutes, "we fell into a convenient and fit harborough." But it was so cold and foggy that they could not "in whole fourteen days together, find the aire so cleare as to be able to take the heighte of sunne or starre. . . ." Fletcher relates the complaints of "those thicke mists and most stinking fogges . . . wherein a blind pilot is as good as the best director of a course. . . ."

[6] Sir Francis Drake, *The World Encompassed,* carefully collected out of the notes by Master Francis Fletcher, preacher (London: Printed by E. P. for Nicholas Bourne, 1635).

In *The World Encompassed,* Fletcher gives an extensive account of the month Drake and his men spent on the California coast. From June 17 to July 23, they worked repairing and refitting the *Golden Hind,* beaching her for a time to caulk a serious leak in the bottom. Like many another Elizabethan, Fletcher is an eloquent writer. He meticulously recorded everything he saw, and possibly added a little enhancement to the narrative. Yet, allowing for this, Fletcher's report is the most comprehensive picture of the Indians of the period, and a generally accurate description of the terrain. Though here, as in the earlier Cabrillo narrative, there is still some difficulty in placing exactly the location of his "harborough." It is generally believed to be the present Drake's Bay north of San Francisco.

No one knows for a certainty. The finding of a brass plate (now in the Bancroft Library at Berkeley) by a motorist in 1936 under a rock in Marin County has only added to the controversy. It bears the following inscription:

BEE IT KNOWNE VNTO ALL MEN BY THESE PRESENTS

IVNE 17 1579

BY THE GRACE OF GOD AND IN THE NAME OF HERR MAIESTY QVEEN ELIZABETH OF ENGLAND AND HERR SVCCESSORS FOREVER I TAKE POSSESSION OF THIS KING- DOME WHOSE KING AND PEOPLE FREELY RESIGNE THEIR RIGHT AND TITLE IN THE WHOLE LAND VNTO HERR MAIESTIES KEEPEING NOW NAMED BY ME AN TO BEE KNOWNE VNTO ALL MEN AS NOVA ALBION.

FRANCIS DRAKE

There is no question that Drake spent the time in California, only a question of precisely where and whether the brass plate was left by him or by some enthusiastic California antiquarian. Fletcher writes:

¶ Before we went from thence, our Generall caused to be set up a monument of our being there, as also of her maiesties and successors right and title to that kingdome; namely a plate of brasse, fast nailed to a great and firme post; whereon is engrauen her graces name, and the day and year of our arrival there, and of the free giving up of the province and kingdome, both by the king and the people, into her maiesties hands: together with her highness picture and armes, in a piece of sixpence current English monie, shewing itself by a hole made of purpose through the plate; underneath was likewise engrauen the name of our Generall.

Drake treated the Indians well, and exchanged gifts with them. Fletcher says with perhaps unconscious humor:

¶ Our Generall having now bestowed upon them divers things, at their departure they restored them all againe, none carrying with him anything of whatsoever hee had received, thinking themselves sufficiently enriched and happie that they had found so free access to see us.

The largest gift of all, "the free giving up of the province and the kingdom," is described by Fletcher in a ceremony which is subject to a variety of interpretations, since neither the English nor the Indians spoke each other's language:

¶ Against the end of three days more . . . were assembled the greatest number of people which we could reasonably imagine to dwell within any convenient distance round about. Amongst the rest the king himself, a man of goodly stature and comely personage, attended with his guard of 100 tall and warlike men, this day . . . June 26, came down to see us. . . . His attire upon his head was a cowl of knitwork, wrought upon somewhat like the crowns. . . . When they were come somewhat near unto us, trooping together they gave us a common or general salutation, observing in the meane time a general silence. Whereupon, he who bare the scepter before the king, prompted by another whom the king assigned to that office, pronounced with an audible and manly voice what the other spake to him in secret, continuing, whether it was his oration or proclamation, at the least half and houre. At the close whereof there was a common *Amen*. . . .

Or, at least, Fletcher thought he heard *amen*. Then he describes a dance by the scepter bearer and the king, followed by the rest of the throng. Now:

¶ After they had satisfied, or rather tired themselves in this manner, they made signs to our Generall to have him sit down; unto whom both the king and divers others made severall orations, or rather, indeed, if we had understood them, supplications that he would take the Province and kingdom into his hand, and become their king and patron: making signs that they would resigne unto him their right and title in the whole land, and become his vassals in themselves and their posterities: which that they might make us believe that it was their true meaning and intent, the king himself, with all the rest, with one consent and with great reverence, joyfully singing a song, set the crowne upon his head, inriched his neck with all his chains, and offering unto him many other things, honored him by the name of *Hyoh*. Adding thereunto (as it might seem) a song and a dance of triumph; because they were not the only visited of the gods (for they still judged us to be), but the great and chief God was now become their God, their king and patron, and themselves were become the only happy and blessed people in the world.

These things being so freely offered, our generall thought not meet to reject or refuse the same, both for what he would not give them any cause of mistrust or disliking of him . . . and chiefly that he knew not to what good end God had brought this to pass, or what honour and profit it might bring to our country in time to come.

Drake in short took everything that was offered and a good deal more. This was, after all, Drake's way. He persuaded himself that there were "riches and treasures thereof (wherewith in the upland countries it abounds)" which "might with great conveniency be transported to the enriching of [Elizabeth's] kingdom at home."

He saw in short what he wanted to see, understood what he wanted to understand; nor was he the last in California to adopt this convenient attitude. There are portions of Fletcher's narrative that help to portray the Indians as they actually were (the notion that they thought in terms of kingdoms, vassals, and so on, is at odds with everything else we know about the California Indians). He describes them:

¶ They are a people of a tractable, free and loving nature, without guile or treachery; their bowes and arrowes (their only weapons, and almost all their wealth) they use very skillfully, but yet not to do any great harm with them, being by reason of their weakness more fit for children than for men, sending the arrowes neither farre off nor with any great force: and yet are the men commonly so strong of body, that which 2 or 3 of our men could hardly beare, one of them would take upon his back, and without grudging carry it easily away, up hill and down hill an English mile together: they are also exceeding swift in running, and of long continuance, the use whereof is so familiar with them, that they seldom go, but for the most part runne. One thing we observed in them with admiration, that if at any time they chanced to see a fish so neere the shore that they might reach the place without swimming, they would never miss to take it.

Drake and his men sailed off in the *Golden Hind,* never to return to New Albion, a brief and colorful chapter in the history of the land. By the 23rd of July, 1579, they were gone.

The Spaniards protested to Queen Elizabeth. She informed them coolly that she found no evidence that Drake had molested any of the subjects of King Philip of Spain, or their property. But the implications of Drake's raids and landings, followed over the years by other corsair activity, was not lost on the viceregal government. California was still, however, regarded as marginal, at best an adjunct of the route from the Philippines. In 1584, a Manila galleon captain named Francisco de Gali reported that the California coast was "a very fair land, wholly without snow, and with many rivers, bays and havens." But he was too careful to attempt a landing, which would involve taking the cumbersome galleon close to shore. Another navigator, Sebastian Rodríguez Cermenho, assigned to make a landing on his return from Manila in 1595, came to grief. His *San Agustín* was driven ashore in Drake's Bay, her cargo scattered and picked up by the Indians. Fortunately, the *San Agustín* carried a prefabricated launch, the *San Buenaventura,* which carried him and his crew on a coastal expedition back to Mexico, a voyage that, though usually neglected by historians, provided a great deal of solid information about the coast of California, and was an accomplishment carried out under the most difficult circumstances. They returned to Navidad exhausted, racked by hunger and disease.

The authorities finally realized that to entrust the exploration to the Manila galleons on that terrible homeward voyage gave little chance of success. And, indeed, they were beginning to doubt the ultimate profit of such a venture. In the sixty years between Cabarillo's voyage and that of Sebastián Vizcaíno, the last of the first group, almost none of the anticipated goals had been reached. There seems little doubt that they were losing heart. Vizcaíno, an experienced mariner, sensed opportunity. For one thing, he appears to have believed in Cortés' earlier project of pearl fisheries; and he may have gotten involved in the project, because he was one of several men who applied for a pearl-fishing license. He won a contract with the viceroy that gave him a twenty-year monopoly of pearl fishing in return for delivering to the king one-fifth of all pearls, gold, and silver he found, and one-tenth of all the salted fish.

A series of unsuccessful voyages ensued. And there were other distractions: the Dutch were raiding in the Pacific; King Philip of Spain had died. By 1602, Vizcaíno won a new contract with detailed instructions from the viceroy. It was apparent that Vizcaíno was not completely trusted. He was to follow the advice of a council of soldiers and a council of navigators sent along with him, to avoid conflict with the natives, to make careful soundings and mappings.

Some hint of his personality appears in the letters he sent to the king. Vizcaíno was an operator, exaggerating his difficulties, quick to ask for money; he had even managed to wheedle a decree ennobling gentlemen who served more than two years on his expedition. On his 1602 voyage, the chronicler was a gifted priest, Father Antonio de la Ascensión, who in his way was the forerunner of another California type, the booster. Father Ascensión's account is written in that hyperbolic style, filled with hints of wealth and enthusiasm for the land. He was even to see in the paint the Indians used on their faces a promise of treasure:

¶ The kind of paint they used looked like a mixture of silver and blue color; and on asking them by signs what it was, they gave them a piece of metallic ore, from whence they made it. . . .[7]

Later, he describes the furs (sables and wild cats), the country itself:

¶ In this harbor [San Diego] is a great variety of fish, as oysters, mussels, lobsters, soles, etc. and in some of the rocks up the country were found geese, ducks, and quail. . . .

The Indians were "robust and well-made," the women "are well-shaped, have fine eyes and features. They have a decent behavior & real modesty . . . are generally very good-natured."

[7] *Documents from the Sutro Collection,* translated and edited by George Butler Griffin (Los Angeles: Franklin Printing Co., 1891).

Vizcaíno had sailed with three ships, the *San Diego*, the *Santo Tomás*, and the *Tres Reyes* from Acapulco, May 5, 1602. It took almost six months to reach San Diego. Between San Diego and Point Concepción, the voyage was easy, with landings along the coast. He erased the traces of Cabrillo's place names, and gave the ones which mainly remain: Santa Catalina, San Pedro, Santa Barbara, Carmel, and Monterey. Father Ascensión, ever sensitive to possibilities, kept recording such things as "golden pyrites . . . , a sure sign that there must be gold in the mountains."

Beyond Point Concepción, things became more difficult. Father Ascensión's charting and descriptions now seem more hurried. His account of Monterey as a "noble harbor," "the best port that could be desired, for besides being sheltered from all the winds, it has many pines for masts and yards, and live oaks and white oaks, and water in great quantity, all near the shore," was only partially accurate, which led later voyagers into difficulty. They found an open roadstead at Monterey, many decades later, but not the great port Vizcaíno had promised. Strangely, the Monterey harbor was a legend that motivated much of the Spanish concern for Alta California. It turned out to be little more than a legend.

One ship filled with the sick was sent back from Monterey. Two proceeded in terrible weather north as far as Cape Mendocino, where the vessels were separated. Scurvy afflicted the crews. On Vizcaíno's ship, "only two sailors . . . could climb the mainmast." Men were thrown from their bunks by the violent pitching of the ship. Vizcaíno himself broke several ribs. They ran for home.

Vizcaíno had found no treasure, and though he praised the land, and suggested strongly that Monterey be settled, his explorations were not immediately useful. Vizcaíno's patron, the Conde de Monterey, was succeeded by a new viceroy, Montesclaros, whose imagination was not engaged by visions of Vizcaíno's California. All he saw was the long death list of the voyage; nearly half the crew had perished in less than a year. The new viceroy was of another generation, more interested in solidifying what was tangible and real than in the pursuit of ephemeral treasure. England and Spain were no longer at each other's throats. The Manila galleons, so close to home by the time they made a California landfall, chose to bear the final ordeal and sail directly to Mexico, running the risk of encountering the corsairs who infested the sea lanes, rather than risk the fate of the *San Agustín* on the rugged coasts of California.

The land to the north receded from the immediate concerns of New Spain, but it had seen the types of men who would come again in the future: men like the quiet, dedicated Cabrillo, the raucous Drake, the aggressive, opportunist Vizcaíno. It was an augury of the future.

2

THE CORSAIRS
IN THE PACIFIC

If the first thrust of Spanish exploration ended with Vizcaíno's expedition at the turn of the eighteenth century, another enterprise had already begun with Drake's depredations some twenty years earlier. The corsairs who invaded the Pacific operated in war and peace; the Manila galleons were too rich a target to ignore. These men were realists above all else.

There was Thomas Cavendish, whose model was Drake himself. Cavendish was a man of Suffolk, of an ancient family that traced its origins to an ancestor who had come to England with William the Conqueror. He inherited a considerable fortune while still a minor, squandered it "in gallantry, and following the court." He accompanied Sir Richard Grenville's expedition to Virginia in a ship equipped at his own expense. The voyage was without profit. In the summer of 1586, Cavendish used his remaining credit to equip a small squadron of three ships, and sailed from Plymouth. By December of that year, Cavendish's fleet had entered the Pacific through the Strait of Magellan.

Sailing north along the coast of Chile, Cavendish intercepted a Spanish packet, which was promptly overhauled and seized. The master of the vessel carried dispatches intended for the viceroy, informing him that an English pirate was operating in the South Sea. The papers had been thrown overboard just prior to the capture, but they were recovered. Cavendish in his efforts to obtain information from the Spanish prisoners hanged one who refused to talk. Another gentle form of torture he employed was the *thumbikins,* in which the thumbs of the prisoners were nearly pulled from their hands by means of a winch.

The English sailed along the coast of South America, raiding ports, burning villages, and acquiring a small amount of treasure. On one occasion they ran upon strong opposition from a Spanish garrison, and in the ensuing fight Cavendish lost a number of his men. He ordered the *Hugh Gallant* scuttled, as he needed all his remaining crew to man his other two vessels. They now sailed for Mexico. In a raid on Guatalco, the English fired a church along with the rest of the town. One of the ships captured as they neared the Mexican coast carried a talkative Frenchman, who described the Manila galleon due shortly from the Philippines. This was the prize Cavendish had been waiting for. After careening his ships for repairs and obtaining water at Mazatlán on the coast of Sonora; the privateers crossed the Gulf of California to Cape San Lucas to wait for the galleon. The ship was sighted on November 4, 1587, as she rounded the tip of Lower California en route to Acapulco. The chase began. Cavendish's *Desire* carried eighteen guns, while the *Content* mounted ten. Their quarry was the *Santa Ana,* a slow-moving galleon of 600 tons, which, strangely, carried no cannon. Later, the galleons would travel heavily armed, but at this period there was so little likelihood of their being intercepted by pirates that the Spaniards had considered heavy guns an encumbrance that would take up valuable cargo space. For the *Santa Ana,* this was to prove a costly mistake. Francis Pretty was master of the *Desire,* and he wrote what took place as the excited English crew closed on the treasure ship:

¶ . . . beating up and down upon the headland of California, which standeth in 23 degrees and ⅔ to the Northward, betwene seven and 8 of the clocke in the morning one of the company of our Admirall which was the trumpeter of the ship going up into the top espied a sayle bearing from the sea with the cape, where upon hee cryed out with no small joy to himselfe and the whole company, A sayle, A sayle, with which cheerefull word the master of the ship and divers others of the company went also up into the maine top, perceiving the speech to be very true gave information unto our Generall of these happy newes, who was no lesse glad than the cause required; whereupon he gave in charge presently unto the whole company to put all things in readiness, which being performed we gave them chase some 3 or 4 houres, standing with our best advantage and working for the winde. In the afternoon we got up unto them, giving them the broad side with our great ordinance and a volee of small shot, and presently layed the ship aboard, whereof the king of Spaine was owner, which was Admiral of the South Sea, called the S. Anna & thought to be 700 tunnes in burthen. Now as we were ready on their ships side to enter her, being not past 50 or 60 men at the uttermost in our ship, we perceived that the Captaine of the said ship had made fights [1] fore and after, and layd their sailes close on their poope, their midship, with their fore castle, and having not one man to be seene, stood close under their fights, with lances, javelings, rapiers, & targets,[2] and an innumerable sort of great stones, which they threw overboard upon our heads and into our ship so fast and being so many of them, they put us off the ship againe, with the losse of 2 of our men which were slaine, & with the hurting of 4 or 5. But for all this we now trimmed our sailes, and fitted every man his furniture, and gave them a fresh encounter with our great ordinance, and also with our small shot, raking them through and through, to the killing and maiming of many of their men. Their Captaine still like a valiant man with his company stood very stoutly unto his close fights, not yielding as yet: Our Generall encouraging his men a fresh with the whole noyse of trumpets gave them the third encounter with our great ordinance and all our small shot to the great discomforting of our enemies raking them through in divers places, killing and spoiling many of their men. They being thus discomforted and spoiled, and their shippe being in hazard of sinking by reason of the great shot which were made, whereof some were under water, within 5 or 6 houres fight set out a flagge of truce and parled for mercy, desiring our Generall to save their lives and take their goods, and that they would presently yield. Our Generall of his

[1] A light screen, probably of wood, used as a defensive measure against small-arms fire and light projectiles.
[2] Shields.

goodness promised them mercy, and willed them to strike sayles, and to hoyse out their boate and to come aboord: which newes they were full glad to heare of, and presently strooke their sailes, hoysed their boate out, and one of their cheife marchants came aboord unto our Generall: and falling downe upon his knees, offered to have kissed our Generals feete, and craved mercie: our General most graciously pardoned both him and the rest upon promise of their true dealing with him and his company concerning such riches as were in the shippe: and sent for the Captaine and their Pilote, who at their comming used the like duetie and reverance as the former did. The Generall of his great mercie & humanitie, promised their lives and good usage. The sayd Captaine and Pilote presently certified the Generall what goods they had within board, to wit, an hundreth and 22 thousand pezos of golde: and the rest of the riches that the ship was laden with, was in silkes, sattens, damasks, with muske & divers other marchandize, and great store of all manner of victuals with the choyse of many conserves of all sortes to eate, and of sundry sorts of very good wines. These things being made knowne to the Generall by the aforesaid Captaine and Pilote, they were commanded to stay aboard the *Desire,* and on the 6 day of November following we went into an harbour which is called by the Spaniards, Aguanda Segura, or Puerto Seguro.

Here the whole company of the Spaniards, both of men and women to the number of 190 persons were set on shore: where they had a fayre river of fresh water, with a great store of fresh fish, foule, and wood, and also many hares and conies upon the maine land. Our Generall also gave them great stores of victuals, of garuansos, peason, and some wine. Also they had all the sailes of their shippe to make them tents on shore, with license to take such store of planks as should bee sufficient to make them a barke. Then we fell to hoysing in of our goods, sharing of the treasure, and alotting to every man his portion in division whereof the eight of this moneth, many of the company fell into a mutinie against our Generall, especially those which were in the *Content,* which nevertheless were after a sort pacified for the time. . . .[3]

The 17th of November being "the queen's day," in honor of the coronation of Her Majesty, the crew celebrated with a display of fireworks and firing of ordnance, which the stranded Spaniards watched from shore. Cavendish then released the captain of the *Santa Ana* after providing him and his men with a supply of swords,

[3] Richard Hakluyt, *The Principal Navigations Voyages Traffiques & Discoveries of the English Nation* (Glasgow: James MacLehose & Co., 1904).

targets, pieces, shot and powder for defense against the Indians. The two English ships weighed anchor and set their course for the Philippines. Before leaving, Cavendish ordered the *Santa Ana,* then lying at anchor offshore, burned so she would be of no use to the Spaniards in furthering their escape. Francis Pretty was abroad the *Desire* with Cavendish. The flagship soon became separated from her consort. Pretty continues his account:

¶ The 19th day of November aforesaid about 3 of the clock in the afternoon, our Generall caused the king's shippe to be set on fire, which having the quantitie of 500 tunnes of goods in her we saw burnt unto the water, and then gave them a piece of ordinance and set sayle joyfully homewardes towardes England with a fayre wind, which by this time was come about the Eastnortheast: and night growing neere, we left the *Content* a sterne of us, which was not as yet come out of the road. And here thinking she would have overtaken us, we lost her companie and never saw her after. . . .

The Spaniards on shore were in luck. The fire burned through the rope anchor cables, and the galleon drifted ashore, where the flames were extinguished. Although the superstructure had been destroyed, the hull was sound enough to be fitted with the sails the English had left them for shelter. The crew and passengers of the *Santa Ana* were able to make their way to Mexico. One of the passengers was reported to have been Sebastián Vizcaíno, who was later to be sent in search of a suitable port in Upper California for the Manila galleons. It is known that he had a considerable number of shares in the *Santa Ana*'s cargo, which was lost to the English. It was a financial disaster that convinced him of the necessity for protecting the sea lanes against further attacks by foreign predators like Cavendish.

The *Desire* stood westward across the Pacific, her hold now weighted with gold and other valuable cargo. In January the ship reached Guam, where the natives were induced to barter fruit and vegetables for pieces of iron. Cavendish's next port of call was in the Philippines, where he sought to avoid trouble with the Spaniards and take on provisions. Unfortunately he was carrying a pilot he had removed from the *Santa Ana,* and the navigator tried to smuggle a letter ashore to his countrymen, describing what had happened to that ship. The message was discovered and Cavendish ordered the man hanged.

From the Philippines the *Desire* headed down to Java, where the Englishmen were well received by the natives and Portuguese, commercial rivals of the Spanish. From there, they sailed for home via the Cape of Good Hope, St. Helena and the Azores, where they learned the news of the startling victory of the English fleet over the Great Armada of Spain.

Cavendish arrived in Plymouth on September 9, 1588, two years and fifty days from the time of his departure. His countrymen gave him a rousing welcome, and his fame spread quickly throughout England. He had been the third to circumnavigate the globe, and he had accomplished his mission in less time than either of his forerunners, Magellan and Drake. It is said that when he entered the harbor, the *Desire*'s sails were made of silk. This is possible, as the ship lost her canvas in a storm upon entering the English Channel, and Cavendish probably ordered his sailmaker to use some of the damasks that were stored in the hold as replacements. Shortly after his arrival, he wrote a glowing report to his patron, Lord Hunsdon, giving an account of his accomplishments. Obviously, the wanton sacking of the Spanish towns the English visited weighed lightly on the admiral-general's conscience. The phrase in which he describes cruising in South America and New Spain, "where I made great spoils," would be his lasting claim to fame. History books have quoted it often, but few have printed the entire text of the report. It is addressed to "the right honourable the Lord Hunsdon, Lord Chamberlaine, one of Her Majesties most honourable Privy Councell":

¶ Right honourable, as your favour heretofore hath bene most greatly extended towards me, so I humbly desire a continuance thereof; and though there be no meanes in me to deserve the same, yet the uttermost of my spirits were clean spent, wishing upon any desert place in the world, to dispose thereof. I am humbly to desire your honour to make knowen unto her Majesty the desire I have had to do her Majesty service in the performance of this voyage. And as it hath pleased God to give her the victory over part of her enemies, so I trust yer long to see her overthrow them all. For the places of their wealth, whereby they have mainteined and made their warres, are now perfectly discovered; and if it please her Majesty, with a very small power she may take the spoile of them all. It hath pleased the Almighty to suffer me to circompasse the whole globe of the world, entring at the Streight of Magellan, and returning by the cape de Buena Esperanza. In which voyage, I have either discovered or brought certeine intelligence of all the rich places of the world that ever were knowen or discovered by any Christian. I navigated along the coast of Chili, Peru, and Nueva Espanna, where I made great spoiles: I burnt and sunke 19 sailes of ships small and great. All the villages and townes that ever I landed at, I burnt and spoiled: and had I not bene discovered upon the coast, I had taken great quantities of treasure. The matter of most profit unto me was a great ship of the kings which I tooke at California, which ship came from the Philippinas, being one of the richest merchandize that ever passed those seas, as the kings register and merchants accounts did shew. . . . Which goods (for that my ships were not able to conteine the least part of them) I was inforced to set on fire. From the cape of California, being the uttermost part of all Nueva Espanna, I navigated to the Islands of the Philippinas hard upon the coast of China; of which countrey I have brought such intelligence as hath not bene heard of in these parts. The statelinesse and the riches of which countrey I feare to make report of, least I should not be credited; for if I had not knowed sufficiently the incomparable wealth of that countrey, I should have bene as incredulous thereof, as others will be that have not had the like experience. I sailed along the Ilands of the Malucos, where among some of the heathen people I was well treated, where our countrey men may have trade as freely as the Portugals, if they will themselves. From thence I passed by the cape of Buena Esperanza, and found out by the way homeward iland of S. Helena, where the Portugals use to relieve themselves: and from that Iland God hath suffered me to returne into England. All which services with my selfe I humbly prostrate at her Majesties feet, desiring the Almighty long to continue her reigne among us: for at this day she is the most famous and victorious prince that liveth in the world.

Thus humbly desiring pardon of your honour for my tediousnesse, I leave your lordship to the tuition of the Almighty. Plimmouth this ninth of September 1588.

Your honours most humble to command,
THOMAS CANDISH

James Burney, in his account of Thomas Cavendish's voyage, casts a critical eye on the privateer's destruction of the Spanish colonies he visited. He writes:

¶ The Commander was sometimes wanting in prudence and vigilance, but the activity and courage displayed by him are conspicuous, and his success has established the reputation of his undertaking. The acts of waste and outrage wantonly committed by him without the smallest shew of remorse, shew equally a rooted hatred against the Spaniards, and a disposition naturally cruel.[4]

Cavendish resumed his campaign against the Spaniards in 1591, when he left England with four ships and entered the Pacific to raid their colonies and search for new prizes. This expedition was doomed to failure from the start. The admiral was at odds with one of his captains who commanded his old ship the *Desire*. The squadron became separated in a storm, and provisions gave out. After pillaging various towns in South America with little success, Cavendish turned his ship back toward England, only after his crew threatened to mutiny if he did not return home. Against this course, Cavendish argued in vain, for he had invested heavily in the expedition, using the gains of his former venture. Now he faced financial ruin and disgrace. Gravely ill, he lay in his cabin giving vent to his bitterness in a letter he wrote to a friend:

¶ . . . with . . . the continual trouble I endured among such hellhounds, my spirits were clean spent, wishing myself upon any desert place in the world, there to die, rather than thus basely return home again. . . .[5]

Cavendish got his wish. He was spared the humiliation of entering Plymouth harbor a defeated and broken man. He died, and like Francis Drake, his weighted body was consigned to the deep.

*   *   *

While California was completely neglected during the seventeenth century, many significant events were taking place nearby, and across the North American continent. The Spaniards settled in New Mexico

---

[4] James Burney, *A Chronological History of the Voyages and Discoveries in the South Sea or Pacific Ocean* (London: Printed by Luke Hansard near Lincoln's Inn Fields, 5 vols., 1803–1817).

[5] Johnstone, Mrs. Christian, *Lines and Voyages of Drake, Cavendish, and Dampier; Including an introductory view of the Earlier Discoveries in the South Sea and the History of the Bucaniers* (New York: Harper & Brothers, 1858), pp. 162–163.

at the turn of the century, and its capital, Santa Fe, served as their major outpost along the frontier from the time of its founding in 1609 until the Pueblo Indians, tiring of Spanish abuses, revolted in 1680, driving the white men from their lands. The Spanish returned in 1690 and hammered the Indians into subjection. In the province of Sonora, the Jesuit fathers extended the area of Spanish control. Later they crossed the Gulf, long known as the Sea of Cortéz, and made a concerted effort to establish colonies in Lower California, a land that remains just as arid, hostile, and primitive today as it was centuries ago.

In Mexico, a new breed succeeded the conquistadores, who had subdued the Indians and conquered the land. Their heirs were indolent weaklings, who established a decadent ruling class similar to that of Spain. The viceroy, as emissary of the king, administered the royal power in Mexico. One of the most notable was Don Luis de Velasco, who made an effort to protect the rights of the Indians; his successors were Don Gaspar de Zuñiga y Acevido, the Count of Monterey, who demonstrated enough interest in the country to the north to send Vizcaíno off on his voyage of exploration; and Francisco Fernandez de la Cueva, viceroy between 1653–1660. He was the Duque de Albuquerque, and has the distinction in history of founding a colony of one hundred families in New Mexico, which is today a city that bears his name.

Mining was the chief interest of the Spaniards in Mexico during the seventeenth century, and the quest for silver extended from New Spain to South America. The metal proved abundant, and much of it was used to purchase goods from Asia, which were being transhipped from Manila to Acapulco and Lima. The trade between these ports and the Philippines far exceeded that which was conducted with the mother country. This had repercussions in Spain. However, whenever the king's regulations were promulgated restricting this trade, ways were devised to circumvent the royal orders.

The Spanish government was already having its troubles on the other side of the American continent, where rivals were vigorously challenging Spain's right to dominate the New World. The London Company had established the first permanent settlement in America at Jamestown, Virginia, on May 13, 1607, where despite the same difficulties encountered that caused Sir Walter Raleigh's prior colony to fail, the little community hung on with sufficient tenacity to weather the first critical years. The following year, Samuel de Champlain explored the St. Lawrence, establishing Quebec for the French on a rugged promontory overlooking the river—a strategic location for a fortress. Champlain added to France's holdings when he founded another trading post known first as Mont Royal. It was later called Montreal.

The period of the 1600's witnessed the founding of colonies that were to provide the nucleus of the future United States. The Pilgrims landed at Provincetown on Cape Cod on November 11, 1620, establishing their settlement at Plymouth. In 1629, the Massachusetts Bay Colony was organized under the leadership of Roger Conant and John White. It became the first haven for Puritans escaping from religious persecution in England, and the population of the new community grew rapidly. Even as these colonists sought to escape intolerance in their homeland, dissension appeared among the leaders in New England. Rhode Island was formed by Roger Williams after he was banished from Massachusetts in 1635 because of his outspoken beliefs on religious freedom and his condemnation of the king's right to grant land patents in a country where Williams claimed the British lacked the authority to do so.

The Dutch were also active. Their West India Company sent a party of settlers to what is now New York in 1624. With characteristic shrewdness, they acquired the island of Manhattan from its Indian inhabitants for a pittance. The English arrived in 1664, and the Dutch lost control. The Dutch continued to harass the Spanish in the Far East during the seventeenth century, surpassing them in explorations and discoveries.

Meanwhile, the French had intensified their explorations in North America. In addition to their fur traders, the Jesuits, who were active in Lower California, were also making important discoveries on the American continent. Two of their order had been informed by Indians of the existence of a great river while exploring on the Sault Sainte Marie in 1641. This was the Mississippi, and for a number of years following, it became the quest of the French traders and Jesuits, who searched the Great Lakes region for its source. Notable during the period were Fathers Joliet and Marquette, who were responsible for the great river's ultimate discovery, and Robert Cavelier de La Salle. He arrived in Canada in 1666, and was accorded the credit for opening the vast Mississippi Valley.

*   *   *

Pacific waters off South America, Mexico, and Lower California continued to be a hunting ground for pirates throughout the seventeenth century. The silver ships sailing between Peru and Mexico, and the galleons returning from the Philippines, provided plenty of incentive for the buccaneers.

William Dampier entered the Pacific in 1704 on an English ship fitted for privateering; and while this expedition accomplished little more than to harass the Spanish, it gave Dampier a knowledge of the seas that was put to good advantage in a subsequent voyage in 1708, when he joined an expedition commanded by Woodes Rogers. This raid was well documented, as Rogers kept a detailed journal of the voyage. It remains one of the most exciting narratives of the gentlemanly pursuit of piracy ever written.

In the year that Rogers began his voyage to raid shipping in the Pacific, England was once more at war with Spain. In the new conflict, known in history as the War of the Spanish Succession, Great Britain formed a grand alliance with Holland, Austria and several German Electors. War was declared against France and Spain.

Captain Rogers was an able seaman and navigator. He also possessed a faculty for recording what he saw in his journal, and much befell the two ships of his squadron, the *Duke* and the *Dutchess,* before they returned to England. The diary was incorporated into a book which Rogers later published under the title *A Cruising Voyage Round the World Begun in 1708 and Finish'd in 1711.*[6] Rogers began his journal August 2, 1708, when

¶ about four in the Afternoon we weigh'd from Kingsroad near Bristol, on board the Duke-Frigot, whereof Capt. Woodes Rogers was Commander, in Consortship with the Dutchess, Capt. Stephen Courtney

[6] London: A. Bell and B. Lintot, 1712.

commander; both private Men of War, bound to Cork in Ireland, and thence to the Southward a cruising. . . .

At Cork, they shipped additional men. En route for the South Atlantic, Rogers decided to pause at Madeira and add to their small stock of spirits. Well supplied now with alcoholic beverages, they continued across the Atlantic. The grog must have proven welcome indeed, for the privateers neared Cape Horn at the worst possible season. It was winter, bitter cold, and heavy seas promised trouble. The *Dutchess* shipped a great deal of water and was finally pooped, but luckily escaped with only minor damage.

Soon after entering the Pacific, the English began to seize prizes along the coast of South America. None carried cargoes of particular wealth, but there were always rumors gleaned from prisoners about other ships carrying great riches. Rogers wrote:

¶ our prisoners tell us they expect the widow of the late vice-roy of Peru, who would shortly embark for Acapulco with her family and riches . . . sailing in one of the King's ships of 36 guns, and that about eight months ago there was a ship with 20,000 pieces of eight aboard. . . .

The lady failed to make her appearance, but by this time Rogers had other plans afoot. He decided to sack the port of Guayaquil in present-day Ecuador. At that time, it was Peruvian territory. Leaving their ships at sea, the privateers entered the harbor in small craft. Their presence was discovered by a Spanish ship lying at anchor, which opened fire. After a brisk action, the Englishmen captured the Spanish vessel. Rogers now pillaged the town, but was disappointed with the results of the raid. He believed the monetary return would have been sizable if the attack had been accomplished with greater stealth. Instead, the English had given the residents and clergy of Guayaquil an opportunity to flee to the mountains with most of the local treasure. Rogers was convinced that he had been deprived of more than 200,000 pieces of eight, and much wrought and much unwrought gold and silver, in addition to many precious gems. Regardless, he had to leave Guayaquil in a hurry. Spanish reinforcements might be on the way, and the English had no desire to be trapped in the harbor.

The two ships set a course for California to await the coming of the Manila galleon.

The privateers arrived off Cape San Lucas, Lower California, on November 3, 1709. By this time, Rogers had three ships in his squadron. One of the prizes he had captured was renamed the *Marquis*. She was manned by a crew from the *Duke* and the *Dutchess*. Elaborate plans were formulated as to what each ship was to do when the treasure galleon appeared:

¶ Nov. 3, 1709 . . . We agreed on signals and stations; and to spread S.W. into the sea, off this Cape that now bore N. by W. from us (Nov. 3). Our stations being concluded, I was to be the outermost ship, the Dutchess in the middle, and the Marquis next the land; with the bark to ply and carry advice from ship to ship . . . by this agreement, we could spread 15 leagues, and see anything that might pass us in the day, within 20 leagues of the shore. And to prevent the ship's passing in the night, we were to ply to windward all day, and drive at night. . . .

One matter plagued Rogers. The galleon would have to make its appearance soon. His ships were short of provisions. Rats had consumed most of their flour, and "the little English bread we had left is eaten as hollow as a honeycomb and so full of worms that it's hardly fit for use." Turtles which had been caught in the Galápagos were the mainstay of the sailors' diet, but it was necessary that men be landed ashore to refill the water casks, which were dangerously low. Indians came out to greet them, paddling on bark logs. They were persuaded to come on board, and accepted small presents. Rogers was convinced that the Spaniards had missionaries ashore, but these Indians were naked and knew no Spanish inhabitants of the region. There were Spanish settlements in Lower California at the time. The English were near La Paz, perhaps some 150 nautical miles from Loreto, where the first Spanish mission was founded in the Californias.

Some of the men went ashore and dined with the Indians, whose principal food was fish. During the time the ships waited for the arrival of the Spanish treasure ship, an artist made sketches in great detail of the flora and fauna found ashore, in addition to a number of drawings depicting the Indians and the way they lived. The captain took time to enter a few observations of his own about Lower California in his log.

¶ It is not yet certainly known whether it [California] be an island or joins to the continent, nor did either our time or circumstances allow us to attempt the discovery. I heard from the Spaniards that some of their nation had sail'd as far up betwixt California and the Main, as Lat. 42 N., where meeting with shoal water, and abundance of islands, they durst not venture any further: so that if this be true, in all probability it joins to the continent, a little further to the northward; for shoal water & islands is a general sign of being near some main land: but the Spaniards having more territories in this part of the world than they know how to manage, they are not curious of further discoveries. The Manila ships bound to Acapulco often make this coast in the latitude of 40 North, and I never heard of any that discover'd it farther to the northward. . . . The Dutch say, they formerly took a Spanish vessel in these seas, which had sail'd round California, and found it to be an island: but this account can't be depended on, and I choose to believe it joins the continent. There is no certain account of its shape or bigness, and having seen so little of it, I shall refer the reader to our common draughts for its situation. What I can say of it from my own knowledge is, that the land where we were is for the most part mountainous, barren and sandy, and had nothing but a few shrubs and bushes, which produce fruit and berries of several sorts. Our men who went in our bark to view the country about 15 leagues to the northward, say it was there covered with tall trees. The Spaniards tell us of several good harbours in this country, but we found none of them near this Cape. We frequently saw smoke in several places, which makes us believe the inhabitants are pretty numerous. The bay where we rode had but very indifferent anchoring ground, in deep water, and is the worst recruiting place we met since I came out. . . .

The natives we saw here were about 300, they had large limbs, were straight, tall, and of a much blacker complexion than any other people that I had seen in the south seas. Their hair long, black, and straight, which hung down to their thighs. The men stark naked, and the women had a covering of leaves over their privates, or little clouts made of silk grass, or the skins of birds and beasts. All of them that we saw were old, and miserably wrinkled. We suppose they were afraid to let any of their young ones come near us, but needed not; for besides the good order we kept among our men in that respect, if we may judge, by what we saw, they could not be very tempting. . . .

Their huts were very low, and made of branches of trees and reeds but not sufficiently cover'd to keep out rain. They had nothing like gardens or provisions about them. They subsisted chiefly on fish while we were here. . . . We saw no nets or hooks, but wooden instruments with which they strike the fish very dextrously, and dive to admiration . . . instead of bread they us'd a little black seed, which they ground with stones, and eat it by handfuls; some of our men thicken'd their broth with it, and say it tastes somewhat like coffee. They have some roots that they eat like yams, a sort of seeds that grow in pods, and taste like green pease, a berry which resembles those of ivy, and being dry'd at the fire, eats like parch'd pease. . . . Their arms are bows and arrows, with which they can shoot birds flying. Their bows are about 7 foot long, and of a tough pliant wood unknown to us, with strings of silk grass; their arrows about four foot and a half made of cane, and pointed with fish bones that they shape for the purpose. Most of their knives and other cutting instruments are made of sharks teeth. . . .

According to Rogers' calculations, the Manila galleon was already a month overdue from the time they regularly fell in with the California coast. The food supply was dwindling rapidly, and he decided to put the matter to a vote among his officers: Would they wait for their quarry, or depart? They gathered in the wardroom of his flagship, and he handed them the following note:

¶ It's plain what flour and bread we have left and the risque we must now run to get to the East Indies, with so mean a stock. This I doubt not will be full satisfaction to our employers that we have prolonged our cruise to the utmost extent, in hopes to meet the rich Manila ship. But since fortune has not favour'd us, we must think of other methods to promote our safety and interest. Except we resolve to take a town here to victual us, 'tis evident we can't cruize, and 'tis my opinion, that now our time is so far spent, we ought to attempt nothing more in these seas. . . . I think it is highly necessary, that from this instant we make all manner of dispatch to fit, and sail hence for the island of Guam. . . . This I give as my opinion aboard the *Dutchess,* this 20th of December, 1709. Woodes Rogers.

The officers concurred with their captain, agreeing that they would no longer wait in California waters for the galleon. Rogers noted that "at signing, this committee all looked very melencholy and dispirited, because so low in provisions, that if we should not reach Guam in the limited time, or accidentally miss it, we shall not have enough till we arrive at any other place."

¶ Necessity forces us to design from hence to Guam, and thence to the East Indies, for if we had provisions to go back round Cape Horn, and to stop in Brazil, and there to sell our Europe prize goods, it might be much more for our advantage, and be sooner at Great Britain.

Dec. 21, 1709. Pursuant to yesterday's agreement we made the best of our way into the harbour call'd by Sir Thomas Cavendish Port Segura, where the *Marquis* [one of the prizes they had captured en route] was re-fitting, but having calms most part of the afternoon, and a current setting to leeward, we rather lost than got ground. Towards morning there sprung up a gale, and we found ourselves to leeward of the port, 'tho we took all advantages of the wind: But to our great and joyful surprise, about 9 o'clock the man at mast-head cry'd out he saw a sail besides the *Dutchess* and bark, bearing west half south of us, distant about 7 leagues. We immediately hoisted our ensign and bore way after her, the Dutchess soon did the same; but it falling calm, I order'd the pinnace to be mann'd and arm'd, and sent her away to make what she was. . . .

Dec. 22. We had very little wind all yesterday afternoon; so that we near'd the ship very slowly . . . [our ship] kept dogging the stranger, tho' at a good distance, which gave us great hopes that 'twas the Manila Ship. . . . We . . . hoisted A French ensign, and fired a gun, which the stranger answer'd. . . .

The English now had two ships in addition to two smaller pinnaces chasing the prize, and there was great excitement aboard their vessels. If this indeed was the Manila galleon, it had arrived at the right moment. Woodes Rogers was after gold, but he also needed food for his men. The chase continued through the night. Rogers paced the *Duke's* quarterdeck, watching the signal fires of his sister ships, which would keep their whereabouts known to him, as well as the fleeing Spanish vessel. There was little that could be done before dawn, at which time he prayed for a fair wind. In this he was to be disappointed, for on the following morning the sea was calm. There was not the faintest trace of a breeze to stir the canvas.

¶ At day-break we saw the chase upon our weather-bow, about a league from us, the *Dutchess* a-head of her to leeward near about half as far. Towards six our boat came aboard, having kept very near the chase all night, and received no damage, but told us the *Dutchess* pass'd by her in the night, and she fired 2 shot at them, but they return'd none. We had no wind, but got out 8 of our ships oars, and rowed above an hour; then there sprung up a small breeze. I order'd a large kettle of chocolate to be made for our ship's company (having no spiritous liquor to give them) then we went to prayers, and before we had concluded were disturb'd by the enemy's firing at us. They had barrels hanging at each yard-arm, that looked like powder barrels, to deter us from boarding 'em. About eight o'clock, we began to engage her by ourselves, for the *Dutchess* being to leeward, and having little wind, did not come up. The enemy fired her stern chase upon us first, which we return'd with our fore chase several times, till we came nearer, and when close aboard each other, we gave her several broadsides, plying our small arms very briskly, which they return'd as thick a while, but did not ply their great guns half so fast as we. After sometime we shot a little a head of them, lay thwart her hawse close aboard, and plyed them so warmly that she soon struck her colours two thirds down. By this time the *Dutchess* came up, and fired about 5 guns, with a volley of small shot, but the enemy having submitted, made no return. We sent our pinnace aboard, and brought the captain with the officers away, and having examin'd 'em found there was another ship came out of Manila with them, of a bigger burthen, having about 40 brass guns mounted, and as many *patereroes;*[7] but they told us they lost her company 3 months ago, and reckon'd she was got to Acapulco before this time, she sailing better than this ship. This prize was call'd by the long name of *Nostra Seniora de la Incarnacion disenganio,* Sir John Pichberty commander; she had 20 guns, 20 patereroes, and 193 men aboard, whereof 9 were kill'd, 10 wounded and several blown up and burnt with powder. We engaged 'em about 3 glasses,[8] in which time we had only my self and another man wounded. I was shot thro' the left cheek, the bullet struck away a great part of my upper jaw, and several of my teeth, part of which dropt down upon the deck, where I fell; the other, Will Powell, an Irish land-man, was slightly wounded in the buttock. They did us no great damage in our rigging, but a shot disabled our mizzen mast. I was forced to write what I would say, to prevent the loss of blood, and because of the pain I suffer'd by speaking. . . .

[7] A small swivel cannon.

[8] These were hour-glasses used for navigational purposes. The sand level varied in them, being sometimes measured for fifteen minutes, a half hour, or longer. It was the duty of the watch to see that they were turned accurately, when the last grain of sand emptied into the lower level.

Rogers ordered his surgeons aboard the prize to care for the Spanish wounded, and all ships made for the harbor. The wound he had received caused considerable discomfort, as he notes:

¶ . . . In the night I felt something clog my throat, which I swallow'd with much pain, and supposed it's a part of my jaw bone, or the shot, which we can't yet give an account of. I soon recover'd myself; but my throat and head being very much swell'd have much ado to swallow any sort of liquids for sustenance. . . .

It was now decided to wait for the larger Manila galleon, for Rogers was certain that it had not as yet passed on its way to Acapulco. The formalities of the capture were concluded with the captain of the prize, who gave Rogers bills of exchange payable in London as ransom, and in payment for a small bark which the English transferred to him for the Spanish to effect their escape from Lower California. According to Rogers,

¶ . . . this was a bargain concluded at their own request, and very much to their own advantage. Sir John Pichberty being, we hope, a man of honour, will not suffer his bills to be protested, since we have so generously trusted him, tho' a prisoner, without a hostage, which is always demanded for less sums.

On December 26th, sentries stationed on a hill overlooking the harbor observed a sail at sea, signaling her approach to the rest of the camp. The privateers raced for their ships, leaving the prisoners under guard on the beach. Soon the *Duke*, Rogers' flagship, the *Dutchess*, and the *Marquis* were under way, standing to the galleon with all the sail they could crowd. The most exciting sea engagement ever fought in California waters was about to commence, and Rogers, despite the painful wound to his jaw, did not neglect to record a running account of the battle in his journal.

The wind was light, and the privateers made little headway. Night fell, and it was not until the following afternoon that the *Marquis*, which had outdistanced the other two ships, was within range of the quarry to open fire.

Rogers wrote:

¶ . . . we saw the *Marquis* come up with the chase and engage her pretty briskly; but soon fell to leeward out of cannon-shot, and lay a considerable time, which made us think she was some way or other disabled. I order'd the pinnace to be mann'd, and sent her away to her, that if what we suspected prov'd true, and we had not wind to get up with them before night, our boat might dog the chase with signals till the morning, that she might not escape us and the other ships; but before the boat could get up with them, the *Marquis* made sail and came up with the chase, and both went to it again briskly for 4 glasses and upwards: then the ship which we took to be the *Dutchess* stretch'd ahead to windward of the enemy, I suppose to fix her rigging, or stop her leaks; meanwhile the other kept her in play till she bore down again, and each firing a broadside or two left off, because 'twas dark: they then bore south of us, which was right in the wind's eye, distant about 2 leagues. By midnight we were pretty well up with them, and our boat came aboard, having made false fires which we answered: They had been on board the *Dutchess* and *Marquis*, and told me the former had her foremast disabled, and the ring of an anchor shot away, with several men wounded, and one kill'd, having receiv'd a shot in their powder room, and several in their upper works, but all stopt. . . .

. . . The chase had made signals to our ship all the day and night, because she took us for her consort, which we had in our possession. . . . In the morning as soon as 'twas day, the wind veering at once, put our ship about, and the chase fired first upon the *Dutchess,* who by means of the wind's veering was nearest the enemy; she return'd it smartly: we stood as near as possible, firing as our guns came to bear; but the *Dutchess* being by this time thwart the Spaniards hawse, and firing very fast, those shot that miss'd the enemy flew from the *Dutchess* over us, and betwixt our masts, so that we ran the risque of receiving more damage from them than from the enemy, if we had lain on her quarters and cross her stern, as I design'd, while the enemy lay driving. This forced us to lie along side, close aboard her, where we kept firing round shot, and did not load with any bar or partridge, because the ship's sides were too thick to receive any damage by it, and no men appearing in sight, it would only have been a clog to the force of our round shot. We kept close aboard her, and drove as she did as near as possible. The enemy kept to their close quarters, so that we did not fire our small arms till we saw a man appear, or a port open; then we fired as quick as possible. Thus we continued for 4 glasses, about which time we received a shot in the main mast, which much disabled it; soon after that the Dutchess and we firing together, we came both close under the enemy, and had like to have been aboard her, so that we could make little use of our guns. Then we fell astern in our berth along side, where the enemy threw a fire-ball out of one of her tops, which lighting upon our quarter-deck, blew up a chest of arms and cartouch boxes all loaded, and several cartridges of powder in the steerage, by which means Mr. Vanbrugh, our agent, and a Dutchman, were very much burnt; it might have done more damage, had it not been quench'd as soon as possible. After we got clear of each other, the *Dutchess* stood in for shore, where she lay brac'd to, mending her rigging, etc. The *Marquis* fired several shot, but to little purpose, her guns being small. We were close aboard several times afterwards, till at last we receiv'd a second shot in the main mast not far from the other, which rent it miserably, and the mast settl'd to it, so that we were afraid it would drop by the board, and having our rigging shatter'd very much, we sheer'd off, and brought to, making a signal to our consort to consult what to do. . . .

We can assume that the galleon was making every effort to depart from these waters with all haste, as Rogers called his other captains aboard the *Duke* for a conference. However, the winds were light, and the heavy Spanish ship was unable to make much headway. Slow and cumbersome she may have been, but the vessel was built like a fortress. The heavy round shot the privateers had hurled at her sides bounced off her hull like so many rubber balls. The unhappy Rogers sat in his cabin discussing the sorry plight of his squadron with the other ship commanders. His jaw was causing him intense pain, and he had received an additional wound in the leg. At the moment, however, his primary concern was about the condition of his ships, and whether to continue the chase:

¶ . . . we consider'd the condition the 3 ships were in, their masts and rigging being much damnified in a place where we could get no recruit, that if we engaged her again, we could not propose to do no more than what we had already done, which was evident did her no great hurt, be-cause we could perceive few of our shot enter'd her sides to any purpose, and our small arms avail'd less, there being not a man to be seen above-board: that the least thing in the world would bring our main-mast, and likewise the *Dutchess'* fore-mast by the board, either of which by its fall might carry away another mast, and then we should lie a battery for the enemy, having nothing to command our ships with so that by his heavy guns he might either sink or take us: That if we went to board her, we should run a greater hazard in losing a great many men with little hope of success, they having above treble the number aboard to oppose us, and there being now in all our 3 ships not above 120 good men fit for boarding, and those but weak, having been very short of provisions a long time; besides we had the disadvantage of a netting-deck to enter upon, and a ship every other way well provided; so that if we had boarded her, and been forc'd off, or left any of our men behind, the enemy by that means might have known our strength, and then gone into the harbour and took possession of the prize in spite of all we could do to prevent it: Besides our ammunition was very short, having only enough to engage a few glasses longer. All this being seriously consider'd, and knowing the difficulty we should have to get masts, and the time and provisions we must spend before we could get 'em fitted, 'twas resolved to forbear attempting her further, since our battering her signify'd little, and we had not strength enough to board her: Therefore we agreed to keep her company till night, then to lose her, and make the best of our way into the harbour to secure the prize we had already took. We engag'd first and last about six or seven hours, during all which time we had aboard the *Duke* but eleven men wounded, 3 of whom were scorch'd with gunpowder. I was again unfortunately wounded in the foot with a splinter, just before we blew up on the quarter-deck, so that I could not stand, but lay on my back in a great deal of misery, part of my heel-bone being struck out, and all my ankle cut abone half thro', which bled very much, and weaken'd me, before it could be dressed and stopt.

The *Dutchess* had about 20 men killed and wounded. The *Marquis* had none kill'd or wounded, but 2 scorch'd with powder. The enemy was a brave lofty new ship, the *Admiral of Manila,* and this the first voyage she had made . . . she was . . . of about 900 tuns, and could carry 60 guns, about 40 of which were mounted, with as many *patereroes,* all brass; her complement of men on board, as we were inform'd, was above 450, besides passengers. They added that 150 of the men on board this great ship were Europeans, several of whom had been formerly pirates, and having got all their wealth aboard were resolved to defend it to the last. The gunner, who had a good post in Manila, was an expert man, and had provided the ship extraordinary well for defence, which made them fight so desperately; they had filled up all between the guns with bales to secure the men. She kept a Spanish flag at her maintop-mast head all the time she fought us: we shatter'd her sails and rigging very much, shot her mizon-yard, kill'd two men out of her tops, which was all the damage we could see we did 'em; tho' we could not place less than 500 shot (6 pounders) in her hull. These large ships are built at Manila with excellent timber, that will not splinter; they have very thick sides, much stronger than we build in Europe. . . .

Rogers departed from Lower California after releasing his prisoners. It was a 6,000-mile journey to Guam, and the men were near starvation when they reached there. Upon arrival, he sent the Spanish governor a polite note. The English were on their way to the East Indies, he informed him; they needed provisions, for which they were willing to pay, but if their request was denied, then "you may immediately expect such military treatment as we are with ease able to give you. . . ."

The governor wisely complied with the request. The English were desperate men, and would undoubtedly have done a thorough job of sacking Guam. An abundance of food was sent to the ships, and Rogers, ever the gentleman, hosted the Spanish authorities aboard the *Duke,* where they were royally entertained, consuming a quantity of the choice wines and liquors Rogers had obtained from the twenty Spanish sail he captured during his long foray in the Pacific. He relates that there were music and dancing on deck. The privateers' recent depredations against Spanish ships and possessions were not discussed. There was no need to spoil a pleasant evening.

Leaving Guam, Rogers sailed on to Batavia, where after receiving additional provisions, the ships of his weary squadron made the long run for the Cape of Good Hope. There, a convoy of English and Dutch ships was formed, and they sailed for Holland. His narrative closes on October 14, 1711. The profits of the voyage turned out to be more than substantial, despite the inability of the English to capture the larger Spanish galleon, some 170,000 pounds being divided, two-thirds to the investors, and one third among officers and men. A tidy fortune of 14,000 pounds went to Woodes Rogers, enabling him to live comfortably in retirement. Honors were conferred upon him, and in 1717 he was appointed Captain-General and Governor-in-Chief of the Bahama Islands, a position that carried profitable economic concessions. He was considered the best qualified man to suppress piracy and restore trade in the West Indies, a problem that beset the British government, and one which the royal navy had been unable to

control. Rogers arrived at Nassau with authority to grant the buccaneers the king's clemency if they would cease their attacks upon
merchant shipping. Some accepted amnesty, while others, including
the notorious Blackbeard, declined. Rogers proved an able adminis-
trator, and did much to restore order in the pirate-infested waters of
the Caribbean. The buccaneers knew he was a man whose word could
be trusted, and they respected him. After all, he had once been a
member of their own brotherhood. He died at Nassau on July 15,
1732.

3

THE JESUIT MISSIONS
IN LOWER CALIFORNIA

The chief interest in colonizing Lower California during the first half of the seventeenth century was a desire among the Spaniards to obtain pearls, which were being discovered in great quantities in the waters off La Paz. As the century neared its close, the militant Jesuit order sent members of its society across the Gulf of California from Sonora to begin the difficult task of establishing a chain of missions on a hostile peninsula. These industrious fathers, led by Juan María de Salvatierra, sowed the first seeds of agriculture and Christianity among the savage inhabitants. Both efforts met with but moderate success. The land was always—and still is—hostile. Rainfall in Lower California is irregular and seldom plentiful. Although the peninsula is some 800 miles long, and from 30 to more than 100 miles in width, there is only one river that touches the entire region, the Colorado, whose delta is at the extreme northeastern border. The interior of the peninsula is mountainous, but little water flows down from the rocky heights. Canyons and other drainage channels are usually dry. The climate is generally warm, and the slim rainfall has resulted in desert-like conditions over much of the terrain. However, when water was available, often from wells, the soil proved fertile. The Indians had no agriculture, other than some natural products of the soil. Fish were abundant, providing their chief form of subsistence. The Jesuits introduced fruit trees and crops from New Spain. Wherever it was possible to irrigate, oranges, lemons, figs, olives, dates, grapes, wheat, barley, and alfalfa were grown successfully. At the southern end of the peninsula, which has a tropical climate, it was possible to grow coconut palms, bananas and pineapples. The date palm was introduced by the Jesuits in 1730, and may still be seen, particularly on the southeastern side of the peninsula.

Miguel Venegas, the Jesuit historian, described some of the events that took place in Lower California during the seventeenth century, commencing with the period immediately following Sebastián Vizcaíno's expedition to Upper California in 1602. Venegas spent considerable time in Lower California during the early 1700's, while it was under Jesuit Control. An English translation of his narrative, *A Natural & Civil History of California,* was published in 1759. He wrote:

¶ During the succeeding years, inconsiderable voyages only were made to California, and these rather to fish for pearls, or procure them by barter, than to make any settlement, and therefore they have been thought below any separate account, especially as in the subsequent royal commissions they are only mentioned in general without any circumstances. At length, in the year 1615, captain Juan Iturbi, obtained a licence for making a new voyage at his own expence. One of his two ships was taken by a set of European pirates, who made themselves famous in America, under the name of Pichilingues, and to the great dishonour of the Spanish power infested the South-seas, till their insolencies clearly proved the necessity of reducing California, as they there securely sheltered themselves: with his other ship Iturbi entered the bay of California; and proceeded to the height of 30 degrees, where he observed that the two coasts of Sinaloa and California gradually approached each other. But the N.W. winds, and the shortness of provisions, hindered him from going any farther. He therefore thought proper to return; but was so distressed for want of provisions, that he and his company must inevitably have perished, without the almost miraculous relief he met in the village of Ahomé in Sinaloa; by means of the missionary father, Andres Perez de Ribas, provincial of the Jesuits of New Spain, who several years afterwards wrote an account of this expedition. From Ahomé he directed his course to Sinaloa, where he received orders from the viceroy, don Diego Fernandes de Cordova, marquis of Guadal-cafar, to make the best of his way to meet and convoy the ship from the Philippine islands, which it was greatly feared would fall into the hands of the Dutch corsairs, who then openly infested those seas under their own colours, and soon afterwards made themselves masters of the greatest part of the trade to the East Indies.

Iturbi accordingly sailed from the gulf into the South-sea, and brought the ship which occasioned so much anxiety, safe into Acapulco: from thence he went to Mexico, where the pearls he brought with him filled the whole city with admiration. He had a great number of them, the most were of a brown tinct, occasioned by the Indians, as we have already observed, putting the shells into the fire, in order to dress the flesh of the oysters. Others he had of a larger sort, and without any damage, which were taken up by his own divers; and so large and clear, that for one only, he paid, as the king's fifth, 900 crowns.

These pearls animated the Mexicans to attempt the conquest and settlement of California; a great many private persons, from the coasts of Culiacan and Chametla, made trips in small boats to the coasts of California, either to fish for pearls, or purchase them of the Indians. And several acts of cruelty and outrage were committed on these poor people; which however did not always escape punishment. A few adventurers enriched themselves by this trade: and there are very surprising accounts of the wealth accumulated by Antonio del Castillo, an inhabitant of Chamelta; which naturally increased the universal impatience for making the conquest. In the year 1628, Philip IV being king of Spain, captain Antonio Bastan came over to Spain for a licence, offering to undertake it at his own expence. The supreme council of the Indies, by a schedule of the 2d of August of the same year, required the marquis de Cerralvo their viceroy to send them further information. The viceroy and council appointed don Juan Alvarez, auditor of the royal audience, to collect proper accounts, and under pretence of greater certainty, and a more particular detail, obtained a licence from the viceroy, for captain Francis de Ortega, to make a voyage thither at his own expence; and he was more fortunate or skillful than his predecessors. He sailed in March 1632, in a vessel of seventy tons, having with him Diego de la Nava, a priest whom the bishop of Guadalaxra had nominated a vicar of California. He landed on the second of May, and having taken a particular survey of the whole coast, from San Barnabe's bay, to Puerto de la Paz, purchased many pearls, and found the Indians generally very friendly and tractable, except in some parts, where they had been injured by those who had come thither to trade for pearls. In June they returned to the coast of Sinaloa, whence they proceeded to lay the whole voyage before the viceroy.

Captain Ortega very probably had found his account in this voyage, as by permission from the viceroy, he made two other trips thither, in the years 1633 and 1634, with an intent of making a settlement. It was his opinion, that the Indians of Puerto de la Paz, might easily be prevailed on to embrace the christian religion, and for the accomplishment of this most desireable end, with the vicar Nava was sent, another priest called don Juan de Zuñniga. In both voyages he took care to lay in as large a quantity of provisions as possible; yet in both, they were all consumed, and he returned to Mexico, having experienced the same melencholy circumstances all the others had felt before him, namely the barrenness and total want of sustenance in the country. . . .

. . . Philip IV, however, a little before his death, which happened on the 17th of September 1665, had ordered the reduction of California to be again completed. And the person nominated to put his order in execution, was don Bernardo Bernal de Piñadero . . . but under certain conditions, both the treasury and nation being exhausted, notwithstanding the importation of so many millions, which had only served to enrich other parts of Europe. But Mexico labouring under that fatal languor, which had pervaded the whole body of the Spanish monarchy, two small vessels built in the Valle de Venderas, were not ready for the expedition till the year 1664, when the voyage took place, and the ships arrived at California, their whole care and employment was to purchase and fish for pearls; compelling with the most barbarous violence, the poor Californians to comply with their demands. As this avarice and cruelty little contributed to the capital intention of their voyage, so it became, in some measure, its own punishment; for the quarrels among the Spaniards, with regard to the riches they found, were carried to such extremity that several were killed and wounded, and the admiral to avoid further confusion, having procured a large quantity of pearls, returned to New Spain. He however met a cold reception from the government, and the affair having been debated in the council of the Indies, the queen mother, then regent, during the minority of Charles II sent order that admiral Piñadero should be obliged, conformable to the treaty made with the king, to attempt another descent. The admiral was not adverse to this, and accordingly in two ships built at Chacale, he sailed on another expedition in the year 1667. Father

Kino mentions it, but all he says is that it miscarried like all the former. . . .

During the first year of the reign and minority of Charles II, no other expeditions were undertaken to California than those we have already mentioned; but the inhabitants of the coast of Culiacan, Sinaloa, Yaqui, Mayo, and New Biscay, were continually going over in little barks to the eastern coast, to procure pearls, either by barter or fishing. In the meantime, the necessity of making a settlement on the coast of California, after a long deliberation in the council of the Indies, was determined, and instructions sent on the 26th of February 1677, to don Francis Payo Enriquez de Rivera, archbishop of Mexico, and viceroy of New Spain that admiral Piñadero should again be employed in the conquest of that country, on his giving security for performing all the articles that should be agreed on; and that if he declined it, the offer should be made to any person that would undertake it at his own expence, and lastly, if no other method could be discovered it should be done at the expence of the crown. The enterprise fell to admiral don Isidro Atondo y Antillón, who signed an instrument for the purpose in December 1678, and which was approved at Madrid, by a warrant of the 29th of December 1679, conferring the spiritual government on the jesuits, and father Eusebio Francisco Kino. On the receipt of his Majesty's approbation, the admiral began his preparations, and put to sea from Chacala, on the 18th of May, 1683, about six years since his majesty's first warrant; and in fourteen days came to Puerto de la Paz. He had with him two ships, very well provided with all kinds of stores, and above one hundred men, three of whom were father Kino as superior of the mission, and the fathers Juan Baptista Copart, and Pedro Matthias Goni. They were followed by a bilander [1] with provisions and other stores; but after several disappointments, she wandered a long time about the gulf, without ever getting sight of the ships.

The admiral and his men continued aboard five days, without seeing any Indians as they expected, on which at last they landed; but on their beginning to form a garrison, they discovered the natives armed, and disfigured with a variety of colours, to strike the greater terror; but seeing a large number of people, they halted and made threatening gestures, intimating that the Spaniards should quit the coast. This proceeded from the abuse their good nature had suffered from other Spaniards, who had landed there. The soldiers drew up, and the missionaries went without any attendants towards them, with a great number of little presents, and some provisions, intimating by signs that they came peaceably. They gave them

[1] A small sloop used for coastal traffic, which carried passengers and cargo.

the presents, which the Indians threw on the ground. But while the fathers were returning, the Indians began to eat what they had first thrown away with disdain, and immediately hastened after the fathers begging for more; and even without any fear or suspicion, followed them into the garrison among the soldiers, where they were so kindly entertained that they went away to their rancherias highly pleased, so tractable and unsuspecting are all these poor Indians in general. The like happened to another company of them, which came two days after to the Spanish camp, and were kindly entertained by admiral Atondo, who came to shew them an experiment of the force of fire-arms, desiring eight of the most robust of them to shoot their arrows against one of the leathern targets which the soldiers carried: which they did but they could not penetrate it. Whereas a musket ball fired off before them, made its way through three targets placed close together. At this, they showed the greatest astonishment. It also inspired them with such terror, that the Spaniards were under little apprehensions of any insults. A church was immediately raised, together with some huts, composed of branches of trees. And the admiral having sent a vessel to Rio Hiaqui for provisions, began to send parties up the country. . . .[2]

Venegas related that little was accomplished by the colonies. The Jesuits believed that they were making progress converting the Indians, but Atondo realized that the country was too barren to support a community. Accordingly, he returned to Mexico and gave his report to the viceroy. Of the royal revenue, 225,000 crowns had been expended in the venture, and after deliberation by a royal council, it was decided that the conquest of California was impractical by those means. However, it was decided to encourage the Jesuits to continue their efforts in converting the Indians, and an investigation was ordered to ascertain the cost of such an undertaking. An Indian revolt in Mexico soon occupied the authorities, while at home in Spain there was trouble with France. Once again, the plan to settle California was postponed.

*　　*　　*

[2] Miguel Venegas, *A Natural & Civil History of California,* translated from the original Spanish edition of 1758 (London: Printed for James Rivington & James Fletcher at the Oxford Theater in Pater-Noster Row, two vols., 1759).

The dream for a Jesuit colonization of Lower California was finally brought to a reality through the efforts of Father Eusebio Francisco Kino, who had been a member of the Atondo expedition. It was he who convinced his superior, Father Juan María Salvatierra, of the project's feasibility. A government warrant was obtained in 1697, granting permission for an expedition, although it would have to be accomplished without the aid of government funds. One of the Jesuits possessed a remarkable talent for fund raising to obtain the necessary revenues. Father Juan de Ugarte conceived the idea of establishing a Pious Fund. Donations were accepted from throughout New Spain to support the plan for settling Lower California. Salvatierra led the expedition, which sailed from Sinaloa, landing at Loreto on October 11, 1697. Kino, who had planned the project, was needed elsewhere. It was an important occurrence in the history of California, for this marked the establishment of the first permanent mission and colony. Venegas described what took place on this memorable occasion:

¶ Father Salva-Tierra's military attendants consisted of five soldiers with their commander; don Luis de Torres Tortolero, ensign, and first captain of the garrison of California. . . . With this small force the father sailed for California on the day above mentioned in the galliot, taking with him the long boat, which soon became necessary; for the galliot had not got above half a league from the harbour, before a furious squall of wind came on and drove her ashore, where she stuck fast in the land, and to all appearance there was little hope of safety. However by the help of the long boat, and the skill of the seamen, she floated with the flood, and was soon out of danger. On the 3rd day they made California; but the long boat being separated from the galliot, and at a loss what coast to steer, they touched at Conception bay, 30 leagues northward of Loreto. They also took a view of the bay of San Bruno, where Atondo had pitched his camp; but this was not approved of, as being far from the sea, and affording only brackish water, especially as Juan Antonio Romere de la Sierpe, captain of the galliot, had offered to shew them a much more convenient place, which he had seen in Atondo's expedition. This was in the bay of San Dionysio ten leagues south of San Bruno, where the coast forms itself into the shape of a half moon near five leagues from point to point. The country near it was covered with trees and other verdure, with a sufficiency of fresh waters not far from the shore. Here they arrived and landed on Saturday the 19th of October, and were received with great joy and affection by above 50 Indians of the neighboring rancheria, and others from San Bruno. A convenient spot near a watering place, about a league and a half from the shore, was chosen for an encampment; the provisions and animals were landed together with the baggage. The father, though the head of the expedition, being first to load his shoulders. The barracks for the little garrison was now built, and a line of circumvallation thrown up; in the center a tent was pitched for a temporary chapel. Before it was erected a crucifix with a garland of flowers; and everything being disposed in the best manner possible, the image of our lady of Loretto,[3] as patroness of the conquest, was brought in procession from the galliot, and placed with proper solemnity. Immediately afterwards, on the 25th of October, of the same year 1697, possession was taken of the country in his majesty's name. Father Salva-Tierra now applied himself to learn the language and instruct the Indians, appointing particular hours for this exercise, when the Indians came and repeated the prayers, and parts of the catechism which he read to them by means of father Copart's papers, after which the father used to listen, and write down their discourse in order to learn the language. He talked to them and the Indians, by that means corrected his mistakes in the words and pronunciation. He used several contrivances for the more speedy instructing the boys in Spanish, though not without being laughed at by them, and the adults for his wrong pronunciation; and their banters are attended with no little art and pleasantry. When all was over, he used to distribute with his own hands among those who attended the exercises, an allowance of pozoli or boiled maize. . . .

Miguel Venegas had an opportunity to observe the Indians at a later date in Lower California. He did not hold them in very high esteem:

¶ Of all the parts of America hitherto discovered, the Californias lie nearest to Asia. We are acquainted with the mode of writing in all the eastern nations. We can distinguish between the characters of the Japanese, the Chinese, the Chinese Tartars, the Mogul Tartars, and other nations extending as far as the bay of Kamfchathka, the learned dissertations on them . . . are to be found in the acts of the Imperial academy of sciences at Petersburg. What discovery would it be to meet with any of these characters, or others like them among the American Indians nearest Asia. But as to the Californians, if ever they were possessed of any invention to perpetuate their memoirs, they have entirely lost it; and all that is now

[3] Venegas uses this spelling for the name of the settlement throughout his narrative. It is spelled "Loreto" on today's maps.

found among them amounts to no more than some obscure oral traditions, probably more and more adulterated by a long succession of time. They have not so much as retained any knowledge of the particular country from which they emigrated; so that both Edues, or Pericues, and Cockimies or Lazmones could give no further account than they had heard their ancestors came from the north, and this might be concluded without their information, California being on all sides environed with the sea; nor can they give any account of the time when they came hither; for their stupidity and ignorance are so great, that they do not appear to have among them any means of distinguishing the years, or the intervals of time, as the Mexicans did, by means of their cycles of fifty years. . . .

. . . But be this as it may, the most probable conjecture [is] that these nations, and all others in America have passed over from Asia since the dispersion of the nations and the confusion of tongues. Tho' it may be at the same time affirmed, that hitherto there has not been found in any of the American nations on either side of the equinox, one single, authentick, and clear monument of their being originally from Asia, or of their supposed transition into America. Nor is there in the furthest parts of Asia, to which the Russians have hitherto penetrated, the least vestige, or tradition that the inhabitants had ever any communication with, or knowledge of the Americans. . . .

The characteristicks of the Californians, as well as of all other Indians, are stupidity and insensibility; want of knowledge and reflection; inconstancy, impetuosity, and blindness of appetite; and excessive sloth and abhorrence of all labour and fatigue; an incessant love of pleasure and amusement of every kind, however how trifling or brutal; pusillanimity and relaxity: and in fine, a most wretched want of every thing which constitutes the real man and renders him rational, inventive, tractable, and useful to himself and society. It is not easy for Europeans, who never were out of their own country, to conceive an adequate idea of these people. For even in the least frequented corners of the globe, there is not a nation so stupid, of such contracted ideas, and so weak both in body and mind, as the unhappy Californians. . . .

The dress throughout the whole peninsula, from Cape San Lucas to the last mission of San Ignacio, was uniform; for the males, whether children or adults, went at all times totally naked. But amidst this naked similarity, there was some diversity in the ornaments used by every nation. The Edue towards Cape San Lucas decorated their heads with strings of pearls braided with their hair: with these they interwove small feathers, the whole forming an ornament, which at a distance resembled in some measure a periwig. Those of Loretto generally wore round their waste a sightly girdle; and on their forehead a curious fillet of net work: to these some added a neckcloth with some well wrought figures of nacar: To compose this, they first detached the mother of pearl from the shell, gave it a fine polish on both sides, and by means of a flint severed it into pieces of six or eight lines in length, or two or three in breadth. At the extremities of these were small holes for forming them into a circular shape adapted to the head; the little bandlets of nacar hanging down on all sides. This kind of diadems was also anciently worn by the Southern Edues, who formed them of small white round shells, resembling pearls, and made a fine appearance. Probably this occasioned the false opinion of Sir Francis Drake, who as father Esquerer relates, believed the Indians offered him the crown and scepter of California. . . .

The women of the northern parts wore a different and meaner garment, (women in the south wore full covering short petticoat and cloak made from palm tree leaves, beated until the thread separates) being covered only from the waist to the knees; before they have a petticoat made of very thin pieces of sedge cut off at the knots, and about the size of a straw. These they fasten together with mescal threads. This petticoat, if it may be called such, hides those parts which nature has taught us to conceal, but does not defend them from the inclemencies of the weather. . . .

Venegas relates that the Indians lived in miserable dwellings and that there was an absence of pottery in their culture; even their marriage habits came under scrutiny:

¶ It is true, they stand in no need of large rooms for depositing their furniture, and the various implements of a wardrobe, for which the greatest part of the houses among us is taken up. With so little furniture and so few utensils do the Indians content themselves, that in removing, they take them all on their shoulders, for they consist of a boat, a dart, a dish, a bowl made in the shape of a high crowned hat, a bone which serves them for an awl in making it, a little piece of touchwood for kindling a fire, a pita net, in which they put their fruit and seeds, another in the shape of a purse or bag, fastened to a kind of prong across their shoulders, in which they carry their children, and lastly, their bow and arrows: to which some, who affect elegancy, add a shell for drinking. Those who live near the coast have also nets for fishing. This furniture the women carry, when they remove from one place to another: the men have only the bow and arrows with their appurtenances, as flints and feathers for the arrows, and nerves for the bows. . . .

It seems strange that they never thought of using clay for these utensils, by hardening it in the sun or fire; but nothing of this was found among them, they being totally ignorant of any such method, till they were taught it. . . . The Edues, or southern Pericues, admitted a plurality of wives, who took care of the sustenance of the family, and were very diligent in bringing to their husbands a sufficient quantity of fruits from the forest to keep them in good temper. For if once they were discarded, which depended wholly on his humour, few were found who would take them so that the more wives a husband had, he was sure to be the better provided for, a particular, which chiefly contributed to keep up this brutal custom. The nation of Loretto were something more moderate, the chief men among them never exceeding two wives, whilst the commonalty contented themselves with one. Adultery was accounted a crime which justly called for revenge, except on two occasions; one at their festivals and routs, and the other at their wrestling matches amongst the rancherias; as on these occasions it was the scandalous privilege of the victor. Among the Cochimies of the north, scarce any such excess was known: and a missionary, speaking of his district says, that amidst the unbounded freedom of these Indians, one does not see among them any debauchery or illegal amours: which he attributes to the uncomfortable life they lead among the mountains in hunger, cold, nakedness and the want of every thing desireable. . . .

The Californians had adopted that absurdity, which is so much laughed at in the accounts of Brazil, that the women after delivery, used immediately to go to some water and wash themselves and the child, and in other particulars to observe no manner of caution, going to the forest for wood and food, and performing every other service the husband wanted; whilst he in the mean time lay in his cave, or stretched at full length under a tree affecting to be extremely ill; and this farce continued for three or four days. Mothers were frequently known to destroy their children, in any scarcity of food, till the venerable father Salva-Tierra to put a stop to this unnatural practice, by ordering that a double allowance should be given to women newly delivered. It was also an established custom among them, like that in the Jewish law, for the widow to marry the brother or nearest relation of the deceased. . . .

Charlatans caused the Jesuits considerable difficulty in their effort to civilize the natives. These were the tribal priests, who exercised rigid control over their people. These also functioned as medical advisors to the ailing, who more often than not died under their administrations. Venegas cites an example of what took place when a patient was desperately ill:

¶ . . . when the distemper arrives at such a height, that herbs, juices, the chicuaco and simarron or tobacco avail nothing, they assemble all the patient's relations, that he might die with the greater uneasiness. In the first place if the patient have a daughter or sister, they cut off the little finger of the right hand, pretending thereby that the blood either saved the patient, or at least removed from the family all sorrow for his death; but was in reality an additional cause of pain and grief: then followed the visits from the whole rancheria, who after talking to him, and being acquainted with his desperate condition, set up a continued howling, sometimes covering their face with their hands and their hair, and repeating this ceremony from time to time divided into separate companies; and all in the presence of the dying person. The women increased the horror of these howlings with passionate cries and exclamations, setting forth the merits of the patient, in order to move the greater compassion. The howling being over, the patient requests the company to suck and blow him in the same manner as the physicians had done: and this last friendly office is performed by everyone; sucking and blowing first the part affected, and afterwards all the other organs of the senses with the utmost forces they are capable of, as this and the force of the cries indicated their degree of affection for the deceased. In the meantime, the doctors thrust their hands into the patient's mouth, pretending to pluck death forcibly out of his body. The women still continuing their outcries, give the patient many severe strokes, in order to awake him, till betwixt one uneasiness and another they deprive him of life: and as soon as he is found senseless they immediately proceed to bury or burn him, making no difference, but chusing the most convenient. The funerals are immediately performed without any preparations, amidst a continuance of the same howlings, and without any singularity, only burying or burning with the patient all his utensils. So little did they enquire into the reality of his death, previously to the burning or interment, that one day father Salva-Tierra, being near San Juan de Londo, and hearing the lamentations and seeing the fire, hastened to the spot, where he found them just going to burn a man, who by his motions he could perceive to have still some remains of life. He snatched him from the fire, and in time recovered him, reproving their inconsiderateness and barbarity. . . .

The efforts of the Jesuits to carry out their plans for founding a chain of settlements in Lower California encountered obstacles from the start. Supplies were constantly short, and more than one vessel was wrecked crossing the Gulf of California, whose waters are treacherous and subject to sudden storms. Charles II of Spain died, and his selection of Philip of Anjou, the grandson of Louis XIV of France, to be the next Spanish monarch, resulted in the War of Spanish Succession (1702–1713). According to Venegas, the new King of Spain "inspired new life and vigor into the languid body of the state . . . and during the first year of his rein, dispatched three warrants strongly in favour of California. . . ."

The ensuing war in Europe made it impossible to carry out the king's requests. Also, there was apathy on the part of the government in Mexico. Jealousy of various officials around the viceroy, directed against the Jesuit order, was evident as early as 1700. It was to undermine the efforts of the mission fathers in Lower California. Venegas gives some of the background:

¶ . . . not the least thing was done at Mexico in favour of the mission on his majesty's account. It is true, that this was in some measure impeded by two conquests, which the government of Mexico had undertaken with great vigor; the first was the garrison of Panzacola, on the gulf of Mexico, in the province of Florida, where it joins to Louisiana in 69 de. W. longitude, according to the famous geographer monsier d'Anville. . . . The second was that of the province of Los Texas, lying north of New Mexico. . . . In the first conquest, above a million dollars was expended in the year 1700, only Panzacola might not fall into the hands of other nations. Great advantages were also expected from the conquest of Los Texas, which was carried on without any regard to the expence. However both diverted the attention of the government from California. But the chief cause of so many delays and obstructions was jealousy, that evil which, from the beginning, has clogged all the plans of the society. . . . The former expeditions to California, though unsuccessful, had served to enrich great numbers, either by the large sums of the royal revenue, which had been expended, or by fishing and trading for pearls. The Jesuits were without any of these advantages. But the report of their being masters of California, had no sooner spread, than many of Mexico conceived and industriously gave out, that the Jesuits found great treasures there . . . the former account of the pearls strengthened these malicious reports, which were carefully disseminated among the people as powerful reasons, and cloathed with the appearance of patriotism, care of the publick money, and zeal for his majesty's service.

There was also another cause which sprung up in the very bosom of the mission, and this was the uneasiness of the captain of the garrison, Antonio Garcia de Mendoza, with whom the fatigues of his employment little agreed. But what he bore still with greater impatience was his sub-ordination to the fathers, who would not allow him to oppress the Indians, by any of those pretences, which, in other parts, have been so successfully practiced by covetousness for obtaining a sudden fortune on the ruin of those unhappy people. Accordingly about this time he wrote several letters to his friends and the viceroy, dated the 22d of October 1700, after be-stowing on the fathers Salva-Tierra and Piccolo, the titles of holy men, apostles, and cherubims, and magnifying their labour, zeal, and disinter-estedness, he inveighs against all inland expeditions, levelings of ways, planting, tilling, and other works, concluding at last "I see no other remedy for putting a stop to these romantick and rash schemes, than to give an account of them to the most reverend provincial of the society, desiring him that he would order from hence these two religious, and secure them in a place where they may receive the punishment they desire: and for my part imprison and chain me in a castle, as a warning to those that come after me, that they may not be carried away by such delusions."

Venegas related that the letter was copied and widely distributed throughout New Spain, and "cooled the hearts of many who before had cheerfully and liberally contributed to the support of the mission, [so] that it became necessary to reduce the garrison of Loreto to only twelve soldiers."

Father Salvatierra, aided by his Jesuit brother of equal tenacity, Juan Ugarte, managed to hold the colony at Loreto together, but with increasing difficulty. The Indians, observing the reduced size of the garrison, became troublesome, refusing to work. The mission was finally completed; the soil was cultivated, horse and sheep were raised, and the padres produced wine. Farming failed to provide an abundant return, and efforts to convert natives living in other areas between Mulege and La Paz achieved but moderate success. Dissatisfaction con-tinued among the soldiers at the various garrisons, who were forbidden to dive for pearls. They disregarded the orders of Father Salvatierra, and as fast as he found them engaged in this activity, he cashiered them from the service. The result was that he was soon without men to guard the new mission communities. Finally, a royal decree was issued in 1702 prohibiting the fishing for pearls, except by duly licensed parties. The king was well aware that indiscriminate diving was depriving him of his fifth of the treasure. Furthermore, no such licenses could be obtained by military personnel. Soldiers and sailors were expressly forbidden to search for pearls. For this royal order, the Jesuits earned the undying hatred of the military.

During the tenure of the Jesuits in Lower California, which lasted for seventy years, fourteen successful missions were founded on the peninsula. These were mostly in the southern section along the Gulf. Progress to the north, and particularly on the Pacific coast, was long impeded by troublesome Indians and mountainous terrain. This frontier would later be extended north to a point near San Diego, when the Dominican order was given the task of completing the colonization of Lower California by a concordat signed between their order and that of the Franciscans in 1772. Under the terms of the agreement, the Franciscans were to have control of the territory from the boundary line just below San Diego, extending northward up through the present State of California. Much of their work was eased by the geographical discoveries made by their predecessors, the Jesuits, and in particular men like Father Eusebio Kino, who had founded twenty-nine missions in Sonora and southern Arizona during his lifetime. Kino had been the first to assert that California was a peninsula along its southern section, and not an island as had long been believed. While exploring from 1687 to 1711, he had traveled over much of the Southwest. Following the Gila River to its juncture with the Colorado, Kino entered Upper California. Another friar, Juan Ugarte, made an extensive exploration of the Gulf of California in 1721, which substantiated Kino's claim, and finally, in 1746, Father Consag made another expedition over the same ground, which dispelled the myth forever.

The first galleon from Manila to stop for aid anchored off Cape San Lucas in 1734, short of water, and with many seamen ill with scurvy. The Black Robes, as the Jesuits were called, came to their assistance, as a mission was located near the cape. A rebellion broke out among the natives that same year, and two of the Jesuit fathers were brutally murdered by the Indians. The revolt was caused, according to Venegas, by the new doctrine depriving the inhabitants of their plurality of wives, and requiring them to live in a regularity and decency incompatible with their "brutish licentiousness."

The hardships of bringing the faith to such an unholy lot of savages in this barren land required men of great perseverance and stamina. At times, it was discouraging work for the most dedicated of men. Herbert E. Bolton, the California historian, relates an anecdote that typifies the attitude of those who were attempting to bring civilization to the peninsula:

¶ The last three Lower California missions were made possible by a Borgian heiress. The tale is told that when she made the gift she was asked in what country she wished the missions established. "In the most outlandish place in the world," she replied. The Jesuits consulted their atlases and returned the answer: "The most outlandish place in all the world is California." So there the new missions were planted.[4]

The Jesuit occupation of Lower California came to an end in 1767, when the order was expelled from the country by a royal decree. Gaspar de Portolá was sent to the peninsula as governor, and the last of the Black Robes were shipped into exile in February of the following year. There were many in Mexico who favored the expulsion of the Jesuits from New Spain, for the missionaries who had labored in Lower California had long been the target of criticism, particularly among the military, who spread false rumors about their activities. The Jesuits were accused of secreting pearls gathered in the waters off La Paz. They were charged with trading with foreign vessels during their occupation of the peninsula, which seems unlikely. The missions had little to barter, being barely able to produce enough to feed and clothe their Indian charges. What goods they needed were sent across the Gulf by the Pious Fund.

Officials in Mexico, however, had little to do with the final order expelling the Jesuits from New Spain. They merely carried out the

[4] Herbert E. Bolton, *Wider Horizons of American History* (New York: D. Appleton-Century Company, 1939).

king's decree. The matter was settled in Europe. To explore the reasons for the ouster of the Jesuits would require a volume in itself, for it would be necessary to trace the history of the order from the time of its founding by Ignatius Loyola in 1534. This was a period when the breach between Romanism and Protestantism was widening. Europe became separated into warring factions, as the conflict between religious ideologies became the underlying cause for numerous wars.

The Jesuits adopted the militant spirit of their founder, who had been a knight, and their influence quickly spread throughout the European continent. Whereas other church orders had neglected education, the Society was composed of scholars, who became the confidants of kings. The great discoveries in the Western Hemisphere opened new doors for converting thousands to the Catholic faith, which would offset the losses the Church was suffering by the Protestant Reformation. Jesuits were sent into every corner of the world—China, India, South America, and Mexico. Members of the order from France settled in Canada, establishing missions along the St. Lawrence River and at Hudson Bay. When Sir George Calvert settled Maryland in 1634 as a haven for persecuted Catholics, Jesuit missionaries accompanied him. Members of the order had been in Mexico as early as 1571, and from here they extended their activities through the states of Durango, Chihuahua, Sinaloa, and Sonora. Their explorations paved the way for future settlements in Arizona and New Mexico, where they were among the first to venture into the vast region of the American Southwest, which was inhabited by nomadic savages, who among all the Indians of North America were later to prove the most difficult to subdue.

By the middle of the eighteenth century, the Jesuit order had acquired many enemies in Europe, a number of whom were in high positions in the governments of various nations. Envy was the paramount reason, though one would have to be quite naïve to wonder how a religious order dedicated to the salvation of men's souls could arouse the jealousy of true Christians—particularly those who supported the Roman Catholic Church. The truth is that by the eighteenth century the Jesuits had progressed far from the period when their primary purpose was to gather converts for the faith. By now they had large mercantile interests and extensive landholdings. The Society engaged in trade, and it was this that proved its undoing, for enemies of the order claimed that the Jesuits were secretively amassing wealth to the detriment of private enterprise, as well as defrauding the royal treasuries of their just share.

The greatest antagonist of the Jesuits was the Portuguese Minister of State, Sebastião José de Carvalho e Mello, who acquired in 1770 the title of Marquis of Pombal, by which he is best known in history. Pombal began his attacks on the order in 1757, by obtaining the support of the Portuguese king, Joseph I, in promulgating a number of measures to suppress Jesuit power, particularly in Portuguese dominions. He charged the Jesuits had hoarded great quantities of mineral wealth in Brazil, and that Portuguese citizens were refused the right to acquire land in their own colony. Brazil was the first quarter in the New World where Pombal struck. Following the partition by Spain and Portugal of certain lands along the Uruguay River in Brazilian territory, he had attempted to displace the Indian residents and seize control of several gold and silver mines. Pombal believed that the Jesuits had been secretly working them. The mines proved nonexistent, and the infuriated minister began a campaign of vilification against the order. He circulated his accusations in pamphlets that were widely distributed. In September, 1757, his efforts began to show results. The King of Portugal dismissed his Jesuit confessor, and other members of the order were banished from his court. Pombal continued his denunciations in Rome, where he succeeded in having Pope Benedict XIV issue an order forbidding the Jesuit order from engaging in trade.

On September 3, 1758, the Portuguese ruler was shot and slightly wounded while returning in the royal carriage from a tryst with one of his paramours. The incident gave Pombal added ammunition. He pursued an investigation to discover the would-be assassin relentlessly. A number of the nobility fell into his net, together with seven Jesuits. They were publicly executed, and the king was firmly convinced that the Jesuit order had been responsible for the attempt upon his life. He ordered their lands confiscated.

Pombal now turned his attention to France and Spain. Louis XV was inclined to be tolerant, but the greatest French enemy of the order was his mistress, Madame de Pompadour. By 1764, the king had signed a decree expelling the Jesuits from France and its dominions. The destruction of the order in Spain proved more difficult, for here the Society had the support of the people. However, there were enough ministers in the government who hated the Jesuits to bring about the final ruin of the religious order. They convinced the Spanish monarch, Charles III, that the order was plotting an insurrection against him after riotings had occurred in various provinces caused by those disillusioned with his reign. Charles signed an order banishing Jesuits from all parts of his realm in February, 1767. He never divulged his reasons, and when Pope Clement XIII tried to intercede, the monarch refused to discuss the matter. Secret orders were dispatched to all corners of the empire. The missionaries were placed aboard ships, which carried them into exile. Many were sent to Rome, but the Papal States were already crowded with nearly 4,000 Jesuits who had been expelled from Portugal. Pope Clement found a refuge for the Spanish friars on the island of Corsica. Their stay there was brief, for in 1768 Corsica became a French possession, and the Jesuits were promptly banished from the island. A haven was finally located in the provinces of northern Italy. Some of these exiles lived to see the final vindication of their order, when in 1814 Pius VII issued a Bull of Restoration authorizing the surviving members to live once more according to the rules set down by Loyola, to found colleges, and accept novitiates into the order long known as the Society of Jesus.

ABOVE: California Indians dressed and painted for a ceremonial dance. BELOW: California Indian girl, late eighteenth century. (*Pictures: State Library, Sacramento*)

An Indian funeral in California. The dead were burned with all their possessions.
(State Library, Sacramento)

Juan Rodríguez Cabrillo, who entered the harbor of San Diego on September 28, 1542, marking the formal discovery of California for the Spanish Crown. *(State Library, Sacramento)*

Antonio de Mendoza, the first Viceroy of New Spain. While he was in power, expeditions were sent out to search for the mythical Seven Cities of Cibola and the kingdom of Quivira. *(Authors' collection)*

Sir Francis Drake, who challenged Spain's authority in the Pacific by raiding her possessions and seizing Spanish vessels along the Pacific coast. *(Bancroft Library, University of California, Berkeley)*

ABOVE: Sir Francis Drake's ship, the *Golden Hind,* in Drake's Bay, north of San Francisco, where the English landed in 1579. Drake called the land Nova Albion, because the terrain reminded him of his native Devonshire. BELOW:. The famed plate of brass, now in the Bancroft Library, which Drake ordered nailed to a post when he took possession of California in 1579. The hole at lower right is where a sixpence bearing the Queen's likeness was inserted. The coin was missing when the plate was found. *(Pictures: By permission of the Director, Bancroft Library, University of California, Berkeley)*

The Monterey Peninsula, with its grove of cypress trees, is considered one of the most beautiful sections of the California coast. Charted by Vizcaíno, later found by Portolá, and finally settled by colonists who came with De Anza, Monterey became the capital of Spanish California. *(Photo by Jo Ella York Murphy)*

José de Gálvez arrived in Mexico in 1761 as Inspector General. Basing his report on intelligence he received, he advised the Spanish government to colonize California to forestall Great Britain and Russia. Gálvez was convinced that both of these nations coveted Spain's neglected possession along the Pacific coast. (*State Library, Sacramento*)

ABOVE LEFT: Juan Bautista de Anza, who led the first Spanish colonists overland to found San Francisco. The picture was drawn from an oil portrait painted by Fray Orsi in 1774. ABOVE RIGHT: Don Gaspar de Portolá and his party as they discover San Francisco Bay. From a painting by Walter Francis. (*Pictures: By permission of the Director, Bancroft Library, University of California, Berkeley*)

The Mission of San Fernando Rey de España at Los Angeles, which was founded on September 8, 1797, by Padre-Presidente Fermín de Lasuén. In the foreground is a statue of Father Junípero Serra, founder of the first nine missions in the chain of twenty-one. Father Lasuén was his successor. During the early nineteenth century the mission supplied tallow, soap, hides, cloth, wine, olive oil, and other products to various missions and presidios. *(Photo by William S. Murphy)*

The Mission of La Purísima Concepción is located near the rural community of Lompoc, north of Santa Barbara. It was established on December 2, 1787, and was the eleventh mission founded in Alta California. Restored, it is today a state park, and attracts thousands of visitors. *(Photo by William S. Murphy)*

ABOVE: Typical dress of the Mexican period. The rancher was fond of colorful garments, and the sash and cape gave him a swashbuckling appearance. Bridles and saddles were often richly trimmed with silver. BELOW: "The Man of Property and His Major Domo." From pictures in the Don Antonio Coronel Collection in the Los Angeles County Museum of Natural History.

The Mexican *vaquero* was the finest horseman of his time. This was the pastoral era in California when cattle grazed across the hills as far as the eye could see. *(Los Angeles County Museum of Natural History)*

Capturing bears was a popular sport in early California. These were matched against equally ferocious bulls in mortal combat, while the spectators wagered on which animal would be the victor. *(State Library, Sacramento)*

A *rodeo,* or roundup of cattle, during the Mexican period. In the background is the Mission San Gabriel Arcángel, founded on September 8, 1771, as a way station en route to the new colony at Monterey. Ten years later, on September 4, 1781, Don Felipe de Neve, governor of California, left this mission with a party of emigrants to establish a new townsite nine miles to the west. This was to become the future city of Los Angeles. *(State Library, Sacramento)*

George Vancouver, the British navigator, who arrived in San Francisco Bay in November, 1792. He later recorded his impressions of California in his book, *A Voyage of Discovery*. *(State Library, Sacramento)*

Richard Henry Dana, who served as a sailor aboard the brig *Pilgrim*, which arrived on the California coast in 1835 to trade for hides. His account of the voyage, *Two Years Before the Mast*, provides one of the best available descriptions of life in California during the era. *(State Library, Sacramento)*

The rolling, hilly region inland from Santa Barbara remains agricultural
today and has changed little since the days of the great Mexican ranchos. Scenes
such as this are typical of the quiet beauty of the countryside.
(Photos by William S. Murphy)

OPPOSITE: The Mission Santa Barbara, founded December 4, 1786, by Father
Fermín Francisco de Lasuén. Today it serves as a Franciscan theological seminary,
and houses the archives of the California missions.

ABOVE: Emigrants bound for California are depicted camping on the plains following a day of travel, in this contemporary print. RIGHT: John Bidwell, California pioneer who arrived in 1841 with an overland party. He became a prominent citizen following statehood, acquiring extensive land holdings in northern California. (*Pictures: State Library, Sacramento*) OPPOSITE: Dana Point on the coast of southern California, south of Laguna Beach. The brig *Pilgrim* anchored off shore in 1835, and from the top of these cliffs, Dana tossed hides brought from the Mission San Juan Capistrano to crew members waiting below. (*Photo by William S. Murphy*)

A VIEW from the SUMMIT of INDEPENDENCE ROCK.
exhibiting the Sweet-water river and Mountains, and
the Washington City Comp.y corralled, at noon,
July 26, 1849.

A view from the summit of Independence Rock, showing the Sweetwater River and mountains in the background. Joseph Goldsborough Bruff made this drawing in Wyoming as the Washington City and California Gold Mining Assocation made camp. This was a group of 64 members, determined to make their fortunes in the newly discovered gold regions of California. The wagons have gathered in a circle for the night, as protection against Indian attack, while at right, across the river, sentries watch over the grazing beef herd that accompanied the caravan. *(Reproduced from the original in the Henry E. Huntington Library and Art Gallery, San Marino, Calif.)*

4

THE FIRST SETTLEMENTS
IN CALIFORNIA

The Spanish government began its long-delayed conquest of California in 1769, when José de Gálvez, the king's *visitador-general* in Mexico, launched a combined sea and land expedition that had as its primary mission the establishment of a line of defense along the Pacific to protect the Crown's holdings from seizure by a foreign power. Vizcaíno's charts, which had been locked away for more than 150 years, were studied, and the port of Monterey, which Vizcaíno had so glowingly described, was selected by Gálvez as the most important point for the establishment of a presidio on the coast of California. Unfortunately, it was to prove difficult for the explorers to find.

Much has been written about why the Spanish government was jolted into an accelerated program of exploration and settlement in California after such a long period of inactivity. The fear of Russian expansion has been generally seen by historians as the motivation for this sudden march north into Alta California. The Russians' activities in the northern Pacific were well known. Vitus Bering, a Dane in the Russian service, had sailed from Kamchatka in 1728 to determine once for all whether Asia and North America were joined together. He clarified this point on future maps, and in 1741 returned with another Russian explorer to the Bering Sea, where they discovered Alaska. A fur trade developed along the Alaskan coast, and the Spaniards knew that it was only a matter of time before the Russians would move southward toward California. According to the intelligence that Gálvez received, that time was now imminent. He therefore formulated his plans for an expedition that would leave Lower California, move north, and locate the port of Monterey.

Marquis Francisco de Croix, the viceroy in Mexico, had received a report from the Spanish Minister of State expressing fear that the Russians already had landed somewhere in North America. "The king has ordered me," the letter read, "to inform Your Excellency of all that has just been set forth, so that you may make it known to the man appointed governor of California, giving him instructions about the vigilance and care that he ought to exercise in order to observe such attempts as the Russians may make there, frustrating them if possible, so that you may report it to His Majesty."

Croix immediately sent this news to Gálvez, causing him to hasten his preparations for an early departure. Gálvez had a remarkable ability for organization. He was meticulous, overlooking no detail in obtaining the necessary supplies for his expedition, even if it meant requisitioning a good quantity from the missions of Lower California. A former Madrid lawyer, Gálvez had been sent to Mexico to seek a method for increasing legal revenues. The new *visitador* had personality traits usually associated with men who are excessively ambitious. He was vain, hot-tempered, and adept at winning the support of those in a position to advance his career. Gálvez was also a remarkable leader, who accomplished the tasks to which he was assigned. As such, he proved the best choice for extending Spain's frontiers at a time when she was making a final bid to maintain her colonial empire in North America.

The Russian threat to California in 1768 has been exaggerated. Actually, in 1768, Russia's Catherine the Great (1762–1796) had numerous problems to occupy her attention. She had succeeded her husband, the ineffectual Tsar Peter III, by having him forcibly deposed. The tsar was strangled, allegedly at his wife's instigation. One of her achievements was to put a former lover on the throne of Poland. In 1768, her meddling in Polish affairs brought about a war with Turkey, where Polish political refugees had fled for sanctuary, only to be pursued within Turkish borders, and arrested.

The real danger to Spanish security in this hemisphere was Great Britain, just as it was her Hudson's Bay Company which would prove a far greater threat to California in the early 1800's by its commercial activities in the Pacific Northwest, than the little colony of Russians struggling to make a success of their settlement.

The English had long had an interest in the Pacific from the time of Drake, Cavendish, and Woodes Rogers. There were other expeditions. In 1740, Commodore George Anson was sent on a predatory four-year cruise by the British Admiralty to attack Spanish possessions in the Pacific. Anson sacked one Peruvian town, missed a galleon off the Mexican coast, but managed to waylay a valuable prize in the Philippines. The British author Arthur Dobbs, writing at about this same time, argued that the Pacific offered untold possibilities for British trade. He attacked the Hudson's Bay Company's lack of initiative in not searching for a northwest passage into the Pacific, which under its charter agreement with the government, the company was obligated to do. Dobbs argued for British bases in the North Pacific, preferably near California, from which to conduct further explorations.

The conclusion of The Seven Years' War (1756–1763), known in America as the French and Indian War, marked the end of French colonial power in this hemisphere. Under the terms of the Peace of Paris, signed February 10, 1763, France ceded to England all Canada, including Nova Scotia, or Acadia, Cape Breton and all other islands in the gulf and river of St. Lawrence, as well as the harbor of Mobile.

Spain also sacrificed considerable territory, relinquishing to Great Britain Florida, and all her other territories east of the Mississippi. As a concession, the British restored to the Spaniards Cuba, which they had seized in 1762, the same year their forces sacked Manila and gained control of the Philippines. This territory was also returned to the Spanish government under the terms of the treaty. Britain had now become the most powerful nation in the world. During this same period, after defeating French forces, England had added India to an ever-growing empire, which also included thirteen colonies on the North American continent.

British explorations in the Pacific were accelerated following the conclusion of the Seven Years' War. Commodore John Byron sailed from England in 1764 with two ships, the *Dolphin* and the *Tamar*. The vessels passed through the Strait of Magellan, setting their course for the South Pacific. This was not a voyage in search of plunder, but one to obtain geographical knowledge. Three months after Byron returned to England, his ship the *Dolphin* was again under way, this time under the command of Captain Samuel Wallis. Two other ships from which the *Dolphin* was later separated took part in the expedition. On this voyage, Wallis found the most romantic island in eastern Polynesia, if not in the entire Pacific—Otaheite, known today as Tahiti. A sister ship, the *Swallow,* which the *Dolphin* had lost contact with, was making additional discoveries. Her captain, Philip Carteret, could add one new landmark to his chart, later destined to play its part in English maritime history—Pitcairn Island. Carteret also made important discoveries in the vicinity of New Guinea.

On August 23, 1768, Captain James Cook sailed from Plymouth in command of the *Endeavour* on the first of several voyages that were to contribute much to the understanding of the geography of vast unknown regions of the world. On this expedition, Cook circled New Zealand and examined the eastern coast of Australia, charting these lands for the benefit of future explorers. It was a time for Spain to rouse itself from its lethargy. The entire Pacific was in danger of slipping from its grasp.

Against this background of international events, the vanguard of Gálvez' expedition arrived in Lower California prepared to begin the quest for Monterey.

*   *   *

Among those gathering in Lower California to prepare the expedition bound for the north was Father Junípero Serra, president of the

Franciscan missions in California, the order which succeeded the ousted Jesuits. He listed the names of those who would lead the various parties when they departed from Loreto:

¶ . . . Don Gaspar de Portolá, Captain of Dragoons, and Governor of California; and second the Captain of said Presidio, Don Fernando Rivera y Moncada—the latter in the first division of Soldiers of the Presidio, to the number of 29; the former with ten leather-jacket Soldiers. They undertook the journey by order of His Majesty (whom God guard) Don Carlos Third. Said expedition was under the protection of St. Joseph.[1]

In addition to the two parties that would march overland, two vessels carrying men and supplies were ready to sail. Serra wrote:

¶ . . . on the 6th day of January of the same year, finding myself in the Port of La Paz with his Eminence the Senor Inspector, I blessed the packet named the "San Carlos," sang Mass aboard her, blessed the Standards; the Litany was sung, and other devotions to Our Lady. And His Eminence made a fervent exhortation with which he kindled the spirits of those who were to go in that vessel to said Ports of San Diego and Montte Rey. These embarked on the 9th, at night, and on the 10th set sail. The Commandant determined upon for the Expedition by sea was Don Vicente Vila, a Pilot famed on the Seas of Europe; the Engineer, Don Miguel Costansó; Chief of the troops of (25 men with the Lieutenant, 26) Don Pedro Fages, Lieutenant of the Company of Catalonian Volunteers. And for Missionary of the Expedition, and for one of the Missions, I fixed upon the Father Preacher Fray Fernando Parron, who had been my companion in Loreto since we arrived in California. And all together they set forth joyfully on the said day of January. . . .

Serra performed the same blessing on the packet *San Antonio,* or *El Principe,* as it was also called. This ship left Cape San Lucas, Lower California, February 15, 1769, managing to arrive in San Diego nineteen days before her sister ship, which ran into adverse winds trying to beat its way up the coast. Aboard the *San Antonio,* Miguel Costansó kept a daily journal of the voyage. A condensed account was published in Mexico in 1770. This was printed in a limited edition, but

[1] This translation from documents in the Spanish archives was published in *Out West* magazine, March, 1902.

a copy was obtained by Alexander Dalrymple, an eminent British hydrographer, who published Costansó's account as a segment of his *An Historical Journal of the Expeditions by Sea and Land to the North of California; In 1768, 1769, and 1770.* The book was printed in 1790. Dalrymple writes in his introduction that he received, in 1783, from an acquaintance, the Spanish manuscript which he had translated into English. He also stated that he knew who the author was, but for some reason he did not give the name. This was outright plagiarism. To set the record straight after more than 175 years, the author was Miguel Costansó. This is his account of the landing at San Diego:

¶ The *San Antonio* having sailed a month after the *San Carlos* had the good luck to make her passage in 59 days, and arrived at San Diego on the 11th of April; but half the crew were equally infected with the Scurvy, having lost also two men in that distemper: in the midst of these troubles there was great joy at their meeting. After mooring the *San Carlos* in a convenient place, the attention of the officers was immediately applied to the care of the sick. The first business was to look out for a watering place, in order to fill the casks with good water for the use of the people; for which purpose, on the 1st of May, the officers, Don Pedro Fages, Don Miguel Costansó, and the second captain of the *San Carlos*, Don Jorge Estorace, with the soldiers and sailors that were most able to undergo the labour, to the number of twenty-five men, disembarked, and keeping the western shore of the port, discovered, at a little distance, a company of Indians armed with bows and arrows, to whom they made signs with a white flag, calling them to make peace; but the Indians measuring their pace by that of our people, would not suffer us to get nearer them, for more than half an hour, neither could our men get on faster, as they had, by being such a long time on board, in some measure lost the use of their legs. The Indians stopped now and then, upon some height, to observe our people, and plainly shewing signs of fear of the strangers, though they seemed to endeavor to hide it. They placed one end of their bows on the ground, and taking the other end in their hand, they danced, turning round with incredible celerity; but on the approach of our men they fled with the same swiftness. At length we contrived to draw near them, by sending a single soldier, who laying his arms upon the ground, and using gestures of peace, was permitted to approach them. He made them some presents, while the rest of our men were coming up, who also recommended themselves by presents of ribbands, beads and toys, asking them by signs where water might be got.

The Indians then making signs towards a wood, at a distance to the NE, gave them to understand that there was a river, or brook, and that they would shew it them. . . . The face of the country was pleasant, and the lands near the banks of the river seemed to be an excellent soil, and capable of producing all sorts of fruits. The river came from very high mountains, in a spacious channel which turned to the east and NE; and about a musket shot from it, towards the mountains, they saw a town, or *Rancheria,* of the Indians, which appeared to be composed of branches of trees, and huts in a pyramidal form, covered with earth. At the sight of their friends, with the company they brought, all the people, men, women and children, came out, inviting the guests to their houses. The women were decently cloathed in their manner, being covered from the waist to the knees with thick nets doubled. The Spaniards entered the town, which contained from thirty to forty families. On one side of it was observed an inclosure, made with boughs and trunks of trees, in which they gave us to understand, they took shelter from their enemies when attacked—a fortification impregnable to such arms as were in use among them.

These natives are of a good size, well made and active; they go naked, without any other cloathing than a girdle, like a net, of *Ixtlé* or very fine *Pita,* which they get from a plant called *Lechuguilla*; their quivers, which they stick between the girdle and the body, are made of wild-cat, coyote, wolf, or deer skins; their bows are two yards long. Besides these arms they use a sort of Macana of very hard wood, the form of which is very like a short and crooked sabre, this they throw at a distance, cutting the air with great violence; they can send it farther than a stone, and never go into the fields without it; if they meet with a viper or other noxious animal they throw their Macana at it, and generally divide it in two pieces, as the Spaniards saw during their intercourse with them: in their nature they are proud, rude in manners, avaricious, great jokers and boasters, though of little courage. They make great account of their strength, and esteem the strongest man the bravest. They are eager for any rags; but after cloathing many of them, on different occasions, the next day they always appeared naked. . . .

The principal food of the Indians that inhabit the shore of this port is fish; they eat much shell-fish, upon the account of the ease with which they gather them. They use boats made of flags, which they manage dextrously with paddles, or oars with two blades; their fish-gigs are of wood, long and pointed with very sharp bone, let into the wood; they are so dextrous in throwing them, that they rarely miss their mark. . . .[2]

Captain Fernando Rivera y Moncada arrived in San Diego on May 14 with the vanguard of the land expedition. They began work on establishing the first colony in Upper California. Costansó described the small settlement:

¶ Near the beach, toward the Eastern part, a small inclosure was made, with a parapet of earth and fascines, which was mounted with two guns, and some of the sails and awnings were landed, with which two large tents were made for an hospital; they put on one side their things, the two officers, the missionaries and the surgeon; and everything being in order to receive the sick, they were brought on shore in the boats, and accommodated in the rooms as conveniently as they could be.

These attentions were not however sufficient to restore their health, medicines and fresh provisions were wanting, being almost entirely consumed during the voyage. The surgeon supplied the want of them, as well as he could, with certain herbs that he searched for with great trouble in the fields, the virtues of which were known to him, and of which he stood in need himself, as much as the sick, finding he was almost overcome with the same distemper as themselves. The cold was felt severely at night in the barracks, and the sun by day; changes which caused the sick to suffer extremely, two or three dying every day, so that the number appointed for the expedition, which was originally more than ninety men, was reduced to only eight soldiers, and as many sailors, in condition to attend to the preservation of the vessels, the management of the boats, and the care of the block-house and the sick. . . .

Don Gaspar de Portolá, the new governor, rode into San Diego with the advance guard of the second land party on June 29th. On July 1, the rest of the expedition reached the settlement. Father Serra accompanied the group. Plans were made for the march north to Monterey, which was commenced on July 14, when Portolá departed with a small company of soldiers, Indians and mule packers. Among them were Lieutenant Pedro Fages, Father Juan Crespi, and Miguel

[2] Alexander Dalrymple, *An Historical Journal of the Expeditions by Sea and Land to the North of California; In 1768, 1769, and 1770* (London: Published by Dalrymple, 1790).

Costansó, the cosmographer and engineer. Father Serra stayed with the remaining members of the party at San Diego, where he founded the first of a chain of twenty-one missions established in Upper California by the Franciscan order. Costansó provided a vivid picture of the Spanish men-at-arms on the march:

¶ The soldiers of the garrison of California, justice and equity oblige us to say, went through infinite labour in the expedition. They make use of two sorts of arms, offensive and defensive; the defensive are a buff-coat and the target; the first of which is made in the fashion of a cassock without sleeves; it is composed of six or seven layers of skins of deer pressed together, and impenetrable to the arrows of the Indians, unless shot from a very small distance. The target has on both sides the raw hide of a bull; it is worn on the left arm, and with it, either clubs or arrows are parried. The horseman defends both himself and his horse; he uses, besides the above, a sort of apron of Neat's leather, hung to the pummel of the saddle, with a fall on each side called arms or fenders, which covers his thighs and legs to save them from hurt when passing through woods. Their offensive arms are the lance, which they manage very dextrously on horseback, the broad-sword, and a short gun which they carry generally in its case.

They are men of great strength, capable of bearing great fatigue, obedient, resolute, nimble, and, we have no doubt in saying, the best horsemen in the world, and the sort of soldiers that best earn and deserve the pay of the August Monarch they serve.

The Portolá party encountered numerous Indians as they walked north. All proved friendly. Many of the sites where the Spaniards camped would later become the leading cities of California. Los Angeles was reached, and so named on August 2 for the feast day of Our Lady of the Angels of Porciuncúla. Ventura, Santa Barbara, and San Luis Obispo were all locales where Portolá and his men built their fires and rested from the day's march. Names were given to these places either to represent a saint, or an incident which had taken place. Gaviota Pass was so called because the soldiers had killed a seagull there. Near San Luis Obispo, a number of bears were sighted. This became Canada de los Osos, and so on. It took three months to reach Monterey, and although Portolá viewed it from a vantage point along the Point of Pines; he failed to recognize it from Vizcaíno's description. The confusion is understandable, for Vizcaíno had referred to the location as "Puerto Monterey." This gave the impression that it would be an enclosed harbor similar to San Diego, instead of an open bay.

Portolá continued north. On November 2, Sergeant José Francisco Ortega sighted inner San Francisco Bay while leading a hunting party in the adjacent mountains. Portolá decided to return to San Diego, as his supplies were exhausted. His tired party reached the new mission Father Serra had established overlooking San Diego Bay on January 24, 1770. Portolá, as evidence indicates, had little interest in the California project, for following completion of his assignment he sailed to Mexico, disappearing from the pages of history—but not before he finished his mission. He was too dedicated a soldier to prove himself a failure in the eyes of his king.

Portolá left San Diego with a new expedition to find the elusive Monterey on April 17, 1770. This time he was successful. He was able to recognize the points that Vizcaíno had described, which he had been unable to do on his former visit. The *San Antonio* sailed from San Diego the day before the departure of the land party to assist in the search. Aboard were Serra and Miguel Costansó. The ship arrived at Monterey on May 31, seven days after the land party had established a base there. Costansó recorded it in his journal:

¶ In this place, according to order, a fort was built, and a Mission established; which was named the Mission of San Carlos; every one cooperating with equal diligence and solicitude, soldiers and sailors, with their respective officers, in the humble beginning of that important settlement; in which were included the particular conveniencies allotted for the Missions, and garrison of the Fort; and the other parts were then marked out, which were to be erected in the future. They then housed the cargo of the packet-boat, and the commandant Don Gaspar de Portolá, resolved to embark in it, with the Engineer Don Miguel Costansó, leaving the command to the Lieutenant of infantry, Don Pedro Fages, as was ordered in his instructions; and, to assist the soldiers in their labours, they left a reinforcement of nine sailors at Monterey.

The *San Antonio* sailed from that port on the 9th July, 1770, and arrived happily at San Blas the 1st August; and the other packet-boat the *San*

Carlos having afterwards arrived at the same port, returning from San Diego, both prepared to proceed on another voyage, in the next month of November, to conduct separately, by the Gulf of California, and by the South Sea, Thirty Missionarys, with a plentiful stock of provisions, cloths, necessaries and ornaments, to provide for the new settlements of San Diego and Monterey, with their respective Missions, and to establish others in the fruitful countries that were traversed by the people of the Land Expedition, from Velicata to the Port of San Francisco, situated in 37° 45′ N. Latitude.

Thus have the desired establishments of San Diego and Monterey had their successful beginnings, and thus may we flatter ourselves that the new Missions, yet to be founded, may encrease, under the protection and auspices of his Excellency the Marquis de Croix, Viceroy, Governor and Captain General of this extensive Empire, whose mild government the subjects applaud, and the towns are grateful: This enterprise, desired for so many years, begun many times with great preparations and expences, will undoubtedly be pleasing to the august Monarch of Spain, whose magnaminous spirit and religious piety, Heaven rewards, by raising in his kingdom great and illustrious men, in every station, Ecclesiastical, Military and Politick; who contend equally in executing the great charges committed to their eminent capacity and talents, never better employed than in the propagation of the Gospel, and the publick felicity of his loyal and beloved Vassals.

Mexico,
October the 24th, 1770

From his presidio at Monterey, Captain Pedro Fages began to explore the surrounding country, accompanied by Father Juan Crespi. In November, 1770, they traveled through the Santa Clara Valley, finally reaching the eastern shore of San Francisco Bay. It is known that they camped somewhere in present-day Alameda, thus becoming the first Spanish exploration party to view San Francisco Bay from its inland side. Mariners had known of its existence for some time, but had never ventured through the Golden Gate.

The Franciscans under Father Serra immediately began work to extend the mission chain. On July 14, 1771, the site for San Antonio de Padua, the third to be founded, was marked out by him in a remote area of Monterey County in the Santa Lucia Mountains near the Salinas River. It is said that Serra had the bells hung in trees, which rang repeatedly as he called out to unseen Indians to come and accept the faith. Soon natives began to gather. They brought pine-nuts and acorns as a token of their friendliness. The padres gave them glass beads in exchange. A church and living quarters were erected with the aid of the Indians. A small community soon developed adjacent to the adobe-walled mission. In time, thousands of cattle grazed in the vicinity. The Mission San Antonio de Padua became noted for the superb stock of horses bred there.

San Gabriel Arcángel, a landmark near Los Angeles today, was founded on September 8, 1771, and the following year Captain Fages left Monterey with Father Crespi for another survey of the San Francisco Bay area. Their route carried them through the Salinas, San Juan Bautista and Santa Clara valleys, pausing in the localities where the cities of Berkeley and Richmond are now located. Before returning to the presidio at Monterey, they became the first white men to view the fertile San Joaquin and Sacramento valleys. In that same year, a royal decree divided the jurisdiction of Upper and Lower California between two missionary orders. The Franciscans would administer the upper region, present-day California, and the Dominican order assumed the responsibility for Baja California, a part of present Mexico. Father Serra also founded the mission San Luis Obispo de Tolosa that year, and then in October sailed for Mexico to settle a jurisdictional argument that had developed between his order and the Dominicans. He persuaded the viceroy, Antonio María Bucareli y Ursúa, to send an overland party from Mexico to California. This resulted in the first expedition of Juan Bautista de Anza, who brought his company from Sonora to San Gabriel Mission near Los Angeles, arriving there on March 22, 1774. Continuing north, De Anza reached Monterey on May 1. Serra also succeeded in having Fages removed as governor, as the two had already clashed. It was the beginning of an endless period of friction between the Franciscan fathers and the military government in California, as the two factions disputed each other's claim to authority. The conflict had a sad outcome, as it brought about the secularization and complete destruction of the mission system, when the Mexican government assumed Spain's role as the supreme political power in California.

The selection of Juan Bautista de Anza as captain of the overland expedition to California was a wise choice. He was an officer of exceptional ability and long experience in dealing with the Indian tribes along the frontiers of New Spain. So eager was Anza to undertake the assignment, he volunteered to defray the costs for supplies and equipment. The offer was declined, the king ordering royal funds made available for the venture. The plan approved by the viceroy was for Anza to make an initial survey of the route as far as Monterey, then return to Sonora and escort a party of settlers to California. Accordingly, he left Tubac, Mexico, on January 8, 1774, with a company of twenty soldiers. They were attacked by Apaches, a number of horses being stolen. This failed to halt Anza. The march north from Sonora into Arizona traversed a desert trail long known as the Camino del Diablo, which was later to be marked by the mounds of hundreds of Americans who perished while trying to reach California along this southerly route in their efforts to avoid Apache war parties roaming the routes farther north.

It required a month for Anza to reach the junction of the Gila and the Colorado rivers near present-day Yuma. Here, his long experience in dealing with the Indians came in to good advantage. Anza found an ally in Palma, chief of the Yumas, whose men assisted the Spaniards in crossing the Colorado. The expedition began its march across the desert, a barren terrain of rolling sand dunes and little water. The absence of wells caused Anza to return to Yuma, where he left most of his pack animals and supplies under a small guard with the Indians. Lightened and trimmed for a fast march, the party made a second venture into the unknown Colorado Desert. They entered California near the site of present-day Calexico. From here, the trail led through Borrego Springs, the Hemet and San Jacinto region, finally ending at San Gabriel Mission on March 22nd. Anza's party was given a warm welcome, for the mission padres and garrison had been on short rations for weeks, welcoming any provisions that the visitors could spare. The march was resumed, the party following the Los Angeles River into the San Fernando Valley. Continuing north, they reached Monterey on April 18th. Anza wasted little time at the presidio. After conferring with Don Pedro Fages, the commandante of California, he was ready to return to Mexico by April 22nd. Six of the soldiers from the Monterey presidio joined his party. Near Santa Barbara they encountered Father Junípero Serra, who had just returned from the Mexican capital. Camp was made for the night in order that Anza and the tireless Franciscan could exchange information and coordinate plans for the future settlement of California. Anza reached Tubac on May 27th, and the recruiting of colonists to found the future city of San Francisco began immediately.

*   *   *

Anza assembled his colonists, mostly destitute families living in Sinaloa. The recruits left Horcasistas on October 23, 1775. There were 240 in the company, and most of the soldiers were accompanied by their wives and children. Three were born during the journey. The procession moved at a slow pace, for more than a thousand cattle were being driven along the trail for them to subsist on, and also form the nucleus for the huge herds that would someday graze across the hills and valleys of California. Another smaller party of settlers under Captain Don Fernando de Rivera y Moncada had sailed for Baja California earlier, reaching San Diego in September, 1774. Rivera had been selected to succeed Fages as the military commandant. Almost from the beginning he clashed over policy with Anza.

On January 4, 1776, Anza reached San Gabriel Mission, learning there that the Indians of San Diego had revolted the prior November, killing one of the mission fathers and two of the soldiers. Taking a detachment of thirty-five men, he hurried south to the presidio. Luckily, it had been reinforced, and Rivera's garrison was in complete control of the San Diego region. Anza returned to San Gabriel, gathered his settlers, and continued on to San Francisco, first pausing at Monterey, where some of the people expressed a desire to remain. In Anza's party was Father Pedro Font, who kept a journal of the 1,600-mile trip from Mexico to California. Leaving Monterey on a March day in 1776, Font accompanied Anza and a small detachment, which rode north to explore San Francisco Bay. He recorded his impressions as the group viewed the magnificent panorama reaching out for miles before them. For the first time the magnitude of the discovery seems to have had an impact upon one of the Spaniards who viewed it:

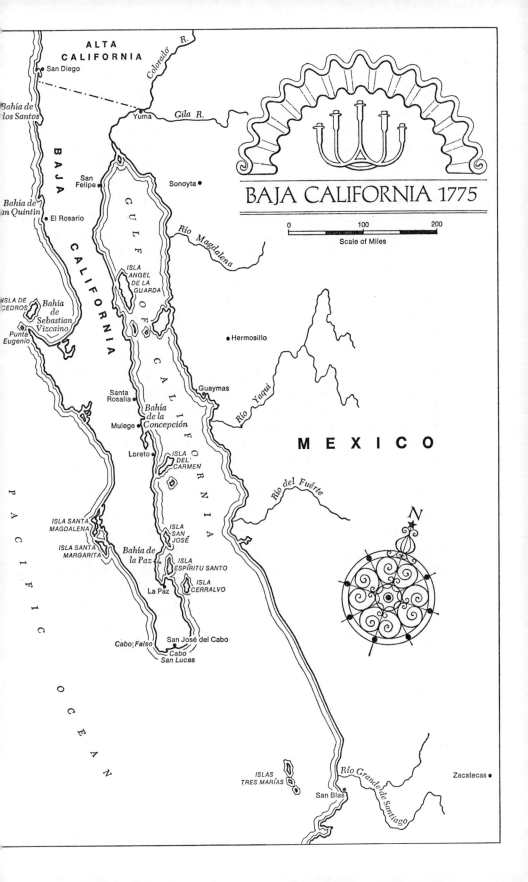

ALTA CALIFORNIA

San Diego

Bahía de
los Santos

Colorado R.

Yuma

Gila R.

BAJA CALIFORNIA

San Felipe

Sonoyta

Bahía de
n Quintin

El Rosario

Río Magdalena

BAJA CALIFORNIA 1775

0   100   200
Scale of Miles

GULF OF CALIFORNIA

ISLA
ANGEL
DE LA
GUARDA

ISLA DE
CEDROS

Bahía
de
Sebastian
Vizcaino

Punta
Eugenio

Hermosillo

Santa
Rosalia

Guaymas

Río Yaqui

Bahía
de la
Concepción

Mulege

MEXICO

Loreto

ISLA
DEL
CARMEN

Río del Fuérte

ISLA SANTA
MAGDALENA

ISLA
SAN
JOSÉ

ISLA SANTA
MARGARITA

Bahía de
la Paz

ISLA
ESPÍRITU SANTO

La Paz

ISLA
CERRALVO

N

PACIFIC

Cabo Falso

San José del Cabo

Cabo
San Lucas

OCEAN

ISLAS
TRES MARÍAS

Río Grande de Santiago

Zacatecas

San Blas

¶ From the interior point of the entrance runs the wonderful port of San Francisco; this consists of a great bay or *estero,* as they call it, which must be some twenty-five leagues in length, and as seen from the entrance, runs about south east and northwest; at the middle is the entrance or mouth. . . . Inside the port I counted eight islands, and I cannot state whether there are more. The first to be met on entering the port—its center, observed from the outer point of entrance, on this side, lies northwest by north in respect to this point, and is about one league from the entrance—is called Isla de Angel, or de los Angeles. . . .

The commander decided to erect the holy cross on the extremity of the white cliff at the inner-point of the entrance to the port, and we went there at eight o'clock in the morning. We ascended a small low hill, and then entered a table-land, entirely clear, of considerable extent, and flat, with a slight slope towards the port; it must be about half a league in width and a little more in length, and keeps narrowing until it ends in the white cliff. This table-land commands a most wonderful view, as from it a great part of the port is visible, with its islands, the entrance, and the ocean, as far as the eye can reach—ever farther than the farallone.[3] The commander marked this table-land as the site of the new settlement, and the fort which is to be established at this port, for, from its being on a height, it is so commanding [that] the entrance of the mouth of the port can be defended by musket-fire, and at the distance of a musket-shot there is water for the use of the people, that is, the spring or pond where we halted. . . .[4]

Font kept a meticulous record of what the party saw, and by means of a graphometer, a surveyor's instrument for measuring angles, he mapped the entire region, denoting the topography on his charts. The site where the explorers viewed the Farallon Islands to the west of San Francisco, as well as the eight islands within the Bay that Font counted, was Fort Point, then called Punta del Cantil Blanco. Leaving here, they traveled southeast to a cove later known as Mission Bay. This site was selected for the first mission, Nuestra Señora de los Dolores. Anza returned to Sonora, and in June, 1776, Lieutenant José Moraga brought the first group of colonists from Monterey to settle San Francisco.

[3] The Farallons, three small islands approximately 25 miles due west of San Francisco's Golden Gate.

[4] *The Anza Expedition of 1775-1776, Diary of Pedro Font,* edited by Frederick J. Teggert (Berkeley: Academy of Pacific Coast History Publications, University of California, March, 1913).

The network was now established: a chain of colonies that would afford Spain a bastion along the shores of the Pacific. They were tiny communities destined to become populous cities—San Diego, Santa Barbara, and San Francisco. Progress was slow, for Spain suddenly found itself drawn reluctantly into a war being fought on the other side of the American continent against an ancient rival, Great Britain.

* * *

The decision of the Spanish government to support the American colonists during the Revolution was reached after considerable hesitation, and would not have taken place without the prodding of France. Spain contributed large sums to the fledgling American government for conducting the war against Great Britain. These financial transactions were made secretly, and were not motivated by any benevolent feeling on Spain's part. It was a matter of political expediency. It may seem incongruous that a nation ruled by a monarchial system would condescend to aid a people in open rebellion against its mother country, but there was the future to be considered. Should the Americans be victorious, Spain would be forced to negotiate with a new government for concessions that would guarantee her sovereignty over possessions on the North American continent. The defeat of the British general Burgoyne by the Americans, and his surrender at Saratoga on October 17, 1777, had a far-reaching effect in Europe. As viewed by France and Spain, it marked the turning point of the war, for it was obvious that the colonists had an excellent chance of achieving final victory. It was an opportune time to destroy England's power, and the French were the first to act.

The British were seeking a way to end hostilities. Representatives were sent to France to meet with the American envoys, Benjamin Franklin, Silas Deane, and Arthur Lee, who had been in Paris soliciting French aid. The French foreign minister, the Comte de Vergennes, was determined that there would be no reconciliation between Great Britain and her colonies that might restore them to England under dominion status. Accordingly, Vergennes initiated the Franco-American treaty signed on February 6, 1778, by which France recognized the independence of America, and agreed to aid the colonies in the war against Great Britain. Spain was not consulted in the move, a gesture that offended the Spaniards, an ally of France. Vergennes now turned his attention toward placating the Spanish government, and bringing that nation into the conflict. He was matched against the Count Floridablanca, Spain's foreign minister, and one of the most brilliant diplomats in Europe. He was determined to extract every concession he could before he would see Spain committed to a war aiding the Americans. Gibraltar, held by the British, had long rankled Spanish pride. Floridablanca first tried to have Britain cede it as the price of Spanish neutrality. When this failed, it became one of the prizes demanded as her price for joining France in her war with Britain. Oddly, it was the one small piece of land Spain failed to obtain.

When Spain entered the war in 1779, a naval force was sent to lay siege to Gibraltar, while other forces were dispatched to seize the Floridas from the British and drive English settlers from Honduras. The wily foreign minister also did his best to obtain future advantages for Spain from the American government. He wanted to ensure that when the rebellious colonies obtained their freedom, Spain's own colonial possessions on the American continent would be recognized, and their boundaries respected. The tide of western migration that followed the Revolution made this an impossibility.

During the month of September, 1781, an American army commanded by General George Washington, aided by French forces under General Rochambeau, had Lord Cornwallis' British army surrounded at Yorktown. A French fleet led by Admiral de Grasse sealed off any avenue of escape by sea. It was also in September that a new Spanish governor of California, Felipe de Neve, marched a party of settlers from the San Gabriel Mission to found a new town, the *Pueblo de Nuestra Señora la Reina de los Angeles*—the Town of Our Lady of the Angels. Eleven men, eleven women, and twenty-two children, who had come overland from Sonora, Mexico, composed the settlement of Los Angeles. They arrived on September 4, as the War for American Independence drew to a close. On October 19, 1781, Cornwallis surrendered, ending hostilities.

The formal peace treaty between Britain and France was not signed until September 3, 1783. In the document was a stipulation that "The navigation of the Mississippi, from its source to the ocean, shall forever remain free and open to the subjects of Great Britain and the citizens of the United States." This paved the way for future troubles with Spain, a recent ally of the American colonies during their struggle for independence. The Mississippi was the boundary line of Spanish territory, and Spain claimed control of its waters. Spain signed a treaty the same day with Great Britain by which she acquired the two Floridas. Spain now held a sizable section of America. Trace a line from southern Georgia around Florida, along the Gulf of Mexico, down across Panama to encompass South America, and then reaching north up the Pacific coast past California as far as Alaska to view the extent of her holdings. In addition, there was a broad region lying just beyond the Mississippi that Spain had acquired from France in 1763—Louisiana, on the Gulf of Mexico. Add to that another huge slice of the continent, a land mainly inhabited by Indians—the great American Southwest.

It is little wonder that Spain had cause to fear what would occur when the population tide moved westward. The remarks attributed to Count de Aranda, the Spanish ambassador at Paris at the time of the signing of the peace treaty in 1783, reflected the thinking among Spanish leaders as they speculated upon the future growth of this new nation:

"This federal republic is born a pygmy. A day will come when it will be a giant, even a colossus, formidable in these countries. Liberty of conscience, the facility for establishing a new population on immense lands, as well as the advantages of the new government, will draw thither farmers and artisans from all the nations. In a few years we shall watch with grief the tyrannical existence of the same colossus."

Floridablanca ordered the Mississippi closed to the United States for navigation in 1784. In addition, he demanded a treaty recognizing Spanish conquests during the Revolution, which in addition to leaving the Mississippi in Spanish control, ceded lands in Georgia, Kentucky, and Tennessee. These terms proved unacceptable to the United States, and Spain relaxed its ban on American navigation along the Mississippi in 1788. Duty was levied on American shipping by the Spaniards at New Orleans.

The frontier boundaries between Spain and the United States remained confused until October 27, 1795, when Thomas Pinckney, representing the American government, signed a treaty at Madrid. By its terms, Americans were given free navigation of the Mississippi, which was recognized as the dividing line between the United States and Spanish Louisiana. The thirty-first parallel of latitude was designated as the boundary of West Florida from the Mississippi to the Apalachicola River. In a monumental diplomatic blunder, Spain ceded Louisiana to France on October 1, 1800. At the same time, American merchants bringing goods down the Mississippi to New Orleans for overseas shipment were forbidden to deposit their cargoes there for transhipment. France's acquisition of Louisiana created a storm in America, for it appeared to be clearly an attempt by Napoleon to establish a new empire in the West. For a time the situation was so volatile that war seemed imminent between France and the United States. Napoleon suddenly offered to sell Louisiana. The agreement was reached on May 2, 1803, and the United States added 865,000 square miles to its territory. The selling price had been reasonable—a mere $12 million.

The next important loss to Spanish holdings in America came some years later, during President Monroe's administration. Seminole Indians from Florida had become increasingly troublesome in Georgia, killing a number of American settlers. Spain at the time was trying to suppress rebellions among its revolted colonies in South America. In addition to the Indians, Florida had become a sanctuary for outlaws and filibusters. During the war that broke out with England in 1812, British forces had landed in Florida with Spanish sanction. General Andrew Jackson stormed their garrison at Pensacola in 1814 with American troops. Four years later, this same general, who had trounced the British at New Orleans, becoming a national hero, once again invaded Florida. It required three months to subdue the Seminoles. Spain objected to Jackson's invasion of its territory, but was flatly informed by the United States either to maintain order in Florida or cede the territory. The Spanish government chose the latter course. The Floridas were acquired by the United States in February, 1819. Under the terms of this agreement, Texas was to be considered as Spanish territory, as well as most of the land encompassing what is now Arizona and New Mexico. Spain's right to California was acknowledged in the Florida treaty, but the United States became a neighbor on the Pacific, for Spain in turn had accepted America's claim to the Oregon country.

*   *   *

The first outsiders began to arrive in California during the latter part of the eighteenth century. Foreign vessels anchored at San Francisco, Monterey, and San Diego, ostensibly for supplies, or to trade. In some cases, the purpose was obviously to spy and assess the Spaniards' capability to defend their possessions along the Pacific against aggression. In addition to the seafarers, the first Americans to travel overland across the continent reached various Spanish settlements along the Pacific coast. Many of these early visitors possessed a remarkable faculty for observation and the ability to record what they saw in their journals and diaries. In a few cases they were professional writers. Some were sea captains or businessmen seeking opportunities to trade, invest, or expand the scope of their commercial enterprises. Several, who were to write some of the most interesting accounts, were rough trappers and hunters, hardened to the frontier and the precarious existence of living among the Indians. The personal narratives began to be published in Europe and the United States. At first these books had but a limited circulation owing to their high cost, but they were read by men of influence in both England and the United States—those with large mercantile interests, as well as the politicians and government officials who formulated national policy. Already, there was considerable interest evidenced in California, particularly by the American and British governments. Beginning with the 1830's, descriptions of California were finding their way into periodicals and newspapers, thus reaching a wider audience, and causing ever greater interest that was soon to lead to a mass migration westward to the Pacific.

By reading these narratives today, we are afforded a description of how California appeared in each period covered by the writers. We learn how the people dressed, the type of homes in which they lived, what they ate, thought about, how they earned their livelihood, and what they did for recreation. Each informant is someone who was on the scene at the time. The authors were generally accurate in what they wrote in their diaries, so their descriptions of what they witnessed is a fairly reliable picture of conditions prevailing at the time. They are not all free from bias or prejudices, which were the result of political or religious convictions.

The so-called pastoral era in California covers a period roughly from the last decade of the eighteenth century to the outbreak of the war with Mexico, and the acquisition of the territory by the United States. During this span of years, a little more than half a century, the Spaniards established their unique system of rule by a military-ecclesiastical government, then lost the land to Mexico during a period of revolution, when Spain's power in the Western Hemisphere was destroyed. Finally, there was that historic moment when the American flag was raised over Monterey, ending Mexico's jurisdiction and tenure. The entire period has been the subject for numerous narratives in saccharine prose describing the idyllic days of the missions and the great ranchos. A myth emerged: under the benevolent eyes of the padres, the Indians labored happily in the fields, while the dons lounged on their verandas, or cavorted nightly at a round of gay fandangos. Such was not quite the case. While the Franciscan system of converting the Indians by having them live and work in the missions was a sound one, and was undoubtedly one of the most successful methods of colonization devised, it also had serious limitations. For one, it reduced the Indian to a state of servitude, and while he learned many useful arts and crafts under the tutelage of the mission fathers, he was entirely dependent upon them for his subsistence. Whatever initiative he may have carried over from his ancestors, who were forced to hunt, dig, and look to the sea for means to clothe and feed themselves, was now lost. The mission provided all the necessities, and thereby weakened the whole social structure of the Indian tribes. When the Mexican government ordered that they be secularized, that is, freed from their bondage to the missions, the final disaster occurred. They were not yet prepared to take their place in society, and so became outcasts, neglected and persecuted by the white man. It was only a question of time until the native races would become virtually extinct.

At the same time, life on the ranchos was not always the serene existence that has been portrayed. Spanish rule over California was apathetic. In fact, it failed completely in fulfilling its obligations to the people who settled in the territory. Soldiers in the garrisons remained unpaid, and essential provisions were always lacking. What began as a noble experiment ended as a colossal failure. Mexican rule over the province failed to improve conditions. If anything they became worse. The coming of a succession of Mexican governors brought graft and political corruption. The bride, the *cohechar,* became the accepted method of transacting business. If there were laws forbidding the citizens to trade with ships of foreign nations, these could be circumvented in this manner. Smuggling along the California coast became a profitable venture.

The advent of the Americans on the scene did not necessarily improve conditions. Although there were many men with lofty ideals, who made important contributions in the establishment of a new society in the West following statehood, there were others who were motivated solely by their greed and personal ambitions. There were many of this breed during the 1850's. It is often the scoundrel who is immortalized in history books. The lives of men who lead prosaic lives generally are dull to read about, regardless of the contributions they may have made to their community, state, or nation in a lifetime. The knave, the renegade from society, continues to capture the public's imagination. What motivated his actions, unless too heinous or barbaric, has always been a matter of universal interest. In the annals of California's history, there is a liberal assortment of both types— good and bad, to furnish us with an account of the state's past.

5

AN ENGLISH VIEW
OF SPANISH CALIFORNIA

Captain George Vancouver was sent to the Pacific by the British government at a time when it appeared that England and Spain would become involved in a new war. The cause was the Nootka Sound controversy, which was precipitated by Spain's decision to exclude foreign vessels from Alaskan waters and fortify Nootka Sound. Differences were reconciled; Spain had no desire at this point to challenge the might of the British navy. A treaty was signed by which Spain agreed that British subjects had the right to make settlements on any part of the Pacific coast that Spain did not already occupy. By this agreement, she surrendered all claims to the territory north of California. Vancouver arrived in San Francisco in November, 1792. En route he was responsible for several important discoveries, which was a secondary phase of his mission.

Vancouver was the most distinguished navigator of his time. Born about 1750, he had served as a midshipman aboard the *Resolution* during Captain James Cook's second voyage of discovery from 1772–

1775. He was also with Cook when the latter lost his life on a follow-ing expedition (1776–1780). After further service in the West Indies, he was assigned by the Admiralty to command the *Discovery* and the *Chatham,* an armed tender. The mission: sail at once to force the Spaniards to capitulate at Nootka, and survey the Pacific coast from the 30th degree of N. latitude, and in particular to search for any rivers, inlets, and lakes from there northward to Canada. He was also to determine the possibility of a northwest passage between the Atlan-tic and the Pacific, not so much as a strait navigable to ships, the exis-tence of which had been disproved earlier; but to discover a river, or series of rivers, that might lead across Canadian territory or the Pacific Northwest and that could open a line of communication to be used by fur traders, who could make the passage by shallow draft boats and canoes. The task occupied several years; Vancouver mapped the coast from San Diego to Cook's Inlet, Alaska. Following the expedition he wrote an account of what he had seen, which was published in 1798, *A Voyage of Discovery to the Pacific Ocean and Round the World.*

We are concerned primarily with his impressions of California, which occupy but a small segment of Vancouver's narrative. Yet, to incorporate only those passages here would fail to present a picture of the writer, as well as some idea of the preparations necessary for such a voyage, a description of the ships and some of the difficulties en-countered during such a lengthy cruise. The geographical knowledge obtained by Vancouver's voyage was to have an ultimate effect upon California's future history. It focused men's attention on an area of the world that still remained a mystery to most Europeans and Ameri-cans. It created international interest in the vast lands of the Pacific Northwest, the Arctic wilderness, and the fabled isles dotting the great South Sea. Vancouver explained the purposes of the voyage:

¶ For some time previous to this period [1790], the Spaniards, roused by the successful efforts of the British nation, to obtain a more extended knowledge of the earth, had awoke, as it were, from a state of lethargy, and had not only ventured to visit some of the newly-discovered islands in the tropical regions of the Pacific ocean; but had also, in the year 1775, with a spirit somewhat analogous to that which prompted their first discovery of America, extended their researches to the northward, along the coast of North-West America. But this undertaking did not seem to have reached beyond the acquirement of a very superficial knowledge of the shores; and though these were found to be extremely broken, and divided by the waters of the pacific, yet it does not appear that any measures were pursued by them for ascertaining the extent, to which those waters penetrated into the interior of the American continent.

This apparent indifference in exploring new countries, ought not, however, be attributed to a deficiency in skill, or to a want of spirit of enterprise . . . because there is great reason to believe, that the extreme caution which has so long and so rigidly governed the court of Madrid, to prevent, as much as possible, not only their American, but likewise their Indian establishments from being visited by any Europeans . . . had greatly conspired, with other considerations of a political nature, to repress that desire of adding to the fund of geographical knowledge, which has so eminently distinguished this country. And hence it is not extraordinary that the discovery of a northwestern navigable communication between the atlantic and pacific oceans, should not have been considered as an object much to be desired by the Spanish court. . . . the Spaniards seem to have considered their former national character as in some measure at stake; and they have certainly become more acquainted than they were with the extensive countries immediately adjoining their immense empire in the new world; yet the measures that they adopted, in order to obtain that information, were executed in so defective a manner, that all the important questions in geography still remained undecided, and in the same state of uncertainty.

Towards the end of April, the *Discovery* was, in most respects, in a condition to proceed down the river,[1] when intelligence was received that the Spaniards had committed depredations on different branches of the British commerce on the coast of North-West America, and that they had seized on the English vessels and factories in Nootka sound. This intelligence gave rise to disputes between the courts of London and Madrid, which had the threatening appearance of being terminated by no other means than those of reprizal. In consequence of this an armament took place, and the further pacific equipment of the *Discovery* was suspended; her stores and provisions were returned to the respective offices, and her officers and men were engaged in a more active service.
. . .

The uncommon celerity, and unparalleled dispatch, which attended

[1] The Thames, where along its banks at the shipyard of Randall and Brent, the *Discovery*, a vessel of 340 tons, was commissioned on January 1, 1790.

the equipment of one of the noblest fleets that Great Britain ever saw, had probably its due influence upon the court of Madrid, for, in the Spanish convention, which was consequent on that armament, restitution was offered to this country for the captures and aggressions made by the subjects of His Catholic Majesty; together with an acknowledgment of an equal right with Spain to the exercise and prosecution of all commercial undertakings in those seas, reputed before to belong only to the Spanish crown. The extensive branches of the fisheries, and the fur trade to China, being considered as objects of very material importance to this country, it was deemed expedient, that an officer should be sent to Nootka to receive back, in form, a restitution of the territories which the Spaniards had seized, and also to make an accurate survey of the coast from the 30th degree of north latitude north-west-ward toward Cook's river; and further, to obtain every possible information that could be collected respecting the natural and political state of that country. . . .[2]

On January 6, 1791, Vancouver was able to enter in his log that "the sails were bent, and the ship got in readiness to proceed." As she beat her way into the open sea, accompanied by the tender, the *Chatham,* Vancouver studied the charts, plotting his course:

¶ Having no particular route to the Pacific ocean pointed out in my instructions, and being left at perfect liberty to pursue that which appeared the most eligible, I did not hesitate to prefer passage by way of the Cape of Good Hope, intending to visit the Madeiras, for the purpose of procuring wine and refreshments. Our course was accordingly directed against winds very unfavorable to our wishes. . . .

The commander's concern for the health of his crew is evident in the precautions he took to prevent sickness by maintaining a clean ship. The *Chatham* proved a terrible sailer, even though ballast had been added to her hold:

¶ April 21, 1791. On our departure from England, I did not intend using any antiseptic provisions, until the refreshments which we might be enabled to procure at the Madeiras should be exhausted; but the light baffling winds, together with the crank situation and bad sailing of the

[2] Captain George Vancouver, *A Voyage of Discovery to the Pacific Ocean and Round the World* (London: Printed for C. G. and J. Robinson, Paternoster-Row; and J. Edwards, Pall-Mall, 3 vols., 1798).

Chatham, having so retarded our progress that by the 21st we were advanced no further than the latitude of 35° 7′ north, longitude 14° 40′ west; sour krout and portable broth had for some days been served on each of the vessels, the store rooms had been cleared, cleaned, and washed with vinegar and the ship had been smoked with gunpowder mixed with vinegar. As I had ever considered fire the most likely and efficacious means to keep up a constant circulation of fresh and pure air throughout the ship; in the forepart of every day good fires were burning between decks, and in the well. Both decks were kept clean, and as dry as possible, and notwithstanding the weather was hot, and the smoke and heat, thence arising was considered as inconvenient and disagreeable, yet I was confident that a due attention to this particular, and not washing too frequently below, were indispensable precautions, and would be productive of the most salubrious and happy effects in preserving the health and lives of our people. . . .

Reaching the Cape of Good Hope, the ships now set sail across the Indian Ocean. The coast of Australia was sighted on September 26th, and the following month Vancouver passed Tasmania, en route to New Zealand, which was duly surveyed and charted. From there they proceeded to the Sandwich Islands—which Vancouver had visited before with Captain Cook.

The natives were friendly, but in obtaining provisions from them, Vancouver refused to trade guns for the food. He had been expressly forbidden to do this by his king. This was resented by the islanders. It happened that Americans had been in the Sandwich group recently, and they had no such scruples about bringing firearms. Indeed, they had built a flourishing trade. Vancouver complained:

¶ The supply of refreshments which the Sandwich Islands on this occasion afforded us, was undeniably a very scanty one. This, however, I did not solely attribute to scarcity, as I had frequently great reason to believe an abundant stock might have been procured had we been inclined to have purchased them with arms and ammunition; with which, through the unpardonable conduct of various traders who have visited these islands, the inhabitants have become very familiar, and use these weapons with an adroitness that would not disgrace the generality of European soldiers . . .

The principal offender, according to Vancouver, was a Yankee trader who had a squadron of some twenty ships engaged in the fur trade on the Pacific coast, gathering pelts that were taken to the Orient, where they brought high prices. This enterprising trader, John Kendrick, discovered that sandalwood, native to Hawaii, brought high prices in India. In payment for cargoes, Kendrick traded fire-arms, probably inexpensive weapons brought from China. His activities were also known in California, and the Spaniards had been just as anxious to curtail his trading there, as this order issued by Governor Fages to Commandant José Arguello on May 13, 1789, attests:

¶ Should there arrive at the port of San Francisco a ship named the *Columbia,* which they say belongs to General Washington of the American states, and which under the command of John Kendrick sailed from Boston in 1787 with the design of making discoveries and inspecting the establishments which the Russians have on the northern coasts of this peninsula; you will take measures to secure this vessel and all the people on board, with discretion, tact, cleverness, and caution, doing the same with a small craft which she has with her as a tender, and with every other suspicious foreign vessel, giving me prompt notice in such cases in order that I may take such action as shall be expedient.

It is evident that Spanish intelligence was efficient as to the destination of the two Yankee vessels, and it is apparent that agents had them under surveillance long before they sailed from Boston. The strange feature is that the ownership of the *Columbia* is attributed to George Washington, unless it was for the purpose of provoking an international incident with the United States. It was well publicized that the voyage was backed by six leading Boston merchants, and there is no evidence in Washington's collected diaries and correspondence that he was interested in such a venture. On one point, however, both the Spaniards and Vancouver were correct in their assumptions. Kendrick turned out to be a scoundrel and a swindler who came to a fitting end. His second in command, Robert Gray, was a better man, and in the course of two voyages discovered the Columbia River shortly before Vancouver entered it. This gave the United States a valid claim to the Oregon territory. As Vancouver was soon to meet Robert Gray after the English ships sailed from Hawaii, a brief account of the Kendrick-Gray voyage is in order, for it ties together with an important series of events that were taking place along the Pacific coast.

The plan for sending two American vessels into the Pacific was conceived by a Boston merchant, Joseph Barrell, who had studied Captain Cook's account of his third voyage, and who saw in the northwest coast of America, with its abundance of fur-bearing animals—the otter in particular—an excellent opportunity for developing a trade with China. There, merchants were willing to pay generous prices for furs. Barrell, together with five associates, outfitted two vessels in 1787 for the voyage. These were the *Columbia,* of roughly 212 tons, and the *Washington,* a 90-ton sloop. John Kendrick, who had commanded a privateer during the Revolution, was placed in charge of the expedition, and acted as master of the *Columbia.* A Rhode Islander, Robert Gray, was selected to be the captain of the sloop.

The two vessels left Boston on September 30, 1787, and while rounding Cape Horn were separated by a storm. Each beat its way northward, heading for a prearranged meeting place in Nootka Sound. Gray passed California, sighting it in August, 1788, in latitude 41° 28′. He reached Nootka on September 17th, and a week later the *Columbia* dropped her anchor nearby. Several hundred fine otter pelts were quickly obtained by trading inexpensive iron chisels with the Indians. Considerable exploring was also done in Alaskan waters, mainly by Gray, who searched for inlets where he could anchor and induce the Indians to come out and trade. He returned to Clayoquot Sound, Vancouver Island, where his furs were transferred aboard the larger *Columbia.* It was decided that he would take the vessel back to Boston, while her commander, Kendrick, would take charge of the sloop and gather an additional cargo of furs. This he accomplished, and then sailed for China. Here he disposed of the otter skins, reportedly for $18,000. Kendrick then absconded on the high seas with both ship and money, and never returned to Boston. He made two voyages between China and the Northwest coast in the stolen sloop until retribution overtook him. While anchoring off Honolulu, December 12, 1794, a nearby ship fired a salute to the King of Oahu with one of her cannon. A negligent gunner forgot to remove a charge of grape beforehand. The shot tore through the ship commanded by Kendrick, killing him and several of his crew.

Robert Gray reached Boston with the *Columbia* in August, 1794, and the owners immediately made plans for another trading expedition, not realizing that they had seen the last of Kendrick and the *Washington,* which would represent a sizable loss on their investment. On September 28, 1790, the *Columbia* was once more outward bound with Captain Gray in command. During 1791, we find him trading along the Northwest coast and then wintering at Clayoquot Sound. With spring, the *Columbia* weighed anchor and went in search of furs. In May, 1792, Gray made his memorable discovery when he entered the mouth of the great river that bears the name of his ship today. He had given the United States a valid claim to an extensive domain in the Pacific Northwest.

* * *

Vancouver sailed from Hawaii late in March, 1792, setting his course for California. He sighted land near Cape Mendocino, but proceeded north without anchoring, as he was anxious to complete the mission he had been assigned. He refers to California as "New Albion," the same name his predecessor Francis Drake had applied to the land. As his ship approached the Strait of Juan de Fuca, the gateway to Victoria in present British Columbia, the British met Robert Gray and the *Columbia.* Vancouver relates what transpired:

¶ At four o'clock, a sail was discovered to the westward standing in shore. This was a very great novelty, not having seen any vessel but our own consort, during the last eight months. She soon hoisted American colours, and fired a gun to leeward: At six we spoke to her. She proved to be the ship *Columbia,* commanded by Mr. Robert Gray, belonging to Boston, whence she had been absent about nineteen months. Having little doubt of his being the same person who had formerly commanded the sloop *Washington,* I desired he would bring to, and sent Mr. Puget and Mr. Menzie on board to acquire such information as might be serviceable in our future operations. . . .

On the return of the boat, we found our conjectures had not been ill grounded, that this was the same gentleman who had commanded the sloop *Washington* at the time, we are informed, she had made a very singular voyage behind Nootka. It was not a little remarkable that, on our approach to the entrance of this inland sea, we should fall in with the identical person who, it had been stated, had sailed through it. His relation differed very materially from that published in England. It is not possible to conceive any one more astonished than was Mr. Gray on his being made acquainted, that his authority had been quoted, and the track pointed out that he had been said to have made in the sloop *Washington*. . . .

Vancouver sailed north for Nootka, where he met with the Spanish commissioner Juan Francisco de la Bodega y Cuadra, who had been sent there by his government to effect a settlement of various issues still unresolved in the treaty signed earlier between England and Spain. Negotiations between Cuadra and Vancouver reached a stalemate at Nootka, although relations between the two men were cordial. Cuadra wished to restore Nootka, and use the Strait of Juan de Fuca as a dividing line between the two nations. Vancouver refused to discuss the boundary question, and it was decided that he would send his lieutenant home to England for further instructions. In the meantime, he would continue his geographical survey.

Vancouver's explorations in the Pacific Northwest resulted in a number of additions to the global map. Entering the Strait of Juan de Fuca, he named the inland sea he found Puget Sound for the second lieutenant of the *Discovery,* who later rose to the rank of admiral. His ship circled what is now called Vancouver Island. A high snowy peak seen in the distance was called Mount Rainier after another naval officer. Vancouver's surveys carried him into many of the inlets between the Strait of Juan de Fuca and Alaska, and his voyage provided the answer for one important question that had remained unsettled for some time. Writing in the opening pages of the three-volume work, John Vancouver, who edited the papers for publication following his brother's death, declared:

¶ . . . the exertions of Captain Vancouver will, I trust, be found to have added the complete certainty, that, within the limits of his researches on the continental shore of North-West America, no internal sea, or other navigable communication whatever exists, uniting the Pacific and Atlantic Ocean.

*   *   *

The British expedition was now ready to sail south for California. The commander was still determined to examine the Columbia River, which Gray had described. At Cape Disappointment, the *Chatham,* his smaller vessel, entered the mouth, and its captain, Lieutenant Broughton, took to her small boats to continue the exploration upriver. The seas were running too rough for Vancouver to effect a passage with the *Discovery,* and he decided to continue to San Francisco, leaving Broughton to follow the course of the river. This the officer did for some eighty-four miles before returning to his ship, which left for Monterey to rendezvous with the *Discovery.* Vancouver's vessel passed the Farallons and entered what would later be known as San Francisco's Golden Gate on November 14, 1792. He writes:

¶ Having passed the inner points of the entrance, we found ourselves in a very spacious sound, which has the appearance of containing a variety of as excellent harbours as the known world affords. The Spanish establishment being on the southern side of the port, our course was directed along that shore, with regular soundings from 9 to 13 fathoms. Several persons were now seen on horseback coming to the s.e. point above mentioned; from whence two guns were fired, and answered by us, agreeably to the signal established between Sen. Cuadra [3] and myself. As the night soon closed, a fire was made on the beach, and other guns were fired; but as we did not understand their meaning, and as the soundings continued regular, we steered into port, under an easy sail, in constant expectation of seeing the lights of the town, off which I proposed to anchor; but as these were not discoverable at eight at night, and being in a snug cove, we anchored to wait the return of day. . . .

Thursday 15 Nov. 1792
Thursday morning discovered our anchorage to be a most excellent small bay within three fourths of a mile of the nearest shore. . . . The herds of cattle and flocks of sheep grazing on the surrounding hills were a sight we had long been strangers to, and brought to our minds many pleasing reflections. These indicated that the residence of their proprietors could not be far remote, though we could perceive neither habitations nor inhabi-

[3] Cuadra was the Spanish commissioner whom Vancouver had met earlier at Nootka.

tants. On hoisting the colours at sunrise a gun was fired, and in a little time afterwards several people were seen on horseback coming from behind the hills down to the beach, who waved their hats, and made other signals for a boat, which was immediately sent to the shore, and on its return I was favored with the good company of a priest of the order of St. Francisco, and a sergeant in the Spanish army to breakfast. The reverend father expressed, and seemingly with great sincerity, the pleasure he felt at our arrival, and assured me that every refreshment and service in the power of himself or mission to bestow, I might unreservedly command; since it would be conferring on them all a peculiar obligation to allow them to be serviceable. The sergeant expressed himself in the most friendly manner, and informed me, that in the absence of the commandant, he was directed on our arrival to render us every accommodation the settlement could afford.

We attended them on shore after breakfast, where they embraced the earliest opportunity of proving, that their friendly expressions were not empty professions, by presenting me with a very fine ox, a sheep, and some excellent vegetables. The good friar, after pointing out the most convenient spot for procuring wood and water and repeating the hospitable offers he had before made in the name of the fathers of the Franciscan order, returned to the mission of St. Francisco, which we understood was at no great distance, and to which he gave us the most pressing invitation.

From these gentlemen we learned, that the station we had taken was far within the general anchoring place of the Spanish vessels, which they said was off that part of the shore where the light was shewn and guns fired the preceding night on the beach, near the entrance into the port. Our situation was however perfectly commodious and suitable to all our purposes, and with the permission of the sergeant, I directed a tent to be pitched for the accommodation of the party employed in procuring wood and water; whilst the rest of the crew was engaged on board in repairing the damages sustained in our sails, rigging &c. during the tempestuous weather with which we had lately contended.

We amused ourselves with shooting a few quails on the adjacent hills, and in the afternoon returned on board to partake of the excellent repast which had been supplied by our hospitable friends. Whilst we were thus pleasantly engaged, our boat brought off father Antonio Danti, the principal of the mission St. Francisco, and Senor Don Heamegildo Sal, an ensign in the Spanish army, and commandant of the port. This gentleman, like those who visited us in the morning, met us with such warm expressions of friendship and goodwill, as were not less deserving our highest commendations, than our most grateful acknowledgments.

The happiness they seemed to anticipate did not appear to arise so much from any pleasure they might derive in our society, as from the comforts and assistance which it was in their power to administer; this was manifested by all their actions, and by their expressing that our arrival had empowered them to execute a talk the most accordant to their own wishes, as well as to the directions of their sovereign, which had been communicated to them and to the neighboring settlements and missions.

From Senor Sal I was made acquainted, that although the situation we had taken might answer our purposes in a certain degree, yet there was one which we had passed by the preceding evening, that we should find infinitely more commodious, as we should then be more immediately in his neighborhood, and more frequent opportunities would be afforded him of rendering service. In addition to the motive of his politeness, I was induced to comply with his wishes by the falling tide discovering to us a very great obstacle to our communication with that part of the shore from whence the wood and water was to be procured. A large bank of mud was found at low water to extend nearly half way between the ship and shore.

I understood from these gentlemen that Senor Quadra still waited our arrival at Monterey; I therefore intrusted to them a letter informing him of our arrival in this port, to which Senor Sal said an answer would most likely be procured in the course of three or four days. Having joined us in drinking the healths of our royal masters, they took their leave and returned to the shore. . . . Whilst engaged in allotting to the people their different employments, some saddled horses arrived from the commandant with a very cordial invitation to his habitation; which was accepted by myself and some of the officers. We rode up to the Presidio, an appellation given to their military establishments in this country, and signifying a *safe guard*.

The residence of the friars is called a Mission. We soon arrived at the Presidio, which was not more than a mile from our landing place. Its wall, which fronted the harbour, was visible from the ships; but instead of the city or town, whose lights we had so anxiously looked for on the night of our arrival, we were conducted into a spacious verdant plain, surrounded by hills on every side, excepting that which fronted the port. The only object of human industry which presented itself, was a square area, whose sides were about two hundred yards in length, enclosed by a mud wall, and resembling a pound for cattle. Above this wall the thatched roofs of their low small houses just made their appearance. . . .

The Spanish soldiers composing the garrison amounted, I understood, to thirty-five, who with their wives, families, and a few Indian servants, composed the whole of the inhabitants. Their houses were along the wall, within the square, and their fronts uniformly extended the same distance into the area, which is a clear open space, without buildings or other interruptions. The only entrance into it, is by a large gateway; facing which, and against the centre of the opposite wall or side, is the church; which, though, small, was neat in comparison to the rest of the buildings. This projects further into the square than the houses, and is distinguishable from the other edifices, by being white-washed with lime made from seashells; as there has not yet been any lime-stone or calcareous earth discovered in the neighborhood.

Vancouver's assessment of the colony was that the people were lazy, and the port was unprotected:

¶ . . . at the expence of very little examination, though not without much disappointment, was our curiosity satisfied concerning the Spanish town and settlement of St. Francisco. Instead of finding a country tolerably well inhabited and far advanced in cultivation, if we except its natural pastures, the flocks of sheep, and herds of cattle, there is not an object to indicate the most remote connection with any European, or other civilized nation. This sketch will be sufficient, without further comment, to convey some idea of the inactive spirit of the people, and the unprotected state of the establishment of this port, which I should conceive ought to be a principal object of the Spanish crown, as a key and barrier to their more southern and valuable settlements on the borders of the north pacific. Should my idea of its importance be over-rated, certain it is, that considered solely as an establishment, which must have been formed at considerable expence, it possesses no other means for its protection than such as have been already described; with a brass three pounder mounted on a rotten carriage before the presidio, and a similar piece of ordnance which (I was told) was at the s.e. point of entrance lashed to a log instead of a carriage; and was the gun whose report we heard in the evening of our arrival. Before the presidio there had formerly been two pieces of ordnance, but one of them had lately burst to pieces. . . .

On our arrival, we were received by the reverend fathers with every demonstration of cordiality, friendship, and the most genuine hospitality. We were instantly conducted to their mansion, which was situated near, and communicated with the church. The houses formed a small oblong square, the side of the church composed one end, near which were the apartments allotted to the fathers. These were constructed nearly after the manner of those at the presidio, but appeared to be more finished, better contrived, were larger, and more cleanly. Along the walls of this interior square, were also many other apartments adapted to various purposes. . . .

Vancouver inspected the mission. In his narrative he frequently refers to the weakness of fortifications in San Francisco and other posts, their inadequate armament, and the small size of their garrisons. This would lead one to conclude that he considered that one of the responsibilities of his mission was to gather information that would have strategic value to his nation should Britain at some future date attack Spanish settlements in California. His Spanish critics, after reading his published account, could claim that his voyage was one more devoted to espionage than to scientific study.

As the party was escorted through the mission, he noted that there was little grain on hand. There was a loom, where wool was manufactured, and although it was coarse, the quality was good. The Indians working at the mission were well fed and better clothed than those who lived in the neighborhood. They were kept clean, instructed, and had every necessary care taken of them. In return for these advantages, they had to submit to certain regulations:

¶ . . . amongst which they are not suffered to go out of the interior square in the day without permission; are never to sleep out of it at night; and to prevent elopements, this square has no communication with the country but by one common door, which the fathers themselves take care of, and see that it is well secured every evening, as also the apartments of the women, who generally retire immediately after supper.

If I am correctly informed by the different Spanish gentlemen with whom I conversed on this subject, the uniform, mild, and kind-hearted disposition of this religious order, has never failed to attach to their interest the affections of the natives, wherever they have sat down amongst them; this is a very happy circumstance, for their situation otherwise would be excessively precarious; as they are protected only by five soldiers who reside under the directions of a corporal, in the buildings of the mission at some distance on the other side of the church. . . .

Vancouver contemplated what would happen if the Indians should ever prove ungrateful and revolt against the padres. There were only three, and there were six hundred Indians living at the mission. They were supposed to have accepted the Roman Catholic faith, but Vancouver was astonished to observe how few advantages had attended their conversion:

¶ They seemed to have treated with the most perfect indifference the precepts, and laborious example, of their truly worthy and benevolent pastors; whose object has been to allure them from their life of indolence, and raise in them a spirit of emulous industry; which, by securing to them plenty of food and the common conveniences of life, would necessarily augment their comforts, and encourage them to seek and embrace the blessings of civilized society. Deaf to the important lessons, and insensible of the promised advantages, they still remained in the most abject state of uncivilization; and if we except the inhabitants of Terra del Fuego, and those at Van Dieman's land, they are certainly a race of the most miserable beings I ever saw, possessing the faculty of human reason. One of their greatest aversions is cleanliness, both in their persons and habitations. . . .

Following a guided tour, the visitors returned to the convent, where they were served an excellent dinner of fish, fowl, and vegetables. Conversation with the padres was carried on with the aid of an interpreter. A statement made by one of them so impressed Vancouver that he had it printed in italics in his book. That was, that this point of California was the northernmost settlement of any description formed by the court of Spain on the continental shore of northwest America. Vancouver was undoubtedly recalling his recent visit to Alaska. If the terms of the Nootka treaty were finally agreed upon, then Spain would relinquish all rights to the territory north of California. This would open the door to the entire northwest coast to Great Britain. He apparently gave little thought to future American aspirations in the same region.

The nearest similar establishment to the mission at San Francisco was Santa Clara, and Vancouver accepted an invitation to visit it the following day. A sergeant accompanied by six soldiers and a drove of horses called for him in the morning. He estimated that they covered forty miles riding to the mission. The extra horses were taken along to

replace those who tired on the trip. Santa Clara was a far more prosperous community than San Francisco. The size of its buildings and
fields under cultivation was larger. Wheat, maize, peas, and beans
were being grown in abundance. In addition, the fathers had planted
peaches, apricots, apples, pears, figs, and grapes. There were also large
herds of beef and sheep grazing near the mission. A feast was given
here in honor of Vancouver and his party, for which a number of
bullocks were slaughtered. When the English returned to San Francisco, the Spaniards refused payment for the supplies purchased from
them. This was a matter that could be settled by their respective
governments. Vancouver insisted that his hosts accept some articles in
exchange, and they were no doubt received with gratitude by the
Franciscans. He notes:

¶ My late excursion into the country had convinced me, that although
its productions, in its present state, afforded the inhabitants an abundant
supply of every essential requisite for human subsistence, yet the people
were nearly destitute of those articles, which alone can render the essentials
of life capable of being relished or enjoyed. On this occasion I experienced
no small gratification, in being able to relieve their wants by the distribution of a few necessary articles and implements, culinary and table utensils,
some bar iron, with a few ornaments for the decoration of their churches;
to which I added one hogshead of wine, and another of rum; and consigned the whole to the care of Senor Sal, with a request that an equal
distribution should be made between the Presidio and the missions of St.
Francisco and Santa Clara. . . .

Leaving San Francisco, the *Discovery* cruised south along the coast
to Monterey. Once again, Vancouver committed his observations to
his journal, and we have an excellent picture of how the town, which
remains today one of the most picturesque of all California cities,
appeared on that day in 1792:

¶ The anchorage . . . is the only situation in the Bay where vessels can
ride with any degree of safety or convenience. In its neighborhood is the
Spanish establishment. The presidio is about three quarters of a mile to the
southward of the spot, where the sandy beach before mentioned commences. This is the landing place, where they have erected a most
wretched kind of house, which they call a store-house, serving for that

purpose, and for the reception of a guard of soldiers generally posted there.

The presidio, like that of St. Francisco, is situated in an open clear plain, a little elevated above the level of the sea; the space, between the presidio and the landing place, is a very low swampy ground. The former does not appear to be much benefitted by its vicinity to fresh water, since in the dry season it must be brought from a considerable distance, as the Spaniards had not been at the pains of sinking wells to insure a permanent supply. There were many delightful situations in the immediate neighborhood of the presidio, with great diversity in the ground to favor the taste of the ingenious, in which our Spanish friends might with equal ease have sat themselves down more comfortable, more convenient, and I should conceive more salutary than their present residence appeared to be.

The most important of all blessings, health, is here treated with great indifference; since not only the climate of Monterey, but the whole of the surrounding country, has the reputation of being as healthy as any part of the world. Other objects of a secondary nature, such as the place of their abode, convenience or comfort, have no greater influence on their consideration, as the present presidio is the identical one that was built on the first establishment of this port in the year 1770, without having undergone the least improvement or alteration since that period. The buildings of the presidio form a parallelogram or long square, comprehending an area of about three hundred yards long, by two hundred and fifty yards wide, making one entire enclosure. The external wall is of the same magnitude, and built with the same materials; and except that the officers' apartments are covered in with a sort of red tile made in the neighborhood, the whole presents the same lonely uninteresting appearance, as already described at St. Francisco. Like that establishment, the several buildings for the use of the officers, soldiers, &c. and for the protection of stores and provisions, are erected along the walls on the inside of the enclosure, which admits but one entrance for carriages or persons on horseback; this, as at St. Francisco, is on the side of the square fronting the church, which was rebuilding with stone like that at St. Carlos. Besides the principal gateway, they have small doors that communicate with the country, nearly in the middle of the side walls, to the right and left of the entrance. One of these, on the right hand, is through the apartments of the commanding officer. These are much more extensive than those at St. Francisco, as they consist of five or six spacious rooms with boarded floors, but under the same disadvantage of wanting glass, or any substitute for it. The window places are open, and only on that side of the houses which looks into the area; as no

apertures, I believe, are allowed to be made in the grand wall of the inclosure, excepting for the doors; which are those already mentioned; with
one at each of the officers' houses contiguous to the governor's, and one
other on the opposite side. These are all the aperture in the wall which
when seen at a distance has the appearance of a place of confinement. At
each corner of the square is a small kind of blockhouse, raised a little
above the top of the wall, where swivels might be mounted for its protection. On the outside, before the entrance into the presidio, which fronts the
shores of the bay, are placed seven cannon, four nine and three three-
pounders, mounted; these, with those noticed at St. Francisco, one two-
pounder at Santa Clara, and four nine-pounders dismounted, form the
whole of their artillery. These guns are planted on the open plain ground,
without any breast work or other screen for those employed in working
them, or the least cover or protection from the weather. Such, I was informed, was also the defenceless state of all the new settlements on the
coast, not excepting St. Diego, which from its situation should seem to be
a post of no small importance.

The four dismounted cannon, together with those placed at the entrance
into the presidio, are intended for a fort to be built on a small eminence
that commands the anchorage. A large quantity of timber is at present in
readiness for carrying that design into execution; which, when completed,
might certainly be capable of annoying vessels lying in that part of the Bay
which affords the greatest security, but could not be of any importance
after a landing was accomplished; as the hills behind it might be easily
gained, from whence the assailing party would soon oblige the fort to surrender; nor do I consider Monterey to be a very tenable post without an
extensive line of works.

The presidio is the residence of the governor of the province, whose
command extends from St. Francisco, southward along the exterior shore,
to cape St. Lucas; and on the eastern side of the peninsula of California,
up that gulph to the bay of St. Louis. The rank in the Spanish service,
required as a qualification to hold this extensive command, is that of lieutenant colonel. Whether the governor interfered in the common garrison
duty I know not. A lieutenant and ensign, sergeants, corporals, &c. resided
also in the presidio; the establishment of which I understand was similar
to all the rest in the province, but was incomplete in consequence of the
recent death of the late commandant. By this event, Lieutenant Arguello,
properly the commander at St. Francisco as being the senior officer, had
taken upon him the government, and had sent the alferez, or ensign, Senor
Sal, to command at St. Francisco; which post we understood they were

severally to retain, until another lieutenant colonel should be appointed by the government.

By what I was able to learn, I did not consider the number of soldiers who composed the garrison as exceeding one hundred, including the non-commissioned officers. From this body detachments are drawn for the protection of the neighboring missions; the remainder, with their wives and families, reside within the walls of the presidio without seeming to have the least desire for a more rural habitation; where garden ground and many comforts might easily be procured, at no great distance from the seat of the establishment. This seemed to be composed entirely of military people, at least we did not see amongst them those of any other description. The few most necessary mechanical employments were carried on in an indifferent manner by some of the soldiers, under permission of the commanding officer. . . .

Vancouver's freedom of movement to observe the defense of California caused a furor when the governor, José Joaquin Arrillaga, learned of it. On the return visit of the British ships, conditions were changed considerably. Vancouver was given a reception that was in marked contrast to the friendly welcome accorded him on his first arrival at San Francisco. While the Spaniards were not openly hostile, Arrillaga made it quite clear that the British were not welcome in California. These difficulties, however, did not arise until his return. At the moment, Vancouver was bidding his Spanish friends at Monterey good-bye. The *Chatham* had by this time joined her sister ship, and their stay in California had been for nearly two months. Before departing from Monterey, a number of sheep and cattle were placed aboard the *Discovery,* as well as a quantity of corn and other seeds. The animals were to be transported to His Majesty's infant colony in New South Wales. Once again the Spaniards declined payment. On January 15, 1793, the *Discovery* and the *Chatham* sailed west from Monterey bound for the Sandwich Islands. From there, with the approach of spring, Vancouver returned to the northwest coast of America to resume his survey. In October, 1793, he turned south for another look at California.

Sal, the military commandant, came aboard in San Francisco, somewhat embarrassed by the news he had to convey to Vancouver. The English were unwanted guests. Sal dined with the British commander aboard the *Discovery,* where he was reluctant to discuss Arrillaga's orders, feeling it would seem discourteous. The picture changed the following day, as Vancouver writes:

¶ After supper Senor Sal retired to the shore, and the next morning I received from him two letters, the one requesting in an official form, that I would acquaint him in writing of our arrival in port St. Francisco, of the supplies we should want, and of the time I intended to remain in that port, in order that he might immediately communicate the same to the governor of the province; the other stating that, under the superior orders by which alone his conduct could be governed, he was obliged to make known to me, that no individual could be permitted to come on shore, but for the purposes of procuring wood and water, excepting myself and one officer, or midshipman, who might pass to the Presidio, where I should be received and attended as on our former visit.

These restrictions were of a nature so unexpected, ungracious, and degrading, that I could not but consider them as little short of a dismission from St. Francisco, and I was left in the greatest perplexity to account for a reception so totally different from what we had experienced on a former occasion, and so contrary to what I had been taught to expect, by the letters with which I had been honored from the viceroy of New Spain, in return to my letter of thanks for the great civilities that had been conferred upon us.

I was given to understand, that a captain in the Spanish infantry, named Arrillaga, had arrived at Monterey some time in the course of the preceding spring; and being senior officer had taken upon himself the jurisdiction of the province, with sentiments apparently not the most favorable toward foreign visitors.

Sailing to Monterey, Vancouver encountered Arrillaga, who would communicate with the British commander only by letter. The Spanish official stipulated that only the commander of a foreign vessel was to be permitted on shore, together with a small work party to gather wood and water, and this was to be accomplished with celerity. After reading these instructions, Vancouver became enraged:

¶ The tenor of these letters being very different from what my conversations with Senor Arrillaga had given me reason to expect, when I visited him at the Presidio; I was reduced to the necessity of sending him the next day a full explanation of the objects of our voyage, and of the motives that had induced me to enter the ports under his jurisdiction. In this I stated, that I had been intrusted by His Brittanic Majesty with a voyage of discovery, and for the exploring of various countries in the pacific ocean; of which the north west coast of America was one of the principal objects. That previously to my departure from England, I had been given to understand, not only that I should be hospitably received on this coast by the subjects of the Spanish crown, but that such information of the progress of my voyage as I might wish to communicate to the Court of Great Britain, would be forwarded by way of St. Blas by officers of His Catholic Majesty residing in these ports; and that I was instructed to make a free and unreserved communication of all discoveries made in the course of my researches, to any Spanish officer or officers whom I might chance to meet, engaged in similar pursuits with myself; and that I now purposed to transmit to Senor Quadra a copy of my charts and surveys, that had been made since our departure from this port the proceeding year. That the voyage in which we were engaged, was for the general use and benefit of mankind, and that under these circumstances, we ought rather to be considered as labouring for the good of the world in general, than for the advantage of any particular sovereign, and the court of Spain would be more early informed of, as much benefited by my labours, as the kingdom of Great Britain. That in consequence of these instructions, I had exchanged some charts with Senor Quadra, and others were ready for his reception. That I had not only been treated on my former visit here with the greatest friendship, and unbounded hospitality; but had received from his Excellency, the viceroy of Mexico, the strongest assurance, that these attentions had been shewn in compliance with the desire of His Catholic Majesty, and of the order he had issued for that purpose; and that I had enclosed his Excellency's letter for his perusal, to certify him, that I did not intend any deception. That our examination and survey would still require another year to complete it; and that I had made choice of this port, or St. Diego, for the purpose of refitting our vessels, unloading the store-ship, and making astronomical observations as were become necessary for prosecuting our researches with correctness. The manner in which these services would require to be performed on shore I particularly pointed out, and hoped that the officers and people would be permitted the same recreation on foot and horseback, with which they had been indulged on our former visit, under such limitations and restriction as he might think proper to prescribe.

On Monday I received from Senor Arrillaga a reply to my letter, in which he was pleased to compliment me upon my ingenuity; and thanked me for having given him the perusal of the viceroy's letters. In vindication of himself he said, that there was no royal order for the reception of our vessel, like that produced by M. de la Perouse. That he did not comprehend that his excellency expected that we should repair a second time to the ports under his jurisdiction; and that even Senor Quadra before his departure had given the commander of the garrison to understand, by a letter which Senor Arrillaga sent me a copy, that the attentions we had received on the former occasion were for that time only; and were not to be considered as necessary to be shewn us in the future. Notwithstanding however all these objections, being desirous of contributing to the public undertaking in which we were engaged, he requested I would inform him of the precise number of days in which the store ship could be unloaded; he offered to give me the key of the warehouse at the landing place, for the reception of her cargo, near which we might erect the observatory; which latter was only to be erected in the day time, as he could not permit any of our people to be on shore between sun-set and sun-rise; and lastly, he had no objection to our recruiting our wood and water, provided all those employed on that service should return on board at night, and that I would engage that the greatest dispatch should take place in these and all our other transactions.

Arrillaga's actions infuriated Vancouver, as he discovered that the place where their stores were to be landed while the *Chatham* was being refitted was along a section of the beach where the surf ran high, and "also it was in the midst of the common slaughtering of their cattle, the neighborhood of which, to a considerable distance in all directions, was rendered extremely offensive and unwholesome, by the offal having never been cleared away, but left from time to time in a continual state of putrefaction."

Vancouver refused to have any more correspondence with Arrillaga, issuing orders for his two ships to get under way. They cleared Monterey and sailed south. Pausing at Santa Barbara, the English were extended a warmer welcome by officials of the garrison and the mission fathers. Arrillaga's stern measures toward excluding Vancouver had apparently not been received by the local officials, or were disregarded. Off San Pedro, today the busy port of Los Angeles, he noted in his log on Sunday, November 24, 1795:

¶ I had . . . been given to understand that a very advantageous settlement is established on a fertile spot somewhere in this neighborhood within sight of the ocean, though at the distance of some miles from the coast called Pueblo de los Angeles; "the country town of the Angels," formed in the year 1781. This establishment was looked for in all directions, but nothing was perceived that indicated either habitations or inhabitants.

The two ships reached Point Loma on November 27th, preparing to anchor in the harbor of San Diego. An officer was sent ashore to determine what kind of a reception was in store for the English. He was taken to Antonio Grajero, a lieutenant of cavalry and the ranking official of the post. The Spanish officer was embarrassed by his governor's orders and tried to make Vancouver and his men welcome to the presidio, but he was expressly forbidden to sell them live cattle or sheep. The Franciscan order offered to send to their mission at San Juan Capistrano for additional supplies, but these Vancouver politely declined, as he was anxious to resume his voyage. He wrote glowingly of the kindnesses extended to him by the missions of California, and before leaving he presented them with a welcome gift:

¶ . . . a handsome barrelled organ, which, notwithstanding the vicissitudes of climate, was still in complete order and repair. This was received with great pleasure and abundant thanks, and was to be appropriated to the use and ornament of the new church, at the presidency of the missions at St. Carlos.

Before leaving California, Vancouver wrote his impressions of San Diego in his journal. Even today, this city at the southern boundary of California has much of the charm and beauty that it possessed during the early days of Spanish rule. This is how it appeared to a visitor in 1793:

¶ The Presidio of St. Diego seemed to be the least of the Spanish establishments with which we were acquainted. It is irregularly built, on very uneven ground, which makes it liable to some inconveniencies, without the obvious appearance of any object of selecting such a spot. . . . During the season, and as long as the rainy weather may continue, a sufficient number [of cattle] are then brought nearer for the use of the Presidio and mission; and such as have not been wanted are again sent back to the interior country when the dry weather commences; which although more productive in point of grass, is not very prolific in grain . . . fruits, roots, or other culinary vegetables. I understood that they are frequently obliged to resort for a supply of these articles to the mission of St. Juan Capistrano, which abounded in vegetables and animal productions, consisting of great herds of cattle, flocks of sheep, and goats; and I was assured it was one of the most fertile establishments in the country.

The pueblos differ materially from either the missions or the Presidios, and may be better expressed by the name of villages, being unsupported by any other protection than that of the persons who are resident in them. These are principally old Spanish, or creole, soldiers; who, having their respective turns of duty in the missions of the Presidios, become entitled to exemption from any further military services, and have permission either to return to their native country, or to pass the remainder of their lives in these villages. Most of these soldiers are married, and have families; and when the retirement of the pueblos is preferred, grants of land, with some necessary articles, are given them to commence their new occupation of husbandry, as a reward for their former services, and as an incitement to a life of industry, which, with the assistance of a few of the friendly and well-disposed natives, they carry into effect with great advantage to their families. Fertile spots are always chosen for planting these colonies; by cultivating which, they are soon enabled to raise corn and cattle sufficient, not only for their own support, but for the supply of the wants of the missions and Presidios in their neighborhood. Being trained to arms, they early instruct the rising generation, and bring them up to the obedience of military authority; under the laws which they themselves continue to be governed. There is no superior person or officer residing amongst them for the purpose of officiating as governor, or as chief magistrate; but the pueblos are occasionally visited by the ensign of the Presidio, within whose particular jurisdiction they are situated. This officer is authorized to take cognizance of, and in a certain degree to redress, such grievances or complaints as may be brought before him; or to represent them, together with any crimes or misdemeanors, to his commanding officer; and also to report such improvements, regulations, or other matters arising in these little societies, as may either demand his permission or assent; from whose decision there is no appeal, but to the governor of the province; whose powers, I understand, were very extensive, though I remained ignorant concerning the particular nature of his jurisdiction.

The pueblos generally consist of about thirty or forty old soldiers with their families, who may be considered as a sort of militia of the country, and as assisting in the increase of its population, which, as far as it respects the Spaniards, is yet in a very humble state.

The mode originally adopted, and since constantly pursued, in settling this country, is by no means calculated to produce any great increase of white inhabitants. The Spaniards in their missions and Presidios, being the two principal distinctions of Spanish inhabitants, lead a confined, and in most respects a very indolent life; the religious part of the society within a cloister, the military in barracks. The last mentioned order do nothing, in the strictest sense of the expression; for they neither till, sow, nor reap, but wholly depend upon the labour of the inhabitants of the missions and pueblos for their subsistence, and the common necessaries of life. To reconcile this inactivity whilst they remain on duty in the Presidio, with the meritorious exertions that the same description of people are seen to make in the pueblos, is certainly a very difficult task; and the contradiction would have remained very prejudicial to their character, had I not been informed, that to support the consequence of the soldier in the eyes of the natives, and to insure him their respect, it had been deemed highly improper that he should be subjected to any laborious employment. This circumstance alone is sufficient to account for habitual indolence and want of industry in the military part of these societies.

The introduction of Christianity amongst the natives, the cultivation of their minds, and making them disciples of the Roman church, being wholly intrusted to the religious of the respective orders; none of those Indians are suffered to be employed in the Presidios but such as are particularly recommended; to whom the officers who give them employ are obliged to pay a certain daily sum of money, according to the service received; whilst, at the same time, the fathers have hundreds at their command, who when employed by them are rewarded with the produce resulting from the labours of such of their own society as are engaged in agriculture, in manufacturing their woolen garments, or in gardening.

These are the payments by which the wages of the carpenter, the smith, the mason, and other mechanics are satisfied; and as they have few persons of these trades amongst themselves, the whole of such business is performed by the Indians, under the immediate instruction and inspection of the Rev. fathers, who by these means alone have erected all their fabrics and edifices. At Santa Barbara a new church was building, and at Buena Ventura the whole was to be rebuilt, both of which when finished, might be justly taken for the workmanship of more experienced artists. These two missions form an entire square; the buildings are more lofty and extensive, and the superior quality of the materials with which they are erected, gives them a decided superiority over all the others.

These benevolent fathers are the corporeal as well as spiritual physicians of all the Indian tribes in the neighborhood of the missions; and they exercise the arts of both surgery and medicine with great success, especially the latter, for the credit of which they may be much indebted to the unimpaired constitutions of their patients, and the natural healthiness of the climate. The scarcity of spirituous liquors, and the great regularity of the inhabitants in food and employment, induces a life of temperance; and consequently, the diseases to which they are liable are seldom of a malignant nature, and in the most instances readily yield to the simplest means of cure.

The number of natives, at this period, who were said to have embraced the Roman Catholic persuasion under the discipline of the Franciscan and Dominican orders of missionaries in New Albion,[4] and throughout the peninsula of California, amounted to about twenty thousand, and they were estimated at an eighth or tenth of the whole native population of those countries. Their progress towards civilization seems to have been remarkably slow; and it is not very likely to become more rapid, until the impolicy of excluding foreign visitors shall be laid aside, and an amicable commercial intercourse substituted in its room; by which system new wants become necessary, new comforts would be introduced; this would stimulate them to industry, their lands would be examined and cultivated, and their stock of cattle would, by attention, soon increase so abundantly, as to enable them to dispose of the surplus produce of their farms to strangers, for such articles of convenience as would tend to facilitate their labours, and otherways render their lives more comfortable. Provisions, timber, and sea otter skins, would be the first commodities for their exportation; and though the sea otter skins obtained in these parts are certainly inferior to those procured further to the north, they could not fail of becoming a profitable article of traffic.

I did not find that New Albion had yet been supposed to contain any valuable minerals, nor is California considered much richer in that respect; though I understood, that about 14 leagues to the north-west of the Presidio of Loretto, which is situated in the 26th degree of north latitude on the shores of the peninsula in the gulph of California, the Spaniards had lately discovered two silver mines that were stated to be tolerably productive. The Presidio of Loretto is on a more extensive plan than any in New Al-

[4] Vancouver persists in using Sir Francis Drake's term "New Albion." He applies the name of California only to the peninsula, what is today Baja California, Mexico.

bion. Its inhabitants amount to about seventy Spaniards and several families of Indians, besides a mixed race, exclusive of the garrison, which is composed of a company of sixty soldiers, with their officers.

The missionaries of the Franciscan order, who extend their functions no further south than St. Diego, act in all cases under the particular direction of their college, a branch of which is established at Mexico; with which a constant correspondence is kept up, and by which their conduct appears, on all occasions, to be regulated; and they seem, in most respects, nearly independent of military subjection.

From this brief sketch, some idea may probably be formed of the present state of the European settlements in this country, and the degree of importance they are of to the Spanish monarchy, which retains this extent of country under its authority by a force that, had we not been eye-witness of its insignificance in many instances, we should hardly have given credit to the possibility of so small a body of men keeping in awe, and under subjection, the natives of this country, without resorting to harsh or unjustifiable measures. The number of their forces, between the port of St. Francisco and St. Diego, including both establishments, and occupying an extent in one line upwards of 420 nautical miles, does not amount to three hundred, officers included; and from St. Diego southward to Loretto, not above one hundred more, exclusive of the garrison and settlers residing at that port. These are all that are employed for the protection of the missions. Those of the Dominican order, to the southward of St. Diego, are sixteen in number, each of which is guarded by five soldiers only. Of the Franciscan order, to the northward of St. Diego, there are thirteen; some guarded by five, whilst others have eight, ten, or twelve soldiers for their protection, in those situations where the Indians are numerous, and likely to prove troublesome. This seems to be more apprehended at La Soledad and St. Antonio than at any other of the establishments. The Presidio of St. Diego and Santa Barbara are each garrisoned by a company of sixty men; out of which number guards are afforded to the missions of the same names. The garrison of Monterey generally, I believe, consists of a company of sixty or eighty men, and that of St. Francisco of thirty-six men only. These soldiers are all very expert horsemen, and, so far as their numbers extend, are well qualified to support themselves against any domestic insurrection; but are totally incapable of making any resistance against a foreign invasion.

The number of vessels that have lately visited the coast of North-West America in new commercial pursuits, have been instrumental in awakening the attention of the Spaniards, and they have made some efforts to show an appearance of a defence. On our last visit to St. Francisco, eleven dismounted brass cannon, nine pounders, with a large quantity of shot, of two different sizes, were lying on the beach. These, we understood, were to be placed on the south-east point of entrance into the harbour, but it is commanded in return by a hill at no great distance, to the south-eastward. Several Spaniards, with a numerous body of Indians, on our late visit on top of the cliff, were employed in erecting what seemed to be intended for a platform, or a barbet battery, but it was not at that time in sufficient state of forwardness for us to decide, whether it might not be designed for a more regular work.

At Monterey the cannon, which, on our former visit, were placed before the Presidio, were now removed to the hill, mentioned at that time as intended to be fortified for the purpose of commanding the anchorage. Here is now erected a sorry kind of barbet battery, consisting chiefly of a few logs of wood, irregularly placed; behind which those cannon, about eleven in number, are opposed to the anchorage, with very little protection in the front, and on their rear and flanks entirely open and exposed.

Santa Barbara is a post of no small consequence, and might be rendered very tenable, by fortifying a hill conspicuously situated for such a purpose on the north-west side of the roadstead; yet they have here only two brass nine-pounders, placed before the entrance into the Presidio, which is situated in the valley or plain beneath, at the distance of about a mile from the eminence. At this post is the key to all the communication between their northern and southern establishments, it was worthy of remark, that they had not attempted to provide an intercourse by some other road, through the mountains, which rise perpendicularly immediately behind the Presidio, and in their present rugged state are inaccessible, lest this station should ever fall into the possession of an invading enemy.

With little difficulty St. Diego might also be rendered a place of considerable strength, by establishing a small force at the entrance of the port; where, at this time, there were neither works, guns, houses, or other habitations nearer than the Presidio, which is at the distance of at least five miles from the port, and where they have only three small pieces of brass cannon.

Such is the condition of this country as it respects its internal security, and external defence; but why such an extent of territory should have been thus subjugated, and after all the expence and labour that has been bestowed upon its colonization turned to no account whatever, is a mystery in the science of state policy not easily explained.

The natives are not, nor can they be, rendered tributary, because they possess no tribute to offer; nor do these territories, though greatly favored by nature, contain, or under the present arrangement seem intended in future to contain, large towns or cities, whose inhabitants could in any respect add to the affluence, grandeur, or dignity of the monarch who upholds them. If these establishments are intended as a barrier against foreign intruders, the object in view has been greatly mistaken, and the most ready means have been adopted to allure other powers, by the defenceless state of what the Spaniards consider as their fortresses and strongholds. Should the ambition of any civilized nation tempt it to seize on these unsupported posts, they could not make the least resistance, and must inevitably fall to a force barely sufficient for garrisoning and securing the country; especially that part which I have comprehended under the denomination of New Albion, whose south-most limits lie under the 30th degree of north latitude. Here the coast, washed by the waters of the Pacific, is not more than 30 leagues (if so much,) from the shore under the same parallel, nearly at the head of the gulph of California. This pass, being once well secured by any power, determined to wrest New Albion from the Spanish monarchy, would inevitably prevent an army by land from coming to the support of the present possessors, or to the annoyance of an invading enemy; for two obvious reasons. The first is, that the natives of the country about the river Colorado, a most daring and warlike people, have from time immemorial been the inveterate and avowed enemies of the Spaniards; who not many years surprized and cut off a Presidio and mission containing near an hundred Spaniards,[5] and still continue to act on all occasions with hostility. The other reason is, that to the westward of the territory of these people, from the banks of the Colorado, the mountainous, barren, and inhospitable state of the country renders it at present so totally impassable, that the Spaniards could never penetrate by land at the back of these their new establishments. These facts were established by many inquiries, and confirmed by the route which the Spaniards pursue for the purpose of avoiding such difficulties, when passing between their settlements in New Albion, and those north-eastward of the river Colorado, which are instances that frequently occur; and on these occasions they are obliged to go as far south as the Presidio of Loretto before they cross the gulf of California, and then proceed along its eastern shores northward to their destination, even though it should be to the city of Santa Fee, the capital of New Mexico.

[5] Vancouver refers here to the Yuma Massacre of July 17, 1781, which took place at Missions San Pedro y San Pablo, and La Concepción. Forty-six Spaniards were killed, including four missionary fathers and Captain Rivera y Moncada.

This city was founded in the beginning of the last century, about the time when the Count of Monterey was viceroy of New Spain; it is garrisoned with five hundred men only, and is said to be situated in the finest country America affords, nearly under the meridian of Loretto and the parallel of port St. Francisco; between which port and Santa Fee, an extent of about 160 leagues, the Spaniards have endeavoured to effect a communication by land, though hitherto unsuccessfully; their labours having been constantly defeated by the obstruction of the lofty range of mountains existing between New Mexico and the sea coast. This project, however, is not entirely abandoned, though little hope was entertained of its accomplishment.

The Spaniards, in doing thus much, have only cleared the way for the ambitious enterprizers of those maritime powers, who in the avidity of commercial pursuits, may seek to be benefitted by the advantages which the fertile soil of New Albion seems calculated to afford. By the formation of such establishments, so wide from each other, and so unprotected in themselves, the original design of settling the country seems to have been completely set aside, and, instead of strengthening the barrier to their valuable possessions in New Spain, they have thrown irresistible temptations in the way of strangers to trespass over their boundary. . . . A certain proportion of the natives have, by the indefatigable labour of the missionaries, been weaned from their former uncivilized savage way of life, and are become obedient to social forms, and practices in many domestic occupations. All these circumstances are valuable considerations to new masters, from whose power, if properly employed, the Spaniards would have no alternative but that of submissively yielding.

That such an event should take place appears by no means to be very improbable, should the commerce of North-west America be further extended. The advantages that have already been derived, and are likely still to accrue, in the prosecution of a well-conducted trade, between this coast and China, India, Japan, and other places, may, on some future day, under a judicious and well-regulated establishment, become an object of serious and important consideration, to that nation which shall be inclined to reap the advantages of such a commerce.

Russia at present time seems principally to engross these benefits, in consequence of the unwise competition between private adventurers of other nations, not only on the coast of America, but also at Canton and in its neighborhood; the only market to which, at present, such adventurers can carry the furs of North-west America.

The importance of such a trade, politically considered, or the value of it, when duly appreciated, to private adventurers, I shall leave to the decision of those who are better informed on such subjects; because I had no opportunity of receiving satisfactory information upon matters of that intricate nature. . . .

This is a remarkable understatement by Vancouver. He was well aware that his report would be read by members of Parliament, the Lords of the Admiralty, and British financiers who dreamed of colonial empires. He had described the richness of the land, the accessibility of its harbors, which could be utilized for developing trade with the Far East. An expert in military affairs, Vancouver had assessed the defenses of the Spanish garrisons and found them inadequate. Here was a great opportunity for a nation that would act. As he wrote, "they have thrown irresistible temptations in the way of strangers to trespass over their boundary." It could be a rich prize for his own nation. The cultivation of the land could be extended, and cattle herds increased. There was room for new settlers. The country was rich in timber that could be exported, and there were opportunities to be found in trade once the "impolicy of excluding foreign visitors" was terminated. Vancouver made only one error in his evaluation of California's rich potential when he wrote: "I did not find that New Albion had yet been supposed to contain any valuable minerals." Gold seekers would prove him wrong at a later date.

The more farsighted Spanish officials viewed Vancouver's visit with alarm. They were aware of the weakness of defenses in California. Soldiers garrisoned there could not be expected to put up a strong resistance against an aggressor. Morale was low, as the troops were seldom paid. Spain's only effort to maintain authority in California was to exclude visitors, a policy that would be continued under Mexican rule, and one that would soon become impossible to enforce.

6

AMERICANS ALONG THE CALIFORNIA COAST

One of the first Americans to realize the advantage of developing trade in the Pacific was a young sea captain, William Shaler, who visited the California coast while searching for a cargo of otter skins to carry to Canton during 1803–1804. Shaler was born in Bridgeport, Connecticut, in 1773. His father, Timothy, was a descendant of a seafaring family, and had been captain of a privateer during the American Revolution. The young Shaler was orphaned at thirteen, and began work at an early age in a New York brokerage firm. He was soon sailing as supercargo on a number of trading voyages to the West Indies, handling the firm's merchandise and negotiating sales and purchases.

Some time around 1799, a ship he was on was captured by privateers off the east coast of Africa. Shaler found himself on the beach at Mauritius, Isle of France, without employment. Here, while enjoying the hospitality of the American consul, he met Richard J. Cleveland, who was searching for a vessel he could buy cheaply, as the port was usually crowded with ships seized as prizes on the high seas. The two pooled their resources with another acquaintance who owned a ship, purchased a cargo of coffee and other commodities, and sailed for Copenhagen. Leaving Denmark following this voyage, Shaler and Cleveland found a suitable vessel for sale at Hamburg. She was the *Lelia Byrd,* a 175-ton schooner built in Portsmouth, Virginia.

In November, 1801, the *Lelia Byrd* made for the open sea. Shaler and his companion were equal partners, but they drew lots to determine who would serve as captain. Shaler won, was designated master, while Cleveland became supercargo, responsible for the trading goods and all financial transactions. Rio de Janeiro was the first port of call. The city was at that time under Portuguese control. Efforts to trade were unsuccessful, and the *Lelia Byrd* next sailed around the Horn, which proved to be a rough passage. One man was swept from the yards and drowned before they reached the Chilean town of Valparaiso. The ship entered the harbor, where its captain was immediately in difficulty with the Spanish officials. Shaler had requested permission to trade and obtain supplies. The Spaniards claimed that he had made such a swift passage to their port that he didn't require any.

Four American ships were lying at anchor. One, the *Hazard* out of Providence, was being detained on suspicion of being English. Two others with valuable cargoes of sealskins were also being held, and were finally confiscated on charges of having supplied English privateers then along the coast. The fourth, a Nantucket whaler, was impounded on a charge of having engaged in illicit trade. Spain distrusted the appearance of foreign ships in their harbors, but while there was constant friction between port authorities and ship captains, there were numerous Spanish officials who were not above enriching themselves when the golden opportunity of a Yankee ship laden with merchandise dropped anchor offshore. Often it was the governor of a province who was involved. Bribery was common practice, and it sometimes happened that in his eagerness to acquire a ship's cargo, orders were issued to confiscate the goods without payment. It was in Valparaiso that Shaler first became aware of the social unrest sweeping through the Spanish dominions in South America. Describing the feelings of several families with whom he became acquainted, Shaler made the following entry in his journal:

¶ They seemed, generally to be awakening to a sense of the abject state of vassalage in which they were held by their European masters; the posts of honor and profit being exclusively in possession of Europeans,[1] to the annoyance of the Creoles. Bursts of indignation, at these other grievances connected with them would sometimes escape them, which were generally accompanied with a hope that the period of emancipation was not very distant.

Such sentiments were met by us with corresponding ones, by drawing a parallel between their country and ours, while each was under a colonial system of government, by advertising to the greater physical means in their possession to enable them to throw off the yoke, than was possessed by the Anglo-Americans, in the beginning of their Revolution, by demonstrating to them the greatly increased value of the products of their soil, and the diminished prices at which they would receive the manufactures of Europe, when their commerce should be freed from the shackles to which tyranny and folly had so long subjected it; and finally, by remarking on the paralyzing and debasing effects on the mind, which are inseparable from a protracted state of dependence and vassalage. For the better promotion of the embryo cause, we gave them a copy of our Federal Constitution, and a translation into Spanish of our Declaration of Independence. . . . The government . . . and particularly the ecclesiastical part of it, are sensible that their power rests on the ignorance of the people; hence the excessive dread of the introduction of all books;[2] the watchfulness of the priests to guard their flocks against possessing any volume which they have not seen and approved, as well as against the contaminating influence and opinions of foreign heretics. The care, anxiety, and efforts made by them to suppress all means of information, do not, however pass unobserved by many of the most sensible Creoles, who seem to be waking up to a sense of their degradation. With these the seed is planted, which, in due time, may be expected to bring forth abundant fruit. . . .[3]

[1] Officials sent directly from Spain. The longtime residents, many of whom were descendants of mixed marriages, i.e., of Spanish-Indian blood, were excluded from all but minor governmental posts.

[2] Despite strict government regulations, the intellectuals of South America were secretly reading the works of the French philosopher Jean Jacques Rousseau (1712–1778). His *Le Contrat social,* published in 1761, which proclaimed the sovereignty of the people, became the handbook of all revolutionists.

[3] William Shaler, *Journal of a Voyage Between China and the North-Western Coast of America Made in 1804, published in The American Register or General Repository of History,* Vol. 3, 1808.

The South Americans had followed the progress of the French Revolution, and yearned for freedom. It was a desire that extended to all classes; the *criollos,* or upper classes, proud of their Spanish ancestry, but already fiercely nationalistic in their love for their own new land; the *mestizos,* of mixed Spanish and Indian ancestry, and finally the lowly Indian, who lived in virtual servitude. Little did Shaler realize that within just a few years from the time of his visit, the wars of independence would erupt in South America. Dynamic leaders were to come forth and lead their people in a successful struggle for liberation—Argentina's José de San Martín and Simón Bolívar of Venezuela. To the north in Mexico, it would be Father Miguel Hidalgo y Costilla who would ignite the flames of revolt in 1810, when he called upon the Indians to take back the lands the Spaniards had stolen from their forefathers. Hidalgo was captured and executed. Many of his followers died, but the fire would not be contained.

The *Lelia Byrd* left Valparaiso after an unsuccessful attempt to trade with the Spanish colony. Shaler, after a discussion with his partner, decided to set a course for the Californias. In July, 1802, their ship anchored at San Blas on the tip of Lower California. At first it appeared that the Americans might receive a friendly welcome. A Spanish commissary officer was happy to trade foodstuffs in exchange for tinplate, which the *Lelia Byrd* carried. The governor of the port learned of the transaction, and there was a violent argument over the commissary's authority to deal with the Americans. Shaler decided to withdraw temporarily, and sailed for the Tres Marías, where the ship's rigging could be overhauled, fuel procured, and a general brushing up of the vessel take place. Meanwhile, an emissary was sent to Mexico to obtain permission to trade along the coast. This mission failed, it was learned when the *Lelia Byrd* returned to San Blas. About this time another ship arrived from Upper California with a valuable cargo of otter skins. Shaler purchased 1,600 of them, and had the pelts loaded aboard his ship. It was now time to get away from the Spanish port before officials realized the value of the cargo he was carrying and decided to delay his departure. Accordingly, as Cleveland later related the story, Shaler "ordered all sails to be loosed, the

topsails to be sheeted home and cable be hove short," [4] as they waited
for the setting in of a sea breeze. When it came, the *Lelia Byrd* was
away under a crowd of sail. Reaching the port of San Diego, Cleveland continues his account of the voyage:

¶ A brisk northerly wind prevented our gaining the anchorage till the
afternoon, when, having passed near the battery without being hailed, we
came to anchor about a mile within it. The next day the Commandant,
Don Miguel Rodriguez, with an escort of twelve dragoons, came down
abreast of the ship, and requested that the boat might be sent for him.
This being done immediately, he crowded the boat with his escort, and
probably regretted the necessity of leaving on shore his horses. We had
been told at San Blas that Don Manuel was an exceedingly vain and
pompous man; and indeed, we found him so, for such a ridiculous display
of a little brief authority, and pompous parade, I never before witnessed.
His dress and every movement evinced the most arrant coxcomb. Having
saluted us on coming over the ship's side, he waited, before proceeding aft,
until his escort were drawn up in two lines, with hats off in one hand, and
drawn swords in the other and then passed between them to the companion way. After ordinary inquiries, of whence we came, whither bound,
and the object of our visit, he called to the officer of the escort, and desired
him to take a minute of the articles we required. With these he said that
he would supply us the next day; on receiving which, he should expect we
would not delay a moment in leaving the port. He counted our men, and
perceiving us to be only fifteen, all told, expressed astonishment at the pre-
sumption of undertaking so long and dangerous a navigation with so few
men. He forbade our going to the town, which is distant about three
miles, but gave us leave to go on shore in the neighborhood of the vessel.
He took leave with characteristic pomp, leaving on board five of his escort,
as he said, to see that we carried on no contraband trade.

In the afternoon we made an excursion on shore; and having rambled
towards the battery, which commands the entry of the port, without meeting with any person to prevent our entering it, we availed ourselves of the
opportunity to ascertain its strength and state. We found eight brass nine-
pounders, mounted on carriages, which appeared to be in good order, and
a plentiful supply of ball; but there was no appearance of their having
been used for a long time. As the examination of a battery belonging to a

[4] Richard J. Cleveland, *Voyages and Commercial Enterprises of the Sons of New
England* (New York: Leavitt & Allen, 1842).

people the most jealous and suspicious on earth was a delicate business, we did not remain long within its precincts, and having had an agreeable excursion, returned on board at sunset. In the evening we made acquaintance with our guard, the sergeant of which appeared to be an intelligent young man. He informed us that only a few days past, the ship *Alexander,* of Boston, Captain Brown, had been there; that he had succeeded in purchasing from the soldiers and people several hundred skins; that information of it had been given to the Commandant, who without first demanding their surrender, boarded the ship with an armed force, made a search, and took away all the skins they could find, together with some merchandise. These skins, he said, were now in possession of the Commandant, which, with what he had of his own, probably exceeded a thousand. These, we made every effort to obtain from him; and, though there is no doubt that he would have been as well pleased to sell, as we would have been to purchase them, if the transaction had been practicable without being known to the people, yet, as this was out of the question, and they were all spies on each other, he dared not indulge his desire of selling them to us. Had Brown negotiated with the Commandant first, it is most probable he would have obtained the whole quantity, and, at the same time, have avoided the humiliating predicament of having his ship taken possession of by the rabble.

It was evident now, that the object for which we came here was unattainable. Having, on the 21st of March, received the supplies we had asked, the Commandant again visited us, in the same pompous style, to receive his pay. On leaving us he made known his expectation, that we would leave the port the next morning, wished us a pleasant voyage, and we parted on the most friendly terms. We had been offered a number of skins in small parcels, in the course of the day, to be delivered to us after dark, and determined to purchase as many as we could that night. Accordingly, between eight and nine o'clock, (the time agreed on) both boats were dispatched to different parts of the harbor, one of which returned in proper time with several skins; but the other, in which was the mate and two men, did not return that night. That some disaster had occurred to prevent her return was presumable, but to attempt ascertaining the cause, in the night, would have been incurring too great a risk. We watched the approach of morning, with a view to seize and act upon any contingency that circumstances might present, before the moving of the people.

The first discovery after dawn, was that of our boat, lying on the beach, abreast of our vessel, with, apparently, no person in her. On seeing this, I went immediately to the boat, and, when there, perceived a group of men at a short distance, among whom ours were discernible. Being without arms, an attempt to rescue them would have been imprudent. I therefore returned on board, taking with me the other boat. It was now very evident, that not a moment was to be lost in deciding on the course to be pursued. The choice presented us was that of submission, indignant treatment, and plunder; or resistance and hazarding the consequences. There was not the least hesitation with Mr. Shaler or myself in adopting the latter alternative. As a preliminary step, the guard on board were disarmed, and made to go below; then I went with four men, each with a brace of loaded pistols, to the rescue of those on shore. On landing, we ran up to the guard and, presenting our pistols, ordered them instantly to release our men from their ligatures; for they had been tied hand and foot, and had been lying on the ground all night. This order was readily complied with by the three soldiers, who had been guarding them; and, to prevent mischief, we took away their arms, dipped them in the water, and left them on the beach. The mate reported, that they were arrested immediately on landing by a party of horse, with the Commandant in person at their head; whence we concluded, that he sent the soldier, with whom we made the agreement for the skins, expressly to decoy us, that he might have an apology to plunder us.

Arriving safely on board, we perceived our men to be so indignant at the treatment of their shipmates, as to be ready for the fight, even had the odds been greater against us. We had, however, a disagreeable and very hazardous task to perform; a failure in which would be attended with ruin to us, besides subjecting us to the humiliating treatment of an incensed petty tyrant. Our position, at anchor, was about a mile within the fort, of which mention has been made. It was necessary to pass within musket-shot of this fort. With a strong wind, the quick passage of the vessel would render the danger trifling; but, unfortunately, we had now but the last expiring breath of the land breeze, sufficient only to give the ship steerage way, and an hour would elapse before we could presume on passing the fort; but no other alternative was left us, that did not prevent a more dreaded aspect.

While making our preparation, we perceived that all was bustle and animation on shore; both horse and foot were flocking to the fort. Our six three-pounders, which were all brought on the side of the ship bearing on the fort, and our fifteen men was all our force, with which to resist a battery of three nine pounders, and, at least an hundred men. As soon as our sails were loosed and we began to heave up the anchor, a gun without shot was discharged from the battery and the Spanish flag hoisted; perceiving no effect from this, they fired a shot ahead. By this time our anchor was up, all sail was set, and we were gradually approaching the fort. In the hope of preventing their firing, we caused the guard in their uniforms to stand along in the most exposed and conspicuous station; but it had no effect, not even when so near the fort, that they must have been heard imploring them to desist firing, and seen to fall with their faces to the deck, at every renewed discharge of the cannon. We had been subjected to a cannonade of three quarters of an hour, without returning a shot, and, fortunately, with injury only to our rigging and sails. When arrived abreast the fort, several shot struck our hull, one between wind and water, which was temporarily stopped by a wad of oakum. We now opened fire, and at the first broadside, saw numbers, probably of those who came to see the fun, scampering away up the hill at the back of the fort. Our second broadside seemed to have caused the complete abandonment of their guns, as none were fired afterwards; nor could we see any person in the fort, excepting a soldier who stood upon the ramparts, waving his hat, as if to desire us to desist firing.

Having passed out of the reach of their cannon, the poor guards, who had been left on board, saw themselves completely in our power, without the chance of rescue, and probably calculated on such treatment as they knew would have been our lot, if equally in the power of their Commandant. Their exhibition of fear was really ludicrous, for, while we were tying up their firearms, so as to prevent their using them, and getting the boat ready to send them harmlessly on shore, they were all the time tremblingly imploring for mercy; nor could they be made to believe, until they were actually on shore, that we intended to do them no harm. When landed, and their arms handed to them, they embraced each other, crossed themselves, and fell on their knees in prayer. As our boat was leaving them, they rose up and cried at the utmost stretch of their voices, *"Vivan, vivan los Americanos."*

Having plugged up the hole made by the shot, near the water, we steered southward for the bay of St. Quintin's, and arrived there on the 24th instant. Here we fell in with Captain Brown, in the ship *Alexander,* who gave us a detail of the rough manner in which he had been treated by the Commandant of San Diego, which confirmed us in the propriety of the measures we had pursued to avoid a similar treatment.

The *Lelia Byrd* continued on to the Sandwich Islands after leaving San Diego. From there she sailed to Canton via Guam, and here

Shaler and Cleveland parted company. Shaler returned to California with a cargo of tea, while Cleveland sailed for Boston on another ship with a consignment of silk. The otter skins had been sold profitably in Canton. The two had become close friends, and although they were to be apart for many years, they kept in contact, and would later be united on Shaler's final venture.

The return voyage to California was a financial loss, for Shaler was unable to dispose of his goods. The ship was sold to a native king in Hawaii following the run, and Shaler took passage for China on another vessel. The *Lelia Byrd* came to an ignominious end. After making several transits between Hawaii and Canton carrying sandalwood, she ended up in the Chinese opium trade.

Shaler recorded some of his observations of his second California trip, which, when published in the *American Register,* caused considerable interest. The emphasis in his essay was the weakness of Spanish rule in California, and how easy it would be for a foreign power to occupy the territory. He was of course thinking in terms of his own nation, and years later there would be men who would recall his words:

¶ The Spanish population of the Californias is very inconsiderable; by the best information I could obtain, it hardly exceeds 3000 souls, including the garrisons, among which, even the latter, the officers excepted, there are very few white people: it principally consists of a mixed breed. They are of an indolent, harmless disposition, and fond of spirituous liquors. That they should not be industrious, is not surprising; their government does not encourage industry. For several years past, the American trading ships have frequented this coast in search of furs, for which they have left in the country about 25,000 dollars annually, in specie and merchandize. The government have used all their endeavours to prevent this intercourse, but without effect, and the consequence has been a great increase of wealth and industry among the inhabitants. The missionaries are the principal monopolizers of the fur trade, but this intercourse has enabled the inhabitants to take part in it. At present, a person acquainted with the coast may always procure abundant supplies of provisions. All these circumstances prove, that, under a good government, the Californias would soon rise to ease and affluence.

The government of this country may be considered as altogether military, although civil causes may be carried before the audience of Guada-laxara, in New Spain. The governor rules everything, and no one under-takes to dispute the legitimacy of his decisions. The missionaries are also under his jurisdiction in civil matters, but he does not interfere with the Indians attached to the missions, except at the request of the fathers, who are their sovereign magistrates. . . .[5]

In his summation of conditions in California, Shaler attacked Spain's attempt to isolate its dominions in the Pacific from the eyes of the rest of the world:

¶ The mutual jealousies and selfish policy of the great European pow-ers have been the causes that some of the most beautiful regions of the universe have long languished under the degrading shackles of ignorance and superstition; and the Spanish monarchy has been so long left to the quiet enjoyment of the finest part of the new world, that they have been at full liberty to extend their conquests there in every direction, without any other obstacle than the feeble opposition of the native savages. Any of the great maritime powers that should determine to give independence to New Spain, or wrest it from the Spanish dominion, would naturally seek to establish themselves in California, from whence, as a place of arms, they might carry on their operations against that defenceless kingdom with a certainty of success. This the Spaniards have doubtless foreseen, and been before hand in occupying it, with a view of forming a barrier to those valuable possessions. The foregoing shows that what they have yet done has had a directly contrary effect. They have, at a great expence and con-siderable industry, removed every obstacle out of the way of an invading enemy; they have stocked the country with such multitudes of cattle, horse, and other useful animals, that they have no longer the power to re-move or destroy them; they have taught the Indians many of the useful arts, and accustomed them to agriculture and civilization; and they have spread a number of defenceless inhabitants over the country, whom they never could induce to act as enemies to those who should treat them well, by securing to them the enjoyments of liberty, property, and a free trade, which would almost instantaneously quadruple the value of their posses-sions; in a word they have done everything that could be done to render California an object worthy the attention of the great maritime powers;

[5] Shaler, *Journal of a Voyage Between China and the Northwest Coast of America.*

they have placed it in a situation to want nothing but a good government to rise rapidly to wealth and importance.

The conquest of this country would be absolutely nothing; it would fall without an effort to the most inconsiderable force; and as the greatest efforts that the Spanish government would be capable of making towards its recovery would be from the shores of New Spain, opposite the peninsula, a military post, established at the bay of Angeles, and that of San Diego fortified and defended by a competent body of troops, would render such an attempt ineffectual. The Spaniards have few ships or seamen in this part of the world; the arsenal of San Blas would be their only resource on such an occasion, and that might be very easily destroyed. But, admitting that the inactivity of the invaders should permit them to transport troops over the peninsula, those that come from New Spain could not be very formidable, either in point of number or courage, and they would have to penetrate through Lower California, where they would not find even water in their march: all the other resources of that desolate country could be easily removed out of their way. . . .

William Shaler later entered the diplomatic service, where he earned an excellent reputation for his efforts in advancing the interests of his nation. President Madison sent him to Algiers in 1815 as consul general for the Barbary States, following a war to suppress piracy in the Mediterranean. For years the Dey of Algiers and neighboring rulers in Tripoli and Tunis had been extracting tribute to permit American shipping in those waters. On March 2, 1815, the United States signed a treaty with Algiers that ended this practice, and Shaler participated in the mission as one of the peace commissioners. Following its successful conclusion, he assumed charge of consular offices at Tripoli, Tunis, and Morocco. During his thirteen-year term of office, he became deeply interested in the culture of the North African people. From youth he had shown a marked desire to become a scholar, and he possessed a remarkable aptitude for learning foreign languages. Now, in his spare time, he mastered Greek and Latin, as well as a number of North African dialects. He wrote essays for the American Philosophical Society, which were published in the organization's journal, and in 1826 *Sketches of Algiers* appeared in book form. Few people were aware that in his younger days he had been a daring sea captain who had defied the Spanish and shot his way out of San Diego harbor. Shaler returned to the United States to be commissioned consul at Cuba in 1829. He remembered his old shipmate of the *Lelia Byrd* adventure. Richard Cleveland joined him at Havana as his vice-consul. William Shaler, mariner, scholar, and diplomat died in March, 1833, after being stricken by cholera during a plague which ravaged Havana. His friend Cleveland was at his bedside.

7

THE RUSSIANS IN CALIFORNIA

The decade 1810–1820 saw the decline of Spanish influence and authority in California, as Spain's colonies from Mexico to South America revolted, and began the long struggle for independence. In the presidios from San Francisco to San Diego pay ceased for the soldiers, the supply ships from Mexico failed to make their appearance, and a succession of military governors waged a losing battle to maintain the royal authority, which was openly ridiculed. The first nation to defy Spain's claim to California was Russia.

Alexander Baranov, an official of the Russian American Company, was the guiding hand of a huge operation engaged in the systematic killing of all the sea otters found in Pacific waters as far south as California. Baranov's company was a Russian fur monopoly operating in Alaska. Beginning in 1803, he contracted with an American sailing master, Joseph O'Cain, to trap otters along the California coast. O'Cain employed Aleut Indians, who searched for them in skin canoes they had brought from Alaska. As the business prospered, a number of American ship captains contracted to perform the same services for the Russian American Company. The sea otters were wantonly destroyed for their skins, which were then shipped to Canton. (It has only been in recent years that the otter has been saved from complete extinction. They are protected by California law, and the herd is growing in the waters off Monterey.)

The zealous Baranov established a Russian colony near Bodega Bay, seventy miles north of San Francisco, on September 10, 1812. This was Fort Ross, and the purpose of the colony, according to the Russian spokesman at the settlement, was to trade with the Spaniards. Baranov was having trouble obtaining food for his fur hunters. He knew the California soil was fertile, and he planned to develop an agricultural settlement that could supply all of his trading posts with grain and other commodities. The community was well planned, consisting of a stockade defended by adequate artillery. One hundred Russians in addition to an almost equal number of Aleutian Indians were assigned to the post. Some writers have stated that this Russian settlement on California soil was a private enterprise. This is undoubtedly true, but at the same time it was sanctioned by the Russian government, and a number of prominent officials were deeply interested in the project. In addition, Baranov held a royal warrant as governor of Sitka and Oonalashka.

The Spaniards refused to trade with the Russians at Fort Ross, but they made no move against the colony. In 1815, a formal order was sent to the Russian commander demanding that the colony be abandoned. The request was ignored.

The Russian-American alliance in the sea-otter trade was short-lived, and the firm was dissolved. The Russian colony in California lasted until 1841, when John A. Sutter purchased the cattle and equipment at Fort Ross. The Russians went home. The settlement could not have survived many years longer, for with the American occupation following the Mexican War, the Russians would certainly have been evicted.

Meanwhile, Pablo Vicente de Solá, the governor of California, complained bitterly in 1817 that he was unable to force the Russians to leave Fort Ross. His artillery was defective, the troops garrisoned in his province were insufficient, and he lacked the most important ingredient for a campaign. There was no ammunition. A year earlier, San Francisco welcomed a Russian visitor, and if the governor was concerned over the presence of Russians at Fort Ross, it did not deter the Spanish inhabitants from extending a hospitable welcome to the foreign vessel in their harbor.

The ship was the *Rurick,* a brig of 180 tons. Her captain, who held a commission in the Russian navy, was Otto von Kotzebue, who headed a scientific expedition to explore in the South Sea, as well as search for a northeast passage through Bering Strait into the Arctic Sea, and from there into the Atlantic Ocean. This part of the voyage failed. On October 2, 1816, the *Rurick* sailed into San Francisco Bay. Von Kotzebue kept a journal, which was later published in book form. What follows are the Russian visitor's impressions of California:

¶ On the 1st of October, at midnight, we descried by moonlight the Cape de los Reyes, and at four o'clock P.M. we dropped anchor in the port of St. Francisco, opposite the government-house. Our *Rurick* seemed to throw the place in no small alarm, for, on approaching the fort of St. Joaquin, situated on a neck of land formed of high rocks, on the southern entrance, we saw several soldiers on horse and foot, and in the fort itself they were loading the cannon. The entrance to the harbour is so narrow, that ships are compelled to sail within musket-shot from the fort. On approaching it, we were asked, through the speaking trumpet, to what nation we belonged, our flag being unknown to them. Having answered that we were Russians and friends, I saluted them with five guns, and were answered by the same number. More than an hour elapsed after we had cast anchor, without any one approaching us, the whole of the military train having left the fort, and ranged themselves opposite our anchorage. At last it occurred to me that Vancouver [1] had not found any boats here; I therefore sent my lieutenant with Mr. Chamisso on shore, to announce our arrival to the commandant, Don Louis d'Arguello, lieutenant of the cavalry, who received them in a friendly manner, promising to provide our ship daily with fresh provisions. A basket of fruit, which he sent me, I found a great treat, not having tasted any so long. He also immediately dispatched a courier to Monterey, to inform the governor of California of our arrival.

The 3d of October. This morning we were visited by the artillery officer

[1] The author refers to the prior visits of George Vancouver, whose account he had obviously read.

of the fort, as a messenger of the commandant, accompanied by a clergyman of the mission. They both offered us every possible assistance; the
former in the name of the commandant, and the latter in the name of the
mission. At noon they sent us a fat ox, two sheep, cabbage, pumpkins, and
a great quantity of fruit; of the latter I made my men eat as much as they
could daily, to counteract any tendency to the scurvy, that might have been
produced in their system. I found the *presidio,* as Vancouver described it;
the garrison consists of one company of cavalry, of which the commandant is the chief, and who has only one officer of the artillery under his
command.

On the 4th we went ashore, in order to ride with the commandant to the
mission-house, whither we had been invited to the feast of St. Francisco.
We were accompanied by ten horsemen, all fine dexterous men, who use
their carbines and lances with the skill of our Cossacks. They owe their
skill to the constant practice in which they are kept, for the military in
California only serve to protect the mission against the attacks of the
savages, and assist the clergy in enlisting Christians among these people,
and to keep the converted in the new faith. We arrived in about an hour,
although above half our road lay among sand and hills, which were
scantily covered with a few shrubs; in the neighborhood of the mission we
came to a delightful country, and recognized the rich vegetation of California. After having rode through a street inhabited by Indians, (for thus
the natives are denominated by the Spaniards,) we stopped at a large building, near the church, inhabited by the missionaries; and here we were
met by five priests, three of whom belong to this mission, and the two
others came from St. Clara, in honour of the solemnity; they led us into
a large room, plainly furnished, where we were received very respectfully. On the clock striking ten we entered the church, built of stone,
and neatly ornamented, where we already found some hundreds half-
naked Indians upon their knees, who, although they neither understand Spanish nor Latin, are not allowed to miss one mass after their conversion. As the missionaries, on their side, do not endeavor to learn the
language of the natives, I cannot conceive in what manner they have been
taught the Christian religion; and the confusion in the heads and hearts of
these poor people, who only know how to mimick some external ceremonies, must indeed be very great. The rage of converting savage nations
is now spreading over the whole of the South-Sea, and produces great mischief, since the missionaries never think to humanize them before they
make them Christians, and thus that which was to have been productive
of happiness and peace, becomes the ground of bloody warfare; for in-

stance, on the Friendly Islands, where the Christians and heathens constantly strive to exterminate each other. It struck me that, during the whole ceremony, the unbaptized were not allowed to rise from their knees; for this exertion, however, they were indemnified by the church-music, which seemed to give them much pleasure, and which undoubtedly was the only part of the ceremony in which they felt interested. The choir consisted of a violoncello, a violin, and two flutes; which instruments were played by little half-naked Indians, who gave us many false notes. From the church we went to dinner, where we found no lack of provisions and wine, the latter of which the missionaries make themselves. After dinner we were shewn the dwelling-places of the Indians, consisting of long, low, clay-built houses, forming several streets. The filthy state of these barracks was beyond conception, which is probably the cause of the great mortality among the inhabitants, since, of the 1000 Indians that are in Fort Francisco, 300 die annually. The Indian girls, of whom there are 400 in the mission, live, separate from the men, likewise in similar barracks; both parties are obliged to work hard. The men cultivate the ground; the produce which is received by the missionaries, who keep it in granaries, from which the Indians receive just enough to subsist on. The soldiers of the settlement are likewise kept from it, but they must pay for the flour with ready cash. The women constantly spin wool and weave a coarse stuff, which is partly used for their ordinary dress, and some sent to Mexico, where it is exchanged for other necessary articles. This being a holiday, the Indians were not at work; and instead of which they were playing at various games, one of which required particular skill: two of them sit opposite each other on the ground, each of them holding in his hand a bundle of sticks; and, while they, at the same time, throw them up in the air with great dexterity, they guess whether the number is even or odd; near each player a person is sitting, who scores the gain and loss. As they are always playing for something, and having nothing besides their clothes, which they are not permitted to stake, they work with great labour small white shells, which are used by them instead of money.

The coast of California is so rich in various tribes, that there are often more than ten tribes together, each of which has its peculiar language. On leaving the mission, we were surprised by two groups of Indians, who also consisted of several nations. They came in battle-array, quite naked, and painted with various colours; the heads of most of them were adorned with feathers and other finery, some had covered their long wild hair with down, and painted their faces in a frightful manner. There was nothing remarkable in the warlike dance, but I regretted I could not understand the words of their song. The physiognomy of these Indians is ugly, stupid, and savage, besides they are well-made, rather tall, and of a dark brown colour; the women are very small and ugly: they have much of the negro in their faces, except that a negro-head, in comparison with theirs, may be called beautiful; what particularly distinguishes them from the negro, is their long straight hair, of the darkest black. The missionaries assured us that their stupidity made it a very difficult task to instruct them; but I rather think that the gentlemen do not trouble themselves much about it; they all told us that the Indians came far from the interior, submitting to them of their own accord (which we also doubted): the religious instruction, they said, was then immediately begun, and, according to their capacities, they were sooner or later baptized. California costs the Spanish government a great sum, without any other advantage than the annual conversion of some hundreds of Indians, but who soon die in their new faith, as they cannot easily accustom themselves to a new mode of life. Twice a-year they are permitted to go home, which short time is for them the happiest; and I have sometimes seen them going, in large numbers, shouting on the road. The sick, who cannot undertake the journey, at least accompany their fortunate countrymen to the shore, where they embark, and remain sitting for days together, casting their sorrowful eyes on the distant hills that surround their habitations; they often stop for several days in this spot, without taking any food, so much are these new Christians attracted by their lost homes. Every time some of those which are on furlough take flight, and probably they would flee away altogether, were it not for fear of the soldiers, who take them, and bring them back like criminals to the mission: but this fear is so great that seven or eight dragoons are enough to keep in check hundreds of Indians.

Two considerable rivers fall in the Bay of St. Francisco, of which that in the north is the largest, and is called by the Spaniards Rio-grande. This river, the missionaries say, is the finest in the world, and is navigable by the largest vessels; at the same time its banks are fruitful, the climate is mild, and the population numerous. The missionaries frequently make excursions upon it in large well-armed boats, in order to get recruits for their faith, in which, however, they seldom succeed, the inhabitants being brave and well-armed. We had just come back to the *Rurick,* when a messenger from the governor of Old California, Don Paolo Vincente de Sola, arrived from Monterey, bringing me a polite letter from the governor, in which, among the rest, he promised to come himself to St. Francisco, as soon as his business would allow. At the same time I obtained permission to send a messenger to Mr. Kuskoff, for some articles I wanted, and which he could immediately supply me, being in trade with American ships. Mr. Kuskoff, an agent of the Russo-American Company, has settled, by order of Mr. Baranof, who is at the head of all these possessions in America, at Bodega,[2] in order to supply the possessions of the colony with provisions from that place. Bodega is half a day's voyage from St. Francisco, and is called by the Spaniards Port Bodega. The harbour is only fit for small vessels. Kuskoff's larger possessions are a little north of Port Bodega.

The 5th.—The *Rurick* required several repairs, which I left to the care of my lieutenant, while I occupied myself with the instruments, which I took on shore under a tent. Our naturalists and draughtsmen were very busy; and, after the days quickly passed in various occupations, we met in the evening to enjoy together the beauty of the climate, in which the officers of the settlement joined us. The military seem to be dissatisfied with the government and the mission, having received nothing for these seven years, and being almost entirely without clothing; at the same time, the inhabitants are entirely deprived of European goods, since no trading vessel is allowed to enter any port of California; and it is truly lamentable to see this beautiful country thus neglected.

On the 16th, the governor arrived in the fort.

On the 17th, a large baydare from Mr. Kuskoff arrived, loaded with all the necessary articles. At noon the governor dined with us in our tent on shore. We found him a very amiable gentleman, and afterwards spent many pleasant days in his company.

On the 18th, I sent word to Mr. Kuskoff, that the governor wished to see him here respecting his establishment at Bodega. The governor told me there were several Russian prisoners in California; they were part of the crew of a vessel belonging to the Company, which had been carrying on trade upon this coast, contrary to Spanish laws, and had been seized by the soldiers while they were on shore, without suspecting any danger, and were thrown into prison. By the express command of the Viceroy of Mexico, the governor was interdicted from surrendering them to Mr. Kuskoff, but he had no objection to give them up to me, if I would carry them away; but my ship being too small, I could only take three of them, and I selected those who had been some time in the service of the Company. Besides these, I took on board Mr. Elliot, with the intention of leaving him, at his own request, on the Sandwich Islands. John Elliot de Castro, a Portuguese by birth, came to Sittka on-board an American vessel, in which he had been engaged by Mr. Baranof, to accompany the ship destined for the coast of California, as supercargo, and had been taken with the rest.

[2] This was the Russian colony at Fort Ross.

On the 23d, the governor amused us with some interesting sport between a bull and a bear; the latter are so frequent in this country, that on going only a mile from the houses into the woods, we could meet with them in great numbers. The species differs from ours by a pointed head, and of an ash-grey colour; they are also more active and daring. Nevertheless, the dragoons here are so dexterous and courageous, that they are sent out into the wood for a bear, as we should order a cook to fetch in a goose. They go on horseback, with nothing but a rope with a running knot in their hands, which is sufficient to overpower a bear. As soon as the enraged animal is about to rush on one of them, another throws the knot, which is fixed to the saddle by a strong curve, round one of his fore-paws, and, galloping off, throws him down; immediately the other throws a knot round his hind-leg, and thus the third is able to tie his forelegs together, after which they carry him home without danger. In this manner, the dragoons had brought one to-day, while others had gone in the same way to fetch a bull. The cattle being, upon the whole, abandoned to themselves, have become savage, and are likewise caught with knots by a few horsemen, when they are wanted to be killed. The battle between these two animals was very remarkable; and, although the bull several times tossed his furious opponent, he was overpowered at last.

On the 29th, the governor returned to Monterey. One of the Russians, whom I had taken here on board, being out a hunting, was so injured by the explosion of his powder-horn, that he died in consequence of it.

On the 1st of November, the *Rurick* being in excellent trim, well furnished with provisions, and my men in perfect health, we heaved anchor, and at ten o'clock A.M. were out of the bay. At a distance of two miles in sea, we heard the piercing howlings of the sea-lions, that lay upon the stones on shore. Sea-otters are very frequently met with upon the shores of California; and, as they had not been seen here at all in former times, it is to be supposed, that they have withdrawn thither from the Alioutskan [Aleutian] Islands, and from the northern parts of America, to escape the persecutions they were exposed to there. . . .[3]

The *Rurick*'s next port of call would be Hawaii. Don Luis de Arguello had protested to Kotzebue that the Russian colony at Fort Ross was in direct defiance to Spanish claims to all of California. The Russian replied that he had no authority to order the colonists to leave

[3] Otto von Kotzebue, *Voyage of Discovery In The South Sea and to Behring's Straits In Search of a North-East Passage; Undertaken In the Years 1815, 16, 17, and 18* (London: Printed for Sir Richard Phillips & Co., 1821).

but that he would bring the matter to the attention of his government. He did one favor for the Spaniards before his departure. Thanks to his generosity, or rather, the agility of the Russians, the Spanish flag was now flying over the presidio. When the *Rurick* entered San Francisco Bay, Arguello found himself in the embarrassing position of not having his nation's colors flying from the flagstaff. The halyards had broken at the top. The leisurely life in California had softened the men of the garrison. No one could climb to the top of the pole to repair it. Kotzebue dispatched one of his sailors to the fort, who quickly reached the tip of the staff and replaced the broken rope. The flustered Arguello regained his composure, ordering the colors run up the staff. A tardy eight-gun salute thundered from the fort, honoring the arrival of the Russian ship.

8

PETER CORNEY'S NARRATIVE

In 1818, Peter Corney, whose antecedents are unknown, had sailed in the fur trade for five years. He found himself on the island of Oahu without a ship. Delighted with the climate of Hawaii, he was content to remain there indefinitely had it not been for the appearance of a South American privateer, which was to alter his way of life and make him an accomplice of Hypolito Bouchard, a pirate who raided the California coast. He wrote an account of his adventures, which appeared in the *London Literary Gazette* of 1821.

Corney had served as chief officer aboard the *Columbia* during 1814, when that ship had visited California to obtain a cargo of sea otters for the China trade. At this time, he discovered that the Russians were also active in Pacific waters, engaging American ships to bring Aleutian Indians and their canoes as far south as California, where the otters were plentiful. A second voyage the following year afforded Corney an opportunity to familiarize himself with much of the Pacific coastline.

In May, 1818, he saw a strange vessel enter Honolulu's harbor. The ship was the *Santa Rosa* out of Peru. The vessel was at first believed to be manned by insurgents fighting for independence against Spain. When her captain sold the *Santa Rosa* and her cargo to the Hawaiian king, Kamehameha, for 6,000 picals of sandalwood, Corney became suspicious, as this was a small price to pay for the ship. He found one of the crew in a waterfront saloon, and after liberally plying him with rum learned that the men had been insurgents, but had mutinied against their officers and put them off the ship. Since that time they had terrorized the South American coast, looting several ports. It had been decided to run the *Santa Rosa* to Hawaii and sell her. The ringleader of the mutiny, the ship's first lieutenant, was named Griffiths. Honolulu proved the wrong port of call for the mutineers, for shortly after their arrival, another vessel, the *Argentina,* anchored offshore. Her captain was Hypolito Bouchard, and his ship flew the insurgent flag of Buenos Aires.

A year earlier, José de San Martín, the liberator of Argentina, had crossed the Andes with an army of 5,000 and invaded Chile, where he smashed a Spanish force at the battle of Chacabuco. While freeing Chile, he granted letters of marque to a number of privateers, who could blockade the coast and prevent Spanish ships from supplying their forces on land. These privateers took it upon themselves to commit a little looting on their own, for they were manned by adventurers and outcasts searching for an opportunity to enrich themselves by plunder. Such a man was Bouchard. He arrived in Hawaii looking for the *Santa Rosa*. Corney was recruited to take part in a raid on California as captain of Bouchard's second ship. It is easy to understand why the French pirate took an immediate liking to the writer. His assistance could prove invaluable. Corney had been to California, was familiar with the harbors there, and—more important—he knew what defenses the Spaniards had erected against a possible attack. Bouchard may have swayed Corney's decision to sail with him by claiming that they were about to bring freedom from Spanish rule to the oppressed people of California. Whatever his motives, Corney signed up for the expedition. What follows is his description of their raid along the California coast:

¶ Captain Bouchard demanded the ship *Santa Rosa* and crew from Tameameah,[1] which was immediately complied with. He forgave the men on a promise that they would behave better in future, and brought both ships down to Woahoo[2] to refit. On their arrival, Captain Bouchard came to our houses, where he spent most of his time, often inviting us on board. He took a particular fancy to me, and asked me to command the *Santa Rosa;* to which I agreed, and in October, 1818, entered on my office. We sailed for Atooi, to take on board some of the *Santa Rosa*'s mutineers, who had been left there by the brig,[3] and got four of them, but could not find Mr. Griffiths. The Commodore being determined to shoot him, told Tamooree (Kaumualii), that if the man was not produced he would destroy the fort and set fire to the village. Three days after Griffiths was sent in a prisoner, tried by a court martial, and sentenced to be shot, having but two hours to make his peace with the Almighty. He was brought down to the beach (where the Patriot colours were displayed) blindfolded, and shot by four marines, belonging to the *Argentina*. Many hundred of the natives were collected to witness the execution. The corpse was buried on the beach at high-watermark; the ships then made sail for Woahoo, for some more of the men who had run away, and found that they had escaped to Mowee;[4] the Commodore being determined not to leave a single mutineer on the islands, proceeded thither in pursuit of them, and on arriving learnt that they had gone to the mountains. Don Hypolito then hired a number of the natives to pursue the fugitives, and they were brought on board in three days. They were tried by a court martial, one was sentenced to be shot, the others to get twelve dozen lashes, they were brought on deck, and the former was reprieved, but the others received the punishment, which tore their backs in a shocking manner. The ships then made sail for Woahoo, where we took on board a supply of hogs and vegetables and a number of natives; and on the 20th of October we took our final leave of those friendly natives, bound for the coast of California, to cruise against the Spaniards. The ship *Santa Rosa* was American built, about 300 tons burthen; mounting eighteen guns, twelve and eighteen pounders; with a compliment of 100 men, thirty of whom were Sandwich Islanders, the remainder were composed of Americans, Spaniards, Portuguese, Creoles, Negroes, Manila men, Malays, and a few Englishmen. The

[1] King Kamehameha.

[2] Oahu.

[3] When the Hawaiian king learned from Corney that the crew of the *Santa Rosa* were mutineers, and the ship he had purchased stolen; he ordered the crew members confined.

[4] Maui.

Argentina had 260 men, fifty of whom were Islanders, the remainder a mixed crew, nearly similar to that of the *Santa Rosa*. On our passage towards California we were employed exercising the great guns, and putting the ship in good condition for fighting, frequently reading the articles of war which are very strict, and punish with death almost every act of insubordination.

After getting a supply of eggs, oil, etc. from the Russians,[5] we made sail towards the bay of Monterey. The Commodore ordered me into the bay, and to anchor in a good position for covering the landing, while he would keep his ship under weigh, and send his boats in to assist me. Being well acquainted with the bay I ran in and came to at midnight, under the fort; the Spaniard hailed me frequently to send a boat on shore, which I declined. Before morning they had the battery manned, and seemed quite busy. I got a spring on the cable, and at daylight opened a fire on the fort, which was briskly returned from the two batteries. Finding it useless to fire at the batteries, the one being so much above us that our shot had no visible effect, the Commodore came in with his boats, and we landed on Point Pinos, about three miles to the westward of the fort; and before the Spaniards had time to bring their field-pieces to attack us, we were on our march against it. We halted at the foot of the hill where it stood for a few minutes, beat a charge and rushed up, the Sandwich Islanders in front with pikes. The Spaniards mounted their horses and fled; a Sandwich Islander was the first to haul down their colours. We then turned the guns on the town, where they made a stand, and after firing a few rounds, the Commodore sent me with a party to assault the place, while he kept possession of the fort. As we approached the town, the Spaniards again fled, after discharging their field-pieces, and we entered without opposition. It was well stocked with provisions and goods of every description, which we commenced sending on board the *Argentina*. The Sandwich Islanders, who were quite naked when they landed, were soon dressed in the Spanish fashion, and all the sailors were employed in searching the houses for money, and breaking and ruining everything. We took several Creole prisoners, destroyed all the guns in the fort, etc. We had three of our men killed and three taken; next day a party of horsemen came in sight, to whom the Commodore sent a flag of truce, requiring the governor to give up our people and save the town. Three days were granted to consider this proposal, and on the third day, not receiving an answer, he ordered the

[5] A curious note; the pirates paused at Fort Ross on Bodega Bay, where they were apparently on friendly terms with the Russians. They then proceeded to sack the ports under Spanish control.

town to be fired, after which we took plenty of live stock on board, wood, water, etc., and on the 1st day of December got under weigh from Monterey, and stood along the coast to the southward.

On the 4th we made a village, called the Ranch (near Point Conception) where we intended to call for provisions, got the boats all ready, landed a party without opposition, and took the town, all the inhabitants flying on our approach. The men remained all night, and next morning the place was plundered. About noon a lieutenant and two seamen having strayed a short distance from the town, a party of horsemen rushed on them, threw the la's-aws (lasso's) over their heads and dragged them up a neighboring hill, before we could render them any assistance. This so enraged Captain Bouchard, that he ordered the village to be fired instantly, and embarked all the men. After dark we again landed a party well armed to try and surprise the Spaniards and make some prisoners, but the next morning embarked without success. We then weighed and made sail along shore to the southward, two miles from shore, a great number of Spanish troops riding along the beach at whom we fired several shot. In the evening of the 8th of December, we were off the town and mission of St. Barbara, in latitude 34° 36′ N. and longitude 119° W.; it falling calm we hoisted the boats out to tow the ships into the bay, where we anchored, the town bearing N. by W. one mile, seemingly deserted. We fired a gun and hoisted the colours with a flag of truce, and sent a boat on shore to say if they would give up our men we would spare the town; to which the governor agreed, and accordingly on the 10th we got our companions on board,[6] weighed the anchor and made sail to the southward. We again ran into a snug bay, in latitude 33° 33′ N.,[7] where we anchored under the flag of truce. The bay is well sheltered, with a most beautiful town and mission, about two leagues from the beach. The Commodore sent his boat on shore, to say if they would give us an immediate supply of provisions we would spare their town; to which they replied, that we might land if we pleased, and they would give us an immediate supply of powder and shot. The Commodore was very much incensed at this answer, and assembled all the officers, to know what was best to be done, as the town was too far from the beach to derive any benefit from it. It was, therefore, agreed to land, and give it up to be pillaged and sacked.

[6] If it is true that all of the sailors returned to the ship, it would dispel the myth concerning the arrival in California of Joseph Chapman, an American who had been supposedly shanghaied by the pirates. According to an often quoted story, Chapman found himself at the end of a lariat held by Don Ortego, owner of a large Santa Barbara rancho. Chapman is said to have married Ortego's daughter, and in 1822 he supervised the construction of the first church in Los Angeles, Our Lady, Queen of the Angels.

[7] This was San Juan Capistrano.

Next morning, before daylight, the Commodore ordered me to land and bring him a sample of the powder and shot, which I accordingly did, with a party of 140 men, well armed, with two field-pieces. On our landing, a party of horsemen came down and fired a few shot at us, and ran towards the town. They made no stand, and we soon occupied the place. After breakfast the people commenced plundering; we found the town well stocked with everything but money and destroyed much wine and spirits, and all the public property; set fire to the king's stores, barracks, and governor's house, and about two o'clock we marched back, though not in the order we went, many of the men being intoxicated, and some were so much so, that we had to lash them on the field-pieces and drag them to the beach, where, about six o'clock, we arrived with the loss of six men. Next morning we punished about twenty men for getting drunk.

On the 23d of December we saw the island of Ceres, and hauled up for the east end of the island; in the afternoon we were boarded by some Russian hunters in bodarkees, assisted by about twenty of which we, at daylight, hoisted the boats out and towed to the anchorage. We came to on the S.E. side of the island, three quarters of a mile from the village: the Russians were landed here by an American brig for the purpose of hunting the sea otter, on this as well as on the other islands about this coast. Their village consisted of about twenty miserable huts, covered with the skins of the sea lion and elephant, which are very plentiful. English and American ships frequently call here to fill up their oil.

We had a party on shore daily hunting the deer, which are the only animals on the island, and killing the sea lion and elephant for the sake of their hearts and tongues, which we found very good. While we lay here five of the former mutineers took the first whale boat in the night and ran away. We sent the launch in pursuit of them, but it returned in three days, without having seen them. Captain Bouchard swore if he caught them he would immediately shoot them.

January 18th, 1819, having completed our wood and water, and refitting the ships, we got under weigh, intending to cruise off St. Blas, for the Manila ships.

January 22nd, we saw Cape St. Lucas, E. by S. about 30 miles, the sea all round was covered with turtles, which we took on board as we wanted them. On the 24th, captured and scuttled a merchant brig.

We sent a party on shore at the Tres Marias to wood and water. We found a root resembling the tarrow of the Sandwich Islands; the Islanders cooked some of it in the island fashion, and immediately after they had eaten of it their bodies and faces became swelled and bloated in a terrible manner, some died in a few days, and others lingered for ten days in the greatest agony. The Commodore lost twelve men in this manner. The Tres Marias are covered with wood, chiefly lignum-vitae, black and white ebony, hard cedar, and many other kinds. There are plenty of parrots, monkeys, snakes, guanas, pigeons, doves, etc., and abundance of fish. We continually kept a party on shore hunting and fishing; in digging for fresh water we found plenty of ore, which our prisoners said was silver; the water is very bad, and brackish.

On the 9th of July we made the harbour of Valparaiso. . . . The *Argentina* arrived in very great distress for provisions and water; she had buried about forty men; the ships were laid up, and most of the crews entered on board the Chilean fleet.

I now applied to Captain Bouchard for my pay and prize-money, and told him I was heartily sick of the service in the Independents, and that I intended to go to England in the first vessel that sailed for that country, the port being then embargoed on account of the expedition going against Peru; he replied that he could not pay me, unless I continued in the service and took the ship to Buenos Ayres; which I declined doing, and left her in charge of Mr. Woodburn, the first Lieutenant. . . .[8]

Corney's narrative appeared in the *London Literary Gazette* the same year. He speculated on America's future plans in the West, mentioning the Treaty of Ghent, which was signed in 1814 between the United States and Great Britain as a formal termination of the War of 1812. Under its terms a boundary commission was formed to work out a settlement of the territorial dispute along the Canadian-American frontier. The British abandoned their fur operations at the mouth of the Columbia River, leaving the station to the Americans. The path westward across the United States was still badly charted. Much of the terrain was unknown, and hostile tribes inhabited the vast wilderness between the western outposts along the Missouri River and the Pacific Ocean. Corney's comments, written in 1820, which discuss American aspirations, are interesting to note:

¶ The fur trade is now totally in the power of Americans, as by the treaty of Ghent the establishment on the Columbia was given up to that republic. The following extract from the *Montreal Herald* of the 18th April, 1820, will show how far they are desirous of profiting by their possessions: "Military Expedition to the Upper Missouri—the 6th regiment of infantry left Bell Fountain on the 4th October. Colonel Atkins commands

[8] Peter Corney, *Voyage in the Northern Pacific* (Honolulu: Thom. G. Thram, 1896).

the expedition. Thus the public have at length the satisfaction to see fairly embarked, this interesting expedition, on the security of which depends the accomplishment of such mighty objects of the American people, viz: —the transfer of the fur trade from the English to the Americans; the extinction of British influence among American Indians, and the opening of a direct intercourse with India by the Columbia and Missouri rivers. . . ."

For several years past it has been a favorite object of the American government to open an easy communication from their western settlements to the Pacific Ocean, and the above paragraph indicated the steps which have been taken to realize this vast project. The most western settlements which the Americans have are on the Missouri, and from the mouth of the Columbia on the Pacific Ocean they are distant about 3,000 miles.[9] This immense space of desert territory, inhabited by Indian tribes, some of whom are hostile, presents obstacles of no ordinary kind to this scheme; while, at the same time, it is this very circumstance of the country being a wilderness, over which the Indian, and the wild beasts of the forest range undisturbed, that offers such peculiar inducement to the American design, not of colonizing the country, though this consequence would undoubtedly follow; but of making an immediate inroad on barbarism, by establishing a chain of posts at the distance of 50 or 100 miles along the great rivers as far as the Pacific Ocean. The fur trade is the great object of attraction to settlers in this wilderness; and so lucrative is this traffic, that it is well calculated to excite a competition amongst rival states. It can only be prosecuted by such nations as have a ready access to these deserts, where the wild animals which afford this valuable article of trade multiply undisturbed by civilized man. These nations are at present British, whose possessions of Canada secures them access to the north-western desert America; the Americans who have free access to the wilderness that lies between their territories and the Pacific Ocean, and the Russians, whose immense empire borders on the north-west coast of America, giving them ample opportunities, which they have duly improved, of establishing settlements on its shores; of cultivating a friendly intercourse with the natives, and of exchanging European articles for the valuable furs which they collect in the course of their hunting excursions. The fur trade has been prosecuted with amazing enterprise and activity by the British and Canadian companies. Every season they dispatch into the wilds a numerous body of their servants, clerks, and boatmen, amounting to about 800, who traveling in canoes across the vast succession of lakes and rivers, which extend northwest nearly 3,000 miles into the American continent, and are connected with the great Canadian lakes of Huron, Superior, and Ontario,

[9] Corney has miscalculated the distance by more than 1,000 miles.

etc., bring back a valuable supply of furs from these remote regions, in exchange for such European articles as are in request among their savage customers. This trade having been prosecuted with such success by the British, the Americans seem in like manner resolved to profit by the vast tract of similar territory to which they have access. By the journey of Captains Lewis and Clark across the Rocky mountains to the Pacific Ocean, the whole of that western region is now laid open. Numerous adventurers have since crossed, by easier and better roads, this mountainous barrier where they found an open champaign country, well wooded and watered, and abounding in game. Captain Lewis and Clark were often astonished by the immense numbers of wild animals which they met with in all directions, consisting of bears, wolves, beavers, hares, foxes, raccoons, etc., and various other animals, which are keenly pursued on account of their furs.

The plan of the Americans seems therefore to be, to form settlements in this country with a view to trade in its great staple, namely fur; and by establishing a port which would gradually grow up into a village or a town at the mouth of the Columbia River on the Pacific Ocean, they could thence transport their cargoes to the great Indian markets, in exchange for the valuable produce of the East. Such is the project contemplated, and if a success, it would have this important consequence, that it would lay the foundation of an American colony on the shores of the Pacific Ocean. The peopling of the American continent is at present going on at a rapid rate; but by this means the seeds of population would be scattered with a more prodigal hand, and having once taken root, the shores of the Pacific would be quickly overspread with civilized inhabitants, drawing their support from the country in which they were settled, and in this respect independent of the parent state. . . .

Peter Corney returned to Hawaii, and few details are known of his later life, although he had married and was raising a family when he made his final voyage. In the preface of the 1896 edition of his work, published on Oahu, the editor states:

¶ . . . The author was well known in Honolulu, and has a number of descendants living here. He died in 1836, on board of the bark *Columbia,* while on his way to what is now called British Columbia, where he was to occupy a responsible position in the service of the Hudson's Bay Company. In consequence of his death his wife and children decided to remain in Honolulu, instead of continuing their voyage to the North-west Coast. . . .

9

CAPTAIN BEECHEY
AND H.M.S. "BLOSSOM"

Mews that the Mexicans had revolted against Spanish rule was
quick to reach California. Governor Sola ordered the royal
flag lowered on April 11, 1822. The colors of the Mexican Empire were
raised, and an oath of allegiance to the new government was recited
by the soldiers of the Monterey garrison. This ceremony was repeated
at San Francisco, Santa Barbara, and San Diego. The changeover
created little excitement. The military had been neglected for so long
that the soldiers hoped that conditions might improve under a new
government. Spain still had its supporters among the mission fathers,
many of whom refused to take the loyalty oath to the Mexican
government. It was too late, however, and the full weight of the new
regime was brought to bear upon the Franciscan order. In July, 1826,
secularization of the California missions was commenced as Governor
José María de Echeandía issued an order that permitted Indians
living at Santa Barbara and Monterey the right to live in towns
and be allotted lands. The breakdown of the mission system had
begun.

The revolt in Mexico that was to change the course of California history had its beginning in the mother country. The Peninsular War erupted into a ferocious contest in 1808. Napoleon placed his brother, Joseph, upon the Spanish throne. The rebellion that started in Mexico was at first a revolt against French domination and the rule of Napoleon, but later under the leadership of patriots like Father Miguel Hidalgo y Costillo and Ignacio de Allende, this grew into a full-scale war against Spanish rule. Of the 6,000,000 people living in Mexico during the first decade of the nineteenth century, only 40,000 were pure Spaniards. The majority were pure-blooded Indians, and mestizos. Mexico erupted in violence. Hidalgo and Allende were executed in 1811, their heads being displayed on pikes at Guanajuato. Their deaths served to intensify the Mexicans' desire for independence, which was achieved in 1821.

On November 6, 1826, a British ship, the *Blossom*, entered San Francisco Bay. It was commanded by Captain Frederick W. Beechey, of the royal navy. Beechey was participating in a government expedition in the Bering Straits. His *Narrative of a Voyage to the Pacific and Beering's Strait* contains an account of California as the author found it shortly after the territory became a part of the Mexican Republic.

Beechey was born in 1796 and entered the royal navy at ten. He was appointed lieutenant in 1815, commander in 1822, and in 1827, while still at sea on the voyage that brought him to California, he was promoted to the rank of captain. He had taken part in the British attack on New Orleans in 1815, and three years later he participated in an expedition sent to the Arctic regions by the British government. The cruise of the *Blossom* occupied three and one-half years between 1825-1828, during which time the ship covered 73,000 miles. His first contact in California was with officers of the presidio at San Francisco, where he found considerable dissatisfaction with the new government:

¶ . . . The reason of this, I believe, was that Mexico was beginning to turn her attention to California, and was desirous of having settlers there from the southern districts, to whom it would be necessary to give lands; and until they could see what would be required for this purpose and for the government establishments, and had the limits of the property already allotted, defined, they did not wish to make any new grants. The real cause, however, was not explained to the soldiers; they merely heard that they would not have the land ceded to them for life as usual, and they were consequently dissatisfied.

The same feeling of discontent that was experienced by the garrison, pervaded the missions, in consequence of some new regulations of the republican government, the first and most grievous of which was the discontinuance of a salary of 400 dollars per annum, heretofore allowed each of the padres: the support the former government had given to the missions amounts, according to Langsdorff, to a million piastres a year. Another grievance was, the requisition of an oath of allegiance to the reigning authority, which the holy men considered so egregious a violation of their former pledge to the king of Spain, that, until he renounced his sovereignty over the country, they could not conscientiously take it; and, much as they were attached to the place in which they had passed a large portion of their lives, and though by quitting it they would be reduced to the utmost penury—yet, so much did they regard this pledge, that they were prepared to leave the country, and to seek an asylum in any other that would afford it to them. Indeed, the Prefect, preferring his expulsion to renouncing his allegiance, has already received his dismissal, and was ready at the seaport of Monterey to embark in any vessel the government might appoint to receive him. A third grievance, and one which when duly considered, was of some importance, not only to the missions but to the country in general, was an order to liberate all those converted Indians from the missions who bore good characters, and had been taught the art of agriculture, or were masters of a trade, and were capable of supporting themselves, giving them portions of land to cultivate, so arranged that they should be divided into parishes, with curates to superintend them, subservient to the conversion of the Indians as usual, and to train them for the domesticated state of society in contemplation.

This philanthropic system at first sight appeared to be a very excellent one, and every friend to the rights of man would naturally join in a wish for its prosperity; but the Mexican government could not have sufficiently considered the state of California, and the disposition of Indians, or they would have known it could not possibly succeed without long previous training, and then it would require to be introduced by slow degrees.

The Indians whom this law emancipated were essential to the support of the missions, not only for conducting their agricultural concerns, but for keeping in subordination by force and example those whom disobedience and ignorance would exempt from the privilege; and as a necessary consequence of this indulgence the missions would be ruined before the system could be brought into effect, even supposing the Indians capable of conducting their own affairs. So far from this being the case, however, they were known to possess neither the will, the steadiness, nor the patience to provide for themselves. Accustomed, many of them from their infancy, to as much restraint as children, and to execute, mechanically, what they were desired and no more, without even entertaining a thought for their future welfare, it was natural that such persons, when released from this discipline, should abandon themselves entirely to their favourite amusements, pastimes, and vices. Those also who had been converted in later life would return to their former habits, and having once again tasted the blessings of freedom, which confinement and discipline must have rendered doubly desirable, would forget all restraint, and then being joined by the wild discontented Indians, they would be more formidable enemies to the missions than before, inasmuch as they would be more enlightened. But I will not anticipate the result, which we had an opportunity of seeing on our return the following year.

The padres, however, dreading the worst, were very discontented, and many would willingly have quitted the country for Manila. The government appeared to be aware of this feeling, as they sent some young priests from Mexico to supplant those who were disaffected, and desired that they should be trained up in the mission, and should make themselves acquainted with the languages and usages of the Indians, in order that they might not promote discontent by any sudden innovation. . . .[1]

Beechey visited the Mission San José during his stay in the San Francisco region, where he found agriculture considerably advanced:

¶ . . . beans, pease, and other leguminous vegetables are in abundance, and fruit is plentiful. The land requires no manure at present, and yields on an average of twenty for one. San Jose reaps about 3,000 fanegas (a fanega is one hundred pounds' weight) of wheat annually.

Hides and tallow constitute the principal riches of the missions, and the staple commodity of the commerce of the country; a profitable revenue might also be derived from grain were the demand for it on the coast such as to encourage them to cultivate a larger quantity than is required by the Indians attached to the missions. San Jose, which possesses 15,000 head of cattle, cures about 2,000 hides annually, and as many *botas* of tallow, which are either disposed of by contract to a mercantile establishment at Monterey, or to vessels in the harbour. The price of these hides may be

[1] Frederick W. Beechey, *Narrative of a Voyage to the Pacific and Beering's Strait,* 2 vols. (London: Henry Coburn & Richard Bentley, 1831).

judged by their finding a ready market on the Lima coast. Though there are a great many sheep in the country, as may be seen by the mission, San Jose alone possessing 3,000, yet there is no export of wool in consequence of the consumption of that article in the manufacture of cloth for the missions. . . .

Captain Beechey walked through the courtyard of the mission. A bell began to ring in the tower overhead, summoning the Indians to mass. He decided to watch the ceremony and entered the church:

¶ Morning and evening mass are daily performed in the missions, and high mass as it is appointed by the Romish Church, at which all the converted Indians are obliged to attend. The commemoration of the anniversary of the patroness saint took place during my visit at San Jose, and high mass was celebrated in the church. Before the prayers began, there was a procession of the young female Indians, with which I was highly pleased. They were neatly dressed in scarlet petticoats, and white bodices, and walked in a very orderly manner to the church, where they had places assigned to them apart from the males. After the bell had done tolling, several *alguazils* [2] with whips, canes, and goads, to preserve silence and maintain order, and, what seemed more difficult than either, to keep the congregation in their kneeling posture. The goads were better adapted to this pose than the whips, as they would reach a long way, and inflict a sharp puncture without making any noise. The end of the church was occupied by a guard of soldiers under arms, with fixed bayonets; a precaution which I suppose experience had taught the necessity of observing. Above them was a choir consisting of several Indian musicians, who performed very well indeed on various instruments, and sang the *Te Deum* in a very passable manner. The congregation was very attentive, but the gratification they appeared to derive from the music furnished another proof of the strong hold this portion of the ceremonies of the Romish church takes upon uninformed minds. The worthy and benevolent priests of the mission devote almost the whole of their time to the duties of the establishment, and have a fatherly regard for those placed under them who are obedient and diligent; and too much praise cannot be bestowed upon them, considering that they have relinquished many of the enjoyments of life, and have embraced a voluntary exile in a distant and barbarous country. The only amusement which my hospitable host of the mission of San Jose indulged in, during my visit to that place, was during

2 Native majordomos, or constables, who were appointed by the padres to maintain order in the mission community.

meal times, when he amused himself by throwing pancakes to the *muchachos,* a number of little Indian domestics, who stood gaping around the table. For this purpose, he had every day two piles of pancakes made of Indian corn; and as soon as the olla[3] was removed, he would fix his eyes upon one of the boys, who immediately opened his mouth, and the padre, rolling up a cake would say something ludicrous in allusion to the boy's appetite, or to the size of his mouth, and pitch the cake at him, which the imp would catch between his teeth, and devour with incredible rapidity, in order that he might be ready the sooner for another, as well as to please the padre, whose amusement consisted in a great measure in witnessing the sudden disappearance of the cake. In this manner the pile of cakes were gradually distributed among the boys, amidst much laughter, and occasional squabbling. . . .

Beechey was not deceived by the serenity of his surroundings. He knew that the mission system was doomed. What disturbed him was that here was a country that was rich, but what would become of the land? Sooner or later, it must pass into other hands:

¶ The more we became acquainted with the beautiful country around San Francisco, the more we were convinced that it possessed every requisite to render it a valuable appendage to Mexcio; and it was impossible to resist joining in the remark of Vancouver, "Why such an extent of territory should have been subjugated, and, after all the expense and labour bestowed upon its colonization, turned to no account whatever, is a mystery in the science of state policy not easily explained."

Situated in the northern hemisphere, between the parallels of 22° and 39°, no fault can be found with its climate; its soil in general is fertile, it possesses forests of oak and pine convenient for building and contributing to the necessities of vessels, plains overrun with cattle, excellent ports, and navigable rivers to facilitate inland communication. Possessing all these advantages, an industrious population alone seems requisite to withdraw it from the obscurity in which it has so long slept under the indolence of the people and the jealous policy of the Spanish government. Indeed it struck us as lamentable to see such an extent of habitable country lying almost desolate and useless to mankind, whilst other nations are groaning under the burthen of their population.

It is evident from the natural course of events, and from the rapidity with which observation has recently been extended to the hitherto most obscure parts of the globe, that this indifference cannot continue; for either

[3] A dish made with boiled meat and vegetable.

it must disappear under the present authorities, or the country will fall into other hands, as from its situation with regard to other powers upon the new continent, and to the commerce of the Pacific, it is of too much importance to be permitted to remain long in its present neglected state. Already have the Russians encroached upon the territory by possessing themselves of the Farrallones, and some islands off Santa Barbara; and their new settlement at Rossi,[4] a few miles to the northward of Bodega, is so near upon the boundary as to be the cause of much jealous feeling;— not without reason it would appear, as I am informed it is well fortified, and presents to California an example of what may be effected upon her shores in a short time by industry.

The tract situated between California and the eastern side of the continent of North America, having been only partially explored, has hitherto presented a formidable barrier to encroachment from that quarter; but settlements are already advancing far into the heart of the country, and parties of hunters have lately traversed the interior, and even penetrated to the shores of the Pacific;—not without the loss of lives from the attacks of the Indians, it is true, but with ease, compared with the labour and difficulty experienced by Lewis and Clarke, who had not the benefit which more recent travellers have derived from the establishment of inland depots by the American fur companies. . . .

The trade of Upper California at present consists in the exportation of hides, tallow, manteca, horses to the Sandwich Islands, grain for the Russian establishments at Sitka and Kodiak, and in the disposal of provisions to whale-ships and other vessels which touch upon the coast, —perhaps a few furs and dollars are sent to China. The importations are dry goods, furniture, wearing-apparel, agricultural implements, deal boards and salt; and silks and fireworks from China for the decoration of the churches and celebration of the saints' days. In 1827 almost all these articles bore high prices; the former in consequence of the increased demand for them; and the latter partly for the necessity of meeting the expenses of the purchase of a return cargo, and partly on account of the navigation act.

The missions and the inhabitants in general complained loudly of these prices, not considering that the fault was in a great measure their own, and that they were purchasing some articles which had been brought several thousand miles, when they might have procured them in their own country with moderate labour only. For example, they were actually living upon the sea-coast and amongst forests of pine, and yet were suffering themselves to buy salt and deal boards at exorbitant prices.

[4] Fort Ross.

With a similar disregard for their interests, they were purchasing sea-otter skins at twenty dollars apiece, whilst the animals were swimming about unmolested in their own harbours; and this from the Russians, who are intruders upon their own harbours; and upon their coast, and are depriving them of a lucrative trade: and again, they were paying two hundred dollars for carts of inferior workmanship, which, with the exception of the wheels, might have been equally well manufactured in their own country. . . .

The *Blossom* was ready to continue her voyage in January, 1827. The ship passed through the Golden Gate, turned south, and anchored first at Monterey, where Beechey recorded his final description of the colorful port:

¶ The village and presidio of Monterey are situated upon a plain between the anchorage and a range of hills covered with woods and pine and oak. The presidio is in better condition than that at San Francisco; still as a place of defence it is quite useless. The fort is not much better, and its strength may be judged of from its having been taken by a small party of seamen who landed from a Buenos Ayrean pirate in 1819, destroyed the greater part of the guns, and pillaged and burnt the town. . . .

We found lying in the port of Monterey an American brig endeavouring to dispose of a cargo of dry goods, and to procure hides and tallow in return; and we opportunely received from her a supply of spirits, as the last cask was abroach. On the 4th a Russian brig, named the Baikal, belonging to the Russian American Fur Company anchored in the bay. This vessel was employed upon the coast, trading between Sitka, Bodega, and several ports in California, either in carrying or arranging the supplies for the Russian settlements to the northward. She was commanded by an officer in the Russian navy, and had on board, Mr. Klebnekoff, the agent. There are several of these vessels upon the coast carrying guns, and wearing pendants. On the 5th we took leave of our hospitable acquaintances, and put to sea on our passage to the Sandwich Islands.

Following the return of the *Blossom* to England, Beechey was assigned to further surveying duties by the British navy along the South American coast and in the Irish Sea. He was promoted to the rank of rear admiral in 1854, and upon his retirement was named superintendent of the marine branch of the board of trade. When he died, on November 29, 1856, Admiral Beechey was president of the Royal Geographical Society of London.

10

VIEWS
OF MEXICAN CALIFORNIA

The years of Mexican rule in California were characterized by mismanagement and political unrest. A succession of inept governors motivated more by personal ambition than by their civic responsibility kept the territory in a constant turmoil. There were revolts and counter-revolts, as rival factions waged a continual struggle for power. The spoils for the victors were considerable. The mission lands were divided among the favored, when those governing California ignored the orders of the Mexican Congress to secularize the mission properties and give the land to the Indians. These officials justified their treatment of the Indians by claiming they were unprepared to accept the responsibilities that freedom from mission authority would require. Captain Beechey had observed what happened to the natives when they were suddenly released from the authority of the Franciscan padres:

¶ . . . these people, who had always been accustomed to the care and discipline of school-boys, finding themselves their own masters, indulged freely in those excesses which it had been the endeavours of their tutors to repress, and . . . many having gambled away their clothes, implements and even their land, were compelled to beg or plunder; in order to support life. They at length become so obnoxious to the peaceable inhabitants, that the padres were requested to take some of them back to the missions, while others who had been guilty of misdemeanors were loaded with shackles and put to hard work. . . .

Efforts by the Mexican government to colonize California during this period had negligible results. In 1829, nearly one hundred convicts were transported from Mexico to California to serve out their sentences. The local residents protested that they did not want their territory transformed into a penal colony. The prisoners were sent home. A more ambitious project was conceived, when a company of three hundred people was recruited to found a colony in California after being granted free passage from Mexico. Alexander Forbes, a British businessman, reported the results of the venture in his *A History of Upper and Lower California*. Forbes arrived in South America in 1825, and later moved to Mexico. He was primarily interested in mining, and news he received from Californians who came to Mexico to transact business prompted him to investigate this promising territory. He describes the unrealistic recruitment program for the new settlers who were sent to the Pacific coast:

¶ . . . They were chiefly from the city of Mexico, and consisted of artizans and idlers who had been made to believe that they would soon enrich themselves in idleness in this happy country. There were to be seen goldsmiths proceeding to a country where no gold or silver existed, blacksmiths to where no horses are shod or iron used, carpenters to where only huts without furniture were erected, shoemakers to where only sandals of raw hide were worn, tailors to where the inhabitants only covered themselves with a blanket, doctors to where no one gets sick; there were also engravers, printers, musicians, gamblers, and other nameless professors, all bound on this hopeful crusade, which their enthusiastic leaders assured them would procure unalloyed felicity and unbounded riches. . . .[1]

According to the author, these colonists settled in the San Francisco Bay region, where they were supported for a time by the missions. In

[1] Alexander Forbes, *A History of Upper and Lower California* (London: Smith, Elder & Co., Cornhill, 1839).

May, 1835, most of the settlers boarded a ship and returned to Mexico. At a later date there would have been opportunities for a number of the trades and professions represented in this group, but at the time of their arrival the need was for competent farmers who would cultivate the land.

The churches and buildings of the mission chain were abandoned and allowed to decay. Many of the Franciscan fathers left California. Their Indian charges were turned adrift into a hostile society. Basically, the mission economy under the guidance of the Franciscan fathers was highly productive. They had planted vineyards, orchards, and had learned to reap bountiful harvests from the land. Their herds of cattle and sheep grazed across the hills as far as the eye could see. It was the missions that fed the presidios and furnished the products that could be exchanged for the necessities obtained from foreign vessels that neither Spain nor Mexico provided. Despite its detractors, the Church system represented order. Its demise, aggravated by the existent political instability, resulted in severe difficulties.

*　　*　　*

George Vancouver had written that the Spaniards were unsuccessful in effecting a juncture with their troops between Santa Fe and the Pacific coast owing to the mountain barrier. There were men, however, who refused to allow the Sierra wall to block their path. These were the trappers—mountain men, as they have come to be called— who roamed the wilderness in search of furs, unknowingly readying the land for future settlement, while at the same time destroying the wildlife. In the decade between 1830–1840, trappers killed the entire beaver population of the Rocky Mountain area. The trails these hunters followed became wagon roads, and their isolated outposts were later the locations for forts and small villages linking the trail west.

The extinction of game was but one of the evils committed by the fur seekers. They also aroused the hostility of the Indians by coercing various tribes to wage war against their neighbors. The trappers carried other vices of civilization, which they scattered with devastating effect among the savages, who prior to the coming of the white predators were unaware of social diseases and the evils of drink. While most of the trappers were coarse, uneducated, and often dissolute wanderers, there were exceptions—men who were educated and who were attracted to the West by a love for the freedom of the outdoors and a zest for adventure. Jedediah Smith was such a man. A Bible-reading veteran of the frontier before he reached thirty, Smith arrived at the Mission San Gabriel near Los Angeles on November 27, 1826, with a company of fifteen trappers. The party had left their trading post near Great Salt Lake the previous August. Smith and his group were hospitably received by the mission fathers, but Governor José María Echeandía declined to permit him to trade.

Smith had served his apprenticeship in the wilderness as an associate of General William H. Ashley, who had established a well-organized and efficient company to hunt for the prized beaver. Jedediah remained at San Gabriel until the following January, when his party returned to Utah. Smith made another trip to California the following year, angering the governor by his presence. The padres at Mission San José jailed him briefly on suspicion of creating unrest among their Indian wards. He shared the fate of many professional hunters of the era. On May 27, 1831, Jedediah Smith was killed by Comanches on the banks of the Cimarron River while leading a trading caravan from St. Louis to Santa Fe.

Among the travelers who came to California during the period of Mexican rule, none seems to have suffered such misfortunes as James Ohio Pattie, nor left behind such an interesting account of life along the coast as he found it. Accompanied by his father, Sylvester, and three other resolute companions, Pattie departed from St. Louis in 1824 to seek his fortune in the West. The strange odyssey finally published in 1833 as *The Personal Narrative of James Ohio Pattie* (Cincinnati: Edited and published by Timothy Flint) is exceedingly rare today.

The Patties reached Santa Fe, and from there roamed across much of the Southwest, hunting for the rapidly disappearing beaver. They explored the Grand Canyon of the Colorado, but near Yuma the party ran into trouble. Their food was gone and there was little game to be found. It was decided to make for California, where the Spaniards had settlements. They had been warmly received in Santa Fe, and believed they would be accorded a similar reception when they arrived at San Diego. The men buried their furs and began the long march to the coast. Much of the country they passed through was desert, but it was no novelty to these wanderers, who had already endured every imaginable hardship.

Entering California through the Imperial Valley, the exhausted group reached the Mission Santa Catalina in Lower California, south of San Diego. Here to their surprise, they were jailed by the Mexican authorities. After being confined for a week, James Pattie, his father and their companions, now numbering six, were marched to San Diego, where the government was to dispose of their case. This was in March, 1828. The order to bring them there from the Mission Santa Catalina had been signed by Governor José María de Echeandía, and as Pattie narrates his story, the Mexican official is cast as a villain. He jailed the Americans, separating them in individual cells. James Pattie contemplated his predicament:

¶ . . . My prison was a cell eight or ten feet square, with walls and floor of stone. A door with iron bars an inch square crossed over each other, like the bars of window sashes, and it grated on its iron hinges, as it opened to receive me. Over the external front of this prison was inscribed in capital letters *Destinacion de la Cattivo*. Our blankets were given us to lie upon. My father had a small package of medicines which he gave in charge to the sergeant, binding him on his word of honor not to part with it to any one. My door was locked, and I was left to reflect upon our position and my past misfortunes; and to survey the dreary walls of my prison. Here, I thought, was my everlasting abode. Liberty is dear to every one, but doubly dear to one, who had been from infancy accustomed to free range, and to be guided by his own will. Put a man, who has ranged the prairies, and exulted in the wilderness, as I have for years, in a prison, to let him have a full taste of the blessings of freedom, and the horror of shackles and confinement! I passed the remainder of the day in fierce walking backwards and forwards over my stone floor, with no object to contemplate, but my swarthy sentinel, through the grate. He seemed to be true to his office, and fitly selected for his business, for I thought I saw him look at me through the grate with the natural exultation and joy of a bad and malicious heart in the view of misery. . . .

The church bell told eight in the morning. The drum rolled. A soldier came, and handed me something to eat. It proved to be dried beans and corn cooked with rancid tallow! The contents were about a pint. I took it up, and brought it within the reach of my nostrils, and sat it down in unconquerable loathing. When the soldier returned in the evening to bring me more, I handed him my morning ration untasted and just as it was. He asked me in a gruff tone why I had not eaten it? I told him the smell of it was enough, and that I could not eat it. He threw the contents of the dish in my face, muttering something which amounted to saying, that it was good enough for such a brute as I was. To this I answered, that if being a brute gave claims upon that dish, I thought he had best eat it himself. On this he flung away in a passion, and returned no more that night, for which I was not sorry. Had the food even been fit to eat, my thoughts were too dark and my mind too much agitated to allow me appetite. In fact, I felt myself becoming sick. . . .[2]

Confinement in a damp cell undermined the health of the elder Pattie, who became gravely ill. Echeandía refused to permit his son to visit him as he lay dying. The only concession he granted James Pattie was to attend his father's funeral:

¶ . . . At eight in the morning, a file of six soldiers appeared at the door of my prison. It was opened, and I once more breathed the fresh air! The earth and the sky seemed a new region—The glare of light dazzled my eyes and dizzied my head. I reeled as I walked. A lieutenant conducted the ceremonies: and when I arrived at the grave he ordered the crowd to give way, that I might see the coffin let down, and the grave filled. I advanced to the edge of the grave, and caught a glimpse of the coffin that contained the remains of the brave hunter and ranger. The coffin was covered with black. No prayers were said. I had scarce time to draw a second breath, before the grave was half filled with earth. I was led back to my prison . . . when I arrived . . . such a horrid revulsion came over me at the thoughts of entering that dreary place again, that I am sure I should have preferred to have been shot, rather than enter it again. But I recovered myself by reflecting that my health was rapidly declining, and that I should be able in a short time to escape from the oppressor and the prison walls, and rejoin my father, and be at rest. . . .

Echeandía later called the young Pattie to his office, asking him to translate some documents he had received, which were written in

[2] James Ohio Pattie, *The Personal Narrative of James Ohio Pattie*, edited by Timothy Flint (Cincinnati, 1833).

English. The prisoner refused and told him he wished to return to his
cell:

¶ . . . bowing, I moved towards the door. He darted a glance at me
resembling that of an enraged wild beast; and in a voice, not unlike the
growl of a wounded grizzly bear, asked me why I did not put myself to
the translation of the letters? Assuming a manner and tone as surly as his
own, I told him my reasons were, that I did not choose to labor voluntarily
for an oppressor and enemy; and that I had come to the determination to
do it no longer. At this he struck me over the head such a blow with the
flat of his sword, as well nigh dropped me on the floor; and ordered the
soldiers to return me to prison, where he said I should lay and rot. The
moment I recovered from the stunning effect of the blow I sprang toward
him; but was immediately seized by the guards, and dragged to the door;
he, the while, muttered abundance of the curses which his language supplies. In return, I begged him to consider how much it was like an officer
and gentleman to beat an unarmed prisoner in his power, but that if I only
had a sword to meet him upon equal terms, I could easily kill as many
such dastards as he was, as could come at me. He bade me be silent, and
the soldiers to take me off. They shoved me violently on before them to
prison. When it closed upon me I never expected to see the sun rise and set
again. . . .

After months of incarceration, Pattie and his companions obtained
their freedom when an epidemic swept through California decimating
the population:

¶ At length the small pox began to rage on the coast, carrying off the
inhabitants by hundreds. Letters from the distressed people were continually arriving, praying the general to devise some mean to put a stop to
the disease, which seemed to threaten the country with destruction. The
general was thus beset by petitions for several weeks, before he could offer
a shadow of relief for them. He was much alarmed, fearing that the disorder might extend its ravages to that part of the coast where he resided.
   One day the soldiers, through mere inquisitiveness, asked the Dutchman [3] if he knew any remedy for the complaint? He answered that he
did; but that he had none of the article that constituted the remedy. He
added, however, that he thought my father had brought some of it
with him, as he recollected his having vaccinated the people at the copper

[3] One of Pattie's companions.

mines. This conversation was communicated to the general immediately, who sent a sergeant to me to inquire if I had any of the remedy. . . . I answered in the affirmative; I then showed him where I had been vaccinated on the right arm, and assured him that it had effectually protected me from the small pox . . . thinking this my only chance for regaining liberty, I refused it to him, saying that I would neither show it to any one, nor apply it, unless my liberty and that of my companions was rendered secure. . . .

Reluctantly, the governor granted the prisoners their freedom, and Pattie began vaccinating the people of California. By the time he completed his work of visiting the chain of missions between San Diego and San Francisco, he relates he had innoculated 22,000 persons against the disease. San Fernando, Ventura, Santa Barbara, San Luis Obispo, and Monterey were some of the communities he visited. The population of these missions consisted mostly of Indians. After leaving the San Gabriel Mission, he visited Los Angeles, at that time a relatively unimportant pueblo. He writes:

¶ My next advance was to a small town, inhabited by Spaniards, called the town of the Angels. The houses have flat roofs, covered with bituminous pitch, brought from a place within four miles of the town, where this article boils up from the earth.[4] As the liquid rises, hollow bubbles like a shell of a large size, are formed. When they burst, the noise is heard distinctly in the town. The material is obtained by breaking off portions, that have become hard with an axe, or something of the kind. The large pieces thus separated are laid on the roof, previously covered with earth, through which the pitch cannot penetrate, when it is rendered liquid again by the heat of the sun. In this place I vaccinated 2500 persons. . . .

Pattie turned down an opportunity to settle in California, when he was offered a large tract of land to repay him for his efforts in preventing an epidemic. The local officials also wanted to give him five hundred cows and five hundred mules for his work. The payment was authorized by Father Juan Cabortes at Mission San Francisco, July 8, 1829. There was one stipulation. He had to become a Catholic and a Mexican citizen. This aroused Pattie's anger, and he hotly

[4] The La Brea Tar Pits on present day Wilshire Boulevard, just east of Beverly Hills.

replied to the priest "that I would not change my present religious opinions for all the money his mission was worth, and moreover, that before I would consent to be adopted into the society and companionship of such a band of murderers and robbers, as I deemed were to be found on this coast, for the pitiful amount of one thousand head of cattle, I would suffer death."

Father Cabortes was merely complying with a government decree, which in 1828 had authorized the granting of lands in California to foreigners who would comply with the requirements of the law by being baptized into the Roman Catholic faith, and becoming naturalized as Mexican citizens. According to Pattie there was already a colony of some forty Americans living at Monterey, mostly seafaring men who had settled there in recent years, as under Mexican rule the restrictions promulgated by Spain were being gradually relaxed. It is here that the migration of Americans had its beginning, although a decade was to pass before the influx reached sizable proportions.

Pattie was anxious to leave California, although before his departure he participated in one of the revolts, which were becoming more prevalent in the stormy Mexican politics following liberation from Spanish rule. Joaquín Solís led a party consisting of many soldiers who, disenchanted with the administration in California of Governor Echeandía, revolted against his rule. Solís, the insurgent general, aroused military elements in the north to establish a new government. This was in November, 1829, and had strong support in Santa Clara, San Jose, San Francisco, and Monterey, a presidio that his forces occupied. An attempt to capture Santa Barbara failed, and Solís made a quick departure. Echeandía recaptured Monterey on January 20, 1830. Oddly, Pattie had supported him during the rebellion instead of backing the insurgents. Considering the harsh treatment he had received at the hands of the California governor, this seems unusual.

Pattie obtained a passport from Governor Echeandía, sailing for Mexico from San Diego on May 9, 1830. It was his intent to seek redress from the Mexican government for false imprisonment and the loss of his furs. His other companions decided to remain in California. Arriving in Mexico City, he was informed by the American consul that an appeal had been made for his release, as well as that of his companions, by President Andrew Jackson. Although an interview

was arranged for him with the Mexican president, Pattie did not press
his claims, possibly at the request of the American consul. He returned to the United States, arriving in New Orleans penniless. He
had been befriended by a fellow passenger, who introduced him to J. S.
Johnston, United States Senator from Louisiana. The senator paid for
the trapper's passage up the Mississippi River to Cincinnati, and also
gave him a letter of introduction to the Reverend Timothy Flint,
editor of the *Western Monthly Review,* published at Cincinnati. Flint
was deeply interested in the exciting events occurring in the unknown
regions of the Far West. He edited and published Pattie's journal,
which appeared in 1831 as *The Personal Narrative of James O. Pattie
of Kentucky.* The book was widely read and discussed. The author
returned to the wilderness. Here he vanished from history.

*   *   *

Zenas Leonard served as a clerk to Joseph Reddeford Walker, the
skilled captain of a band of fur seekers that came to California in
1833–1834. The mountain men had rendezvoused near Great Salt
Lake during the summer of 1833. At this gathering were trappers of
the American Fur Company, the Rocky Mountain Fur Company, and
the organization headed by Captain Benjamin L. E. Bonneville.
Walker belonged to this company, and it was decided to send him
and a party across the Sierra toward the Pacific, trapping beaver en
route. If unsuccessful, the men were to return to the Great Salt Lake
the following year.

The route they followed has a number of landmarks bearing this
great pathfinder's name—Walker Lake and Walker Pass, the trail
they opened through the Sierra Nevada, losing many of their pack
animals in the passage. It was during this journey that they became
the first white men to enter the Yosemite Valley, where they viewed
the magnificent spectacle of its great waterfall, lofty mountain domes
and pinnacles. From there they followed the Merced River to the San
Joaquin, searching for beaver as they headed for the coast. The San
Joaquin River flowed into Suisun Bay near the present town of
Martinez. The party passed San Pablo and San Francisco Bay, making
camp at Point Año Nuevo about twenty miles northwest of Santa

Cruz. Here an exciting meeting took place. An American ship was anchored offshore. When the sailors and mountain men met along the beach, a riotous reunion took place, and the celebration lasted throughout the night. They of course did not realize the significance of the meeting. For the first time, Americans who had crossed the Sierra Nevada and those who had come by sea to California joined hands in a land which within a few years would become a part of the United States.

Leonard's journal was printed as the *Narrative of the Adventures of Zenas Leonard a Native of Clearfield County, Pa who spent five years in Trapping for Furs, Trading with the Indians, &c., of the Rocky Mountains. Written by Himself.* Here he describes that historic rendezvous in November, 1833, on the shores of the Pacific Ocean:

¶ . . . About noon of the third day after we arrived here, the attention of the company was directed to an object which could be dimly seen at a distance riding on the water, which was immediately judged to be a ship, but no one knew from whence it came, where it belonged or where going. It was now our curiosity to know more of this singular object and if possible to attract their attention and bring them ashore. Accordingly we fastened two white blankets together and hoisted them into the air on a pole: This had the desired effect. It was not long until we could tell that the distance between us was fast diminishing, and our joy and surprise may be imagined when we beheld the broad stripes and bright stars of the American flag waving majestically in the air at the mast head. The ship anchored some distance from the shore and the boats were dispatched to see what nation we belonged to, and what our business was. Their astonishment was equally as great as ours when they ascertained that we were children of the same nation as themselves. On making this discovery, and a signal to that effect being given by the boats, the ship fired several salutes of cannon in honor of our meeting, which made the welkin ring.—

On further acquaintance we ascertained this ship [the *Lagoda*] to belong to Boston, commanded by Capt. Baggshaw.[5] After exchanging civilities by shaking hands all round, Capt. Baggshaw strongly insisted on us going on board and partaking of the ship's fare, stating that he had a few casks of untapped Coneac. This was an invitation that none of us had the least desire to refuse, and accordingly 45 of us went on board the

5 The master of the *Lagoda* was John Bradshaw. Leonard misspelled his name.

Lagoda, leaving the remainder to take care of the camp &c. When arriving on the ship Capt. B. had a table spread with the choicest of liquors & best fair the ship would afford, which was immediately surrounded with hungry . . . Mates, Clerks, Sailors and greasy trappers—after eating, the glass was passed around in quick succession, first drinking after the fashion of brave Jack Tars, and afterwards in the mountain style, mixed with something of the manners of the natives, in order to amuse the sailors.

After we got on board, the sea became very rough, causing the vessel to pitch and plunge a great deal as she lay at anchor and consequently I was compelled to return to shore from sea sickness. The balance remained and kept up the celebration until daylight. The next morning . . . they all returned to land, accompanied by the ship's crew to taper off on the harder fare of the trapper and hunter. The feast on the vessel was far superior to anything we could give them, although they appeared perfectly satisfied with the reception they met with from us, as it was a long time since they had tasted any fresh meat, or anything but salted victuals; and theirs was the first bread, butter, cheese, &c., that we had seen for more than two years.

After the feasting was at an end, Capt. Baggshaw gave us a description of the country to enable us to lay our plans accordingly. He said the nearest settlement was the town of St. Francisco, about forty miles north of our present encampment, situated on the south side of the Francisco Bay, formed by the river which we descended, which he calls Two Laries,[6] or Bush River. It is about three-fourths of a mile wide at its mouth, and is considered a safe harbor for almost any quantity of vessels; and within 60 or 70 miles south of us is the town of Monterey, also Spanish, the capital of this province, which is called Upper California. He also informed us that about 60 or 70 miles north of St. Francisco, and about 100 miles from our present position was a Russian settlement, which consists of about 150 families who settled in this country a few years ago for the purpose of catching sea otter, which are of great value, on account of the quality of the fur. They also cultivate the ground to a considerable extent. Capt. Baggshaw went and examined the carcass of the whale which our men had found, and pronounced it to be the Sperm whale, the oil of which is of the most valuable kind. He supposed it had been washed here when the sea was rough during a storm, and was unable to make his way back over the sand bars. From him we also learned some further particulars concerning the mountain which had caused us so many hardships in crossing,

[6] The Tulare, or San Joaquin, River.

parts of which was visible from the ocean, particularly the snow covered peaks. This he called the California mountain, as it runs parallel with the coast for a great distance, commencing at the mouth of the Columbia river, and extending along the coast to mouth of the Red river, or Gulf of California, forming a beautiful country from the sea shore to the base of the mountain, and extending north and south a distance of about 6 or 700 miles of rich soil, well timbered and abundantly watered by innumerable small streams heading in the mountain and flowing toward the Father of Waters.

Most of this vast waste of territory belongs to the Republic of the United States. What a theme to contemplate its settlement and civilization. Will the jurisdiction of the federal government ever succeed in civilizing the thousands of savages now roaming over these plains, and her hardy free-born population here plant their homes, build their towns and cities, and say here shall the arts and sciences of civilization take root and flourish? Yes, here, even in this remote part of the great west before many years, will these hills and valleys be greeted with the enlivening sound of the workman's hammer, and the merry whistle of the plough-boy. But this is left undone by the government, and will only be seen when too late to apply the remedy. The Spaniards are making inroads on the South—the Russians are encroaching with impunity along the sea shore to the North, and farther North-east the British are pushing their stations into the very heart of our territory, which even at this day, more resemble military forts to resist invasion, than trading stations. Our government should be vigilant. She should assert her claim by taking possession of the whole territory as soon as possible—for we have good reason to suppose that the territory *west* of the mountain will some day be equally as important to a nation as that on the *east*.[7]

Following the Walker expedition to California, Leonard returned to his home in Clearfield, Pennsylvania, arriving there in the fall of 1835. Six months later he was on the move again. He opened a store in present Sibley, Missouri, where he sold goods to settlers passing through on their way west. He also obtained furs from the Indians, which he shipped by riverboat to St. Louis. Leonard married and became the father of three children. His narrative was first published

[7] Zenas Leonard, *Narrative of the Adventures of Zenas Leonard a Native of Clearfield County, Pa who spent five years in Trapping for Furs, Trading with the Indians, &c., of the Rocky Mountains. Written by Himself* (Clearfield, Pa.: Printed by D. W. Moore, 1839).

in installments by the *Clearfield Republican*. The great interest shown by his readers caused the newspaper's publisher to bring it out in book form. Copies of the original 1839 edition are extremely rare today. Leonard died on July 14, 1857. He was forty-eight.

*   *   *

For a young man troubled with poor vision, Richard Henry Dana possessed the most observant eyes of any visitor to California. On August 14, 1834, Dana shipped out of Boston on the brig *Pilgrim,* bound for Cape Horn and a voyage into the Pacific. Suffering from weak eyesight which forced him to discontinue his studies at Harvard, he had signed aboard the trading vessel as a common seaman. He was nineteen.

A sailor's life in Dana's day was one of privation and hardship. Tyrannical captains flogged their men for the slightest infraction of an archaic code of regulations. The master of the *Pilgrim* was no exception. When Dana wasn't aloft or attending to his shipboard duties, he entered his impressions of the voyage in a journal. These provided the notes for his *Two Years Before the Mast,* a remarkable account of life at sea during the age of sail. In addition, his book contains one of the best descriptions available of California and its inhabitants during the final decade of Mexican rule.

The *Pilgrim* reached Monterey, where her cargo of merchandise was bartered for the hides that the cattle-raising Mexicans had in abundance. Wide-eyed, they came aboard to stare at the goods on display. Dana wrote:

¶ . . . Our cargo was an assorted one; that is, it consisted of everything under the sun. We had spirits of all kinds (sold by the cask), teas, coffee, sugar, spices, raisins, molasses, hardware, crockery-ware, tin-ware, cutlery, clothing of all kinds, boots and shoes from Lynn, calicoes and cottons from Lowell, crapes, silks; also, shawls, scarfs, necklaces, jewelry, and combs for the women; furniture; and, in fact, everything that can be imagined, from Chinese fireworks to English cart-wheels—of which we had a dozen pairs with their iron tires on . . .[8]

[8] Richard Henry Dana, *Two Years Before the Mast—A Personal Narrative of Life at Sea* (New York: Harper & Brothers, 1840).

Like so many of the industrious Yankees who visited the Pacific coast, Dana was critical of the indolence he discovered among the people he encountered:

¶ The Californians are an idle, thriftless people, and can make nothing for themselves. The country abounds in grapes, yet they buy, at a great price, bad wine made in Boston and brought round by us, and retail it among themselves at a *real* (12½ cents.) by the small wine-glass. Their hides, too, which they value at two dollars in money, they barter for something which costs seventy-five cents in Boston; and buy shoes (as like as not made of their own hides, which have been carried twice round Cape Horn) at three and four dollars, and "chicken-skin boots" at fifteen dollars a pair. Things sell, on an average, at an advance of nearly three hundred per cent upon the Boston prices. This is partly owing to the heavy duties which the government, in their wisdom, with an idea, no doubt, of keeping the silver in the country, has laid upon imports. These duties, and the enormous expenses of so long a voyage, keep all merchants but those of heavy capital from engaging in trade. . . .

The owners of the *Pilgrim* had several other vessels gathering hides along the California coast. Dana was assigned to work in one of the company's warehouses and curing plants at San Diego, where he spent several months. He was anxious to return home to continue his studies. Friends in Boston arranged for him to be transferred to the *Alert,* which was scheduled to leave California before the *Pilgrim.* He boarded the ship at San Diego before she sailed north toward San Francisco. The *Alert* left Monterey on January 8, 1836. Her destination was Santa Barbara, and here Dana did not find the people idle. Ashore, there was great activity and excitement. A wedding was to take place. This was sufficient reason—or excuse for the pleasure-loving Californians to organize a celebration of the sort they enjoyed most—a *fiesta.* There would be music, dancing, a great feast, and although the temperate young Dana refrained from reporting the matter, the local brandy reserves were generally depleted. A *fiesta* could last several days; on occasion, the festivities continued for a week. Describing how the *Alert* rounded Point Conception and entered the Santa Barbara Channel, Dana writes:

¶ . . . It was a bright, sunny day, and the wind, though strong, was fair; and everything was in striking contrast with our experience in the same place two months before, when we were drifting off from a north-wester, under a fore and main spencer. "Sail ho!" cried a man who was rigging out a top-gallant studding-sail boom. "Where away?" "Weather beam, sir!" and in a few minutes a full-rigged brig was seen standing out from under Point Conception. The studding-sail halyards were let go, and the yards boom-ended, the after yards braced aback, and we waited her coming down. She rounded to, backed her maintop-sail, and showed her decks full of men, four guns on a side, hammock nettings, and everything man-of-war fashion, except that there was no boatswain's whistle, and no uniforms on the quarter-deck. A short, square-built man in a rough grey jacket, with a speaking-trumpet in hand, stood in the weather hammock nettings. "Ship ahoy!" "Hallo!" "What ship is that, pray?" etc., etc. She proved to be the brig *Convoy,* from the Sandwich Islands, engaged in otter-hunting among the islands which lie along the coast. Her armament was because of her being a contrabandista. The otter are very numerous among these islands, and, being of great value, the government require a heavy sum for a licence to hunt them, and lay a high duty upon every one shot or carried out of the country. This vessel had no licence, and paid no duty, besides being engaged in smuggling goods [onto] other vessels trading on the coast, and belonging to the same owners. . . . Our captain told him to look out for the Mexicans, but he said they had not an armed vessel of his size in the whole Pacific. This was without doubt the same vessel that showed herself off Santa Barbara a few months before. These vessels frequently remain on the coast for years, without making port, except at the islands for wood and water, and an occasional visit to Oahu for a new outfit.

Sunday, January 10th. Arrived at Santa Barbara, and on the following Wednesday slipped our cable and went to sea, on account of a south-easter. Returned to our anchorage the next day. We were the only vessel in the port. The *Pilgrim* had passed through the canal and hove-to off the town, nearly six weeks before, on her passage down from Monterey, and was now at the leeward. She heard here of our safe arrival at San Francisco.

Great preparations were making on shore for the marriage of our agent, who was to marry Dona Anita de le Guerra de Noriego y Corillo, youngest daughter of Don Antonio Noriego, the grandee of the place, and the head of the first family in California. Our steward was ashore three days making pastry and cake, and some of the best of our stores were sent off with him. On the day appointed for the wedding, we took the captain ashore in the gig, and had orders to come for him at night, with leave to go up to the house and see the fandango. Returning on board, we found preparations making for a salute. Our guns were loaded and run out, men appointed to each, cartridges served out, matches lighted, and all the flags ready to be run up. I took my place at the starboard after-gun, and we all waited for the signal from on shore. At ten o'clock the bride went up with her sister to the confessional, dressed in deep black. Nearly an hour intervened, when the great doors of the mission church opened, the bells rang out a loud discordant peal, the private signal for us was run up by the captain ashore, the bride, dressed in complete white, came out of the church with the bridegroom, followed by a long procession. Just as she stepped from the church door, a small white cloud issued from the bows of our ship, which was full in sight, the loud report echoed among the surrounding hills and over the bay, and instantly the ship was dressed in flags and pennants from stem to stern. Twenty-three guns followed in regular succession, with an interval of fifteen seconds between each, when the cloud blew off, and our ship lay dressed in her colours all day. At sundown another salute of the same number of guns was fired, and all the flags run down. This we thought was pretty well—a gun every fifteen seconds—for a merchantman with only four guns and a dozen or twenty men.

After supper the gig's crew were called, and we rowed ashore, dressed in our uniforms, beached the boat, and went up to the fandango. The bride's father's house was the principal one in the place, with a large court in front, upon which a tent was built, capable of containing several hundred people. As we drew near, we heard the accustomed sound of violins and guitars, and saw a great motion of the people within. Going in, we found nearly all the people of the town—men, women, and children—collected and crowded together, leaving barely room for the dancers; for on these occasions no invitations are given, but every one is expected to come, though there is always a private entertainment within the house for particular friends. The old women sat down in rows, clapping their hands to the music, and applauding the young ones. The music was lively, and among the tunes we recognized several of our popular airs, which we, without doubt, have taken from the Spanish. In the dancing I was much disappointed. The women stood upright, with their hands down by their sides, their eyes fixed upon the ground before them, and slid about without any perceptible means of motion; for their feet were invisible, the hem of their dresses forming a circle about them, reaching to the ground. They looked as grave as though they were going through some religious ceremony, their faces as little excited as their limbs; and on the whole, instead of the spirited, fascinating Spanish dances which I had expected, I found the Californian fandango, on the part of the women at least, a lifeless affair. The men did better. They danced with grace and spirit, moving in circles round their nearly stationary partners, and showing their figures to advantage.

A great deal was said about our friend Don Juan Bandini, and when he did appear, which was toward the close of the evening, he certainly gave us the most graceful dancing that I had ever seen. He was dressed in white pantaloons, neatly made, a short jacket of dark silk, gaily figured, white stockings and thin morocco slippers upon his very small feet. His slight and graceful figure was well adapted to dancing, and he moved about with the grace and daintiness of a young fawn. An occasional touch of the toe to the ground seemed all that was necessary to give him a long interval of motion in the air. At the same time he was not fantastic or flourishing, but appeared to be rather repressing a strong tendency to motion. He was loudly applauded, and danced frequently toward the close of the evening. After the supper the waltzing began, which was confined to a very few of the *gente de razon,* and was considered a high accomplishment, and a mark of aristocracy. Here, too, Don Juan figured greatly, waltzing with the sister of the bride (Dona Augustia, a handsome woman and general favorite) in a variety of beautiful figures, which lasted as much as half an hour, no one else taking the floor. They were repeatedly and loudly applauded, the old men and women jumping out of their seats in admiration, and the young people waving their hats and handkerchiefs. The great amusement of the evening—owing to its being the Carnival—was the breaking of eggs filled with cologne or other essences, upon the heads of the company. The women bring a great number of these secretly about them, and the amusement is to break one upon the head of a gentleman when his back is turned. He is bound in gallantry to find out the lady, and return the compliment, though it must not be done if the person sees you. A tall, stately Don, with immense grey whiskers, and a look of great importance, was standing before me, when I felt a light hand on my shoulder, and, turning round, saw Dona Augustia (whom we all knew, as she had been up to Monterey, and down again, in the *Alert*), with her finger upon her lip, motioning me gently aside. I stepped back a little, when she went up behind the Don, and with one hand knocked off his huge *sombrero,* and at the same instant, with the other, broke the egg upon his head, and springing behind me, was out of sight in a moment. The Don turned slowly round, the cologne running down his face and over his clothes, and a loud laugh breaking out from every quarter. He looked round in vain for some time, until the direction of so many laughing eyes showed him the fair offender. She was his niece, and a great favourite with him, so old Don Domingo had to join in the laugh. A great many such tricks were played, and many a war of sharp manuvring was carried on between couples of the younger people, and at every successful exploit a general laugh was raised.

Another of their games I was for some time at a loss about. A pretty young girl was dancing, named—after what would appear to us an almost sacrilegious custom of the country—Espiritu Santu, when a young man went behind her and placed his hat directly upon her head, letting it fall down over her eyes, and sprang back among the crowd. She danced for some time with the hat on, when she threw it off, which called forth a general shout, and the young man was obliged to go out upon the floor and pick it up. Some of the ladies, upon whose heads hats had been placed, threw them off at once, and a few kept them on throughout the dance, and took them off at the end, and held them out in their hands, when the owner stepped out, bowed, and took it from them. I soon began to suspect the meaning of the thing, and was afterwards told that it was a compliment, and an offer to become a lady's gallant for the rest of the evening, and to wait upon her home. If the hat was thrown off the offer was refused, and the gentleman was obliged to pick up his hat amid a general laugh. Much amusement was caused sometimes by gentlemen putting hats on the ladies' heads without permitting them to see whom it was done by. This obliged them to throw them off, or keep them on at a venture, and when they came to discover the owner the laugh was turned upon one or the other.

The captain sent for us about ten o'clock, and we went aboard in high spirits, having enjoyed the new scene much, and were of great importance among the crew, from having so much to tell, and from the prospect of going every night until it was over; for these fandangos generally last three days. The next day two of us were sent up to the town, and took care to come back by way of Señor Noriego's, and take a look into the booth. The musicians were again there, upon their platform, scraping and twanging away, and a few people, apparently of the lower classes, were dancing. The dancing kept up at intervals throughout the day, but the crowd, the spirit, and the *élite* come in at night. The next night, which was the last, we went ashore in the same manner, until we got almost tired of the monotonous twang of the instruments, the drawling sound which the women kept up, as an accompaniment, and the slapping of the hands in time with the music, in place of castanets. We found ourselves as great objects of attention as any persons or anything at the place. Our sailor

dresses—and we took great pains to have them neat and ship-shape—
were much admired, and we were invited, from every quarter, to give
them an American dance; but after the ridiculous figure some of our
countrymen cut in dancing after the Mexicans, we thought it best to leave
it to their imaginations. Our agent, with a tight black swallow-tailed coat
just imported from Boston, and a high stiff cravat, looking as if he had
been pinned and skewered, with only his feet and hands left free, took the
floor just after Bandini, and we thought they had had enough of Yankee
grace.

The last night they kept it up in great style, and were getting into a high
go, when the captain called us off to go aboard, for, it being south-easter
season, he was afraid to remain on shore long; and it was well he did not,
for that night we slipped our cables, as a crowner to our fun ashore, and
stood off before a south-easter which lasted twelve hours, and returned to
our anchorage the next day.

Dana returned to Boston in September, 1836, tanned and hardened
from his voyage, and the problem he had had with his eyesight had
vanished. He reentered Harvard, graduating the following year at the
head of his class. As a lawyer, he had a long and distinguished career.
Although not identified as an active Abolitionist, he defended a
number of clients involved in the anti-slavery movement. During
1867–1868, he was co-counsel for the United States in treason proceedings brought against Jefferson Davis, president of the Confederacy
during the Civil War. These were dropped after the general amnesty
proclamation of December 26, 1868. Dana never lost his love for the
sea, and was fond of travel. He died in Rome of pneumonia on January 6, 1882.

Dana Point, south of Laguna Beach, marks one of the landing
places of the *Pilgrim* along the Southern California Coast. It was here
young Richard Dana landed with members of the crew to gather
hides brought from the mission at San Juan Capistrano. From the
steep cliffs, he hurled the hides to others waiting below:

¶ There I stood . . . throwing off the hides, and watching them pitching and scaling to the bottom, while the men, dwarfed by the distance,
were walking to and fro on the beach, carrying the hides, as they picked
them up, to the distant boats, upon the tops of their heads . . .

On any day of the year you will find visitors who come to the Point to stand in the cupola which overlooks the steep cliffs and affords a panoramic view of the Pacific. For many, Richard Henry Dana is just a name on the bronze plaque that marks the site, but there are those who recall his lines that so eloquently describe the beauty of the setting, and which has not changed:

¶ . . . there was a grandeur in everything around, which gave a solemnity to the scene, a silence and solitariness which affected every part! Not a human being but ourselves for miles, and no sound heard but the pulsations of the great Pacific! and the great steep hill rising like a wall, and cutting us off from all the world but the "world of waters!" I separated myself from the rest, and sat down on a rock, just where the sea ran in and formed a fine spouting horn.

Compared with the plain, dull sand-beach of the rest of the coast, this grandeur was as refreshing as a great rock in a weary land. . . .

11

THE MIGRATION BEGINS

As knowledge of the lands across the Rockies and the Sierra Nevada spread through settled regions of America, emigrant trains began their arduous trek across the wilderness. John Bidwell was a member of the first party of American settlers to arrive in California. He kept a diary of his journey, which was printed in St. Louis in 1842, following the long journey.

The book contained useful information sought by those who would follow in the author's path. The Mexicans were allowing American settlers to enter California, but Bidwell advises "that all who would come into this country must bring passports from the Governors of their resident state." In his book, Bidwell has some pertinent words for those who would travel west:

¶ . . . If I were to come to this country again, I would not come with wagons, but would use pack animals, either mules or horses—mules are rather better than horses generally for packing, but the latter for riding— as I have come by one route to this country, I cannot recommend any other. This journey with packed animals could be performed in three months, provided the Company have a pilot (and surely no other Company than ours ever started without one.)

Allowing a person to be 3 months on the route, he will need in the provision line 100 lbs. of flour, 50 lbs. of bacon, and if a Coffee drinker 20 lbs. of sugar and coffee to his taste—a few other things, dried fruit, rice, etc. would not come amiss. With all these he would have to be prudent, and before passing the mountains of Buffalo range, it will be necessary to lay in 140 lbs. of dried buffalo meat. A person will need one animal to pack his provision, one to carry his clothing and one to ride—it would be well to bring some kind of mountain goods in order to traffick in the mountains, provided one was so unlucky to have a horse stolen by the Indians or lose one otherwise. A person if fond of sporting or intends to hunt, will require 5 lbs. powder and 10 lbs. of lead, if the gun is a cap lock one, he should be provided with fire works—flint, steel, lint &c, if a few extra boxes of caps they will sell well—should bring a good supply of clothing (a hunter should wear nothing but buckskin) clothes being very dear here. Persons coming here with the intention of settling, will do well to bring an extra animal laden with guns or dry goods, as they are more current than money. If however any large quantity were brought into the country, duties would be required, which would overun the profit. . . .[1]

Bidwell suggested in his book that there would be many advantages in coming to California by ship, which was the means of transportation used by thousands who followed later during the gold-rush period:

¶ . . . so many things could be brought, such as ploughs, wagons &c. Surely no American could reconcile himself to the awkward utensils of the Spaniards. . . .

In later years, Bidwell contributed several articles to *The Century Magazine.* An account of his overland journey appeared in the November, 1890, issue as *The First Emigrant Train to California.* In the article, he looked back on the day when as a young man he decided to join with the thousands of other restless wanderers who formed an endless procession that moved in the direction of the setting sun—across prairies and over mountain barriers in a search for new opportunities:

[1] John Bidwell, *A Journey to California with Observations About the Country, Climate and the Route to This Country* (St. Louis, 1842). By permission of the Director, the Bancroft Library, University of California.

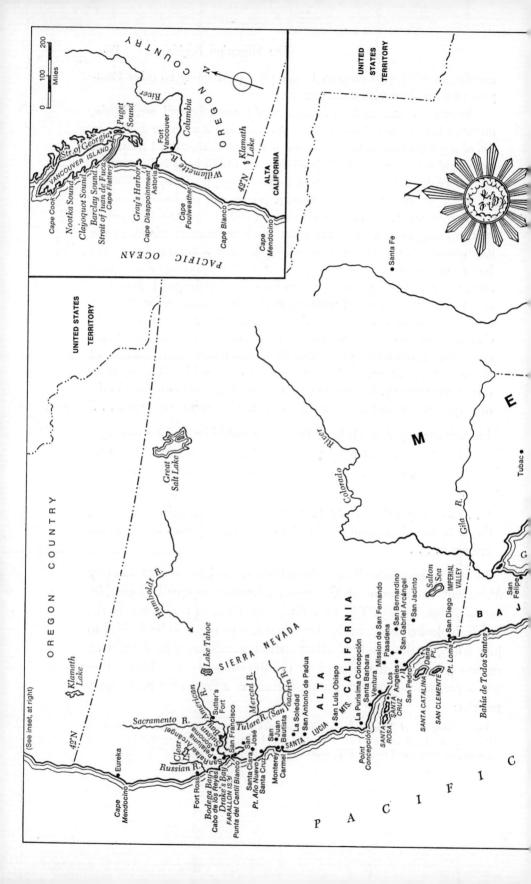

CALIFORNIA
AND THE
NORTHWEST
IN 1840

Scale of Miles

0 100 200 300 400

¶ In the spring of 1839,—living at the time in the western part of Ohio,—being then in my twentieth year, I conceived a desire to see the great prairies of the West, especially those most frequently spoken of, in Illinois, Iowa, and Missouri. Emigration from the East was tending westward, and settlers had already begun to invade those rich fields.

Starting on foot to Cincinnati, ninety miles distant, I fortunately got a chance to ride most of the way on a wagon loaded with farm produce. My outfit consisted of about $75, the clothes I wore, and a few others in a knapsack which I carried in the usual way strapped upon my shoulders, for in those days travelers did not have valises or trunks. Though travel was considered dangerous, I had no weapon more formidable than a pocket-knife. From Cincinnati I went down the Ohio River by steamboat to the Mississippi, up the Mississippi to St. Louis, and thence to Burlington, in what was then the Territory of Iowa. Those were bustling days on the western rivers, which were then the chief highways of travel. The scenes at the wood landings I recall as particularly lively and picturesque. Many passengers would save a little by helping to "wood the boat," i.e., by carrying wood down to the bank and throwing it on the boat, a special ticket being issued on that condition. It was very interesting to see the long lines of passengers coming up the gang-plank, each with two or three sticks of wood on his shoulders. . . .

Bidwell settled in a small community, the westernmost settlement in Missouri, where he found employment as a teacher. Here he might have remained had he not encountered a trapper returned from California. He addressed a gathering, creating considerable excitement with his description of the land to be found on the far side of the mountains.

¶ In November or December of 1840, while still teaching school in Platte County, I came across a Frenchman named Roubideaux, who said he had been to California. He had been a trader in New Mexico, and had followed the road traveled by traders from the frontier of Missouri to Santa Fe. He had probably gone through what is now New Mexico and Arizona into California by the Gila River trail used by the Mexicans. His description of California was in the superlative degree favorable, so much so that I resolved if possible to see that wonderful land, and with others helped get up a meeting at Weston and invited him to make a statement before it in regard to the country. At that time when a man moved out West, as soon as he was fairly settled he wanted to move again, and naturally every question imaginable was asked in regard to this wonderful country. Roubideaux described it as one of perennial spring and boundless fertility, and laid stress on the countless thousands of wild horses and cattle. He told about oranges, and hence must have been at Los Angeles, or the mission San Gabriel, a few miles from it. Every conceivable question that we could ask him was answered favorably. Generally the first question which a Missourian asked about a country was whether there was any fever and ague. I remember his answer distinctly. He said there was but one man in California that had ever had a chill there, and it was a matter of so much wonderment to the people of Monterey that they went eighteen miles into the country to see him shake. Nothing could have been more satisfactory on the score of health. He said that the Spanish authorities were most friendly, and that the people were the most hospitable on the globe; that you could travel all over California and it would cost you nothing for horses or food. Even the Indians were friendly. His description of the country made it seem like a Paradise.

The result was that we appointed a corresponding secretary, and a committee to report a plan of organization. A pledge was drawn up in which every signer agreed to purchase a suitable outfit, and to rendezvous at Sapling Grove in what is now the State of Kansas, on the 9th of the following May, armed and equipped to cross the Rocky Mountains to California. We called ourselves the Western Emigration Society, and as soon as the pledge was drawn up every one who agreed to come signed his name to it, and it took like wildfire.

The enthusiasm for the project was short-lived. The merchants of Platte County did their best to break up the movement by pointing out how foolish it was for five hundred people to pull up stakes, leave that beautiful country, and move to a region that people knew little about. A letter was widely circulated in which the writer claimed that Americans were oppressed by the native Californians and it was dangerous for them to go there. When Bidwell reached the rendezvous point in May, 1841, he was worried that he might have to continue across the plains alone. There was only one other wagon waiting to make the trip. But there were people who were determined to make the journey:

¶ For the next few days one or two wagons would come each day, and among the recruits were three families from Arkansas. We organized by electing as captain of the company a man named Bartleson from Jackson County, Missouri. He was not the best man for the position, but we were given to understand that if he was not elected captain he would not go; and as he had seven or eight men with him, and we did not want the party diminished, he was chosen. Every one furnished his own supplies. The party consisted of sixty-nine, including men, women, and children. Our teams were of oxen, mules and horses. We had no cows, as the later emigrants usually had, and the lack of milk was a great deprivation to the children. It was understood that every one should have not less than a barrel of flour with sugar and so forth to suit; but I laid in one hundred pounds of flour more than the usual quantity, besides other things. This I did because we were told that when we got into the mountains we probably would get out of bread and have to live on meat alone, which I thought would kill me even if it did not the others. My gun was an old flint-lock rifle, but a good one. Old hunters told me to have nothing to do with cap or percussion locks, that they were unreliable, and that if I got my caps or percussion wet I could not shoot, while if I lost my flint I could pick up another on the plains. I doubt whether there was one hundred dollars in money in the whole party, but all were enthusiastic and anxious to go.

In five days after my arrival we were ready to start, but no one knew where to go, not even the captain. Finally a man came up, one of the last to arrive, and announced that a company of Catholic missionaries were on their way from St. Louis to the Flathead nation of Indians with an old Rocky Mountaineer for a guide, and that if we would wait another day they would be up with us. At first we were independent, and thought we could not afford to wait for a slow missionary party. But when we found that no one knew which way to go, we sobered down and waited for them to come up; and it was well we did, for otherwise probably not one of us would ever have reached California, because of our inexperience. Afterwards when we came in contact with Indians our people were so easily excited that if we had not had with us an old mountaineer the result would certainly have been disastrous. The name of the guide was Captain Fitzpatrick;[2] he had been at the head of trapping parties in the Rocky Mountains for many years. He and the missionary party went with us as far as Soda Springs, now in Idaho Territory, whence they turned north to the Flathead nation. The party consisted of three Roman Catholic priests—Father DeSmet, Father Pont, Father Mengarini—and ten or

[2] Thomas Fitzpatrick, a famous guide known on the frontier as "Broken Hand."

eleven French Canadians, and accompanying them were an old mountaineer named John Gray and a young Englishman named Romaine, and also
a man named Baker. They seemed glad to have us with them, and we
certainly were glad to have their company. . . .

In general our route lay from near Westport, where Kansas City now is,
northwesterly over the prairie, crossing several streams, till we struck the
Platte River. Then we followed along the south side of the Platte to and a
day's journey or so along the South Fork. Here the features of the country
became more bold and interesting. Then crossing the South Fork of the
Platte, and following up the north side for a day or so, we went over to the
North Fork and camped at Ash Hollow; thence up the north side of that
fork, passing those noted landmarks known as the Court House Rocks,
Chimney Rock, Scott's Bluffs, etc., till we came to Fort Laramie, a trading
post of the American Fur Company, near which was Lupton's Fort,
belonging, as I understood, to some rival company. Thence after several
days we came to another noted landmark called Independence Rock, on a
branch of the North Platte called the Sweetwater, which we followed up
to the head, soon after striking the Little Sandy, and then the Big Sandy,
which empties into Green River. Next we crossed Green River to Black
Fork, which we followed up till we came to Ham's Fork, at the head of
which we crossed the divide between Green and Bear rivers. Then we
followed Bear River down to Soda Springs. The waters of Bear Lake discharged through that river, which we continued to follow down on the
west side till we came to Salt Lake. Then we went around the north end
of the lake and struck out to the west and southwest.

For a time, until we reached the Platte River, one day was much like
another. We set forth every morning and camped every night, detailing
men to stand guard. Captain Fitzpatrick and the missionary party would
generally take the lead and we would follow. Fitzpatrick knew all about
the Indian tribes, and when there was any danger we kept in a more
compact body, to protect one another. At other times we would be scattered along, sometimes for half a mile or more. We were generally together, because there was often work to be done to avoid delay. We had to
make the road, frequently digging down steep banks, filling gulches,
removing stones, etc. In such cases everybody would take a spade or do
something to help make the road passable. When we camped at night we
usually drew the wagons and carts together in a hollow square and
picketed our animals inside in the corral. The wagons were common ones
and of no special pattern, and some of them were covered. The tongue of

202 WEST OF THE WEST

one would be fastened to the back of another. To lessen the danger from Indians, we usually had no fires at night and did our cooking in the daytime.

The first incident was a scare that we had from a party of Cheyenne Indians just before we reached the Platte River, about two weeks after we set out. One of our men who chanced to be out hunting, some distance from the company and behind us, suddenly appeared without mule, gun, or pistol, and lacking most of his clothes, and in great excitement reported that he had been surrounded by thousands of Indians. The company, too, became excited, and Captain Fitzpatrick tried, but with little effect, to control and pacify them. Every man started his team into a run, till the oxen, like the mules and horses, were in full gallop. Captain Fitzpatrick went ahead and directed them to follow, and as fast as they came to the bank of the river he put the wagons in the form of a hollow square and had all the animals securely picketed within. After a while the Indians came in sight. There were only forty of them, but they were well mounted on horses, and were evidently a war party, for they had no women except one, a medicine woman. They came up and camped within a hundred yards of us on the river below. Fitzpatrick told us that they would not have come in that way if they were hostile. Our hunter in his excitement said that there were thousands of them, and that they had robbed him of his gun, mule, and pistol. When the Indians had put up their lodges Fitzpatrick and John Gray, the old hunter mentioned, went out to them and by signs were made to understand that the Indians did not intend to hurt the man or take his mule or gun, but that he was so excited when he saw them that they had to disarm him to keep him from shooting them; they did not know what had become of his pistol or of his clothes, which he said they had torn off. They surrendered the mule and the gun, thus showing that they were friendly. They proved to be Cheyenne Indians. Ever afterwards that man went by the name of Cheyenne Dawson.

As soon as we struck the buffalo country we found a new source of interest. Before reaching the Platte we had seen an abundance of antelope and elk, prairie wolves and villages of prairie dogs, but only an occasional buffalo. We now began to kill buffaloes for food, and at the suggestion of John Gray, and following the practice of Rocky Mountain white hunters, our people began to kill them just to get the tongues and the marrow bones, leaving all the rest of the meat on the plains for the wolves to eat. But the Cheyenne, who traveled ahead of us for two or three days, set us a better example. At their camps we noticed that when they killed buffaloes they took all the meat, everything but the bones. Indians were never wasteful of the buffalo except in winter for the sake of the robes, and then only in order to get the whisky which traders offered them in exchange. There is no better beef in the world than that of the buffalo; it is also very good jerked, i.e., cut into strings and thoroughly dried. It was an easy matter to kill buffaloes after we got to where they were numerous, by keeping out of sight and to the leeward of them. I think I can truly say that I saw in that region in one day more buffaloes than I have seen of cattle in all my life. I have seen the plain black with them for several days' journey as far as the eye could reach. They seemed to be coming northward continually from the distant plains to the Platte to get water, and would plunge in and swim across by thousands—so numerous were they that they changed not only the color of the water, but its taste, until it was unfit to drink; but we had to use it. One night when we were encamped on the South Fork of the Platte they came in such droves that we had to sit up and fire guns and make what fires we could to keep them from running over us and trampling us into the dust. We were obliged to go out some distance from camp to turn them: Captain Fitzpatrick told us that if we did not do this the buffaloes in front could not turn aside for the pressure of those behind. We could hear them thundering all night long; the ground fairly trembled with vast approaching bands; and if they had not been diverted, wagons, animals, and emigrants would have been trodden under their feet. . . .

Here was an example of the deep tragedy wrought by the western migration. For ages, the Indians who roamed the great plains depended upon the buffalo for their existence, and as Bidwell pointed out, they wasted nothing. The animal provided food, clothing, and shelter. The trappers found the buffalo tongue a delicacy. The rest was abandoned as carrion. Later, Americans would simply slay these giant slow-moving beasts for sport. The herds disappeared. In the Indian villages, drums beat as painted figures bobbed in the shadows of countless campfires, their moccasins tracing the steps of the Ghost Dance, the red man's final pathetic effort to recall the buffalo and a return of the old days, before white men violated the land.

The wagon train separated near present-day Pocatello, Idaho. Thirty-two of the emigrants followed their guide, Fitzpatrick, to the Columbia River. Bidwell and the remaining members of the party struck out for California, following an unknown trail. Before reaching their destination, it became necessary to abandon the wagons in favor of pack animals. The young pioneer fared well in California. For a time he was employed by John Sutter, the baron of the vast Sacramento Valley, whose fort became a gathering place and refuge for the first emigrants coming across the Sierra. Following the discovery of gold, he mined at Bidwell's Bar, and in 1849 was able to purchase a 22,000-acre ranch. Settling in Chico, Bidwell became a leading citizen of the new state, being elected to California's first legislative senate. He was elected to Congress in 1864, was three times an unsuccessful candidate for governor, and in 1892 became the Prohibition party candidate for President. As a former teacher, he was deeply interested in education, donating the land for the Chico Normal School, and also serving as a regent of the University of California. He died on April 4, 1900.

12

THE WILKES EXPEDITION
TO THE PACIFIC

It is one of the ironies of history that the achievements of some men are given little acclaim, while others engaged in similar pursuits are immortalized. The overland expeditions of John C. Frémont made him the darling of the nation. Later, he was discredited and even vilified by his detractors. Oddly, a man who shared with Frémont in the opening of the Pacific Coast to America has almost been forgotten. He was Charles Wilkes, USN, commander of an exploring expedition sent out between 1838–1842 to conduct surveys of the Antarctic continent, the Pacific islands, and the territory along the Pacific coast. Wilkes was recommended for the assignment by J. R. Poinsett, Secretary of War under President Martin Van Buren. Poinsett had also been one of Frémont's principal supporters, and it was part of the overall plan in the explorations along the west coast of North America that Frémont would connect his explorations, which began in 1843, with those of Commander Wilkes. As Wilkes later described the objectives of the voyage:

¶ In May, 1836, the law of Congress was passed, authorizing an exploring expedition to be sent out. The purpose of the instructions were as follows, "To explore and survey the Southern Ocean, having in view the important interest of our commerce embarked in the whale fisheries, as well as to determine the existence of all doubtful islands and shoals; and to discover and accurately fix the position of those which lie in or near the track pursued by our merchant vessels in that quarter, and may hitherto have escaped the observation of scientific navigators.

"Although the primary object of the expedition is the promotion of the great interest of commerce and navigation, yet all occasions will be taken, not incompatible with the great purpose of the undertaking, to extend the bounds of science, and to promote the acquisition of knowledge. For the more successful attainment of these, several scientific gentlemen will accompany the expedition, for the departments of philology, zoology, conchology, geology, mineralogy, and botany, with suitable artists, and a horticulturist, and are placed under your direction. . . ." [1]

By the time this expedition returned to New York on the 9th of June, 1842, after an absence of three years and ten months, Wilkes and his men had surveyed 1,600 miles of coastline in the Antarctic, and nearly 300 islands in the Pacific. Several months were spent in Hawaii, where Wilkes became so enchanted with Moana Loa, that he spent three weeks camping on top of the crater, making topographical drawings. From here the explorers proceeded to the present State of Washington, where Wilkes raised the American Flag—the first to be unfurled west of the Rockies. Two overland parties were organized while the squadron was on the Pacific coast. One was to conduct explorations on the Columbia River, while the other was ordered to pass through the Willamette Valley, strike the headwaters of the Sacramento River at its source, and pass down through its valley to San Francisco, where it would rendezvous with the ships of the squadron. In August, 1841, Wilkes sailed through the Golden Gate. What he observed was later published in his *Narrative of the United States Exploring Expedition During the Years 1838, 1839, 1840, 1841, 1842.* This is how he found San Francisco:

[1] *Synopsis of the Cruise of the U.S. Exploring Expedition During the Years 1838, 39, 40, 41 and 42,* delivered before the National Institute by its commander, Charles Wilkes, Esq., on the 20th of June, 1842 (Washington: Printed by Peter Force, 1842).

¶ . . . Although I was prepared for anarchy and confusion, I was surprised when I found a total absence of all government in California, and even its forms and ceremonies thrown aside.

After passing through the entrance, we were scarcely able to distinguish the Presidio; and had it not been for its solitary flag-staff, we could not have ascertained its situation. From this staff no flag floated; the building was deserted, the walls had fallen to decay, the guns were dismounted, and every thing around it lay in quiet. We were not even saluted by the stentorian lungs of some soldier, so customary in Spanish places, even after all political power as well as military and civil rule has fled. I afterwards learned that the Presidio was still a garrison in name, and that it had not been wholly abandoned; but the remnant of the troops stationed there consisted of no more than an officer and one soldier. I was not able to learn the rank of the former, as he was absent, and appeared, at least among the foreigners, to be little known.

At Yerba Buena there was a similar absence of authority. The only officer was the alcalde, who dwells at the mission of Nostra Señora de los Dolores, some three miles off. He was full of self-importance, making up for what he wanted in the eyes of others by a high estimate of his own dignity. I could find no one who could furnish me with his name, which must be my apology for not recording it in this place. Some excuse may be offered for his inattention to his duties, as I understood that he had just been united in wedlock to a lady of one of the distinguished families of the country; and after such an event in California much gaiety and rejoicing usually follow, until the hilarity at times becomes so uproarious as to end in fighting and bloodshed. . . .

I found it very difficult to obtain accurate information in relation to Upper California. The country, at the time of our visit, and for several years previous, had been in a state of revolution; and, as is often the case under similar circumstances, was involved in anarchy and confusion, without laws or security of person and property. It is undergoing such frequent changes, that it is difficult to understand or to describe them. . . .

Upper California may boast one of the finest, if not the very best harbour in the world,—that of San Francisco, as before described. Few are more extensive or could be as readily defended as it; while the combined fleets of all the naval powers of Europe might moor in it. This is, however, the only really good harbour which this country possesses; for the others so called may be frequented only during the fine season, being nothing more than roadsteads, affording little safety and but few supplies to vessels.

Among these bays are that of Monterey, the capital of Upper California, and that of Santa Barbara and San Pedro. The two last are partly protected from the swell of the Pacific Ocean by the islands that cover them. They are, however, but seldom used, there being comparatively little trade upon all this coast; for the hides and tallow which formerly abounded and made the business profitable for vessels, are no longer to be procured. The destruction of the missions, and the onerous laws, duties, and prohibitions, have nearly destroyed the little traffic that once existed, and it is now all transferred to the bay of San Francisco. There a few hulks may be seen lying, furnished with every needful article: these keep up an illicit intercourse by the connivance of the officers of the customs, by whose cupidity the revenue laws are openly infringed, and what of right belongs to the government, goes to enrich the governor and his officers.

The principal articles imported, are cotton cloths, velvet, silks, brandies, wines, teas, &c.; in return for which they receive hides and tallow, skins, wheat, and salmon. The attention of the inhabitants has been principally directed to the raising of cattle, and the greater part of the wealth of California may be considered as consisting of live-stock. . . . From four to five hundred sea-otter skins are brought in by the American hunters, which are valued at thirty dollars each. Wheat has been exported to the Russian posts, to the amount of twelve thousand bushels. . . .

. . . As respects trade, it may be said there is scarcely any, for it is so interrupted, and so much under the influence of the governor and the officers of the customs, that those attempting to carry on any under the forms usual elsewhere, would probably find it a losing business. Foreigners, however, contrive to evade this by keeping their vessels at anchor, and selling a large portion of their cargoes from on board. Great partiality is shown to those of them who have a full understanding with his excellency the governor; and from what I was given to understand, if this be not secured, the traders are liable to exactions and vexations without number. The enormous duties, often amounting to eighty per cent. ad valorem, cause much dissatisfaction on the part of the consumers: the whole amount raised is about two hundred thousand dollars per annum, which is found barely sufficient to pay the salaries of the officers, and defray the costs of the government feasts, which are frequent, and usually cost a thousand dollars each. These emoluments are shared among the heads of departments at Monterey, whilst the soldiers are often for months without their pay, and are made to take it in whatever currency it may suit the government to give. Besides the above duties, there is a municipal tax on many things: thus, a dollar is demanded on every gallon of spirits imported; fifty cents on each beaver or otter skin, and on other articles in the same ratio. Next come the church tithes, which are enormous. I heard of a farmer who was made to pay one hundred and ninety dollars as the tithe on his produce, although he lives far removed from either church or priest. All these things are bringing the government into great disrepute, and the governor is every day becoming more and more unpopular; so much so, that his orders have not been complied with, and have been treated with contempt, particularly when he desires to recruit his forces. A short time before our arrival, he sent a list to a pueblo of the young men to be drafted as soldiers; when it was received, they in a body refused to go, and sent back the disrespectful and defying message, that he might come and take them.

Nothing can be in a worse state than the lower offices, such as the alcaldes, &c. They are now held by ignorant men, who have no ideas of justice, which is generally administered according to the alcalde's individual notions, as his feelings may be enlisted, or the standing of the parties. To recover a debt by legal means, is considered as beyond a possibility, and creditors must wait until the debtor is disposed to pay. Fortunately, and to the honour of the country, a just claim is rarely or never denied; and, until lately, the word of a Californian was sufficient to insure the payment of claims on him; but, such has been the moral degradation to which the people have fallen since the missions have been robbed by the authorities, and the old priests driven out, that no reliance can be placed now upon their promises, and all those who have of late trusted them, complain that engagements are not regarded, and that it is next to impossible to obtain any returns for goods that have been delivered. The state of the country, is, however, some excuse, as it has been impossible for any one to make calculations under the existing anarchy and confusion. . . .

. . . The situation of Upper California will cause its separation from Mexico before many years. The country between it and Mexico can never be any thing but a barren waste, which precludes all intercourse except that by sea, always more or less interrupted by the course of the winds, and the unhealthfulness of the lower or seaport towns of Mexico. It is very probable that this country will become united with Oregon, with which it will perhaps form a state that is destined to control the destinies of the Pacific. This future state is admirably situated to become a powerful maritime nation, with two of the finest ports in the world,—that within the straits of Juan de Fuca, and San Francisco. These two regions have, in fact, within themselves every thing to make them increase, and keep up an intercourse with the whole of Polynesia, as well as the countries of South

America on the one side, and China, the Philippines, New Holland, and New Zealand, on the other. Among the latter, before many years, may be included Japan. Such various climates will furnish the materials for a beneficial interchange of products, and an intercourse that must, in time, become immense. . . .[2]

Wilkes traveled extensively throughout California while his ships were in port. His description of one of the vacqueros he encountered remains one of the most colorful to be found in the literature of the period. Accompanied by one of the large landowners, he had gone out to inspect the rancher's herd, when they met the rider:

¶ . . . We had not proceeded far before we were overtaken by the person who had them in charge, coming at a furious gallop. He was mounted on the best horse I had seen in the country, and dressed after the Californian fashion, in a dark brown cloth jacket, thickly braided, both before and behind, with slashed sleeves, showing his shirt elegantly embroidered, both on the breast and sleeves; velvet breeches of bright blue, secured around his waist with a red sash, and open at the sides, ornamented with braid and brass bells, in abundance; below the knee he wore leather leggins, fastened with garters, worked in silver, and below these, shoes, over which were fastened large silver spurs, with the heavy rowels of the country; on his head was tied a red bandana handkerchief, and over that a huge broad-brimmed sombrero, with peaked crown, covered with an oil-silk cloth; the whole decorated with cords, aiguillettes, and ribands, with a guard-cord passing under the chin. His horse was equally well caparisoned, the bridle being decked with silver, as were the tips of his large wooden stirrups; with pillions and saddle-cloths in abundance. Few riders had so gay an air, or seemed to have so perfect a command of the animal he rode; and until we arrived at the wood where his Indians were looking out, he was an object of great attraction, assuming all the airs and graces of a person of high rank. . . .

While the garb and manners of the typical California don seemed to impress Wilkes, this was an exception. His overall opinion of the people was far from favorable:

¶ The health and robustness of the white inhabitants seem remarkable, and must be attributed to the fine climate, as well as to their simple diet.

[2] Charles Wilkes, *Narrative of the United States Exploring Expedition During the Years 1838, 1839, 1840, 1841, 1842* (Philadelphia: Lea & Blanchard, 1845. Five volumes and atlas).

This consists of beef roasted upon the coals, a few vegetables, and the tortilla, which is a thin cake, made of corn-meal, and baked upon a sheet of iron. Throughout the country, both with the rich and poor, this is the general fare; but some few luxuries have been lately introduced, among which are rice and tea. The latter is used so sparingly, that the discoloration of the water is scarcely perceptible. At the missions they live more after the Spanish fashion. The children are, for the most part, left to take care of themselves, and run about naked and dirty. They are generally robust, and their relative number seems to be very great; thus, it is by no means uncommon to see families of fourteen or fifteen children; and an instance was mentioned to me of a woman near Yerba Buena, who had had twenty-six. A large number die from accidental falls from horses, with which from their earliest childhood they are accustomed to be engaged. They early become expert and fearless riders, and this skill is not confined altogether to the male sex; the women are almost equally expert. Families with numerous members are seldom met with who have not had to mourn the loss of several of their number from casualties of this sort.

Although the Californians are comparatively few in number, yet they have a distinctive character. Descended from the old Spaniards, they are unfortunately found to have all their vices, without a proper share of their virtues; they are exceedingly fond of gambling, which is equally in favour with the male and female portion of the community. Their games consist in cards, dice, &c.

Their amusements are cock-fighting, bull and bear-baiting, and dancing; these are the predominant occupations of their lives, always accompanied with excessive drinking. Parties of amusement, to which the surrounding population is invited, are frequent; these generally last for three days, and rarely break up without some quarrel. Weddings are particularly liable to these disorders, and at each of the three last that took place at and in the vicinity of Yerba Buena, previous to our visit there, a life was lost by the *cuchillo* [knife]. This weapon is always worn, and is promptly resorted to in all their quarrels.

The female portion of the community are ignorant, degraded, and the slaves of their husbands. They are very fond of dress, and will make any sacrifice, even their own honour, to gratify it. The men have no trades, and depend for every thing upon the Indians at the missions, some of whom are quite ingenious, both as carpenters and blacksmiths. The whites are so indolent, and withal have so much pride, as to make them look upon all manual labour as degrading; in truth, they regard all those who work as beneath them; they, in consequence, can never be induced to labour. . . .

Commander Wilkes appears to have been somewhat of a martinet. Following his return to the United States, he was court-martialed and reprimanded for illegally punishing some of his men. Later, he was to achieve a small measure of fame in that he nearly involved the United States in a war with England. On November 8, 1861, while commanding a federal vessel during the Civil War, he overhauled a British mail steamer, forcibly removing the two Confederate commissioners, James H. Mason and John Slidell, who were en route to England to plead the cause of the South and enlist foreign aid. The North was jubilant about Wilkes' zeal, but the English came close to commencing hostilities over the incident. It took considerable persuasion to placate the aroused British, and President Lincoln was forced to release the two prisoners. Wilkes retired from the navy as a rear admiral in 1866.

13

THE HUDSON'S BAY COMPANY EYES CALIFORNIA

Sir George Simpson, governor-in-chief of the Hudson's Bay Company's Territories in North America, arrived in San Francisco in 1841, not long after the departure of Wilkes and his squadron. He had met the American naval commander when Wilkes paused with his expedition at Vancouver before sailing south to California.

George Simpson was a dedicated servant of the Hudson's Bay Company, eager to promote British colonial expansion in whatever territories his company could secure a foothold. Simpson was equally at ease among royalty or with the Indians and the hard-drinking *voyageurs,* who gathered furs for his company.

Simpson's *Narrative of a Journey Round the World* is a fascinating travel book of the period, for it is not only a masterpiece of carefully documented observation; the narrative also sparkles with wit and the dry humor characteristic of the cultured British gentleman of the era. In fact, the account is so interesting and entertaining that it has been asserted that he employed a ghost writer, Adam Thom, a Montreal lawyer working for the Hudson's Bay Company, to complete the book.

Simpson's travels took him around the world; he was knighted by Queen Victoria, and retired with noteworthy achievements to his credit. He had organized an expedition to the Arctic, and lifted the fur trade out of the depths into which it had fallen.

Simpson began his around-the-world journey in March, 1841. After arriving at his company's headquarters at Montreal, he proceeded by canoe and pack train westward across the continent. After a journey lasting some six weeks, the party arrived on the Columbia, continuing downriver to Fort Vancouver, where Hudson's Bay had a large post. He next sailed to Sitka, Alaska, to confer with Russian traders, with whom the British were on amicable terms. From here, his ship turned south for San Francisco. His visit to California was not prompted by idle curiosity. Hudson's Bay had an agent in the town, and the company was engaged in trapping along the Sacramento River.

The dispute over the Oregon question was yet to be resolved between the United States and Great Britain, for a treaty was not concluded until 1846, which left the territory in America's possession. The settlement of Oregon began several years earlier, when Americans began to arrive in large parties to found farming communities in Oregon's rich valleys. Since the earliest negotiations for the title to the Pacific Northwest between Great Britain and the United States, the Hudson's Bay Company had vigorously opposed the surrendering of Oregon to America. It had a powerful lobby in Parliament; although the concern was privately owned, some of the most influential men in England had financial interests in it.

Simpson readily perceived the weakness of the Mexican government in California. It was inevitable that the country would soon be occupied by a foreign nation. But which—the United States or his own? Doubtless, Sir George furnished his own government with confidential information following his return to England. In his narrative, Sir George refrains from speculating on future international disputes over California. He confines his book to providing a description of the lands he visited during his long journey. The result is an account of a region that was at that time a remote outpost of Mexico, where a new culture that was neither Spanish nor Mexican—but distinctively Californian—was emerging.

Sir George was also witnessing the last of an era. The pastoral days that had characterized the period of Mexican rule were soon to come to an end. In December, 1841, Simpson entered San Francisco Bay aboard the bark *Cowlitz*. He recorded his first impressions in his journal:

¶ The world at large has hitherto made nearly as little use of the peculiar facilities of San Francisco as the Californians themselves. Though at one time many whaling-ships, as the name of Whaler's Harbor would imply, frequented the port, yet, through the operation of various causes, they have all gradually betaken themselves to the Sandwich Islands. In the point of natural capabilities for such a purpose, the Sandwich Islands are, on the whole, inferior to San Francisco. If they excel it in position, as lying more directly in the track between the summer-fishing of the north and the winter-fishing of the south, and also as being more easy of access and departure by reason of the steadiness of the trade-winds, they are, in turn, surpassed in all the elements for the refreshing and refitting of vessels by a place where beef may be had for little or nothing, where hemp grows spontaneously, where the pine offers an inexhaustible supply of resin, and where suitable timber for ship-building invites the axe within an easy distance. But though nature may have done more for San Francisco than for the Sandwich Islands, yet man has certainly done less to promote her liberal intentions. The Sandwich Islands afford to the refitting whaler an ample supply of competent labor, both native and foreign at reasonable wages, while San Francisco, turning the very bounty of Providence into a curse, corrupts a naturally indolent population by the superabundance of cattle and horses, by the readiness, in short, which idleness can find both subsistence and recreation. . . .

Moreover, even on the score of fiscal regulations, the savage community has as decidedly the advantage of the civilized as in point of industrious habits. In the Sandwich Islands the whaler can enter at once into the port which is best adapted for his purposes, while in San Francisco he is by law forbidden to remain more than forty eight hours, unless he has previously presented himself at Monterey and paid duty on the whole of his cargo. What wonder, then, is it that with such a government and such people Whaler's Harbor is merely an empty name.

Few vessels, therefore, visit the port, excepting such as are engaged in collecting hides or tallow, the tallow going chiefly to Peru, and the hides exclusively either to Great Britain or the United States. It was in the latter branch of the business that most of the vessels which we had found at anchor were employed, the mode of conducting it being worthy of a more detailed description.

To each ship there is attached a supercargo, or clerk, who, in a decked launch, carries an assortment of goods from farm to farm, collecting such hides as he can at the time, and securing, by his advances, as many as possible against the next *matanza,* or slaughtering season, which generally coincides with the months of July and August. The current rate of a hide is two dollars in goods, generally delivered beforehand, or a dollar and a half in specie, paid, as it were, across the counter; and the great difference arises from the circumstance that the goods are held at a price sufficient to cover the bad debts which the system of credit inevitably produces, the punctual debtor being thus obliged, in California as well as elsewhere, to pay for the defaulter. . . .[1]

Sir George quoted Richard Henry Dana's *Two Years Before the Mast,* first published in 1840, for a description of the hide-and-tallow trade as seen by the young American sailor who wrote the celebrated book, and to which Simpson added a few of his own personal observations:

¶ The trade of the bay, and in fact of the whole province, is entirely in the hands of foreigners, who are almost exclusively of the English race. Of that race, however, the Americans are considerably more numerous than the British, the former naturally flocking in greater force to neutral ground, such as this country and the Sandwich Islands, while the latter find a variety of advantageous outlets in their own national colonies. At present the foreigners are to the Californian in number as one to ten, being about six hundred out of about seven thousand, while, by their monopoly of trade and their command of resources, to say nothing of their superior energy and intelligence, they already possess vastly more than their numerical proportion of political influence, and their position in this respect excites the less jealousy, inasmuch as most of them have been induced, either by a desire of shaking off legal incapacities or by less interested motives, to profess the Catholic religion, and to marry into provincial families. . . .

[1] Sir George Simpson, *Narrative of a Journey Round the World* (London: Henry Colburn, 1847. 2 vols.).

Sir George, like many of the foreign visitors to California, did not have too high a regard for the Mexicans he encountered. He writes:

¶ . . . the population of California in particular has been drawn from the most indolent variety of an indolent species, being composed of super-annuated troopers and retired office-holders and their descendants. In connection with the establishment of the missions, at least of those of the upper province, there had been projected three villages or pueblos[2] as places of refuge for such of the old soldiers as might obtain leave to settle in the country; but as the priests were by no means friendly to the rise of a separate interest, they did all in their power to prevent the requisite licenses from being granted by the crown, so as to send to the villages as few denizens as possible, and to send them only when they were past labor, as well in ability as in inclination. These villages were occasionally strengthened by congenial reinforcements of runaway sailors, and, in order to avoid such sinks of profligacy and riot, the better sort of functionaries, both civil and military, gradually established themselves elsewhere, but more particularly at Santa Barbara, while both classes were frequently coming into collision with the fathers whose vexatious spirit of exclusiveness, even after the emancipation of the veterans, often prompted them nominally to preoccupy lands which they did not require.

Such settlers of either class were not likely to toil for much more than what the cheap bounty of nature afforded them, horses to ride and beef to eat, with hides and tallow to exchange for such other supplies as they wanted. In a word, they displayed more than the proverbial indolence of a pastoral people, for they did not even devote their idle hours to the tending of their herds. As one might have expected, the children improved on the example of the parents through the influence of a systematic education, an education which gave them the lasso as a toy in infancy and the horse as a companion in boyhood, which, in short, trained them from the cradle to be mounted bullock-hunters, and nothing else and if anything could aggravate their laziness, it was the circumstance that many of them dropped, as it were, into ready-made competency by sharing in the lands and cattle of the plundered missions.

Sir George was invited to call upon Mariano Guadalupe Vallejo, the *comandante-general* of California. Vallejo was a native son, who had

[2] Los Angeles, at this time a relatively unimportant town, was one of the designated pueblos.

fared well in California politics. Born at Monterey, on July 7, 1808, he entered the military service as a cadet in 1824. He achieved rapid promotion in the army, and in 1832 married one of the most beautiful women in California, Francisca Benicia Carrillo of San Diego. Vallejo became one of the most affluent men in the territory. At Petaluma, he owned a ranch stocked with thousands of cattle. Another rancho was located at Sonoma, where he was fond of entertaining on a lavish scale. Although Vallejo objected to the presence of the Russians in California, he became one of the earliest benefactors of the American settlers, who in turn repaid his kindness by jailing him during the war with Mexico. Nevertheless, after American acquisition, Vallejo became a dedicated citizen of the United States, participating in the first constitutional convention prior to statehood. He was also elected to the California Senate. He died at Sonoma, January 18, 1890. The town of Vallejo near San Francisco was named for him.

Vallejo was living at the Mission San Francisco Solano at the time of Simpson's visit. En route there with his local agent, Forbes, Sir George describes meeting Timothy Murphy, who worked as an aide to Vallejo. And here we gain an insight of how the *comandante-general* of California enriched himself at the expense of the deposed Franciscan order:

¶ Timothy Murphy, who unconsciously played the part of so inhospitable a landlord on this occasion, resides at the Mission San Rafael as administrador in behalf of General Vallejo, to whom, as one of the prime movers in the revolution of 1836, there fell the lion's share of prize-money, in the shape of two nice snuggeries of San Rafael and San Francisco Solano. The general, who shows his sagacity by systematically allying himself with foreigners, selected Mr. Murphy as a fitting mate for one of his sisters, the prettiest girl of the family, giving him, in advance, as an earnest of the bargain, the management of San Rafael, with a good slice of the booty for his private use. The lady, however, could not, or would not, fancy Timothy, and the matter ended by the general's acquisition of two foreigners instead of one, Mr. Leese having obtained the dona's hand and Mr. Murphy having kept her dowry.

But the jilted administrador is not without his share of pleasant society, in the person of one of the few priests who remained in the country after the confiscation of their establishments. Father Quijas is one of those jovial

souls who show that, in the New World as in the Old, power and wealth
are more than a match for monastic austerities; nor has the removal of the
corrupting influences rendered his reverence a more rigid observer of his
vows, excepting always (thanks to Murphy and Vallejo) the single
article of poverty. The two friends lately led each other into trouble in a
way which forcibly illustrates the state of government in general and the
character of Vallejo in particular.

As the Bay of San Pablo is separated by a ridge of green hills from the
valley of Santa Rosa, in which are situated the settlements of Bodega and
Ross, Murphy and Quijas, whether it was that the former was in search of
stray bullocks, or that the latter wished to ease the schismatics of a little of
their brandy, fell into the snare of visiting the Russians, against all rule
and precedent. The treason soon came to the general's ears, and on the
very evening after their return the delinquents were politely invited to
attend at headquarters, by a sergeant and five troopers. As the night was
wet and stormy, they tried to bribe the soldiers with their best fare into a
respite of a few hours, pleading at the same time the want of horses. But,
while the sergeant disclaimed all official knowledge of wind and weather,
the troopers caught the requisite number of nags, and the next morning
the luckless wights were thrown, all drenched and splashed, into the
general's calabozo or dungeon, to chew the cud, in hunger and thirst, on
the contraband hospitalities of Bodega and Ross. So much for the freedom
and equity of Californian republicanism. . . .

Sir George and his interpreter reached the mission at Sonoma,
where the *comandante-general* resided. He found Vallejo to be a good-
looking man of about forty-five, and soon was seated at his dinner
table. Undoubtedly Sir George was polite to his host, but later in print
he proceeded to deprecate the cooking of the Californians in no uncertain terms:

¶ . . . on the table was placed an array of five dishes—two kinds of stewed
beef, rice, fowls, and beans. As all the cooking is done in outhouses, for the
dwellings, by reason of the mildness of the climate, have no chimneys or
fireplaces, the dishes were by no means too hot when put on the table,
while being served out in succession to a party of about twenty people they
became each cooler than the other before they reached their destinations. It
was some consolation to know that the heat must once have been there, for
everything had literally been seethed into chips, the beans or *frijoles* in

particular having been first boiled and lastly fried, with an intermediate stewing to break the suddenness of the transition. Then every mouthful was poisoned with the everlasting compound of pepper and garlic, and this repast, be it observed, was quite an aristocratic specimen of the kind, for elsewhere we more than once saw, in one and the same dish, beef and tongue and pumpkin and garlic, and potatoes in their jackets, and cabbage and onions and tomatoes and peppers, and Heaven knows what besides, this last indefinite ingredient being something more than a mere figure of speech, considering that all the cookery, as one may infer from the expenditure of so much labor, is the work of native drudges, unwashed and uncombed. When to the foregoing sketch are added bad tea and worse wine, the reader has picked up a perfect idea of a Californian breakfast, a Californian dinner, and a Californian supper. . . .

One of the guests at the dinner was Commandant Prado of the presidio, "a very fierce paunchy little man enveloped in an immense cloak." Describing this hotspur, who seemed always ready for either an amorous adventure or an argument that might invoke sword-play or a sharp-bladed knife, one gains some idea of the explosive temperament of the native Californians:

¶ Besides having been engaged in many skirmishes against both Californians and Indians, he has had several narrow escapes with his life in private brawls. About two years ago a religious festival was celebrated at the Misión San Francisco de Asís in honor of the patron saint, passing through all the usual gradations of mass, bullfight, supper, and ball. In the course of the evening, Don Francisco Guerrero, the steward of the Mission, stabbed Prado with the ever-ready knife for presuming to interpose in an altercation between himself and his mistress; but the corpulent commandant was not to be so easily run through, for though breadth of beam is not generally an advantage to a soldier, yet on this occasion Prado's fat did succeed in saving his bacon. Such a termination of a religious festival is so much a matter of course that at one which took place a few months back one of Prado's numerous enemies came up to him, and, drawing his knife, said "What! here's daylight, and no one yet stabbed!" and it required all the influence of Vallejo, who happened to be present, to nip so very promising a quarrel in the bud. On such occasions the cloak is often invaluable as a shield, and in fact, when both parties are on their guard, there is commonly far more of noise than of mischief. . . .

Before his departure, Sir George was to contribute the final chapter to California's most famous romance—the tragedy of the Doña Concepción Argüello. When Georg Heinrich von Langsdorff, a Russian engineer who left an account of his visit, arrived in San Francisco on April 5, 1806, he was accompanied by Nikolai Rezanov, an official of the Russian American Fur Company. Negotiations to establish trade produced negligible results, as the colony was forbidden by law to engage in commerce with foreign vessels. For the Russians, this was a serious blow. Their settlement at Sitka, Alaska, was desperate for food. Something had to be done—and then Rezanov caught the eye of the military commander's daughter, Concepción Argüello.

Langsdorff described her as "distinguished for her vivacity and cheerfulness, her love-inspiring and brilliant eyes and exceedingly beautiful teeth, her expressive and pleasing features, shapeliness of figure, and for a thousand other charms. . . ." Rezanov was duly smitten. He wasted no time in proposing, and the lovely Concepción accepted. The dour Langsdorff injects a callous note when he declared that his companion "decided to sacrifice himself, by wedding Doña Concepción, to the welfare of his country, and to bind in friendly alliance both Spain and Russia." Judging from his description of the girl's beauty, Rezanov's ardor could hardly have been motivated by patriotism.

Concepción's parents found the Russian suitor unacceptable, his chief fault being that he was a member of the Orthodox faith. The distraught girl argued with her parents. She loved the handsome Nikolai. Moved by her tears, the Argüellos consented. It grieved them to surrender their daughter, who would sail away to a far-off land, but they had fourteen other children living in California to console them. A betrothal agreement was drawn up, but there was one stipulation: a consent for the marriage must be received from the Pope in Rome. Rezanov left for his homeland, vowing to return to his loved one. He never reached his destination. En route, he fell from a horse, and died from the injuries he sustained. No one bothered to write Concepcíon. She moved to Santa Barbara, and, as legend says, maintained a lonely vigil, gazing seaward from a rocky point that bears her name, and where numerous vessels, including a squadron of United States Navy destroyers, have run aground in the fog that often drapes itself shroud-like along the coast. Concepción was still waiting for her lover to return thirty-five years later when Sir George Simpson arrived at Santa Barbara. Having read Langsdorff's book, he was aware of Rezanov's death. Here he tells of his meeting with the broken-hearted Concepción:

¶ Among the persons whom we met this afternoon, was a lady of some historical celebrity. Von Resanoff, having failed . . . in his attempt to enter the Columbia in 1806, continued his voyage as far as San Francisco, where, besides purchasing immediate supplies for Sitka, he endeavored, in negotiation with the commandant of the district and the governor of the province, to lay the foundation of a regular intercourse between Russian America and the Californian settlements. In order to cement the national union, he proposed uniting himself with Donna Conception Arguello, one of the commandant's daughters. . . .

The chancellor, who was himself of the Greek Church, regarded the difference of religion with the eyes of a lover and a politician; but, as his imperial master might take a less liberal view of the matter, he posted away to St. Petersburg with the intention, if he should there be successful, of subsequently visiting Madrid, for the requisite authority to carry his schemes into full effect. But the Fates, with a voice more powerful than that of emperors and kings, forbade the bans; and Von Resanoff died, on his road to Europe, at Krasnoyarsk in Siberia of a fall from his horse.

Thus at once bereaved of her lover, and disappointed in her hope of becoming a pledge of friendship between Russia and Spain, Donna Conception assumed the habit, but not, I believe, the formal vows, of a nun, dedicating her life to the instruction of the young and the consolation of the sick. This little romance could not fail to interest us; and, notwithstanding the ungracefulness of her conventual costume and the ravages of an interval of time, which had tripled her years, we could still discover in her face and figure, in her manners and conversation, the remains of those charms which had won for the youthful beauty Von Resanoff's enthusiastic love and Langsdorff's equally enthusiastic admiration. Though Donna Conception apparently loved to dwell on the story of her blighted affections, yet, strange to say, she knew not, till we mentioned it to her, the immediate cause of the chancellor's sudden death. This circumstance might, in some measure, be explained by the fact, that Langsdorff's work was not published before 1814; but even then, in any other country than California, a lady, who was still young, would surely have seen a book, which, besides detailing the grand incident of her life, presented so gratifying a portrait of her charms. . . .

Doña Concepción entered the Dominican Sisters' order on April 11, 1851. She received the name of María Dominga. She resided at their Benecia convent in the San Francisco Bay area until her death on December 23, 1857. Bret Harte, the celebrated author, read Sir George's account, and it captured his imagination. He envisioned an entirely different setting where Simpson would meet Concepción. He also altered the time lapse, and called her Concha when he wrote these lines:

¶ Forty years on wall and bastion swept the hollow idle breeze,
  Since the Russian eagle fluttered from the California seas;
  Forty years on wall and bastion wrought its slow but sure decay,
  And St. George's Cross was lifted in the port of Monterey;
  And the citadel was lighted, and the hall was gayly drest,
  All to honor Sir George Simpson, famous traveler and guest.
  Far and near the people gathered to the costly banquet set,
  And exchanged congratulations with the English baronet;
  Till the formal speeches ended, and amidst the laugh and wine
  Someone spoke of Concha's lover—heedless of the warning sign.
  Quickly then cried Sir George Simpson: "Speak no ill of him, I pray.
  He is dead. He died, poor fellow, forty years ago this day—
  Died while speeding home to Russia, falling from a fractious horse.
  Left a sweetheart, too, they tell me. Married, I suppose, of course!
  Lives she yet?" A death-like silence fell on banquet, guests, and hall,
  And a trembling figure rising fixed the awe-struck gaze of all.
  Two black eyes in darkened orbits gleamed beneath the nun's white
      hood;
  Black serge hid the wasted figure, bowed and stricken where it stood.
  "Lives she yet?" Sir George repeated. All were hushed as Concha drew
  Closer yet her nun's attire. "Señor, pardon, she died too!" [3]

[3] Mary Graham (ed.), *Historical Reminiscences of One Hundred Years Ago—Maria de la Concepcion Arguello* (San Francisco: P. J. Thomas, Printer, 1876).

14

FOLLOWING
THE EMIGRANT TRAIL

The movement west by hundreds of settlers, which began in the spring of 1843, spearheaded the drive for the American acquisition of California. Initially intent upon settling in Oregon, there were a number of the more venturesome who turned to the south, following the few rough trails into California. At first they were welcomed by the Mexican authorities, until it became obvious that the territory would be overrun by Yankee settlers.

Independence, Missouri, became the assembly area and gateway to the Oregon Trail. There, small parties from Ohio, Tennessee, Indiana, Kentucky, Illinois, Iowa, and other states gathered with their wagons. Companies were formed, and the caravans began the long march with herds of cattle being driven along the flanks of the wagon column. Outriders encircled the train, for there was always the danger of a sudden attack by Indians. Mountain men, who were familiar with the wilderness and who had abandoned the dying fur trade, served as guides for the emigrants bound for the new lands in Oregon and

California. After a trip averaging ninety-eight days, the company would reach Fort Hall, a trading post on the eastern border of the Oregon country. By this time, they had covered two-thirds of the distance. From there, in ten days they would reach Fort Boise. An additional ten days of travel and the emigrants would discover the beauty of the Grand Ronde, that sprawling valley of the Blue Mountains. A brief pause and the teams were once again hitched, the grazing cattle driven in close to the train, and the wagons rolled on to the rich Willamette Valley.

The mass migration to Oregon in 1843 accelerated the settlement of the boundary dispute that had long been a matter of controversy between Great Britain and the United States. When the treaty was finally concluded in 1846, thousands of Americans were already living in the territory.

One of the accounts written on this emigration was *Route Across the Rocky Mountains with a Description of Oregon and California* by Overton Johnson and Wm. H. Winter. The authors came west in one of the caravans, a sizable community of six hundred persons. In the first chapter, they write:

¶ In the latter part of 1843, we left Independence, a small town in the Western part of the State of Missouri, situated six miles South of the Missouri River and twelve miles from the western line of the State, and now the principal starting point for all the companies engaged in the Western and New Mexican trade, and place of general rendezvous of persons from all parts of the United States, wishing to emigrate or travel beyond the Rocky Mountains. . . . We were traveling here in the great Santa Fe trace and again and again, we passed long trains of Merchant wagons, laden with the products of our Manufactories and other Merchandize, and bearing them afar across the deserts, to be exchanged for the gold and silver of the provinces of Mexico. This trace is large, and as well beaten as many of the most important highways in the States. . . .[1]

Arriving in the valley of the Willamette, the two joined a smaller party bound for California:

[1] Overton Johnson and Wm. H. Winter, *Route Across the Rocky Mountains with a Description of Oregon and California* (Lafayette, Ind.: John B. Semans, Printer, 1846).

¶ We left the rendezvous near the Methodist Mission, on the Upper Willamette, on the 18th day of June, 1844, for Upper California. Our company consisted of thirty-seven persons; of which number, thirteen were women and children; the rest were made up of Americans, English, French, Mexicans, and Indians of four different tribes. We took our baggage, entirely with pack animals, as the route will admit of being traveled in no other way. . . .

After a hard journey over the mountains, Johnson and Winter reached the fort of Captain John A. Sutter, who in those early days was a benefactor to the first settlers arriving in California. The authors describe the settlement as they found it in 1844:

¶ One hundred and sixty miles from the head of the valley, we came to the Fort of Captain Sutter, a large trading establishment, built of dobies. Capt. Sutter's Fort is situated on the East side of the Sacramento River, about fifty miles above its entrance into the Bay of St. Francisco, at the head of the tide water, and some distance below the affluence of the Rio de los Americanos, or the American River, a stream which has its source in the Mountains to the East. It is in latitude 38 deg. 35 min. North, and is the principal place in the Sacramento Valley, and one to which the foreigners who are residing in Upper California, look for refuge and protection, in case of an outbreak by the Indians, or an attempt on the part of the Spaniards to expel them from the country. The Fort is a quadrangular wall, built of large sundried brick, and has bastions in the corners, in which are mounted several pieces of artillery. It is garrisoned by about forty Indians; one of whom, constantly stands sentry, during the day, as well as the night, and apprises those in the fort, of the approach of any party, whether friends or foes. It covers a large area, and is probably capable of containing a garrison of one thousand men. Within the walls, are the shops, and the residences of the officers, mechanics, and servants; and there is, also, connected with the establishment, a horse mill, a distillery, and a tannery. Captain Sutter, at first, had difficulties with the Indians; but by the promptness, and severity with which he had frequently chastised them; whether he acted against tribes or individuals, against Chiefs or subjects; has at length brought them to fear, and respect him; and now they seldom molest his property or the men in his employ.

The Indians cultivate, and improve his farms, attend to his large herds of animals, make a portion of his trapping parties, and do all the drudgery about the Fort: hundreds of them are ready, also, to defend him against any emergency. The government of California was, at first, suspicious of him, on account of the strength of his fortifications, and the influence which he was acquiring over the Indians; but he has since been appointed an officer of Justice by them. It is, however, very doubtful, whether their former feelings towards him are changed; were it not for the insufficiency of their power, it is believed, that they would yet banish him from the country. Capt. Sutter is a native of Switzerland, and came from Missouri to his present location, and has been in California about five years; he purchased the cannon and other portions of the establishment of the Russian Company, then in the country; and having obtained, of the Mexican Government, a grant of land along the Sacramento River, of some thirty or forty square leagues; he removed to his present situation. Besides the fur trade, he carried on an extensive business in farming, stock raising, and manufacturing. He has a very large farm, and large bands of cattle, horses, sheep, and hogs, and constantly keeps employed, mechanics of different descriptions—He is spoke of by all who visit him, as being very accommodating, hospitable, and altogether, much of a gentleman; nor have we any disposition, to differ with the general impression. Here our company disbanded; some going to one, and some to another part of the province. . . .

John Sutter lived like a medieval lord in his Sacramento fort. He was always ready to aid the newly arrived emigrants, employing many of them. Unfortunately, during the American military occupation of California, he found himself caught in the middle of the conflict. He had been appointed an official of the Mexican government to which he owed an allegiance, while at the same time he was sympathetic toward the Americans. John Charles Frémont, the explorer who was to play one of the chief roles in the conquest, found Sutter's attitude vacillating, and despised him for it. Ironically, it was an employee of Sutter, James W. Marshall, who while constructing a sawmill that the two were to operate as a partnership, made the first discovery of gold in May, 1847, on the American River. In the great rush that followed, Sutter, the long-time friend of the emigrants, was deprived of his lands and robbed of his wealth by the gold seekers who flocked to California. For years he waged a battle in the United States courts to keep the lands granted him by the Mexican government, encompassing nearly 141,000 acres. Sutter was finally granted two large tracts; one was of 8,800 acres near the American River; the other included the site of California's capital city, Sacramento. Mismanagement and the steady influx of settlers stripped Sutter of all his holdings. Nearly penniless, he was in Washington trying to secure redress from Congress for his losses when he died on June 18, 1880, at the age of seventy-seven.

*   *   *

For those who read the Johnson and Winter account, California would appear to be the Promised Land. The authors praised the climate, and the productiveness of the soil, predicting Americans would soon outnumber the Mexican inhabitants:

¶ There are now about five hundred foreigners residing in the country, and the principal portion are from the United States. Emigration from the United States is rapidly increasing, and it is probable that our citizens will possess themselves of this beautiful and healthy country, with its many vales of fertile land. They will soon outnumber the Spaniards, and gain the ascendency over them. The consequence will be, to throw off their present form of government, establish a Republic of their own, and render this portion of our globe, what nature has seemed to design it should be, a prosperous and happy country. . . .

The Government is under the direction of a Governor, appointed by the authorities of the Mexican Government, and the officers of justice are the same as in her other Provinces; they are called Alcaldes, are elected by the people, and have powers very similar to our Justices of the Peace; but the influence of bribery and favoritism affects, in a great degree, the principles of justice, and almost entirely defeats the administration of the laws; and its remoteness from the Capital renders the influence and control of the National Government very limited. . . .

The authors concluded their account:

¶ . . . It requires about five months to make the journey, under ordinary circumstances; but difficulties and detentions may, in some instances, increase the time to six months; it will therefore be the safest, and most prudent, for emigrants to lay in provisions for six months. . . . The rough manner of living, which it is necessary for the traveler to adopt, together with the purity of the atmosphere, the consistent and wholesome exercise, and the various scenes and incidents daily presented, which tend to divert the mind, all have a great tendency to promote uncommon good health, and consequently, uncommon good appetites. . . . With but few exceptions it is only things which are the most substantial and nutritious that should be taken; such as flour, middlings of bacon, because they are free from bones, rice, sugar, coffee, salt, pepper, &c. The quantity of flour for each individual, should not be less than two hundred pounds, unless the company be entirely made up of pack-men, who intend to make the journey in as short a time as practicable. Where a company carries their provisions, packed on mules, they can generally make the trip about a month sooner, than those who go with wagons can, and therefore the quantity of provisions should be proportionately reduced; one hundred and fifty pounds of flour will be an abundant supply for a packman. . . . Wagons should be selected with the greatest care; those should be taken which are made out of the best material, well put together, and properly proportioned. The irons on the wheels should be as tight as possible, without breaking or straining the wood; and the whole wagon should only be heavy enough to bear the required load. It is necessary to have the tires tight on the wheels, on account of the hot dust and sand through which they have to go, and which is very liable to loosen them from the wood.

It will also be well for those who wish to be provided against every circumstance that is liable to come in the way, to construct the beds of their wagons in such a manner that they can be corked and converted into boats. It matters not about the shape of the former. The covering of the wagon should be of strong and very close material, or painted so as to render it impervious to the heavy rains, which are likely to be encountered on the waters of the Kansas, and on the Platte. . . .

Taking every thing into consideration, oxen are preferable to any other animals for teams. It is true they cannot endure the heat, the want of sufficient food, and other hardships incident to the journey, quite so well as mules; neither can they travel with the same speed: but with moderate traveling, and proper care, they will make the trip, and may be kept in good traveling condition. They are the kind of teams generally used, and are not likely to be stolen by the Indians; and, in addition, they are more serviceable to a farmer improving in a new country. . . .

Every male person who is of sufficient age to bear arms, should be provided with a gun, and a good supply of ammunition. The kind of guns which are preferable for such a trip, are large and strong rifles: their balls should not be less than one fiftieth of a pound, and they would be better if they were larger. The stock, which is very liable to be broken, should be made uncommonly strong at the breech, and all parts of the piece which are liable to wear or break, should be effectually tried before leaving the settlements. This is also a matter which should not be disregarded. It is necessary to be properly armed, to insure safety; those who are not, have no business in an Indian country. Five pounds of powder will be an abundant supply for those who intend to hunt a great deal; for those who do not intend to hunt much, half that quantity will probably be sufficient. The amount of lead, it will be remembered, should be four times that of the powder. Emigrants generally supply themselves over-abundantly with these articles.

It will be impossible for great numbers to travel together in the same company. It is necessary that the companies should be as small as will be consistant with their safety, in order that they may not be so much delayed in traveling, and that the animals of the several companies may be supplied with grass. It will not be difficult for any one to imagine how delays will occur, where a great number of wagons are traveling together. And grass is found in many places, in quantities sufficient for small companies, but not for large ones.

One hundred men well armed, may travel in safety, by conducting themselves properly, through the most dangerous part of the country, that is, the country laying between Big Blue River, one of the main branches of the Kansas River, and Green River, of the Gulf of California, which is to be crossed, a few days travel beyond the summit of the Rocky Mountains. From Green River to the settlements in Oregon, fifty men will make a company sufficiently strong, to avoid or repel all danger.

The character of the Indians will be learned from our preceding remarks. The manner in which they are treated, will, of course, make a great difference in their disposition towards those who chance to meet with them. They should never be trusted, nor should they, if it can be avoided, be allowed to have the advantage in any particular. And while every thing that would be calculated to give them offence, should be carefully avoided by those who wish to go in peace, they should at the same time be constantly held at a distance. The emigrants should refrain from all familiarity himself, and discourage it in them. In trading with them he should make use of few words; never attempt to deceive, and be prompt to the letter, in fulfilling every promise. Few presents should be given them, and those few should appear to be given rather as an expression of friendship, than to conciliate their favor. Under all circumstances, the least expression of fear should be sternly avoided. From the late difficulties with the Shoshone Diggers, and with the Walawalas . . . these tribes will not likely be well disposed towards emigrants. Previously, those who have gone into Oregon have become, after traveling thus far, impatient and careless; have separated into very small companies, and poorly armed, have hastened on, regarding nothing but the termination of the journey. What these have been compelled to submit and endure, should be a warning to others. Companies passing through these tribes should consist of not less than thirty well armed men.

The time of leaving the United States will vary with the season. Companies should start as soon as the grass will admit, which will vary from the latter part of April through the month of May. The road is so well marked that there will be no difficulty in finding it, and a pilot would only be useful to direct the manner of traveling, &c., and to point out the best places for encampment. . . .

15

JOHN CHARLES FRÉMONT AND THE CONQUEST OF CALIFORNIA

During the spring of 1845, diplomatic relations between the United States and Mexico had reached such an unfriendly state that the two nations were on the verge of war. With the inauguration of James Knox Polk as President on March 4 of that year, an era of American expansion commenced, and the new Chief Executive was its most vigorous champion. One object of Polk's program was the planned annexation of Texas to the United States. This aroused the fury of the Mexicans, who refused to recognize the independence from Mexican rule that the Texans had proclaimed March 2, 1836.

Polk's term of office was an active one. The United States Naval Academy was founded. Texas, Iowa, and Wisconsin were added to the Union as states. A treaty was signed between Great Britain and the United States, settling the Oregon boundary controversy. A war with Mexico was fought, and the long dream of the expansionists, the proponents of "Manifest Destiny," among whom were such leaders as Senator Thomas Hart Benton of Missouri, came true. California was acquired by the United States. In his Inaugural Address, President Polk declared:

❡ The Republic of Texas has made known her desire to come into our Union, to form a part of our Confederacy and enjoy with us the blessings of liberty secured and guaranteed by our Constitution. Texas was once part of our country—was unwisely ceded away to a foreign power—is now independent, and possesses an undoubted right to dispose of a part or the whole of her territory and to merge her sovereignty as a separate and independent state in ours. . . .

I regard the question of annexation as belonging exclusively to the United States and Texas. They are independent powers competent to contract, and foreign nations have no right to interfere with them or to take exceptions to their reunion. . . . Our Union is a confederation of independent States, whose policy is peace with each other and all the world. . . . The world has nothing to fear from military ambition in our Government. . . . Foreign powers should . . . look on the annexation of Texas to the United States not as the conquest of a nation seeking to extend her dominions by arms and violence, but as the peaceful acquisition of a territory once her own, by adding another member to our confederation, with the consent of that member, thereby diminishing the chance of war and opening to them new and ever-increasing markets for their products. . . .

The annexation of Texas did not take place as peacefully as the President had hoped. Hatred for the Mexicans had been intense throughout Texas for years, and it was an attitude that became widespread in the United States. During the war for Texan independence, Americans were shocked by the news of the annihilation of the besieged garrison at the Alamo in March, 1836. Antonio López de Santa Anna's Mexican troops had soaked the bodies of the valiant defenders in oil, then jubilantly burned them. A short time later, several hundred Texans who surrendered at Goliad were shot by orders of Santa Anna. And now, a decade later, thousands of Americans were eager to cross the Rio Grande and seek revenge.

The time came in March, 1846, when troops commanded by General Zachary Taylor began to move from their staging area at Corpus Christi. The Rio Grande, the river that had long been an uneasy boundary, was crossed on April 24 near Matamoros by a cavalry patrol led by

Captain Seth Thornton, sent out by Taylor to scout the terrain. The following day Thornton and his dragoons found themselves surrounded by Mexican soldiers. In the quick fire fight that took place, eleven Americans were killed. The remainder of the patrol, consisting of some sixty-three dragoons, including Thornton, were captured. Hostilities had commenced.

In the general orders, Taylor confidently informed his troops that if they obeyed his commands and instructions, he had no doubt of the result, regardless of their numbers. He reminded the infantry that "their main dependence must be in the bayonet." The invasion of Mexico was at hand.

As part of the overall strategy of the war, a plan was formulated by the United States to seize California. John C. Frémont, already a celebrated explorer, was west of the Rockies on a military topographical expedition. Earlier, President Polk had selected a young Marine Corps lieutenant, Archibald Gillespie, to carry dispatches to Frémont and the American consul at Monterey, Thomas O. Larkin, advising them of the possibility of war and instructing Frémont to cooperate with American settlers in case of hostilities. The main concern was to prevent California from falling into British hands. Larkin had written to the President that the Hudson's Bay Company had intrigued in California with insurrectionists against the Mexican governor, Manuel Micheltorena. The British had been liberal with funds and weapons. This was enough for Polk. Commodore John Drake Sloat, commander of the Pacific Squadron, was sent racing to California, backed by an additional task force under Commodore Robert F. Stockton. In New York, a regiment of volunteers commanded by Colonel Jonathan Drake Stevenson was soon to embark for California, and later General Stephen Watts Kearny would march a force of dragoons west across the continent, only to be soundly thrashed in an ambush staged by the Californians at San Pascual in present San Diego County.

Gillespie, who was fluent in Spanish, began his cloak-and-dagger mission to find Frémont in 1845, sailing from New York to Vera Cruz, Mexico, where he was certain that his luggage would be searched. He memorized his orders and destroyed them. After crossing Mexico, he rendezvoused with Commodore Sloat at Mazatlán. One of the ships of the Pacific Squadron, the *Cyane,* carried him to Monterey, the Mexican capital of Alta California. From here, the government agent followed Frémont to Klamath Lake, Oregon, where he delivered his message from the President.

On July 7, 1846, a crowd of curious residents assembled in front of Monterey's Customs House at ten o'clock in the morning to witness the landing of Captain William Mervine and a party of marines and sailors from the sloop-of-war *Cyane,* then lying at anchor in the harbor. Ships of the American squadron thundered a twenty-one-gun salute across the bay, and the Stars and Stripes were soon snapping in the breeze, announcing the occupation of California by the United States. A proclamation signed by Commodore John Drake Sloat, commanding the naval forces, was read before the inhabitants present at the ceremony. Most of them could not understand English. For their benefit, it would later be printed in Spanish. Sloat stated:

> ¶ The central government of Mexico having commenced hostilities against the United States of America by invading its territory and attacking the troops of the United States on the north side of the Rio Grande, that he was therefore hoisting the Standard of the United States immediately, and shall carry it throughout California. . . .[1]

*   *   *

Among the men participating in the acquisition of California, John C. Frémont emerges as the central figure. From the military viewpoint this distinction seems unearned, as he participated in no major engagements. He arrived with his command too late to take part in the minor skirmish fought at Los Angeles, but he did accept the surrender of the Mexicans. This was only because their leader, Andrés Pico, was afraid to tender his sword to Frémont's superiors, Commodore Robert F. Stockton and General Stephen Watts Kearny. They would have hanged him. Pico had been captured earlier and had broken his parole by again bearing arms against the United States. Frémont was acclaimed by the nation for his discoveries. He became known as the Pathfinder, the explorer who charted the trail to the Far West. It was Frémont who had surveyed the route beyond the Mississippi as far as Wyoming's South

---

[1] Hubert Howe Bancroft. *History of California,* Vol. 5 (San Francisco: The History Company, Publishers, 1886).

Pass in 1842, and a year later his explorations brought him to the mouth of the Columbia River. But it was his third march to the West that involved him in the California adventure, and the first of the many controversies that would extend throughout his lifetime. Allan Nevins in his distinguished biography of Frémont refers to the explorer's life as one of the stormiest, most erratic, and most adventurous of American careers. He writes:

¶ There are two great elements of interest in Frémont's biography. One lies simply in the unfailing drama of his life; a life romantically wrought out of the fiercest tempests and most radiant bursts of sunshine. From birth to death fortune gave him one sustained adventure. His fate carried him along our wildest frontiers, into the clash of national ambitions in the Far West, up to the higher reaches of party politics, through the thick of the Civil War, and into the thorniest jungles of post-bellum finance. It was no mean destiny. To explore more of the West than any other single man, to be a leading figure in the conquest of California, to be the first candidate of a great party for the Presidency, to pen a book that helped in molding now-populous communities, to rise from poverty to millions and sink to poverty again, to leave a name written across the geography of one third of the continent—this constitutes an absorbing story. It tells us much of the United States as well as of Frémont. . . . Whether we dislike or like the man, whether we applaud or condemn his acts . . . his life will always touch our imagination.[2]

In later years, Frémont's widow wrote an article recalling the excitement of the first expeditions before he crossed the Sierra into California. The story of Jessie Benton Frémont's romance with the famed explorer has been well chronicled, and it was a romance that reads like fiction. Jessie's father, the powerful Senator Thomas Hart Benton of Missouri, was deeply interested in the plans to acquire California and settle the Oregon boundary question. He was a dedicated expansionist and had considerable influence in Washington politics. It was natural that the senator should become interested in the young John Charles Frémont and invite him to his home. Here he was to meet Jessie, then sixteen, and the most beautiful girl in Washington. It was

[2] Allan Nevins, *Frémont, Pathmarker of the West* (New York: D. Appleton-Century Company, 1939).

love at first sight. Benton did his utmost to intervene, as he considered Frémont a poor match for his daughter, despite the explorer's growing reputation. The angered father's efforts were to no avail, as the couple married secretly. When the pair announced their troth to Jessie's father, the senator became enraged, ordering Frémont from the house. It was at this point that Jessie invoked the words of Ruth—and it was a story she was fond of relating in later years. Taking her place beside her husband, she ignored the protests of Senator Benton, and said:

"Whither thou goest, I will go; and where thou lodgest, I will lodge; thy people shall be my people, and thy God my God!"

The senator relented. Frémont moved into the house.

Jessie outlived her husband by twelve years, residing in Los Angeles with her daughter. She contributed articles to numerous magazines, and became a prolific writer. In 1890, the women of Los Angeles presented her with an attractive cottage at 28th and Hoover streets, adjoining the present-day campus of the University of Southern California. This article of Jessie's concerning her husband's role in the western exploration was a favorite subject with her, for she delighted in retelling how she chose to ignore an order recalling her husband's expedition—sending a messenger on to him, urging the party to leave at once. The following account, entitled "The Origin of the Frémont Expeditions," appeared in *The Century Magazine* in 1891. Jessie died at her Los Angeles home on December 27, 1902. She was seventy-eight. Her obituary published in the Los Angeles *Times* the following morning read in part:

¶ ". . . the brilliant and beautiful woman so long associated with the early history of the state is no more. Only a memory is left of her beauty, her wit, her gracious use of power, her influence for good. . . ."

¶ Long before the words carried their meaning I was familiar with "Oregon occupation" and the "India trade." They connected themselves with big English law-books in my father's library, whose Hogarth-like pictures were a delight to my childhood when there were no picture-books made for children. Many a pleased hour I puzzled over these in that sunny library where I was free to come on condition that I would be "as quiet as a mouse." One of these illustrations, together with my father's many and patient explanations tempered to a child's mind, gave me some ideas which have never faded, but, emerging from childish imaginings and confusings, became strangely interwoven into the very substance of my real life. This favorite picture was that scene of which Macaulay has made so vivid a word-painting, the "Impeachment of Warren Hastings." It became an endless theme between my father and myself, and through it from him came my earliest impressions of India and Oriental life, and of England's power—her love of justice as well as her love of gain; her daring conquests, and her crushing mastery of a race that were to me then the people of the Arabian Nights, only more warlike, and more splendid. The peacock throne of gold and gems seemed as real to me as the living peacocks that at sunset spread their feathers and screamed on the lawn at my grandfather's house in Virginia. And on the long gallery of our own home in St. Louis, where in the pleasant way of the old French town much life went on in the open air, again England was a household theme. For the British Fur Company, its enmity to the American Fur Company, its harassing opposition to Americans settling in Oregon, were matters of personal interest and necessary consideration to those meeting there.

Chief of the unusual figures frequenting that tree-shaded gallery was the stately and venerable General William Clark, who was ending his honorable days in St. Louis, where he held superintendency over all the Indians of the West. He who had first explored the Columbia to the Pacific, and carried through Jefferson's once defeated plan, was, of right, chief of this informal council. There met the heads of the fur trade—the many Chouteaus, and Ramsay Crooks, who brought Washington Irving when he was collecting material for his "Astoria." At times came picturesque Mexican merchants in gold-embroidered velvet riding dress and great ringing silver spurs; waiting under the shade of our old trees were their horses glittering with silver-mounted saddles and trappings. Nobody walked. There waited also horses with military saddles belonging to officers up from Jefferson Barracks, their riders, in well-worn uniforms and with thinned, sun-burned faces, freshly in from prairie chase and sharp skirmish with Black Hawk and his turbulent Indians—these too kept in enmity by the opposing British Fur Company. Black-robed Italian and Belgian dignitaries of the Catholic Church, keeping to their traditions as pioneer travelers, would bring some humble devoted missionary priest who has his tale to tell and his valuable addition to make to the little known geography of plain and mountain. Wiry French *voyageurs* in their fringed buckskin, keen-witted and light of heart; and wealthy citizens, Spanish, French, and American, interested in the trade which, crossing Mexico, stretched to the "Sea of Cortez," as the Gulf of California was called, met there in council, all animated by a common purpose to free our way westward.

Year after year this small but forceful council met with my father in the vacations of Congress, and he carried up to their friends in Washington the knowledge gained among them as an impelling force towards our more energetic occupation of Oregon. In this interest he had visited Mr. Jefferson in his mountain home in Virginia, and gained deeper insight and further purpose from the mind to which we owe our expansion westward.

When in 1840 there came to Washington M. Nicollet, a French *savant* and traveler, and Mr. Frémont, who had been with him on the northwestern geographical surveys, it was of keenest interest to my father to know them, and to follow their travels on their maps in course of construction. This resulted in Mr. Frémont's becoming a part in his long-cherished work for the occupation of Oregon. Now, to his own accumulated knowledge and the increasing public interest and political reasons, could be joined the experience and love of adventurous travel, the youth and proved endurance, such as Jefferson so long before had secured for Oregon exploration in the traveler Ledyard. And to this was soon added personal and family identity in work and aim, for I by marriage had become their connecting link.

It would have needed only a request from my father to obtain for Mr. Frémont duty which should keep him in Washington in place of the long absences and dangers of these expeditions; but self-renunciation lies at the root of great work, and this was to be my part in being of use to my father; so that it was but a few months after my marriage that the first of the planned series of expeditions (that of 1842) was in the field. As that proved successful and of sudden and large interest (that of 1843–44) was started off without delay.

The winter of 1842–43 had been used to make out the maps and write the report. In this I was secretary and amanuensis, and had full knowledge of the large scope and national importance of these journeys—a knowledge as yet strictly confined to the few carrying out their aim. Even to the Secretary of War, and to Mr. Frémont's immediate commander, the colonel of the Topographical Engineers, they were only geographical surveys to determine lines of travel. This, the second, was to connect with the survey of the bay of San Francisco made by Captain Wilkes, U.S.N.

President Harrison, being both a Western man and a soldier, would have been friendly to their larger aim, but his death reversed this. Events justified the wisdom of silence until the fast-going hour. War with Mexico was nearing, and in that event the ownership of the bay of San Francisco would be open to the chances of war.

In the month of March, 1843, I accompanied Mr. Frémont to St. Louis, where the second expedition was fitted out; that through, he left for the frontier, where the men and animals were gathered. Following my duty of secretary, I was to open the mail and forward to the camp at Kaw Landing, now Kansas City, all that in my judgment required Mr. Frémont's attention. One day there came for him an official letter from his colonel, the chief of the Topographical Bureau; it was an order recalling him to Washington, whither he was directed to return and explain why he had armed his party with a howitzer; saying that it was a scientific, not a military expedition, and should not have been so armed. I saw at once that this would make delays which would involve the overthrow of great plans, and I felt there was a hidden hand at work. Fortunately my father was absent from St. Louis, and I could act on my instinct. Without telling any one of the order I put it away and hurried off a messenger to Mr. Frémont—one of his men, Basil Lajeunesse, who was to join him with the last things. I feared a duplicate letter might have been sent on to the frontier; but the river mail was very irregular and slow, and I charged Basil to make all haste, for much depended on that letter. I wrote Mr. Frémont that he *must not ask why,* but must start at once, ready or not ready. The animals could rest and fatten at Bent's Fort. "Only GO." There was a reason, but he could not know it; my father would take care of everything. And as we acted together unquestioningly, he did go immediately.

We were in that older time when there was no telegraph to paralyze individuality. Else the grand plan with its gathered strength and fullness, ripening and expanding from Jefferson's time to now, almost its culminating hour, would have fallen before petty official routing. I suspected some obscure intrigue, such as had recalled the young traveler Ledyard when he had already crossed Russia into Siberia in carrying out the design of Mr. Jefferson, then minister to France, for opening up the Columbia River—an intrigue that had thus balked and overthrown the foresight of Jefferson, the friendly assistance of the Empress Catherine, and the energetic ambition of Ledyard. It was now my happy privilege to be of use in counteracting a like evil interference. With the distance and the slow mails between the frontier and Washington I could count on gaining time enough for a good start for the party.

Not until after I received the good-by letter did I write in answer to his colonel who had sent the order of recall. Then I wrote him exactly what I had done: that I had not sent forward the order because it was given on

FORT HALL near the Shoshoni of snake river.

Fort Hall, near the Snake River in what is today Idaho, was a way station on the overland journey to California. Joseph Goldsborough Bruff sketched it when his party paused there on their way to the California gold fields in 1849. *(Reproduced from the original in the Henry E. Huntington Library and Art Gallery, San Marino, Calif.)*

ABOVE: Cross-country travel was not without its hazards. This drawing in *Harper's Weekly,* September 16, 1876, shows early pioneers under attack by Indians. The emigrants are using single-shot cap and ball rifles, which were slow to load. Each charge had to be pushed down the bore with a ramrod. BELOW: *Harper's Weekly* published in its issue of September 14, 1867, this drawing entitled "The Last Shot." The trained scouts were a fearless breed who depended upon their weapons and a fast horse for safety, but there was always the risk of an ambush by the Indians.

John Charles Frémont, from
a photograph by Brady taken
in 1850. *(State Library,
Sacramento)*

Jessie Benton Frémont. This
portrait was painted by T.
Buchanan Read in 1856, and
today hangs in the research
library of the Southwest
Museum at Los Angeles.
*(Reproduced by permission of
the Southwest Museum)*

ABOVE: Monterey in 1846. Reproduced from J. W. Revere's *A Tour of Duty*, published in 1849. BELOW: John C. Frémont is depicted here entering Monterey, California, with his volunteer force during the war with Mexico. In the foreground are the Indian scouts who always accompanied the famed Pathfinder. From *Frémont's Life, Explorations and Public Services* (1856). *(Pictures: State Library, Sacramento)*

UPPER LEFT: Thomas O. Larkin served as United States consul for the Mexican port of Monterey in 1843. He acted as a confidential agent for his government and played an important role in the American acquisition of California. *(State Library, Sacramento)* UPPER RIGHT: Commodore John Drake Sloat, commander of the Pacific squadron during the early days of the war with Mexico. He anchored off Monterey with his flagship, the *Savannah,* and on July 7, 1846, landed with 250 men, raising the American flag over California. *(Authors' collection)* LOWER LEFT: Commodore Robert E. Stockton, who succeeded Sloat as commander of the Pacific squadron. Known to his men as "Fighting Bob," he was a flamboyant personality, who quickly alienated the Mexican population by his autocratic methods of governing California. *(State Library, Sacramento)* LOWER RIGHT: John B. Montgomery was in command of the United States sloop of war *Portsmouth* when the Americans occupied San Francisco, July 9, 1846. *(State Library, Sacramento)*

The battle at San Pascual, near San Diego. Kearny's dragoons were led into an ambush by General Andrés Pico. Arriving on the field with powder dampened by rain, the Americans' sabers were no defense against the lances of the hard-riding *Californios. (By permission of the Director, Bancroft Library, University of California, Berkeley)*

ABOVE: Battle of San Gabriel near Los Angeles. The Americans formed a square as they marched on the Californians during the final days of the Mexican War in California. *(From Gleason's Pictorial Drawing Room Companion, courtesy of State Library, Sacramento)* BELOW: Pío Pico, the last governor of California under Mexican rule. With him in the picture, from left, are Marianita Alvarado, his wife's niece; Mrs. Pico; and another niece of hers, Trinidad Ortega. The photo was taken in 1845. *(Los Angeles County Museum of Natural History)*

RIGHT: Major General Stephen Watts Kearny, who marched west from Santa Fe with a column of dragoons. Defeated at San Pascual, he united with Commodore Stockton for the final campaign against Los Angeles which ended the war in California. *(State Library, Sacramento)* BE-LOW: Many of the dragoons who marched with Kearny during the Mexican War in California settled in southern California following the signing of the peace treaty at Cahuenga Rancho. These four veterans visited a Los Angeles daguerreotype studio in 1850. Unfortunately the photographer who made this interesting study did not record their identities. *(Los Angeles County Museum of Natural History)*

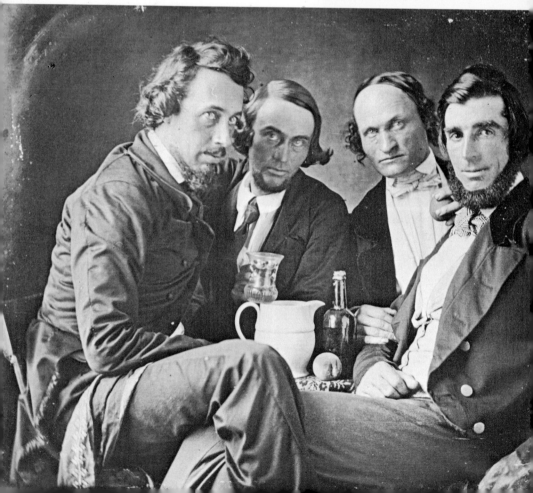

Donner Lake, looking east across the Sierra range toward Nevada from Donner Summit. The Donner party, prevented by heavy snows from crossing the mountains from which this photograph was taken, camped along the lake shore during the winter of 1846-1847. Thirty-four persons died of cold and starvation before rescue parties reached them from Sutter's Fort at present-day Sacramento. Some ate the bodies of their companions to survive. *(Photo by William S. Murphy)*

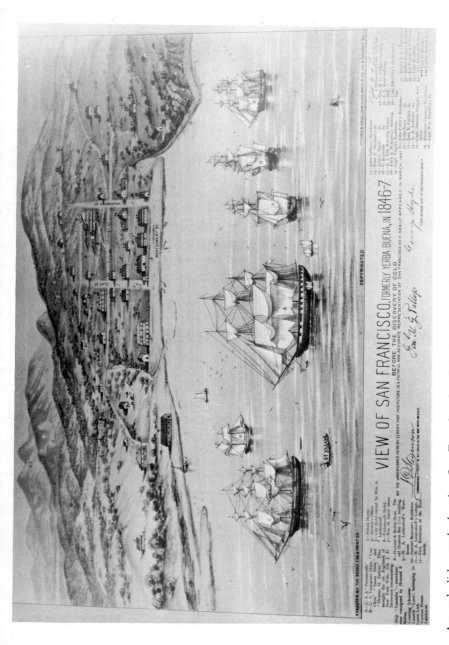

An early lithograph showing San Francisco in 1846-1847, before the discovery of gold. (*State Library, Sacramento*)

John Augustus Sutter, baron of the vast Sacramento Valley, who aided many of the early American settlers. Following the discovery of gold, which ironically was found by one of his employees, his lands were overrun by those searching for the yellow metal. His empire in California was swept away, and he died penniless.

Richard Barnes Mason, colonel of dragoons, who became military governor of California, succeeding General Kearny on May 31, 1848. Gold was discovered while he was in office, and his report to the President contributed heavily to the migration that followed. *(Pictures: State Library, Sacramento)*

VIEW OF
SUTTER'S MILL
OR PLACE WHER
THE FIRST GOL
HAS BEEN DISCOVE

Drawings reproduced in an old lithograph depict *(upper left)* James Marshall, who made the initial discovery of gold in California while constructing a sawmill for John Sutter on the American River; *(above)* the mill itself, where Marshall first sighted gold nuggets in the tailrace. *(State Library, Sacramento)*

The crowded port of San Francisco, June 1, 1849. This drawing was published in the New York *Tribune* in August of that year, and shows a portion of the two hundred vessels that were detained in the harbor, their crews having deserted to join the rush to the gold fields. The caption on the original states that the view is from Rincon Hill looking northwest. The Marin hills are in the distance and at the left is the embryo city flanked by Telegraph and Russian Hills. *(State Library, Sacramento)*

ABOVE: A typical miners' camp in the Mother Lode during the Gold Rush era. From a contemporary print. BELOW: Gold miners shown at work. The men with pick and shovel are digging earth near the riverbank in which placer gold is found. In the background, others are shown panning similar dirt in the river. (Pictures: State Library, Sacramento)

Mining operations—in one case a family affair—at Spanish Flat in the California Mother Lode during the 1850s. These photographs show sluice boxes being used to trap the particles of placer gold being washed down the river. *(Pictures: State Library, Sacramento)*

ABOVE: Hydraulic mining near Columbia, one of the richest regions of the Mother Lode, where millions of dollars in gold was recovered. An aqueduct completed in 1854 carried water for more than 60 miles through the mountains to where this picture was made during the period. This system of mining eroded the land, leaving scars which are still visible today. BELOW: The first quartz-crushing mill in California was constructed at Amador City in 1850. The builder is pictured in front of the equipment. (Pictures: State Library, Sacramento)

insufficient knowledge, and to obey it would break up the expedition, that the journeys to and from Washington, with indefinite delays there, would lose to the animals the best season for grass and throw them, underfed, into the mountains in winter; that the country of the Blackfeet and other fierce tribes had to be crossed, and that Indians knew nothing of the rights of science, but fought all whites; that these tribes were in number and the party not fifty men, therefore the howitzer was necessary; that as I knew a military order must be obeyed, I had not let it be known to any one, but had hurried off the party.

When my father returned he entirely approved of my wrong-doing, and wrote to the Secretary of War that he would be responsible for my act, and that he would call for a court martial on the point charged against Mr. Frémont. But there was never any further question of the wisdom of his arming the party sufficiently. In fact it had been but a pretext, for which the colonel, a quiet man, had been used. I had so grown into my father's purpose that now, when my husband could be of such large aid to its accomplishment, I had no hesitation in risking for him all consequences. Upon this second expedition hinged great results. It made California known in a way which roused and enlisted our people and led directly to its being acquired during the third expedition (that of 1845–47), and this time there were no "foes in the rear."

With the election of President Polk the way was made free to western expansion, and his having for Secretary of the Navy the historian Bancroft was of determining advantage. Then my father could say in that Senate where so long ago his voice had plead to dull ears for attention to our Pacific coast, "Now we own the country from sea to sea,—from the Atlantic to the Pacific,—and upon a breadth equal to the length of the Mississippi and embracing the whole temperate zone." From his own hearth had gone the one who carried his hopes to fullest execution and aided to make true his prophetic words, afterward cut into the pedestal of his statue in St. Louis, whose bronze hand points west—

There Is The East,
There Is The Road To India.[3]

Frémont wrote an article describing his part in the conquest of California that was also published in *The Century Magazine* in 1891. The editors had asked him to describe his role during the period. This pleased him, for he had recently been attacked by a historian of the

[3] Jessie Benton Frémont, "The Origin of the Frémont Expeditions," *The Century Magazine*, March, 1891.

period, deprecating his contributions in the acquistion of the territory. This was not the first time he had been assailed for his part in the conquest. Now he wanted to set the record straight. He finished the article and sent it to Jessie for editing. For a long while, he had been dependent upon the earnings of his devoted wife, who had become an established author. His friends had rallied to his aid by managing to have a bill introduced in Congress, that would restore him to the army as a major-general and place him on the retired list. This would qualify him for a pension. The bill was passed by Congress in April, 1890. Frémont would receive an annual pension of $5,625. For the first time, he was freed from financial worry. A few months later, on July 13, 1890, he succumbed to peritonitis suddenly in a New York rooming house. Jessie Benton Frémont was in Los Angeles at the time. In part, this is how he recalled his role in California during the war with Mexico:

¶ . . . the covert struggle between England and the United States on the Oregon question had ripened into positive antagonism. In 1845 I was sent out at the head of a third and stronger expedition, for which the plans and scope had been matured on my return from the second. The geographical examinations proposed to be made were in greater part in Mexican territory. But in arranging this expedition the eventualities of war had to be taken into consideration. My private instructions were, if needed, to foil England by carrying the war now imminent with Mexico into its territory of California. At the fitting moment that territory was seized, and held by the United States.

During the winter preceding it the coming third expedition was an engrossing subject to Senator Benton and me, also to others who had interest in its scientific and its possible results; largely so to General John A. Dix, then senator from New York, and to the Prussian Minister, Baron von Gerolt, an intimate friend of Humboldt, by whom he had been selected as Minister to Mexico. Baron von Gerolt had lived there some twenty years, was well acquainted with Mexican affairs, and had maintained active personal relations with men in power in that country. He was fully informed of their movements in this critical period. His intimacy with Senator Benton and his family and me had increased the interest with which he had followed the course of the previous expeditions, of which he kept Humboldt informed fully, giving him also personal details. Now the Baron, knowing from his correspondents in Mexico that there was to be interference by that government which would place me in peril and break up the expedition if it should enter California, came to give us warning.

It may be well to remind the reader that Senator Benton, not only from his political associations, but from his position as chairman of the Senate military committee,—a post he held for twenty-eight years,—was fully informed of every military measure of the Government. Mr. Benton had many clients from among old Spanish families in Florida and Louisiana, and his knowledge of their language led to friendships with them. He had always held that towards Mexico our relations should be that of the great Republic aiding a neighboring state in its early struggles; he belonged with those who preferred the acquiring of Texas by treaty and purchase, not by war; this he opposed and denounced, and he now held the same views concerning California.

President Polk entered on his office in March, 1845, with a fixed determination to acquire California, if he could acquire it in an honorable and just manner. The President and Cabinet held it impossible for Mexico, situated as things were, to retain possession of California, and therefore it was right to negotiate with Mexico for it. This it was hoped to accomplish by peaceful negotiation; but if Mexico, in resenting our acceptance of the offer of Texas to join us, should begin a war with us, *then, by taking possession of the province.* Relations with Mexico soon became critical and threatened war, leaving no room for further negotiations.

The Secretary of State, Mr. Buchanan, and Senator Dix of New York came frequently to confer with Mr. Benton. Mr. Buchanan had discovered a leak in his department, and, not knowing the Spanish language himself, brought his confidential letters and documents from Mexico to be read to him by Mr. Dix and Mr. Benton, who knew the language well. For the whole of his senatorial term Mr. Dix was a near neighbor, a member of the military committee, and also personally intimate with Mr. Benton. In the security of Mr. Benton's library these despatches were read and discussed and many translations made for Mr. Buchanan's use by Mrs. Frémont and her elder sister. These frequent discussions in our homes among the men who controlled the action of the Government gave to me the advantage of knowing thoroughly what were its present wishes, and its intentions in the event of war. . . .

To Mr. Benton and other governing men at Washington it seemed reasonably sure that California would eventually fall to England or to the United States, and they were firmly resolved to hold it for the United States. The instructions early sent, and repeatedly insisted upon, to the officers commanding our Pacific squadron, gave specific orders *to be strictly followed in the event of war*. For me no distinct course or definite instruction could be laid down, but the possibilities were made known to me, as well as what to do when they became facts. The distance was too great for timely communication, but failing this, *I was given discretion* to act. And for this, as soon as war was sure between Mexico and ourselves, Lieutenant Gillespie was despatched with instructions and with letters which, if intercepted when crossing Mexico, would convey no meaning to others, while to me they would be clear.

The first and second expeditions had their political as well as their geographical objects; both were successfully accomplished. The route to Oregon through to the mouth of the Columbia was definitely surveyed and mapped and its features were fully described for the use of the emigration. And the intended political effect was created of awakening the Government's interest in and protection to the emigration to Oregon. The third expedition had also its underlying political intention. Its chief geographical feature was very interesting. It was to explore and open what had hitherto been believed to be an uninhabitable desert—thence to find nearer passes through to the Pacific.

Our journey was continuously in Mexican territory from the head of the Arkansas River, and through all of the Salt Lake Valley. I found the beds of mineral or rock salt where Humboldt had marked them on his map of New Spain, "Montagnes de Gemme," to the eastward of the Salt Lake. He had so placed them from the journal of Father Escalante, who towards the close of the last century attempted to penetrate the unknown country from Santa Fé in New Mexico to Monterey, California. Father Escalante did not get beyond the southeastern rim of the lake. It was believed to be a desert without water. None of my men knew anything of it; not even Walker or Carson. The Indians declared that no one had ever crossed the immediate plain of sagebrush stretching westward to the stony, black, unfertile mountains which ran in range north and south in jagged saw-teeth profile.

Early in November we reached a river to which I gave the name of Humboldt,[4] who did me the honor to write and thank me for being the first to place his name on the map of the continent. Both the river and the mountain to which I gave his name are conspicuous objects, the river stretching across the basin to the foot of the Sierra Nevada, and the mountain standing out in greater bulk and length than its neighbors. Here

[4] The Baron Friedrich Heinrich Alexander von Humboldt, famed German naturalist and world traveler. Frémont was an admirer of his work.

I divided the party: the main body with Walker, who knew the southern part of the California mountains well, as their guide, had a secure southerly line in following the Humboldt River, which was to be surveyed by Mr. Kern. For myself I selected ten men, among them some of my Delawares. Leaving the main party, I started on a line westward directly across the basin. This journey determined a route passable for wagons from eight to nine hundred miles shorter than any known, and through a country abounding in game and fine grasses and wood.

Passing over details of the separation of the party and its wanderings and hardships on the Sierra Nevada, I come to my arrival at Sutter's Fort on the 9th of December, 1845. On the 15th of January, 1846, I set out with Mr. Liedesdorff, American vice-consul, for Monterey, and on arriving went directly to the house of our consul, Mr. Larkin. My purpose was to get leave to bring my party into the settlements in order to refit and to obtain the supplies that had now become necessary. All the camp equipment, the clothes of the men, and their saddles and horse gear, were either used up or badly in want of repair.

The next morning I made my official visits. I found the governor, Don Pio Pico, absent at Los Angeles. With Mr. Larkin I called upon the commanding general, Don José Castro, and upon the prefect, the alcalde, and Ex-Governor Alvarado. I informed the general and the other officers that I was engaged in surveying the nearest route from the United States to the Pacific Ocean. I informed them further that the object of the survey was geographical, being under the direction of the Bureau of Topographical Engineers, to which corps I belonged; that it was made in the interests of science and of commerce; and that the men composing the party were citizens and not soldiers. The permission asked for was readily granted, and during the two days I staid I was treated with every courtesy by the general and the other officers. By the middle of February my party was all reunited in the valley of San José, about thirteen miles south of the village of that name on the main road leading to Monterey, which was about sixty miles distant.

The place I had selected for rest and refitting was a vacant rancho called the "Laguna," belonging to Mr. Fisher. I remained here until the 22d, occupied in purchasing horses, obtaining supplies, and thoroughly refitting the party. It was the delightful spring season of a most delightful climate, and many Californians visited the camp, and very friendly relations grew up with us. I established the rate of the chronometer and made this encampment a new point of departure.

March 1 we resumed our progress southward along the coast, and

March 3 encamped at the Hartwell rancho. We were now passing Monterey, which was about twenty-five miles distant. The Salinas Valley lay outside of the more occupied parts of the country, and I was on my way to a pass opening into the San Joaquin Valley at the head of a western branch of the Salinas River.

In the afternoon the quiet of the camp was disturbed by the sudden appearance of a cavalry officer with two men. This officer, Lieutenant Chavez, was abrupt and disposed to be rude. He brought me peremptory letters from the general and the prefect, ordering me forthwith out of the department and threatening force if I should not instantly comply with the order. I desired the officer to carry as my answer that I peremptorily refused to comply with the order, which was an insult to my Government. My men, like myself, were roused by the offense, and were eager to support any course I saw fit to adopt.

Near by was a mountain called the Gavilan (or Hawk's) Peak. Early the next morning I moved camp, following the wood-road to the summit, and camped in a convenient position. It afforded wood, water, and grass, gave a view over the surrounding country, including the Salinas plain and the valley of San José, and opened in case of need a retreat to the San Joaquin. Here we built a rough but strong fort of logs. A tall sapling was prepared, and on it the American flag was raised amid the cheers of the men. The raising of this flag proved a premonition of its permanent raising as the flag over California.

I remained in possession, the flag flying, for three days, during which I received information from Mr. Larkin, our consul, and from citizens of what was going on below. Late in the afternoon of the second day we discovered a body of cavalry coming up our wood-road; with about forty men I went quickly down this road to where a thicket among the trees made a good ambush, and waited for them. They came to within a few hundred yards of us and halted, and after some consultation turned back. Had they come on they would have had to come within a few paces of our rifles.

The protecting favor all civilized governments accord to scientific expeditions imposed on me, even here, corresponding obligations, and having given Castro three days' time in which to execute his threat, I slowly withdrew. Besides, I always kept in mind the object of the Government to obtain possession of California, and would not let a proceeding which seemed personal put obstacles in the way. In a letter written soon after to Mrs. Frémont, telling of this, I made an allusion she would fully comprehend.

Sacramento River,

Latitude 49°, April 1, 1846.

. . . . My sense of duty did not permit me to fight them, but we retired slowly and growlingly: they had between three and four hundred men and three pieces of artillery, and were raising the country against me on a false and scandalous proclamation. I had my own men, and many Americans would have joined me, but I refrained from a solitary hostile or improper act, for I did not dare to compromise the United States, against which appearances would have been strong. . . .

We made a stop of a week near Sutter's Fort to recruit the animals on the fine range, and then continued to travel slowly towards the Oregon line. One night I was standing alone by my camp-fire and thinking these things over, and how best to meet the expectations intrusted to me in case of war, when suddenly my ear caught the faint sound of horses' feet, and as I listened there emerged from the darkness into the circle of the firelight two horsemen riding slowly, as though horse and man were fatigued by traveling. They proved to be two men from Sutter's whom I knew, named Neal and Seigler. They had ridden nearly a hundred miles in two days, having been sent forward by a United States officer, Lieutenant A. H. Gillespie, who was on my trail with despatches for me. He had been sent to California by the Government across Mexico to Mazatlan, and had letters for me. He had been directed to find me wherever I might be. Accordingly on landing from the United States steamer *Cyane* he had started from Monterey, and had been looking for me on the Sacramento. Learning at Sutter's Fort that I had gone up the valley, he had made up a small party and had followed my trail for six hundred miles, the latter part of the way through great dangers from Modoc and Klamath Indians.

Then I knew the hour had come. Neal knew the danger from these Indians, and his party becoming alarmed and my trail being fresh, Lieutenant Gillespie had sent forward Neal and Seigler on their best horses to overtake me and inform me of their situation.

I selected ten of the best men, Kit Carson, Stepp, Dick Owens, Godey, Basil Lajeunesse, and Crane with four other Delawares, and at early dawn we took the backward trail, and after a ride of about forty-five miles we met Lieutenant Gillespie and greeted him warmly. It was now eleven months since any tidings had reached me.

Lieutenant Gillespie informed me that he had left Washington in

November (1845), under orders from the President and the Secretary of the Navy, and had been directed to reach California by the shortest route through Mexico to Mazatlan. With many detentions on the way he had followed his instructions to find me wherever I might be, and under Neal's guidance had now overtaken me.

It was a singular coincidence that I was informed by Neal of Gillespie's coming on the 8th of May and met him on the 9th—the days on which were fought the first battles of the Mexican war, Palo Alto and Resaca de la Palma.

Lieutenant Gillespie brought a letter of introduction from the Secretary of State, Mr. Buchanan, and letters and papers from Senator Benton, and family.

This officer informed me also that he was directed by the Secretary of State to acquaint me with his instructions to the consular agent, Mr. Larkin, which were to ascertain the disposition of the California people and conciliate their feelings in favor of the United States. This idea was no longer practicable, as actual war was inevitable and immediate; moreover, it was in conflict with our own instructions. We dropped this idea from our minds, but falling on others less informed, it came dangerously near losing us California. The letter of Senator Benton, while apparently only one of friendship and family details, was a trumpet giving no uncertain note. Read by the light of many conversations and discussions with himself and other governing men in Washington, it clearly made me know that I was required by the Government to find out any foreign schemes in relation to California, and to counteract them so far as was in my power. His letters made me know distinctly that at last the time had come when England must not get a foothold; that we *must be first.* I was to *act,* discreetly but positively.

Some years ago, when publishing a volume of memoirs, I wished to be especially accurate on the subject of Lieutenant Gillespie's coming to me from the Government. Gillespie had been directed to commit his dispatches to memory before reaching Vera Cruz, then destroy them. I asked Mr. George Bancroft, who as an accurate and reliable historian kept the data of this California period, which was solely in his charge, for his recollections, and he was so kind as to take much trouble to verify the subject. He sent me full and distinct memoranda to use, marked "Not to be printed." With his consent, I have used the following extracts from these official and personal papers; now such of them as are needed here are given to show how subsequent events were governed by these instructions brought me by Gillespie. They were to be known only to Gillespie and myself. Commodore Sloat had his separate, repeated, definite orders.

¶ FROM MEMORANDUM BY THE HONORABLE
  GEORGE BANCROFT (SECRETARY OF THE NAVY),
  MADE FOR GENERAL FRÉMONT.

Newport, R.I., 2d September, 1886.

Very soon after March 4, 1845, Mr. Polk one day, when I was alone with him, in the clearest manner and with the utmost energy declared to me what were to be the four great measures of his administration. He succeeded in all the four, and one of the four was the acquisition of California for the United States. This it was hoped to accomplish by peaceful negotiation; but if Mexico, in resenting our acceptance of the offer of Texas to join us, should begin a war with us, then by taking possession of the province. As we had a squadron in the North Pacific, but no army, measures for the carrying out this design fell to the Navy Department. The Secretary of the Navy, who had good means of gaining news as to the intentions of Mexico, and had reason to believe that its government intended to make war upon us, directed timely preparation for it.

In less than four months after the inauguration, on the 24th day of June, 1845, he sent orders to the commanding officer of the United States naval forces on the Pacific, that, if he should ascertain that Mexico had declared war against the United States, he should at once possess himself of the port of San Francisco and such other ports as his force might permit. At the same time he was instructed to encourage the inhabitants of California "to adopt a course of neutrality." The Secretary of the Navy repeated these orders in August and in October, 1845, and in February, 1846. On one of these occasions (October, 1845) he sent the orders by the hands of an accomplished and thoroughly trustworthy officer of the navy [5] as a messenger, well instructed in the designs of the department and with the purposes of the administration, so far as they related to California. Captain Frémont having been sent originally on a peaceful mission to the West by way of the Rocky Mountains, it had become necessary to give him warning of the new state of affairs and the designs of the President. The officer who had charge of the despatches from the Secretary of the Navy to

[5] Lt. Archibald Gillespie, USMC.

Commodore Sloat, and who had purposely been made acquainted with their import, accordingly made his way to Captain Frémont, who thus became acquainted with the state of affairs and the purposes of the Government. Being absolved from any duty as an explorer, Captain Frémont was left to his duty as officer in the service of the United States, with the further authoritative knowledge that the Government intended to take possession of California.

The Navy Department had no cause for apprehension that the movement upon California would lead to a *conflict* with any European power, and yet it was held that the presence of armed ships of any other power in the California harbors before annexation might be inconvenient. Therefore no orders were given to use force against any European powers; but the utmost celerity was used by the Navy Department in conveying to the commander of the American naval forces on the California coast orders in the event of war by Mexico to take instant possession of San Francisco and as many other places in California as the means at his disposal would permit. The information which the department possessed made it reasonably certain that if the United States commander in California should act with due celerity on receiving his orders, California would be occupied before any European government or any armed ship in the Pacific could be in motion.

My motive in sending so promptly the order to take possession was not from any fear that England would resist, but from the apprehension that the presence of an English man-of-war in San Francisco harbor would have a certain degree of inconvenience, and that it was much better for us to be masters there before the ship should arrive; and my orders reached there before any English vessel was off California. The delay of Sloat made a danger, but still he took possession of San Francisco before the British ship arrived. . . . After your interview with Gillespie you were absolved from any orders as an explorer, and became an officer of the American army, warned by your Government of your new danger, against which you were bound to defend yourself; and it was made known to you on the authority of the Secretary of the Navy that a great object of the President was to obtain possession of California. If I had been in your place I should have considered myself bound to do what I saw I could to promote the purpose of the President. You were alone; no Secretary of War to appeal to; he was thousands of miles off; and yet it was officially made known to you that your country was at war; and it was so made known expressly to guide your conduct. It was further made known to you that the acquisition of California was become a chief object of the President. If you had letters to that effect from the Secretary of War, you had your warrant. If you were left without orders from the War Department, certainly you learned from the Secretary of the Navy that the President's plan of war included the taking possession of California. The truth is, no officer of the Government had had anything to do with California but the Secretary of the Navy so long as I was in the Cabinet. . . .

With this necessary digression to make clear my subsequent acts, I return to our camp of May 9 (1849) on the Klamath Lake. We had talked late, but now, tired out, Gillespie was asleep. I sat far into the night, alone, reading my home letters by the fire, and thinking. I saw the way opening clear before me, and a grand opportunity was now presented to realize fully the far-sighted views which would make the Pacific Ocean the western boundary of the United States. I resolved to move forward on the opportunity, return forthwith to the Sacramento Valley, and bring all the influence I could command. This decision was the first step in the conquest of California. . . .

On the 24th of May we reached again Lassen's (near Sutter's Fort), and in the evening I wrote to Senator Benton a guarded letter. Until the arrival of Commodore Sloat my own movements depended on circumstances, and of them I could say but little. But I told him of the arrival of Lieutenant Gillespie, of the Klamath fighting [6] and the men we had lost, and how we fought that nation from one border to the other, "and have ever since been fighting until our entrance into the lower Sacramento Valley," and in phrases he would understand let him know I was to go the whole length of California; why, he knew.

Gillespie's arrival at Sutter's, and his taking the men to help him overtake me, had quickly spread among the people, and I found the settlers anxiously awaiting the result of his risky journey, and hoping to see me return with him. The Government vessels at San Francisco, the coming of a Government messenger to follow and find me, together with thick-coming rumors of war, were more than enough for our intelligent, quick-witted Americans. I found myself welcomed, and saw I should find support in carrying out my instructions.

The California authorities, under their orders from Mexico, had on their side given offense and alarm to old settlers and the incoming immigra-

[6] A description of this surprise attack by Indians follows in an account by Frémont's topographer, Edward M. Kern.

tion—requiring all foreigners to be naturalized or expelled, interfering with long acquired property rights, and fomenting disturbances by the Indians. I saw we must meet these Indian menaces and make them realize that Castro was far and I was near. And I intended to leave no enemy behind to destroy my strength by cutting off my supply of cattle and breaking communication with the incoming emigrants. So we raided all their rancherias on the western bank of the Sacramento, finding the men with feathers in their heads, faces painted black, and on the midst of their war ceremonies, and we did this so effectually as to put an end to the burning of wheatfields and intended attack on whites. It was a rude but necessary measure to protect the whites.

Then I began my preparations for carrying out my instructions. Except myself, then and for many months afterward, there was no other officer of the army in California. The citizen party under my command was made up of picked men, and though small in number was a formidable nucleus for frontier warfare, and many of its members commanded the confidence of the immigration. I wrote to Captain Montgomery, commanding the United States ship *Portsmouth,* then at Yerba Buena (San Francisco), asking for needed supplies from his ship's stores. With this was also an official letter from Lieutenant Gillespie,—who was well known to him,— which ended as follows:

Hoping you will be able to make the supply, I will only add that in the event of the party receiving from you the assistance requested, you may be sure the same will not only be highly appreciated by the President and departments, and confer an obligation upon Captain Frémont and myself, but will receive the heartfelt thanks of some of the bravest and most determined men, who are happy in suffering privations while serving their country with unsurpassed zeal and fidelity.

ARCHIE H. GILLESPIE
First Lieut., U.S. Marine Corps, and special and confidential Agent
for California.

Gillespie visited Captain Montgomery on his ship, and brought me in answer all I required—lead, powder, percussion caps, as well as camp supplies, and fifteen hundred dollars, to be repaid by an order on the proper department in Washington.

Soon after, when urgently appealed to for powder to sustain his party by Mr. William B. Ide, who had raised the flag of independence, the Grizzly

Bear flag, at Sonoma, Captain Montgomery, while answering with perfect courtesy, had to decline. . . .[7]

Frémont refers here to the celebrated Bear Flag Revolt that took place when a number of American settlers living in the Sacramento Valley decided that they would establish an independent republic in California. Frémont stated that Montgomery could not aid a citizen movement but that he knew through Gillespie enough of his secret instructions to realize that Frémont represented the army and the flag. Frémont later maintained that he adopted a policy of neutrality concerning the Bear Flaggers, but it is plausible to assume that he was furnishing them advice when they decided to overthrow the existing Mexican government.

Among the group, the leaders were Robert Semple, William B. Ide, and Ezekial Merritt. Riding into Sonoma, they surrounded Colonel Mariano Vallejo's rancho, and after drinking amply from the hospitable Mexican official's brandy cellar, marched him off to Sutter's Fort, where he was locked in a miserable cell. The enthusiastic Americans raised a flag featuring a crudely painted bear in the design, which one observer said looked more like a shoat. This was on June 14, 1846. William Ide read a proclamation in which he claimed the people had been persecuted and cheated by the Mexican government. He called upon them to rally around their new banner of "The California Republic."

After the Americans had raised their new banner, Frémont took a more active role in the conquest. He proceeded to San Jose, gathering a volunteer force, which was to aid the military units arriving in California. He left the topographer of his expedition, Edward M. Kern, in charge of Sutter's Fort, appointing him First Lieutenant of United States Volunteers, a rank later confirmed by Commodore Stockton. The Kern River and Kern County are named after him. Kern addressed this letter to his brother, Richard, living in Philadelphia. It is a rather colorful account of the Bear Flag Revolt and correlated events. The letter is in the manuscript collection of the Huntington Library:

---

[7] John Charles Frémont, "The Conquest of California," *The Century Magazine,* April, 1891.

¶ U.S. Fort Sacramento July 29, 1846

DICK:

By the favor of Com. Sloat I am enabled to send you a few lines of the doings in this newly acquired Terr. of the U.S. Little did I think when sitting at home in our office in G St. that I would ever be raised to be a Mil. character a (real) commandant of a fort with power to do as I pleased & shoot people if they do not obey me and all that sort of thing. "But there is a time in the affairs of men which when at the turn may lead to glory." Anyhow, strange as you may think it here I am, vested with the aforesaid authority and surrounded by a garrison of run away seamen & Indians. (I would not march through country with them) & the most ungodly hord of hard biting putting-your-finger-on-and-not-to be found fleas that have ever worried man since the days of Adam. They are a staple production of the country—before entering upon my blood & thunder narrative of the wars I will give you a sketch of some of the people concerned therin. . . .

Portion of Edward M. Kern's letter to his brother describing the Bear Flag Revolt. (*Reproduced from the original in the Henry E. Huntington Library and Art Gallery, San Marino, California.*)

. . . From that place [8] we had taken up our line of march for home and had got as far as the head of Klamath Lake when an express arrived for

[8] The reference here is to the last time he had written his brother, which was from

our immediate return to [California]. We lost 3 of our men. They were murdered in bed. We revenged ourselves on the Indians by killing and burning wherever an opportunity offered. Liet. Gillespie the courier had been followed some days by the native Indians. When a party was sent from our camp to meet him. On the night they came up with them was the intended time of attack. It came, and we lost 3 of our best men—it was an exchange of 3 for 4. Had the Lieut missed us that night it is more than likely in this reaching you I should have been at home.

What we were to return to Cal. for no one knows (but to return was sure of creating a row with the yellow belly [9]) we had been ordered out on March last, and abused by a Proclamation [10] (a copy enclosed) and left the country without a fight. When fairly down in the valley—couriers were running here and yon & nobody knew what for. At last word was sent to Jose Castro that we had returned. Then came a rumor that he was marching against us with a force of 300 men. Then the foreigners living round the upper part of the country, about 20 or 25, were called into camp—as a Proclamation had been issued stating that all foreigners—Americans in particular should leave the country at once or abide by the consequences—Indians were bribed to burn the crops as soon as they should be ripe enough, thereby cutting off all supplies for the Emigrants when they should arrive this fall. A gun had been given to an Indian to shoot Capt. Sutter, owner of this fort & all such unmanly means that none but a cowardly Spaniard would think of. Now to the commencement of hostilities. Having collected what forces could be raised in the upper country [we] moved from the Buttes towards the fort. The Spaniards were reported to be on the W. side of the Sacramento River. We supposed they would move upwards and sweep the country down—attacking us in the rear, defeat [us] (of course easily) and have possession of the whole upper country. But there was no army following. It turned out to be a corporal with 12 men driving a band of horses for the use of Castro. Here was an opening to commence business & Merritt, a Mountain man at the head of 12 men started and returned with the whole (cavellarda) not a blow struck. He sent word to Castro that he was there, he took the horses & that if he (C) wanted them to come and get them if he was a man.

---

the Oregon Camp, where he had been with Frémont and where the explorers were nearly murdered to the last man. Kit Carson is reported to have sounded the alarm in time to save most of the men. This is where Gillespie delivered the President's message to Frémont.

[9] Kern's term for Mexicans.

[10] The Frémont party was unceremoniously ordered to leave California by the Mexican governor.

The next move was the attack & taking of Sonoma a bold and beautifully managed affair. Our information that this post was garrisoned with about 80 or 100 men & about 200 Indians. We had every reason to suppose that they were on the alert as the business had commenced. Merritt started with 25 men to the place, his forces increasing to 45 all told when he arrived there. The charge was made that there was no resistance simply because there was no one to resist. Here a garrison was stationed under the command of one Ide a Mormon. While a party returned bringing with them as a proof of victory Gen. M. G. Vallejo, Col. S. Vallejo, Victor Prudhomme, a frenchman & I. Please, an American. They made no resistance, but when the head is cut off legs can't go. I have them at present under my charge. The next move of the insurgents, for they had it all to themselves . . . was the issue of a proclamation from the headquarters at Sonoma signed by said Ide calling on the people who love their liberty to fly to arms, etc. This produced a counter one from Castro calling everybody thieves etc. in the country and ordering the people to arm themselves in defence of their firesides which were about to be invaded by a party of Barbarians and that he particularly believed himself the chosen of God to avenge their wrongs. A movement was made a few days after taking of S. [Sonoma] by the Spaniards to regain so desireable position and the arms contained therein. Supposing the garrison to consist of but 15 men, a force of 70 were crossed below under the command of Joaquin Torres. They had come upon 3 of the boys unaware & taken them prisoners. When they were met by 15 of the garrison whom they surrounded, the boys let loose on them killing an ensign and wounding 2 more, one mortally. A retreat was the consequence leaving their prisoners behind them. You may judge of their valor from this act. The next thing was catching a couple of Americans who were riding peaceably along the road. After detaining them for an hour or 2 . . . then butchered them in cold blood, cutting to pieces with their sword etc. proceedings that would disgrace a Pi-Ute. But such is their nature. Beat them and they will love you. Treat them well and they'll kill you. I should never allow myself to be taken by them alive. This produced an order from our side to take no one prisoners. Capt. F. now marched to the assistance of the garrison. Martial law proclaimed throughout the country. Our next attack was on San Raphael, but like Sonoma there was no one to fight so of course it was taken. Two spies were killed on the road & asked no questions.[11] It is the

[11] The killing of these two harmless Mexicans, whom Kern calls spies, was long held against Frémont. Kit Carson is supposed to have been the trigger man in the brutal affair.

only way to bring them to their senses. Frémont is now camped at Monterey with a force of 200 men. Castro has gone down the country with an equal force. Desperation may drive a fight out of him, he knowing in the field he will receive no mercy. At present he is camped at the Rincon on the coast—the strongest position in California. Surrounded by bluffs on one side and the ocean on the other its impassable. 10 men would be good against a 1000. On the highway with no other road to pass to the lower settlements . . . On the 7 of Jul. Com. Sloat took possession of Monterey and the U.S. Flag is now flying at the principal 3 places in the upper country. To take or kill Castro will close the affair. Com. Stockton has relieved Sloat in the command of the Pacific Squadron. This is about all that has occurred in the way of war. Had the revolutionists been left to themselves a few weeks would have settled the business by their defeating themselves. A few honest & well disposed persons among them who really intended the movement for the best, but the majority moved by nothing but the chance of plunder without the slightest principles of honor to guide them, they must have defeated the cause—

CASTRO'S PROCLAMATION

The citizen José Castro—Lieut. Col. of the Mexican Army and commander in chief of the department of California: Fellow citizens: a band of robbers commanded by a captain of the U.S. Army, J. C. Frémont have without respect to the laws and authority of the department daringly introduced themselves into the country & disobeyed both the orders of your commander in chief & of the Prefect of the district by which he was required to march forthwith out of the limits of our territory. Without answering their letters he remains encamped at the farm "Natividad" from which he sallies forth committing depredations and making scandalous skirmishes.

In the name of our native country, I invite you to place yourselves under my immediate orders at headquarters where we will prepare to lance the ulcer which (should it not be done) would destroy our liberties & independence for which you ought to sacrifice yourselves as will your friend and fellow citizen,

José Castro

Headquarters at San Juan
8 March 1846

As pretty a piece of bombast as was ever written. We have had two other proclamations from the same Gent. and of the same nature. . . .

Matters turning out as they have it will be almost impossible for us to reach home this winter, as it will be so late before we get through this business here that the snows will have set in & though we could cross the Cal mts. the route will be impassable. We would have to winter somewhere. I am in hopes of getting a furlough when I am relieved and then have a chance of seeing something more of the settlements. I'm so far away from any place at this fort that it is only now and then when an explorer comes that I am enabled to know what is going on at all. There is a large emigration expected this fall from the states led by one Hastings, author of the Emigrants Guide and as big an ass as runs. There is a party of Mormons reported to be on their way here from N.Y. . . . The Lord knows where they will settle as there are so many rumors of their doings that the people are opposed to their entrance. A kind of Catholic religion is the religion of the country—among the foreigners. What a field this country will be for those miserable priests the missionaries. Here they can find the untutored child of the forest in a perfect state of nature. Women preachers could do a better business than the men. . . .[12]

Frémont and his men moved into action following the Bear Flag Revolt. They hurried to the San Francisco Bay area, and in his *Century* magazine article, Frémont relates what followed:

¶ In answer to urgent appeals made by the settlers I went to Sonoma on the 25th of June. On what I learned there I hurried back to head off advancing troops under De la Torre, a Mexican cavalry officer, but found he had retreated to Saucelito. At Saucelito I found an American vessel, the *Moscow,* Captain Phelps, of Worcester, Massachusetts. Before daylight next morning he was at the landing with one of his large boats. I took twelve of my men, my best shots; Captain Phelps and his boat's crew were excited and pleased to aid in the work on hand. On his ship were a quantity of rat-tail files, with which we supplied ourselves. It appeared that there was little or no guard maintained at the fort, which was at the point on the southern side of the gate which makes the entrance to the bay, and to which I gave the name of Golden Gate. Pulling across the strait or avenue of water which leads in from the gate, we reached Fort Point in the gray dawn and scrambled up the steep bank in time to see horsemen escaping towards Yerba Buena. We promptly spiked the guns,—fourteen, —nearly all long brass Spanish pieces. The measures which I had taken

[12] Edward M. Kern, letter in the manuscript collection of the Henry E. Huntington Library & Art Gallery, San Marino, Calif.

and the retreat of De la Torre freed from all Mexican authority the territory north of the bay of San Francisco from the sea to Sutter's Fort.

On the fourth day of July I was back in Sonoma, where the day was celebrated by salutes, and in the evening by a ball. During that and the following day the settlers were organized into a battalion consisting of four companies, numbering 244 men. The force with which I had recently been acting was 160 men. It was now necessary to concentrate the elements of this force. Naturally, the people desired me to take charge of it. Its existence was due to my presence in the valley, and upon my withdrawal it would have collapsed with absolute ruin to the settlers. They saw the co-operation between me and the naval forces, and Carson, and some of my most trusted men, had enough information from me to assure them of my having the support of the Government. Accordingly, the settlers having met to offer me this command, I accepted it. In accepting I urged them to remember the responsibility which I had assumed as an officer of the United States army, and said I trusted them to do nothing which would discredit it, themselves, or their country's flag.

This placed the settlers' movement under our flag, and made the necessary condition which both Mexico and foreign nations were bound to respect under the law of nations.

I sent out parties for horses to mount the battalion, and bring in cattle for their support. The fine immigration coming in was full of enthusiasm for the lovely land of California. A picked body of men was also hastening down from Oregon, and we only waited the arrival of Commodore Sloat.

On the 10th the express from Captain Montgomery roused us to enthusiasm by the news that Commodore Sloat had raised the flag at Monterey, that he had hoisted one at Yerba Buena, and sent one to Sonoma to be hoisted at that place. Montgomery also sent one with the request to have it hoisted at Sutter's Fort, and accordingly, with great satisfaction, I had this done at sunrise the next morning with a salute of twenty-one guns and amid general rejoicing. This paralyzed all opposition. . . .

A long letter from Commodore Sloat to me, dated July 9, followed, in which he requested me to bring my force to Monterey, saying, "I am extremely anxious to see you."

Going down to Monterey by way of the Salinas Valley, we gave on the way a marching salute to Gavilan Peak, where four months before we had hoisted the flag.

It was a day of excitement when we entered Monterey (July 19). Four of our men-of-war were lying in the harbor, and also the *Collingwood,* 80 guns, flagship of Admiral Sir George Seymour. She had come in on the

16th, and on her arrival the vessels of the American squadron had been signaled to prepare for action. I learned from Midshipman Beale, who was on shore at the time with a party building a blockhouse on the hill, that the signal was also made recalling to their ships all officers and men, and when he reached the *Congress* he found the men at quarters. . . .[13]

The British ship that caused such consternation among the Americans was on a peaceful mission. Fred Walpole was an officer serving aboard the vessel. Watching the parading and excitement ashore, he commented:

¶ The war of the United States with Mexico no doubt justifies them in seizing any part of her territory they can; if the war itself be justifiable, is another question; but for a long while they had been secretly intriguing for California, and that in a time of peace between the two countries.

Walpole had an opportunity to witness the arrival of Frémont and his men at Monterey. Later, he would include a description of the Americans in his *Four Years in the Pacific in Her Majesty's Ship Collingwood from 1844 to 1848.*

¶ During our stay Captain Frémont and his party arrived, preceded by another troop of American horse. It was a party of seamen mounted, who were used to scour the country to keep off marauders. Their efficiency as sailors, they being nearly all English, we will not question. As cavalry they would, probably, have been singularly destructive *to each other.* Their leader, however, was a fine fellow, and one of the best rifle-shots in the States. Frémont's party naturally excited curiosity. Here were true trappers, the class that produced the heroes of Fenimore Cooper's best works. These men had passed years in the wilds, living on their own resources: they were a curious set. A vast cloud of dust appeared first, and thence in long file emerged this wildest wild party. Frémont rode a-head, a spare active-looking man, with such an eye! He was dressed in a blouse and leggings, and wore a felt hat. After him came five Delaware Indians, who were his body-guard, and have been with him through all his wanderings: they had charge of two baggage-horses. The rest, many of them blacker than the Indians, rode two and two, the rifle held by one hand across the pommel of the saddle. Thirty-nine of them are his regular men, the rest are loafers picked up lately; his original men are principally backwoods-

13 *The Century Magazine,* April, 1891.

men from the State of Tennessee, and the banks of the upper waters of the Missouri. He has one or two with him who enjoy high reputations in the Prairies. Kit Carson is as well known there as the Duke is in Europe. The dress of these men was principally a long loose coat of deer-skin, tied with thongs in front; trousers of the same, of their own manufacture, which, when wet through, they take off, scrape well inside with a knife, and put on as soon as dry; the saddles were of various fashions, though these and a large drove of horses, and a brass field-gun, were things they had picked up about California. The rest of the gang were a rough set; and perhaps their private, public, and moral characters had better not be too closely examined. They are allowed no liquor, tea and sugar only; this, no doubt, has much to do with their good conduct, and the discipline too is very strict. They were marched up to an open space on the hills near the town, under some large firs, and there took up their quarters in messes of six or seven in the open air. The Indians lay beside their leader. One man, a doctor, six foot six high, was an odd-looking fellow. May I never come under his hands!

The party, after settling themselves, strolled into the town, and in less than two days passed in drunkenness and debauchery, three or four were missing. . . .[14]

The initial phase of the conquest had taken place with little bloodshed. California appeared to be securely in the hands of the Americans. John Bidwell later recalled, "The first conquest of California, in 1846, by the Americans, with the exception of the skirmish at Petaluma and another towards Monterey, was achieved without a battle. We simply marched all over California from Sonoma to San Diego and raised the American flag without opposition or protest. We tried to find an enemy, but could not."[15]

Commodore Robert F. Stockton succeeded John Drake Sloat as senior naval officer in California waters on July 23, 1846. Though short in stature, Stockton was a dynamic, if somewhat pompous officer. He was idolized by his men, who called him "Fighting Bob," a sobriquet acquired during the War of 1812. General Stephen Watts Kearny arrived later with a small force of regular army troops from Santa Fe, and was involved in the one major engagement of the war

[14] Fred Walpole, *Four Years in the Pacific in Her Majesty's Ship Collingwood from 1844 to 1848* (London: Richard Bentley, 1850. 2 vols.).
[15] *The Century Magazine,* January, 1891.

in California. At San Pascual in present San Diego County, Kearny led his dragoons into a clever ambush staged by the Mexican general Andrés Pico, and his hard-riding legion of Californians.

A conflict developed between Stockton and Kearny as to who exercised supreme military authority. The commodore was enough of a diplomat to treat the veteran army officer with courtesy. Frémont failed to act with similar discretion. He refused to accept Kearny in the role of commanding officer. Instead, he recognized Stockton's authority. This may seem incongruous, considering that Frémont and the general were fellow army officers. However, it is easy to perceive why Frémont favored the commodore. Stockton, obviously forewarned by the Marine Corps courier Gillespie, was aware that Frémont had strong support for his actions in Washington, and the fact that he was the son-in-law of the powerful Senator Thomas Hart Benton undoubtedly influenced his thinking. Regardless of the motives, he did aid Frémont; promoting him in rank, and later designating him as military governor of the territory. Kearny, on the other hand, resented Frémont as a young upstart, and he succeeded in having the explorer court-martialed later for his insubordination. Although Frémont was cleared by presidential intervention and the influence of Senator Benton, he resigned from the army, bitter at the treatment he had received for his efforts.

Frémont, a brash young man at the period, found Stockton's predecessor vacillating and overly cautious. Commodore Sloat mistrusted him, primarily because he was without credentials. Frémont writes of their first meeting aboard the *Congress* at Monterey:

¶ I was accompanied by Lieutenant Gillespie. Commodore Sloat was glad to see me. He seemed excited over the gravity of the situation, in which he was the chief figure, and now wholly responsible for its consequences. After a few words he informed me that he had applied to Lieutenant Gillespie, whom he knew to be an agent of the Government, for his authority; but it had been declined. He then asked to see my instructions. "I do not know by what authority you are acting; I can do nothing. Lieutenant Gillespie has told me nothing; he came to Mazatlan and I sent him to Monterey, but I know nothing. I want to know by what authority you are acting."

I informed him that I had been expected to act, and had acted, largely on my own responsibility, and without written authority from the Government to justify hostilities.

He was greatly disturbed by this, and distinctly told me that in raising the flag at Monterey he had acted upon the faith of my operations in the north.

He had expected to find that I had been acting under such *written* authority as would support his action in raising the flag. He was so discouraged and offended that he terminated the interview abruptly, quitting the cabin and leaving me. I should have been glad to explain, and to satisfy him that the taking of California would exactly meet the wishes of the Government, but he closed his mind against anything short of "the written paper." He declined to see me again; and, as a much younger officer, I could not urge myself upon one of his rank and present command. Knowing the instructions to all officers on the coast, I could not suppose that the officer commanding the squadron was relying on me to justify his action. . . .[16]

Sloat refrained from mentioning his conference with Frémont in the carefully detailed report he sent to Secretary of the Navy George Bancroft. He sailed from California satisfied that he had performed his assignment efficiently. The Mexicans had been subjugated, and the British threat had proved non-existent. California was safely in American hands.

¶ Flagship "Levant" At Sea, July 31, 1846.

SIR: I have the honor to report that, on the 7th June, I received at Mazatlan information that the Mexican troops, six or seven thousand strong, had, by order of the Mexican Government, invaded the territory of the United States north of the Rio Grande, and had attacked the forces under General Taylor, and that the Squadron of the United States were blockading the Coast of Mexico on the Gulf.

These hostilities, I considered, would justify my commencing offensive operations on the west coast. I therefore sailed on the 8th in the "Savannah" for the coast of California, to carry out the orders of the Department of the 24th June, 1845, leaving the "Warren" at Mazatlan to bring me any

---

[16] *The Century Magazine,* January, 1891.

despatches or important information that might reach there. I arrived at Monterey on the second of July, where I found the "Cyane" and "Levant," and I learned that the "Portsmouth" was at San Francisco, to which places they had been previously ordered to await further instructions.

On the morning of the 7th, having previously examined the defenses and localities of the town, I sent Captain Mervine with the accompanying summons (A) to the military commandant at Monterey, requiring him to surrender the place forthwith to the forces of the United States under my command. At 9 o'clock 30 minutes A.M., I received his reply (B), stating that he was not authorized to surrender the place, and referred me to the Commanding General of California, Don José Castro.

Every arrangement having been made the day previous, the necessary force (about 250 seamen and marines) was immediately embarked in the boats of the Squadron, and landed at 10 o'clock under cover of the guns of the ships, with great promptitude and good order, under the immediate command of Captain Wm. Mervine, assisted by Commander H. N. Page as second.

The forces were immediately formed and marched to the Custom House, where my Proclamation to the inhabitants of California (C) was read, the standard of the United States hoisted amid three hearty cheers by the troops and foreigners present, and a salute of 21 guns fired by all the ships. Immediately afterwards, the Proclamation both in English and Spanish, was posted up about the town, and two Justices of the Peace appointed to preserve order and punish delinquencies; the Alcaldes declining to serve.

Previous to landing, the accompanying "General Order" (D) was read to crews of all the ships; and I am most happy to state, that I feel confident that the inhabitants of Monterey, and all other places where our forces have appeared, will do them and myself the justice to say that not the least depredation, or slightest insult or irregularity, has been committed from the moment of our landing until my departure.

Immediately after taking possession of Monterey, I despatched a courier to General Castro, the military commandant of California, with a letter and a copy of my Proclamation, to which I received a reply. On the 9th, I despatched a letter by a courier to Señor Don Pio Pico, the Governor at Santa Barbara.

On the 6th of July, I despatched orders by sea to Commander Montgomery, to take immediate possession of the Bay of San Francisco, etc., and on the 7th a duplicate of that order by land, which he received on the evening of the 8th; and at 7 A.M. of the 9th, he hoisted the flag at San

Francisco, read and posted up my Proclamation, and took possession of that part of the country in the name of the United States. . . .

On the 13th, at the request of the foreigners at the Pueblo of San Jose, I furnished a flag to be hoisted at that place (about 70 miles interior from Monterey), and appointed a Justice of the Peace to preserve order in the town; the Alcaldes declining to serve. The flag was hoisted on the 16th.

Deeming Purser D. Fauntleroy well qualified for such service, I directed him, on the 8th, to organize a Company of 35 Dragoons from volunteers from the ships and citizens on shore to reconnoiter the country, keep open the communication between Monterey and San Francisco, and to prevent the people of the country from being robbed, etc., and directed him to purchase the necessary horses and equipments to mount them. . . .

On the afternoon of the 15th July, the "Congress" arrived, and Commodore Stockton reported for duty.

On the 16th, the British Admiral, Sir Geo. F. Seymour, arrived in the "Collingwood," 80. An officer was immediately sent to tender him the usual courtesies and the facilities of the port. He was subsequently furnished with a set of top-gallant masts and other spars for his ship, and sailed on the 23d for the Sandwich Islands.

The visit of the Admiral was very serviceable to our cause in California, as the inhabitants fully believed he would take part with them, and that we would be obliged to abandon our conquest; but when they saw the friendly intercourse subsisting between us, and found that he could not interfere in their behalf, they abandoned all hope of ever seeing the Mexican flag again.

On the 23d, my health being such as to prevent my attending to so much and such laborious duties, I directed Commodore Stockton to assume command of the forces and operations on shore, and, on the 29th, having determined to return to the United States, via Panama, I hoisted my broad pennant on board the "Levant," and sailed for Mazatlan and Panama, leaving the remainder of the Squadron under his command, believing no further opposition would be made to our taking possession of the whole of the Californias (as General Castro had less than one hundred men), and that I could render much more important service by returning to the United States with the least possible delay, to explain to the Government the situation and wants of that country, than I could by remaining in command, in my infirm state of health. At the time of my leaving Monterey, the United States were in quiet possession of all "Alta California" north of Santa Barbara. . . .[17]

[17] Executive Document, 2d Session, 30th Congress, p. 1006, Vol. I.

The situation did not remain tranquil for long following Sloat's departure. Upon assuming command, Stockton issued a proclamation that served to rouse the fury of many Mexican residents, particularly those living in the south. Reading the commodore's bombast, it is easy to understand why it would have incurred the resentment of a proud people. The figures citing the number of Mexicans and Americans involved is misleading. Stockton had a tendency to exaggerate in his reports. He wanted to enhance his military reputation in California, and was disappointed that the opportunities were limited. The War with Mexico created a scramble for glory among senior officers of both the United States Army and Navy. California had little to offer as far as achieving a combat record was concerned. The real fighting took place in Mexico, and much of the battling was between various American generals. There was considerable jealousy, for every officer was aware that future promotion in a peacetime military establishment would be predicated upon his war record. Accordingly, competition for battle honors was keen and often vindictive. In Los Angeles, the opposition to Stockton's decree was openly hostile. Angered Mexicans gathered in the town Plaza, to read the proclamation:

¶ Californians—The Mexican government and their military officers have without cause, for a year past, been threatening the United States with hostilities.

They have recently, in pursuance of these threats, commenced hostilities by attacking, with 7,000 men, a small detachment of 2,000 United States troops, by whom they were signally defeated and routed.

General Castro, the commander-in-chief of the military forces of California, has violated every principle of international law and national hospitality, by hunting and pursuing with several hundred soldiers, and with wicked intent, Captain Frémont, of the United States army, who came here to refresh his men (about forty in number), after a perilous journey across the mountains on a scientific survey.

For these repeated hostilities and outrages, military possession was ordered to be taken of Monterey and San Francisco until redress could be obtained from the government of Mexico. . . .

On assuming the command of the forces of the United States on the coast of California, both by sea and land, I find myself in possession of the ports of Monterey and San Francisco, with daily reports from the interior of scenes of rapine, blood, and murder. Three inoffensive American residents of the country have, within a few days, been murdered in the most brutal manner; and there are no California officers who will arrest and bring the murderers to justice, although it is well known who they are and where they are.

I must, therefore, and will, as soon as I can, adopt such measures as may seem best calculated to bring these criminals to justice, and to bestow peace and good order on the country.

In the first place, however, I am constrained by every principle of national honor, as well as a due regard for the safety and best interests of the people of California, to put an end at once, and by force, to the lawless depredations daily committed by General Castro's men upon the persons and property of peaceful and unoffending inhabitants. . . .

The present general of the forces of California is a usurper, has been guilty of great offenses, has impoverished and drained the country of almost its last dollar, and has deserted his post now when most needed.

He has deluded and deceived the inhabitants of California, and they wish his expulsion from the country. He came into power by rebellion and force, and by force he must be expelled. Mexico appeared to have been compelled, from time to time, to abandon California to the mercies of any wicked man who could muster one hundred men-in-arms. The distances from the capital are so great that she cannot or will not punish or control the chieftains who, one after the other, have defied her power and kept California in a constant state of revolt and misery.

The inhabitants are tired and disgusted with this constant succession of military usurpers and this insecurity of life and property. Therefore, upon them, I will not make war. I require, however, all others, civil and military, and all other persons, to remain quiet at their respective homes and stations, and to obey the orders they may receive from me, and by my authority; and, if they do no injury or violence to my authority, none will be done to them.

But notice is hereby given, that if any of the inhabitants of the country either abandon their dwellings or do any injury to the arms of the United States, or to any person within this territory, they will be treated as enemies and suffer accordingly.

No person whatever is to be troubled in consequence of any part he may heretofore have taken in the politics of the country, or for having been a subject of General Castro. And all persons who may have belonged to the government of Mexico, but who, from this day, acknowledge the authority of the existing laws, are to be treated in the same manner as other citizens of the United States, provided they are obedient to the law and to the orders they shall receive from me or by authority.

The commander-in-chief does not desire to possess himself of one foot of California for any other reason than as the only means to save from destruction the lives and property of the foreign residents and the citizens of the territory, who have invoked his protection.

As soon, therefore, as the officers of the civil law return to their proper duties, under a regularly-organized government, and give security for life, liberty, and property, alike to all, the forces under my command will be withdrawn, and the people left to manage their own affairs in their own way.

R. F. STOCKTON
Commander-in-chief, etc. etc.[18]

That many of the Mexicans were resisting the American occupation of California because they were patriotic and were trying to repel an invader was a factor that Stockton ignored. He did find acceptance among those residents who were tired of the political corruption that had long existed under the Mexican regime. Perhaps a statesman more skilled in diplomacy could have pursued a more moderate course. However, these were turbulent times, and Stockton felt the measures he adopted were necessary. As a military commander, his first obligation to his government was the subjection of the territory and its inhabitants to United States authority. It was not a time for moderation. Diplomacy could be exercised by others at a later date. It is little wonder that many of the citizens were uneasy, particularly those of Mexican descent. They found no assurance in the closing words of the proclamation, which declared that American forces would retire once civil government was restored. It was feared that one corrupt system had merely been exchanged for another.

Commodore Stockton proceeded in the conquest of California, quickly consolidating all of the territory. He left the Marine Corps lieutenant Archie Gillespie in charge of the garrison at Los Angeles. This was a mistake. While Gillespie had performed a creditable job in carrying dispatches to Frémont, he proved to be an autocrat, and angered the Mexican populace. In a short time the marine officer, now

---

[18] A copy of Stockton's proclamation is in the Gillespie papers collection, University of California, Los Angeles.

designated as military commandant of the southern district, would have a revolt on his hands. Stockton was anxious to convey the news that California had been pacified to Washington as quickly as possible. He sent Kit Carson, Frémont's able scout, east with a message to the President that California had been conquered. Carson was intercepted by General Kearny, who was then marching west from Santa Fe. What took place is recorded in this statement Carson made to Senator Benton, who had little affection for Kearny. The account was appended in a note to Benton's speech, on July, 1848, on the brevet nomination of General Kearny:

¶ I met General Kearny with his troops on the 6th of December, a short distance below Santa Fé. I had heard before of their coming, and, when I met them, the first thing I told them was that they were "too late"—that California was conquered, and the United States flag raised in all parts of the country. But General Kearny said he would go on, and said something about going to establish a civil government. I told him a civil government was already established, and Colonel Frémont appointed governor, to commence as soon as he returned from the North, some time in that very month, (October.)

General Kearny said that that was no difference,—that he was a friend of Colonel Frémont, and he would make him governor himself. He began from the first to insist on my turning back to guide him into California. I told him I could not turn back; that I had pledged myself to Commodore Stockton and Colonel Frémont to take their despatches through to Washington city, and to return with them as far as New Mexico, where my family lived, and to carry them all the way back if I did not find some one at Santa Fé that I could trust as well as I could myself; that I had promised them I would reach Washington in sixty days, and that they should have return despatches from the government in one hundred and twenty days. I had performed so much of the journey in the appointed time, and, in doing so, had already worn out and killed thirty-four mules; that Stockton and Frémont had given me letters of credit to persons on the way to furnish me with all the animals I needed, and all supplies to make the trip to Washington and back in the one hundred and twenty days; and that I was pledged to them and could not disappoint them; and besides, that I was under more obligations to Colonel Frémont than any other man alive. General Kearny would not hear any such thing as my going on. He told me he was a friend to Colonel Frémont and

Senator Benton, and all the family, and would send on the despatches by Mr. Fitzpatrick, who had been with Colonel Frémont in his exploring party, and was a good friend to him, and would take the despatches through and bring them back as quick as I could.

When he could not persuade me to turn back, he then told me that he had a right to make me go with him, and insisted on his right; and I did not consent to turn back till he had made me believe that he had a right to order me; and then, as Mr. Fitzpatrick was going on with the despatches, and General Kearny seemed such a good friend of the Colonel's, I let him take me back; and I guided him through, but with great hesitation, and had prepared every thing to escape in the night before they started, and made known my intention to —— Maxwell, who urged me not to do so. . . .

This statement I make at the request of Senator Benton, but had much rather be examined in a court of justice, face to face with General Kearny, and there tell at once all that I know about General Kearny's battles and conduct in California.[19]

Stockton returned to San Francisco confident that the pacification of California had been achieved. Upon his arrival, he reported that "The inhabitants of San Francisco, on my arrival, received me *en masse,* with every demonstration of joy on the conquest of the country, and with every manifestation of personal respect as the governor of the territory and commander-in-chief of the United States forces." On September 30th, he received a surprise:

¶ A courier arrived from Captain Gillespie, despatched by that officer to convey to me the information that an insurrection had broken out at Ciudad de los Angeles, and that he was beseiged in the government-house at that place by a large force. I immediately ordered Captain Mervine to proceed in the *Savannah* to San Pedro for the purpose of affording aid to Captain Gillespie. Major Frémont was at Sacramento when the news of the insurrection reached him, and having formed the determination to march against the insurgents with the force he could muster, amounting to about one hundred and twenty men, was preparing to move. I sent a request to him forthwith to join me at San Francisco with his command, and to bring with him as many saddles as he could procure. . . .

Frémont arrived in San Francisco, and Stockton ordered him to proceed by ship to Santa Barbara, where he was to procure horses and

[19] Appendix to the *Congressional Globe,* 1848.

march on Los Angeles. Accordingly, he boarded the *Sterling* with 160 men. The ship set a course for the south. Stockton followed with another force in the *Congress,* but paused at Monterey to land troops, as it had been reported that insurgents were planning to attack the town. Continuing to San Pedro, he discovered that the victorious insurgents had occupied Los Angeles, and Gillespie had been driven from the town. Frémont failed to arrive. Stockton writes:

¶ On my arrival . . . about the 23d of October, I found the *Savannah* frigate. Captain Mervine informed me that Captain Gillespie, with the volunteers under his command, was on board his vessel, having left Ciudad de los Angeles under a capitulation entered into with General Flores, the leader of the insurrection,—one of the Mexican officers who, having been made prisoner of war, had been released on parole.

Captain Mervine further informed me that, about two weeks before, he had landed with his sailors and marines for the purpose of marching in conjunction with Captain Gillespie and his detachment of volunteers to Ciudad de los Angeles. He had not carried any artillery with him; that about twelve miles from San Pedro he encountered a party of the insurgents with one piece of artillery; a battle ensued; that several charges had been made upon the insurgents' gun, but it was impossible to capture it, as whenever he approached, they hitched their horses to it and retreated. Having sustained a loss of several men killed and wounded, he retired with his force and re-embarked.

Proper arrangements having been made during the night, in the morning we landed a strong force with several pieces of artillery, once more hoisted the flag of the United States at San Pedro, and formed our camp there. The insurgent force in the vicinity was supposed to number about eight hundred men. Our authority was necessarily limited to the portion of territory in our actual possession or within the range of our guns. The insurgents, in the undisturbed occupancy of the interior, and watchful of our every movement, could, at their pleasure threaten us with an attack by night or day, and had the precaution to remove beyond our reach every horse and all the cattle which might have been available either for food or transportation.

The roadstead at San Pedro was also a dangerous position for men-of-war, being exposed to the storms which at that season of the year rage with great violence upon the coast.

This consideration decided me to proceed to San Diego, which, although the entrance was obstructed by a bar which had never been passed by a vessel of equal draught of water with the *Congress,* might, I hoped be crossed; and if the passage should prove practicable, would be found a convenient and safe harbour. We did not, however, leave San Pedro until I had been compelled to relinquish all expectation of the co-operation of Major Frémont, from whom I had not heard a word since we parted off San Francisco, nor until the officers and men had become completely exhausted by their incessant duties on shore, in guarding the camp from attack and pursuing small parties of the insurgents who approached us. Having embarked the men belonging to the squadron, and volunteers under Captain Gillespie, I sailed for San Diego in the *Congress.*

On my arrival off the harbour of San Diego, I received information from Lieutenant Minor that the town was besieged by the insurgents, that his stock of provisions was small, and that he was in want of an additional force. He gave it as his opinion that the *Congress* might be got over the bar. In attempting this, however, the ship struck, and her position was so dangerous that we were compelled to return to the anchorage outside.

On the following day the *Malek Adhel,* a prize to the United States ship *Warren,* arrived from Monterey with despatches from Lieutenant-Colonel Frémont. I thus received information from that officer that on his way to Santa Barbara he met the merchant-ship *Vandalia* from San Pedro, by whom he was informed of the state of affairs at the South; that it would be impossible for him to procure horses at Santa Barbara, in consequence of which he had proceeded to Monterey, and would employ all diligence in preparing his force for Ciudad de los Angeles.

Lieutenant Minor was directed to send the ship *Stonington,* then lying in the harbour of San Diego, with as many volunteers as could be spared, to Ensenada, about ninety miles below San Diego, for the purpose of procuring animals, which he was instructed to have driven into San Diego. Without a supply of horses and beeves, it was not prudent to commence our march. Captain Mervine was despatched in the *Savannah* to Monterey, to aid Lieutenant-Colonel Frémont in his preparations to march, and, having myself gone to San Pedro, returned with all convenient speed to San Diego.

About thirty or forty miles from the place our progress was arrested by a calm. My anxiety on account of Lieutenant-Colonel Frémont, and my desire to go to his assistance was so great, that a boat was immediately despatched with Lieutenant Tilghman, the bearer of a communication addressed to Lieutenant George Minor, in command at San Diego, apprising that officer that on my arrival I would be ready to take the field in person, and with an additional force of two hundred men from the ship, to take up the line of march for Ciudad de los Angeles. Lieutenant Minor was directed to arrange with Lieutenant Tilghman, the commanding officer of the artillery, and Mr. Southwick, commanding officer of the engineers, to have the horses necessary for the transportation of the guns and ammunition. Notwithstanding my first unsuccessful attempt to get into the harbour of San Diego, it was an object of too great importance to be abandoned, unless from the absolute impossibility of effecting it. The bar and channel were again, on my return, examined and buoyed, and a second attempt made. After crossing the bar, the ship grounded, and in such a situation that it became expedient to prepare her spars to shore her up, to prevent her from tumbling over. While thus occupied, the insurgents commenced an attack upon the town, and notwithstanding the perilous condition of the frigate and the necessity of employing the crew in extricating her from her position, a portion of them was simultaneously engaged in landing from the ship in boats to take part in the fight. In executing my orders in reference to those two distinct objects at the same time, the conduct of the officers and men under my command was such as to command my warmest commendation. Everything was performed with the regularity and order of the ordinary duties of the vessel. Having accomplished a landing of the men from the ship, the attack of the insurgents was successfully repelled by the combined force under the command of Lieutenant Minor and Captain Gillespie.

The situation of the place was found to be most miserable and deplorable. The male inhabitants had abandoned the town, leaving their women and children dependent upon us for protection and food. No horses could be obtained to assist in the transportation of the guns and ammunition, and not a beeve could be had to supply the necessary food; some supplies of provisions were furnished from the ship. The expedition to the southward for animals, under the command of Captain Gibson, of the battalion, had succeeded in driving about ninety horses and two hundred head of beef-cattle into the garrison.

The horses were, however, much worn down, and it was supposed a fortnight's rest would be required before they would be fit for service. During the time required for resting the horses, we were actively employed in the construction of a fort, for the more complete protection of the town, mounting guns, and in making the necessary harness, saddles, and bridles. While the work of preparation necessary for our march to meet Lieutenant-Colonel Frémont at Ciudad de los Angeles was thus going on, we sent an Indian to ascertain where the principal force of insurgents was encamped. He returned with information that a body of them, about fifty strong, was encamped at San Bernardo, about thirty miles from San Diego. Captain Gillespie was immediately ordered to have as many men as he could mount, with a piece of artillery, ready to march for the purpose of surprising the insurgents in their camp. Another expedition under command of Captain Hensley of the battalion was sent to the southward for animals, who after performing the most arduous service returned with five hundred head of cattle and one hundred and forty horses and mules. About the 3d of December, two deserters from the insurgents, whose families lived in San Diego, came into the place and reported themselves to Lieutenant Minor, the commander of the troops. On receiving information of the fact, I repaired to Lieutenant Minor's quarters with my aide-de-camp, Lieutenant Gray, for the purpose of examining one of these men. While engaged in this examination, a messenger arrived with a letter from General Kearny of the United States army, apprising me of his approach, and expressing a wish that I would open a communication with him and inform him of the state of affairs in California.

Captain Gillespie was immediately ordered to proceed to General Kearny's camp with the force which he had been directed to have in readiness, carrying a letter which I wrote to General Kearny. Captain Gillespie left San Diego at about half-past seven o'clock the same evening, taking with him one of the deserters to act as a guide in conducting General Kearny to the camp of the insurgents. . . .[20]

Gillespie and his force, numbering thirty-nine men, with a small brass four-pounder, trotted across San Diego County, meeting Kearny's dragoons near Warner's Ranch. It is said that Gillespie passed the house of a sister of the Mexican leader, Andrés Pico, with his men, and she sent a message to her brother alerting him that the hated former military commandant at Los Angeles was in the vicinity. Rain had been falling for several days, and the combined American contingent bivouacked in a muddy campsite, shivering in their soaking blankets, for cold added to their misery. It also dampened their powder. On the following day, many would ride into battle with carbines and pistols that misfired. On the morning of December 6th, the men answered the bugler's call "To Horse," and rode off down into the serene valley of San Pascual. A report of the furious encoun-

[20] This and subsequent correspondence of Commodore Stockton is taken from Executive Document No. 1, accompanying the President's message at the 2nd Session of the 30th Congress, December, 1848.

ter that followed was written by Captain Archie Gillespie to Commodore Stockton following the action:

¶ . . . The gray light of the moon appeared as we approached the valley. We were marching by twos, and as the advance commanded by Capt. Johnson reached the plain, the general gave the order to "trot," which Capt. Johnson misunderstood for "charge." A shout and off dashed the dragoons at the charge. . . .

As we came up, I saw a party of some 25 or 30 dragoons slowly turning before a superior force of the enemy. Sword in hand, I dashed forward to them crying, "Rally, men, for God's sake rally, show a front, don't turn your backs, face them, face them, follow me," but to no effect. Their brave leader had fallen, pierced by many lances.

I fell upon the center of the enemy, and was immediately saluted with the cry of recognition, "Ya, es Gillespie, adentio, hombres, adentio. There is Gillespie. At him men, at him!"

Four lances were darted at me instantly, which being parried, the fifth and sixth quickly followed, accompanied by the discharge of an Escopeta, almost into my face. At this moment, I noticed a lance "in rest" coming from the front, and when leaning over the neck of my horse, parrying the charge, I was struck on the back of the neck by another lance at the collar of my coat with such force, as to be thrown clear from my saddle to the ground with my sabre under me.

As I attempted to rise, I received a thrust from a lance from behind me, striking above the heart, making a severe gash open to the lungs. I turned my face in the direction of my assailant, when one of the enemy riding at full speed charged upon me, dashed his lance at my face, struck and cutting my upper lip, broke a front tooth and threw me upon my back as his horse jumped over me. . . .[21]

Gillespie, bleeding profusely from his wounds, staggered to his feet, sabering his way through the melee to one of the American howitzers. If he could get the cannon into operation, the enemy might be routed:

¶ Dragoons and a few riflemen were flying across the field, fighting singlehanded against overpowering numbers; the carbines of the dragoons (Hall's breech-loading) had become utterly useless from the rain the night previous and were in many instances clubbed, the men having

[21] The original of this document, together with most of Gillespie's papers, is in the library of the University of California, Los Angeles. They were discovered in a Sacramento rooming house just prior to the outbreak of World War II.

apparently lost confidence in their sabres. The dead and wounded were lying in every direction, whilst the yell and clash of arms with the firing of rifles from an elevation on the right, proved the bravery and desperation with which our men fought against such odds. . . .

Gillespie reached the cannon, which several soldiers were trying to fire:

¶ I heard the cry—"Where is the match?" "There is none," someone answered. Lt. Warner fired his pistol upon the powder without success. Quick as a thought, I lit my Segar Match, ordered a dragoon to put on more powder and instantly fired the gun. As I handed the match to a dragoon, I fainted.

The Californians retreated. Kearny had lost twenty-one men. In addition, many of his soldiers were wounded—the general being one of the casualties. The column fought off an attempted ambush during the march to San Diego, where they joined forces with Stockton. The commodore ordered the assault on Los Angeles to be made without delay. He was anxious to bring the war in California to a successful conclusion. Stockton appointed Kearny commander of the troops, but he reserved the title of commander-in-chief of the expedition for himself. There was friction between the two from the start. As the column approached Los Angeles, Stockton received a message from Gillespie, who was ahead with the advance guard, informing him that two commissioners had arrived with a flag and a message for him. Stockton continues his account:

¶ Repairing to the front, I received the commissioners, who bore a letter signed by General Flores as governor and commander-in-chief, addressed to the commander-in-chief of the American forces. Upon reading it, and ascertaining from whom it emanated, I replied to the commissioners, substantially, that I perceived the letter was written by General Flores, whom I had captured and held as a prisoner, but whom I had released on his parole of honour; that in appearing now in hostile array he had violated his parole, and could not be treated as an honourable man; that I had no answer to return to his communication but this:—that if I caught him I should shoot him. . . .
. . . Our men were badly clothed, and their shoes generally made by

themselves out of canvas. It was very cold and the roads heavy. Our animals were all poor and weak, some of them giving out daily, which gave much hard work to the men in dragging the heavy carts, loaded with ammunition and provisions, through deep sands and up steep ascents, and the prospect before us was far from being that which we might have desired; but nothing could break down the fine spirits of those under my command, or cool their readiness and ardour to perform their duty; and they went through the whole march of one hundred and forty-five miles with alacrity and cheerfulness.

During the day of our march to the cayotes [Los Coyotes], we learned that some of the enemy were in our rear following us; and as we approached the cayotes several of them made their appearance in front of the house upon the hill, and waved their lances in angry defiance; but on the approach of the advance guard they rode off and left us to encamp on the hill without molestation.

Being quite satisfied that we were in the neighborhood of the enemy, during the night a confidential person was sent to ascertain, if possible, their position; he returned, and informed me that the enemy were in force between us and the Rio San Gabriel, and I was satisfied that the enemy intended at last to make a stand against us, and to fight us on the 8th day of January (1847). The day suited me. Before moving that morning, the arms were fired and reloaded and each officer and man was assigned to his position for the fight, and was reminded it was the 8th day of January and the anniversary of the battle of New Orleans.

We marched at nine o'clock. Immediately on reaching the plain we formed a square, our baggage-packs, spare oxen, and beef cattle in the centre. . . .

When within about two miles of the Rio San Gabriel, the enemy appeared in sight upon the hills on the opposite side; they were six hundred in number, in three divisions, their right about two miles down the river. As we approached, our column closed up and moved steadily on towards the ford, when within a quarter of a mile of the river, a halt was ordered and disposition made to meet the enemy.

A detachment of marines, under Lieutenant H. B. Watson, was sent to strengthen the left flank of the square. A party of the enemy, one hundred and fifty strong, had now crossed the river and made several ineffectual attempts to drive a band of wild mares upon the advance party. We now moved forwards to the ford in broken files; Captain Hensley's command was ordered to dismount, and acting as skirmishers, it deployed to the front and crossed the stream, (which is about fifty yards in width,) driving before them a party of the enemy which had attempted to annoy us. The enemy had now taken their position upon the heights, distant six hundred yards from the river and about fifty feet above its level; their centre or main body, about two hundred strong, was stationed immediately in front of the ford, upon which they opened a fire from two pieces of artillery, throwing round and grape shot without effect. Their right and left wings were separated from the main body about three hundred yards. Our column halted upon the edge of the stream; at this time the guns were unlimbered to return the enemy's fire, but were ordered again to be limbered and not a gun to be fired until the opposite bank of the river was gained. The two nine-pounders, dragged by officers as well as men and mules, soon reached the opposite bank, when they were immediately placed in battery. The column now followed in order under a most galling fire from the enemy, and became warmly engaged on the opposite bank, their round shot and grape falling thickly among us as we approached the stream, without doing any injury, our men marching steadily forward. The dragoons and *Cyane's* musketeers, occupying the centre, soon crossed and formed upon a bank about four feet above the stream. The left, advancing at the same time, soon occupied its position across the river.

The rear was longer in getting across the water; the sand being deep, its passage was delayed by the baggage carts; however, in a few moments the passage of the whole force was effected with only one man killed and one wounded, notwithstanding the enemy kept up an incessant fire from the heights.

On taking a position upon the low bank, the right flank under Captain Zeilin was ordered to deploy to the right; two guns from the rear were immediately brought to the right; the four-pounder under Acting Master Thompson, supported by the riflemen under Lieutenant Renshaw. The left flank deployed into line in open order. During this time our artillery began to tell upon the enemy, who continued their fire without interruption. The nine-pounders, standing in plain view upon the bank, were discharged with such precision that it soon became too warm for the enemy to remain upon the brow of their heights; eventually a shot told upon their nine-pounder, knocked the gun from its trail, astounding the enemy so much that they left it for four or five minutes. Some twenty of them now advanced, and hastily fastening ropes to it, dragged the gun to the rear. Captain Hensley's skirmishers now advanced and took the hill upon the right, the left wing of the enemy retreating before them. The six-pounder from the rear had now come up; Captain Hensley was ordered to support it, and returned from the hill. This movement being observed, the enemy's left made an attempt to charge the two guns; but the right flank of the marines, under Captain Zeilin, being quickly thrown back, showed too steady a front for the Californians to engage, who wheeled to the left and dashed to the rear across the river. At this time the enemy were observed collecting on our left and making preparations to charge our left flank. General Kearny was now ordered to form a square with the troops on the right flank, upon which the left flank, in case of being worsted, might rally. . . .

The dispositions for charging the heights were now made. The troops having been brought into line, the command forward being given, on they went, (the artillery in battery,) charging the heights, which the enemy's centre contested for a few moments, then broke in retreat, their right wing charging upon the rear, under Captain Gillespie, encumbered with packs, baggage, horses, and cattle; but, receiving a well-directed fire from the guard, which hurled some of them from their saddles, they fled at full speed across the river we had just left. The other portion of their forces retreated behind their artillery, which had taken position in a ravine, and again opened its fire upon our centre; our artillery was immediately thrown forward, the troops being ordered to lie down to avoid the enemy's cannon-balls, which passed directly over their heads.

The fire from our artillery was incessant, and so accurate that the enemy were from time to time driven from their guns, until they finally retreated.

We were now in possession of the heights, where a short time before the insurgents had so vauntingly taken strong position; and the band, playing "Hail Columbia!" and "Yankee Doodle," announced another glorious victory on the 8th day of January.

Our loss in this action was ascertained to be two killed and nine wounded. The enemy's loss we could not ascertain with any certainty, as they carried away both killed and wounded upon their horses.

We moved down the heights until they brought us near the river, where we encamped, having our cattle, horses, and mules under the bank, safely protected. Tattoo was beat at an early hour, and the camp retired to rest. At about twelve o'clock, the picquets having been fired upon, the camp was soon under arms in the most perfect order. Finding the enemy made no further demonstration, after remaining under arms a short time, we again sought our blankets, and nothing disturbed our repose until the sounding of the reveillé on the 9th told us to be stirring.

At daylight, Captain Zeilin was despatched with a party of thirty marines to a rancho about three-quarters of a mile from camp, to ascertain if there were any persons concealed about it, or whether there was any barley or provisions to be found there; finding none, he returned with his party about sunrise, without meeting any of the enemy.

At nine o'clock our column commenced its march, taking a direct course over the plain of the Mesa towards Ciudad de los Angeles. We had advanced some six miles when the enemy appeared in front, deployed in open order, their line extending nearly across our road. Approaching a ravine to the left of their line in front, the enemy opened a fire from their artillery, masked upon the edge of the bank, but with no other effect than killing an ox and mule in the centre of the square. Our artillery soon returned the fire, while still continuing the march; the enemy now brought up two other pieces of artillery; our column halted; our artillery on the two flanks in front was now placed in battery. The six-pounder under Acting Master Thompson . . . now opened its fire upon the enemy's nine-pounder, the shot telling upon it and cutting away the fixtures about the gun at every fire. . . .

A reinforcement now joined them, and soon after they came upon us, charging upon the left flank, front and rear. A shower of lead from the musketry under Renshaw and Guest, and Passed Midshipman Duncan's carbineers . . . did so much havoc that their courage failed, and caused them to draw off more to the rear, which had until this moment stood firm without firing a shot. The four-pounder now poured forth a charge of grape upon a party of the enemy about thirty yards distant, hurling four from their saddles, and they again retired.

The Californians now retreated, and we pursued our march along the Mesa and crossed the Rio San Fernando about three miles below the town, where we encamped for the night.

During the day we lost but one killed and five wounded, notwithstanding the shot from the enemy, both round and grape, and from the carbines of the horsemen, fell thick among our men. . . . On the 10th our tents were struck at an early hour; but the morning being cold and the town distant but three miles, our march was delayed until about ten o'clock.

We entered the City of the Angels, our band playing as we marched up the principal street to the square, our progress being slightly molested by a few drunken fellows who remained about the town. The riflemen, having been sent to the heights commanding the town, were soon followed by Lieutenant Tilghman, with two pieces of artillery, supported by the marines under Captain Zeilin, the enemy, in small force retiring out of sight upon their approach.

Captain Gillespie, having received the order, now hoisted the same flag upon the government-house of the country which he hauled down when he retreated from the city in September last. . . .

Our loss was three men killed and fourteen wounded; that of the enemy between seventy and eighty, besides many horses. . . .

The Californians retreated through the Cahuenga Pass into the San Fernando Valley, and here they encountered John Charles Frémont, who had finally arrived from Santa Barbara. He had missed the fighting, but would now become involved in a battle royal with General Kearny over who was to become governor of the new province. Reflecting on the consequences of that argument many years later, Frémont wrote:

¶ On the 24th of July, Commodore Stockton received full command, succeeding Sloat. He asked me to join him with the men under me, and act with him and under him, I on land, he by water, as long as he was in possession of the territory. To accept the proposal of Commodore Stockton was to abandon the strong and independent position in which I had left Washington and under which I knew I would have the support of the Government. Knowing, however, that the men under me would go only with me, I accepted Stockton's proposal to take service under him as long as he required my services; and I adhered to this engagement at the cost of my commission in the army. As I was an officer in the army, he could not command me. Gillespie was also independent, being on special service. Stockton therefore asked us to volunteer. There was no longer for me the clear initiative. The new situation was forced upon me, and for the general good I gave up my independent position which had led only to success, and in that way became later involved with the rivalries of Stockton and Kearny, who threw upon me the decision they could not make themselves, as to which should command. Each gave me the order to act under him. I remained with Stockton as I had agreed. When Stockton sailed for Mexico I was made to feel the revenge of Kearny. . . .[22]

General Andrés Pico found Frémont and expressed his willingness to surrender to him. Jose María Flores, the Mexican commander, had delegated his authority to Pico before fleeing to Sonora, knowing that a noose or firing squad would be his fate if captured by Stockton. Pico had also broken parole, but he remained. Frémont's policy was one of

[22] *The Century Magazine,* April, 1891.

conciliation. There would be no reprisals against those participating in the revolt against American authority. He describes the closing scene of the war in California:

¶ . . . I had led the battalion a second time to the south; carefully making the people sure of our good-will and protection, and arriving near Los Angeles in good time to make with the insurgent Californians there a treaty of peace. They had been irritated by injudicious and petty restrictions which many resented. Their fine horsemanship, their inherent love of combat, and their great familiarity with the country enabled them to carry on a guerrilla warfare as harassing as it was successful. They were succeeding in confining their enemy near his ships when we bore down on them inland. This, and the friendship of some leading Californians, brought about a capitulation to me, arranged during Christmas week at Santa Barbara and compiled on the plains of Cahuenga,[23] January 13, 1847. This was signed by me as Military Commandant representing the United States, and by Don Andrés Pico, Commander-in-Chief of the Californians.

With this treaty of Cahuenga hostilities ended and California was left in our possession, to be finally secured to us by the treaty of Guadaloupe Hidalgo in 1848, thus becoming ours by purchase as well as by conquest and by treaty. . . .

That night brandy flowed liberally in Los Angeles. A guardhouse was soon filled with the reveling soldiers, all riotously drunk. Even the noncommissioned officers assigned to guard them succumbed to the fiery *aguardiente*. In the disturbances that took place throughout the night, two Mexicans were shot by the exuberant conquerors. American rule had arrived in California.

[23] In present Universal City, a Los Angeles suburb located in the San Fernando Valley. A small park marks the site.

16

THE TRAGEDY
AT DONNER LAKE

Motorists driving between Reno and Sacramento follow a modern freeway that crosses the Sierra wall in a gentle ascent. At its summit, the altitude is more than 7,000 feet. This new highway replaces a road that once passed Truckee, and then spiraled up over the mountains in a series of curves that were often hazardous during the months when snow blanketed the Sierra country. During the winter of 1846–1847, that road—then but a wagon trace—became a trail of terror for a party of emigrants, who had left Independence, Missouri the previous spring, bound for a new life in California. George Donner had been elected captain of this company. Donner's selection had been a poor choice, for he was utterly lacking in the qualifications needed to guide nearly 100 men, women, and children through the wilderness.

The Donner party was a mixed lot, drawn from various states in the East and assembled as a traveling community only because of the necessity for seeking protection in numbers while crossing the continent. Some, like Donner, were affluent; others were people of modest means. But to the west was a land that offered equal opportunity for all. They had read this in the cheap circulars that had been widely distributed, but these often contained inaccuracies and conjectures, rather than substantiated facts. South of the Great South Lake, Donner and his followers relied on such misleading information with fatal consequences.

An opportunist named Lansford Hastings, who had been over the route before, later writing a book on his travels, recommended a shortcut into California that would eliminate many miles from the journey. The Donner party elected to follow this cutoff. Lacking a competent guide, they were soon lost. Cattle upon which the emigrants depended for subsistence strayed and were stolen by Indians. There was dissension in the group, and tension mounted as tempers flared. During an altercation, James Reed killed one of the party and was banished from the train. One elderly man found himself unable to walk. The others left him sitting by the trail, knowing he would perish.

It was late November when this slow moving procession finally crossed into California, reaching a small lake that now bears Donner's name. The emigrants gazed fearfully at the towering Sierra which lay ahead, its summit white with snow. They stood shivering in a cold wind, the first sign of an impending storm. Crude shelters were constructed near the lake, as the party decided to wait for help. By the time aid arrived, many of them would be dead.

A number of the men fashioned snowshoes and attempted to climb the mountain barrier. Trapped in a blinding snowstorm, eight died. The survivors ate their bodies. Word had reached Sutter's Fort of the tragedy taking place on the eastern slope of the Sierra. As early as January 30, 1847, the *California Star* published an account of the trapped party which shocked its San Francisco readers. Funds were raised and relief parties organized to rescue those camped at Donner Lake. Blizzards and impassable snow drifts hindered their efforts until spring.

In its May 22 edition, the *Star* printed the journal of Patrick Breen, who had recorded the sufferings of those camped by the lake. His early entries describe how some of the men prepared to make an attempt to reach the settlements on the other side of the mountains and bring help. As the days pass, his daily log becomes a diary of despair. The makeshift settlement is plagued by hopelessness, sickness, starvation, and death:

¶ Truckey's Lake, Nov. 20, 1846. Came to this place on the 31st of last month; went into the Pass, the snow so deep we were unable to find the road, and when within 3 miles from the summit turned back to this shanty[1] on Truckey's Lake. . . . We now have killed most part of our cattle, having to remain here until next Spring, and live on lean beef without bread or salt. It snowed during the space of eight days with little intermission, after our arrival here, though now clear and pleasant, freezing at night, the snow nearly gone from the valleys.[2]

Nov. 21, Fine morning, wind N W, 22 of our company about starting to cross the mountains this day. . . .

Nov. 23, Same weather, wind W, the expedition across the mountains returned after an unsuccessful attempt.

Nov. 25, Cloudy, looks like the eve of a snow storm, our mountainiers are to make another trial tomorrow, if fair—froze hard last night.

Nov. 26, Began to snow last evening, now rains or sleets, the party does not start to-day.

Nov. 29, Still snowing, now about 3 feet deep, wind W—killed my last oxen to day, gave another yoke to Foster[3]—wood hard to be got.

Nov. 30, Snowing fast, looks as likely to continue as when it commenced, no living thing without wings can get about.

Dec. 1, Still snowing, wind W, snow about 6 or 6 1-2 feet deep—very difficult to get wood and we are completely housed up—our cattle all killed but two or three, and these, with the horses, and Stanton's[4] mules all supposed to be lost in the snow, no hopes of finding them alive. . . .

Dec. 6, The morning fine and clear—Stanton and Graves[5] manufacturing snow-shoes for another mountain scrabble—no account of mules. . . .

Dec. 9, Commenced snowing about 11 o'clock, wind N W—took in

[1] A small shack that had been constructed by a prior emigrant party.

[2] *California Star*, May 22, 1847. A copy of this newspaper is in the manuscript collection of the Henry E. Huntington Library and Art Gallery, San Marino, Calif.

[3] George Foster, who later died.

[4] Charles T. Stanton, a native of Chicago.

[5] Franklin W. Graves. Traveling with him was his wife, eight children, a married daughter and her husband. They were from Illinois.

Spitzer [6] yesterday so weak that he cannot rise without help, caused by starvation. . . .

Dec. 10, Snowed fast all night with heavy squalls of wind, continues to snow, now about 7 feet in depth. . . .

Dec. 21, Milton [7] got back last night from Donners camp, sad news, Jacob Donner, Sam'l Shoemaker, Rhinehart and Smith are dead, the rest in a low situation—snowed all night with a strong S W wind. . . .

Dec. 25, Began to snow yesterday, snowed all night, and snows yet rapidly—extremely difficult to find wood, offered our prayers to God this Christmas morning, the prospect is appalling but we trust in Him.

Dec. 27, Cleared off yesterday, continues clear, snow 9 feet deep—wood growing scarcer, a tree when felled sinks in the snow and is hard to be got at. . . .

Dec. 31, Last of the year—may we with the help of God spend the coming year better than we have the past, which we propose to do if it is the will of the Almighty to deliver us from our present dreadful situation. Amen. Morning fair but cloudy, wind E by S, looks like another snow storm—snow storms are dreadful to us, the snow at present very deep.

Jan. 1, 1847—We pray the God of mercy to deliver us from our present calamity if it be His holy will. Commenced snowing last night and snows a little yet—provisions getting very scant, dug up a hide from under the snow yesterday, have not commenced on it yet. . . .

Jan. 15, Clear day again, wind N W—Mrs. Murphy blind,[8] Lanthron [9] not able to get wood, has but one axe between him and Kiesburg [10]—it looks like another storm, expecting some account from Sutters' soon.

Jan. 17, Eliza Williams came here this morning, Lanthron crazy last night, provisions scarce, hides our main subsistence—may the Almighty send us help.

Jan. 21, Fine morning, John Battise came this morning with Eliza, she will not eat hides; Mrs.——— sent her back to live or die on them.[11]

Jan. 26, Cleared up yesterday, to-day fine and pleasant, wind S, in hopes we are done with snow storms—those who went to Sutters' not yet re-

---

[6] August Spitzer. All were not as hospitable as Reed, some refusing to share their rations with the others unless paid for them.

[7] Milton Elliott. The shelters of the various families were scattered over a wide area, the snow making communications difficult.

[8] Mrs. Lavinia Murphy, died in the Sierra.

[9] Lanthron Murphy.

[10] Louis Keseberg, who was later branded as the villain in the party, having survived by eating the flesh of those who died.

[11] Eliza Williams died of starvation.

turned, provisions getting scant, people growing weak, living on small allowance of hides.

Feb. 5, Snowed hard until 12 o'clock last night, many uneasy for fear we shall all perish with hunger, we have but a little meat left and only three hides. . . . Eddy's child died last night . . .[12]

Feb. 8, Fine clear morning, Spitzer died last night, we will bury him in the snow, Mrs. Eddy died on the night of the 7th. . . .

Feb. 10, Beautiful morning, thawing in the sun. Milton Elliot died last night at Murphy's shanty, Mrs. Read (sic) [13] went there this morning to see after his effects. J. Denton trying to borrow meat for Graves, had none to give, they had nothing but hides, all are entirely out of meat but a little we have, our hides are nearly all eat up, but with God's help spring will soon smile upon us.

Feb. 25, To-day Mrs. Murphy says the wolves are about to dig up the dead bodies around her shanty and the nights are too cold to watch them, but we hear them howl.

Feb. 26, Hungry times in camp, plenty of hides but the folks will not eat them, we eat them with tolerable good appetite, thanks be to the Almighty God. Mrs. Murphy said here yesterday that she thought she would commence on Milton and eat him, I do not think she has done so yet, it is so distressing, the Donners told the California folks four days ago that they would commence on the dead people if they did not succeed that day or next in finding their cattle, then ten or twelve feet under the snow, and did not know the spot or near it, they have done it ere this.

March 1, Ten men arrived this morning from Bear Valley with provisions, we are to start in two or three days and cache our goods here, they say the snow will remain until June.

The *Star* carried a postscript to this diary, signed by one of the men who organized the rescue parties:

¶ The above mentioned ten men started for the valley with seventeen of the sufferers, they traveled 15 miles and a severe snow storm came on; they left fourteen of the emigrants, the writer of the above journal and his family, and succeeded in getting in but three children. Lieut. Woodworth [14] immediately went to their assistance, but before he reached them

[12] William H. Eddy survived, but his wife and two children died before the arrival of rescue parties.
[13] Mrs. James F. Reed.
[14] Lieutenant Selim Woodworth.

they had eaten three of their number, who had died from hunger and fatigue; the remainder, Lieut. Woodworth's party brought in. On the 29th of April 1847, the last number of that party was brought to Capt. Sutters Fort; it is utterly impossible to give any description of the sufferings of the company—Your readers can form some idea of them by perusing the above diary Yours&c.

GEORGE McKINSTRY JR.

Fort Sacramento, April 29, 1847.

Various writers have disagreed as to the exact number of persons who died during the long winter at Donner Lake. The most creditable figure is that out of 79 members of the party, only 45 reached the settlements in California. Patrick Breen was one of the survivors.

Oh, Sally, dearest Sally!
Oh, Sally fer your sake.
I'll go to Californy.
An' try to raise a stake.
    —from "Joe Bowers from Pike," a song popular during the Gold Rush period

17

"SOMETHING SHINING IN THE BOTTOM OF THE DITCH"

William Tecumseh Sherman arrived in California during the war with Mexico, a first lieutenant, Company F, Third Artillery. He was twenty-six. His company was part of a contingent of troops sent by sea from New York, reaching Monterey Bay on January 26, 1847, after a voyage of 198 days. The peace treaty had been signed, and the new arrivals were assigned to the routine tasks of occupation duty. Colonel R. B. Mason was in command of all military units ashore, and in this capacity also acted as governor until the territory could be placed under the administration of civil authorities. He selected Sherman to be his adjutant general. The young officer found the duties boring. He longed to be in Mexico where his fellow West Point graduates were winning brevet promotions for deeds of valor on many battlefields. Sherman may have missed the brief skirmishes that had taken place a short time earlier, but he was to be a witness to the most significant event that ever took place in the future state's history. It was to touch off a mass migration westward such as the nation had never known. Sherman recalled the incident that resulted in the Gold Rush:

¶ I remember one day, in the spring of 1848, that two men, Americans, came into the office and inquired for the Governor. I asked their business, and one answered that they had just come down from Captain Sutter on special business, and they wanted to see Governor Mason *in person*. I took them in to the colonel, and left them together. After some time the colonel came to his door and called to me. I went in, and my attention was directed to a series of papers unfolded on his table, in which lay about half an ounce of placer-gold. Mason said to me, "What is that?" I touched it and examined one or two of the larger pieces, and asked, "Is it gold?" Mason asked me if I had ever seen native gold. I answered that, in 1844, I was in Upper Georgia, and there saw some native gold, but it was much finer than this, and that it was in phials, or in transparent quills; but I said that, if this were gold, it could be easily tested, first, by its malleability, and next by acids. I took a piece in my teeth, and the metallic lustre was perfect. I then called to the clerk, Baden, to bring an axe and hatchet from the backyard. When these were brought, I took the largest piece and beat it out flat, and beyond doubt it was metal, and a pure metal. Still, we attached little importance to the fact, for gold was known to exist at San Fernando, at the south, and yet was not considered of much value.

Colonel Mason then handed me a letter from Captain Sutter, addressed to him, stating that he (Sutter) was engaged in erecting a saw-mill at Coloma, about forty miles up the American Fork, above his fort at New Helvetia,[1] for the general benefit of the settlers in that vicinity; that he had incurred considerable expense, and wanted a "preëmption" to the quarter-section of land on which the mill was located, embracing the tail-race in which this particular gold had been found. Mason instructed me to prepare a letter, in answer, for his signature. I wrote off a letter, reciting that California was yet a Mexican province, simply held by us as a conquest; that no laws of the United States yet applied to it, much less the land laws or preëmption laws, which could only apply after a public survey. Therefore it was impossible for the Governor to promise him (Sutter) a title to the land; yet, as there were no settlements within forty

[1] Sacramento.

miles, he was not likely to be disturbed by trespassers. Colonel Mason signed the letter, handed it to one of the gentlemen who had brought the sample of gold, and they departed. . . .[2]

Colonel Mason was mistaken in his belief that Sutter would not be disturbed by trespassers. For the baron of the Sacramento Valley, the discovery of gold in California was a calamity that caused the downfall of his land empire. Sutter had engaged James Marshall to build a sawmill, and when he discovered pieces of the shiny metal in the tailrace, Marshall brought the nuggets to his employer, who tried to keep news of the find secret. This failed, and thousands flocked to California in search of wealth. They butchered Sutter's cattle, overran his lands, and stole his property. He was an easy victim for scheming speculators who tricked him into a succession of disastrous business ventures. Bankrupt, he was stripped of his holdings. James Marshall tells of the initial discovery on the American River:

¶ One morning in January,—it was a clear cold morning; I shall never forget that morning,—as I was taking my usual walk along the race after shutting off the water, my eye was caught with the glimpse of something shining in the bottom of the ditch. There was about a foot of water running then. I reached my hand down and picked it up; it made my heart thump, for I was certain that it was gold. The piece was about half the size and of the shape of a pea. Then I saw another piece in the water. After taking it out I sat down and began to think right hard. I thought it was gold, and yet it did not seem to be of the right color: all the gold coin I had seen was of a reddish tinge; this looked more like brass. I recalled to mind all the metals I had ever seen or heard of, but I could find none that resembled this. Suddenly the idea flashed across my mind that it might be iron pyrites. I trembled to think of it! The question could soon be determined. Putting one of the pieces on a hard river stone, I took another and commenced hammering it. It was soft, and it didn't break; it therefore must be gold, but largely mixed with some other metal, very likely silver; for pure gold, I thought would certainly have a brighter color.

When I returned to our cabin for breakfast, I showed the two pieces to my men. They were all a good deal excited, and had they not thought that

[2] *Memoirs of General William T. Sherman by Himself* (New York: D. Appleton and Co., 1875), Vol. I.

the gold only existed in small quantities they would have abandoned every-thing and left me to finish my job alone. However, to satisfy them, I told them that as soon as we had the mill finished we would devote a week or two to gold hunting and see what we could make out of it.

While we were working in the race after this discovery we always kept a sharp lookout, and in the course of three or four days we had picked up about three ounces—our work still progressing as lively as ever, for none of us imagined at that time that the whole country was sowed with gold.

In about a week's time after the discovery I had to take another trip to the fort; and, to gain what information I could respecting the real value of the metal, took all that we had collected with me and showed it to Mr. Sutter, who at once declared it was gold, but thought with me that it was greatly mixed with some other metal. It puzzled us a good deal to hit upon the means of telling the exact quantity of gold contained in the alloy; however, we at last stumbled on an old American cyclopedia, where we saw the specific gravity of all metals, and rule given to find the quantity of each in given bulk. After hunting over the whole fort and borrowing from some of the men, we got three dollars and a half in silver, and with a small pair of scales we soon ciphered it out that there was no silver nor copper in the gold, but that it was entirely pure.

This fact being ascertained, we thought it our best policy to keep it as quiet as possible till we should have finished our mill. But there was a great number of disbanded Mormon soldiers in and about the fort, and when they came to hear of it, why it just spread like wildfire, and soon the whole country was in a bustle, I had scarcely arrived at the mill again till several persons appeared with pans, shovels, and hoes, and those that had not iron picks had wooden ones, all anxious to fall to work and dig up our mill; but this we would not permit. As fast as one party disappeared another would arrive, and sometimes I had the greatest kind of trouble to get rid of them. I sent them off in different directions, telling them about such and such places, where I was certain there was plenty of gold if they would only take the trouble of looking for it. At that time I never imag-ined that the gold was so abundant. I told them to go to such and such places, because it appeared that they would dig nowhere but in such places as I pointed out, and I believe such was their confidence in me that they would have dug on the very top of yon mountain if I had told them to do so. . . .[3]

[3] This account was taken down by an unidentified correspondent for *The Century Magazine* (February, 1891). He accompanied Marshall to the scene.

Colonel Mason was interested enough in the discovery to undertake a personal investigation. Accompanied by Lieutenant Sherman, he left for the gold fields. Upon his return, he sent the following report to the Secretary of War:

¶ Headquarters, 10th Military Dept.
  Monterey, California, Aug. 17, 1848.

Sir—I have the honor to inform you that, accompanied by Lieut. W. T. Sherman, 3d Artillery, A.A.A. General, I started on the 12th of June last to make a tour through the northern part of California. My principal purpose, however, was to visit the newly discovered gold "Placer," in the valley of the Sacramento. I had proceeded about forty miles, when I was overtaken by an express bringing me intelligence of the arrival at Monterey of the United States ship *Southampton* with important letters from Commodore Shubrick, and Lieut. Col. Barton. I returned at once to Monterey, and despatched what business was most important, and on the 17th resumed my journey. We reached San Francisco on the 20th, and found that all, or nearly all, its male inhabitants had gone to the mines. The town, which a few months before was so busy and thriving, was then almost deserted. On the evening of the 24th, the horses of the escort were crossed to Sausalito in a launch, and on the following day we resumed the journey, by way of Bodega, and Sonoma to Sutter's Fort, where we arrived on the morning of the 2d of July. Along the whole route, mills were lying idle, fields of wheat were open to cattle and horses, houses vacant, and farms going to waste. At Sutter's there was more life and business. Launches were discharging their cargoes at the river, and were hauling goods to the fort, where already were established several stores, a hotel, &c. Captain Sutter had only two mechanics in his employ, a wagon-maker and a blacksmith, whom he was then paying $10 a day. Merchants pay him a monthly rent of $100 per room; and, whilst I was there, a two story house in the fort was rented as a hotel, for $500 a month.

At the urgent solicitation of many gentlemen, I delayed there to participate in the first public celebration of our national anniversary at that fort, but on the 5th resumed the journey, and proceeded twenty-five miles up the American fork to a point on it now known as the Lower Mines, or Mormon Diggins. The hill sides were thickly strewn with canvas tents and bush arbours; a store was erected, and several boarding shanties in operation. The day was intensely hot, yet about two hundred men were at work in the full glare of the sun, washing for gold—some with tin pans, some with close woven Indian baskets, but the greater part had a rude machine, known as the cradle.

This is on rockers, six or eight feet long, open at the foot, and at its head has a coarse grate or sieve; the bottom is rounded, with small cleets nailed across. Four men are required to work this machine; one digs the ground in the bank close by the stream; another carries it to the cradle and empties it on the grate; a third gives a violent rocking motion to the machine; whilst a fourth dashes on water from the stream itself. The sieve keeps the coarse stones from entering the cradle, the current of water washes off the earthy matter, and the gravel is gradually carried out at the foot of the machine, leaving the gold mixed with heavy fine black sand above the first cleets.

The sand and gold mixed together are then drawn off through augur holes into a pan below, are dried in the sun, and afterwards separated by blowing off the sand. A party of four men thus employed, at the lower mines, averaged $100 a day. The Indians and those who have nothing but pans, or willow baskets, gradually wash out the earth, and separate the gravel by hand, leaving nothing but the gold mixed with sand, which is separated in the manner before described. The gold in the lower mines is in fine bright scales, of which I send several specimens. . . .[4]

Reporting on Marshall's discovery, Mason described how Sutter tried to keep the news a secret, but failed in his efforts:

¶ He (Marshall) then went to the fort, told Captain Sutter of his discovery, and they agreed to keep it secret until a certain grist-mill of Sutter's was finished. It, however, got out, and spread like magic. Remarkable success attended the labours of the first explorers, and in a few weeks hundreds of men were drawn thither. At the time of my visit, but little more than three months after its first discovery, it was estimated that upwards of four thousand people were employed. At the mill there is a fine deposit or bank of gravel, which the people respect as the property of Capt. Sutter, although he pretends to no right to it, and would be perfectly

[4] Mason's report appeared in a book which contributed to the rush of gold seekers to California, *Geographical Memoir Upon Upper California*, by John Charles Frémont (Philadelphia: Published by William McCarty, 1849). The volume contained the explorer's address to the U.S. Senate in 1848. The publisher added extracts from letters of other officials describing the gold discovery, including Mason's; the President's Message to Congress, December 5, 1848; and an account by Thomas O. Larkin, the former U.S. consul general at Monterey. The 80-page, paperbound volume was priced at twenty-five cents and had wide distribution in the East.

satisfied with the simple promise of a preemption, on account of the mill, which he has built there at considerable cost.

Mr. Marshall was living near the mill, and informed me that many persons were employed above and below him, and they used the same machines at the lower washings, and that their success was about the same—ranging from one to three ounces of gold per man daily. This gold, too, is in scales a little coarser than those of the lower mines. From the mill, Mr. Marshall guided me up the mountain on the opposite or north bank of the south fork, where in a bed of small streams and ravines, now dry, a great deal of coarse gold has been found. I saw there several parties at work, all of whom were doing very well; a great many specimens were shown me, some as heavy as four or five ounces in weight, and I send three pieces. . . .

On the 7th of July I left the mill, and crossed to a small stream emptying into the American fork, three or four miles below the saw-mill. I struck this stream (now known as Weber's creek) at the washings of Sunol & Co. They had about thirty Indians employed, whom they pay in merchandise. They were getting gold of a character similar to that found on the main fork, and doubtless in sufficient quantities to satisfy them. . . . From this point we proceeded up the stream about eight miles, where we found a great many people and Indians—some engaged in the bed of the stream, and others in the small side valley that put into it. These latter are exceedingly rich, and two ounces were considered an ordinary yield for a day's work. . . .

President James Knox Polk discussed the importance of California's mineral wealth in his message to Congress on December 5, 1848. The publicity given his remarks intensified the rush to reach the gold fields. Thousands booked passage on every available vessel bound for California. Polk said:

¶ . . . The accounts of the abundance of gold in that territory are of such an extraordinary character as would scarcely command belief, were they not corroborated by the authentic reports of officers in the public service, who have visited the mineral district, and derived the facts which they detail from personal observation. Reluctant to credit the reports in general circulation as to the quantity of gold, the officer commanding our forces in California visited the mineral district in July last, for the purpose of obtaining accurate information on the subject. His report to the War

Department of the result of his examination, and the facts obtained on the spot, is herewith laid before Congress. When he visited the country, there were about four thousand persons engaged in collecting gold. There is every reason to believe that the number of persons so employed has since been augmented. The explorations already made warrant the belief that the supply is very large, and that gold is found in various places in extensive districts of country.

Information received from officers of the navy, and other sources, though not so full and minute, confirm the accounts of the commander of our military force in California. It appears also, from these reports, that mines of quicksilver are found in the vicinity of the gold region. One of them is now being worked, and is believed to be among the most productive in the world.

The effects produced by the discovery of these rich mineral deposits, and the success which has attended the labours of those who have resorted to them, have produced a surprising change in the state of affairs in California. Labour commands a most exorbitant price, and all other pursuits but that of searching for the precious metals are abandoned. Nearly the whole of the male population of the country have gone to the gold district. Ships arriving on the coast are deserted by their crews, and their voyages suspended for want of sailors. Our commanding officer there entertains apprehensions that soldiers cannot be kept in the public service without a large increase of pay. Desertions in his command have become frequent, and he recommends that those who shall withstand the strong temptations, and remain faithful, should be rewarded. . . .

Desertions among the poorly paid regular troops were plaguing Mason. After watching the mass exodus to the mining districts, many enlisted men found it difficult to resist the temptation to go "over the hill." They shed their uniforms, heading for the rugged Sierra country, where they would be difficult to apprehend. Mason reported:

¶ The discovery of these vast deposits of gold has entirely changed the character of Upper California. Its people, before engaged in cultivating their small patches of ground, and guarding their herds of cattle and horses, have all gone to the mines, or on their way thither. Labourers of every trade have left their workbenches, and tradesmen their shops. Sailors desert their ships as fast as they arrive on the coast, and several vessels have gone to sea with hardly enough hands to spread a sail. Two or three are now at anchor in San Francisco, with no crew on board. Many desertions, too, have taken place from the garrisons within the influence of these mines; twenty-six soldiers have deserted from the post of Sonoma, twenty-four from that of San Francisco, and twenty-four from Monterey. For a few days the evil appeared so threatening, that great danger existed that the garrisons would leave in a body; and I refer you to my orders of the 25th of July, to show the steps adopted to meet this contingency. I shall spare no exertions to apprehend and punish deserters, but I believe no time in the history of our country has presented such temptations to desert as now exist in California. The danger of apprehension is small and the prospect of high wages is certain; pay and bounties are trifles, as labouring men at the mines can now earn in one day more than double a soldier's pay and allowances for a month, and even the pay of a lieutenant or captain cannot hire a servant. . . . No officer can now live in California on his pay—money has so little value. The prices of necessary articles of clothing and subsistence are so exorbitant, and labour so high, that to hire a cook or a servant has become an impossibility, save to those who are earning thirty to fifty dollars per day . . . if the government wish to prevent desertions here, on the part of the men, and to secure zeal on the part of their officers, their pay must be increased very materially. Soldiers, both of the volunteers and regular service, discharged in this country, should be permitted at once to locate their land warrants in the gold district. Many private letters have gone to the United States, giving accounts of the vast quantity of gold recently discovered, and it may be a matter of surprise why I have made no report on this subject at an earlier date. The reason is that I could not bring myself to believe the reports that I heard of the wealth of the gold district, until I visited it myself. I have no hesitation now in saying that there is more gold in the country drained by the Sacramento and San Joaquin rivers than will pay the cost of the present war with Mexico a hundred times over. No capital is required to obtain this gold, as the labouring man wants nothing but his pick, shovel, and a tin pan, with which to dig and wash the gravel, and many frequently pick gold out of the crevices of rocks, with their butcher knives, in pieces from one to six ounces. . . .

Thomas O. Larkin, the former American consul in California, added his comments on the excitement in a letter he sent to the Secretary of State on November 16, 1848:

¶ The digging and washing for gold continues to increase on the Sacramento placer, so far as regards the number of persons engaged in the business, and the size and quantity of the metal daily obtained. I have had in my hands several pieces of gold, about twenty-three carats fine, weighing from one to two pounds, and have it from good authority that pieces have been found weighing sixteen pounds. Indeed, I have heard of one specimen that weighed twenty-five pounds. There are many men at the placer, who in June last had not one hundred dollars, now in possession of from five to twenty thousand dollars, which they made by digging gold and trading with the Indians. Several, I believe, have made more. A common calico shirt, or even a silver dollar has been taken by an Indian for gold, without regard to size; and a half to one ounce of gold—say eight to sixteen dollars—is now considered the price of a shirt, while from three to ten ounces is the price of a blanket. One hundred dollars a day, for several days in succession, was and is considered a common remuneration for the labour of a gold-digger, though few work over a month at a time, as the fatigue is very great. . . .

Commodore Thomas Ap C. Jones, Commander-in-Chief of the Pacific Squadron, was experiencing difficulty in keeping the sailors aboard his ships because of the gold fever. He sent the following message to the Secretary of the Navy. Jones failed to elaborate on what preventative measures he had taken to halt desertions, but it is conceivable that a number of his men were confined in the brig:

¶ Nothing, sir, can exceed the deplorable state of things in all Upper California at this time, growing out of the maddening effects of the gold mania. I am sorry to say that even in this squadron some of the officers are a little tainted, and have manifested restlessness under moderate restrictions, imperiously demanded by the exigencies of the times. . . . I am, however, happy to say that I have not been disappointed in the good effects of the means employed to prevent desertion, and to maintain order in the squadron, as but one desertion has taken place since the rush of eight from this ship on the evening of the 18th instant; and that the views and opinions of the few officers who were skeptical as to the right or efficacy of the means employed to prevent offences and to punish crime have undergone a most favourable change, whereby I shall be enabled to keep on this coast until the whirlwind of anarchy and confusion confounded is superseded by the establishment of some legal government, potent enough to enforce law and to protect life and property, which at this time are in great jeopardy everywhere outside our bulwarks. . . .

The commerce of this coast may be said to be entirely cut off by desertion. No sooner does a merchant ship arrive in any port of California, than all hands leave her—in some instances, captain, cook, and all. At this moment, there are a number of merchant ships thus abandoned at San Francisco, and such will be the fate of all that subsequently arrive. The master of the ship "Izaak Walton," that brought stores for the squadron to this port, offered, without success, fifty dollars per month to Callao, and thence twenty dollars per month home, to disbanded volunteers, not seamen. We were obliged at last to supply him with four men, whose term of service was drawing to a close. This state of things is not confined to California alone. Oregon is fast depopulating; her inhabitants pour into the gold diggings, and foreign residents and runaway sailors from the Sandwich Islands are arriving by every vessel that approaches this coast. . . .

A pamphlet by J. B. Hall, *An Account of California and the Wonderful Gold Regions* (1849), was widely read. Its author advised the prospective gold seeker to take the longer route via Cape Horn, instead of attempting to travel across Panama, because of the shortage of vessels plying the Pacific coast:

¶ This route is the most acceptable as far as cost and facilities are concerned, but loss of time balances the difference in the price of passage, &c., which varies from one hundred to three hundred dollars, according to accommodations.

The distance from New York to San Francisco, via Cape Horn, is about 18,000 miles, and will occupy nearly five months in making the passage. Notwithstanding this appears to be a long voyage, yet it is, (in the present amount of travel across the Isthmus, and the probable want of vessels from Panama to San Francisco,) the surest route. . . .[5]

For those who would attempt to make the overland journey, Hall had some advice. Despite his negative approach, and his warning of the hardships that would be encountered, those determined to make the trip refused to be discouraged:

¶ A long dreary road of more than 2000 miles lies before you, without houses, without meat or flour, and in many places without wood, water or

[5] J. B. Hall, *An Account of California and the Wonderful Gold Regions* (Boston, 1849).

grass. You that start across the plains, by the time you reach Santa Fe—a distance of not less than 1200 miles from St. Louis—will find your ambition and courage fail; and yet . . . Santa Fe is a paradise to what you will see afterward. By the time you have been fifty days out—which will be the time you will be in going there, or kill all your oxen and mules—you will wish yourselves back again in your native town at work—mark my words. You must cook your own meals, which will be fun and sport for a few days, where wood, water and grass are plenty; but after you get one hundred miles beyond Council Grove, you will hunt in vain for wood, and often for water and grass. . . .

Two men will use a barrel of flour before getting to Santa Fe; and two hundred pounds of good bacon, about thirty pounds of coffee, and if you drink whiskey, (a very necessary article, by the way,) two men cannot do with less than ten gallons. You can travel on foot better than be troubled with a horse, for you certainly can keep up with an ox wagon, and in a few days become used to it, which will harden you for the labor, when called to use the pick, crowbar, spade or shovel.

You want a good axe, hatchet, pick-axe, crowbar, spade and shovel; an auger, and an inch chisel or two. You will want tin or pewter plates, tin cups, a good knife or two, a spoon or two, coffee boiler, tea-kettle, frying pan, spider, bake oven and canteen; a little salt, pepper, saleratus, mustard, red pepper, plenty of pickles, and a good supply of vinegar; molasses tastes quite sweet on the plains. Get plenty of matches, both lucifer and wax. Get two large blankets as your bedding; a cap is better than a hat. It matters not about the sun, you'll get used to it. . . .

Another guidebook offering advice to the prospective miners was *Journals of Travels from St. Joseph to Oregon Together with Some Description of the Gold Mines* by Riley Root. The author lamented about the conduct of the treasure hunters on Sundays:

¶ There is a consideration in relation to spending the Sabbath amongst the gold mines of California. The reader may greatly wonder what is the mode of spending the Sabbath there, when I say to him that the Sabbath appears as silent as the house of mourning. Seldom is a man seen with his implements in his hands, laboring for gold. All around is quiet, except now and then a few horsemen are passing from one little town to another for purposes best known to themselves. What then, is the wonderful employment or idle condition of miners upon that day? Alas! every public tent through the whole mining region is resorted to for gambling. In each of these tents stands from one to four or six monte tables, around which miners of all classes assemble to risk their fortunes. These tables are arranged with small or large sums of money, by one or more persons, according to the ability of the person or persons that establish them. The sums of money so arranged are called monte banks. On the opposite side of the table, sit two men, who managed the affairs of the bank, and deal the cards by which the fate of bettors is determined. This game at cards is carried on from morning till night, and often through the following night till twilight breaks upon them, with the stillness and quiet of a religious assemblage. . . .[6]

One of the best reports about California during the tumultuous period following the discovery of gold was written by Bayard Taylor, a rising young reporter sent to the West Coast by Horace Greeley, publisher of the New York *Tribune*. Taylor had already established himself as a journalist of considerable talent before he undertook his California adventure. In later years, he achieved his greatest fame as world traveler, lecturer, poet, and author. He earned a reputation as a scholar following his translation in 1870 of Goethe's *Faust*. In 1878, President Hayes appointed him minister to Germany, where he died that same year.

Taylor sailed for California in June, 1849, crossing the Isthmus of Panama to another ship, and finally reached San Francisco in August. He returned to New York in 1850, where he completed his famed *Eldorado*. No other account is comparable to this in capturing the turmoil and excitement prevalent in San Francisco at the height of the gold-rush period. As Taylor left his ship, he wrote:

¶ We scrambled up through piles of luggage, and among the crowd collected to witness our arrival, picked out two Mexicans to carry our trunks to a hotel. The barren side of a hull before us was covered with tents and canvas houses, and nearly in front a large two-story building displayed the sign: "Fremont Family Hotel."

As yet, we were only in the suburbs of the town. Crossing the shoulder of the hill, the view extended around the curve of the bay, and hundreds of tents and houses appeared, scattered all over the heights, and along the shore for more than a mile. A furious wind was blowing down through a

---

[6] Riley Root, *Journals of Travels from St. Joseph to Oregon Together with Some Description of the Gold Mines* (Galesburg, Illinois: 1850).

gap in the hills, filling the streets with clouds of dust. On every side stood buildings of all kinds, begun or half-finished, and the greater part of them were canvas sheds, open in front, and covered with all kinds of signs, in all languages. Great quantities of goods were piled up in the open air, for want of a place to store them. The streets were full of people, hurrying to and fro, and of as diverse and bizarre a character as the houses: Yankees of every possible variety, native Californians in sarapes and sombreros, Chilians, Sonorians, Kanakas from Hawaii, Chinese with long tails, Malays armed with their everlasting creeses, and others in whose embrowned and bearded visages it was impossible to recognize any especial nationality. We came at last into the plaza, now dignified by the name of Portsmouth Square. It lies on the slant side of the hill, and from a high pole in front of a long one-story adobe building used as the Custom House, the American flag was flying. On the lower side stood the Parker House—an ordinary frame house of about sixty feet front—and towards its entrance we directed our course . . .

.   .   .

A better idea of San Francisco in the beginning of September 1849, cannot be given than by the description of a single day. Supposing the visitor to have been long enough in the place to sleep on a hard plank and in spite of the attack of innumerable fleas, he will be awakened at daylight by the noises of building, with which the hills are alive. The air is temperate, and the invariable morning fog is just beginning to gather. By sunrise, which gleams hazily over the Coast Mountains across the Bay, the whole populace is up and at work. The wooden buildings unlock their doors, the canvas houses and tents throw back their front curtains; the lighters on the water are warped out from ship to ship; carts and porters are busy along the beach; and only the gaming-tables, thronged all night by the votaries of chance, are idle and deserted. The temperature is so fresh as to inspire an active habit of body, and even without the stimulus of trade and speculation there would be few sluggards at this season.

As early as half-past six the bells begin to sound to breakfast, and for an hour thenceforth, their incessant clang and the braying of immense gongs drown all the hammers that are busy on a hundred roofs. The hotels, restaurants and refectories of all kinds are already as numerous as gaming-tables, and equally various in kind. The tables d'hôte of the first class, (which charge 2 dls. and upwards the meal,) are abundantly supplied. There are others, with more simple and solid fare, frequented by the large class who have their fortunes yet to make. At the United States and California restaurants on the plaza, you may get an excellent beef-steak, scantily garnished with potatoes, and a cup of good coffee or chocolate for 1 dl. Fresh beef, bread, potatoes, and all provisions which will bear importation are plenty; but milk, fruit and vegetables are classed as luxuries, and fresh butter is rarely heard of. On Montgomery street, and the vacant space fronting the water, venders of coffee, cakes and sweet-meats have erected their stands, in order to tempt the appetite of sailors just arrived in port, or miners coming down from the mountains.

By nine o'clock the town is in the full flow of business. The streets running down to the water, and Montgomery street, which fronts the bay, are crowded with people, all in hurried motion. The variety of characters and costumes is remarkable. Our own countrymen seem to lose their local peculiarities in such a crowd, and it is by chance epithets rather than by manner, that the New Yorker is distinguished from the Kentuckian, the Carolinian from the Down-Easter, the Virginian from the Texan. The German and Frenchman are more easily recognized. Peruvians and Chilians go by in their brown ponchos, and the sober Chinese, cool and impassive in the midst of excitement, look out of the oblique corners of their long eyes at the bustle, but are never tempted to venture from their own line of business. The eastern side of the plaza, in front of the Parker House and a canvas hell called the Eldorado, are the general rendezvous of business and amusement—combining 'change, park, club-room and promenade all in one. There, everybody not constantly employed in one spot, may be seen at some time of the day. The character of the groups scattered along the plaza is oftentimes very interesting. In one place are three or four speculators bargaining for lots, buying and selling "fifty varas square" in towns, some of which are canvas and some only paper; in another, a company of miners, brown as leather, and rugged in features as in dress; in a third, perhaps, three or four naval officers speculating on the next cruise, or a knot of genteel gamblers, talking over the last night's operations.

The day advances. The mist which after sunrise hung low and heavy for an hour or two, has risen above the hills, and there will be two hours of pleasant sunshine before the wind sets in from the sea. The crowd in the streets is now wholly alive. Men dart hither and thither, as if possessed with a never-resting spirit. You speak to an acquaintance—a merchant, perhaps. He utters a few hurried words of greeting, while his eyes send keen glances, on all sides of you; suddenly he catches sight of somebody in the crowd; he is off, and in the next five minutes has bought up half a cargo, sold a town lot at treble the sum he gave, and taken a share in some new and imposing speculation. It is impossible to witness this excess and dissipation of business, without feeling something of its influence. The very air is pregnant with the magnetism of bold, spirited, unwearied action, and he who but ventures into the outer circle of the whirlpool, is spinning, ere he has time for thought, in its dizzy vortex.

But see! the groups in the plaza suddenly scatter; the city surveyor jerks his pole out of the ground and leaps on a pile of boards; the venders of cakes and sweetmeats follow his example, and the place is cleared, just as a wild bull which has been racing down Kearney-street makes his appearance. Two vaqueros, shouting and swinging their lariats, follow at a hot gallop; the dust flies as they dash across the plaza. One of them, in mid-career, hurls his lariat in the air. Mark how deftly the coil unwinds in its flying curve, and with what precision, the noose falls over the bull's horns! The horse wheels as if on a pivot, and shoots off in an opposite line. He knows the length of the lariat to a hair, and the instant it is drawn taut, plants his feet firmly for the shock and throws his body forward. The bull is "brought up" with such force as to throw him off his legs. He lies stunned a moment, and then, rising heavily, makes another charge. But by this time the second vaquero has thrown a lariat around one of his hind-legs, and thus checked on both sides, he is dragged off to slaughter.

The plaza is refilled as quickly as it was emptied, and the course of business is resumed. About twelve o'clock, a wind begins to blow from the north-west, sweeping with most violence through a gap between the hills, opening towards the Golden Gate. The bells and gongs begin to sound for dinner, and these two causes tend to lessen the crowd in the streets for an hour or two. Two o'clock is the usual dinner-time for business men, but some of the old and successful merchants have adopted the fashionable hour of five. Where shall we dine today? the restaurants display their signs invitingly on all sides; we have choice of the United States, Tortoni's, the Alhambra, and many other equally classic resorts, but Delmonico's, like its distinguished original in New York, has the highest prices and the greatest variety of dishes.

We go down Kearney street to a two-story wooden house on the corner of Jackson. The lower story is a market; the walls are garnished with quarters of beef and mutton; a huge pile of Sandwich Island squashes fills one corner, and several cabbage-heads, valued at two dollars each, show themselves in the window. We enter a little door at the left of the building, ascend a dark, narrow flight of steps and find ourselves in a long, low room, with ceiling and walls of white muslin, and a floor covered with oil-cloth.

Downieville, from a lithograph made in 1854. Located on the Yuba River, it was one of the richest mining communities in the Sierra country. It has changed little since this drawing was made, and today is one of the most picturesque towns of the Mother Lode. Gold is still found in its vicinity. *(State Library, Sacramento)*

LEFT: Bad whiskey and the intemperate climate of the mining communities was a volatile mixture during the Gold Rush. This drawing published in *Harper's New Monthly Magazine,* January, 1861, depicts a rather exuberant Saturday night gathering. BELOW: For those who had gold dust to wager, there were many professional gamblers operating in the mining towns anxious to acquire it. This drawing which appeared in *Harper's Weekly,* October, 1857, shows a faro game in progress. *(Pictures: State Library, Sacramento)*

ABOVE: The clipper ship *Flying Cloud* shown taking on supplies. In 1854, the vessel sailed from New York to San Francisco in 89 days, a record passage. From *Gleason's Pictorial Drawing Room Companion,* May, 1851. BELOW: Crossing the Isthmus of Panama from the Atlantic coast to reach the San Francisco steamers was not without its dangers. This picture shows an accident which occurred near Gatun Bridge in 1856. From *Frank Leslie's Illustrated Newspaper,* May, 1856.

RIGHT: Brigadier General Bennett Riley, governor of California while it was under military rule. He encouraged the American settlers to establish a civil government that would pave the way for statehood. BELOW: Fires plagued San Francisco. This one, in 1851, was the sixth to leave the city in ashes. From *Gleason's Pictorial Drawing Room Companion,* August 30, 1851. *(Pictures: State Library, Sacramento)*

Colton Hall, Monterey, where California's first constitutional convention was held, was the prelude for the new territory to be admitted to statehood. *(Photo by William S. Murphy)*

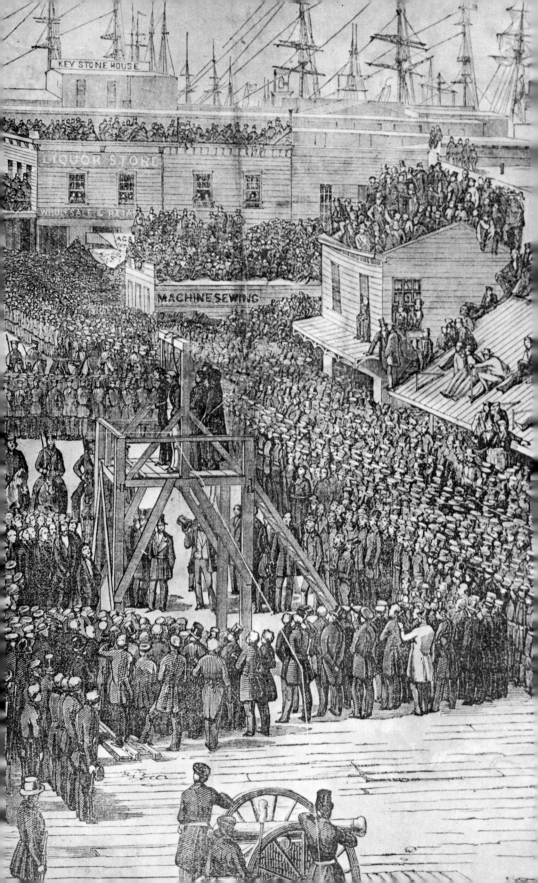

ABOVE: James King of William had slandered James P. Casey by bringing the latter's unsavory past to the attention of readers of his San Francisco newspaper. Casey accosted King, and without warning shot him. When the crusading editor died, Casey paid for the murder with his life. From *Frank Leslie's Illustrated Newspaper*, July, 1856. OPPOSITE: Vigilante justice. Two men condemned by the citizens' committee in San Francisco stand on the gallows awaiting execution. BELOW: The San Francisco Committee of Vigilance removing Casey and Charles Cora from jail to be tried and hanged. *(Pictures: State Library, Sacramento)*

The Committee of Vigilance took no chances on there being any attempt to free those they had sentenced to die on the gallows. Judging from this militant array of sentries guarding the scaffold, it would have taken an army to interrupt the proceedings. *(State Library, Sacramento)*

ABOVE: The hot-tempered Judge David S. Terry, a member of the State Supreme Court, is depicted in this early drawing, stabbing a member of the San Francisco Vigilance Committee who sought to arrest him. Terry later killed U.S. Senator David C. Broderick in a duel. BELOW: A detachment of the Committee of Vigilance in San Francisco seizes the "Law and Order" armory, June 21, 1856. From a rare daguerreotype. (Pictures: State Library, Sacramento)

Bret Harte, one of California's most distinguished men of letters. As a young man, he wrote an editorial denouncing the murder of a number of Indians near Arcata by unknown Americans. When it appeared in the local newspaper, Harte was forced to flee to San Francisco to escape a possible lynching. He achieved literary fame in the Bay area, when his first fiction appeared in a magazine he edited, the *Overland Monthly*. *(State Library, Sacramento)*

A Pony Express rider, on his way over the Rocky Mountains, meets a packtrain and is obliged to dismount to pass the heavily loaded mules on the narrow trail. From the *New York Illustrated News,* June 2, 1860. *(State Library, Sacramento)*

ABOVE: Arrival of the Pony Express at Sacramento following its inaugural run. From the *New York Illustrated News*, May 19, 1860. *(State Library, Sacramento)* BELOW: A Butterfield Mail cover, typical of those used by those sending letters east via the stage line. *(Authors' collection)*

The Overland stage crossing the mountains during a blizzard. From a contemporary print. (*State Library, Sacramento*)

The Wells Fargo Express being attacked by Indians while crossing the plains.
From the *Aldine,* published in 1878-1879 *(State Library, Sacramento)*

Los Angeles as it appeared in 1859. *(Title Insurance & Trust Co., Los Angeles)*

ABOVE: San Jose in 1857. From *Harper's New Monthly Magazine,* June, 1863. *(State Library, Sacramento)* BELOW: Drum Barracks, San Pedro, during the Civil War. This camp near the present Port of Los Angeles served as a training ground for the California volunteers, who later marched to Tucson, where they restored federal authority in Arizona following the collapse of the Confederate invasion of the Southwest. Camels were used briefly crossing the desert to Fort Yuma, but this method of transportation proved impractical and was discontinued. *(Authors' collection)*

There about twenty tables disposed in two rows, all of them so well filled that we have some difficulty in finding places. Taking up the written bill of fare, we find such items as the following:—

Soups

Mock Turtle 0 75
St. Julien 1 00

Fish

Boiled Salmon Trout, Anchovy sauce 1 75

Boiled

Leg Mutton, caper sauce 1 00
Corned Beef, Cabbage 1 00
Ham and Tongue 0 75

Entrees

Fillet of Beef, mushroom sauce 1 75
Veal Cutlets, breaded 1 00
Mutton Chop 1 00
Lobster Salad 2 00
Sirloin of Venison 1 50
Baked Macaroni 0 75
Beef Tongue, sauce piquante 1 00

So that, with but a moderate appetite, the dinner will cost us five dollars, if we are at all epicurean in our tastes. There are cries of "steward!" from all parts of the room—the word "waiter" is not considered sufficiently respectful, seeing that the waiter may have been a lawyer or a merchant's clerk a few months before. The dishes look very small as they are placed on the table, but they are skillfully cooked and very palatable to men that have ridden in from the diggings. The appetite one acquires in California is something remarkable. For two months after my arrival, my sensations were like those of a famished wolf.

In the matter of dining, the tastes of all nations can be gratified here. There are French restaurants on the plaza and on Dupont-street; an extensive German establishment on Pacific-street; the *Fonda Peruana;* the Italian Confectionary; and three Chinese houses, denoted by their long three-cornered flags of yellow silk. The latter are much frequented by Americans, on account of their excellent cookery, and the fact that meals are one dollar each, without regard to quantity. Kong-Sung's house is near the water; Whang-Tong's in Sacramento-street, and Tong-Ling's in Jackson-street. There the grave Celestials serve up their chow-chow and curry, besides many genuine English dishes; their tea and coffee cannot be surpassed.

The afternoon is less noisy and active than the forenoon. Merchants keep within doors, and the gambling-rooms are crowded with persons who step in to escape the wind and dust. The sky takes a cold grey cast, and the hills over the bay are barely visible in the dense, dusty air. Now and then a watcher, who has been stationed on the hill above Fort Montgomery, comes down and reports an inward-bound vessel, which occasions a little excitement among the boatmen and the merchants who are awaiting consignments. Towards sunset, the plaza is nearly deserted; the wind is merciless in its force, and a heavy overcoat is not found unpleasantly warm. As it grows dark, there is a lull, though occasional gusts blow down the hill and carry the dust of the city out among the shipping.

The appearance of San Francisco at night, from the water, is unlike anything I ever beheld. The houses are mostly of canvas, which is made transparent by the lamps within, and transforms them, in the darkness, to dwellings of solid light. Seated on the slopes of its three hills, the tents pitched among the chapparal to the very summits, it gleams like an amphitheatre of fire. Here and there shine out brilliant points, from the decoy-lamps of the gaming-houses; and through the indistinct murmur of the streets comes by fits the sound of music from their hot and crowded precincts. The picture has in it something unreal and fantastic; it impresses one like the cities of the magic lantern, which a motion of the hand can build or annihilate.

The only objects left for us to visit are the gaming-tables, whose day has just fairly dawned. We need not wander far in search of one. Denison's Exchange, the Parker House, and Eldorado, stand side by side; across the way are the Verandah and Aguila de Oro; higher up the plaza the St. Charles and Bella Union; while dozens of second-rate establishments are scattered through the less frequented streets. The greatest crowd is about the Eldorado; we find it difficult to effect an entrance. There are about eight tables in the room, all of which are thronged; copper-hued Kanakas, Mexicans rolled in their sarapes, and Peruvians thrust through their ponchos, stand shoulder to shoulder with the brown and bearded American miners. The stakes are generally small, though when the bettor gets into "a streak of luck," as it is called, they are allowed to double until all is lost or the bank breaks. Along the end of the room is a spacious bar, supplied with all kinds of bad liquors, and in a sort of gallery, suspended under the ceiling, a female violinist tasks her talent and strength to minister to the excitement of play.

The Verandah, opposite, is smaller, but boasts an equal attraction in a musician who has a set of Pandean pipes fastened at his chin, a drum on his back, which he beats with sticks at his elbows, and cymbals in his hands. The piles of coin on the monte tables clink merrily to his playing, and the throng of spectators, jammed together in a sweltering mass, walk up to the bar between the tunes and drink out of sympathy with his dry and breathless throat. At the Aguila de Oro there is a full band of Ethiopian serenaders, and at the other hells, violins, guitars, or wheezy accordeons, as the case may be. The atmosphere of these places is rank with tobacco-smoke, and filled with a feverish, stifling heat, which communicates an unhealthy glow to the faces of the players.

We shall not be deterred from entering by the heat and smoke, or the motley characters into whose company we shall be thrown. There are rare chances here of seeing human nature in one of its most dark and exciting phases. Note the variety of expression in the faces gathered around this table! They are playing monte, the favourite game in California, since the chances are considered more equal and the opportunity of false play very slight. The dealer throws out his cards with a cool, nonchalant air; indeed, the gradual increase of the hollow square of dollars at his left hand is not calculated to disturb his equanimity. Two Mexicans in front, muffled in their dirty sarapes, put down their half-dollars and dollars and see them lost without changing a muscle. Gambling is a born habit with them, and they would lose thousands with the same indifference. Very different is the demeanour of the Americans who are playing; their good or ill luck is betrayed at once by involuntary exclamations and changes of countenance, unless the stake should be very large and absorbing, when their anxiety, though silent, may be read with no less certainty. They have no power to resist the fascination of the game. Now counting their winnings by thousands, now dependent on the kindness of a friend for a few dollars to commence anew, they pass hour after hour in those hot, unwholesome dens. There is no appearance of arms, but let one of the players, impatient with his losses and maddened by the poisonous fluids he had drank, threaten one of the profession, and there will be no scarcity of knives and revolvers.

There are other places, where gaming is carried on privately and to a more ruinous extent—rooms in the rear of the Parker House, in the City Hotel, and other places, frequented only by the initiated. Here the stakes are almost unlimited, the players being men of wealth and apparent respectability. Frequently, in the absorbing interest of some desperate game, the night goes by unheeded, and morning breaks upon haggard faces and reckless hearts. Here are lost, in a few turns of a card or rolls of a ball, the product of fortunate ventures by sea or months of racking labour on land. . . .[7]

The gold region encompassed much of the Sierra Nevada. As miners gathered near the richer diggings, communities were soon established. Downieville, located on the Yuba River, was at the extreme northern tip of the bonanza country. Today, there are more gold deposits remaining in this vicinity than in any other section of the state. Additional towns were built on the Feather and American rivers in the north, and the Stanislaus and Tuolumne rivers in the south. Coloma, near the site of Marshall's initial discovery, became the first sizable mining center. Following the Mother Lode south was Placerville, originally named Hangtown; Auburn, Columbia, Sonora, and, at the extreme southern end, Mariposa. Scattered between all of these major outposts were locales somewhat more colorfully named: Helltown, Bedbug, Shinbone Peak, Poker Flat, Murderer's Gulch, and Delirium Tremens, to name but a few.

During the months following the finding of gold, there was little lawlessness in the mining camps, despite the fact that there was no clearly defined system of jurisprudence. Instances of claim jumping were rare, and although men frequently had large quantities of gold in their possession, there was little banditry. The only evil influence in the camps was the prevalence of gamblers, and an abundance of bad whisky. By 1849, however, conditions changed as the population grew. Many of the men coming to the gold fields were social misfits— outcasts from society, who frequently had criminal records. Incidents of armed robbery and theft began to be reported. Worse, a number of miners were murdered for their gold. Retaliation was swift, and lynch law became the acceptable method of dispensing justice.

Benjamin Butler Harris arrived in California during this period. He

[7] Bayard Taylor, *Eldorado, or Adventures in the Path of Empire; comprising a Voyage to California via Panama; Life in San Francisco and Monterey; Pictures of the Gold Region, and Experiences of Mexican Travel* (New York: George P. Putnam; London: Richard Bentley, 1850).

had come overland by horseback from Texas in 1849, traveling with a party of prospective miners. Crossing the desert, they entered the territory from the south, pausing briefly in Los Angeles before continuing north to the Sierra country. He described the future metropolis as a town "containing 2000–3000 people. . . . Its houses were one story adobe—roofed with thatch smeared over with brea which during the heat of day dripped from the eaves like ropy tar. Only 3 or 4 Americans lived there—one was Don Benito Wilson at whose store we replenished supplies for the journey to the mines. . . ." Harris reached his destination on September 29, 1849, after six months of travel, and began his search for wealth:

¶ Agua Fria, Mariposa County witnessed my first effort to wring the golden treasure from reluctant state crevices. My first crowbar, pick, shovel and battered second hand property of a disgusted miner were purchased for sixteen dollars. My diggings were about eighteen inches of bedrock. I managed to crevice and dig out about a dozen pans full per day from which about an ounce was daily realized. Out of this it required about $10 per day to supply my food which was usually beef or pickled pork, hard bread and coffee. By extra economy I sometimes managed to subsist on $8 per day. About this time my fancy was caught by a widely circulated caricature of the return of two ragged, famished prospectors having washpans heaped with shining gold—voraciously regarding a lot of Irish potatoes at a trading booth and balancing in the scales their weight in gold. One of them is saying "this yer gold dust looks mighty yeller, but them thar' taters looks yeller-er."

. . . Sudden disappointment on reaching the mines not only did sink the heart but sometimes the minds of the gold seekers. The abrupt dashing of expectations—the sudden wrecking of gorgeous visions that possessed and illumined the imagination were as falling resurrectionless like Lucifer from gilded Heaven into the gulf of dark despair. Such a victim was a promising young physician from New Orleans, who, engaged to the lady of his choice, had abandoned a fine practice in hope of sudden wealth in California for an early marriage dowry. Stern reality, the appalling difficulties of the mines, the sudden descent from Utopia to Sahara, overturned reason and he became a maniac, requiring the oversight of a guard. He conceived himself to be in hell, insisting that the friends and miners about him were devils—and the mountain sides the wall of the infernal prison. Generosity soon harvested a liberal sum from the miners which paid for returning him with guard to his home. . . .

My preparatory in a newly created country and county site in Texas fitted me for the wild administration of Justice in the Sierras. The aforesaid county had been created a month or two before the first session therein of the District Court. There was not a building at the County Seat or within 7 miles of it nor a road cut through the woods to it. The sheriff had caused to be constructed under a shady tree a raised platform of split logs, split side up, for judge's seat, also a few split half logs similarly arranged for jury seats. The only civilization signs in and about the court were the "citizen dress" worn by some of those present (the majority being in buckskin a la Indian) and a barrel of whiskey, in the split of a cart tongue hauled by an enterprising backwoodsman with great difficulty through the roadless forest. The Judge, a highly accomplished scholar and brilliant man, early paid frequent visits to the barrel. After causing court to be opened and the grand jury empaneled, the Judge thus addressed them, "Gentlemen of the Jury: the Grand Jury is an ancient institution. It originated among our liberty loving Anglo Saxon forefathers, the bulwarks of English and American liberty. They, gentlemen, were the Anglo Saxon Jurors by G—d. Gentlemen, you can retire to your (imaginary) room. During business hours you will not be allowed any refreshments, but may partake during recess—and, Gentlemen, the Court will have no objection to taking a social glass with you." Is it any wonder that in the trial of the Civil Case immediately following, the plaintiffs' and defendants' counsel, during the deep slumber of the judge, from wrangle and insult got into a fight, were separated and fined by the jury $25 each for contempt—not allowed to proceed until its payment. . . .[8]

Harris proceeded to Sonora in Tuolumne County. Here at a nearby mining camp he witnessed the havoc caused by the arrival of an itinerant liquor seller:

¶ Next day came to Yorktown which the day before had "broken out" into diggings by a Mexican finding 19 pounds of gold mixed with quartz forming the image of a tenpin. It was said that 7000 people were then on the ground. A city of store and miners' tents were already erected and gold was said to be found everywhere. . . . Spirituous liquids for several days in October 1849 had run short in Yorktown—whose "dry diggins" to

[8] Benjamin Harris, in the manuscript collection of the Henry E. Huntington Library and Art Gallery, San Marino, Calif.

many seemed very dry. At length a wagon loaded with several barrels came upon the scene. Then there was "hurrying in hot haste" to and fro. Men with camp kettles, skillets—coffee pots—tin plates, wash pans and bowls, canteens, and one man having nothing else but an empty whiskey barrel scurried toward the wagon. The demand was so pressing that the consignee was not allowed to unload, but had to retail the whole of the calamity water from the wagon. Imagine if you can the pandemonium that ensued for the next two or three days. Mining became almost suspended. Nearly all of our fellow citizens became mellow citizens— Satan staggered to and fro wandering up and down "the diggins." Whiskey was King; another Yorktown surrendered to Corn-Wallowers. Little did they comprehend that it required more vigilance for safety against this dangerous Devil than constant watch against the most vicious wild Indians. . . .

At Yorktown I voted at the election adopting the first constitution of California. Ballots were received from natives—foreign born, Indians, peons, from everyone. No challenges put in, no qualifications or questions were suggested or deemed requisite. It was a voting Saturnalia, but nearly all on the affirmative side. . . .

A Sunday in Sonora, then having several thousand population, had its main street about its entire length blocked to impassiveness from many Monte tables at intervals piled with gold dust and thronged with bettors. Late in the afternoon, after most of the day's sights had been taken in, I asked D. G. L., now a member of the Pioneers of San Bernardino, how much gold dust he had seen that day in Sonora. He replied that he thought he had seen about "ten barrels of it."

The recollections of Benjamin Harris are somewhat disjointed in their editorial organization. He read them before the San Bernardino Society of California Pioneers on February 17, 1890. They are written in pencil on narrow sheets of foolscap. It is evident that he was simply attempting to recall the more colorful vignettes of that exciting period in the long ago that were still vivid in his memory. Here he continues with his account of life at Sonora in the Mother Lode country:

¶ In November 1849, a physician felt a teamster's pulse for which he charged one ounce of gold ($16), and prescribed for him charging five ounces. The same day the doctor engaged the teamster as part of his back-load to haul a trunk a dozen miles to Montezuma on the Stockton road, for which the teamster charged 6 ounces. The charges in each were not demurred to, or considered exorbitant.

Rough two dollar cowhide boots were sold for six ounces. Lumber shipped from Maine hauled to the mines or lumber whip sawed in the vicinity readily brought $1 per foot. About this time I read of a New Englander who wore buck skin clothes in the mines returning home with his "pile" and throwing away the old suit from which his thrifty wife gleaned from pockets and seams $13 in gold dust. The profits from the mines so possessed men's imaginations that United States private soldiers and sailors on this coast deserted on every opportunity, often with much risk. They were encountered everywhere in the Sierras. No one seemed to blame their yielding to the irresistible temptation. Luck seemed to smile on them more than on others and with these were verified the proverb that "Sailors make money like horses—but spend it like asses."

Rewards were in many instances circulated throughout the camps for return of deserters. Either the amounts proposed were ridiculously insignificant, or sympathy for the escapees too strong to tempt recapture. Lieut. P. with a detail of soldiers was ordered to recapture "a host of these deserters" ascertained to be mining in Sullivan's Creek. The gold fever early struck his men, who also deserted, leaving him like "the guest that treads alone, some marble hall deserted." The infection caught the Lieutenant. His resignation was forwarded, and when I saw him he was a hired hand pumping water at $20 per day and "grub" in the rich claim of the very men he was sent to arrest—and whom he before commanded.

.   .   .

In the spring of '50 a flood of scoundrels—many said from Tasmania, polluted the mines. Too mean or lazy to work, they loafed about the camps, ascertained who had gold dust, and prowling at night, robbed and murdered the unsuspecting victims. Such occurrences were almost daily. The guilty not being detected—these unseen oft recurring atrocities generated a public frenzy, so much so that a slight suspicion of being one of the thugs would have occasioned instant execution. The Civil power completely mystified and baffled could do nothing. At length a traveller in a remote place reported 3 or 4 Yaqui Indian miners burning the corpses of two white men. Immediate arrest and collection of excited men took place. Men were in hot haste to have the Yaqui's blood. They were forcibly taken from the Sonora jail and hung up without opportunity to say aught explanatory or in vindication. The new County Judge (Tuttle) with some others rushed up, cut down the Yaquis and the Judge by dint of much hard persuasion induced the lynchers to desist and await the session of the next District Court then but a few weeks off, first pledging his head for safe custody of the prisoners meanwhile. When the day arrived for the trial armed delegations of mobs from all parts of the surrounding country instructed to kill the prisoners anyhow assembled at Sonora. The miners organization at Pasala—Pina . . . ordered out 100 armed men under Capt. Short, instructed to protect the Yaquis if innocent, to help hang them if guilty. The trial opened—the jury was empaneled, the court room packed densely with men armed with rifles—hundreds like armed, being outside unable to get entrance. All noisy and threatening. "Hang 'em—Hang 'em" resounded in the court and among jurors all over town. Whenever the sheriff at recess conducted the jury through the dense throng many voices threatened that if they failed to hang, the crowd would hang the jury. The evidence exonerated the prisoners, it having been clearly established—that it was customary among those people to bury the dead—that the dead bodies, from the maggots found in them at their burning and from other elicited facts, must have been killed several days prior.

The case was submitted—the jury retired for making a verdict to a room over the court room. Amid this frenzied scene, Dr. Shepherd, ex-secretary of the navy for the Texas Republic, having several days imbibed Bacchus excessively, a large brawn, stalwart, handsome man; mounted the Judge's rostrum and kicked a table over the Judge's head. The Judge withdrawing through a side door went to the front entrance—instructed the District Attorney to pacify the crowd with a speech—retired to his hotel. Dr. Shepherd, bowie knife in hand, eyes glaring, face and hair awry, faced the crazy mob—making the following remarks: "I want to fight, I want to fight, I won't disgrace myself by fighting one man or a dozen—I will fight fifty—yes, a hundred—bring them—mighty little difference it makes on God's books whether my name was there a thousand years ago or now."

At this stage a rifle held in a man's hand resting on a bench, slipping exploded, sending the ball through the ceiling grazing a jury man. Instantly a hundred mouths yelled, "A Mexican has shot an American." The hundreds outside repeated the cry. Mexicans who formed two thirds of the population ran to cover. Many retreating out of town over the hills were the targets of long irregular volleys from the insane multitude.

Narrow escapes were numerous—none were hurt. Pandemonium subsided a little. Two of the jurors acknowledging the defendants' innocence advocated a verdict of guilty on the grounds that if acquitted the frantic people would hang the jury. After a little they were won over—then a message was dispatched to Capt. Short to know if the jury could rely on him for protection. He replied favorably. The verdict was announced. Capt. Short's hundred men surrounded the prisoners and jury, guarding them safely away. Excitement speedily collapsed and calm retrieved her throne . . .

.   .   .

The 4th of July in 1850 was unique. For days preparations were made up and down the Tuolomne River by miners then preparing to mine the bed of the stream by damming and turning its water through canals. About a fourth of a mile of parallel tables lain upon stakes driven into the earth groaned under rough but relishable viands, mainly beef, pickled pork, coffee, beans, bread, scarcely leavened hard bread—all in or partaken from tin plates, dishes, cups, etc.

Red, blue, grey shirts, pants foxed before, pants foxed behind with flower sacks showing "self raising" Haxhall—Chili brands, etc. Stuffed into the coarse cow skin boots of the wearers, slouch wool hats—bowie knives—long straggling beards and whiskers, graced everywhere these descendants of the sires of Seventy-Six. Whiskey there was no end of; ladies and boiled shirts were as rare as stove pipe hats and no stove pipe hats were there. But the eagle and atmosphere of Bunker Hill—Yorktown and Brandywine were there in all their glory.

The uppermost question then was damming the river. When all arranged at the table preparatory to attacking the dinner the President of the day in stentorian tone opened the ceremony with his toast:

"Here's to Benedict Arnold and the Tuolomne River, the one a traitor to his country, the other about to become master to his country. May they both be most effectually damned."

.   .   .

. . . A man who for some years had been a sea farer was hung by a mob at Georgetown for murders. His two motherless, and soon to be fatherless little children lived with him. At the hanging the ex-sailors, full of solicitude less he should not die game and thereby disgrace the profession, comforted him with such expression as "Jack, die like a sailor, old Toppy," "Shipmate, don't shame the craft." A box fastened to a nearby tree labeled, "For the Orphans" received a small fortune in shape of gold dust from the men that carried out the father's execution.

About a thousand miners assembled one Sunday at Fiddletown on Dry Creek suddenly precipitated themselves into a mob—caused by a miner while gambling after losing his purse of gold dust—grabbing and pocketing it. He and the dealer had altercations over it. Somebody's pistol exploded, accidentally, doing no harm. The cry went forth that "A gambler had shot a miner."

"Hang him, hang him!" resounded everywhere. Ropes enough to hang every "gay gambolier" in California were seized from adjacent stores by crowds rushing to the scene. The gambler slipped through the throng, escaping a gust that rose and subsided in five minutes. On another occasion for a wounding shooting . . . impudent Bill Gardiner, then riding the usual gambling circuit, was ordered by a suddenly evoked mob to permanently leave the camp in ten minutes or be hung on the stroke of the eleventh. Promptly mounting his mule tied near, he bade the angry multitude good afternoon, adding that five minutes notice was sufficient for him. . . .

. . .

The first political convention I witnessed in California was for nominating a state Senator and two Assemblymen. It was a mass meeting. A hat was handed around for ballots. On announcement of the results the majority became wroth at the nomination for Senator. The entire crowd, chairman excepted, peace makers included, engaged in fisticuffs—commencing in the playful sparring of 2 Jack Tars. A one-half acre of ground had men striking at nearest heads—friends pomelling friends or foes. What gouging, kicking, tumbling, squirming, piling—rolling down hill, not knowing or heeding whom they hit. It was Donny Brook Fair many times magnified. At length by tacit understanding the tumult ceased—then quietly resuming seats the convention serenely proceeded to nominate the two Assemblymen, then placidly dispersed. Never before or since have I known men to fight just for the fun of the thing. It evinced a high degree of metal and readiness at least. . . .

In the early days of mining, it was difficult for public speakers to obtain audience room under shelter. Store tents or shanties had the largest space and these were invariably accompanied with a bar and tables rent to gamblers. Often have I witnessed merchandising, whiskey selling and drinking, preaching and gaming all going on in the same tent on a Sunday and other days. It looked queer at first to see quiet men listening to the "divining of the word" rise orderly from their goods box seat, softly approach the bar, take a drink, and as orderly resume listening to the sermon. On one of these occasions while two or three monte tables were running and Preacher P—— who had an unpleasant rancous, rasping voice was holding forth; Yank Humphreys was annoyed thereby in the matter of ruining his game. He approached the preacher saying, "Money is what you are preaching for—you are interupting my game. Here's $2 I'll give you, if you'll dry up and quit preaching."

The preacher meekly pocketing the lucre remarked, "The Lord sent it but the Devil brought it," continued preaching as before. Such a guffaw went up as was rare in those "diggins." Discomfitted, Yank also continued his game—preaching to the contrary—notwithstanding $2 loser in the operation. . . .

The bonanza was short-lived. Within a few years, the placer gold scattered along the riverbanks and lodged in bedrock had been gleaned. Washed along countless streams from the snow-capped Sierra summits, an accumulation of the yellow metal that had been gathering for centuries vanished as thousands combed through every productive region in a frantic quest for instant wealth. In their haste, they built flumes to divert the rivers and expose rich sandbars. This eroded the soil. Hydraulic machinery was introduced that utilized intense water pressure to level hillsides. Throughout the Mother Lode, the scars are visible today. The land is barren.

As the Americans moved away from diggings no longer profitable, the patient Chinese moved in, sifting and panning the few remaining particles of gold. There was still untapped millions to be discovered, but this treasure was only to be located by following rich veins deep into the mountains. It would take machinery and organization. Great mining companies were yet to be formed—companies such as the Idaho-Maryland at Grass Valley, which would sink its shafts more than five thousand feet underground and produce millons of dollars in bullion in the next hundred years, until finally rising operational costs weighed against a fixed government price of $35 an ounce made it impossible to continue operations. The Idaho-Maryland shut down. Its subterranean levels were allowed to flood, leaving the untapped ore deposits for the ages. In 1966, the Sixteen-to-One Mine at Alleghany was forced to close. This was the last large gold-mining corporation operating in California. An era had come to an end.

By the time Marshall's discovery became known throughout the nation, and thousands of prospectors rushed west, they would be called Forty-niners, for this was the epoch year. As time progressed, many became disillusioned as it became apparent that whatever wealth was to be obtained had passed into the hands of earlier arrivals. Times had been difficult in the East, and many men left their families to make the long journey to California with the hope that they would strike it rich. Most had no intention of remaining. There were many personal tragedies among those who became obsessed by the dream of achieving great wealth. They had read the pamphlets, accounts published in the press, and even books printed during the period, which portrayed, often erroneously, the monetary awards awaiting those who would seek them. Few more poignant accounts are to be found than one related by Ananias Rogers, who kept a diary in a cheaply covered ledger book.

It is difficult to summarize Rogers' background, because many of the entries in his journal are vague and elusive. He was a man in his forties or fifties who had married children at home. Rogers left Wisconsin to follow his dream, joining a band of men who came west with wagons drawn by oxen. After many hardships they reached California. Near Bidwell's Bar, scene of a prior strike, he set up a crude rocker, or sluice box, along the river, and joined several men who had accompanied him. They worked on an equal-share basis. On October 28, 1849, Rogers noted in his journal:

¶ Mr. B. & myself . . . found we had made $46.00 the last day we had worked the cradle. Pretty fair, as it is only the 2nd day we have worked it. . . .[9]

With the approach of winter, there was considerable discomfort among those working the diggings along the river:

¶ Nov. 6. Rain, rain, nothing but rain & mud for this & the most part of the day. I am witness to much suffering. Many of the emigrants are much worse off than we are. Having no shelter, whilst our tent keeps most of the rain from us, but it is very damp & chilly. Many are troubled with Bloody Flux. . . .

12th. Yesterday was fair & Mr. B & self washed for gold as we had only been able to work but 2 days in the past week, and probably made less than 2 ounces. We have worked for 2 days where we first commenced &

[9] Ananias Rogers, journal in the manuscript collection of the Henry E. Huntington Library and Art Gallery, San Marino, Calif.

have probably made over two ounces per day & the weather is fair. Flour has risen to 75 cents per lb. Many are leaving. I fear provisions are going to be scarce. We are now paying $1.00 per lb. for pork and 50 cents for sugar, 50 cents for fruit, potatoes $1.00, mackerel from 38 to $1.00 each. . . . On the 23rd Mr. B and self washed $68.67 worth of gold. This is the largest amount we have procured. . . . I have bought 2 flannel shirts for $14.00, one pocket knife for $2.00 & 2 pr. socks $3.00, 16 quart tin pan $4.00 & 2 lbs tobacco $2.00. Such are the prices at this place. There were no cabins or houses on the river previous to my coming up. Now there are several tolerable respectable cabins. Most have cloth roofs, but some have quite decent clapboard roofs. Some are covered on the outside with green hides. Others have dug holes in the ground & covered them with pine brush & dirt. They are not as good buildings as the Indians make and must be very unhealthy. . . . I hear that many who came through the past summer have procured sufficient gold to satisfy them and are ready to return to the States. My expenses are such that I fear that it will be long before I shall get enough to satisfy, although it would not take a large sum to do so. . . . I have more goods and chattels, arms & ammunition than I will know what to do with, so I traded my double barrel for a revolver & a rifle. I can carry the revolver & they are worth more here than guns on that account. This country is certainly better supplied with arms & ammunition than any I ever had knowledge of. Where I shall be in a week from this time I know not. This much I know from experience—that it is very disagreeable living in a tent at this time and place. My feet never feel like they were dry and frequently are so cold that I cannot sleep. For several days, more have left the river than have arrived. . . . I purchased a claim on Bidwell's Bar for $10.00. Packed my tools up the river & ferried over and worked about 2½ hours. Made about $5.00. I fear my purchase is not a rich one, but I can't lose much. . . .

Nearly three years passed, and Rogers was still pursuing his dream—searching, but never finding what had compelled him to make the long journey across the continent. He received infrequent letters from one of his daughters, Mary. His wife seldom wrote. What little gold he acquired went for subsistence, and the price of food and other essentials was exorbitant. Like so many of his fellow gold seekers, Rogers realized that the quest had been futile, and his efforts a failure. On March 16, 1852, he made the following entry in his journal:

¶ I am solitary & alone. Am I never to see my loved ones again. If I had determined to make a permanent residence in this valley I might now have been well off and have had the means to bring my family out, but disliking the country that I was in & firmly believing that it was a poor country to settle in, my whole anxiety was to make a sudden raise and return to my family. This I undertook to do by mining. This is certainly the most uncertain of any business in the world. Twice in my life have I found it so. Here & in the lead mines. But I hoped to draw a prize & really thinking there were few blanks ventured my all. From Mary's letter I fear that my family may not be in very good circumstances. . . . Indeed I do not know what to do. Oh that I could once more be with my family. Alas, I fear this never may be. Oh me, I am weak in body & I fear worse in mind. . . .

A letter finally arrived from his wife. There was news that the family might cross the plains the following year and join him in California. The thought of seeing his loved ones failed to dispel a feeling of despondency that is apparent in Rogers' diary:

¶ I can look back & see the thousand mistakes that I have made, but I can't see ahead. All is misty—darkness & confusion. If I knew that my family would come, I would try & find a claim & try & fix a home for their reception. How can I without means? One reflection gives me satisfaction. I intended all for the best. I wish I could keep the recollection constantly in my mind. . . .

I fear they are in straightened circumstances and have too long forborn letting me know it. Had I received the letter in due season I could have forwarded a small sum that would have sufficed to buy seed for the season.

One wonders what became of Ananias Rogers, and whether he was ever reunited with his family. Unfortunately, after making his last troubled entry, Rogers put the journal aside. He never wrote the ending.

18

CALIFORNIA
AND STATEHOOD

If the gold camps had their own rough forms of government, the rest of California went through a period of political confusion. Frémont had served as military governor for a period of fifty days, arrogating that position over the objections of Kearny. Orders from Washington settled the controversy in Kearny's favor, and he promptly court-martialed Frémont, accusing him of disobedience, mutiny, and of "most cruelly and shamefully" treating the native Californians.

By the end of the Mexican War, California was ruled by military government and a succession of fairly enlightened officers who attempted to meld the *alcalde* system with American ideas of local government. It satisfied neither group. There were language difficulties, collisions between the military and civilians, bitter feelings between the native Californians and the newcomers. General Bennett Riley, military governor in 1849, was a reasonable and enlightened man. Both groups wanted self-government. A congressional emissary, Thomas Butler King, sent by the President to encourage sentiment for statehood, saw that it already existed. San Francisco's troublesome "Legislative Assembly," representing the most powerful elements in its community, sought a civil government. General Riley, whose army of occupation had been reduced to practically a skeleton crew, called for an election of representatives to a constitutional convention. Accordingly, on October 2, 1849, the delegates convened at Monterey's Colton Hall to draft the document. Forty-eight answered the first roll call, as Dr. Robert Semple, president of the first constitutional convention rapped a huge bony fist against a table and shouted for order. Among the elected representatives were six Californians who fought against the United States during the Mexican War of 1846–1847. They would unite with their former conquerors to prepare the framework for statehood, and then demand that California be admitted to the Union.

"We have discussed many problems here," Dr. Semple told the gathering after it had been in session some hours. "What are to be the boundaries of our proposed state? There is the question of slavery, taxation, and education. There is even the task of selecting an appropriate coat of arms. I believe that Mr. Lyon has a final sketch to submit to the convention."

Caleb Lyon, a settler from New York, and assistant secretary of the convention, arose. He held up a drawing that had been made by Major R. S. Garnett, U.S.A.

"Major Garnett has made a few changes in compliance with the wishes of some of our earlier settlers," he announced. "You will note he has added a grizzly bear guarding Minerva's shield."

A number of delegates applauded, recalling the short-lived Bear Flag Republic, the Americans' first bid for freedom from Mexican rule in 1846. Delegate Mariano Vallejo from Sonora had been a Mexican general during those days. He well remembered that the Bear Flag enthusiasts had arrested and imprisoned him.

"I suggest that if we retain the bear," he cried, "its neck be encircled by a lariat held in a vaquero's hands."

His proposal was ignored, and Caleb Lyon explained the final design. Around the ring were thirty-one stars, being the number of states comprising the Union upon the admission of California. The foreground figure was the Goddess Minerva having sprung full grown from the brain of Jupiter. She would represent the political birth of the State of California, which would not go through the customary probation of a territory. At Minerva's knee would be a grizzly bear feeding upon a cluster of grapes. The grapevine and a sheaf of wheat illustrated the agricultural interests of the future state. A miner is shown at work with a rocker and bowl at his side, depicting the golden wealth of the Sacramento upon whose waters is seen shipping, typical of commercial greatness. The snow-clad peaks of the Sierra Nevada comprised the background.

The Great Seal of California

"We have added the word 'Eureka,'" Lyon said, "which, if you don't know your Greek, means 'I have found it.' You can apply that to the principle involved in the admission of the state, or the success of the miner at work."

The Honorable Myron Norton addressed the chair:

"I should like to offer a resolution that the words 'The Great Seal of California' be added to the design."

Cheers greeted his request and the emblem was adopted. The convention completed its work. Slavery was outlawed, and even the former Southerners failed to object to this section. The constitutions of New York and Iowa were followed extensively in preparing California's official charter. A provision was adopted that would disfranchise anyone who should fight a duel. It would have little effect on a number of voters, who would continue to settle their disputes in a cloud of gunsmoke. The constitution was completed and signed on October 13, 1849. The weary delegates voted themselves an elaborate ball in honor of the occasion, while Monterey's fort boomed a thirty-one-gun salute. A popular election ratified the document.

The Californians lost no time in establishing legislative machinery to put their new constitution into operation. Peter H. Burnett, a Democrat, was elected the first governor, and the legislature selected two United States senators—this before statehood was ratified by Congress. They were John C. Frémont, the explorer and popular hero of the hour, and William M. Gwin, a Southerner who had lived in Tennessee and Mississippi. His knowledge of parlimentary procedure had brought him acclaim during the convention at Monterey. He was a scholar, a persuasive speaker, and had learned his skills in the rough-and-tumble arena of Jacksonian politics. For a decade during the turbulent 1850's, Gwin was the major political force and manipulator in California. As a Southerner, he elected to support the Confederacy during the Civil War, and, like many fellow losers in that conflict, ended his days in obscurity.

While the exuberant residents clamored for statehood, the politicians reacted slowly in Washington. There was much criticism of the brash manner in which the upstarts on the West Coast had the effrontery to send two new senators to the nation's capital with the demand that they be seated. One of California's greatest champions was James K. Polk, eleventh President of the United States. As a North Carolinian, he was at odds with his fellow Southerners on this issue, most of whom wanted no part of a new state entering the Union, which was not favorable to the extension of slavery. When Californians met at Monterey for the purpose of forming a civil government, they were vehement in their denunciation of a system that permitted thousands of unfortunate people to be held in bondage. Unfortunately, the President was no man to placate the South. He lacked the personality of the skilled politician who could attract a wide popular following. He was drab, austere, and dedicated to his work. Historian Allan Nevins describes him as "a man to command respect, but neither liking nor awe. In person he was spare, of middle height, angular in his movements, with a small head, long grizzled hair brushed stiffly behind his ears, penetrating and rather chilly grey

eyes, and a stern mouth. His countenance was usually sad, but sometimes lightened by a genial smile. . . . He was intense, laborious,
humorless, pedestrian, immensely aware at all times of the responsibilities which he bore, and inclined to make everyone with whom he
came in contact aware of them. . . ." [1]

Few Presidents have achieved such a monumental record during a
four-year term of office. He added more than 500,000 square miles of
territory to the United States; the Oregon boundary question was
settled with Great Britain; and his dream of acquiring California
became a reality. It is significant that President Polk died at fifty-
three, several months after leaving office. Overwork unquestionably
was the contributing factor. The entry in his diary on Saturday,
January 20, 1849, reflects James Polk's eagerness in securing the
ratification of California as the thirty-first state in the Union:

¶ . . . The Cabinet met at the usual hour; all the members present. The
Secretary of the Navy read a despatch received last night from Commodore Jones, commander of the Pacific squadron; the Secretary of War
read a letter to the Paymaster-General from Paymaster Rich serving in
California; and the Secretary of State read a letter from Mr. Larkin,
formerly United States consul at Monterey in California. These several
communications represent the increased richness of the gold region recently discovered in California, the rage which prevails among all classes
to go in pursuit of it. Commodore Jones and Paymaster Rich represent the
desertions from the squadron and the army to go in pursuit of gold to be
such as to destroy all efficient service in both arms of the service. They
represent also the state of anarchy and confusion existing in California,
where, without any regularly organized government, there is no security
for life, liberty, or property, and they represent the urgent necessity for the
establishment of the authority of the United States by the organization of
some kind in that Territory. It occurred to me at once that it would be
proper for me to transmit these communications to Congress with a
message urging the establishment of civil Government for the inhabitants
of California at the present session, and I submitted two questions to the
Cabinet, 1st, whether these communications should be sent to Congress,
and if so what the recommendations of my message should be. The views
of all the members of the Cabinet were freely given. Mr. Marcy and Mr.

[1] *Polk, the Diary of a President 1845–1849* edited by Allan Nevins (New York: Longmans, Green and Company, 1929), pp. xv–xvi.

Walker advised that the communications be sent to Congress with a message. Mr. Buchanan, Mr. Mason, Mr. Johnson, and Mr. Toucey advised against it. The latter gentlemen thought that they should be published without delay in the *Union* newspaper, and that if called for by Congress, as they probably would be, they should then be transmitted. They assigned their reasons for this opinion. Among other reasons they said that I had already in my annual message said all that could be said to induce Congress to act, and that exception might be taken by the Whig members, and perhaps some Democrats, if I repeated my views. After their views were expressed Mr. Marcy expressed his willingness to acquiesce in them, though he rather preferred that the papers should be sent to Congress with a message. Finding that Mr. Walker alone concurred fully with me in my first impressions, I stated that I would for the present yield to the views of the majority of the Cabinet. I then directed that copies of the communications, or of the material parts of them, should be furnished to the editor of the *Union* for publication. I then stated to the Cabinet that I had become perfectly satisfied that no bill to establish a territorial government could be passed through the House of Representatives without having the Wilmot Proviso [2] attached to it as a condition, that with this provision the bill would probably be rejected by the Senate, and that if it was not, and the provision was made to apply to the territory South of 36° 30′ I must veto it, and in either event the people of California would be left without a government. I expressed to them the opinion that the only hope of providing a government for California at the present session was to admit her as one of the States of the Union, as had been proposed in the Senate by Senators Downs of Louisiana and Douglas of Illinois. In this opinion all the members of the Cabinet concurred, and expressed their desire that such a proposition might pass. I expressed my fears that the extremes of the South headed by Mr. Calhoun and the extremes of the North headed by Hale and Giddings might unite to prevent

[2] On August 8, 1846 a bill was introduced in Congress that would appropriate $2,000,000 to be allocated to the President in negotiating a peace treaty in Mexico. Representative David Wilmot, a Democrat from Pennsylvania, sponsored an amendment that "Provided . . . as an express and fundamental condition to the acquisition of any territory from the Republic of Mexico by the United States, by virtue of any treaty which may be negotiated between them, and to the use by the Executive of the moneys herein appropriated, neither slavery nor involuntary servitude shall ever exist in any part of said territory, except for crime, whereof the party shall first be duly convicted." The measure passed in the House, but died together with the bill when the Senate adjourned. At the next session, it was reintroduced, with the appropriation being upped to $3,000,000, and broadened in scope to include all territory that might be acquired by the United States. Once again the bill passed the House, but the Senate refused to enact the measure into law. The proviso failed to be adopted by Congress.

such a measure from passing and thus keep the subject of slavery open for political agitation.

I expressed my strong desire that California might be admitted as a State, because I believe if this was not done at the present session the danger was imminent that the inhabitants of this fine country would, before the next session of Congress, set up an independent government for themselves, and that of the Whig party, who would then be in power, would suffer the country to be lost to the Union. I gave my reasons at some length for this opinion. I expressed my disapprobation of any further proceeding of the Southern members of Congress on the slave question in caucus.[3]

After night I sent for Senator Douglas and held a long conversation with him in relation to his bill to admit California into the Union as a State, and the prospect of passing it. I told him confidentially that I and every member of my Cabinet were in favour of his bill, as the only thing that could probably be done at the present session so as to provide a government for California, and thus secure that valuable country to the Union and put an end to the slavery excitement. He expressed himself as much gratified, and thought there was a fair prospect for passing the bill. . . .[4]

The legislation was not enacted by Congress until the following year. It had become the chief topic in Washington, and the main objection to California being admitted to the Union was that it would disturb the balance of power in the Senate to the prejudice of the slaveholding states of the South. Despite the protests of the Southerners in Congress, California was designated as the thirty-first state, but the storm of controversy the issue raised fanned the smouldering passions that flamed into the great Civil War some ten years later. President Fillmore signed the bill on September 9, 1850. The event

[3] Polk, *Diary,* p. 371. Allan Nevins explains this as follows: "Polk, vigorously supported by Alexander H. Stephens of Georgia, tried to prevent action by the caucus of Southern members led by Calhoun. He failed. The caucus issued an address to the Southern people. This dwelt upon the growing antagonism between North and South, attacked the North for its failure to render up fugitive slaves and for its lack of respect for the Missouri Compromise, declared that the North was trying to refuse the South its due share of the Mexican cession, and lamented the attacks by Northern Congressmen upon slavery. It called for unified action by the South to meet these affronts and aggressions. This Congressional address to the South found loud echoes in the resolutions drawn up by various Southern legislatures and mass meetings. Polk's administration was closing amid a rising storm of sectional dissension."

[4] *Ibid.,* pp. 370–371.

created considerable excitement at the nation's Capital, but the people who were directly affected were unaware of the news for more than two weeks until a ship sailed into San Francisco Bay carrying the first official word. Express riders quickly spread it to every corner of California. How the growing city of San Francisco reacted to the news is recorded in the *California Daily Courier* of October 19, 1850:

¶ Yesterday, at about half past ten, A.M., the booming of cannon was heard in the bay, and in a few minutes the beautiful steamship *Oregon* hove in sight, completely covered with flags of all nations, the starry flag of our country proudly waving over all. She came up in fine style, in front of the city, firing her heavy guns in quick succession, which were answered by the ships in the harbor, and from cannon on shore, as also by the vessels at Saucelito.—The news flew from mouth to mouth, that California was now one of the States of our glorious confederacy. The hills and housetops were soon covered with multitudes of people, who uttered cheer upon cheer as the *Oregon* swept up towards her anchorage at Rincon Point. In the course of the afternoon a grand salute was fired from the Plaza, and groups filled the streets, congratulating each other upon the happy event. The roof of Wells's splendid banking house on Montgomery street was covered by a large party of gentlemen who had assembled for the same purpose. Bonfires were kindled on the hills and in Happy Valley. A grand salute was fired from the Revenue Cutter in the harbor in the evening, and the whole night was spent in every manner of rejoicing—great guns and little ones—rockets and crackers—drums, trumpets, and trombones—all were brought into requisition to celebrate this great event.

Many of the public houses of the city were illuminated in the most beautiful style. Among these we noticed first, and most prominent were, Delmonico's, Ross's Merchants' Exchange, Cronin & Markley's, the El Dorado, City Hotel, *Alta California* and *Courier* offices. The show from some of the houses was most brilliant.

Every one seemed happy—and we do not believe that the news of a brilliant victory was ever received by any people with greater joy, than was the news of yesterday, that California is now one of the brightest stars in our glorious galaxy of States. Thanks to a tardy but patriotic Congress—thanks to our brethren of the Atlantic States—thanks to an Administration which has shown itself true to California, and true to the Union! Long may our heaven-blessed, united country be preserved for the glory of our times and the pride of unborn generations.

19

VIGILANTE JUSTICE AND VIOLENCE

The influx of gold seekers to California overtaxed the inexperienced authorities, who were vainly trying to enforce newly enacted laws. By the end of 1849, San Francisco's population had increased by more than 80,000. Unfortunately, the new arrivals were not all model citizens. The promise of sudden wealth had attracted the refuse of the world to the Pacific coast. Among the worst were discharged soldiers, who had served in Colonel Stevenson's New York regiment of volunteers. They formed a band under one Sam Roberts, calling themselves Hounds or Regulators. This gang terrorized citizens, particulary those in the Latin-American minority. Another source of trouble was the arrival of numerous ex-convicts from the British penal colonies, notably Australia. These felons were offered conditional pardons with the stipulation they go to any country other than England. At San Francisco they found a haven in a growing underworld, where they were dubbed Sydney men, sometimes referred to as "Sydney Ducks." Vice flourished. Professional gamblers arrived in droves to fleece those returning from the gold fields of their hard-earned dust in crooked card games.

The criminal element in San Francisco grew bolder as the danger of prosecution lessened. Corrupt politicians controlled the city, and the payoff became an acceptable method of persuading public officials to turn their backs upon the most heinous depredations of the lawless. Honest citizens were appalled, but instead of relying upon popular elections to remedy the existing evils in civic government, they decided to take the law into their own hands. Their reluctance to pursue a democratic course to improve conditions, namely, by placing the issues before the voters, is understandable. Few elections were conducted honestly, and ballot-box stuffing was a common procedure. Accordingly, a number of angry citizens met to lay preliminary plans for administering justice. The group had its leaders: Sam Brannan, a preacher who had come to San Francisco with a colony of Mormons in 1846; William T. Coleman, a Kentuckian who arrived in California in 1849; and James King of William, a banker, later turned newspaper publisher, who would be shot to death by a politician he denounced in print. On their third meeting, the members adopted a constitution, which was to govern their actions. Its opening paragraph reads:

9th June, 1851

¶ Whereas it has become apparent to the Citizens of San Francisco that there is no security for life and property either under the regulations of Society as it at present exists or under the laws as now administered, —therefore, the Citizens whose names are hereunto attached do unite themselves into an association for the maintenance of the peace and good order of Society and the preservation of the lives and property of the Citizens of San Francsico and do bind ourselves each unto the other to do and perform every lawful act for the maintenance of law and order to sustain the laws when faithfully and properly administered, but we are determined that no thief, burglar, incendiary or assassin shall escape punishment, either by the quibbles of the law, the insecurity of prisons, the carelessness or corruption of the Police, or a laxity of those who pretend to administer justice. . . .

The name of the new organization would be "the Committee of Vigilance for the protection of the lives and property of the Citizens and residents of the City of San Francisco." It was a frightening compact. The extremists would soon be in control of the community. The terror of vigilante justice spread to the mining communities of the Mother Lode and south to Los Angeles, an unimpressive little settlement, which during the decade of the 1850's earned a reputation as one of the most notorious and crime-infested settlements of the West—a rather inauspicious beginning under American rule for a town called the City of the Angels.

In their eagerness to hang the guilty, the members of the San Francisco Committee made no pretense at observing due process of law. The culprits were tried by kangaroo courts and executed in a most barbaric manner. The members of the two committees formed in 1851 and 1856 were respected citizens of their community in later years, possibly with the exception of Sam Brannan, who died penniless in San Diego County in 1889, reported to have become the victim of drink.

A small book was printed in San Francisco in 1858 chronicling the activities of the two committees. Its author preferred to remain anonymous, and considering his narrative was not always laudatory, this is understandable. The book was not widely circulated and is therefore little known. It is reasonably certain that the author was not a member of the committee. The little volume is entitled *Judges and Criminals: Shadows of the Past—History of the Vigilance Committee of San Francisco, Calif.* Its chapters provide a rational appraisal of a violent era. The following account describes the swift course of justice that took place when a suspect was taken into custody by the committee:

¶ About the beginning of June, 1851, another of the tragedies so disgraceful to the State occurred in San Francisco. A man named Jenkins had been taken in the act of conveying away a small safe which he had stolen. The safe was placed in a boat by him, and he was conveying it away, when some members of this organization pursued him. Jenkins in the meantime threw the safe overboard into the Bay. It was however, fished up by his pursuers. He was arrested, and after having been put through a mock trial, was sentenced to die, which the Committee carried out upon the morning of the 11th of June, by putting a noose around the prisoner's neck some distance from the place where they intended to execute him, and having fastened a rope around a cross-beam of an adobe building which stood near the north-western corner of the plaza, a number of men pulled at the rope with such violence that the unfortunate man must have been dead before his body was suspended from the beam. There was an attempt made to stop this brutal exhibition, but it was of no use; the thirst for blood which was created had to be satisfied, and the friends of law and order were pained to witness such an outrageous violation of the rights of even a felon without the forms of law. It was the first time in the nineteenth century that the crime of larceny brought with it the death penalty. It was the commencement of an encroachment upon the constitution and laws which but a year preceding, those same violators of law had formed and guaranteed to abide by; and yet before the ink became dry upon the statute book, they commenced a series of outrages which gave strong proof of an insurbordination which speaks but badly for a capacity for self-government. . . .

The hanging of Jenkins was witnessed by a reporter for the San Francisco *Herald*. His story appeared in the June 11, 1851, edition:

¶ . . . About midnight the bell of the California Engine House commenced to toll and struck upon the ear with awful solemnity in the silence of the night. It was the death knell of the prisoner. His judges had condemned him to be hung. Thus was the silence of the night broken by these melancholy sounds, while the Society within preserved the most impenetrable silence, and those without had but vague rumor to found a judgment upon.

Immediately after sentence of death was passed upon the prisoner, who gave his name as John Jenkins, he was asked if he had anything to say, he replied, "No, I have nothing to say, only I should wish to have a cigar." A cigar was handed him, and he afterwards asked for brandy and water, which was given him. He betrayed not the slightest trepidation or compunction. It is probable he expected to be rescued up to the moment the rope was placed around his neck.

At a quarter before one o'clock, A.M., Mr. Brannan came out and ascended the mound of sand to the east of the Rassette house. The crowd followed and Mr. Brannan addressed them, stating that he was deputed to inform them of the action of the committee. They had taken the evidence against the prisoner, and that evidence was clear as to his guilt of the crime of which he was charged. They had before them the persons who saw him drop the safe into the water. The committee, after hearing the evidence, had decided he should then be punished, and the punishment be death by hanging—the execution to take place on the Plaza in an hour. He called on them as they valued the importance and gravity of the occasion to make no rush or disturbance—The committee would conduct all things to the entire satisfaction of the citizens. They had sent a request to the clergymen to come and assist the unfortunate man in his preparation for death. He asked the people whether the action of the committee was satisfactory?

A tumultuous cry, mingled with cheers, and some "noes" was the response.

Voice in the Crowd,—"Who is the speaker?"

Mr. Brannan was named.

Another Voice,—"Who are the committee?"

This was answered with the cry of "no names! no names!" and the crowd broke up and the greater portion repaired to the Plaza, some remaining behind to see the prisoner taken out. . . .

A clergyman was sent for who remained with the prisoner about three quarters of an hour. A little before two o'clock the committee came from the building, having the prisoner with his arms pinioned, in a ring formed by a rope around which those entrusted with the execution closely clustered to prevent a rescue. Two men were within the ropes having hold of the arms of the condemned.

The procession was formed and the crowd moved slowly up Sansome street to California, thence through Montgomery up to Clay street, thence to the Plaza, where the necessary preparations for the execution had been previously made.

Arrived at the flag-staff, some were climbing up it to arrange the halter, when an earnest cry was raised by some present "for God's sake not to hang him on the liberty pole." The appeal was heard, and those in charge of the execution mounted the beams on the south porch of the adobe—a rope was stretched across between two of the supporters, to the middle of which a block and pulley were fastened, another rope was run through this with a noose at one end. Volunteers were called for to man the other end. The prisoner, who had not spoke a word as far as we could hear during the whole march and dreadful preparations going on before him, was taken by his guard beneath the beam, the noose adjusted around his neck, and in an instant, at ten minutes past two o'clock, he was jerked high into the air and hung dangling from the beam.

He was a very tall, stout, heavy man, and his struggles were violent and continued several minutes. Gradually they ceased, and he swung slowly round and round. Those who were executing him held steadfastly on the end of the rope—keeping it tense and allowing no interference. They held him thus for twenty minutes, when, no doubt, the effort being very great, or the rope stretching, the hanging wretch imperceptibly lowered until his feet hung several inches below the top of the railing. No effort was made to avert his fate. Several hundred persons were on the ground at the time of his execution. When we left at half-past 2 o'clock, he was still hanging, and a proposition had been offered to appoint a committee to hold him there until day-light. He is probably dead at the time of writing this.

Four O'Clock—He is still hanging—dead.

The anonymous author of *Judges and Criminals: Shadows of the Past* describes another hanging. The executions were beginning to assume the grisly carnival atmosphere of the *auto-da-fé* practiced by the Spanish Inquisition centuries earlier, when suspected heretics were burned at the stake.

¶ Upon the 24th of August, another of those violations of law occurred in San Francisco. Two prisoners named Whittaker and McKenzie, who were charged with robbery, and had been taken out of their hands by the constituted authorities were in the County Jail. It was a Sabbath morning, and it was the custom of the prisoners to be admitted to the jail yard, for the purpose of hearing public worship. While thus engaged a band of armed men suddenly surrounded the jail, and having broken it open, captured the two men, and after hurrying them into a carriage, they proceeded with them to a street called Battery. The unfortunate men were conveyed into the upper story of a building, where they were speedily pinioned; ropes were next adjusted out of two beams which protruded over the outside of the building. The noose of these ropes was placed around their necks and they were thrust out of the windows which overlooked the street. The ropes were pulled violently by members from inside of the building, which nearly dashed the brains of the doomed men against the beams of which they were suspended. The crowd which had thronged about the building at this time was immense. The curses, jeers, and imprecations which were heard on every side; the loud laugh and the obscene joke which was cracked in the crowd below; with the evident glee and humor with which the members of the Committee carried out their bloody purpose, will long remain vivid in the memories of those who witnessed those occurrences of blood, those violations of law—those violent outbursts of popular passion. . . .

The First Vigilance Committee had its desired effect upon the lawless element in San Francisco. There was a decrease in the amount of crime. There were fewer robberies, but the disregard for law and order took on more subtle forms. The judiciary of the city continued corrupt, and there were numerous scandals involving bribery of officials and thefts of public monies. Finally, in 1856, the murder of a crusading editor who was not above slandering his adversaries acted as a catalyst that touched off a new wave of vigilante terror. *Judges and Criminals: Shadows of the Past* records what transpired during the tenure of the Second Vigilance Committee:

¶ The disastrous results attending the failure of several of the prominent banking houses of the State of California, the frauds practised upon the citizens of the State by bankrupt traders, which in turn were followed by State peculation, had ruined numbers of persons and produced a want of confidence and an universal panic, which only needed some irritating course to make it produce disorder.

An ex-banker, who had been lately employed by the banking and express firm of Adams & Company—one of the firms which had closed its doors against its depositors, whether with the desire to wreak his vengeance upon his late employers, or for the purpose of benefiting the public by the exposure of their frauds—commenced the publication of a newspaper called the "Evening Bulletin," in the city of San Francisco, a city which had been before this, surfeited by journalism.

Mr. King set out with the new idea of opening his journal to personal assaults upon the reputation of private citizens as well as upon public men, and more particularly to assault upon the attaches of the house of Adams & Company. This method of assault was new, and found a multitude of sympathizers among those classes who had been injured by the numerous failures of the banks. Attack upon one side in the columns of this paper was met by counter defence and assault, until the press, instead of being a medium of intelligence and the faithful guardian of the rights of the people, was suddenly converted into a vehicle for private vengeance. . . .

An attack was made upon the brother of James King, the editor of the Bulletin, in the columns of a Sunday paper, called the "Times," by a correspondent; this paper was published by a man of the name of Casey, who had been elected, some time before, as one of the Supervisors of the city. The correspondent who wrote the article which appeared in the columns of the Times, charged therein that certain violent language which was used in the Bulletin against the United States Marshal of the Northern District of California—McDuffie—was instigated by the fact that King's brother had been a candidate for that office himself, and that was the motive for his attacks upon the Marshal, McDuffie, in the Bulletin. Upon the appearance of the article in the Times newspaper, King's brother demanded of Casey the name of the author, which Casey refused, stating that the author was a married man, and that he would take upon his shoulders the responsibility of the act, if any responsibility was attached to it.

A short time before this event, it appears that some violent enemies of Casey had obtained from New York, some evidence of his early indiscretions; to wit: the judicial record of his conviction, sentence, and subsequent pardon for a crime—gave them to the editor of the Bulletin for insertion, and he proposed to publish the same. In the meantime, Casey got notice of the intention of Mr. King to publish these papers, and was aware of the malicious motives of the men who had thus sought to ruin him in the estimation of every man, in the same manner that they before this time sought to take his life, and imagining that the editor of the Bulletin was somewhat governed by the like spirit of revenge owing to the refusal of Casey to surrender up the name of his correspondent, who had attacked his brother, Thomas S. King, in the columns of the Times, Casey called upon the editor of the Bulletin and requested, nay, begged of him not to publish the record of his past indiscretions, intimating to the editor that he was doing his best to retrieve his character, and to sustain a good name amongst his fellow men. It is said that Mr. King demanded of Mr. Casey, in a boisterous tone, to leave his office, never to present himself there again; at which, Mr. Casey told him that he would defend himself from attacks, and make the editor responsible for them. The Bulletin, shortly after, contained in its columns what purported to be the record of a felony, which it was said Casey had been some years before convicted of.

Upon the appearance of this expose of Casey's character, he determined to attack King in the streets, when he should meet him; and for this purpose he armed himself with a pistol. The opportunity soon presented itself. Mr. King, upon the afternoon of the 14th of May, 1856, had left his office, in Montgomery street, and was passing diagonally across it near the corner of Washington street, while Casey, watching his opportunity for a meeting, observed the former approaching towards him.

Casey called upon Mr. King to defend himself; he did not notice the warning, but, wrapped up in a cloak, passed onwards. In the meantime,

Casey had drawn and cocked his pistol, levelled it at King and fired, the ball taking effect in his left breast. The wounded man continued his way across the street and entered the office of the "Pacific Express," where his wound was attended to. Casey, in the meantime, had surrendered himself to the authorities, and was conveyed to the office of the Chief of Police in the basement of the city hall.

By turning himself in voluntarily, Casey was certain that he would be in safe custody and be acquitted, for he was among friends. It was a feeling shared by a dissolute gambler named Charles Cora, who had shot United States Marshall William Richardson, and was subsequently freed by a split jury that had been tampered with. Both Casey and Cora were wrong. A new Vigilance Committee was formed, and the two were both soon to be tried by a jury of vigilantes in a manner reminiscent of the days of 1851. During the few days the wounded publisher lived, San Francisco was a bedlam. A group in opposition to vigilante justice was organized. Its members were known "law and order men," and were pledged to maintaining the existing judiciary system. They were in the minority, and their efforts were swiftly curtailed by the powerful Committee of Vigilance. The elected authorities petitioned Governor J. Neely Johnson to aid them in suppressing the vigilantes with the use of the state militia and federal troops if necessary. For a time, San Francisco was on the verge of civil war. The Vigilance Committee was victorious without a struggle. It had some 9,000 men under arms, fully trained and organized into military units. On May 19, 1856, King's newspaper, the *Evening Bulletin,* published this description of the surrender of Casey and Cora to the Committee of Vigilance:

¶ Sunday, the 18th of May, 1856, will long be remembered as a day on which, emphatically, the People arose, and, as one man in sentiment and feeling, in defiance of the officers of the Government, aided as these were by innumerable gamblers, shoulder-strikers and ruffians of every description, struck a blow that, it is hoped, will rid our community of all the pests of society which have disgraced the community for the last few years. The execution of the law has reverted back to those from whom the law first emanated. The People have taken the initiatory step to drive from among them that horde of desperadoes and villains of every grade that has so long cursed this city.

Perhaps on no occasion mentioned in history has the uprising of a whole people been made in a better cause, or has it been reached by more unanimity, and quiet, irresistible force, than were manifested yesterday. Early in the morning parties of armed men were seen in every direction, each marching to their distinct rendezvous, appointed by the Vigilance Committee. At ten o'clock the crowd had accumulated in such numbers that a passage in some parts of Sacramento and Sansome streets was absolutely impossible. At eleven o'clock, everything being in readiness, the Committee commenced forming in the streets, and soon after began their march. Each company was in excellent drill, and their evolutions showed plainly that their two days' drill, under the most competent military leaders, had prepared them to meet any emergency. At a quarter past eleven o'clock the march commenced, the main body of the Committee passing along the following streets, viz: up Sacramento to Montgomery, through Montgomery to Pacific, up Pacific to Kearny, through Kearny to the jail in Broadway.

Other companies passed through different streets; and all united in Broadway. When on the ground there were twenty-four companies of one hundred men each, the great majority armed with rifles or muskets and bayonets, and revolvers. Those who had not the larger weapons were armed with small firearms. A piece of artillery, a large brass cannon, was placed in the street, pointing to the door of the jail. The gun was loaded and ready to do execution at an instant's notice. Companies were posted so as to surround the jail, rendering an attack from those in the building absolutely impossible, without the certainty of being at once shot down. On the tops of the neighboring houses, companies of riflemen were placed to clear if necessary the roof of the jail of the armed guard of the prison. After everything was in readiness a committee, consisting of our most influential citizens, waited upon Sheriff Scannell.

They requested the surrender into the hands of the Vigilance Committee of the person of James P. Casey. After some consultation, the jail door was thrown open, and the Committee entered the building. Casey, when apprised of the fact, drew a knife which he had concealed and swore that no irons should be put upon his limbs. Marshall North being present, having mentioned to him the impossibility of a rescue, he submitted to be handcuffed; then, attended by Marshall North and two members of the Committee, he entered a carriage and was driven, attended by about two hundred of the armed citizens, to the headquarters of the Committee on Sacramento street, where he was placed in close confinement, under a sufficient guard of people.

The Special Committee then returned to the jail and demanded the person of Cora, accused of the murder of the late Gen. Richardson. There was some delay at this time, and an hour was consumed before Cora made his appearance. He was then accompanied by those who had taken him in their custody.

Cora was placed in a carriage along with three members of the Committee. Two other carriages followed with the other members, and two companies of the Committee Guards, walked by the side of the carriages. These were followed by the body of the Vigilance Committee. They marched to their Armory and placed Cora with Casey in the custody of an efficient detailed guard, and then adjourned to meet again when called upon, at a moment's notice. . . .

James King of William died from his wound. The next day the columns of his newspaper were heavily ruled in black. On the day of his funeral, the Vigilance Committee made preparations to hang Casey together with Charles Cora. An hour before the pair were placed on an improvised gallows, Cora married his paramour, Belle Cora. A newspaper reported that the unfortunate woman remained with her husband until his final moment. The execution is described in *Judges and Criminals: Shadows of the Past:*

¶ James P. Casey and Charles Cora were hung yesterday, by the Vigilance Committee, at half-past one o'clock, at the Head-Quarters of the Executive Committee, on Sacramento street, near Davis.

Both prisoners had been tried before the Committee, or a portion of it, and had been found guilty. These trials were in secret, and the reporters of the press were refused admittance, and were unable to acquire information from those present, who, as it appears, were sworn to secrecy. A promise had been made to Casey before he was taken, that he should have a fair trial, and be permitted to speak ten minutes. These conditions were strictly observed. Casey was informed on Wednesday afternoon that he had been condemned to be hung. While under charge of the Vigilance Committee, his spirit appeared to be unbroken. When awakening after a sleep, he would frequently strike the floor with his handcuffs and swear fiercely at his fate. On Wednesday afternoon, a young married woman, his cousin, was permitted to visit him. They had some conversation together. He told her that he was to be executed, and she swooned on hearing it. During the evening, the Right Rev. Bishop Allemany attended Casey, who had been educated in the Catholic religion.

During the night he was restless, and passed a portion of the night pacing up and down. He was heard to exclaim, "Oh, my God! has it come to this! Must I be hung like a dog! During the first two or three days I might as well have escaped from the jail as not, and I only stayed there for Scannell's [1] sake." Casey made a will, the particulars of which are unknown to us. He had considerable property to dispose of, estimated by rumor to be worth $30,000. Casey was thin and pale, and his expression was haggard. His face appeared coarse for the want of shaving, no razor having been allowed him for shaving.

✱At eight o'clock yesterday the General Committee was notified that Casey would be executed at half-past one, and ordered to appear under arms. During the morning, preparations were made for the execution. Beams were run out over two of the windows of the Committee room, and platforms about three feet square extending out under each beam. These platforms were supported next the house by hinges, and outside by ropes extending up to the beams. Along the streets for a considerable distance on each side of the place of execution were ranged the Committee, more than 3,000 in number, some on foot with muskets and others on horseback with sabres. No outsiders were permitted to approach within a hundred yards. Beneath the place of execution were several cannon and caissons ready for use if necessary. The houses in the vicinity were covered with spectators, and in the streets were collected probably not less than eight or ten thousand persons.

At a quarter past one o'clock, Casey and Cora were brought out upon the platforms. The former was attended by the Rev. Father Gallagher. The arms of both were pinioned at the elbows, and both wore white caps intended to be drawn over the eyes before the drop fell. Cora walked composedly, and stood stiffly while his companion addressed the crowd. The two were about ten steps apart, Cora occupying the position nearest Davis street. Casey spoke in a very loud and clear voice, as follows:

"Gentlemen, fellow-citizens—I am not guilty of any crime. When I am dead, when I am laid in my grave, let no one dare traduce my character or asperse my memory. Let no man exult over me, or point to my grave as that of an assassin. I only acted as I was taught—according to my early education—to avenge an insult. Let not the *Alta,* the *Chronicle,* and the *Globe,* persecute my memory; let them no more proclaim me a murderer to the world. Let them not insult me after death. I have an aged mother in the Atlantic States, and I hope she will never hear how I died. I trust she will never know that I am executed on a charge of murder. I am not guilty of any such crime."

[1] Scannell was the sheriff, and Casey's jailkeeper.

About this time Father Gallagher touched Casey and said, "Pray to God to pardon your crime; pray God to save your soul."

Casey after a moment's hesitation, spoke again:

"Oh, God, pardon and forgive me. Oh, my mother! my mother! I hope she will never hear of this. Oh, God! have mercy on my mother; comfort her in her affliction. Oh, God! have mercy on my soul! Oh, my God! my God! I am not guilty of murder—I did not intend to commit murder."

Some one here said, "It is not necessary to repeat that again." Casey was confused at this, and mentioning the name of his mother again in a low tone of voice, he drew back. As he did so, the drop beneath Cora was withdrawn, and his body fell a distance of about five feet. He did not move; his neck was no doubt broken by the shock, and there was one soul less in the land of the living. The rope was adjusted around Casey's neck, and he weakened in the knees so that a committee man had to support him. He was placed on the platform; a moment afterwards it fell beneath him. He struggled a little, but at the end of about three minutes he ceased to move, and he too was dead.

The bodies continued to hang for nearly an hour as they were executed. Although a great many persons were in sight at the time, awaiting the climax of the tragedy, there were many others scattered about town who supposed that the affair would be postponed. The news spread rapidly through the city, and ten minutes after the death of Casey, great numbers of men were to be seen rushing down Clay and Washington and Commercial streets, as though it were a matter of life and death to get a sight of the spectacle. At half-past two o'clock, the Coroner, having been notified, sent his clerk with a wagon and removed the bodies.

An interesting essay exploring Vigilante justice appeared in *A History of the Bench and Bar of California*. John G. Jury pictures what took place in some of the northern California mining communities. Here justice was meted out at an even swifter pace than at San Francisco, and the manner in which executions were performed reflected greater brutality: ·

¶ Lynch law appears to be rooted in the theory of the guilt of the accused from the time of his arrest. That most salutary rule of law that the defendant is presumed to be innocent until the contrary is proved, is subverted, and the door is thereby thrown open to prejudice, unfairness and error. When a hearing is given the accused by a lynching party it is conducted in the most perfunctory manner, and without regard for those principles of evidence founded in justice, and designed to clear the pathway to truth. The character of the punishment to be inflicted is left to the spontaneous and often cruel ingenuity of the crowd. . . .

One of the first instances of the application of lynch law in California was in proceedings taken in January, 1849, from which Hangtown, now Placerville, derived the former name. The facts appear to be about as follows: Five men had been caught in the act of attempted robbery and larceny. The feeling of the miners ran high, as it generally did in cases of robbery, larceny and murder. No court, it seems, was organized in the town, hence, a provisional judge and jury were called to try the case. The proceedings were conducted in an orderly manner and the sentence rendered that the prisoners should be given thirty-nine lashes each. Hardly had the sentence been executed before other charges were presented against three of the men for robbery and attempt to murder, committed on the Stanislaus River in the previous autumn. A jury of all the miners in camp, about two hundred in number, heard the evidence and sentenced the unhappy prisoners to be hanged. Only one man seems to have protested against the sentence, but his protests were quieted under threats of death. The defendants suffered the penalty thus imposed upon them. The man who strenuously protested against the execution was Lieut. E. G. Buffum. The attitude of the miners toward Lieut. Buffum was prompted by anger and impatience, due perhaps to the fact that in their view, the prisoners had as fair a trial as the circumstances would warrant, and when the sentence was pronounced they would brook no delay. . . .

Ford's Bar, on the middle fork of the American River, had, as early as May, 1849, acquired a reputation of being the worst place on the river. In the month indicated a drunken row between two of the miners occurred at this place. One of the combatants was struck so violently with a crowbar that he fell into the stream. The other followed, and the two infuriated men fought in the water. The fight almost resulted in a general combat between the friends of both parties. Better judgment prevailed, and after calm was restored, seeing that recurrence of such disgraceful scenes should be prevented, the men called a meeting and voluntarily agreed upon a few simple rules calculated to secure the peace and quiet of the camp. The code of laws thus improvised provided for the trial of certain specified offenses by a jury consisting of three persons. It is amusing to read the first application of the law, thus devised, to the case of a tinker who had been arrested for assaulting a party with a junk bottle. His antagonist retaliated by drawing a knife and with it inflicting several severe cuts and gashes upon the tinker. Both men were arrested and taken before Alcalde Graham, who evidently was the leading spirit in the administration of justice in the camp. The tinker, although the offending party, was acquitted "because there was no law against using a bottle as a weapon," while his antagonist was convicted of unlawfully drawing a knife, an offense which had been expressly legislated upon in their simple code of laws. . . .

The feverish haste exhibited at lynch law proceedings may be illustrated by a case which occurred in Columbia, Tuolumne County, on Wednesday, October 10th, 1855. A man named John H. Smith became involved in a quarrel with the proprietress of a saloon, during which quarrel he was fatally shot by the husband of the woman, who, on coming from an adjoining room into the barroom where the quarrel was going on, fired upon and killed Smith. John S. Barclay was the name of the murderer. The direction given to the trial and other events which followed was determined principally by the attitude of James W. Coffroth, a popular man in the camps, who had just been elected to the State senate. Coffroth, in his regard for his deceased friend, allowed his passions to dominate. He vehemently demanded that vengeance be meted out to Barclay for the crime. The mob was stirred to frenzy by Coffroth. No thought, however, was entertained of visiting punishment upon the offender without a show at least of fairness. The crowd gathered about the jail, and a judge, marshall and jury of twelve persons were impressed into service. The iron doors were then forced open and Barclay, who had hoped to make his escape through the crowd, was seized and carried off by the excited people amid cries and imprecations. In the impromptu trial, Coffroth acted as the prosecuting attorney, and John Oxley, a man of firm and noble purposes, defended the prisoner. Coffroth was insistent upon revenge, and in his shrewd way invoked in behalf of the people, the law quoted at the head of this paper: "An eye for an eye; a tooth for a tooth; a life for a life." The text, "Whoso sheddeth man's blood, by man shall his blood be shed," was also used to lend strength and the semblance of sanctity to his case. Despite the protests of Oxley and his appeals to the people asking them to reflect on what they were about to do, amid cries for the life of the prisoner, Barclay was told to prepare himself for the execution which awaited him according to the sentence. The sheriff of the county, J. M. Stewart, made an ineffectual attempt to rescue the prisoner, but was beaten back and hustled away from the scene. While the sheriff was thus being fought off the prisoner was hanged. His arms were left unpinioned. His convulsive clutching at the rope while hanging in mid-air, were greeted with derisive cries and yells from those who looked on. This in brief is the story of one of the most barbarous cases in the annals of lynch law.[2]

Violence in California during this period was not confined to the methods of the vigilantes. It extended to the body politic. The ward boss, the party machine, and corruption of officeholders were just a few of the evils in California government during the first decade of American occupation. Elections were conducted by fraudulent methods. Ballot-box stuffing continued to be the acceptable method for ensuring victory at the polls. The voter was expected to endorse the straight ticket of his party's choice. Failure to comply generally brought prompt retribution. Hubert Howe Bancroft, the California historian, is not noted for injecting humor into the numerous volumes he wrote. Pondering elections that took place in the 1850's he observed: "Human faces appeared the next day which had been mashed into the shape of a squeezed orange." A journal of the period complained:

¶ On election day, a lawless horde of brawling scamps are let loose to browbeat, to bully, to put in fraudulent votes and to take the ballot box, if necessary, in order to suppress anything like legitimate sentiment, and in this way are chosen delegates to a convention that pretends to give us Congressmen and state officers. . . .

Although John C. Frémont had been elected as a United States senator by the first state legislature, he never became a significant figure in California politics, as did his fellow senator, William M. Gwin. Frémont became the first presidential candidate of the newly organized Republican party in 1856, when he polled 1,341,000 votes, only to be defeated by James Buchanan. Later, he was to become a liability to the Lincoln administration during the Civil War, first as an inept general, who had to be relieved of his command. When Lincoln was up for reelection in 1864, the famed Pathfinder challenged the popularity of the President as a candidate of the radicals. This bid for the nation's highest office ended like everything else in Frémont's later life, and proved a failure.

Democrat William M. Gwin was the complete opposite. He was a

[2] John G. Jury, *A History of the Bench and Bar of California,* edited by Oscar T. Shuck (San Francisco: The Occident Printing House, 1888).

dedicated politician—dedicated not necessarily to the service of the electorate, but certainly to the advancement of his own interests and those of his friends, for Gwin was a favorite at Washington, particularly with President Buchanan. Following the President's inauguration, on March 4, 1857, Gwin was awarded the privilege of dispensing federal patronage in California, a powerful weapon for controlling a political machine, and this he did with consummate skill. Gwin had arrived in California with the express intent of becoming a United States senator. There is ample evidence that he regarded the office as his God-given due, and considered the rank and file of the electorate fortunate to have a man of his brilliance representing their interests. He remained at heart a Southerner, and as such was proslavery in a period when antagonism toward this social evil was reaching growing proportions.

The senator's political leadership was challenged by David C. Broderick, a brawling young Irishman who arrived in San Francisco in 1849, attracted by the discovery of gold. Digging for the metal was not to his liking, but he opened an assay office and began making gold slugs having values ranging from four to eight dollars. These coins proved highly popular with the early residents of San Francisco, and are still prized by collectors. Broderick had some training in New York politics as a Tammany Democrat. He organized a fire company in San Francisco patterned after one he had served as foreman in New York. This was at a time when the Bay city suffered from several devastating fires. It also served as the nucleus for his political organization, which soon emerged as a major force in state politics.

Broderick was elected to the state legislature in 1850, and at the age of thirty-one he was serving as president of the state senate. He was vigorously opposed to slavery. In 1854, his position was so strong in the legislature that he launched a drive to unseat Gwin in the United States Senate, although the scheduled selection of a man to fill this office wasn't to take place for some time. Gwin's forces were able to defeat this proposal by a slim margin. One of Gwin's most powerful allies at a convention held at Sacramento was David S. Terry, Chief Justice of the California Supreme Court, who headed the opposition against Broderick. Terry was a firebrand who had once been in trouble with the San Francisco Vigilance Committee in 1856, when he stabbed one of their members. Only his high office saved him from the gallows. In 1857, Broderick managed to have himself elected to the United States Senate. Gwin also requalified, but only after he conceded Broderick's power in California. In a document later to be known as "the scarlet letter," Gwin offered Broderick control of federal patronage in payment for his political support. The junior senator accepted, and rallied enough legislative votes to reelect Gwin. The selection of the two United States senators was not decided by popular election at this time.

After reaching Washington, Broderick discovered that he had been undermined. President Buchanan disliked him intensely, as he was well aware that Broderick opposed his view on Kansas, where a bitter argument raged as to whether the Territory would be admitted to the Union as a slave state. Representatives meeting there at Lecompton who were proslavery enacted a law that called for a state constitutional convention that would be thoroughly in accord with their views. The decision of whether slaves were to be admitted to Kansas was not to be left to the voters. The rigged convention would merely forward a request to Congress that Kansas be admitted as a slave state. A majority of Kansas settlers were against the measure. Nevertheless, the President favored the Lecompton constitution. Broderick hated slavery, and was outspoken. Buchanan made certain he had nothing to say about how federal patronage would be dispensed in California, despite Gwin's written promise. Broderick returned to California in 1859 to discover his political hold was slipping. He had been unable to deliver government posts to those who had supported him. The bitter senator retaliated by launching a vitriolic campaign against Gwin. His opponent had his supporters, mainly the Chief Justice. Judge Terry had denounced Broderick before the Democratic state convention held at Sacramento in 1859 to discuss the Lecompton issue.

"Broderick is an arch-traitor," Terry thundered. "The men who follow him are personal chattels of a single individual who they are ashamed of. They belong heart, body, and breeches to David C. Broderick. . . ."[3]

Senator Broderick replied caustically to this speech in a conversation with D. W. Perley, an attorney and friend of Gwin. He stated that he had once called Terry the only honest man on the Supreme Court bench. This was at a time when Terry had been incarcerated by the

[3] Ben C. Truman, *The Field of Honor* (New York: Fords, Howard & Hulbert, 1884).

Vigilance Committee for stabbing one of their officers. Further, Broderick informed the attorney that he had contributed two hundred dollars to a San Francisco newspaper to defend the Chief Justice in its columns. Now, however, he was retracting his statement about Judge Terry being honest. Perley was infuriated. He challenged Broderick on the spot. The senator turned him down with the curt reply that he fought only with gentlemen of his own position in society. The angered Perley hurried to Judge Terry. Correspondence was exchanged between the Chief Justice and Broderick, and a duel was arranged. The two adversaries, accompanied by their seconds, met on a cold September morning at Lake Merced in San Mateo County. What took place is reported in the Sacramento *Democratic Standard* of September 14, 1859:

¶ THE DUEL

Our telegraphic reporter has furnished us with a detailed account of the circumstances of the late duel, from which we make the following extracts. After detailing the circumstances of meeting, with which our readers are already familiar, he goes on to say:

As the second stepped back and Mr. Coulton gave the word, the principals raised their pistols, which they had held pointed to the ground. On the rise, Mr. Broderick's weapon went off, the ball striking the ground a few feet short of his opponent. The next instant, Terry, who had fully raised his weapon, discharged it. Mr. Broderick suddenly turned a few inches, and was seen to brace himself for a moment, then gradually lowered himself down to a reclining position on the ground, and then fell at full length. He did not speak a word during this time.

While Mr. Broderick thus fell, still clasping his pistol, Judge Terry stood with his arms folded, till his seconds advanced, and with them he left the field unharmed.

It is supposed that he has gone to some unknown place to await the news of the result of the shot.

The surgeons who were present, Drs. Loehr, Hammond and Aylett, together with Broderick's seconds, advanced immediately upon his fall, and tearing off his coat, examined the wound, which was found to be in the breast. The ball entered near the right nipple, passed across the front part of the body, and lodged in the left side. It seems to have entered the cavity of the chest, or, at least, scored and cut the breast bone; and, though subsequently extracted, has produced a wound which, it is supposed, will prove fatal.

A mattress litter was placed in an express wagon, and Mr. Broderick was conveyed, at his own request, around the western part of the city, to the residence of Mr. Haskell, near Fort Point. While coming in he sat up a portion of the way, and evidently did his utmost to conceal the great pain which the wound caused him; he was fully conscious, and complained of the great weight of 1,000 pounds, as he expressed it, weighing upon his breast. This feeling was caused by the internal hemorrhage, which had become very great, and dissolution was expected to take place every few moments. Drs. Loehr, Sawyer and Rowell were present and afforded all the aid in their power, but Mr. Broderick continued to sink, and became weaker apparently with every breath. He is surrounded by a number of his friends. He is unable to write, both arms being paralyzed. His surgeons inform us that his recovery would be a miracle, and it would seem impossible for him to survive many hours. Not more than half a dozen personal friends of Mr. Broderick were at the meeting, both principals requesting that the affair might be conducted as privately as possible.

A profound sensation pervades the community. It is understood that Judge Terry, immediately after his antagonist had fallen, started for his home in Sacramento.

The above are all the particulars that have been made public.

Mr. Broderick's Condition—Latest—A telegraph dispatch was received by a friend of Mr. Broderick, (stopping at the Union Hotel,) last evening, at half-past nine o'clock, which stated that the bullet had been extracted from Mr. Broderick's wound; that he was at that time sleeping; and that strong hopes were entertained of his recovery.

David Broderick did not survive his wound. He died on September 16, 1859, and was widely mourned throughout the state. Terry, who had resigned his office before fighting the duel, came under considerable fire. There is some evidence that he had previously practiced with the pistols used by the two adversaries. The one which Broderick was handed had a hair-trigger causing the gun to discharge prematurely. Normally a good shot; on the morning of the encounter Broderick was suffering from fatigue caused by overwork, and was visibly nervous.

Terry met his death in a similar violent manner some thirty years later, when he assaulted a jurist on a train. A marshal accompanying the judge shot him down. Senator Gwin's popularity declined rapidly throughout the state following Broderick's death. The Democratic party was now hopelessly divided, permitting the new Republican organization to make inroads in California. In the national election of 1860, the state's four electoral votes went to Abraham Lincoln. The Civil War soon followed, and California was pledged to defend the Union. The disgusted Gwin and some of his followers departed for the South to offer their services to the Confederacy.

The Indians, too, were the victims of violence. As thousands of settlers moved into California during the years following the Gold Rush, it was inevitable that there should be conflict between the Americans and the Indian inhabitants. Many of the new residents were of the belief that the best method for dealing with the Indian problem was to eliminate it by decimating the tribes. In a more enlightened era we would call this genocide, or to express it with greater candor: mass murder. One of the most merciless slaughters took place on February 26, 1860 near the small town of Arcata, then called Union, which is located on the northern California coast near the Oregon boundary.

For some time, Indians living in the nearby mountains had been stealing livestock from settlers in the region. The Americans retaliated, but instead of searching out the guilty Indians, they selected as objects of their vengeance a harmless tribe of Wiyot Indians who had a colony on Gunther Island in Humboldt Bay. It had been rumored that the Wiyots had been supplying arms and ammunition to the renegade Indians living in the mountains. Night riders gathered near Arcata. Boats were obtained and the men rowed toward Gunther Island. Landing, they found many of the males absent, apparently away on a hunting or fishing expedition. The Indians discovered in their huts were mostly women and children. The ranchers began their grisly work.

News of the tragedy reached Arcata the following day. Among those gathering on the shore to watch the dead being removed from canoes was the young assistant editor of the *Northern Californian*, a four-page weekly founded in 1858. The newspaperman was only twenty-four, but he had already demonstrated his talent as a writer. Two years earlier he had begun his career as a printer's devil, but had been quickly promoted from the back shop to his editorial post. The publisher was away on a business trip, so the responsibility for determining what news stories were to appear in the next edition of the *Northern Californian* was the assistant's. Quickly, he made his decision, returning to the newspaper's office, where he wrote an editorial that shocked the community when it was published on February 29, 1860:

¶ INDISCRIMINATE MASSACRE OF INDIANS
WOMEN AND CHILDREN BUTCHERED

Our Indian troubles have reached a crisis. Today we record acts of Indian aggression and white retaliation. It is a humiliating fact that the parties who may be supposed to represent white civilization have committed the greater barbarity. But before we review the causes that have led to this crowning act of reckless desperation, let us remind the public at a distance from this savage-ridden district, that the secrecy of this indiscriminate massacre is an evidence of its disavowal and detestation by the community. The perpetrators are yet unknown.

The friendly Indians about the bay have been charged with conveying arms and ammunition to the mountain tribes, and receiving slaughtered beef as a reward. A class of hard-working men who derive their subsistence by cattle raising have been the greatest sufferers, and if in the blind fury of retaliation they spare neither age or sex, though they cannot be excused, a part of the blame should fall upon that government which places the responsibility of self defense on the injured party. . . .

If the deed was committed by responsible parties, we will give place to any argument that may be offered in justification. But we can conceive of no palliation for women and child slaughter. We can conceive of no wrong that a babe's blood can atone for . . . What amount of suffering it takes to make a man a babe-killer, is a question for future moralists. What will justify it, should be a question of present law. . . . And what assistance can be expected from a legislature already perplexed with doubts and suspicion, in the face of the bloody record we today publish.

. . . when the facts were generally known, it appeared that out of some 60 or 70 killed on the Island, at least 50 or 60 were women and children. Neither age or sex had been spared. Little children and old women were mercilessly stabbed and their skulls crushed with axes. When the bodies were landed at Union, a more shocking and revolting spectacle never was exhibited to the eyes of a Christian and civilized people. Old women wrinkled and decrepit lay weltering in blood, their brains dashed out and dabbled with their long gray hair. Infants scarce a span long, with their faces cloven with hatchets and their bodies ghastly with wounds. We gathered from the survivors that four or five white men attacked the ranches at about four o'clock in the morning, which statement is corroborated by people at Eureka who heard pistol shots at about the same time, although no knowledge of the attack was public. With the Indians who lived on the Island, some thirty from the mouth of Mad River were staying, having attended a dance the evening previous. They were all killed with the exception of some few who hid themselves during the massacre. No resistance was made, it is said, to the butchers who did the work, but as they ran or huddled together for protection like sheep, they were struck down with hatchets. Very little shooting was done, most of the bodies having wounds about the head. The bucks were mostly absent, which accounts for the predominance of female victims.

On Monday we received a statement from our Senior,[4] at Eureka en route for San Francisco. He says that about nine o'clock he visited the Island, and there a horrible scene was presented. The bodies of 36 women and children, recently killed, lay in and near the several ranches. They were of all ages from the child of but two or three years to the old skeleton squaw. From appearance most of them must have been killed with axes or hatchets—as the heads and bodies of many were gashed, as with such an instrument. It was a sickening and pitiful sight. Some five or six were still alive and one old woman was able to talk, though dreadfully wounded. Dr. Lee visited them and dressed the wounds of those alive. . . .

It is not generally known that more than three bucks were killed, though it is supposed there must have been 15 or 20. It is thought that the bodies of the men were taken away by Indians early this morning as four canoes were seen to leave the Island.

On the beach south of the entrance it is reported that from 30 to 50 were killed. It is also reported, that at Bucksport, all were killed that were there. I passed in sight of them about 11 o'clock and saw the ranches on fire. It is also said that the same has been done at the several ranches on Eel River.

No one seems to know who was engaged in this slaughter, but is supposed to have been men who have suffered from depredations so long on the Eel River and vicinity.

Indian Island is scarcely one mile from Eureka, the County seat of Humboldt County. With the exception of the conjectures that the Indians on this Island offer aid and assistance to mountain Indians, they are peaceful and industrious, and seem to have perfect faith in the good will of the whites. Many of them are familiar to our citizens. "Bill," of Mad

---

[4] The reference here is to Col. S. G. Whipple, co-owner of the newspaper.

River, a well known and intelligent fellow, has proven a faithful ally to the white men on several occasions and has had his wife, mother, sister, two brothers, and two little children cruelly butchered by men of that race whom he had learned to respect and esteem.

Reaction to the editorial in Arcata and surrounding towns was clearly against the newspaper's condemnation of the white man's inhumanity toward the Indians. There were some who advocated lynching the editor and destroying the *Northern Californian*'s printing plant. Friends warned the writer of the editorial that he had best leave Arcata as quickly as possible. Francis Bret Harte packed his bags and departed for San Francisco. Here he was to become a distinguished man of letters. He contributed articles and stories to various publications during the years that followed. His first real opportunity came when Anto Roman, a San Francisco bookseller, founded the *Overland Monthly,* an excellent literary magazine from the time of its first issue. Harte was named editor. He began writing the stories and poems that made him famous as they appeared in subsequent issues of the *Overland*—"The Luck of Roaring Camp," "Tennessee's Partner," and "The Heathen Chinee," were among those which would be reprinted in numerous anthologies.

Harte's second story to appear in the magazine, "The Outcasts of Poker Flat," reveals his compassion for the underdog. The protagonist is John Oakhurst, a professional gambler who is banished with several others from a mining community in the Sierras. Among the expatriates expelled by an indignant community preoccupied with self-righteousness are two prostitutes and the town drunkard, who steals their horses and deserts them. Trapped in a blizzard and lacking provisions, the women perish in the snow, while Oakhurst is attempting to break through the mountains for aid.

The nearest place he can go for help is the one they had been ordered to leave—Poker Flat. They had been told never to return under penalty of death. Oakhurst shoots himself, first pinning his epitaph to a pine tree with a bowie knife. It is written on a card from his deck—the deuce of clubs, and in its simplicity is a moving protest against intolerance. Perhaps Bret Harte recalled another community, where a number of citizens had decided that among them were those who were also undesirable neighbors.

20

OVERLAND MAIL
AND THE PONY EXPRESS

While irate citizens were hanging the lawless element of the new state, there were those who were working to further the economic growth of California. Some of the most industrious were in Washington, where congressional approval was needed to further some of the more ambitious projects. The most pressing was a railroad that would unite the nation, but although several surveys had been made, the actual construction was not to begin until the Civil War period, when its need became a military necessity for the North. In 1857, John Butterfield, one of the founders of the American Express Company, presented a plan for establishing a stage route to San Francisco. To many, this seemed like an impossible undertaking, but Butterfield was a determined man. The first step was to secure a federal contract to carry the mail. This he and an associate accomplished, obtaining a $600,000 annual subsidy, which was to run for six years. There was one stipulation. The company had to be in operation within a year.

Butterfield immediately began the task of constructing way stations, buying wagons, horses, mules, and other equipment to stock his line, which stretched for more than 2,700 miles across the wilderness from St. Louis to San Francisco. In addition to St. Louis, then the western-most extension of the railroad coming from the East, Memphis was also designated as a major terminal for the line. That the postmaster general lived in that city may have had some influence on this choice.

When the overland stage left St. Louis on September 16, 1858, for its first western trip across the continent, one of the passengers was Waterman L. Ormsby, Jr., correspondent for the New York *Herald*. Ormsby's articles were brought to light through the curiosity of Lyle H. Wright, head of the reference department of the Huntington Library. In a collection of early newspapers acquired by the library, he discovered one of the original timetables published by the Butterfield company. One of Ormsby's stories also caught his eye, and he began a long search to assemble all of the reporter's articles. These he found in the Library of Congress. The complete series was finally published in book form.[1] It is from this volume that excerpts from Ormsby's account of his travels are taken. The reporter gave this description of the advance planning necessary to ready the line for operation:

¶ An exploring party had been sent over the road to lay out the details of the line, consuming nearly eight months time; that during this time over 100 wagons had to be built, nearly 1500 horses and mules bought and stationed, corrals and stations built and men employed. . . .

Leaving St. Louis, the stage traveled to Fort Smith, Arkansas, then through Indian territory—now Oklahoma, Texas, New Mexico, and Arizona. At Fort Yuma, on the Colorado River, the stagecoach crossed into California:

¶ We now came to a patch of wood, through which the road was tortuous and stony. But our driver's ambition to make good time overcame his caution and away we went, bounding over the stones at a fearful rate. . . .

[1] Waterman L. Ormsby, *The Butterfield Overland Mail*, edited by Lyle H. Wright and Josephine M. Bynum (San Marino, Calif., The Huntington Library, 1960).

This excessive rate of speed was at its best around five miles per hour. Meals were furnished at stations along the way, but the menu was limited. At one stop, the newspaperman noted:

¶ Breakfast was served on the bottom of a candle box. . . . The edible, for there was but one—consisted of a kind of shortcake, baked on the coals, each man breaking off his "chunk" and plastering on butter, which is a rare luxury between Red River and the Rio Grande—at least on this route at present. . . .

The first trip was peaceful, but violence had preceded the stage. Three employees had been murdered by bandits at one of the way stations seventy-five miles from Tucson, called Dragoon Springs:

¶ It appears that the bandits waited until the men were asleep, and then attacked them with axes, killing the three almost instantly. They then attacked a fourth man, Silas B. St. John, who defended himself with his pistol, though severely wounded, and drove them off. . . .

St. John lost an arm, but recovered. The first stagecoach was late for another meeting, which might have marked the end of the journey and curtailed Ormsby's literary career. The party had paused briefly for a change of horses at a remote stopover in the Arizona wastelands, appropriately named Soldier's Farewell. Moving across the plain to the next station, Stein's Peak, Ormsby reported:

¶ We had learned on our way that this station was a favorite camping ground for the Apache Indians, and that but a few days before a band of 250, headed by Chief Mangas, had gone to the station and demanded the gift of 20 sacks of corn, telling the men they had better hurry it up d———d quick. . . .

The Apache chief was Mangas Coloradas, the dreaded Red Sleeves, whose hand was raised against all white men.

Los Angeles was almost bypassed in planning the route, for originally it was not intended to be a stopover. Butterfield at first had selected San Bernardino as a station, and from there the stage would proceed to San Francisco. At the last moment it was decided that the desert was too hazardous and the road too difficult to follow. The route was diverted into San Diego County, where it paused at

Warner's Ranch near Escondido before coming on to Los Angeles. From Warner's the road passed through the southwestern corner of San Bernardino County. Here the *Herald* correspondent described the land as rich and capable of producing anything, but it was used principally for grazing. After leaving the extensive Chino ranch, the stagecoach entered El Monte, "a beautiful little town which is ranged along the road for nearly five miles, and is composed of a series of neat looking houses built of wood, and considerable cultivated land."

What Ormsby wasn't aware of was that the Monte, as it was called, was a haven for some of the most desperate criminals in southern California. During the Civil War it became a gathering place for Confederate sympathizers. The Butterfield Stage reached Los Angeles, drawing up before a livery stable at Second and Spring streets, now the site of the Mirror Building in Times Mirror Square. Regarding Los Angeles, Ormsby wrote in his notebook:

¶ Los Angeles city is about twenty-seven miles from the coast, on the San Pedro River. It contains about 6,000 inhabitants, and has a number of fine buildings. The people are mostly Mexicans, Spanish, and Indians, but since the acquisition of the state by the United States, the Americans have been increasing in numbers. There is a weekly paper published there, and the town, as I passed through it, looked thrifty and business-like. On the outskirts of the city are vineyards, covering many acres and producing the most luscious grapes, from which the wines are made which have a world-wide celebrity. Celebrated sparkling wines are made here. The fruits of the neighborhood are of the largest kind. I saw some pears which would take premiums at our agricultural fairs. Their flavor was, however, inferior to the Bartlett pear.

We arrived at Los Angeles in five days and four hours from Tucson, making nearly six miles an hour on the average, in spite of the sandy desert and craggy hills. As we entered the town we met the sixth mail from San Francisco, which left on Monday, October 4, with two through passengers. We stopped only long enough to change coaches, and started on our way again. . . .

The arrival of the Butterfield Stage for the first time was duly noted in the weekly edition of the Los Angeles *Star,* which came out on October 9, 1858:

¶ ARRIVAL OF THE MAIL FROM MEMPHIS
AHEAD OF THE TIME
THROUGH IN TWENTY-ONE DAYS
HUNDRED GUNS FOR THE OVERLAND MAIL

On Thursday at 1 o'clock P.M. the first through stage of the Overland Mail Company arrived here, from Memphis in twenty one days. Ormsby, a reporter of the New York *Herald,* was the only passenger. He speaks in the highest terms of the road and all the appointments. He left New York on the 10th and St. Louis on the 16th; he had private dispatches to the 17 ult. There was no mail for this city. No papers received by this arrival. No inconvenience was felt from the heat during the journey. Passengers easily became accustomed to sleeping on the stages, and are subject to no fatigue for want of sleep. . . . The prescribed time for running is 26 days, but the first trip will be made in 24 days, being two days less than schedule time. Mr. Ormsby is of the opinion that the trip can be made in twenty days.

The joyful and important event of the arrival of the first through stage from Memphis was hailed with great satisfaction by our citizens, and a salute of a hundred guns was fired, in honor of the event, during the afternoon.

The stage navigated the steep trail which is today called the Ridge Route leading from Los Angeles to Bakersfield. Motorists who now drive along a modern freeway pass Fort Tejon, which is a state monument. It once served as a stopover for the Butterfield mail, after the coach left the San Fernando Mission. From Fort Tejon, it proceeded down into the great San Joaquin Valley. At Gilroy, near San Jose, and on the final leg to San Francisco, Ormsby recorded the following conversation as the villagers gathered around the stage, asking numerous questions:

¶ Have you got the States mail?
  What is the news from the States?
  Have you any through passengers?
  Only the correspondent of the *Herald.*
  Why then, we shall hear all about it.
  How did you like your trip, sir?
  Very well.
  How did you manage to sleep?

What, slept in the wagons?

Did you ride day and night?

Well, I declare, I should think you would be tired.

Have plenty to eat?

What, beans and jerked beef? . . .[2]

The arrival at San Francisco was the highlight of the trip, and this is Ormsby's colorful account of the final dash into the Bay City:

¶ It was just after sunrise that the city of San Francisco hove in sight over the hills, and never did the night traveller approach a distant light, or the lonely mariner descry a sail, with more joy than did I the city of San Francisco on the morning of Sunday, October 10. As we neared the city we met milkmen and pleasure seekers taking their morning rides, looking on with wonderment as we rattled along at a tearing pace.

Soon we struck the pavements, and with a whip, crack, and bound, shot through the streets to our destination, to the great consternation of everything in the way and the no little surprise of everybody. Swiftly we whirled up one street and down another, and round the corners, until finally we drew up at the stage office in front of the Plaza, our driver giving a shrill blast of his horn and a flourish of triumph for the arrival of the first overland mail in San Francisco from St. Louis. But our work was not yet done. The mails must be delivered, and in a jiffy we were at the post office door, blowing the horn, howling and shouting for somebody to come and take the overland mail.

I thought nobody was ever going to come—the minutes seemed days—but the delay made it even time, and as the man took the mail bags from the coach, at half-past seven A.M. on Sunday, October 10, it was just twenty-three days, twenty-three hours and a half from the time that John Butterfield, the president of the company, took the bags as the [railroad] cars moved from St. Louis at 8 A.M. on Thursday, 16th of September, 1858. And I had the satisfaction of knowing that the correspondent of the New York *Herald* had kept his promise and gone through with the first mail—the sole passenger and the only one who had ever made the trip across the plains in less than fifty days. . . .

The excitement that swept San Francisco over the arrival of the Butterfield Stage spread to every corner of the state. At the capital, the Sacramento *Union* published the following article on October 12, 1858, datelined San Francisco:

[2] Ormsby, *The Butterfield Overland Mail.*

¶ There is great enthusiasm in town about the Overland Mail. A national salute was fired this afternoon. Musical Hall is densely crowded this evening pursuant to a call, to take measures for celebrating the event. W. L. Ormsby, special correspondent of the New York *Herald,* addressed the assembly, giving a favorable description of the route. . . .

A San Francisco newspaper commented on the increased speed with which it would be able to furnish worldwide news to its readers by the use of the Butterfield Overland Mail:

¶ The magnitude of the work is better exhibited in the fact that we shall be within considerably less than thirty days of Europe. . . . our news items of events transpiring at New York, for instance, on one day, will be accompanied by those which transpired on the previous day in England and on the Continent,[3] all of which, though necessarily condensed into as brief a space as possible, will serve to keep the public constantly posted as to the news transpiring on the other side of the Rocky Mountains, instead of being compelled to take on board an immense load at one sitting after the arrival of each steamer, of what has taken place during the interval of a fortnight . . .[4]

The parting of that Union, when the country was divided by the Civil War, marked the end of the Butterfield line. Confederates streaming up the Rio Grande overran Arizona and New Mexico territories. The route had to be abandoned. Following the war, railroads took its place. For newspaperman Ormsby, the great adventure was over. He returned to New York by ship. As he sailed through the Golden Gate, recalling his exciting race across the continent, he no doubt dreamed of a future time when better roads and improved service would shorten the Butterfield Stage's time schedule. They would be making the 2,700-mile journey in twenty days. That would be a speed record to achieve.

*   *   *

The need to establish a faster system of mail communication between East and West during the latter part of the 1850's became urgent as

[3] Messages were now being transmitted by telegraph between London and New York over the newly laid Atlantic Cable.

[4] *The San Francisco Weekly Alta California,* October 16, 1858.

the economic and political importance of the new state became more evident. While the Butterfield Stage was still operating successfully with several overland mail systems, it was a slow means of carrying mail. For those who relied upon ships to transport their correspondence, the service was far from satisfactory. The first regular mail to reach California by this means from the Atlantic seaboard arrived in 1849, carried by a vessel from New York to Panama. From there it was packed by mules and horses across the jungle to the Pacific coast, where it remained in a storehouse before a passing ship delivered it to San Francisco. This sometimes resulted in a letter taking as long as three months to reach its destination. Even with the completion of a rail line across Panama in 1855 to facilitate the transferring of mail and passengers from Atlantic to Pacific steamers, the best service between New York and California averaged a month.

An answer to the problem of how to speed delivery appeared with the inauguration of the Pony Express. The man responsible for this novel and daring experiment was William H. Russell, owner of a San Francisco freighting firm. With the aid of two partners, he raised sufficient funds to underwrite the venture. Russell also had the aid of Senator Gwin of California. They laid out an elaborate courier system that would run between St. Joseph, Missouri, and Sacramento, a distance of 1,980 miles. Russell mapped a network of nearly two hundred stations, just as Butterfield had done. These were to be staffed with men who were used to the wilderness. Five hundred of the best horses were obtained, and then there were the riders to be found. Eighty were employed. Those selected were all young, light, and familiar with the rough life of the frontier.

On April 13, 1860, the first rider dashed from St. Joseph. His name was Johnny Frey. Another messenger, Harry Roff, left Sacramento at the gallop, racing east. Two minutes was the average time allowed at each station to transfer saddle and mail pouch to a fresh mount. The total weight carried by each horse was limited to twenty pounds of mail. The cost for carrying a letter across the continent was $5.00 for each half ounce. The price was later reduced to $1.00. The average time to cover the route was eight days. Indians nearly disrupted the system, when they began raiding the company's stations only a few months after service started. Several employees were murdered, and many of the swift ponies Russell had obtained had new Indian owners. It was necessary to close the line for a number of weeks while the stations were rebuilt and Russell secured more horses, as well as some new recruits to man the stations. There was no shortage of riders, who had become adept at outrunning the Indians who attempted to ambush them.

An average ride for each man was supposed to be thirty-five miles, using three ponies in succession, but it was not unusual to have to cover far greater ground than this. The Pony Express lasted for eighteen months. The Pacific Telegraph, which linked both coasts by wire, doomed the service. William Russell and his two partners, Majors and Waddell, had pumped $700,000 into the Pony Express system. The Indian depredations, which had caused a temporary halt to operations, caused a $75,000 debit in the ledger. When the books were closed, the firm showed a loss of $200,000.

The arrival of the first Pony Express rider in Sacramento with his leather mail satchel touched off a spontaneous celebration in the capital. Later, both horse and rider were carried by steamer to San Francisco, where jubilant residents went wild with excitement over this historic event. The following day, April 14, 1860, the Sacramento *Daily Union* described the arrival in its columns. Another story reports the rider's reception at San Francisco. The account opens as a large crowd excitedly waits for the courier to come dashing through the streets of Sacramento:

¶ . . . Flags were run up on all the public buildings and engine houses, flags were hung out from various awning posts along J street and to more perfectly illustrate the unflagging zeal of parties, flags were stretched across the street at the corner of J and Third (from the State Telegraph office) and, further down, from the windows of the *Union* office. So J street was, for the first time in its history, tolerably well flagged; but it was intolerably dusty for all that.

There were other indications of the swelling of popular enthusiasm. Various quaint devices and appropriate mottoes began to appear in front of the stores on J street. Lorye's crockery establishment had a hobby horse mounted before the awning posts, decored with flags and inscribed "Pony Express. Russell, Majors & Co. take the skates!" Dale & Co., nearly opposite, thought the idea a good one, and rigged out their largest doll (a perfect bouncer) on a wooden pony, stuffed letters and papers in his hand, mounted a soldier cap on his head and set him off with the motto, "Pony Express, forever!" Genella's crockery store (the crockery men are in favor of a smashing business in overland news) hung out their banners with "Hurrah for the Pony Express!" "Hurrah for the Central Route!" emblazoned upon their ample folds (of brown paper). McDonald's tool and hardware store was a little cutting in its emblems and comparisons. "Pike county vs. Butterfield & Co," was the legend that attracted curious eyes in that quarter, while little flags waved their salutations to the coming Pony. It will be seen by our St. Louis letter that Butterfield & Co. started a rival Pony Express half an hour before this one started by the Central route.

The question is, whether that Pony has been cut up by Comanches or caught up among the Celestial lines of the rainbow on that route, or whether he had "gone to grass," where there is more pasture than along the line of that Butter-field.

But the more earnest part of the pony welcome had been arranged early in the day. This was a cavalcade of citizens to meet the little traveler a short distance from the city and escort him into town. Accordingly, late in the day, a deputation of about eighty persons, together with a detachment of fifteen of the Sacramento Hussars, assembled at the old Fort, and stretched out their lines on either side of the road along which the express was to come. Some of the horsemen carried small flags, and one banner (borne by the marshal elected for the occasion), welcomed the "Pony" in set phrase and with appropriate compliments. The company waited long and patiently for the appearance of their expected guest. Meantime the excitement had increased all over the city and J street was lined from Tenth street to the levee with watchers. The balconies of the stores were occupied by ladies, and the roofs were taken possession of by the more agile of the opposite sex, straining to catch the first glimpse of the Pony.

At length—5:25—all this preparation was rewarded. First a cloud of rolling dust in the direction of the Fort, then a horseman bearing a small flag, riding furiously down J street, and then a straggling, charging band of horsemen, flying after him heralding the coming of the Express. Almost simultaneously, from the church towers and engine houses in all parts of the city rang out a merry peal of bells. A cannon planted on the square at Tenth street, and served by the boys of Young America, No. 6, sent forth its noisy welcome. It was answered by an anvil chorus from one of those implements placed at the corner of Ninth and J and fired by "No. 2's boys," and another, managed also as a piece of ordnance, by Holmes and

Andrews, on Sixth street, near J. The latter fired first nine, and then thirteen guns. Each of the other pieces above mentioned gave nine guns as a salute. Amidst the firing and shouting, and waving of hats and ladies' handkerchiefs, the pony—the veritable pony—was seen coming at a rattling pace down J street, surrounded by about thirty of the citizen deputation. The little fellow stretched his neck well to the race, and came at a rattling pace down the street which was wild with excitement. A thick cloud of dust rolled over the heads of the party as it came dashing on in the most hopeless confusion. Such a scene—both for comicality and becoming enthusiasm—our city has never, perhaps, witnessed. Here and there were riderless steeds, and yonder were steeds that might as well have been riderless for all the control those who sat astride could exercise over them. But out of this confounded confusion, mingled fun and earnestness, "rider and horse, friend and foe in *dusty* burial blent," emerged at last the Pony Express, trotting up to the door of the agency (Alta Telegraph office), and depositing its precious mail in ten days from St. Joseph to Sacramento. Hip, hip, hurrah for the Pony Carrier!

Our pioneer rider at this end of the line—Sam Hamilton—informs us that he left Sportsman's Hall at 1¼ p.m., left Placerville at 1:35, had the first relay at Mud Springs, the second at Mormon Tavern, the third at the Fifteen Mile House, and the fourth and last at the Five Mile House. The last five miles was made in twenty minutes, notwithstanding obstructions of which we make especial mention. He complains, naturally, that the cavalcade, which met him at the Fort to escort him into town soon after starting in generally put spurs to their fresh animals and took the lead, creating a great dust, which was not only annoying to him, but exceedingly injurious to his pony—possibly simply for the purpose of boasting that they had beaten the "Pony Express," but probably thoughtlessly during the excitement of the occasion. Hamilton states that the Express can be carried through in much less time by several days, at a more favorable season. In consequence of late rains the road was in very bad condition, compelling him to ride zig zag, as though traveling a snake fence. Hamilton is the rider who carried the first Express to Placerville on the 4th inst., in four hours three minutes. The pony—a roan—which has thus distinguished itself, belongs at Rightmire's stable on K street. Being somewhat obese from the inaction and high feeding, two hostlers were employed several hours in rubbing him down. By this prompt attention he is regarded as being fully able to repeat the performance today, and do even more. The Express brought through about eighty letters for this city and San Francisco.

. . .

¶ BY TELEGRAPH TO THE UNION
By the State Telegraph Line

Arrival of the Pony Express in San
Francisco—Impromptu Celebration

San Francisco, April 18th.

The General Committee on celebrating the arrival of the Pony Express met this evening at the Merchants' Exchange. It was decided to have a preliminary celebration tonight on the arrival of the steamer Antelope.[5] A band of music was ordered, and a supply of fireworks. Telegraph men, firemen, newspaper men, and citizens at large were invited to participate.

At 11 o'clock a large assemblage was gathered at the corner of Merchant and Montgomery streets, and preceded by the band, proceeded to Broadway wharf, where they awaited the arrival of the steamer, which came handsomely into her berth shortly after 11 o'clock. Immediately on the steamer heaving in sight several port-fires were lighted and rockets sent up; the band played a national air, and general enthusiasm ensued. After the landing of the Express, a procession was formed, consisting of delegations from the Fire Companies, with torches, and citizens generally. The line of march was enlivened by the discharge of blue-lights, Roman candles and other fireworks; and on arrival at the corner of Merchant and Montgomery streets, the Monumental Fire Company fired a salute on the Plaza of nine guns. The horse was handsomely decorated, and on the dismounting of the rider, the Express bag was handed to the Agent, who immediately opened it and distributed the letters as directed to persons present. The greatest excitement prevailed, and several impromptu addresses were made, after which the various parties who had participated in the celebration adjourned, pleased with themselves and the rest of mankind, and the Pony Express in particular. All took a drink at their own expense. It is understood that a general meeting of citizens will be held in a day or two to make a more extended celebration of this great event.

[5] Both pony and rider were transported to San Francisco for the occasion. As Sacramento served as the western terminus for the mail service, future letters bound for San Francisco were carried aboard the river steamers plying between the two cities.

21

CALIFORNIA AND
THE CIVIL WAR

O n the grounds of the State Capitol building at Sacramento is a memorial grove that was dedicated on May 1, 1897, in honor of the Californians who fought in the Civil War. Actually, there were only five hundred who went east to participate in the fighting, but they took part in some of the bloodiest encounters of the four-year conflict. The trees in this grove were sent as young saplings from the various battlegrounds where the Californians engaged the Confederates. Today, many of these trees reach a lofty seventy-five feet in height. They were contributed by people of the South to demonstrate that the bitterness that had once divided the nation no longer existed. The war wounds had healed. There is a fir from Cold Harbor, a white oak from Vicksburg, a tulip tree from Five Forks, and an American elm from Gettysburg. Few visitors who wander through this shady arbor are probably aware of the exploits of the California five hundred, or for that matter, what did take place within the state during this stormy era.

Following the firing on Fort Sumter and the outbreak of hostilities in April, 1861, the California legislature adopted the following resolution on May 17th:

¶ Resolved by the Senate, the Assembly concurring, that the people of California are devoted to the Constitution and Union of the United States, and will not fail in fidelity and fealty to that Constitution and Union now in the hour of trial and peril. That California is ready to maintain the rights and honor of the National government at home and abroad, and at all times to respond to any requisition that may be made upon her to defend the republic against foreign or domestic foe.[1]

California's loyalty to the federal government during the struggle was thus assured, but the Confederates had many sympathizers, particularly in the southern section of the state. A number of newspapers were prosouthern in their sentiments, so much so that they had to be excluded from the mails. These included the San Jose *Tribune,* the San Joaquin *Republican,* the Stockton *Argus,* and the Merced *Express.* In Visalia, when the *Expositor* printed a poem containing offensive references to Abraham Lincoln, soldiers destroyed the publishing plant. Los Angeles was the hotbed for secessionists. Henry Hamilton, the fiery editor of the *Star* was particularly vitriolic in his attacks upon the Lincoln administration. The military locked him up temporarily, and he was sent to San Pedro to be shipped to the federal military prison on Alcatraz Island. Friends interceded, and he was freed. A picnic was held in the editor's honor at nearby El Monte, where he received a tumultuous welcome.

Southern California was thinly populated at the time. Many of the people who settled there had emigrated from Missouri, Arkansas, and various southern states. There was considerable agriculture in the region, but the principal occupation was the raising of sheep and cattle. Sympathy ran strong for the southern confederacy, and it became necessary to dispatch several companies of cavalry to Los Angeles to ensure proper respect for federal authority. A worried resident wrote the following letter to General E. V. Sumner, who

---

[1] *Records of California Men in the War of the Rebellion, 1861 to 1867,* revised and compiled by Brigadier General Richard H. Orton, Adjutant General of California (Sacramento: State Printing Office, 1890).

succeeded General Albert Sidney Johnston as commanding general of the Department of the Pacific:

¶ Los Angeles, August 10, 1861

GENERAL E. V. SUMNER,
   Commanding Pacific Division, San Francisco.

SIR: I feel it my duty as an old resident of this place to apprise you that all of us who are loyal and devoted to the Stars and Stripes, and that have something to lose in this section of the country, feel that we are in the greatest insecurity as to the public interest as well as to our lives and property. No part of your command is composed of such discordant and menacing elements as it. Within we have open and avowed secessionists and Southern sympathizers, and I am sorry to say that they are chiefly composed of those who exercise most political influence with the native population, and already they have not failed to poison their minds against the Puritan fanatics of the North. We are threatened with rebellion across the plains by people of the Van Dorn stripe, if we are to credit the repeated reports of the Texan emigration and in these disordered times it is not well to discredit them. Lower California, the asylum of cut throats and robbers, is on our immediate border. We are surrounded to a great extent by barbarous and hostile Indian tribes, that may at any moment be excited against us, and the Government by rebels or marauding Mormons. I not only consider it necessary, but the part of prudence and timely vigilance to station a lookout cavalry force at the Cajon Pass, or at some point close thereto. Please to receive my suggestions with indulgence, being made in a spirit to subserve public and private interests.

Your most obedient servant,
Matthew Keller [2]

Immediate steps were taken to prevent any Confederate sympathizers from causing disturbances within the state. Recruiting began for volunteer troops, and during the war more than sixteen thousand men were under arms in California, and were mustered into the federal service. With the exception of the cavalry legion that served in the East, these troops did not participate in the great battles of the

[2] *The War of Rebellion. A Compilation of the Official Records of the Union and Confederate Armies.* Series I, Volume L, Part I (Washington: Government Printing Office, 1897).

war, but they performed valuable service in preserving order in the Southwest and along the Pacific coast. Brigadier General Richard H. Orton, Adjutant General of California in 1890, and a captain of the First California Cavalry during the Civil War, pointed out the important role of these Californians in the preservation of the Union when he wrote:

¶ . . . the service they rendered was of as great importance as that rendered by those from other states. It was as severe, entailing long and fatiguing marches across burning deserts and among almost inaccessible mountains. They were engaged in hundreds of fights with Indians and small forces of Confederate troops on the frontier, in Texas and Mexico, and they never knew defeat. It was a constant source of regret among them that they were never ordered East, and the question was continually asked: "When are we to be ordered to the seat of the war?" The Government deemed it wisest to keep them on the Pacific Coast and in the Territories. They occupied nearly all the posts from Puget Sound to San Elizario, Texas, and they did their duty faithfully, notwithstanding their disappointment. By their loyalty they preserved peace in these western states and Territories, and the flag of rebellion was soon driven beyond the Rio Grande.[3]

At the outbreak of hostilities the Department of the Pacific was commanded by Brigadier General Albert Sidney Johnston, a native Texan who was considered one of the best military strategists in the army. Abraham Lincoln wanted him for a top command in the Union Army, but it was soon evident that his sympathies were with the South, and Brigadier General Edwin V. Sumner relieved him at San Francisco on May 3, 1861. Johnston was accused at the time of being party to a plan to aid the Confederacy in California. A secret organization known as the Knights of the Golden Circle hoped to take the state from the Union and form a Pacific republic. They claimed a membership of twenty thousand, who were well armed. Johnston's name was associated with this group. Such accusations proved false. It has been documented that Confederate supporters approached the general with a plan to surrender the government arsenal at San Francisco. He made it clear that he would defend

[3] *Records of California Men in the War of the Rebellion.*

government property entrusted to him with his life if necessary. Johnston's personal feelings were expressed in a letter he wrote to one of his sons, Louis, which is now in the possession of Justin Turner, a prominent Los Angeles collector of rare documents. The general wrote this early in 1861 before resigning his commission:

¶ Yesterday the San Francisco newspapers announced that Texas has completed all arrangements contemplated as necessary to separate her destiny from the General Government. . . . To continue to hold my commission after being apprised of the final action of my state to whose partiality in a great measure I hold my position, could find no justification in my own conscience, and I have therefore this day forwarded the resignation of my commission for the acceptance of the President, which I hope may be promptly accepted.

I have asked that my successor be appointed to relieve me as soon as practicable. You probably have seen a paragraph in the papers to the effect that the evidence is in the possession of the War Department that Gen. Johnston and other officers are conspiring to establish a Pacific Republic.

I say the whole charge is false in every particular and there is not the slightest ground for it. I am a stranger here and have had no conversations ever with any one who desires such a result or entertains such views. If the War Department has such information, why don't they order an investigation and not give it to letter writers to damage the reputation of officers?

My escutcheon is without a blur upon it and never will be tarnished. I shall do my duty to the last and when absolved take my course. . . .

After being relieved by General Sumner, Johnston went to Los Angeles, where he stayed with his family in the home of his brother-in-law, Dr. J. S. Griffin. He was constantly being watched by the Union authorities, who waited for a final order to arrest him. Johnston had planned to take his wife and children to New York by ship, but received information that he would be taken prisoner upon his arrival. There was only one course open. He had to leave his family and make his way overland to Virginia, where he could offer his services to the Confederate government. He had a small band of followers who would accompany him. They permitted information to circulate that they would depart for the East on June 29, 1861. Two weeks before that date they left Los Angeles, riding from the town at night to avoid detection, because Johnston was being watched by federal agents. The group reached Warner's Ranch in San Diego County, and from here followed the trail for the East.

The party crossed into Arizona, now swarming with Texas Confederates who had clashed with Union forces in the desert wastelands. Marauding Apaches, who ambushed troopers wearing either blue or gray, added to the hazards of the road. Federal troops under Colonel E. R. S. Canby narrowly missed capturing Johnston and his followers at Dragoon Springs at the junction of the Fort Buchanan road and the Tucson Trail to the Rio Grande River. Canby had just received orders from Washington to arrest the general. The party evaded the federal troops, arriving safely in Virginia, where Jefferson Davis, president of the Confederacy, offered Johnston an important military command. At Shiloh, one of the bloodiest battles of the Civil War, Albert Sidney Johnston was killed leading southern troops. A ball struck his boot, severing an artery. He bled to death on the field because he had ordered his personal physician to go to the aid of wounded Union prisoners.

*   *   *

Early in the fall of 1861, men began arriving at San Pedro from throughout the state to undergo training at a newly established base, Drum Barracks, which was located at Wilmington, not far from present Los Angeles Harbor. General George Wright succeeded Sumner, who returned east, as commanding officer of the Department of the Pacific. Taking his place in southern California was a highly qualified major, James Henry Carleton. He was destined to rise swiftly to the rank of brigadier general, and be responsible for the training of thousands of volunteers at Drum Barracks. It would be Carleton who would plan the expedition that would march into Arizona and restore federal authority. This did not occur until the following year, when the California Column, as it came to be known, was ready to move from Los Angeles.

The problem of logistics required intensive planning. Some 1,600 men would be marching through desert and mountain regions. Wells had to be marked and cleaned by advance scouts. Food would be a considerable problem. How much pork, sugar, coffee, vinegar, beans, and pickles a small army could consume from San Pedro to Fort Yuma had to be calculated with slide-rule accuracy, and anyone who takes time to study the official records compiled under the title of *The War of the Rebellion* will find that Carleton overlooked nothing, not even the smallest item. His signature appears on countless orders and reports, and it is obvious he was a stickler for detail and discipline. This order was sent to a colonel commanding a base at San Diego:

¶ Headquarters District of Southern California
Los Angeles, Cal. February 21, 1862.

LIEUT. COL. J. R. WEST,
First Infantry California Volunteers,
Commanding at Camp Wright,
San Diego County, Calif.

COLONEL: I have the honor to acknowledge the receipt of yours of the 19th instant in relation to the refusal of certain privates in Company A, First Infantry California Volunteers, to carry their knapsacks on drill. I have always regarded that company as one of the finest I have ever seen in service—one of the first I should have chosen to follow me into any battle where the integrity of the country or the glory of the flag was to be maintained; so you can judge how greatly I have been disappointed. It is hardly possible that it is a settled purpose on the part of that whole company to set military authority at defiance and constitute itself a judge of what shall be done and what not. The men are intelligent men, and can at once see to what all this would tend. Nor can it be possible the men refuse to obey orders for the purpose of remaining behind to gain by the delays incident to a trial before a general court-martial immunity from the fatigues of a hard march and from the danger of facing an enemy. The men are hardy and brave and patriotic; such a thought, therefore, would be unjust to them. Now, the infantry require the soldiers of that arm to drill with knapsacks on at the quickstep, and even at the run. To accustom them to this weight, to carry out and perfect them in their instruction, was one purpose of General Orders, No. 3, requiring the First Infantry, my own regiment, to drill with knapsacks on. Another purpose was this, and I want the soldiers to know it: We are about to commence a movement with limited means of transportation over a desert country. Unless the soldiers carry their knapsacks at the commencement of the march, it will be impossible to transport a sufficiency of food, of ammunition, of clothing, or of hospital stores. So the purpose of the expedition will have to be abandoned, or the men, like good soldiers, must be willing to sacrifice personal convenience for a short time to attain an important object. Read all this to those men. Read the Articles of War to them. Remind them of their paths. Give them one hour to reflect on the unhappy consequences of such conduct. Let them see how unworthy it is of them as soldiers, how degrading to themselves as men, how much it reflects upon their company and regiment, how disgraceful it is to California, to the flag, to the country. If, then, any one man amongst them does not feel ashamed of such conduct, and feel willing to obey orders promptly and cheerfully, the only alternative left is to have that man at once mustered out of the service without pay. The country has plenty of soldiers, and California has enough of them even here, who stand ready to take his place and obey orders. Depend on that. I have taken some pains to explain this matter, and have exercised a forebearance in the case unusual in our profession, because I feel an attachment to the men of my regiment, and I do not wish to see them dishonor the flag or disgrace themselves if I can help it. But I leave the issue to them, feeling confident that the determination to which they will come, after a sober second thought, will be such as to cause them no regrets hereafter. There is one thing they can count upon: The colors of the First Infantry of California will go forward, even though every man in the regiment but one refuses to go with them.

> I have the honor to be, very respectfully,
> your obedient servant,
> JAMES H. CARLETON,

Colonel First Infantry, California Volunteers, Commanding.[4]

Carleton's words had their effect. The men stopped grumbling. They carried their knapsacks at drill, and when they began the long hike to Fort Yuma, there would be a lot more to tote along. These are some of the items specified in Carleton's general orders, dated February 12, 1862:

¶ The infantry companies which may be required to take the field in this district, unless otherwise ordered, will always march with knapsacks

[4] *The War of Rebellion. A Compilation of the Official Records of the Union and Confederate Armies.*

on. Each soldier will carry one greatcoat, one blanket, one forage cap, one woolen shirt, one pair of drawers, one pair of stockings, one towel, two handkerchiefs, one fine and one coarse comb, one sewing kit, one piece of soap, one toothbrush. Each soldier will wear his uniform hat without trimmings, one blouse, one pair of trousers, one pair of stockings, one woolen shirt, one pair of drawers, and may wear a cravat in lieu of the leather stock. Each soldier, whether of cavalry or infantry, will have one canteen, one haversack, and one tin cup. In his haversack he will carry one fork, spoon, and plate. He will wear a good sheath knife. . . .

It is clear that Carleton was a perfectionist. Nothing escaped his attention. It was his responsibility to see that his men would survive in a hostile wilderness. And this they would do. The casualties were few.

*   *   *

While the Californians trained and readied themselves for the campaign in the Southwest, the territory had already become the scene of a violent contest between federal and Confederate forces. The outcome was decided before Carleton's men had an opportunity to participate in the fighting. Early in the fall of 1861, Confederate troops overran New Mexico and much of Arizona. Most of these men were a hard-riding, hard-fighting lot recruited in Texas. Their commander was Brigadier General Henry Hopkins Sibley, CSA. He marched up the valley of the Rio Grande from El Paso with 2,600 men on a daring mission for the South. The success of Sibley's invasion was being watched with concern by the fledgling Confederate government at Richmond. Whoever controlled New Mexico held the key to California, with its gold mines, two splendid harbors, and unlimited resources. The Confederate acquisition of California would undoubtedly have brought rapid recognition and aid from various European powers for the southern government.

The federal commander opposing Sibley was General E. R. S. Canby. He was garrisoned at Fort Craig with 3,800 men. This outpost was located 130 miles south of Albuquerque and seven miles south of Valverde in a desolate corridor leading to Santa Fe. Canby was aware of Sibley's movements, but he was in no position to attack. The garrison was short of supplies, and twice it had been necessary to suppress mutinies among his unpaid troops. In addition, a number of his officers had resigned to join the Confederacy.

The rebel force bypassed the fort, following the eastern bank of the Rio Grande to a ford at Valverde. Canby decided to engage the enemy. Both sides arrived at this point at the same moment. Sibley launched a cavalry attack on the federals' left flank, which was held by Colorado volunteer troops. The charge was halted at a heavy cost to the Texans. A well-placed federal battery pinned the Confederates down. Suddenly, one of their officers ran forward shouting for his men to take the battery. The assault succeeded, and the Confederates overwhelmed the gun position. Canby ordered his troops to fall back on Fort Craig. As they struggled across the Rio Grande, they were cut down by their own guns, now in the possession of the Texans.

The dead and wounded were removed under a flag of truce. Sibley ignored Fort Craig and pushed on to occupy Albuquerque and Santa Fe. His victory was complete, but the tide began to turn against him. Coloradoans mauled the Texans in two later encounters. The final calamity for the Confederates occurred when their supply train was captured and burned. Retreat was inevitable. Sibley's men began the long march home, following the Rio Grande. When the Texans finally reached San Antonio, they had lost more than 1,700 men.

*   *   *

The nearest town to California that the Confederates reached in their drive to the West was Tucson, Arizona. Captain Sherod Hunter entered the pueblo on February 28, 1862, with one hundred Texans, following the Southerners' victory at Valverde. A few weeks later a small patrol of California calvary, members of Carleton's advance guard now in Arizona, skirmished with a rebel detachment at Pichacho Pass. Three of the California cavalrymen and two Confederate soldiers were killed in the encounter. In May, 1862, Carleton was at Fort Yuma with most of his troops, ready to move on Tucson. He issued orders to his officers on how they should instruct their men to conduct themselves when they met the enemy:

¶ Have your sabers very sharp, that they may readily cut through clothing. Cavalry recently mounted on California horses cannot use any kind of firearms with success. The men should practice dismounting to fight on foot a great deal. If a rush is made by Texans on horseback with revolvers upon your cavalry while mounted, if the sabers are sharp I would recommend closing in with them as quick as thought. The cold steel will win against the pistol, but with our men well kept together and well in hand, or they will not succeed. In closing with cavalry against cavalry in hand-to-hand encounters on horseback, it is well to get your enemy in your power by cutting off his reins, killing his horse, etc. If your cavalry happen to be on foot and the Texans happen to be on foot, and attempt to make a rush upon your men with their revolvers, as is their custom, teach your men to use their side-arms until the shots are exhausted and then the carbine. It is my opinion that a judicious use of the saber on foot or on horseback will tell very much in your favor. Pray teach your men not to despise their enemy. Those men whom they go to encounter are determined men and will fight with desperation. . . .

A major engagement did not take place, however, between Carleton's men and the Confederates. When Sherod Hunter learned of Sibley's losses, he abandoned Tucson, realizing he would soon be surrounded by Union forces. The Texans had learned to their dismay that they could not live off the land. The settlers did not come to the assistance of the invaders, as the Confederates believed they would do. Sibley had claimed they would welcome the Stars and Bars flag of the Confederacy. He was mistaken. Instead of providing food for his men and forage for their horses, the people of New Mexico and Arizona hid what they possessed. In some cases they went so far as to destroy it. Sibley's miscalculations in logistics had cost him and the Confederacy the loss of an army. Carleton's careful planning brought results. In June, 1862, his troops entered Tucson. He issued a proclamation:

¶ The Congress of the United States has set apart a portion of New Mexico and organized it into a territory complete in itself. This is known as the territory of Arizona . . . the undersigned as military governor assumes control of the territory until such time as the president of the United States shall otherwise direct . . . the territory of Arizona is hereby under martial law. . . .

The Californians had restored order in Arizona and would continue to preserve it for the duration of the war. The Confederate threat to the Pacific coast was ended. In military posts throughout the South-west, the Stars and Stripes flew once again, with many of these forts being occupied by California troops. For the remaining years of the conflict they would be relegated to the boredom of routine garrison life, generally in isolated desert regions far from civilization. An occasional patrol against the unruly Indians relieved the monotony, and couriers brought the Los Angeles and San Francisco newspapers with their official dispatches. These were eagerly read, for there was plenty of activity on the home front. William M. Gwin, the United States Senator from California, and the most important political figure in the state for nearly a decade, had departed to serve in the Confederacy. He had been reported arrested while en route to Havana, where he was supposed to have rendezvoused with the Confederate commissioners Mason and Slidell, the same pair who were later intercepted by the United States Navy on the high seas, and forcibly removed from an English vessel—an incident which nearly precipitated a war between Great Britain and the United States. Gwin was held briefly after being removed from a ship at Panama by federal authorities. Following his release, he went to Paris on a mission for the Confederate government. He remained there until his death in 1885, and was known to Frenchmen as the Duke de Gwin.

The secessionists were still active, but they had lost ground. In Stockton, someone raised Confederate flags over the main public buildings, but they were quickly removed. At Los Angeles, Assembly-man E. J. C. McKewan was arrested in October, 1862, for making treasonable remarks against the federal government, and shipped to the military prison on Alcatraz Island. Two weeks later, he was released after taking the oath of allegiance and paying a fine of $5,000. Pro-Union sentiment heavily outweighed that accorded to the Confederate government in California. Men such as the tireless minister Thomas Starr King traveled throughout the state making speeches exhorting the people to support the Union. And this they did by such acts as raising funds for the Sanitary Commission, an organization that was a forerunner for the Red Cross. The news the people were most interested in was what was occurring on the opposite side of the continent, where the war was being fought. They had a contingent representing them there, and the story of this battalion is one of the most colorful episodes of the state's history. The battalion had already participated in numerous engagements. In *Records of California Men in the War of the Rebellion,* Brigadier General H. Orton describes how this battalion was organized:

¶ THE CALIFORNIA HUNDRED AND BATTALION

These organizations were raised under the following circumstances; There were a large number of men in the State who desired to go East and enter the army, and when it was found that the California Volunteers were being kept on this coast, a proposition was made to the State of Massachusetts to raise a company here, take it East, and credit it to the quota of that State, if the expenses of its organization and transportation were guaranteed. The State of Massachusetts was paying large bounties for volunteers; this bounty, it was decided, should be paid into the company fund and used for the purpose of paying the expenses of the company.

On the twenty-seventh day of October, 1862, Captain J. Sewell Reed received the necessary authority from Governor Andrews of Massachusetts, and on the following day recruiting commenced. Assembly Hall, located on the northwest corner of Kearny and Post Streets, San Francisco, was made headquarters, and the first private enrolled was H. H. Fillebrown. In three weeks, more than five hundred men had offered themselves for enrollment. One hundred were selected, and they were mustered into the United States service by Lieutenant-Colonel George H. Ringgold, U.S.A., at Platt's Hall, December 10, 1862. The next day, the company sailed for the East on the steamer *Golden Age.*

The company went to Readville, near Boston, Massachusetts, where it arrived January 4, 1863. The company was designated as Co. A of the Second Massachusetts Cavalry, then consisting of a battalion of four companies. The Californians were soon mounted and ordered to the front, arriving at Yorktown, Virginia, in February, 1863. The battalion was under the command of Major Caspar Crowninshield. After its arrival at Yorktown it performed picket and scouting duty, and had its first battle at South Anna Bridge, where seventy Californians and twenty Massachusetts men captured one hundred and twenty-three of the Forty-fourth North Carolina Infantry, in a dismounted charge upon their earthworks. In the fight the company lost Joseph B. Burdick, killed, and two seriously wounded.

The success attending the raising of the "California Hundred," and the large number presenting themselves for enlistment, induced others to offer to raise four more companies under the same conditions. After considerable negotiation with the authorities in Washington and Massachusetts, permission was received by Major D. W. C. Thompson to raise a battalion of four companies, which were rapidly recruited. Upon the arrival of these companies at Readville they were also attached to the Second Massachusetts Cavalry, and became Companies E, F, L, and M, of that regiment.[5]

One of the men who was to join this second contingent was Charles Roberts. He kept a diary of his adventures; a well-worn small leather-covered journal that he carried in his saddlebags while his regiment was hunting elusive bands of John Singleton Mosby's Confederate guerrillas in Virginia. The diary was acquired by the Huntington Library several years ago. In the opening pages, he writes that on January 1, 1863, he started work in Empire City, Nevada Territory, as a hostler for forty dollars a month. Entries note his decision to enlist and his subsequent departure from San Francisco:

¶ Wed. April 8, 1863. Have a great notion of going east with the cavalry that goes from San Francisco . . . am studying very deep the questions. I will be leaving a situation here to go, but that's nothing to what is at stake.
April 9. Have concluded to go and join my comrades in battling for our country. Settled up with my employer, and started on foot to Carson City.[6]

Roberts reached Sacramento by stage, then boarded the steamer for San Francisco. Upon arriving in the city, he hurried to the recruiting office, took his oath, and was sworn into the service of the United States for a three-year enlistment. The recruits were placed aboard a Panama-bound steamer, and after a rough passage reached the Isthmus, where the men boarded trains for the Atlantic coast. Here they were marched aboard a federal vessel. This ship sailed in convoy with an escort, as there were Confederate privateers on the high seas. The Californians landed at New York, where they traveled by train to

[5] *Records of California Men in the War of the Rebellion.*
[6] Charles Roberts, diary in the manuscript collection of the Henry E. Huntington Library and Art Gallery, San Marino, Calif.

Readville, Massachusetts, and went into bivouac. The new arrivals joined the first hundred that had sailed for the East in December, 1862. Their first assignment was to scout in front of the forts defending Washington. Their patrols ranged along the upper Potomac, looking for the anticipated movement of Lee's army into Maryland. About this time the battalion made its first raid, crossing the Potomac at White's Ford, and marching through Loudon and Fairfax counties, Virginia, in search of Mosby's guerrillas.

Roberts writes that he went on this patrol. The men carried three days' rations, "which was our haversacks full of hard bread and salt pork." The troopers covered 150 miles on the scout with negligible results. It was a tiresome pursuit. On June 28, 1863, Roberts noted, "we layed down with our bridles in our hands and slept." They were deep in Confederate territory. The danger of surprise was so great that the horses were not unsaddled. They stood by, while their tired riders would sleep for a few brief hours, the reins tied to the wrists to prevent the animals from straying.

On the 26th of June, near Edwards' Ferry, the Californians joined the Army of the Potomac, then under the command of General Hooker, and marched toward Gettysburg. A few days afterward, Stuart's cavalry having crossed the Potomac at Muddy Branch Ford, the battalion was sent to watch the movements of these Confederates. The men who rode with the famed Jeb Stuart were ranked as some of the best fighters in the entire Confederate Army. By a forced march, the Californians came up with the enemy, engaging their rear guard near Brookville, Maryland, on the first day of July, continuing to follow them into Pennsylvania, capturing stragglers and harassing the Southerners' column. Orders to join Lee's army then at Gettysburg made Stuart's cavalry hurry forward without bothering to attack the small forces about them.

The curious feature of Roberts' narrative is that the most decisive battle of the war was being fought between July 1st and July 4th at Gettysburg, Pennsylvania, but he was not aware of it. Pickett's long gray line had been shattered by federal guns during the fatal Confederate charge at Gettysburg on July 3rd, which marked the high-water mark of the southern invasion of Union soil. It was the beginning of the end for Lee's once magnificent army. Stuart was too late to be of aid to his commander, who had been deprived of his cavalry during the engagement, which could have served as the eyes for his infantry—gathering the intelligence that might have prevented the costly debacle. Lee and his defeated army began their long retreat into Virginia.

Roberts, who was spared the fury of the great battle fought at Gettysburg, jotted down the following entry in his diary on Wednesday, July 1, 1863:

> ¶ Fine morning. The Col. sent me down to the Monacacy the first thing to tell the teamsters or wagon masters to go to Poolsville with the wagons. I started not knowing the road, but felt sure of finding it. I stopped on the way and ate cherries for breakfast, as I could find them while riding along in a strip of woods. Something took my attention to the right of me. I took the second look and saw a man crouched down behind a stump. Thinking I had a reb to deal with, I out with my pistol and ordered him out. . . .

Roberts' prisoner was apparently a deserter or straggler, but the young cavalryman was anxious to complete his mission and did not wish to be encumbered with a prisoner to watch. He freed his captive, not knowing whether he was a rebel or Union soldier. Subsequent entries in his journal during this period state that the Californians had no news about what was going on around them, which would account for their being ignorant of the historic events taking place at Gettysburg. The men were on short rations, but berries were plentiful, as was milk and pork. Roberts had demonstrated an aptitude for soldiering. He was promoted to corporal.

The California battalion formed the right of a cavalry force that started on July 8th to make a reconnaissance into Virginia, east of the Blue Ridge Mountains and through Ashby's Gap into the Shenandoah to discover the position and watch the movements of Lee's army then retreating up the valley. On the morning of July 12th, a sharp action took place at Ashby's Gap between four companies of the California battalion and a detachment of the enemy that was strongly posted, resulting in the Confederates' being driven from the gap and up into the valley. There were several casualties among the Californians during the skirmish. Roberts' entry for that day reads:

¶ July 12, 1863. Leesburg. Stopped there for two hours in the rain. Looked in some stables for horse feed, but could find none and our poor horses, having had nothing but grass since we started, . . . I started in search of some for myself. I went into a hotel and told the proprietor to give us some milk, bread, butter and beef for myself and one or two men. He gave me quite a lot of grub and a canteen of milk. I told him I had no money and to charge it to the U.S. Everyone here is a rebel to the backbone. They shut up their houses, stores, and everything looks deserted. . . .

On July 17th, the battalion was attached to a mixed command of cavalry, artillery, and infantry, detailed to protect the line of communication between Washington and the Army of the Potomac, then concentrating near Culpepper, and to operate against the partisan troops of the enemy east of the Blue Ridge. While on this duty, the battalion made regular camps at Falls Church, Vienna, Fairfax Court House, and Centreville, scouting through most of the Virginia countryside bounded by the Blue Ridge Mountains and the Rappahannock and Potomac rivers. Roberts' diary continues:

¶ July 19, 1863. Coffee and pork cooked. . . . Caught four rebels, one of them was Gen. Stuart's messenger. . . . Went back, crossed Bull Run and took the road up to Centreville. I have been in the advance and rear guard all day. We pitched camp on the hill where the first battle of Centreville commenced just across the creek from the fortifications old Beauregard threw up there. . . . Have not had the saddles off our horses since we left Alexandria.

Tuesday, July 21st, 1863. Fine morning. Started off another road with three days rations. We went through Centreville and up the pikes towards Warrenton. Passed over the old Bull Run battlegrounds. The looks of the country told plainly what transpired here. Saw human skulls and bones laying on the ground. Also spent cannon balls. Pieces of shells and plenty of lead bullets.[7]

Friday, July 24, 1863. Couple of gentlemen came into camp today selling paper, pens, etc. They found the boys had not been paid and could not sell it and they give it all out. Said they were soldiers once themselves, and

[7] Roberts was visiting the Bull Run battlefield almost two years to the day after the initial encounter of the Civil War was fought. Known in the South as the First Manassas, the battle ended in a rout for the Union Army, which fled from Virginia back to Washington.

knew what it was to be out of money . . . Heard firing yesterday and it proved to of been an engagement between Meade and Lee. Gen. Meade, the Union commander, drove the rebels through Warrenton.

Tuesday, July 29th, 1863. One of our men was arrested on charge of drawing a saber on the orderly sergeant. Case is his name. Corporal Harkins has entered charges against Captain Adams, our squadron commander, for using abusive language . . . quite an excitement . . . all at once they report a cavalry fight going on close here. All hands saddled up in a terrible hurry. The order came to unsaddle. It was the picket firing.

The following day, July 30th, the Californians were in for a real skirmish, and there was plenty of action for all. They tangled with Mosby's guerrillas near Aldie, Virginia, recapturing a train of thirty-three wagons taken by the Confederates the previous day on the Warrenton Pike. It was a blow for the Southerners, who needed the supplies they had been fortunate enough to seize from the Union Army. Roberts was in the midst of the action, and it provides some of the most interesting reading in his diary:

¶ Friday, July 21st, 1863. Halted about two o'clock in the woods near the old church near Aldie. Myself with two men was detailed on picket. Posted one of the men. Told him to wake the other when he would have been on an hour. They was on an hour each. Waken me up. I was on but a short time when I heard firing down the pike a short distance. I woke the boys that was on post with me. An outside picket came in and informed the Col. of the firing. In a few minutes every one was in his saddle. We formed platoons and marched to the edge of the woods close to the pike. We soon saw the rebels coming down the road screaming at the top of their voices after some of our men, when they caught sight of us they retraced their steps very quickly, then the Col. ordered ten of us to follow him and the balance of the command to follow by platoons. We went on the pike, then galloped after them as fast as our horses could go, four or five of us passing the Col. at a good speed until we came to where the road was blocked with sutler wagons, mules and horses (these were Mosby's booty that he had captured at Fairfax Court House). We drove them away from the wagons very hasty. We got past the wagons and followed them down the pike for two miles, when they scattered in all directions like so many sheep. We retook the wagons from them and came to the place where we could see the effects of the shooting that we heard.

There had been a detachment of our command sent off under Lieutenant Manning soon after we left Centreville to come on to the pike lower down or nearer Fairfax Court House than we did. They camped beside the road and the rebels coming on to them first, they engaged one another but Lieut. Manning only having twenty men could not hold his ground against eighty or a hundred men. They killed two of the Lieuts men, captured four and wounded two severely, and drove the balance up the pike till they saw us, when we drove them back, they got away with three prisoners. The Col. with part of the men stopped and had the dead men buried. I had charge of digging the grave. Dug it under a locust tree—had an old axe to use as a pick. The ground was very hard—in a man's dooryard. When the sutler wagons came up (there being twenty-seven of them), the Col. had a detachment of thirty men go in with them as guard and left three men to bury the dead men, then took the advance of the command and followed in pursuit of the rebels again. We got a man for a guide. We went up towards the Bull Run Mountains. Got on their track, followed them up through the mountain. The road was very narrow and timber thick. The ascent was very steep. When we got near the top every one was called to the front that had carbines and ordered to dismount. We finally found the rendezvous (or one of them). There was four or five rebs laying down together. When the rebs saw us they took for the woods. Fired a few shots at them and gave chase, but the woods was their game. They knew it better than we did and we didn't get them, but we retook all the prisoners and a lot of horses they had.

The elated Californians rode back to Centreville, where a victory feast took place, thanks to the provisions carried on the sutlers' wagons, which had originally been following the Union Army until Mosby's men caught them by surprise. Roberts writes:

¶ When we were digging the grave in the man's dooryard they brought us out a pan of milk and some bread. We got some ripe pears off a tree close by. Then the sutlers gave the boys cakes, wine, cigars, tobacco, and everything they wanted. They felt so good at being recaptured from the rebs. It appears that the Col. had been apprised of Mosby's taking this train and had layed a good plan to recapture them with Mosby and his command and would of done it, had Lieut. Manning's party not attacked the rebs or engaged them.

Friday, Aug. 7. Everybody is faring sumptuously on the retaking of the sutlers' wagons, having cakes, pies, cigars, etc. Some got plenty of clothes. I got a good cap. Some of the boys got pickles, cheese, cakes, wine, and in fact everything good in the eating line. . . .

Roberts recorded in his diary the following day that "he feels somewhat unwell. Got a severe headache." Mosby was having his difficulties with the Californians. It had developed into a personal war between the two opponents. The Confederates were desperate for food and clothing, but as fast as the guerrilla leader seized a supply train belonging to the enemy, the men from California were at his heels. On the 17th of August, they relieved him of thirteen wagons he had taken near Annandale on the Fairfax Pike. Roberts was having some excitement of his own on that particular day. That night he made the following entry in his diary by the light of a campfire:

¶ Mon. Aug. 17. Went down through the woods. Searched some houses near the creek. Halted by an old church. . . . When near Aldie we saw fifteen or twenty rebs come up over the hill. We started after them at full speed. Drove them across the creek through a strip of woods, when we found them brought up against a fence, one of them letting it down. They fired a volley at us. We returned it and followed these rebs. After we got in the open field we kept nearing them. Captured two while going up the hill. They was making for the woods on the hill. . . . When they got to the fence near the woods, we was too close on them to let the fence down. So they left their horses, jumped the fence and got off in the woods. We got one in a barn close to where they went through the fence. When going up the hill I had to dismount. When half way up my horse gave out. I took my carbine and went up at double quick on foot. . . . We took three prisoners, six horses and equipment. Our captain complimented us highly for our bravery, but we did not act much like soldiers in scattering about.

Monday, Aug. 31. Cleaning up for inspection. This is muster day, with everyone having to be present to get their pay when the paymaster comes. Major Forbes in examining one of Co. D's new pistols came near getting shot as he held it up for inspection—he in cocking put his finger on the trigger. It went off and the ball passed through the major's cap visor.

On the 25th of August, there was a lively firefight with Mosby's command near Coyle's Tavern. Three of the Californians were killed and several wounded and captured. In this skirmish, Mosby was severely wounded, being put out of action for several months.

Roberts closed his diary the following January, for some reason failing to detail events that followed. An account of actions the Californians participated in subsequently until Robert E. Lee's surrender of the Confederate Army at Appomattox Court House was written by D. W. C. Thompson, who served as a major in the California Cavalry Battalion. It was published in the 1890 edition of *Records of California Men in the War of the Rebellion*. Thompson forwarded his report to the state's adjutant general in 1867, at a time when the events he described were still vivid in his memory. This is a summary of his report from the point where Roberts ceased to make further entries in his journal:

¶ A detachment of cavalry, of which two companies belonged to the battalion, were surprised and defeated near Dranesville, on the twenty-second of February, by a larger force under Mosby. The commanding officer, Captain Reed, of the California Hundred, and thirteen enlisted men were killed, and a larger number wounded and captured; Captain George A. Manning and Lieutenant William C. Manning were disabled and taken prisoners. This affair was the most disastrous that occurred to the battalion during its long and eventful service.

During the spring of 1864 considerable skirmishing took place in the vicinity of Upperville, Rectortown, and Manassas Gap, between the battalion and partisan troops of the enemy, but no decisive action could be forced from them, though in their own country.

On the eighth of June, 1864, two companies of the battalion formed part of a cavalry force detailed to protect a train of ambulances sent from Washington to remove our wounded from the battlefield of the Wilderness.

Early on the morning of the eleventh the column crossed the Rappahannock at United States Ford, and after passing over the old battlefield of Chancellorsville, soon reached the scene of the more desperate battle of the Wilderness, fought a short time before. The badly wounded of both armies were still in field hospitals, and the dead lay in lines, or scattered through the woods, unburied as they fell in the fight. The command visited Parker's Store, Locust Grove, Wilderness Tavern, and other parts of the field, and collected all our wounded that were able to be removed in ambulances.

On the twelfth the train and escort recrossed the Rappahannock in our return, and passing through Brentsville, Manassas Junction, and Centreville, reached Alexandria on the fourteenth. During this march some skirmishing took place, a few guerrillas were captured, and a superior force of the enemy, sent from Orange Court House to take the ambulances, was avoided.

A part of the battalion, with small details from other regiments, while out scouting, were attacked near Aldie, on the sixth of July, by a superior force under Mosby, and compelled to retire with considerable loss.

This was the last affair between the Californians and the guerrillas in Virginia. For a year they had been pitted against Mosby's, White's, Imboden's and Gilmore's men; they had hunted them summer and winter, night and day, mounted and dismounted, together and in squads, from the Blue Ridge to the Potomac, on every road and in almost every house in London, Fairfax, Prince William, and Fauquier Counties. When a fair, square fight could be obtained, the Californians were never beaten. If a small scouting party or isolated picket post could be pounced upon or a detachment ambushed in the woods, or going through a pass, the wily enemy were often successful in such operations. Eigenbrodt's and Manning's companies, on the sixth of March, 1864, were attached to the cavalry forces on the upper Potomac, camped near Edwards' Ferry, and were employed in picketing along the river and scouting between Washington and Harper's Ferry. They made frequent raids into Virginia, and assisted in surrounding and searching Leesburg and other towns for guerrillas and furloughed Rebel soldiers. These companies continued on this active duty until the fifth of July, when they were moved to watch Early's army, then crossing into Maryland. At Point of Rocks, on that day, part of them were engaged skirmishing with the enemy's advance.

During the battle of Monocacy Junction, fought on the ninth of July, between General Wallace's forces from Baltimore, and Early's army, Captain Eigenbrodt's company held the fords below on the Monocacy River, and Captain Manning's company, under Lieutenant Partridge, was placed on the Frederick Pike, to watch the enemy's movements toward Washington. Both companies were employed in skirmishing in front and on the flanks of the enemy's column, during the tenth and on the eleventh, until forced up to Fort Stevens on the Seventh Street Road, a few miles from the Capital. They were there dismounted and engaged on the skirmish line and in the rifle pits of the fort until the enemy retreated on the morning of July thirteenth.

On the tenth of July, Adams and De Merritt's companies, that had remained on duty in Virginia, near Fairfax Court House, were ordered over to the defense of Washington. On the morning of the eleventh they took position in the Tanallytown Road and Rockville Pike, to oppose a demonstration of the Rebels on that road. As Early's army advanced against the forts, they were placed on the skirmish line, in front of Fort Reno, and were on duty there until the enemy retired.

The battalion, mounted, had the honor of the right and leading the advance in driving Early's army out of Maryland. At Rockville on the thirteenth, it made a dash on a Rebel brigade, and with its seven-shooters did the enemy considerable damage. At Darnestown, on the morning of the fourteenth, a small skirmish took place, resulting in capturing an officer and several men from the enemy's rear guard; and at Poolsville, on the afternoon of the same day, the battalion, dismounted and deployed, took part in an action against infantry and artillery, lasting some two hours, until the arrival of the Sixth Army Corps, when the enemy retired over the Potomac.

On the fifteenth, the two companies that had been stationed on the Potomac, near Edwards' Ferry, resumed their former position and duties along the river, and the two companies from Fairfax Court House continued to follow up the enemy in advance of the Sixth and Nineteenth Army Corps, through Loudon County and Snicker's Gap into the Shenandoah Valley, skirmishing with their rear guard or flankers at every favorable opportunity. Soon after reaching the valley they were ordered to return to their former camp and duties near Fairfax Court House.

Early's army having threatened another invasion of Maryland, these companies, on the twenty-fifth of July, moved over the river again and proceeded up the Frederick Pike to South Mountain and Harper's Ferry. Eigenbrodt's and Manning's companies, which had been picketing on the Potomac, were stationed at Poolsville on the thirty-first day of July, when Mosby's guerrillas crossed the river at Nolan's Ford for the purpose of capturing a wagon train on its way from Washington to Harper's Ferry. Before the enemy could reach the prize the Californians interfered, and coming on the guerrillas near Sugar Loaf Mountain, drove them in a running fight back over the Potomac and scattered them in the woods beyond. The companies continued to cover the communications and protect the trains going to Harper's Ferry until the ninth of August, when they moved to Halltown and joined the Army of the Shenandoah under the command of General Sheridan. There the four companies of the battalion were again united and formed a part of the Third Brigade, First Division of Cavalry, under the command of General Merritt.

At daylight on the morning of the tenth of August, 1864, the battalion marched with Sheridan's army up the valley towards Winchester, commencing on that day those brilliant and successful operations and almost daily battles against the enemy that resulted, on the evening of the memorable nineteenth of October, at Cedar Creek, in the ruin and almost total annihilation of Early's army.

In this particular battle, the Confederates launched the attack. Sheridan was away on official business, and as the assault began, Union troops retreated. It was then that Sheridan made his twenty-mile dash from Winchester to rally his men, who, cheering their general, returned to the field and delivered a smashing defeat to the forces of the Confederate leader Jubal Early. It was the final major battle fought in the Shenandoah Valley. Union forces lost 644 killed and more than 3,000 were wounded. Among them was the author of the diary, Charles Roberts. The roster printed in the *Records of California Men in the War of the Rebellion* is brief regarding his war record. Nothing is known of his later life. It reads:

¶ Roberts, Charles, served in Company F, Second Massachusetts Cavalry. Promoted to Corp.; subsequently to Sergt. Severely wounded in Sheridan's battle of Cedar Creek, Octo. 19, 1864. Promoted to 1st Lieut., July 9, 1865. Mustered out July 20, 1865.

The Californians participated in many additional battles as the war neared its end in 1865. There were raids into Confederate territory, and months of constant marching, fighting, and skirmishing. The casualties mounted. A number of their best officers were killed. As the closing scenes of the long war took place, the Californians were in the field. Major Thompson describes the final days of the four-year conflict.

¶ On the morning of the memorable ninth of April, Sheridan's cavalry having formed in line of battle across Lee's line of retreat, the battalion was dismounted and deployed as skirmishers immediately in front of the enemy. When the army of Northern Virginia attempted to advance that morning it found every foot of ground stubbornly contested. For some time this spirited engagement was kept up, the Rebels expecting to break through the cavalry and escape. While this was going on, the Fifth, Twenty-fourth, and part of the Twenty-fifth Corps came up and formed in rear of the cavalry, which gradually moved to the right flank to allow them to come into action. When their long line of battle advanced under

General Ord, the veterans of the best Rebel army, who had fought for four years vainly, but too well, saw that their doom was sealed. They stopped firing and slowly fell back around Appomattox Court House, the Union troops following and hemming them in on all sides. Soon a white flag, a token of surrender, was presented to Sheridan's cavalry—an honor they well merited—and hostilities ceased. Early in the afternoon the battalion had the pleasure of witnessing the meeting of the General-in-Chief of the armies of the United States and the General-in-Chief of the Rebel armies, and soon after the formal surrender of the army of Northern Viriginia.

. . .

Four hundred officers and enlisted men were mustered into the battalion at San Francisco,[8] of which number only one hundred and forty-eight remained to be mustered out at its final discharge from the service. Many were killed in battle or died in the service; some were missing and unaccounted for; a large number were discharged from time to time on account of wounds or disability, and thirty of the enlisted men were promoted to commissioned officers in various regiments.

The veterans of the California Cavalry Battalion and California Hundred, organized in this State, have inscribed on their colors the names of the following engagements in which they have participated: Brookville, Ashby's Gap, Cyle's Tavern, Little River Pike, Dranesville, Rectortown, Point of Rocks, Aldie, Frederick Pike, Tanallytown, Fort Reno, Fort Stevens, Rockville, Poolsville, Leesburg, Snicker's Gap, Nolan's Ford, Shepardstown, Whitepost, Middletown, Strasburg, Kearnstown, Winchester, Berryville, Pike, Charlestown, Summit Point, Halltown, Smithfield, Opequan Creek, Knoxford, Front Royal, Snake Mountain, Luray Court House, Five Forks, South Side Railroad, Devil's Ford, Sailor's Creek and Appomattox Court House. Many skirmishes that the Californians were in, with the guerrillas in Virginia, with Early's forces in the Valley, while on the march to Petersburg, and during the ten days campaign before the surrender of Lee's army, have not been mentioned.

Today these tattered battle flags, which are a testimonial to the valor of a fighting legion of Californians, are on permanent display in the rotunda of the State Capitol at Sacramento.

---

[8] This was in addition to the first hundred men, who were sent east from San Francisco. The remaining four hundred are referred to as the California Cavalry Battalion.

22

BUILDING THE
FIRST TRANSCONTINENTAL
RAILROAD

As the Civil War raged, work began on a project that had more effect on the future history of California than any other enterprise. Construction started on a railroad that would span the nation. The first Pacific Railroad Act was passed July 1, 1862. It provided for the construction of a railroad and telegraph line from the Missouri River to the Pacific Ocean, a distance of about two thousand miles, and crossing the Rocky and Sierra Nevada Mountains. By its terms, the Central Pacific Railroad, a corporation organized in California, was authorized to build that portion starting at the Pacific coast and stretching from there eastwardly until a meeting and connection should be formed with the road in construction from the East. This was to be built by the Union Pacific Railroad Company. The Central Pacific—later to become the great Southern Pacific Company of California—had been incorporated on June 28, 1861. Four of its founders were to become the best-remembered personalities in the state's history. Leland Stanford, soon to be elected governor, was named president of the railroad. The vice-president was Collis P. Huntington, a Sacramento storekeeper, and the most dynamic and controversial figure in the group. His partner, Mark Hopkins, was designated secretary, while Charles Crocker, who had once carried freight to the gold mines by mule team, would serve as superintendent of construction. There were several others on the board of directors, but this quartet dominated the affairs of the company. They had become interested in the dream of Theodore D. Judah, a brilliant engineer, who had surveyed the western portion of the proposed transcontinental system, and perceived the feasibility of the plan, where others had scoffed at his proposals. The first publication to narrate in detail the long struggle to build the first transcontinental railroad was a San Francisco magazine, *The Overland Monthly,* a periodical of exceptional literary merit. The magazine's first issue was released while the railroad was still under construction in July, 1868. The editor, Bret Harte, had intended to include a short story of his own in the initial edition, but missed the deadline. He ran *The Luck of Roaring Camp* the following month. It made him famous. Harte assigned one of his writers to do an in-depth study, tracing the difficulties that had to be surmounted before a line could be extended across the formidable Sierra wall. The article appeared in the May, 1869, issue:

¶ . . . Judah's survey extended no farther than 128 miles east of Sacramento, to a point about five miles down the valley of Truckee River; but within this distance all the difficulties of the route were overcome; a mere reconnaissance through the valleys of the eastern slope showing that they afforded an easy railroad grade, while on the plateau beyond the base of the Sierra, as far as Salt Lake, the survey and estimates of Lieutenant Beckwith were a sufficient temporary guide. The main object was to demonstrate the practicability of crossing the Sierra by the most direct route between San Francisco, the commercial entrepôt of California, Sacramento, the capital of the State, and Virginia, the heart of the silver mines of Nevada. . . . Lower passes to the northward offered less obstacles from winter snows, but necessitated a longer line. The projectors of the Central Pacific Railroad preferred taking the chances of winter obstructions to those of losing a share of the profitable business that would help pay for the extension of the road toward Salt Lake. They were convinced that the snow difficulty was much exaggerated. Judah's survey crossed the State at nearly its narrowest part. It demonstrated that an elevation of 7,000 feet, with a base of only seventy miles, could be overcome with a maximum grade of one hundred and five feet per mile; that the western flanks of the Sierra, being at right angles to the northwesterly and southeasterly trend of the chain, could be ascended along an unbroken ridge from base to summit, in the general direction of the streams; that the necessary tunnelling would be comparatively easy and inexpensive. . . .

Judah died before the completion of the route, and while his engineering was accurate—Southern Pacific trains still follow the same roadbed across the mountains—the work was not easy. Today, driving along a modern freeway between Sacramento and Reno, Nevada, one crosses the Donner Summit at 7,135-feet of elevation. Paralleling the highway to the south, the long diesel-powered Southern Pacific trains thread their way down through Donner Pass toward Truckee. Much of the roadbed rests on shelves chiseled into the mountainside. It passes across trestles and disappears through tunnels that were bored through solid rock. When the original road was constructed, there were no power tools for digging and grading. Charles Crocker accomplished the task by importing an army of thousands of Chinese laborers from Canton. They worked with pick, shovel, and wheelbarrow to do the job. Nitroglycerin was the only modern innovation for moving mountains, and on a number of occasions the charges inflicted casualties among workers slowly laboring across the rugged Sierra Nevada, as a number of coolies were blown sky-high. In a statement forwarded to the President and the Secretary of the Interior by Central Pacific describing progress on the railroad, the importance of the use of Chinese labor was cited:

¶ . . . A large majority of the white laboring class on the Pacific Coast find more profitable and congenial employment in mining and agricultural pursuits, than in railroad work. The greater portion of the laborers employed by us are Chinese, who constitute a large element in the population of California. Without them it would be impossible to complete the western portion of this great national enterprise, within the time required by the Acts of Congress. As a class they are quiet, peaceable, patient, industrious and economical—ready and apt to learn all the different kinds of work required in railroad building, they soon become as efficient as white laborers. More prudent and economical, they are con-

tented with less wages. We find them organized into societies for material
aid and assistance. These societies, that count their number by thousands,
are conducted by shrewd, intelligent business men, who promptly advise
their subordinates where employment can be found on the most favorable
terms. No system similar to slavery, serfdom or peonage prevails among
these laborers. Their wages, which are always paid in coin at the end of
each month, are divided among them by their agents, who attend their
business, in proportion to the labor done by each person. These agents are
generally American or Chinese merchants, . . . under the just and liberal
policy pursued by the Company, it will be able to procure during the next
year, not less than 15,000 laborers. With this large force, the Company will
be able to push on the work so as not only to complete it for within the
time required by the Acts of Congress, but so as to meet the public
impatience.[1]

The fact that the Chinese laborers were "contented with less
wages," was a subject close to the heart of Collis Huntington and his
associates. He spent most of his time in the East raising funds for the
construction of the road, and there were times when the shaky Central Pacific was pressed for cash. The widespread use of Chinese
workers was to have serious repercussions in later years, when American labor fighting for higher pay considered the presence of Orientals
a threat to their livelihood. Financing for such a giant undertaking
was a complicated procedure, but the government was generous. The
bill passed in 1862 granted bond subsidies of three classes at the rate
respectively of $16,000, $23,000, and $48,000 per mile, according to the
nature of the country. The bonds were a lien upon the road and its
fixtures, and eventually repayable to the government. This was later to
result in a heated controversy, when Collis Huntington, the surviving
member of the Big Four, and then head of Southern Pacific, fought a
losing battle with Congress to avoid payment on these obligations. In
addition, the government awarded the railroad builders a liberal share
of the public domain in land grants amounting to 12,800 acres per
mile. The value of this real estate was calculated at the time to be in

---

[1] This report, dated October 10, 1865, and addressed to President Andrew Johnson
and Secretary of the Interior James Harlan, is signed by Leland Stanford, president of
the Central Pacific. It was later printed in pamphlet form (Sacramento: H. S. Crocker
& Co., printers, 1865). Collection of Henry E. Huntington Library and Art Gallery,
San Marino, Calif.

the neighborhood of $32,000 per mile. The estimated aggregate cost of the 1,851-mile railroad from Omaha to San Francisco was $100,000,-000. Considering that Central Pacific's founders, with the exception of Stanford, were men of moderate means, they had undertaken a financial venture of considerable magnitude. These, however, were four determined men, and each contributed his particular talent to the enterprise.

Collis Huntington was the money raiser and expediter of the necessary supplies and rolling stock. Mark Hopkins, noted for his frugality, kept one eye on the ledger, and the other on the cash drawer. Stanford, the politician, was an ideal front man for the organization. A gifted orator, he could charm the crowds, and after he became governor he was in a position to exert considerable influence on the state for passing favorable legislation. Crocker, a huge, restless man, and the most energetic of the foursome, exhorted his Chinese to greater efforts, as they swarmed like ants across the Sierra Nevada. It was said of Crocker that, had he lived in the time of the Pharaohs, he would have had the great Pyramids constructed in record time.

Central Pacific began the work of grading from Sacramento in January, 1863. Leland Stanford, now governor, gave a stirring speech before taking a shovel and turning the earth for the railroad's embankment. The crowd cheered as he declared:

¶ We may now look forward with confidence to the day, not far distant, when the Pacific will be bound to the Atlantic by iron bonds, that shall consolidate and strengthen the ties of nationality, and advance with great strides the prosperity of our State and of our country. The blessings which are to follow the completion of the work which we this day inaugurate can not be fully estimated. Agriculture, commerce, manufactures, wealth and population, will feel its influence, and will commence with it a new era in progress. . . .[2]

The first shipment of rails reached Sacramento in October, 1863. By June, 1864, thirty-one miles of track had been set down in the foothills of the Sierra. Huntington was having financial problems in the East. The California legislature had passed laws authorizing several counties to issue bonds for subscription to the stock of the company. While

[2] Sacramento *Union,* January 9, 1863.

the railroad was a private enterprise, all Californians would benefit by it. It was logical that municipalities such as San Francisco, which would derive the most advantages by being the western terminus of the route, should support the company financially. Yet the issue of San Francisco bonds was prevented by hostile suits, which were carried to the Supreme Court in 1865. Central Pacific had many enemies, generally financial groups that had failed to see the possibilities of the railroad in the beginning. A rumor that the road would not proceed beyond Dutch Flat, sixty-seven miles from Sacramento, injured Central Pacific's credit. It was discouraging for Huntington and his associates, but despite delays the work went on. By September, 1866, they were seventy miles east of Sacramento, and working at an altitude of more than five thousand feet in the mountains. The company was sending out iron by nearly every vessel leaving New York for San Francisco.

Union Pacific began grading work on the eastern end of the route in the summer of 1865. Its task was easier, as there was a five-hundred-mile stretch of prairie ahead of them, and the road building proceeded rapidly. Union Pacific also had the advantage of sufficient capital backing its operations. Snow in the mountains brought a halt to Central Pacific's progress in 1866. In the spring of the following year, work was resumed and the summit of the Sierra was reached. Fifteen tunnels had been completed, embracing a length of 6,262 feet. Ten thousand men were engaged in building the grade down the eastern slope. The race between the two railroads continued. The author of *The Overland Monthly* article wrote:

¶ . . . The woods of the Sierra and Rocky Mountains rang with the strokes of axmen and the click of steel in the quarries. The streams were bordered with camps of lumbermen and choked with floating logs. At one place on the Truckee River, twenty-five saw-mills went into sudden operation. Lumber, iron and material of every description lined the road, and the wake of the advancing workmen was marked by the odd debris of deserted camps. On the Central road alone from seventy to one hundred locomotives and several hundred cars were constantly passing to and fro with material, supplies and laborers. The wharves at San Francisco and Sacramento were piled with iron bars. At one time thirty vessels were en

route from New York via Cape Horn with iron and rolling stock for the
road, and locomotives and rails were even ordered by way of the Isthmus.
The forest solitudes of the Sierra Nevada thundered to the roar of falling
trees or passing trains. The desert spaces of the plains were populous. On
the eastern end the buffalo was scared from his pasture range, and even
the more savage red man dared only a few sneaking acts of resistance that
were more like thievish murders. Track was laid at the rate of two, three,
four, five and six miles a day by each company. Within a few weeks the
Central company have laid seven miles in one day. It is a literal fact that
more ground was ironed in some days, by the two companies together,
than the ox teams of 1849 averaged for a day's journey. By September 30th,
1868, the Central track extended 350 miles, and the graders were fifty miles
ahead, while another grading party was coming one hundred miles
westward from Salt Lake. . . .

The competition increased as the two roads neared each other;[3] but
when winter again set in, the operations of the Union Pacific were
seriously interrupted. Along the four hundred miles of track, from the
Black Hills to the Wasatch Mountains, where the country has an elevation
of from five thousand to eight thousand feet, the road was blocked with
snow for nearly two months. Mails, material, and supplies were stopped,
and passengers suffered great hardships. Serious defects in construction
were revealed, leading to complaints and investigation before Congress.
The Central road was stopped but one week. It had no snow difficulty
except in the Sierra, and twenty-two of the forty or fifty miles of deep
snow belt had been roofed in with heavy hewn timbers. Where this protection had not been furnished the track could have been kept clear by snow-
ploughs, but for the fall of some trestle work which prevented the passage
of the engine for a few days. . . .

The Central had enough iron, ties, and other material over the mountains to keep up the work of construction steadily. The train was stopped
in the vicinity of Ogden, within eighty miles of the head of Salt Lake, by
an obstinate rock tunnel, which is even yet not quite finished. A temporary
track was laid around it, and this gave rise to more complaints.

The competition between the two companies was transferred to Washington, where charges and counter charges were made, and an imbroglio

[3] It was more than competition. A bitter rivalry had developed between the two companies. For a time, Union Pacific and Central Pacific were grading roadbed side by side
for two hundred miles in Utah and eastern Nevada. Each hoped to lay its rails first and
collect the mileage subsidy from the government. Officials in Washington settled the dispute by designating the joining point as Promontory Point, Utah.

created which has not yet been cleared up. The Central wished Ogden fixed as the point of junction, claiming that the Union was working west of that place off the official line; and the Union wished Monument Point named for the junction, though there was a time when its managers expected to reach the California State line, and actually made surveys that far.

But with these disputes the *Overland* has nothing at present to do. It has only to rejoice that the work so long prayed for by denizens of the Pacific coast, on which so many hopes have centered, and which is really of great importance to the whole Republic, is at last about completed. One thousand miles of track have been laid within twelve months past: the larger proportion of that amount within six months. For a year, the iron road across "The Plains" has been growing at the rate of nearly two and three-quarter miles a day; a line of telegraph following it. The whole work of laying 494 miles of track, from Chicago to Omaha, and 1,727 miles, from Omaha to Sacramento—2,221 miles in all—has been accomplished in less than seven years since Congress passed the Pacific Railroad Act, and in a little over six years since California began work on the main line. . . .

As the railroad neared completion in the spring of 1869, the San Francisco *Alta California* published a special edition on May 8th, containing a round-up of stories describing the final stages of work, and the mounting excitement as Union Pacific and Central Pacific crews and officials prepared to rendezvous at Promontory Point, Utah, to drive the final spike. As the gap narrowed, Central Pacific established an all-time record for rail laying. It nailed down ten miles of track in one day. A reporter for the *Alta* was on the scene:

¶ The Central Pacific Railroad—The Front—Wednesday, April 28. It is daybreak. The scene is in the Valley of Salt Lake. Around the edge of what at some remote period must have been the shore of that great inland sea, is to be performed a day's work for which no parallel can be found in the history of the world—the laying of ten miles of rail. Standing here upon the rising ground, a view of the whole field may be obtained. Yonder is the Lake, glistening in the morning sun. Along the line of the road may be seen the white camps of the Chinese laborers, and from every one of them squads of these people are advancing to the great battle with that old enemy of mankind—space. There is a jaunty air about the

Oriental as he marches along; he has a woolen peaked cap, with ear flaps. He brings up rather the idea of an ancient Crusader more than that of a coolie laborer. The enthusiasm of the occasion has evidently brought even him within its influence, and the Caucasian part of the force is worked up to the highest pitch of excitement.

HOW THE RAILS ARE CARRIED FORWARD

AND LAID DOWN

The failure of the day before, caused by one of the engines attached to the train conveying the iron to the front running off the track just as two miles had been laid, nerved every man of them to such careful exertion that no accident could possibly occur. See that car loaded with iron coming up the track. It is wheeled along by a pair of horses, tandem fashion, after the manner of canal boats, the horses galloping at the side of the track. They are met by another car of a similar pattern coming down, after leaving its load at the front. This latter is bowled along (for the grade descends) by the men on each side, using their feet like oars. Surely this must be *contretemp,* for vehicles cannot pass on a single track—but stop—the down platform car stopped in an instant, it is lifted up, standing on the edge, and the loaded car passes on to the front without interruption. Arrived there, two men throw a wooden bar across the wheels to stop the motion, the horses are detached and gallop back to the rear. The two outer rails of the road on either side are seized, with iron nippers, hauled forward by four men, and laid on the ties over them; the car goes forward, and at it comes a gang of men, who half drive the spikes and screw on the fresh bolts. At a short interval behind them comes the first party of Chinamen, who drive home the spikes and add others. Behind them again, advances a second squad of Chinamen, two deep, on either side of the track. The inner line with shovels, the outer with picks. The pickaxe men loosen a shovelful of earth; it is picked up by the inner line and thrown about the ends of the ties. An idea of the speed attained may be obtained from figures. I timed the movement twice, and found the speed to be as follows: First time, 240 feet of rail laid in one minute and twenty seconds; second time, 240 feet in one minute and fifteen seconds. This is about as fast as a leisurely walk—as fast as the early ox teams used to travel over the Plains. It may seem incredible, but it is nevertheless the fact, that the whole ten miles of rail were handled and laid down this day by eight white men.

But we have here only taken in a portion of the scene. Along the line are overseers galloping up and down, seeing that everything is properly done. Right at the front sits Mr. Charles Crocker, the General Superintendent.

. . . The eye of Mr. Crocker takes in every detail of the operation, and his merry laugh when anything amusing takes place awakens the long-slumbering echoes.

By six o'clock two miles are laid, and a train containing two more miles of rails is pushed forward from the rear. It steams up to the last rail just laid; a squad of men rush at it; it took exactly ten minutes to unload it. There are one hundred tons of iron to the mile, so that two hundred tons of iron, together with ten tons of spikes were unloaded within the time stated. Then the iron cars are loaded, and are started off one after another, as already described. While this advance is made along the line, the ties are being hauled along by a parallel road on the right, while the water-carts and tool wagons move on the left.

By noon there is no longer any doubt that the great feat will be successfully accomplished. In six hours and forty-two minutes six miles of track were laid, but here are these 1,200 or 1,400 men to be fed. They have advanced six miles from a home from which they started. Look far to the rear and behold a strange phenomenon; it looks like a village of one street in motion. This is the boarding-house train, composed of a number of plain wooden-house cars with peaked roofs. Here are the bunks of the workmen, arranged after the manner of the steerage of a ship; and likewise their dining-rooms. I have seen the men at their meals and inspected their food. They are fed like fighting cocks. Their bread and meat are of the very best description, and as soon as the implements are thrown down the boarding-house train is at hand, and the white laborers retire to their dinner. The Chinamen bring their food with them and dine on the line of work.

So far as I have been able to observe there was not the slightest antagonism between the two races engaged on the works of the Central Pacific. Passing along this line of Chinamen, I hear the Caucasian commander of the gang singing out, "Hurry up there, ye devils, shure we have no time to lose," and the answer comes from the whole squad, in a laughing manner, "Tach I Yah," which I inferred meant, "Ready and begorra, we do that same," for a closing up of the ranks, a brisker gait and a livelier movement of shovels and pick-axes immediately followed.

·   ·   ·

Onward the army of workers advance. The engines puff; the platform cars whirl; "klink, kling," go the hammers; there is no pause or cessation. Before the night comes on the great job is completed. The last two rails are laid, the last spike is driven, and the conquering army returns to its quarters. No such feat has ever before been accomplished in the history of railroading. In making up opinions upon it, it is necessary to bear in mind that nearly an hour was lost after dinner in the bending of the rails for the great curve which completed the day's work. The rails are placed on blocks, and with the blows of heavy hammers are forced into the desired form. If the line had been perfectly straight and level the men who laid ten miles of rail today would have easily accomplished fifteen.

It was delightful to witness the congratulations which passed from one to the other when the great job was done. . . . The Pacific General Super-intendent, Mr. Charles Crocker, makes no secret of all his wishes; his merry laugh was heard all day along the line; nothing appears to depress him. On Tuesday, a quarter of an hour after the failure of the first attempt to lay ten miles of rail in a single day, I found him shooting at the end of a cigar box set up on the ground a hundred yards distant. He sent a bullet through it five times out of nine; one of the shots was almost in the center. His face clouded for a moment when he heard the engine had got off the track, and for that day the great feat was an impossibility; but it soon assumed its jovial aspect. His merry laugh was ringing out as clearly as if nothing to annoy him had recently occurred. And now as to what remains to be done. The work of today leaves but four miles to be laid on the Central Pacific. These four miles are almost graded. The calculation now is that the last rail will be laid on Thursday by Gov. Stanford. . . .

. . .

Sacramento, May 4th—The Pacific Union Express tonight was the scene of great excitement and crowded by people to look at the last tie to be laid on the Pacific Railroad. It was uncovered in the presence of a throng of people, and in form is a splendid piece of California laurel-wood. In length it is over six feet, six inches wide and seven deep. In the centre of the tie is a plate of solid silver, seven inches by six, on which are the names of the Directors and officers of the Company on either side. The plate also bears the name of West Evans, who has prepared most of the ties issued on the road.

William Seddon has put in order the well known cannon "Union Boy," which was fired 875 times during the last campaign in honor of Grant, besides announcing victories during the rebellion. It has been put in the best condition—the Railroad Company having demanded that it go to the front—and from it will be reported the completion of the notable event of the age. A large transparency has been prepared, which on one side bears the following:

"I announced its opening Nov 9, 1863," "I proclaim its completion, May, 1869."

The original Board of Directors of the Company, which still remains consists of Leland Stanford, C. P. Huntington, E. B. Crocker, Mark Hopkins, A. P. Stanford, E. H. Miller and Charles Marsh. The gold spike, which is to be driven by the President of the road, has arrived, and with the tie will go forward in the morning. Quite a number of people are going out to the front in the morning to witness the closing of the road.

· · ·

From the Railroad Front—Victory, Head of Great Salt Lake, May 4—Left there for the front at one P.M. and stopped six hours at Rosebud, waiting for the arrival of trains from the eastward with men from the front coming back to ballast up and put in complete order portions of track hastily laid during the last winter. One of these trains consisted of twenty-seven long platform cars, loaded with dirt carts, tools, company utensils and other implements of a division of the Asiatic contingent of the Grand Army of Civilization. The cars contained 557 Chinese, all laughing and shouting in high glee at the approaching completion of the great work and their return from the end of the sage brush. . . . Thirty-five horses were also on the train. A similar train, loaded with white laborers, followed. The first of these trains was bound for the vicinity of Twelve Mile Cañon, to finish the work there. These Chinese expect to be sent north to work on the Northern Pacific Road. One train had 300 soldiers of the Twelfth U.S. Infantry, from the south under Col. Wallace, bound for California with the entire Twenty-first Regiment en route between here and Omaha, and will reach here Saturday.

The weather is very warm and hazy.

The first view of Salt Lake, with its dark-blue water, reflecting as from a mirror the purple and snow-clad mountains around the eastern, southern and western borders, is wonderfully picturesque and beautiful.

Reaching here at 5 P.M., I found the Central Pacific road all completed, save the laying of two rails, which are reserved for the final ceremony. The camp and construction trains moved back eight miles to this point. Passengers in from Ogden report that only four miles of the Union Pacific road are uncompleted. It is generally understood that the junction will be formally made with fitting ceremonies in the presence of the officers of both roads and guests from the Atlantic and Pacific slopes, now en route on Friday, or Saturday at the furthest.

The Pacific Mail Steamer burns en route to San Francisco from Panama in 1862. There were a number of similar sea tragedies from the time of the Gold Rush on, in which the boilers of the vessels either exploded, or the ships ran aground along the often fog-shrouded Pacific coast. *(State Library, Sacramento)*

This signal tower was a familiar landmark in San Francisco. Vessels entering the harbor were noted by the lookout with his glass long before they anchored in the bay. Sketch of the city was made in 1863. *(State Library, Sacramento)*

When President Abraham Lincoln was assassinated, obsequies were held at San Francisco. Hundreds of California troops paraded, not only as a gesture of sympathy, but as an act of reaffirmation that the state had remained loyal to the Union. *(State Library, Sacramento)*

A track-laying crew at work on the Central Pacific Railroad in 1868. *(Southern Pacific Company)*

While en route to the Last Spike ceremonies held at Promontory, Utah, the special Central Pacific train encountered a covered wagon train westbound with emigrants. Both caravans halted while a photographer recorded this historic moment in 1869. With the advent of the first transcontinental rail system, the slow-moving wagons with their sun-bleached canvas tops would vanish from the prairies, becoming symbols of a bygone era. *(Southern Pacific Company)*

ABOVE: On May 10, 1869, trains from east and west met as the first transcontinental railroad was completed. The last section of track was laid at Promontory, Utah. For the Far West, this was a momentous occasion, and the beginning of a new era of expansion. BELOW: This early photograph shows eight Central Pacific locomotives pushing a snow plow across Donner Summit in the High Sierra. The Southern Pacific follows these same rails across the mountains today, and at times it is still necessary to use giant rotary snowplows to clear a passage for the trains. *(Pictures: Southern Pacific Company)*

Los Angeles' first volunteer fire department turned out for a July 4 parade in 1871, marching behind their newly acquired fire engine. The volunteers were an exclusive group, whose headquarters was a local saloon. The event was the biggest celebration since the American flag had been raised on Fort Moore Hill, overlooking the Civic Center, for the first time on July 4, 1847. The scene is near the present City Hall. *(Los Angeles County Museum of Natural History)*

ABOVE: *Frank Leslie's Illustrated Newspaper* published this sketch of San Diego in its June 28, 1873, edition, with the following caption: "The new town or city of San Diego is said to contain about 2,000 inhabitants; and judging from the number of immigrants that we now see entering with their goods and families, the population is likely to assume important dimensions speedily. The shipping, too, that we see crowding the bay is significant in the extreme, and would seem to engender the idea that this little center may soon rival San Francisco."

RIGHT: Workers preparing to go belowground in a Nevada silver mine are shown passing the paymaster's window as they check in before beginning their shift. From *Harper's Weekly,* August 25, 1877. *(Pictures: State Library, Sacramento)*

Los Angeles, 1889. The city had a population of 50,000 when the new cable car line opened. This is one of the cars on Broadway, just north of Second Street near the present Civic Center. (*Authors' collection*)

OPPOSITE: California Street, San Francisco, August 26, 1875, following the announcement that the Bank of California had closed its doors. (*State Library, Sacramento*)

A bull team and logging crew near Fort Bragg in the 1880s. *(Union Lumber Co., Fort Bragg, Calif.)*

LEFT: Captain Jack, the renegade Modoc chief, who led his band in a wave of terror against settlers and the U.S. Army in the northeastern section of California during the war of 1873. He was finally captured in the Lava Beds and hanged. *(State Library, Sacramento)* BELOW: Canby's Cross marks the spot on the Lava Beds National Monument where General E. R. S. Canby sat down to parley with the Modoc Indians and was shot to death. *(Photo by William S. Murphy)*

THE BIG FOUR

ABOVE LEFT: Leland Stanford, one of the organizers of the Central Pacific Railroad, who became governor of California. ABOVE RIGHT: Charles Crocker, another member of the Big Four in building the Central Pacific Railroad. He had been a dry-goods merchant before joining the combine that built the route across the Sierra that joined with Union Pacific to become the nation's first transcontinental rail system. BELOW LEFT: The frugal Mark Hopkins was the Central Pacific's secretary and watched the cash drawer. BELOW RIGHT: Collis P. Huntington, from first to last the major figure of the Big Four, who pioneered the Central Pacific, later to become the mighty Southern Pacific rail network (*Photos: Southern Pacific Company*)

ABOVE: Volunteers leaving Los Angeles during the war with Spain in 1898, for San Francisco, where transports would carry them to the Philippines. *(Authors' collection)* BELOW: A packed transport sails from San Francisco for the Philippines. *(State Library, Sacramento)*

One of the most striking photographs taken following the disastrous earthquake and fire that leveled San Francisco on April 18, 1906. This view was taken from the Ferry Building tower, looking up Market Street. (*Southern Pacific Company*)

OPPOSITE: The San Francisco *Call* building in flames following the earthquake of 1906. (*Los Angeles* Times *collection*)

Martial law was declared in San Francisco following the earthquake and fire
of 1906. U.S. troops were assigned to the city to prevent looting and preserve order.
The photographer apparently asked them to draw their pistols for effect. A
number of looters were shot during the days following the disaster. *(State Library,
Sacramento)*

The New York *Daily Tribune* carried an account of the formal ceremonies uniting the two railroads in its May 11, 1869, edition:

¶ Washington, May 10—The announcement having been made here about noon today that the driving of the spikes in the last rail which would complete the line of railroad between the Atlantic and Pacific Oceans would be communicated to all the telegraph offices in the country the instant the work was done, a large crowd gathered in the main office of the Western Union Telegraph Company here to receive the welcome news. Mr. Tinker, the manager of the office here, placed a magnetic bell in a conspicuous place, where all present could witness the performance, and connected the same with the main lines.

At about 2:27 P.M., many of the offices in different parts of the country began to make all sorts of inquiries of the office at Omaha, from which point the circuit was to be started. That office replied:

"To everybody: Keep quiet. When the last spike is driven at Promontory Point we will say 'Done.' Don't break the circuit, but watch for the signals of the blows of the hammer."

After some little trouble in the Chicago office, and the closing of a circuit west of Buffalo, the instrument here was adjusted, and at 2:27 P.M., Promontory Point, 2,400 miles west of Washington, said to the people congregated in the various telegraph offices:

"Almost ready. Hats off; prayer is being offered."

A silence for the prayer ensued. At 2:40 the bell tapped again, and the office at the Point said:

"We have got done praying. The spike is about to be presented."

Chicago replied: "We understand. All are ready in the East."

Promontory Point—"All ready now, the spike will soon be driven. The signal will be three dots for the commencement of the blows."

For a moment the instrument was silent, and then the hammer of the magnet tapped the bell, one, two, three—the signal. Another pause of a few seconds, and the lightning came flashing eastward, vibrating over 2,400 miles, between the junction of the two roads and Washington, and the blows of the hammer upon the spike were delivered instantly, in telegraphic accents, on the bell here. At 2:47 P.M. Promontory Point gave the signal, "Done!" The announcement that the continent was spanned with iron.

23

THE TURBULENT SEVENTIES

The railroad brought thousands of new residents into California, and with the growing population came severe social and economic problems. Southern Pacific needed buyers for its extensive landholdings. The purchasers were chiefly farmers. These were the type of settlers the railroad was interested in bringing to the state. Farmers were shippers, and shipping brought freight revenues. Agriculture began to assume the significant role it occupies today in California's economy. Unfortunately, the relationship between the farmers and the railroad soon deteriorated. Growers complained that Southern Pacific's tariff structure for carrying agricultural products was excessive, and that the railroad granted special concessions in the form of rebates to favored shippers.

There was trouble in the ranks of labor during this decade, as workers increased their demands for better wages; and then a financial disaster occurred that shattered the economy of the nation. In 1873, the banking firm of Jay Cooke and Company failed. The firm had been underwriting the financing of the Northern Pacific Railroad. The route crossed through unsettled regions of the Pacific Northwest. When the rails were finally laid, Northern Pacific discovered that there was little traffic, and revenues were inadequate to defray operational costs. The banking firm was unable to sell its bonds. The failure of Cooke and Company came as a shock to the public. It had been considered the most reputable financial institution in America. A panic followed. Stocks tumbled, and the New York Exchange was forced to suspend operations for ten days. There were thousands of business failures. Nearly a hundred railroads defaulted on their bonds. All railroad construction ceased in 1874, and a half a million men were out of work. There was widespread unemployment throughout the United States, and the Chinese question became the most vital problem of the day. Thousands had been recruited to build the Central Pacific, and they later found employment on other railroads and in various industries. They were still arriving at San Francisco from Canton by the shipload. The Chinese worked for low wages. They maintained their own culture and demonstrated little inclination to learn American ways. To American organized labor, they were a threat, and agitation for the exclusion of the Chinese was increased in Congress. Owing to the pressures exerted in California, a law was passed in Washington in 1879 that made it illegal for a vessel to bring more than fifteen Chinese into an American port. This law was a violation of the Burlingame Treaty, which permitted unrestricted immigration into the United States, and when it was placed on President Hayes' desk for signature, he vetoed the bill, arousing considerable wrath in California.

In 1880, the treaty was changed. Revised, the document permitted the United States to regulate the immigration of Chinese. Congress then slammed the door by enacting a law that suspended immigration from China for twenty years. This time it was President Arthur who vetoed the bill. An amended version proved acceptable to the President in 1882. This was enacted into law. It suspended Chinese immigration for a period of ten years.

In San Francisco, and in other cities of the nation, the bigoted rantings of Dennis Kearney, the sandlot orator, contributed in some measure to the barring of Chinese from American soil, but there were others who also helped to evoke a feeling of contempt for the Orientals. People were amused at the first illustrated edition of Bret Harte's *Heathen Chinee* published in 1870. The caricature of Ah Sin, the character depicted in the poem, shows a grinning coolie with a long pigtail. Ridicule was subtle, but it is evident when you read Dan De Quille's account of silver mining in Virginia City and his description of an opium den, what an impact it must have had upon the reader. Every Chinaman, as they were called, became in the eyes of the public a depraved drug addict.

During these troubled times, there was suddenly a golden ray of hope, as the neighboring State of Nevada became the setting for a frantic scramble for riches that affected the lives of thousands of Californians. The tapping of the fabulous Comstock Lode near Virginia City touched off a wave of excitement unmatched since the days following the first discovery of gold on the American River. Interest in silver mining had its origins as early as 1863, when stock in several Virginia City mines was sold in San Francisco. In 1872, the California Stock Exchange Board was organized, and speculation became widespread in the Nevada mines. The value of these securities soared from seventeen to eighty-four millions. The population of Virginia City climbed to 25,000, and it became the mining capital of the world. The community also developed a reputation as the wildest town in the West, and judging from the presence of more than one hundred saloons, there was little chance that any of the residents would go thirsty.

The mining era produced its financial giants, a few who towered over the thousands buying shares in the silver mines with every available dollar they possessed, often mortgaging their homes to purchase additional stocks. Such a man was William C. Ralston, the most flamboyant, daring, and imaginative of all the silver barons.

Ralston reached California in 1853. With several others, he organized the Bank of California and was soon its president. This bank became a financial institution known through the world. Ralston invested bank funds in the Comstock mines, but he also developed a number of industries in his effort to make San Francisco one of the leading cities of the world. Firms he owned manufactured furniture, carriages, watches, repaired ships, wove wool into fabrics, and refined sugar, to name but a few of his financial interests. A patron of the arts, Ralston built the California Theater in the Bay City. He lived and entertained in the manner befitting a silver king. His villa at Belmont, twenty-two miles south of San Francisco, was built and furnished at a cost of more than a million dollars. When Ralston's financial empire suddenly crashed in 1875, as the bullion that had seemingly poured in an endless stream from Nevada's Washoe Valley began to slow to a trickle, the Bank of California closed its doors. Ralston's creditors had called their loans, causing the bank's failure. Ralston drove his carriage out to North Beach, where he was in the habit of taking a daily swim in San Francisco Bay. He plunged into the water and was a considerable distance from shore, when he disappeared. His drowning was considered a suicide, but Ralston's physician disputed this theory, claiming the financier became overheated and suffered a cramp.

There were others who made and lost fortunes in the Comstock: William Sharon, who was associated with Ralston, managing his Nevada mines; Adolph Sutro, who engineered a huge tunnel to drain the water from the deeper levels of the lode, thereby reaching veins of ore the miners had been unable to extract, because the areas were flooded. There were John W. Mackay, James Fair, Jim Flood, William O'Brien, all powerful figures in the Comstock, but Ralston was the most colorful of them all. Much has been written about them by George D. Lyman[1] and others. There is little material available, however, about what it was like to work in the mines, where an army of perspiring workers chipped and blasted deep in the earth to remove the valuable metal. On the scene during the era was William Wright, better known to his readers as Dan De Quille, for thirty years a reporter and mining editor of the *Territorial Enterprise* in Virginia City. Early in his career, he had helped a fledgling writer on this same newspaper—Samuel L. Clemens, who adopted a pseudonym under which name he became famous: Mark Twain. The two became lifelong friends, and Twain contributed a foreword to Wright's book describing the exciting period of Virginia City's brief moment of glory, when it was the silver center of the West. In these excerpts from

[1] *Ralston's Ring—California Plunders the Comstock Lode* (New York: Charles Scribner's Sons, 1937).

History of the Big Bonanza: An Authentic Account of the Discovery, History, and Working of the World Renowned Comstock Silver Lode of Nevada, Dan De Quille takes the reader on a tour of one of the mines, visits an opium den, and recounts the frenzied speculation in mining stocks that went on around him:

¶ In the winter of 1874–75, owing to the wonderful developments made in the Consolidated Virginia and California mines, there was a grand stock excitement throughout the towns of the Pacific Coast. San Francisco and Virginia City, however, were the two great centres of excitement. As the vast and astonishingly rich deposits of ore in the California mine began to be drifted into and opened to view, the stock of the company rapidly and steadily advanced from about fifty dollars per share to nearly one thousand dollars. Consolidated Virginia stock advanced in about the same ratio, as in the mine of that company the width and richness of the ore was far beyond anything that had ever before been seen on the Comstock lode. In the Ophir mine, the next north of the California, large and rich bodies of ore were being opened, and the stock of that company advanced with almost bewildering rapidity. Persons who happened to have twenty, fifty, or one hundred shares in either of these mines suddenly found themselves rich. The investment of a few hundreds of dollars had brought them thousands, and the investments of thousands brought them tens of thousands of dollars.

The great strike in the "bonanza" mines started up the stocks of all the adjoining mines, and, indeed, of all the mines along the Comstock range. The stock of mines that were rich in "great expectations" only were as eagerly sought for and as briskly dealt in, as were those in which ore was already being extracted, for many said: "It is just as well for us to double our money in a stock that costs but one or two dollars per share as in stocks that cost from one to five hundred dollars." And many did double and more than double their money in such stocks; indeed, in some instances they sold for five or ten times what their stocks cost them.

Every day there is a morning and an afternoon session of the San Francisco Stock Board, and the reports of the sales are telegraphed to Virginia City, Gold Hill and other Nevada towns as fast as the stocks are called. Thus, as soon as the Stock Board is in session and business begins, reports of sales begin to arrive in Virginia City and are placed in the windows or on the bulletin-boards of the various stock-brokers of the town, where all interested may see them. Therefore during a big stock excitement the bulletin-boards are the centres about which are seen large crowds of anxious dealers—and nearly everybody in the city dabbles more or less in stocks, women as well as men.

On very critical occasions, either when stocks are rapidly rushing or when they are rapidly "tumbling," then is a grand charge made upon all the bulletin-boards as soon as it is known that the reports have arrived. Dry-goods clerks—yardstick in hand and scissors peeping from vest-pocket—come running out bare-headed and bald-headed to catch a glimpse of the bulletin; bar-keepers in their white aprons come; bare-headed, bare-armed, and white-aproned butchers smelling of blood, come; blacksmiths, in leather aprons and hammer in hand, flour-dusted bakers, cooks in paper caps, cobblers, tinkers, and tailors all come to learn the best and the worst. The miner on his way to or from work, carrying his dinner-pail and candlestick, halts for a moment to see how fares his favorite stock, and the teamster stops his long string of mules opposite one of the centres of attraction and, thrusting his "black snake" under the housing of his saddle-mule, marches to the board to read his fate. Ladies linger as they pass the groups at the bulletin-boards and try to catch some word of hope, or ensconce themselves in the nearest shops, and hence send messenger-lads to bring tidings of their favorite gamble. . . .

.   .   .

In the Consolidated Virginia Mine, and in all other leading mines, three shifts of men are employed, each shift working eight hours.

The morning shift goes on at 7 o'clock. Before descending the shaft the men go to the office of the time-keeper, situated in the hoisting works, and give their names at a window which resembles the ticket-office at a railroad-station. These men come up out of the mine at 3 o'clock P.M., and again go to the window of the time-keeper's office, and give their names. . . .

When the shifts are being changed the men do not rush promiscuously to the shaft, but form in a line and march up to the cages in single file, just as men are seen to form in line in front of the window of a post-office or at the polls on the occasion of an election. On the levels below, when the men are coming up, they form in lines in the same way in front of the shaft. No crowding or disorder of any kind is permitted. . . .

In a silver-mine it is not all dark and dismal below, as many persons suppose. On the contrary, the long drifts and cross-cuts are lighted up with candles and lamps. It is only the little-used drifts, in parts of the mine distant from the main workings, that absolute and pitchy darkness prevails.

In the principal levels candles and lamps are always burning. When it is midnight above, and storms and darkness prevail throughout the city, whole acres of ground, hundreds of feet below in the bowels of the earth, are lighted up; and down there all is calm and silent, save when sounds peculiar to the place break the stillness.

In a mine there is neither day nor night; it is always candlelight. If we go into a mine late in the afternoon and remain below for some hours, a gloomy feeling is experienced when we come to the surface and find it is everywhere night above. We almost wish ourselves back in the lower levels of the mine, for when we are there it seems to be always daylight above.

On the principal levels of a mine we have long drifts, galleries and cross-cuts which intersect each other, much as do the streets and alleys in some old-fashioned, overcrowded village—some village seated in a confined place, where encroaching precipices seem to crush it out of shape.

Our underground streets are not wanting in life. As we pass along the highways and byways of the lower levels, we meet with the people of the place at every turn. One mine connects with another, and so we have streets 3 miles long. There are employed in a single mine from 500 to 700 men; a number sufficient to populate a town of considerable size. Men meet and pass us—all going about their business, as on the surface—and frequently a turn brings us in sight of whole groups of them. We seem to have been suddenly brought face to face with a new and strange race of men. All are naked to the waist, and many from the middle of their thighs to their feet. Superb, muscular forms are seen on all sides and in all attitudes, gleaming white as marble in the light of the many candles. We everywhere see men who would delight the eye of the sculptor. These men seem of a different race from those we see above—the clothes-wearers. Before us we have the Troglodytes—the cave-dwellers. We go back in thought to the time when the human race housed in caverns; not only far up the Nile, as the ancients supposed, but in every land, at a certain stage of their advancement in the arts of life.

Not infrequently, while travelling along a lonely passage in some remote section of the mine, we are suddenly confronted by a man of large stature, huge, spreading beard, and breast covered with shaggy hair, who comes sliding down out of some narrow side-drift, lands in our path, and for a moment stands up and gazes curiously upon us, as though half inclined to consider us intruders upon his own peculiar domain. We seem to have before us one of the old cave-dwellers and we should not be at all surprised to see him cut a caper in the air, brandish a ponderous stone ax, and advance upon us with a wild whoop.

The only clothing worn by the men working in the lower levels of a mine are a pair of thin pantaloons or overalls, stout shoes, and a small felt hat or a cap such as cooks are often seen to wear. Not a shirt is seen. From the head to the hips each man is as naked as on the day he was born. All are drenched with perspiration, and their bodies glisten in the light of the candles as though they had just come up through the waters of some subterranean lake.

In places, in some of the mines, the heat is so great that the men do not even wear overalls, but are seen in the breech-clout of the primitive races. Instead of a breech-clout, some of the miners wear a pair of drawers with the legs cut off about the middle of the thighs. Something must be worn on the head to keep the falling sand and dirt out of the hair, and shoes must be worn to protect the feet from the sharp fragments of quartz which strew the floors of the levels. One may be well acquainted with a miner as he appears upon the streets, yet for a time utterly fail to recognize him as found attired in the underground regions of a mine. . . .

No fighting is allowed among the miners while in the lower levels. No matter how angry they may become, not a blow must be struck. The penalty for a violation of this rule is the immediate discharge of both parties to the quarrel.

It very frequently happens that two men who have had a serious mis-understanding while in the mine, repair to some quiet place when they come to the surface and have their fight out, friends on both sides being present and the rules of the prize ring being observed.

Fights growing out of wrangles in the mines are always thus settled with fists; knives or pistols are never used on such occasions. However, there is much less quarrelling in the mines than would be supposed, the large number of men and their various and antagonistic nationalities being considered. The fact that nearly all are members of the same society,—the Miners Union—doubtless has much to do with keeping peace among all the large underground families along the Comstock lode.

.   .   .

In Virginia City, as in all other places where there is a considerable Chinese population, are found opium-dens. These are sometimes on the first floor, but are generally in a cellar or basement. We will take a look at one not in any building: it is a subterranean opium-den—a cave of oblivion:—

In the side of a little hill in the eastern part of the Chinese quarter of Virginia City is to be seen a low door of rough boards. An open cut, dug in the slope of the hill and walled with rough rocks, leads to the door. The boards forming the door and its frame are blackened by smoke, particularly at the top, for the den has neither chimney nor flue. The surface of the hills forms its roof. All that is to be seen on the outside is the door and the walled entrance leading up to it. Not a sound is heard within or about the place. The cave of the Seven Sleepers was not more silent. But gently pushing the door, it opens—opens as noiselessly as though hinged in cups of oil.

At first we can see nothing, save a small lamp suspended from the centre of the ceiling. The lamp burns with a dull red light that illuminates nothing. It seems more like a distant fiery star than anything mundane. Though at first we see nothing but the lamp, gradually our eyes adapt themselves to the dim light, and we can make out the walls and some of the larger objects in the place. A voice says: "What you want?" Looking in the direction whence proceeds the inquiry, we see a sallow old Mongolian seated near a small table. He is the proprietor of the den. "What you want?" he repeats. We feel that we have no business where we are, but to speak the truth is always best, therefore we simply say in pigeon-English: "Me comee see your smokee saloon." The old fellow settles one elbow on the table before him, and makes a remark which appears to be the Chinese equivalent for "Humph!"

Before this taciturn dispenser of somnial drugs are a number of little horn boxes of opium, several opium-pipes, small scales for weighing, with beam of bone, covered with black dots instead of figures; small steel spatulas, wire probes, and other smoking-apparatus.

We now observe that two sides of the den are fitted up with bunks, one above the other, like the berths on shipboard. A cadaverous opium-smoker is seen in nearly every bunk. These men are in various stages of stupor. Each lies upon a scrap of grass mat or old blanket. Before him is a small alcohol lamp burning with a blue flame which gives out but little light—only enough to cast a sickly glare upon the corpse-like face of the smoker, as he holds his pipe in the flame, and by a long draught inhales and swallows the smoke of the loved drug. These fellows are silent as dead men, and seem unconscious of our presence. Occasionally, at a sign, the proprietor arises and furnishes the customer a fresh supply of the drug. The peculiar sweetish-bitter odor of the burning opium fills and saturates the whole place—one can almost taste it.

While the majority, lying upon their sides, and propped on one elbow, are calmly inhaling their dose, a few appear to have had enough. These lie with their heads resting upon short sections of bamboo, which serve this curious people as pillows, and move no more than dead men. The eyes of some are wide open, as in a fixed stare, while those of others are partially or wholly closed. If they have any of those heavenly visions of which we are told, they keep them to themselves; as, save in a few somniloquous mutterings, they utter no sound. The door is gently opened, and a gaunt, wild-eyed Mongolian slips stealthily in. The old man at the table merely elevates his eyes. The newcomer steps out of sandals and, making no more noise than a cat, crosses the earthen floor of the room and creeps into a vacant bunk. The boss of this cavern of Morpheus now raises his elbows from the table, takes up a pipe and its belongings, sleepily lights one of the small alcohol lamps, and then places the whole before his customer. The old man then returns to his table and sits down. Not a word is spoken.

Thus the business of the cavern goes on, day and night, and this is all of opium-smoking that appears on the surface, tales of travellers to the contrary notwithstanding. What shapes may appear to the sleepers, or what flight their souls may take into interstellar regions, we know not. To a looker-on it is all vapid, vacuous stupefaction.

Not a few white men in Virginia City—and a few women—are opium smokers. They visit the Chinese opium dens two or three times a week. They say that the effect is exhilarating—that it is the same as intoxication produced by drinking liquor, except that under the influence of opium a man has all his senses, and his brain is almost supernaturally bright and clear. An American told me that he had been an opium-smoker for eighteen years, and said there were about fifty persons in Virginia City who were of the initiated. In San Francisco he says there are over five hundred white opium-smokers, many women among them. . . .[2]

* * *

Charles Nordhoff was a talented newspaperman who visited California in 1871–1872, and wrote *California: For Health, Pleasure and Residence*. It became a popular travel book of the period. In journalistic parlance, the volume is clearly a puff book on Collis P. Huntington and the Southern Pacific Railroad. It is rather apparent that the shrewd Huntington subsidized the publication and its distribution, for

[2] Dan De Quille (William Wright), *History of the Big Bonanza: An Authentic Account of the Discovery, History, and Working of the World Renowned Comstock Silver Lode of Nevada* (San Francisco: Hartford Publishing Co., A. L. Bancroft & Co., 1876).

the book was intended to draw prospective farmers into the state. This does not lessen the readability of Nordhoff's account, for his narrative contains a most detailed description of what California was like in 1871.

Nordhoff, who was born in 1830, left a life at sea in 1853 to become a journalist. He had served in the navy and aboard merchant, whaling and fishing vessels. Writing, however, was his chief interest. He had a brief introduction to journalism as a boy of fourteen, when he worked for a Philadelphia newspaper before joining the navy. From 1853 to 1871, he was employed by newspapers in Philadelphia, Indianapolis, and New York, where he was on the editorial staff of the New York *Evening Post*. Later he contributed to the New York *Herald*. Following Nordhoff's California trip, he visited Hawaii in 1873. The following year he was hired by the New York *Herald* as its Washington correspondent, a position he held until his retirement in 1890. He spent the final years of his life at Coronado, California, and died at San Francisco on July 14, 1901. His grandson, Charles Bernard Nordhoff, became a well-known author, who is best noted for his *Mutiny on the Bounty* trilogy, on which he collaborated with James Norman Hall.

This is part of Nordhoff's introduction to his account of California as he saw it after riding one of the Southern Pacific's trains across the continent, when the railroad was still new enough for the trip to be regarded as an exciting adventure:

¶ California is to most Eastern people still a land of big beets and pumpkins, of rough miners, of pistols, bowie-knives, abundant fruit, queer wines, high prices—full of discomforts, and abounding in dangers to the peaceful traveler. A New Yorker, inefficient except in his own business, looking to the government, municipal, State, or Federal, for almost every thing except his daily dollars; overridden by a semi-barbarous foreign population; troubled with incapable servants, private as well as public; subject to daily rudeness from car-drivers and others who ought to be civil; rolled helplessly and tediously downtown to his business in a lumbering omnibus; exposed to inconveniences, to dirty streets, bad gas, beggars, loss of time through improper conveyances; to high taxes, theft, and all kinds of public wrong, year in and year out—this New Yorker fondly imagines himself to be living at the center of civilization, and pities the unlucky friend who is "going to California." He invites him out to dine before he sets out, "because you will not get a good dinner again until you return, you know;" he sends him his parting blessing, a heavy navy revolver; and shudders at the annoyances and dangers which his friend, out of a rash and venturesome disposition, is about to undergo.

Well, this New Yorker is mistaken. There are no dangers to travelers on the beaten track in California; there are no inconveniences which a child or tenderly reared woman would not laugh at; they dine in San Francisco rather better, and with quite as much form, and more elegant and perfect service, than in New York; the San Francisco hotels are the best and cheapest in the world; the noble art of cooking is better understood in California than anywhere else where I have eaten; the bread is far better, the variety of food is greater; the persons with whom a tourist comes in contact, and upon whom his comfort and pleasures so greatly depend, are more uniformly civil, obliging, honest, and intelligent than they are anywhere in this country, or, so far as I know, in Europe; the pleasure-roads in the neighborhood of San Francisco are unequaled anywhere; the common country roads are kept in far better order than anywhere in the Eastern States; and when you have spent half a dozen weeks in the State, you will perhaps return with a notion that New York is the true frontier land, and that you have nowhere in the United States seen so complete a civilization—in all material points, at least—as you found in California. Moreover, the cost of living is today less in California by a third than in any Eastern State; it is, at this time, the cheapest country in the United States to live in. . . .

Certainly in no part of the continent is pleasure-traveling so exquisite and unalloyed a pleasure as in California. Not only are the sights grand, wonderful, and surprising in the highest degree, but the climate is exhilarating, and favorable to an active life; the weather is so certain that you need not lose a day, and may lay out your whole tour in the State without reference to rainy days, unless it is in the rainy season; the roads are surprisingly good, the country inns are clean, the beds good, the food abundant and almost always well cooked, and the charges moderate; and the journey by rail from New York to San Francisco, which costs no more than the steamer fare to London, and is shorter than a voyage across the Atlantic, is in itself delightful as well as instructive. . . .

The traveling time from New York to San Francisco, if you go through without stopping is seven days. . . .[3]

[3] Charles Nordhoff, *California: For Health, Pleasure and Residence* (New York: Harper & Brothers, 1872).

The author was enthusiastic about the comforts of the train, his drawing room, and in particular the meals served in the dining car:

¶ It is now the custom to charge a dollar per meal on these cars; and as the cooking is admirable, the service excellent, and the food various and abundant, that is not too much. You have your choice in the wilderness— eating at the rate of twenty-two miles per hour—of buffalo, elk, antelope, beef-steak, mutton-chops, or grouse. . . .

Nordhoff informed his readers that roughly $500 would cover the cost of a tour of California and return. Good hotel accommodations were to be had for $3.50 per day, and horses and guides could be hired for a trip to view the wonders of Yosemite for $5.00 per day. He advised the prospective traveler to take a ship from San Francisco to Los Angeles:

¶ To Los Angeles you go by steamer; fare $18 each way, which includes meals and state-rooms. The sail is a lovely one, with land in sight all the way. Try to secure a berth on the land side, as the coast affords continuously fine views. The steamer lands you at San Pedro. Thence by cars to Los Angeles. The fare is $2.50. From Los Angeles you should drive to the Mission San Gabriel, where are the finest orange orchards. The drive will cost you from three to five dollars. At San Diego you see a fine bay and a growing city, which now waits for railroad connections. . . .

You will find good hotels everywhere, though often in the country, plainly furnished. The bread is good, food is always abundant, and generally well cooked, and the beds are clean, and almost always good. The stage-drivers, landlords, and others with whom a traveler has to do are civil and obliging, and I have never heard of attempts at extortion.

Nordhoff did not seem to be impressed by Los Angeles. At the time of his visit, the town had not been connected to San Francisco by the Southern Pacific Railroad. This event occurred on September 5, 1876, when the railroad crossed the Tehachapi barrier, and gave Los Angeles a link with the transcontinental system. This greatly accelerated the city's growth. In 1871, Los Angeles was still regarded as a small pueblo, dwarfed in size and importance by the more glamorous metropolis to the north—San Francisco. Nordhoff wrote:

¶ The Puebla de Los Angeles—the town of the angels—is not in its present state, a very angelic place. It is irregularly built, the older part having but one principal street, at one end of which, however, stands a building which is both for size and excellence of architecture, worthy of San Francisco or New York. If you will walk down this street, you will be surprised at the excellence of the shops, and the extent of some of the warehouses, and will see abundant signs of a real and well-founded prosperity, which will surprise you if you have listened to the opinion of the San Franciscan about this metropolis of Southern California.

In fact Los Angeles has many signs of a prosperous business centre; it has excellent shops, and a number of well-built residences; it sends its exports to the sea by a well-managed and prosperous railroad [4] and expects to be connected within a year with San Francisco by the Southern Pacific Railroad, by way of Bakersfield. It is chiefly noted for the production of wine and oranges; but in its neighborhood there is a large tract of fine corn land, El Monte, where large crops are raised every year. Los Angeles is the trade center of a considerable region, which includes San Bernardino to the east, and reaches to the Inyo and Owen's River mines to the northeast.

The old Spanish town, nicknamed Sonora, lies at one end near the mission church, the somewhat discordant clangor of whose bells startles you out of your sleep early in the morning as they summon the faithful to prayers. Next to this come the business streets, and beyond these the American part of the town. Orange-groves surround the town almost, and vineyards are numerous.

The architecture of this region will remind you that you are in a land where it is never very cold. The dwelling is a secondary matter here, and it results that many people are satisfied to live in very small and slight houses. Muslin and paper inside walls are common; a barn is like Jack Straw's house, neither wind-tight nor water-tight. In the Pico House at Los Angeles, you must walk across an open, brick-paved court, containing a fountain and flowers, to get from your room to the dining-room; at San Bernardino, most of the rooms in the hotel have no entrance from within at all; you go on to an open corridor, and enter your chamber from that; and, as the stores and shops are mostly without chimneys, at San Bernardino I saw clerks and shop-keepers on a cool day warming their coat-tails by a fire built in the mildle of the broad business street. . . .

[4] As part of the terms for building the connecting rail line to Los Angeles, Southern Pacific demanded and received title to this line, which extended from Los Angeles to San Pedro Harbor.

The price of land at first strikes the stranger as high. Near Los Angeles they ask from thirty to a hundred dollars per acre for unimproved farming land. I thought they were already discounting the railroad which is coming to them, and which will no doubt cause this part of the country to increase rapidly in population and wealth. Everybody is "talking railroad." A corps of engineers of the Southern Pacific Company was near the town completing surveys for the road; and as I had seen in the East, the raise in prices following the mere announcement of a new railroad, it was natural for me to think that prices here had been affected by the same cause. But I am satisfied that they are, on the whole, not too high. . . .

Nordhoff found San Francisco more appealing than Los Angeles. The atmosphere was cosmopolitan and sophisticated. It resembled New York City, and he extolled its wonders to the prospective visitor:

¶ The tourist will find San Francisco one of the pleasantest and most novel of all the sights of California. The hotels are admirably kept; the streets are full of strange sights; the Cliff House will make one of your pleasantest experiences; at Woodward's Gardens a good collection of grizzly bears, and other wild beasts native to California, will amuse and instruct children from fifteen to fifty years of age; the Chinese and Japanese shops have curiosities at all prices, from twenty-five cents to five hundred dollars; and the Chinese quarter will occupy your leisure several days, if you are at all curious.

Your first drive in San Francisco is likely to be the Cliff House. You may breakfast there if you like; and as all outdoor amusements in this place are controlled by the climate during the spring and summer months, the cold seabreeze making the afternoons uncomfortable, it is a pretty and sensible thing to rise at six some morning, and see the sea-lions while it is yet warm, and you take it on the verandah, with all China, and Japan, and the King of the Cannibal Islands, looking at you across the broad Pacific. . . . The greater part of San Francisco is smoothly laid with wooden pavement; and the city is approached from every side over admirable roads. A New Yorker boasts of Central Park roads till he has driven thirty miles in a brief forenoon, forty or fifty miles in a day here, over the best ways I ever saw. Go where you will, within fifty miles of the city, and you find smooth, hard roads, broad avenues, often, as at Santa Clara, lined with long, double rows of fine shade trees—roads over which you may drive at the rate of ten or twelve miles per hour and do no harm to your horses nor tire yourself.

A prominent and wealthy citizen of San Francisco drives into town daily from his country place, twenty-four miles distant, and does it in one hour and fifty minutes. . . .

You will find the streets in San Francisco devoted to the Chinese. They occupy a considerable part of the heart of the city; and their shops, in Sacramento, Dupont, and other streets, are open to visitors . . . Ladies and children may safely and properly walk in the main streets in the Chinese quarter by day. The tourist who wishes to investigate farther should get a policeman stationed among the Chinese to show him around after dark. He will see some strange and unpleasant sights; and ladies and children must be excluded from this tour. . . .

Among the sights in California most attractive to the tourist, the groves of Big Trees and the wonderful Yosemite Valley, are of course, the chief.

Travelers who come for but a hurried stay will economize time by seeing first San Francisco and its neighborhood, in which I include the San Jose Valley, the Almaden mine,[5] and Santa Cruz, and on the north the Geysers, Clear Lake if you have the time, the Napa Valley, Santa Rosa, and the Sonoma country. Having "done" the coast, you can turn your face eastwards, and, leaving your luggage at the hotel at Stockton or Merced, begin the tour of the Trees and the Valley.

Those who mean to see Los Angeles, San Diego, San Bernardino, or Santa Barbara should, of course, take the steamer trip also before leaving for the interior. . . .

Charles Nordhoff's description of Los Angeles as "not a very angelic place" was a rather accurate assessment. Perhaps he was thinking about a recent occurrence—the wanton lynching of a number of Chinese during a massacre by a mob, which blackened the community's reputation throughout the world. Charles Dwight Willard was critical of the period from 1850–1870 in his *The Herald's History of Los Angeles City:*

¶ The people of Los Angeles seem, from the very beginning, to have adopted the principle that whatever they undertook to do they must do thoroughly. During the Spanish regime their chief purpose was to avoid work; and indolence was practiced until it became almost an art. Probably there was at that time no city within the boundaries of the Union where

---

[5] The New Almaden was a quicksilver mine reached by coach from San Jose.

more work was left undone than at Los Angeles. In the quarter of a century of Mexican rule the pueblo leads as the great rallying point for revolutions. Here again a comparison with other cities of the United States need not be feared. When California was brought under American rule, however, revolutions became dangerous and impracticable. If the city was to continue to be preeminent, it must be for some other characteristic than political turbulence.

This brings us to the darkest chapter in the history of Los Angeles; for, during the period from 1850 to 1870, it was undoubtedly the toughest town of the entire nation. During most of this time it contained a larger percentage of bad characters than any other city, and for its size had the greatest number of fights, murders, lynchings and robberies. This long era of violence and contempt for law had its culmination in 1871, in the brutal slaughter of nineteen Chinamen and the looting of Chinatown by a mob of 500 men. The number of lynchings during this period (not including the Chinamen) is estimated at thirty-five, which is more than four times the number credited to the famous vigilance committees of San Francisco. In addition to the executions that were done in the name of order, if not the law, there were legal hangings almost twice a year. As to the number of killings, it is impossible to make an estimate, as no record was kept. There is no complete file of the earliest newspapers, all having been destroyed in a fire in 1880,[6] but such copies as are still in existence contain here and there brief items, two or three lines in length, that show by the very absence of comment what the state of things was. A murder which in these days would be given half a page of newspaper space, with the pictures of the victim and all his family, and a lurid diagram of the spot and its surroundings, was dismissed with a few short sentences, accompanied by no comment. The Los Angeles *News* of March, 1866, contains these three items, for example:

"The verdict of the coroner's jury on the body of Seferino Ochoa returned that he came to his death by the discharge of a gun loaded with powder and balls.

"A party of Salt Lake and Montana teamsters had a lively row in the Monte [7] on Monday night; several shots were fired, from the effects of which one man died.

"A shooting affray occurred recently between Mr. T. Baldwin and Mr.

[6] The author is in error. Files of the Los Angeles *Star* and *Semi-Weekly News* dating back to the Civil War period, and in some cases earlier, may be found at the Los Angeles City Library. Other copies, though in broken dates, can be seen at the Huntington Library and at the Los Angeles County Museum Library.

[7] The present city of El Monte, near Los Angeles.

Adam Linn. Mr. Baldwin was shot through the heart, but unloaded his pistol before he expired, dying without speaking. Mr. Linn was uninjured."

The *Southern Californian* of March 7 remarks: "Last Sunday night was a brisk night for killing. Four men were shot and killed and several wounded in shooting affrays."

This lawlessness had its beginning in the years California was without a regular government—the interim between Mexican and American authority. The semi-military government that prevailed through part of this time served to hold things in check, but it was withdrawn before the new authority was firmly in its seat. The changed order brought inevitable confusion in the effort to accommodate Spanish law to American customs and Spanish customs to American law, and this confusion was suddenly confounded by the arrival of a hundred thousand newcomers in the state—the gold hunters. In such a vast number, coming for such a purpose, it was to be expected that representatives of the criminal and desperate classes should be included. When the vigilance committees of San Francisco and the northern mining camps began to drive these bad characters out, many of them drifted south to Los Angeles, and the latter city soon took on the character of a frontier town of the toughest type.

The situation was more complicated in Los Angeles than in most other portions of the state, because of the presence in that city of many hundred native Californians of the lowest class. These were idle, shiftless and addicted to drink, but up to the time of the American occupation they had not shown contempt for the law, nor were they given to crimes of violence. The change of government seemed to bring a radical change in the character of many of these men. It may have been that they were merely imitative, and that they were undertaking to do as they saw the American frontier outlaws doing; or it may have been that having lost their country and—many of them—their vague claims to land, they became desperate, and defied all authority; at all events, a large percentage of the killings recorded for this period, particularly the murders done for money, are to be charged to the native Californians, and many of the fiercest and most reckless highwaymen were of this class. . . .

The most terrible page in this dark chapter of the city's history is that on which is recorded the massacre of the Chinamen. The Los Angeles of today is so far removed from anything like mob sentiment, its population, 90 per cent of which comes from older eastern states, is so thoroughly conservative and law-abiding, that it is hard to understand how, only thirty years ago, such a horrible outrage came to be committed in the city.

As a mere exhibition of mob rule, however, it was no worse than has been seen since that period in various eastern cities, notably Cincinnati, Pittsburg, Kansas City and St. Louis. If the number of lives taken was greater than in any of these latter instances, that may be accounted for by the fact in those days nearly everyone in Los Angeles was accustomed to go armed, and know how to shoot to kill, and by the further fact that public sentiment at that time placed a very low estimate on the value of the life of a Chinaman. This is not offered in extenuation of the crime, but merely to help explain something that seems at first sight difficult of comprehension.

The affair took place on the 24th of October, 1871, and succeeded the great Chicago fire as a topic of news most under discussion throughout the country. This was for many thousand eastern people, their first introduction to Los Angeles, and the incongruity of the name as the location for such an awful deed was frequently commented upon. The riot grew out of a war between rival Chinese societies—or "tongs"—that had been in progress for several days, one faction shooting across "Nigger Alley" at the other from time to time. A city policeman attempting to make an arrest met with resistance and summoned to his aid a well-known citizen, named Robert Thompson. Some Chinamen concealed in a building on the corner of Arcadia street and "Nigger Alley" shot through the door and mortally wounded Thompson. He was carried to an adjoining drug store, and died within an hour.

The fatal shot had been fired just at dusk. By night time a great crowd of angry men had gathered in the alley and surrounded the building. Several of the Chinamen undertook to escape, but were shot down or captured and hung. The mob finally broke open the building, which the Chinamen had barricaded on the inside, and dragged eight Chinamen out into the street, where they were beaten and kicked and pulled about with ropes tied around their necks, and finally taken over to a corral on New High Street back of the Downey block and hanged to a high cross-bar above its gate. This was about 9 o'clock in the evening.

In the meantime a gang of thieves and toughs, who had joined the mob for purposes of plunder made the most of the confusion to break open several stores belonging to Chinamen who could not be supposed to have had any part in the murder of Thompson. Some seized the goods and began to carry them off, while others wrecked the buildings and the store fixtures. All Chinamen that came into the hands of the mob were dragged out into Nigger Alley and hung or shot to death. The crowd was beside itself with rage against the race, and spared neither youth nor old age.

Two of the victims were very young boys, and one, an old physician, a man of good education, who begged for his life, and offered over $2000 in money to those who had captured him. The money was taken, but he was hanged with the rest. The amount of cash taken by the mob was estimated at $40,000.

There were in all nineteen Chinamen put to death, some with great cruelty. The affair lasted only about an hour. News of what was going on had by this time spread over the town, and a party of brave and law-abiding citizens, accompanied by the sheriff, went down into Chinatown and compelled the mob to desist. A few arrests were made, and when the grand jury met, indictments were found against 150 persons for participation in the massacre. Only six of these were convicted in the trial that followed, and they after a short imprisonment, were given their freedom on a technicality. The jury severely censured the officers of the city and county for neglecting their duty. From the evidence taken afterward it was established that only one of the nineteen Chinamen killed was concerned in the original conflicts between the "tongs." The guilty parties had all made their escape before the mob came on the scene.[8]

[8] Charles Dwight Willard, *The Herald's History of Los Angeles City* (Los Angeles: Kingaley-Barnes & Neuner Co., 1901).

24

THE MODOC WAR

In the northeastern corner of California is a remote, lonely region that bears the scars of a prehistoric age. Here, molten lava once covered a 43,000-acre tract bordering Tule Lake. When this liquid fire cooled, it left a charred and distorted crust on the earth's surface. Huge cinder cones rising several hundred feet are scattered across the blackened plain. These small volcanoes erupted in an ancient era, spreading lava like molasses along the valley floor. Fissures were torn in the earth, and the slaglike rock flowed from deep cracks in the earth's crust, leaving a pattern of serpentine trenches and a labyrinth of caves and chasms.

This region was designated as the Lava Beds National Monument by the United States Department of the Interior in 1925. To the early settlers, who followed the overland trails into California, the land had a more terrifying name. They called it the Dark and Bloody Ground. It was here in 1872–1873 that a small band of Modoc Indians, led by their chieftain, Keintpoos, who adopted the name of Captain Jack, defied an army sent by the President of the United States to subdue them.

During the administration of Ulysses S. Grant, which was characterized by political corruption and mismanagement, the Modocs were taken from their hunting grounds in California and placed on a reservation at Fort Klamath, Oregon. This proved to be a tragic mistake, for the Klamath Indians, who were in the majority on the reservation, were the traditional enemies of the Modoc. A year later, in 1870, Captain Jack gathered his people, numbering nearly four hundred, and left the reservation. They returned to their old lands near Tule Lake. Settlers had moved into the country, and friction followed between the Indians and the white intruders. This was to last for two years. Alfred B. Meacham, appointed by President Grant as Indian superintendent in Oregon, had for some time been attempting to negotiate with Captain Jack to return to the reservation. Finally, in the fall of 1872, Captain James Jackson was sent to bring in the Modocs and their recalcitrant leader. The military troop entered the Modoc village accompanied by a party of settlers in a show of force. One of the Modocs, named Scarfaced Charley, opened fire on the soldiers, and in the melee that followed, Jackson had eight casualties. He ordered his bugler to sound the retreat, while the Modocs fled into the Lava Beds, where the numerous caverns and hidden rocky trails offered a natural fortress that would be difficult for an enemy to invade. Before settling down in this sanctuary, the Indians murdered a number of settlers living in the vicinity.

In retaliation for this wave of terror, additional troops were sent to the lava beds. Lieutenant Colonel Frank Wheaton was assigned as commander of the Department of the Lakes. His headquarters were at Fort Klamath in Oregon's Upper Klamath Lake region. The more important phase of his command was taken from him and assigned to Colonel Alvan C. Gillem, First Cavalry, who was placed in charge of the active theater of operations running along the California-Oregon boundary. This consisted of Lower Klamath Lake, Lost River, Tule Lake, and Clear Lake. Most of the fighting would be confined to the Lava Beds area south of Tule Lake, which came to be known as Captain Jack's Stronghold.

Gillem owed his rank to political connections dating back to his

Civil War days. Although a West Point graduate, he had served for some time in the Marine Corps. He was not popular with his officers and this dislike filtered down through the enlisted ranks. Among the troops who went into camp along the Lava Beds were regulars and a number of volunteer companies recruited in Oregon. They were poorly trained and badly disciplined. Privates received thirteen dollars a month for their services, and a good percentage of their pay soon went to the sutlers who set up shop near the soldiers' bivouac, and began dispensing cheap whisky. There was no *esprit de corps* typical of the calvary regiments that fought on the plains and that is best illustrated by the caliber of men who died with Custer three years following the Modoc uprising. As a result of their lack of morale, courage, and discipline, a number of men were destined to lose their lives in the Lava Beds. For the moment, the President desired to settle the Modoc question by continued negotiations rather than by force. In the West, the settlers preferred a policy of exterminating the Indians. In the East, however, there were a number of organizations that were protesting the inhuman treatment of the American Indian. These groups exerted considerable pressure at Washington.

A commission was organized consisting of Alfred Meacham, the Oregon Indian agent, who had gained valuable experience dealing with the Modocs; the Reverend Eleaser Thomas, an idealistic Methodist minister, and L. S. Dyar, the Indian subagent from Oregon. Added to this group was the key man on the commission—Brigadier General E. R. S. Canby, commanding the Department of the Pacific. He was a man with long-proven ability in dealing with Indians dating back to his service in the Seminole War. It was Canby who helped to turn back the Confederate tide in New Mexico at the outbreak of the Civil War, and during that conflict he later held important commands. Both President Grant and the army's commanding general, William T. Sherman, as military men, had more confidence in Canby than in the three civilian commissioners. Canby, as head of the group, would make the final decision on what course to pursue. After several overtures to Captain Jack, the Indian leader agreed to a meeting in the Lava Beds. Canby and the commissioners went out to confer with the Modoc chief. They sat down in front of a tent that had been set up for the peace parley. The general opened a box of cigars and passed them around. After all but the Reverend Eleaser Thomas, a nonsmoker, were puffing contentedly, the commissioners and the Indians shook hands. The peace talks were ready to commence. Suddenly, Captain Jack drew a pistol and fired. The ball struck Canby in the face. He rolled over on the ground, mortally wounded. The other Indians opened fire. Thomas died quickly. Commissioner Dyar made his escape, but Meacham was severely wounded. Miraculously, he survived.

Official correspondence relating to the subsequent war with the Modocs affords a rather graphic account of how a small band of defiant Indians held off an army of several thousand troops.

¶ Headquarters Modoc Expedition,
  Camp South of Tule Lake, April 11, 1873.

Sir: It is with the most profound sorrow that I have to inform you of the death of Brigadier-General E. R. S. Canby, U.S.A., which occurred today at 1:30 P.M. about one mile in front of this camp, under the following circumstances: For a day or two, communication between the Indians and the peace commission had been virtually suspended. Yesterday morning an Indian (Boston Charley) came into camp, and informed the commission that Captain Jack would "talk." In order to avoid all misapprehension, the commission sent their interpreter (Frank Riddle and his squaw) into the Indian camp; they returned in the evening and reported that Captain Jack said he would *not* meet the commission, nor come out of his stronghold again until the troops were removed from his vicinity. An Indian returned with Riddle and confirmed his statement. This morning, however, this Indian (Bogus Charley) asserted that Riddle (the interpreter) had not told all that Captain Jack had said, and asserted that Jack had agreed to meet General Canby, myself, and the commission at a tent that had been pitched about a mile in front of this camp. In order to reconcile these conflicting statements, the two Indians (Boston and Bogus) were sent back to the Indian camp. They soon returned and said that Jack would meet five of us—General Canby, myself, and three commissioners, at the tent. After duly considering the subject, it was determined to accept the proposition. I was too ill to accompany the party, and before leaving the interpreter brought the commissioners to my bed-side, and asked me to bear witness that he had warned them that there was danger in going out; however, it was decided to go.

At 11.06 A.M. the party left camp. I directed the signal officer to keep a strict watch on the tent and to inform me of everything that occurred. At 1.30 p.m. the signal-officer brought me information that Major Mason's camp on the east side of the Lake had been attacked and two officers probably captured. (This afterward proved to be incorrect.) Convinced that treachery was intended, I sent for Assistant-Surgeon Coburiss, who volunteered to take a note to General Canby. I could not send a verbal message, as many of the Indians understand English. I had written but a few words when shots were heard, and officers from the signal-station brought me information that General Canby and the peace commissioners had been murdered. The troops were under arms at once and advanced. I found the bodies of General Canby and the Rev. Doctor Thomas about seventy yards from the tent. Mr. Meacham was near, severely, if not mortally, wounded; all were stripped. Mr. Dyar, one of the commissioners, escaped unhurt, having a small pistol which he drew on his pursuer.

The remains of General Canby and Mr. Thomas will be sent to Yreka tomorrow, in charge of Lieut. H. R. Anderson, A.D.C. to the General.

Very respectfully, your obedient servant,

ALVAN C. GILLEM,
Colonel First United States Cavalry
Commanding Modoc Expedition.

The Adjutant-General, U.S.A.[1]

¶ TELEGRAM.

Headquarters Army of the United States,
Washington, D.C., April 13, 1873.

GENERAL J. M. SCHOFIELD,
Commanding Military Division, San Francisco:

Your dispatch of yesterday is this moment received. Last night about midnight General Townsend came to my house with a dispatch from General[2] Gillem to the same effect as yours, which dispatch he had shown to the President, and I answered General Gillem direct, with a copy of the answer to you. The President now sanctions the most severe punishment of the Modocs, and I hope to hear that they have met the doom they so richly have earned by their insolence and perfidy. This is Sunday. I will see

---

[1] This and other quoted materials in this chapter are from the War Department pamphlet, *Official Copies of Correspondence Relative to the War with Modoc Indians in 1872–73*, prepared by the Adjutant General's Office (Washington, D.C.: Government Printing Office, January 7, 1874).

[2] Probably a brevet rank.

the President this evening, and tomorrow will notify you of any change in the existing commands, if made, but you may be sure that any measure of severity to the savages will be sustained.

W. T. Sherman,
General.

Sherman moved a qualified officer in to succeed General Canby: Colonel and Brevet Major General Jefferson C. Davis, a veteran of the Mexican and Civil wars. The fact that he had the identical name of the former president of the Confederacy had been a cause of constant irritation to him. Sherman's orders were explicit: End the war and annihilate the Modocs. Meanwhile, the quarry sat in their caves in the Lava Beds, confident in the strong medicine of their shaman, Curley Headed Doctor. By killing Canby and the commissioners, the Modocs believed that they would frighten the white soldiers into giving up the fight and going away, leaving the Indians in peace. Besides, there was the new faith that had spread in 1871 among the tribes of Nevada, northern California, and southern Oregon. This was known as the Ghost Dance Cult. It had its origins in 1869, when an elder of the Paiute tribe then living at Walker Lake, Nevada, claimed to have had a dream in which he visited the land of the dead. Here he was told that all the departed Indians would return to life and destroy the white men. By dancing and chanting, the living would let the dead know they were ready to welcome them. In the glare of blazing fires, the Indians worked themselves into a frenzied state to the accompaniment of war drums. The Modocs chanted in their hidden caves deep in the Lava Beds. Shadows leaped on the walls as they performed the ghost dance with wild abandon. They failed to summon the spirits—only more of the hated soldiers. Colonel Gillem describes what followed in his report to the Assistant Adjutant General:

¶ . . . After such perfidy, there remained but one course for me—to administer the punishment so richly merited—and preparations for an advance were at once made. Knowing the confidence of the Indians in their position, and the great difficulty of taking it by assault, I determined, if possible, to surround them, not only to save my own men but to prevent the escape of the Indians. On the 14th Major Mason, Twenty-first Infantry, whose command consisted of three companies of his regiment . . . Mc-

Kay's company of Warm Spring Indians, and a section of mountain-howitzers under Lieutenant Chapin, Fourth Artillery, was directed to move up as near as possible to the Indian position under cover of the darkness. Captain Perry, First Cavalry, with Troops "F" and "K," First Cavalry, was ordered from the camp on the south side of the lake to make a similar move at 2 A.M. on the 15th. Both movements were successful, and the respective parties took their positions without loss. At 8 A.M. on the 15th Maj. John Green, First Cavalry, who commanded the troops south of the lake, moved out with Batteries "E," "K," and "M," Fourth Artillery, and companies "E" and "G," Twelfth Infantry. Thomas's Battery ("A," Fourth Artillery) remained in camp with the Coehorn mortars ready packed on mules, to advance when he should receive the signal to do so.

The skirmishing began about a mile in front of the Indian position. The ground, or rather rocks, being exceedingly difficult to get over, our progress was very slow; the Indians contested every foot of ground, and having every advantage often succeeded in checking the troops. At 1.30 P.M. the battalion of the Fourth Artillery and Twelfth Infantry made a beautiful charge, driving the Indians back several hundred yards, to a very strong position near the crest of the lava-bed. The mortars were then ordered up, and in order to secure a good position for them in reach of the caves, Troops F and K, First Cavalry, were ordered to drive the Indians from the northern point of the lava-bed, and did so in a handsome charge. The mortars were then placed in position, and began shelling the Indians. It was now nearly dark, the lines were straightened and strengthened, and operations suspended for the night, except the mortars, which continued firing during the night, having secured the range and position of the Indian camp. The troops on the east side of the lava-bed advanced as directed on the night of the 14th, and at daylight on the 15th the howitzer battery opened fire on Jack's camp, and the infantry advanced as far as possible, endeavoring to unite their left with Major Green's right, and thus inclose the Indians, but it was found impossible to effect the junction without weakening the line too much. Our loss on this day was one officer (Lieutenant Eagan, Twelfth Infantry) wounded, three (3) enlisted men killed, and nine (9) wounded.

Early on the morning of the 16th our entire line advanced, but owing to the almost impassable nature of the ground, and the stubborn resistance of the Indians, the progress was slow; the mortars and howitzers continued shelling, and one most important advantage was gained—the left of Major

Green's and the right of Major Mason's commands succeeded in forming a junction, and thus cut off the communication of the Indians with the water. During this day the command advanced to within the immediate vicinity of the caves held by the Indians; in some places so near as to render it necessary to fall back in order not to interfere with the shelling. During the night of the 16th the firing was almost continuous, the Indians endeavoring to pass through our lines in several places, evidently for the purpose of procuring water. None of these efforts succeeded.

On the morning of the 17th the troops cautiously advanced. Now and then a shell was thrown in, and it was soon evident that the great part of the Indians had abandoned the place, leaving a rear-guard to keep the troops in check. These were driven away by a charge, and retreated south among the rocks.

The troops at once took possession of the celebrated stronghold of the Modocs. As yet, I have been unable to definitely locate the Indians; a part of them—it is possible all—are in the southern portion of the lava-bed, and they may make another stand. A small party was seen to come to the lake for water.

On the morning of the 18th, all the cavalry and the Warm Spring Indians were sent to the south of the lava-bed to ascertain whether or not the Indians had taken that direction. On the return of this force, I shall be governed in my movements by the information it brings. If the Indians are still in the rocks, we will attack them again. . . .

So far, in his efforts to ferret the Modocs from their underground caves, Gillem had lost one officer and six enlisted men. Nineteen men were wounded. The Indians never had more than seventy men in their stronghold, while Gillem had hundreds of troops deployed, and his batteries were pounding the Modocs with mortar fire. The colonel's plans were not as brilliantly executed as his report would indicate. The officers, particularly Major Edwin Mason, seemed to have disregarded the colonel's orders and functioned independently on their own. The artillery did no damage, and when the slow-moving infantry finally reached the stronghold, they discovered that the Modocs had slipped away. A search was launched to discover the Indians' new redoubt, and it was soon located. Aiding the troopers was a company of Warm Springs Indians from a reservation neighboring that of the Klamath tribe. They had been enlisted as scouts and trackers, and as they hated the Modocs, they made formidable allies. The attacking force had accomplished one tactical advantage, however, that was to be the major factor in ending the campaign—establishing a line that cut the Modocs off from their water supply at Tule Lake. The Indians were still defiant and soon retaliated by inflicting a stunning defeat on the attacking force. The worried Colonel Gillem sent in his report detailing this new fiasco. He knew that when Jeff Davis arrived on the field there would be hell to pay. General Schofield read the dispatch in San Francisco and relayed it to Sherman in Washington:

¶ To GENERAL SHERMAN:

The following distressing intelligence is just received: "Lava-Beds, April 28, 1873; to Major General Schofield, San Francisco. On the 26th instant, Major Green, commanding the camp on the west side of the lava-bed, ordered Captain Thomas, Fourth Artillery, with batteries A and K, Fourth Artillery, Company E, Twelfth Infantry, and a party of Warm Spring Indians, about seventy soldiers and fourteen Indians, to make a reconnaissance in a southeasterly direction to a point about four miles from camp. The party left camp at 7 A.M.; at 12 M. the party reached the designated point, and were resting. No Indians had been seen. Suddenly, the party was fired upon by Indians, when a portion of the command seem to have become panic-stricken, and organization seems, in a great measure, to have ceased. Stragglers arrived in camp at about half-past 1 P.M. Major Green at once went to assistance of Major Thomas; arriving on the scene, he found Thomas's command entirely disorganized and scattered. Upon searching the lava-chasms the bodies of Capt. E. Thomas and Lieut. A. B. Howe, Fourth Artillery, and Lieut. Thomas F. Wright, Twelfth Infantry, were found; First Lieut. Arthur Cranston, Fourth Artillery, has not been found. He is undoubtedly killed. Lieut. George M. Harris and Acting Asst. Surg. B. Semig seriously, though I hope not dangerously wounded. Thirteen enlisted men killed, and sixteen wounded . . . The Indians occupy a position in the rocks, about four miles south of their old caves. It will be impossible to surround them with the force at or en route to the place. The circumference of the lava-beds is about thirty miles; all of it is very much of the same character. General Davis is expected tomorrow.

"ALVAN C. GILLEM,
"Colonel First Cavalry, Commanding."

When General Jefferson Davis arrived on the field and learned of the debacle, he erupted with the fury of one of the long-dormant volcanoes that he saw in the distance as he surveyed the dismal battleground, a region often shrouded by fog. The general's anger was directed chiefly at the enlisted men who had fled the field when the patrol was ambushed by the Modocs. Gillem, as commanding officer, had to accept responsibility for the mismanagement of the campaign. As soon as Davis familiarized himself with conditions in the Lava Beds, he relieved the unfortunate colonel and had him transferred to San Francisco.

Briefly, what had occurred was that a party had been sent on a reconnaissance mission. Their orders were not to attack, which seems unusual, as the patrol was encumbered by two batteries of artillery. The men were nervous as they moved into the Lava Beds, as there was no sign of the Indians. In their fear, they bunched up, contrary to the basic rules of infantry tactics, which would make them easy targets should they encounter the enemy. No flankers protected the main body of the column. The patrol was inviting an ambush, and that is what took place. A halt was called, and the men opened their rations and began to eat. They were sitting in a ravine, unaware that they were being watched by the Modocs from their positions along a rocky butte above them. The Indians opened fire at long range, but narrowed the gap as they moved quickly down the slopes toward the ravine.

When the Modocs began to enfilade the patrol from both flanks, a number of the soldiers became terror-stricken, and fled. The officers and a few seasoned noncoms tried to hold their position, and became casualties. Some of the stragglers were easily picked off by sharpshooting Indians as they ran blindly over the pock-marked lava beds. Davis sent the following report to headquarters. His contempt for the cowardice of the men who fled when fired upon is quite evident:

¶ Headquarters Lava-Beds, May 4, 1873.

SIR: For the information of the general commanding the division, I have the honor to state that I arrived here on the evening of the 2d instant; have visited all the camps, and find affairs here about as follows: The troops are in very good health, being well located, well fed and clothed, but owing to the heavy losses they have sustained in their recent conflicts with the Indians and the little successes gained by them, there is a very perceptible feeling of despondency pervading the entire command.

It was my intention on my arrival here to make another effort to dislodge the Indians from their stronghold, but the disaster of the 26th ultimo made such an attempt too hazardous to be thought of for the present.

Owing to the fact that all the commissioned officers, who accompanied the disastrous reconnaissance being killed or so badly wounded as to be unable to make statements, I cannot obtain a very satisfactory account of the affair.

The party, consisting of six commissioned officers, sixty-four enlisted men and fourteen Indian scouts, all under the command of Capt. Evan Thomas, Fourth Artillery, started out on the reconnaissance about 8 o'clock A.M. on the 26th. The object of the reconnaissance was to ascertain the practicability of taking a pack-train and the mortar-battery through the lava-bed to a sand-hill near the center of the lava-bed, about five miles distant from the camp. The objective point was reached without difficulty by noonday, and the party halted for rest and refreshment. No Indians had been met, no resistance seems to have been expected, and a general feeling of security seems to have prevailed among the officers. The signal-sergeant was preparing to send a message back to camp, announcing the result of the reconnaissance, when a few shots in close proximity announced the presence of the enemy.

The officers, though surprised, immediately sprang up and prepared for action. A well-directed fire, however, by this time, from the Indians, caused a large number, probably two thirds, of the enlisted men to break and run away in the most cowardly manner. The officers, thus deserted by their men, rallied the few brave spirits—mostly noncommissioned officers—and fought the foe with undaunted courage. They and the brave men who stood by them were all found killed and wounded where they so nobly but ineffectually fought.

The reconnaissance was ordered by Major Green, of First Cavalry, from his camp, with the authority of Colonel Gillem. Its object was an important one, and I think the party was quite sufficient in number and appointments.

An error was made by the officer in command in not pushing his skirmish-line further to the front and on the flanks before halting, but this mistake could have been easily and quickly remedied had the men, as a few did, stood by the officers and obeyed orders. This they did not do. The result was conspicuous cowardice on the part of the men who ran away, and conspicuous bravery and death on the part of the officers and men who stood. The lesson taught by this affair is that a great many of the enlisted men here are utterly unfit for Indian fighting of this kind, being only cowardly beef-eaters. My recommendation is, however, that they be kept here, trained, and made to fight. I shall take such steps while here as I think will insure this training.

I am, very respectfully, your obedient servant,

JEFF C. DAVIS

Bvt. Major-General, Commanding

The Assistant Adjutant-General,
Military Division of the Pacific, San Francisco, Cal.

General Davis needed no urging to bring the war to a quick conclusion. His career was at stake. Already, the long and costly campaign was being subjected to considerable criticism by the press, which derided the army for being unable to defeat a band of less than a hundred Indians. In Washington, General Sherman was furious over the delays in ending the uprising. He was ready to commit the entire army if necessary to crush the rebellious Modocs. This wouldn't be necessary, for the Indian revolt was rapidly disintegrating. The Indians were without food and water. There was little ammunition left. Several of the leaders were dead. Clearly, the medicine of their shaman, Curley Headed Doctor, was bad. The men quarreled with Captain Jack over continuing the war. The Modoc chief remained defiant, but his braves were weary. A number defected and deserted their leader, surrendering to the soldiers. Four of them, Bogus Charley, Hooker Jim, Shacknasty Jim, and Steamboat Frank, betrayed Captain Jack by leading troopers to the hideout of the diehards who refused to capitulate. The Modoc chief was captured and placed in irons. The war had come to an end. Sherman reported the victory to the Secretary of War, and in reading the correspondence it is apparent that the same general whose troops during the Civil War had ravaged the South in their march through Georgia to the sea was now determined to exterminate the tribe by hanging its leaders, and removing the rest of the Modocs to a remote reservation far from the land that had been their home for centuries. Here, in a climate to which they would be unaccustomed, they could be expected to die off quickly. This was the easy solution to the Indian problem:

¶ Headquarters Army of the United States,
   Washington, D.C., June 3, 1873.

GENERAL: I have the honor herewith to inclose copies of the two dispatches of June 2 from General Schofield, commanding Military Division of the Pacific, announcing the capture of the last of the Modocs, including the chief, Captain Jack. I understand them all to be now in military custody, and most respectfully ask order for their disposition. I inclose also a copy of my dispatch to General Schofield in reply.

It is so important that some just and lawful rule of action should be prescribed in advance of these Indian matters, (which must arise from time to time), that I most earnestly beg that the present case shall receive the consideration of the highest law-officer of our Government, before some agent makes a fatal promise, such is now urged for turning loose the convicted murderer, Satanta, that I most respectfully ask the President to sanction my present orders for General Schofield to hold all the Modoc prisoners in military custody until they are disposed of according to the judgment of some competent tribunal or the orders of the President himself. And further, I earnestly recommend that Captain Jack, Schonchin, and the others who were present at the peace council when General Canby and the Rev. Mr. Thomas were murdered, be tried by a general court-martial as violators of military law; that such of the other prisoners as are indicted for murder by the civil courts of Oregon and California be surrendered to the sheriffs of the respective counties on the proper requisition of the governors of said States; and, finally, that the rest of these Indians be transported east, and be distributed among a tribe easily guarded, say the Winnebagos of Lake Superior.

Thus the tribe of Modocs would disappear, and the example would be salutary in dealing with other Indians similarly disposed and similarly situated.

With great respect, your obedient servant,
W. T. SHERMAN,
General.

General W. W. Belknap
Secretary of War.

Captain Jack and the ringleaders were taken to Fort Klamath under heavy guard. The Indians who had been present at the shooting of

General Canby and the peace commisioners would be tried by a military court-martial as Sherman had recommended. The trial was a mockery of justice. In their denial of rights to the accused, the proceedings were far more despicable than the drumhead decisions rendered by the Vigilantes. The Indians had no legal counsel to defend them, and the tribunal neglected to appoint one. The accused understood little English. They were unable to comprehend what was taking place. The trial moved quickly, and arrangements were made to transfer the tribe to the Quapaw agency in present Oklahoma, then Indian Territory.

The most damaging testimony against Captain Jack and the other Indians charged with the murder of General Canby and the Reverend Eleaser Thomas, was that given by Commissioner Meacham, who recovered from his wounds. When the firing began at the peace parley, Meacham tried to escape. One bullet clipped off a piece of his ear. Another ricocheted off a rock, struck him in the head, and knocked him senseless. The Modocs stripped him of his clothes. Boston Charley began cutting along his forehead with a knife to remove his scalp, but the fact that Meacham was nearly bald made the task difficult. The Indian gave up. He fled with his companions, leaving the commissioner naked and bleeding, where he was found by the soldiers when they reached the scene of the shooting. Here, before the military tribunal, he describes his harrowing experience under questioning of the prosecutor:

¶ . . . While Schonchin was talking, Captain Jack had risen and turned his back and was walking off a few steps, perhaps behind Mr. Dyar's horse, or toward it; he was coming again toward the circle at the time the Indians rose up; he was rather facing it, but when the Indians made their appearance I asked the question of Captain Jack, "What does that mean?" but he made no reply to me directly; he put his right hand under the left breast pocket and drew his pistol, and sung out some word in Indian that I did not then understand.

Q. Had you seen the pistols before? A. I had seen the shape of them, not the pistols themselves; I became satisfied they were all armed some time before that.

Q. You think the two men who appeared from the rocks came into sight before the first pistol was fired?—A. I know it, sir.

Q. You saw them come out?—*A.* Yes.

Q. What next took place?—*A.* Captain Jack and Schonchin John changed places, bringing Captain Jack in front of General Canby and Schonchin in front of me; and Captain Jack drew his pistol and the cap bursted but did not discharge.

Q. Whom did he aim at?—*A.* At General Canby, and within less than three feet—pointed toward General Canby's head.

Q. Had the commissioners done anything to justify or excite the attack?—*A.* There had been no angry words.

Q. Or motions?—*A.* No acts of any kind that could have provoked hostilities that I know of; on the contrary, we were sedulously careful to avoid it; and I believe we all appreciated the necessity of being careful in our conversation and in our action. But after the assault of Captain Jack with the pistol on General Canby, what I remember most distinctly was that Schonchin John drew his pistol from this (left) side of him.

Q. You saw it?—*A.* Yes; within not to exceed 3 or 4 feet from me; he discharged it at me, aiming evidently at my head. After drawing the pistol, almost at the same time or very nearly, he drew a knife which he held in his left hand.

Q. Did he hit you?—*A.* Not at that time. He subsequently did shoot me. This ball which struck me in my face (showing) was discharged from the pistol in the hands of Schonchin John, within 15 or 16 feet of me, after I had taken the cover of a rock.

Q. Did you notice whether there was any more firing?—*A.* There was; the firing was very hot and they were all very active, making hostile demonstrations on the peace-commission party. One man was after Dyar, I know, but I cannot tell who.

Q. You saw that?—*A.* Yes; I saw Dyar running and Riddle running, and I saw some men chasing him; but I cannot designate the men who did it, only they were of the party who were in the council.

Q. Did you still retain your senses after this ball had struck you in the forehead?—*A.* For a very short time afterward. Very soon afterward I received a shot in my wrist, and within a few seconds after I lost my consciousness, probably from the grazing shot on my temple. I remained unconscious until the skirmish-line of rescuers came up.

Q. What other wounds did you have?—*A.* I received a shot on my left hand, my right wrist, my face, the end of my ear and side of my head, and a knife-cut of four or five inches in length on the side of my head, besides bruises.

Q. Do you say the party of Indians, as soon as Jack fired, sprang simultaneously up?—*A.* Sprang up and commenced firing; all drew arms, or they were engaged in it some way. I didn't see General Canby after Captain Jack had cocked his pistol to shoot the second time—I have no recollection of seeing him. I did see Dr. Thomas after he had received the first shot, and my memory is that Boston was shooting at him. Dr. Thomas got on his right hand without falling entirely to the ground.

Q. After this did you become unconscious?—*A.* Yes. I fell back thirty or forty steps from where the firing began; I succeeded in running that distance.

Q. When did you recover your senses?—*A.* When the skirmish line, Colonel Miller's command, came up. I suppose it must have been the time that it required to march from headquarters on double-quick. I came to consciousness when the line came up, hearing the voice of Colonel Miller straightening his line; that is the first sound I remember.

Q. Do you have any doubt that the Indians intended to kill and murder you?—*A.* None.

Captain Jack and five of his companions were found guilty by the court-martial board and sentenced to be hanged. The execution was set for October of 1873 at Fort Klamath. A gallows was erected and six graves were dug, which the prisoners could view from their cells. The sentences of two, Barcho and Slolux, had been commuted by the War Department. They were to be imprisoned for life on Alcatraz Island. However, the pair was purposely kept uninformed of their reprieve until the final moment, when they were to climb the ladder leading to the gallows. The others, Captain Jack, Boston Charley, Black Jim, and Schonchin, were escorted to the platform. They sat on stools while the ropes were adjusted. Gathered below were members of the Modoc tribe, the entire garrison on parade, reporters, and other witnesses. An officer read the verdict of the court-martial, which was translated. At that time he also read the commutation of the death sentences of Barcho and Slolux, who sat puzzled in a wagon, wondering why they had not been taken to the platform. They had been saved because the military did not regard them as participating in the conspiracy to murder the peace commissioners. They had merely followed orders. At an officer's signal, a soldier severed the rope holding the drop-board with an ax. Captain Jack and his three lieutenants plummeted into eternity. The Modoc War was thus concluded amidst an atmosphere of violence, the same way that it began.

25

COLONY BUILDERS
AND BANDITS

The danger of being scalped by Indians failed to slow the tourist trade or deter prospective settlers from coming to California. While Modoc country offered little inducement to the newcomer as a place to acquire land—it remains today a sparsely settled county—people were beginning to discover that there were regions other than the San Francisco Bay area that offered many advantages, particularly for those interested in farming. Much of this interest was centered in southern California, although the influx of settlers did not reach its peak until the following decade.

D. M. Berry was sent west by a group organized in Indiana that desired to establish a colony in California. He was searching for a suitable tract of land that could be purchased. Berry took a ship from San Francisco to San Diego. He jotted down his observations of the coastal cities he visited, intending to send them to the newspaper, but they were never published. Berry found land suitable for the Indiana colony near Los Angeles—in Pasadena. His report, dated September 1, 1873, reads in part:

¶ Our passage out of the harbor of San Francisco and over the much dreaded bar, was made at the most favorable time of the tide, so we were spared the usual discomforts of that sometimes rough and tumultuous passage. The Golden Gate exhibited all colors except gold as the good ship *Orizaba* steamed out into the beautiful waters of the Pacific Ocean. From the rocks about the cliff the mournful barking of a large drove of sea-lions mingled with the dull dashing of the surf. One of the largest lions sunning himself on the rock is called General Grant because he is a big lion and makes the spray rise like his namesake's smoke as he leaps into the water after a savory fish. A lion of still larger corporosity is named General Butler, but it is possible his name may be changed after the next election in Massachusetts.

Some of the hills and canyons along the coast for two hundred miles are well timbered with pine and redwood, and some veins of coal have been discovered, all of which will be of great advantage to the timberless region of the southern counties. This is the usual place for correspondents to speak of the pleasures of seasickness, but as the writer never experienced those interesting sensations a description is the next thing omitted. The next day we passed Point Conception and at once were translated from the chill and discomfort of a San Francisco climate into the charming temperature and smooth sea of the semi-tropics, a temperature both agreeable and exhilarating. Near Santa Barbara vast quantities of petroleum rise to the surface of the sea and overspread and perfume a large area. Our recollections of good Saint Barbara will be that she was a messenger of peace pouring oil upon the troubled waters.

This circumstance relieves somewhat the barbarous construction of her name. From the seacoast in Santa Barbara county to the eastward as far as the Sierra Madre mountains this yield of petroleum continues to exhibit itself and large quantities of asphaltum are found in the same range and are being used in the manufacture of gas and in the construction of pavements. . . .

In the afternoon we landed at the pleasant town of Santa Barbara and visited the old Mission with its sturdy adobe walls and quaint adornments, the monument of the labors of the zealots of a former century. Next morning we anchored in the harbor of Wilmington or San Pedro.[1] If this is

---

[1] Berry was critical of the harbor, and he viewed with disdain the aspirations of the local citizens to dredge and construct a more navigable shelter for visiting ships. It was not until 1899 that the first carload of rock for a new breakwater was dropped into San Pedro Bay, and work was commenced to make this one of the finest harbors in the world. Today it is known as the Port of Los Angeles.

a harbor it is certainly the largest your correspondent ever enjoyed, as it extends from the bluffs at the mouth of the San Gabriel River back to Japan. A breakwater is nearly completed from the south bank of the river to Dead-Man's Island, and this structure it is claimed will make the harbor smooth and safe. But if the soft banks continue sliding down under the friction of the waves, the small body of water to flow out at ebb tide will hardly be able to keep the channel open, and the hopes of the people may be realized in having the harbor "smooth" and solid also. It is very kind of our good Uncle to allow these hopefuls to experiment with appropriations to build this uncertain wall. . . .

After "rocking the cradle of the deep" but not very deep, of this horrible harbor all day, we bore away for San Diego. Next morning a shout on the starboard announced whales in sight and a rush of excited passengers was made to see these giants of the deep in their sporting and spouting. This interesting sight brought out the usual number of marvellous stories of whales and whaling in the Pacific sea. About ten o'clock we sighted Point Loma which protects the entrance to the harbor, and at one o'clock rounded the point and steamed into the spacious and beautiful bay of San Diego.

This charming spot is destined to form an important feature in the future trade of the United States. It is the only safe and spacious harbor for seven hundred miles of coast of Southern and Lower California, and the terminus of the great Texas and Pacific railroad which is now being rapidly built from Shreveport to this place. . . .[2]

Each section of the United States has had some brigand in its past, whose exploits were so notorious that he became a part of the folklore of the region. Among them are Jesse James, the Dalton gang, Billy the Kid, Sam Bass, and other members of the quick-trigger set, who have been popularized in books written about the West, varying from the lurid paperbacks published in the latter part of the nineteenth century to more scholarly studies authored in recent years.

California had its outlaw who became a legend during his lifetime, and this was perpetuated following his death by the repeated mention of his name in many history books which have been written about the state. Tiburcio Vasquez never achieved the notoriety of some of his counterparts, but he was well known throughout the State of Cali-

[2] D. M. Berry, in the manuscript collection of the Henry E. Huntington Library and Art Gallery, San Marino, Calif.

fornia, where he and his followers rode for a time unchecked—creating more of a nuisance than a reign of terror until lawmen finally brought him to bay. There was nothing spectacular in the criminal record of Vasquez. He would undoubtedly have gone unnoticed had he not finally become involved in the senseless killing of three unlucky citizens during a small-time robbery.

This crime made him the object of the greatest manhunt in the state's history. As a quarry with a price on his head, Tiburcio eluded his pursuers, shot his way out of more than one ambush, and continued to enhance his reputation as a highwayman by staging a series of robberies, which, while not highly renumerative, were boldly committed and kept his name in print, for the press meticulously reported his forays in various communities. It was his role as a fugitive that brought him fame. Readers marveled at his daring—that is, everyone but tired peace officers like Sheriff Harry Morse of Alameda County, who had doggedly trailed the outlaw with a posse across more than two thousand miles of the state. When California finally sentenced the celebrated criminal to the gallows, spectators in the courtroom wept. Vasquez, like another highwayman of a later era, John Dillinger, had become a popular hero.

Tiburcio Vasquez was born in Monterey, California, in 1835. His family was respected in the town, and he received enough of an education to enable him to read and write. Tiburcio came to age during an era that witnessed the transition from Mexican to American rule, and this was not so easily accomplished as some writers claim. Not all the Americans who flocked into California were as tolerant as the early settlers who had arrived before the war with Mexico. They had intermarried, adopting the religion and faith of the local inhabitants. This changed during the 1850's. Many of the newcomers looked down on the Mexicans. They cheated them in numerous ways, such as loaning money to the Mexican landowners, for which they charged usurious rates of interest. When the ranchers were unable to meet the payments, the money lenders foreclosed on the property. Some of the largest ranchos in California passed into the hands of shrewd and unscrupulous Yankee businessmen in this manner.

Vasquez resented these *gringo* spoilers, but it was not his reason for embarking upon a career of crime. His trouble seems to have been in the choice of companions. At the age of seventeen, he attended a lively *fandango* at Monterey with two friends. An altercation occurred, which was commonplace at these gatherings, when an excessive intake of brandy was likely to touch off the volatile tempers of some of the more high-spirited guests. A constable arrived to quiet the celebrants. He was either shot or stabbed to death by one of Tiburcio's associates—the story is somewhat clouded. At any rate, young Vasquez deemed it prudent to hide in the mountains rather than risk questioning. His career as an outlaw had begun. First he tried his hand at robbing stagecoaches and unwary travelers. In 1857, after stealing and attempting to sell a herd of horses near Los Angeles, Tiburcio was apprehended by the law. He pleaded guilty to the charge and was sentenced to serve five years in San Quentin. In a mass break staged in 1859, Vasquez went over the wall. His freedom was brief. He was back in custody within three months. Released in 1863, he teamed up with two notorious felons, Tomas Redondo, alias Procopio, and Juan Soto. Authorities picked Tiburcio up once again, this time for cattle rustling. Vasquez went back to San Quentin. The door was unlocked for him in June, 1870, after he had served three and one-half years. By this time Tiburcio was a hardened criminal, with little respect for the law, and he certainly had no love for the *gringos*.

Northern California roads were plagued with a new outbreak of banditry, as Vasquez pursued his depredations. Every stagecoach driver kept his shotgun handy while passing through the more sparsely settled regions. A marshal managed to corner the bandit near Santa Cruz, but Vasquez escaped with a bullet wound in the shoulder, leaving a dead confederate behind.

On August 26, 1873, Vasquez and his gang committed a robbery that aroused the wrath of the entire state. He and four accomplices entered Snyder's Store at Tres Pinos, a small community near Hollister and northeast of Monterey. The gang leader ordered the customers and the owner, Andrew Snyder, to raise their hands. They complied and were quickly tied. A local sheepherder named Bernal Berhuri approached the store, where he was spotted by the gang's lookout, a thug known as Moreno. The gunman shot Berhuri down. Another customer arrived in a wagon in front of the store. Vasquez ran outside, pointing his rifle at the startled shopper, whose name was

Redford. Instead of obeying Vasquez's order to throw up his hands, Redford made a dash for the barn at the rear of the store. Tiburcio opened fire. Redford staggered to the door, clutching at the latch. He turned slowly and fell dead. The bandit leader now turned his attention to the adjacent hotel, where owner Leander Davidson had come out on the porch to find out what was taking place. One look was enough. Davidson ran inside and slammed the door. Vasquez snapped a shot after him. The heavy slug bored through the wood panel, striking Davidson in the chest. He dropped dead before the horrified eyes of his wife. The gang looted the store. They rounded up the horses in the stable, and galloped out of town. They had left three dead men in Tres Pinos.

Governor Newton Booth called a special meeting in his Sacramento office. Sheriff Harry Morse was selected to direct the search for the killers, and the Legislature provided funds to finance the expedition. A liberal reward was offered for the capture of Vasquez.

Tiburcio had gone into hiding at the house of a friend on the La Brea Rancho, about eight miles northeast of Los Angeles. Once the local sheriff had come close to capturing him, but the wily outlaw had escaped in a running gunfight. But time was running out for Tiburcio Vasquez. A posse acting on a hunch of Sheriff Billy Rowland of Los Angeles, who had probably been tipped by an informer, entered the canyon on the La Brea Rancho, surrounding the house where Vasquez was believed to be hiding. The place was owned by a known acquaintance of the bandit, who was called Greek George. Accompanying the posse was a reporter for the San Francisco *Chronicle*, George A. Beers. The newsman spotted a horse tied behind the house and stationed himself where he could intercept anyone running toward the animal. It was Greek George who was the first to discover the deputies dashing for the building. He shouted for Vasquez to run for it. The fugitive plunged through a glass window at the rear of the house. Stumbling, he tried to reach his horse. Reporter Beers shot him through the shoulder, and Los Angeles Police Chief F. Hartley opened up on the bandit with a double-barreled shotgun, inflicting additional wounds in Vasquez's shoulder, while some of the pellets penetrated his arm. Overpowered, the elusive desperado was at last in custody. He was carried to Los Angeles, treated for his wounds, and lodged in the city jail. Here he became a celebrity, with a crowd gathering to catch a glimpse of the famed outlaw. In May, 1874, Vasquez was transported by steamer to San Francisco. His trial was scheduled to be held in the District Court of Santa Clara County at San Jose the following January.

George Beers, the reporter who aided in the capture of Vasquez, also covered the bandit's trial. Vasquez was found guilty of his crimes and sentenced to the gallows. Tiburcio had no ill feelings toward his captors, for Beers interviewed him frequently during the trial and was with him during the final hours before the execution. Later, Beers wrote a book in which he gives an account of the highwayman's life and trial following the capture—*Vasquez or the Hunted Bandits of the Joaquin—Containing Thrilling Scenes and Incidents Among the Outlaws and Desperadoes of Southern California.* Two nights before Vasquez's death, the newspaperman was with him in his cell. The bandit had dictated several messages of farewell to his relatives:

¶ . . . After completing the dictation of the documents, Vasquez expressed a desire to retire, and bidding a pleasant good-night to his visitors, was left alone with his guard. It had been a scene never to be forgotten. The cold moon shone dimly down through the dusty skylight, rendering the gloomy apartment only more ghastly. It was the bandit's last night but one on earth; and yet—save in lulls in the conversation, when he would gaze abstractedly into the expiring embers of the little box-stove—typical of his own fleeting spark of life—he seemed the most cheerful one of the little party.

Early on the following morning G. D. Hoppes and L. Whittier, of Sacramento, builders of the scaffold on which Mortimer, Estrada, and Cotta [3] were hanged, began the erection of the gallows in the southwestern corner of the jail yard. The structure was visited by over a thousand visitors during the day, and merits a description. It consisted of a platform about ten feet square, supported ten feet above the ground by a stout frame of timbers; eight feet above the platform, and supported on the north and south ends by strong posts reaching eighteen feet from the ground, extended the beam from which depended the fatal noose over the trap. The latter consisted of two doors opening downward and apart—a convenient arrangement for a man who is compelled to "step down and out." Underneath the eastern door were bolted two stout wooden bars of

[3] Other bandits executed earlier.

sufficient length to reach across underneath the opposite door when both were lifted to a level with the floor of the platform. Back of this second door, and running parallel with it underneath the platform, was a stout piece of timber with mortises, well oiled, through which worked the two ears of a strong flat bar of iron, and when the doors were in position these ears, when shoved forward, caught under the ends of the wooden bars, and held the trap-doors firmly in place on a level with the platform. To the centre of the iron bar was attached a rope which ran over a pulley and down a narrow box affixed to a post in the rear of the scaffold, and was there fastened to a heavy iron weight. A smaller cord was also attached to this weight, and, when the trap was set, it supported the weight, and was exposed at the height of the railing in the rear of the scaffold. The cutting of this cord, at the proper signal, of course instantly drops the weight upon the other cord or rope, jerks back the iron bar and ears which support the wooden bars, and the doors open, ushering the unfortunate wretch into eternity. The whole action is instantaneous. Cords are also fastened to the underside of the doors, and, running over pulleys, support weights, and the moment the trap is sprung, the doors are drawn back against the posts, which are so padded that there is scarcely a particle of noise, and the witnesses are spared the disagreeable spectacle of loose doors banging against the writhing body of a dying man. It is the most perfect machine of the kind probably ever invented; a fall of seven feet is given, and death is almost invariably instantaneous. When Mortimer fell through the trap he hung motionless. There was absolutely not a particle of swaying of the body, no heaving of the chest, no twisting of the rope. He hung as motionless as though he had been hanging there for a thousand years.

About ten o'clock, A.M., the prisoner was visited by his counsel, Mr. Collins, and the dying statements prepared from Vasquez's dictation of the previous evening, were carefully translated to him by Deputy Selman, and, listening intently, he approved sentence after sentence by an affirmative nod of the head or an occasional word expressive of approval. Some additions were made at the suggestion of his counsel, and with the prisoner's hearty concurrence. His heart-broken sister, Mrs. Laria, was present, and when Mr. Collins came to the concluding paragraph of the "Address to Parents," [4] where he says: "Farewell, sisters dear," the bandit

---

[4] Vasquez had a word of warning for all parents. They should prevent their offspring from seeking the degrading companionship of the immoral and vicious. He dictated: "I wish the children throughout the world, who may read the incidents of my life, to take warning in time of the example before them of me, and to realize the force of the saying: 'The way of the transgressor is hard!'—the truth of which is now being verified to me."

for the first time showed emotion. A sudden change swept across his countenance. His eyes were moistened, and he drew forth his handkerchief, and removed the evidence of emotion as quickly as possible. All present were much affected, and for some moments Mr. Collins was unable to proceed.

At the conclusion of the reading, Vasquez declined to sign the statements, saying that he should never again take a pen in his hand; but authorized his name to be attached, repeating his declaration that the sentiments were those he wished to go forth as his dying expressions. His signature was attached, and witnessed by most of those present. Vasquez insisted, however, that before publication, they should be submitted to Father Serda. His request was complied with, and the Rev. gentleman gave his approval without suggesting any changes.

During the day, a large number of representatives of the press, officers from adjoining counties, and other invited guests arrived, and were admitted to the jail to see the prisoner and to inspect the arrangements for his execution.

Following is the form of invitation cards issued:

Sheriff's Office,
County of Santa Clara,
San Jose, March 16th, 1875.

To ——:

Sir—Pursuant to the statute in such cases, you are hereby invited to be present at the execution of Tiburcio Vasquez, at the jail of said county, in San Jose, on the 19th day of March, A.D., 1875, at 1:30 P.M.

J. H. Adams, Sheriff.

Present at jail entrance. Not transferable.

The bandit's relatives were with him nearly all the forenoon. . . . The women exhibited the most intense grief at the parting, but the prisoner bore himself with composure throughout. . . .

Throughout the afternoon there was a constant rush of visitors, and although all were respectful and gazed on the condemned man with no indication in their demeanor of a feeling of vindictiveness, I realized, as I looked upon the coming and going throng, as I never realized before, the horrible ordeal of the death penalty. I had looked upon many a scene of blood and carnage; had moved away the dead and dying upon the battlefield; and had learned that the majority of men, when they know they *must die,* arouse manhood enough to face the mysterious and terrible ordeal with wonderful fortitude. Even the unfortunate victims of the battle-field, mutilated and suffering untold agony, as a rule suffer and die in silence. The "shrieks and groans" of the wounded, as thrillingly and with horrible eloquence depicted in works of romance and even in histories, are things of the imagination. The thousands who survived Antietam, Chancellorsville, Gettysburg—all the great battles and skirmishes of our late war, will testify to the truth of this statement. But the condemned man—the man in full health, who knows that tomorrow he must die! At a moment when he would wish to be with his relatives and immediate friends only, or alone with his own thoughts, or communing with his God; or if possible to compose himself, to sleep, to rest, preparing himself for the dread ordeal. It is terrible, in those supreme last hours, to be the constant centre of searching, piercing eyes—to be scanned hour after hour by curious and experienced eyes—to feel that he is being searched to the heart, and to hear whispered comments, hour after hour, on his "nerve" and bearing! I can imagine nothing but the tortures of the inquisition more terrible, more trying! But this man was in the fullest sense of the expression, "equal to the occasion." For each and every visitor he had a manly, affable and self-possessed reception, replying pleasantly and without bravado to all remarks and inquiries.

Having expressed a strong desire to examine the coffin his friends had prepared for him, Sheriff Adams directed Messrs. Truman and Woodson, the undertakers, to gratify his wish; and accordingly about 8 o'clock in the evening of the 18th Mr. Woodson brought the fine casket to the jail, and Vasquez viewed it with great curiosity. The lid having been opened at his request, he examined the satin lining, pressed the cushions and remarked, "I can sleep here forever very well!"

After trying on his pantaloons and finding them a little tight, he found fault, but immediately apologized, and remarked that they would answer, as he "should not have to use them much."

... He retired shortly before midnight, but afterwards remarked to young Adams, the sheriff's son, who remained as guard, that he did not feel very sleepy, lighted a cigar, and conversed as he smoked for half or three-quarters of an hour, and then fell into a sound slumber.

.   .   .

Vasquez's last morning on earth found him as imperturbable and cheerful as ever. He arose early, dressed himself tidily for the solemn event so near at hand, and ate a substantial breakfast. At eight o'clock his relatives and friends came to pay their last visit, most of them remaining until nearly noon.

Soon the usual throng of visitors began to pour in, and during the whole morning, up to the moment of the execution, a dense crowd of people occupied the space in front of the high fence which shuts out the jail-yard from view. In the saloons about town the principal topic of discussion was Vasquez's "courage," and—to the discredit of "human nature"—bets were offered and taken as to whether the bandit would die "game." Vasquez's counsel, Mr. Collins, spent some time with his unfortunate client, and about an hour and a half before the execution, Father Serda called for the last time, and was occupied in religious services with the prisoner until the time arrived to read the death warrant.

Sheriff Adams, deeming it unnecessary cruelty to compel the unfortunate man to stand upon the scaffold during the tedious reading of the document, which had to be translated as the reading proceeded, decided to go through the ceremony within the prison. The newspaper representatives, sheriffs, physicians and a few others only were admitted.

As the solemn document was read by Under-Sheriff Winchell, and translated sentence by sentence, all present narrowly watched the expression of the prisoner's countenance, and could not detect the slightest indication of weakness.

At the conclusion of the reading, Sheriff Adams said, "Vasquez, the time has come to march to the scaffold."

"All right!" was the quick reply, and shaking hands calmly with those present, and saying, with an affable bow, to each one, "Good-bye!" signified his readiness for the ordeal. Under-Sheriff Winchell, and Deputy Selman led the way, followed by the condemned, supported on either side by Sheriff Adams and Father Serda. Various sheriffs and reporters brought up the rear. So densely was the jail-yard crammed with spectators, that the solemn procession had to crowd the way to the gallows.

Vasquez bore a small crucifix before him as he moved forward and ascended the scaffold. Taking his place on the drop, some moments of respite were granted to allow him the last rites of the Catholic church, a white robe or shroud being first thrown over his shoulders. The prisoner gave his responses in a calm, distinct tone, and did not exhibit the slightest agitation. The dense throng of spectators gazing upon the solemn scene preserved the most perfect silence. On the scaffold besides the sheriff and his deputies, Father Serda, and one or two reporters, were Sheriff B. F. Ross, of Hollister, Sheriff H. N. Morse, of Alameda; ex-Sheriff Harris, of

Santa Clara; Sheriff Orton, of Santa Cruz; ex-Sheriff Wasson, of Monterey, and one or two others.

The religious ceremony ended, Vasquez quickly pulled off his coat, and handing it to Winchell, proceeded calmly to remove his collar, and bared his neck for the rope. He was then pinioned with straps, at the elbows, wrists (buckled to a strap securely fastened around the hips), at the knee, and again at the ankles. Under-Sheriff Winchell then placed the fatal noose over the bandit's neck.

Even at this supreme and appalling moment, Vasquez maintained the most absolute command of nerve—the most perfect composure, turning his neck to assist the officer in working the knot closely under the left ear. Winchell made no mistake or blunder, as often does happen in such cases; but the hangman's knot does not always slip easily and in this case the rope was somewhat stiff, and in using the necessary force it suddenly slipped so tight to the neck as to impede the circulation. Within a few minutes suffocation would have ensued.

The doomed bandit simply turned his head, and giving Winchell a meaning look, exclaimed in Spanish:

"Pronto!" (quick!)

It was his last word!

The next moment the black cap was drawn over his head.

Winchell stepped back, the sheriff gave the signal, and the next instant the soul of Tiburcio Vasquez passed from time to eternity!

The time was 1:35 P.M.

The same phenomenon that occurred in Mortimer's case was repeated here. The body fell perpendicularly seven feet, dislocating the cervical vertebra and snapping the spinal cord, and the body remained as still and immovable as though it had been hanging for a month.

Death was instantaneous. . . .[5]

[5] George Beers, *Vasquez or the Hunted Bandits of the Joaquin—Containing Thrilling Scenes and Incidents Among the Outlaws and Desperadoes of Southern California* (New York: Robert M. DeWitt, Publishers, 1875).

26

CALIFORNIA
IN THE EIGHTIES

William Henry Bishop, a writer for *Harper's New Monthly Magazine,* left New York in March, 1881, for a leisurely tour of Mexico and her lost provinces. One of these was California. Arriving at San Francisco, the first observation he wrote in his notebook was the arrival of a shipload of Chinese, whose emigration into the state was a continuing matter of concern:

¶ A China steamer . . . had come in along-side just before us, and supplied a novel element of foreigners. Almond-eyed Celestials, in blue blouses, swarmed her decks and poured down her side. Groups were loaded into express wagons, and driven away uptown in charge of friends come down to meet them. Others trudged stoutly on foot, with their effects deposited in a pair of wicker baskets, at the end of a long bamboo on their shoulders. . . .[1]

[1] The articles written by Bishop were later published in book form—*Old Mexico and Her Lost Provinces—A Journey in Mexico, Southern California, and Arizona by Way of Cuba* (New York: Harper & Brothers, 1883).

The writer described San Francisco as a city having a population of three hundred thousand, "not extraordinary now, as populations go, but there are certain things which make San Francisco cosmopolitan beyond its actual size. An entirely new commercial situation gives rise to a new milieu. San Francisco faces toward Asia, the great English-speaking colonies of Oceanica and the islands of the sea, as New York faces Europe. It enjoys already a trade with the Orient amounting to ten millions per annum in imports and eight millions in exports. The possibilities of this trade extended among the teeming population in the cradle of the human race seem almost limitless."

Bishop was quick to realize that the state was destined for greater achievements than those of the short-lived mining booms in California gold and Nevada silver. He predicted that the real wealth was in the land and what it would ultimately produce. He wrote:

¶ Physical and commercial conditions are changing. Life hereafter will depend less upon spasmodic "finds," and more on the humdrum and legitimate industries. Mining, though the supply of treasure, with improved machinery, still holds out in a uniform way, takes a lesser rank. Agriculture and manufactures come every day more to the front. California produces an annual wheat crop of $50,000,000, a wool crop of $10,000,000, wines to the amount of $40,000,000, and fruits worth as much more, though these last two branches are but in their infancy. Of the greater part of all this San Francisco is the *entrepôt*. . . .

After a stay in San Francisco, Bishop set out to learn what southern California was like. His description is included in his previously cited book, but it was first published as a series of three articles in the October, November, and December, 1882, issues of *Harper's New Monthly Magazine*.

Bishop had unknowingly timed his visit to California at the end of an era. The great wave of expansion that was destined to bring thousands of settlers into southern California was still a few years distant. Life hadn't visibly changed much since the leisurely days of the Spanish ranchos. The people had, for they were predominantly of other than Mexican descent. Indeed, even the Chinese, whom Bishop discovered in great numbers, seemed to fare better economically than the Mexican, who had either sold or been deposed from the land that had been his birthright.

One observation of Bishop's would have been carefully noted by every prospective land buyer in the East, and that was the information that southern California was a land of little rain. Water to irrigate the ranchos was hard to obtain. Later years would witness the completion of giant engineering projects—the Hetch Hetchy Dam, with its 186-mile aqueduct carrying water from the Tuolumne River to San Francisco; the Owens River aqueduct completed in 1913, a pipeline from the eastern slope of the Sierras to Los Angeles that set off a bitter controversy within the state while it was under construction. Settlers of the Owens Valley watched helplessly as the course of their valuable river was diverted to satisfy the needs of thousands living miles to the south. The biggest project of all was the construction of the Hoover Dam, completed in 1935. An elaborate system of pumping stations brings Colorado River water to much of the southern-California region. Even today as work proceeds on the Feather River project, which will provide an additional source for southern California, water remains one of the state's biggest problems. An atomic-powered plant for the conversion of salt water is to be constructed near the southern-California coast under federal and state auspices. The constant quest to discover new ways to secure water for an ever-burgeoning population has created conflicts between the counties of the northern and southern sections of the state. An even more touchy problem is California's relations with neighboring Arizona and Mexico over the continued use of waters from the Colorado.

William Henry Bishop traveled south by train, buggy, and horseback. Near San Francisco, he visited Belmont, the luxurious estate of the late William Ralston, who drowned in San Francisco Bay following the collapse of his financial empire. Ironically, the property was now owned by William Sharon, United States Senator from Nevada. Sharon had at one time been an employee of Ralston's, managing the Nevada branch of the Bank of California, where he became the most influential figure in the Comstock. When Ralston lost his fortune, Sharon, although a director in the bank that was forced to close its doors, weathered the financial crisis that bankrupted thousands of others.

Bishop continued his journey, pausing in the rich Santa Clara Valley. He took time to visit a winery, still a popular outing in various sections of the state. At Monterey, he discovered that whaling was still an industry. On ranchos he passed while crossing the San Joaquin Valley, he observed at work the last of the *vaqueros,* the colorful horsemen who were once the caretakers of the great cattle herds roaming across southern California. There were strange little communities to be seen, and the Southern Pacific Railroad now crossed the Tehachapis to Los Angeles. The great Loop engineered by William Hood, by which the trains would circle the 4,000-foot mountain barrier by a series of tunnels, making a gradual ascent to the summit without exceeding a 2.64 percent grade, was one of the wonders of its time when completed in 1876. It remains the route of Southern Pacific trains following the inland route from the San Joaquin Valley today.

The writer visited the picturesque city that had once, under Spanish and Mexican rule, been the most important community in California:

¶ Monterey, which is now not even a county seat, was the Spanish capital of the province from the time it was first thought necessary to have a capital, after the landing here of the missionary father Junipero Serra in the year 1770. It was next a Mexican capital under eleven successive governors. Then it became the American capital, the first port of entry, the scene of the first Constitutional Convention of the State, and an outfitting point for the southern mines. . . .

. . . the place seems nearly as desirable a resort at one time of the year as another. The quaint town is always here; so are the wild rocks with their gossiping families of gulls and pelicans, and the romantic drives through extensive forests of pine and cypress.[2] There are varieties of these two trees—the latter of which is like the Italian stonepine—peculiar to Monterey alone. They are hoary with age and hanging moss. They are contorted into all the fantastic shapes imagined in Doré's illustrations to the "Inferno," and they stand by the most savage points of rock, where the breakers toss up handfuls of white spray to them, forty feet in the air, as if in amity and greeting.

Along the beach at this remote point of the great Pacific Ocean is a lonely Chinese settlement. The veritable Celestials, with hardly a word of English among them, paste crimson papers of hieroglyphics on their shanty residences, burn tapers before their gods, and fish for a living in such junks and small boats as are seen at Hong Kong and Canton. They

[2] The scenic grandeur is still to be found along this section of the California coast. It attracts thousands of visitors to the Monterey Peninsula each year.

prepare, too, the avallonia [abalone] meat and avallonia shells for their home market. We shall find that the Chinese element, which one had thought of as confined to San Francisco, constitutes a feature of exceeding quaintness and picturesqueness throughout all of Southern California as well. . . .

The large Chinese communities have largely disappeared in southern California, but when Bishop visited the state there were sizable Chinese populations in each city. Here he visits one of the richest agricultural centers of the San Joaquin Valley:

¶ Separated from the main part of Fresno, as by a wide boulevard, is seen a long row of low wooden houses and shops, as clearly cut out against the encompassing desert as a row of bathing houses on a beach. This is the Chinese quarter. Its isolation tells the story of the peculiar people who tenant it; and of the feeling of social ostracism entertained toward them on one hand, and their own unconquerable clannishness on the other.

There is now hardly any hamlet so insignificant, even down in the wastes of Arizona, that the Chinese have not penetrated to it, in search of labor and opportunities for profit. Almost every settlement of the Pacific slope has its Chinese quarter, as mediaeval towns had their Ghetto for the Jews. It is not always set without the rest of the place, as at Fresno; but wherever it be, it constitutes a close corporation and a separate unit, unencroached upon by any other. Its people, in dress, language, and habit of life, adhere as closely to Oriental tradition as their new conditions will permit.

Whoever is gifted with an eye for the picturesque very soon puts the Chinese in the foreground in almost every prospect in California. They have not introduced a national style of architecture, and build little but shanties themselves. They rather adapt what they find to their own purposes, distinguishing their handiwork with such emblems and devices that the character of the dwellers within can not thereafter be mistaken. There is a great incongruity between the common little Yankee wooden dwellings tenanted by the Chinese in this rural life and the tasselled lanterns, gilded signs, and hieroglyphics upon red and yellow papers with which they are so profusely overspread. Here are Ah Coon and Sam Sing, keeping laundries like the usual Chinese laundry the world over. Yuen Wa advertises himself as a contractor for laborers. Hop Ling, Sing Chong, and a dozen others have miscellaneous stores. In their windows are junk-shaped slippers, opium pipes, bottles of saki (a rice brandy), dried fish, goose livers, gold and silver jewelry, and packets of face-powder, and hair ornaments for the women. The pig-tailed merchants sit within on odd-looking chests and budgets, and gossip in an animated cackle with friends, or figure gravely in brown-paper books, using a pointed brush as a pen. Some women—who are much more numerous in proportion to the men than is commonly supposed—occasionally waddle by. Their black hair is very smoothly greased, and kept in place by long silver pins. They wear wide jackets and pantaloons of cheap black "paper cambric," which increase the natural awkwardness of their short and uncomely figures.

Upstairs in some unpainted, cobwebby second stories are found the joss-houses or temples, which the rustic Chinamen, even with the disadvantages under which they labor, do not neglect to establish. Here the hideous but, it must be confessed, extremely decorative idols grin as serenely as if in the centre of their native Tartary, and as if there were no snug little spires of Baptist and Methodist meeting-houses rising in severe reproach across the way. There are pastilles burning before these idols, and some crimson banners draped about; and there are usually a few pieces of antique bronze upon which the eye of the connoisseur can not but rest enviously.

Other interiors are cabarets, which recall those of the French working classes in the great air of animation reigning within. The air is thick with tobacco smoke of a peculiar Chinese odor. Games of dominoes are being played with a magpie-like chatter by excited groups of men clustered around long stout wooden tables. Most of those present wear the customary blue cotton blouse and queer little back felt hat, and all have queues, which either dangle behind them or are coiled up like the hair of women. Some, however—teamsters perhaps from place to place, and here only temporarily—are dressed in the slop clothing and cowhide boots of ordinary white laborers. The Chinamen are servants in the camps, the ranches, and the houses of the better class; they are track-layers and section hands on the railroad, and laborers in the factories and fields. What Southern California, or California generally, could do without them just at this time it is difficult to see. They are found, for the most part, capable, industrious, honest, and neat. One divests one's self rapidly of any prejudice against them with which he may have started. Let us hope that laborers of a better class, by whom they are to be succeeded, may have at least as many praiseworthy traits.

Not everyone would agree with Bishop. Many believed the Chinese were a threat to organized labor. Their champion had achieved prominence a few years earlier, speaking from a sandlot across from the San Francisco City Hall. This was Denis Kearney, a brawling Irishman who emerged as the titular head of the Workingmen's Party, which was organized to protect the rights of the wage earner and advocate labor reform. Kearney's angry diatribes brought him widespread recognition, and he was asked to address other groups of workers in various eastern cities. He gladly complied. His principal target was the Chinese emigrant. They were usurping jobs which should rightfully be filled by Caucasians. They worked for a wage that no decent American could support his family on. Kearney hammered this theme home in his speeches. Standing before a large gathering in Boston, he shouted:

¶ By the heavens above and the stars that are in it; by the moon, that pale empress of the night; by that sun that shines by day; by the earth and all its inhabitants, and by the hell beneath us, the Chinese must go . . . it will be well for you to know some of the issues that deceive the Democratic thief and Republican robber out of sight in California. The workingmen of California are becoming overpressed. The capitalistic thief and land pirate of California, instead of employing the poor white man of that beautiful and golden State, send across to Asia, the oldest despotism on earth, and there contracting with a band of leprous Chinese pirates, brought them to California, and now used them as a knife to cut the throats of honest laboring men in that State. A Chinaman will live on rice and rats. They will sleep one hundred in a room that one white man wants for his wife and family. . . .

. . . The question is, are the Chinese to occupy this country? (Cries of "No," and a vote taken resulted in an almost unanimous response in the negative.) The Chinese Government has sent an Embassy to this country to establish Consulates in California. We can take care of the Chinaman. It is designed to distribute Chinese throughout the United States. They have a population of 450,000,000 in China, and I can smell them afar off. I said there was one within 100 rods of me when I landed in Boston, and I ran against one within 50 rods (Laughter). Let me caution workingmen not to employ Chinese laundrymen. They are filthy; they spit on clothes, and if these have any disease it is transmitted to men and women through such washed clothing when the body perspires. Do you want leprosy here? (Cries of "No.") By not employing them you can drive them from the country.

They call this a barbarous country, and us barbarians. If our forefathers
101 years ago voted to throw tea overboard, let us take and throw the
teamakers overboard. (Laughter) . . .

In conclusion, fellow workingmen. Awake! Arise! Your work begins
anew! We will teach these thieves and bondholders what workingmen can
do. We will do it with our bullets if our ballots fail. We will drive these
moon-eyed lepers back by steamship and by sail. . . .[3]

Kearney returned to California, where considering his growing
popularity, he disappeared suddenly from the political scene. No
longer were crowds treated to his thundering outbursts on the sandlot,
where he had achieved his early popularity and begun his spectacular
rise. The labor movement at that time was not a lucrative field for
earning a living. Kearney had addressed an audience of twelve hundred people in St. Louis. When the hat was passed for contributions
to support the cause, it proved a disappointment. Only $5 had been
collected. There were a number of business leaders who preferred
that the fiery orator remain silent. Collis Huntington, who ran the
Southern Pacific Railroad with an iron fist, once remarked that every
man had his price. In countless San Francisco saloons, where workingmen gathered to discuss the departure from the scene of the man whom
they had regarded as a messiah, it was said that gold in the palm had
silenced the gifted tongue of Denis Kearney.

*   *   *

Bishop managed to visit every city in southern California as far
south as San Diego. He arrived there aboard a steamer:

¶ . . . A low hand-car running on a track upon the long wharf conveys
our baggage up into the town while we walk beside it. The town on being
reached is found to be a place of loose texture. It has a disproportionately
large hotel, the Horton House, which was built in anticipation of future
greatness, and proved a loss to its proprietors. The blue shades are down
and the plate-glass windows dusty also in much of the "Horton Block,"
opposite, which still wears an expectant look. After '73, it is said, half the
shutters in San Diego were nailed up. They have now come down, however, no doubt to stay. There is a charming view of the harbor and of deep

[3] From a pamphlet printed in 1878, in the manuscript collection of the Henry E.
Huntington Library and Art Gallery, San Marino, Calif.

blue ocean beyond from the upper slope. A part of the view is a group of Mexican islands, particularly the bold Coronado. . . .

The chronic condition of shutters in San Diego "Old Town" is to be nailed up—that is to say, so far as it can be said to have shutters still remaining. It dates from 1769. Having been found disadvantageously situated as regards the bay, it began to be deserted in favor of the newer site about ten years ago. Nothing is more desolate now. The usual old mission, with a few palms and olives about it, stands in a valley up the pretty San Diego River, and the earth-works of Commodore Stockton, who threw them up one night before the enemy knew he was ashore, are seen on the hill. . . . The plaza has a toppling flag-staff, a decayed music stand, and vestiges of a number of burned-down edifices which it has never been worth anybody's while to build up again. The broken "Merchants' Exchange" will never supply cocktails to thirsty souls again; the Cosmopolitan Hotel, though wrecked only financially, is without a guest; whole rows of weather-beaten adobe houses—whole quarters of them— stand vacant. It should be a famous place for ghosts.[4]

Bishop arrived in Los Angeles, and here he noted a strange attitude on the part of many people he interviewed. They felt that they were isolated from the northern part of the state. There were proponents for a division of California—a new state that would be called South California. Its proposed capital would be Los Angeles. One of the separatists had maintained in the *Californian* magazine: "We are different in pursuits, in tastes, manner of thought and manner of life . . . our hopes and aspirations for the future are different. The restless, uneasy population of the north, ever drifting, without local attachments, has no counterpart in Southern California; neither has the wild spirit of mining speculation ever flourished here. With this peaceable life, possibly in part as a result of it, there has grown up in the people an intense love of their land. And it is for their own section of the State that this love exists. We call ourselves, not Californians but Southern Californians. . . ."

The writer hired a buggy and was given a tour of the town. He made numerous notes that were incorporated into his articles:

[4] William Henry Bishop, *Old Mexico and Her Lost Provinces—A Journey in Mexico Southern California, and Arizona by Way of Cuba* (New York: Harper & Brothers, 1883).

¶ The City of Angeles is, in general effect, another San Jose, only upon a more hilly site. Its population must be about fourteen thousand. The long thoroughfare of Main Street proceeds, from the depot, at first through a shabby Spanish quarter, locally known as "Sonora," consisting of one-story, whitewashed, adobe houses. But presently—after passing a small Spanish plaza set out with sharp-pointed cypresses, and the principal hotel, the Pico House—it is lined with excellent buildings of the modern pattern, and becomes the principal street of the town. The handsome Baker Block is particularly notable. Continuing on to the ornate Los Angeles Bank, it is found that Spring Street diverges at this point at a small angle, and contributes, with Main Street, to give to what may be called the commercial skeleton of the town the shape of a Y with a very long stem. On Spring Street you find the common little post-office, the municipal offices, and a brown Dutch-looking brick building, standing free, which was originally constructed for a market, and is now the County Courthouse. You may also look into the lobby of a small adobe jail, which lobby some leisurely prisoner of the frescoer's trade has been allowed to convert into a resemblance to the dungeon scene at a theatre. These two streets, with another shorter one, Los Angeles Street, parallel to Main, and containing fruit and other produce, commission houses, comprise all of the commercial portion of the city worth mentioning.

New buildings are going up. The shops are large and well-appointed. On all sides are read placards offering goods in the usual shibboleth of enterprising traders: "To Reduce Stock!" "At a Wholesale Slaughter," and "For the Next Sixty Days." A serious depression afflicted Los Angeles in 1875, at the time of the general depression throughout the State, but that has been succeeded by a new reign of activity. Trim large residences for the more prosperous merchants are seen in the outskirts of the town. Further out yet they become villas, set down in the midst of plantations of orange and lemon, which are ruled off into formal plots by the ditches for irrigation. The class of more modest means are housed along the side streets in frame cottages. The German Turn-hall serves as the principal theatre.

It is held that Los Angeles, with its port of Wilmington, thirty miles away, should be, and will be, now upon the completion of the Southern Pacific Railroad, the entrepôt and Pacific terminus respectively of a new commerical system. San Francisco has too long sat at the Golden Gate, as it is picturesquely put, "levying toll on every pound of freight that passes through." This selfish greed on the part of San Francisco is to be properly rebuked by the diversion of a part of its trade to the places named. Enthusiastic San Diego too expects to have its share. The wickedness seems to depend largely upon who it is that takes the toll. Los Angeles, it is held, is to be the Lyons, and San Diego the Marseilles, of the State, this theory still leaving San Francisco its Paris. . . .

We had not expected to find Los Angeles wholly foreign, but we were surprised to find it in so many respects very much like other towns in the United States. There is Spanish Town, however, and that should be important. Come, let us go through Sonora.

The Mexican element must be something like one-third of the entire population of the place. In Sonora the recollection of Mexico is revived, but of a very shabby and provincial Mexico. You may find *mescal* and *tequila* —the two varieties of intoxicating liquors distilled from the *maguey,* or aloe—to drink. The dingy little adobe shops contain dingy little stocks of goods, samples of which are set in the shuttered loop-holes of windows. A few swarthy, lantern-jawed oldtimers hang about the corners, gossiping in a bad patois, and women with black shawls over their heads pass by. Much of the quarter is in a ruinous condition. There remain in it the vestiges of an arcade system of the kind known in some form to travellers in most tropical or semi-tropical countries. The arcades in Sonora are not of massive brick and stone, but wooden roofs, such as are sometimes put out by our corner grocers, supported on light posts. Here and there only the battered skeletons of these awnings remain attached to the ruinous houses. Most California municipalities have borrowed something of this Spanish idea. At Sacramento, for instance, the thriving but flat and not overattractive capital of the State, one can walk nearly all over the business part of the town under cover.

There is a very respectable-looking Mexican restaurant—a vine-embowered cottage—opposite the Pico House, where the familiar *tortillas,* or pancakes, and *frijoles,* or stewed beans, may be had. Alongside it is an adobe church, quaint in pattern, but modern and devoid of interest, with a belfry, from which chimes jangle several times a day in true Mexican fashion. Out of Sonora, too, emerges on the 15th of every September a military company, the Juarez Guard. It escorts a triumphal car bearing the national tri-color of red, white, and green. There is an escort also of dark little maids in white muslin and slippers. The whole proceed to celebrate with appropriate ardor the anniversary of Mexican independence.

But this is a people which has gone to the wall. They wear no very pathetic aspect in their adversity. They are for the most part engaged in the coarser kind of work; they are improvident, and apparently contented with their lot. It is only here and there that a Spanish name—a Pacheco,

Sepulveda, Estudillo—rises into prominence in the State of which they were once owners. Old Don Pio Pico, the last of the Spanish Governors, resides here, impoverished, in a little cottage, in sight of property of much value which was formerly his, and the plaza which was once the centre of his authority.

Don Pio is one of the picturesque sights of Los Angeles. With his history and circumstances, he would be esteemed an interesting figure anywhere. Above eighty now, with his stocky figure, square head, and bright eye, contrasting with his bronzed skin and close-cropped white hair and beard, he has a certain resemblance to Victor Hugo. He has a rather florid taste in jewelry, and carries himself about town, in his short overcoat with velvet collar and cuffs, with a bearing still erect and stately. It seems strange to tell, but it is true, and evidence of the conservatism and lack of adaptability in this peculiar race, that the old gentleman, though once Governor of the State, and a continuous resident in it as an American citizen since he surrendered it to Frémont and Stockton in 1847 [5]—strange to tell, I say, that he does not speak a syllable of anything but his own language. The talk of this historic personage suggests but a rude picture of the advantages to be enjoyed in the state of society existing during his youth. Was there anything in the world so remote as the California of the years 1810–30, or thereabouts?

"I am a plain person," the old man says, "who had the chance to learn but little from books. My father did not leave me a mule nor a vara [yard] of ground. I worked for the fathers at the old San Gabriel Mission when I was a boy."

He disclaims even being an authority on the events of his fall and the encroachments of the conquering Americans. "There are many," he says, "who have a better head for all these things than I, who will tell you better than I. I was a just man, however," he naively admits. "I aimed to judge a rich man who came before me no better than if he were poor. When it was asked who should be Governor, who was *lo mas justo y honrado*—the most just and honest man—for that place, it was answered that it was I, Don Pio Pico."

Pio Pico had declared during the days when American settlers were moving into California, although it was still a province of Mexico, "We find ourselves suddenly threatened by hordes of Yankee emi-

---

[5] The writer is in error. Frémont accepted the surrender of the Mexican forces from the gallant Andrés Pico, the governor's brother. Pio Pico made a hasty departure to Mexico, where he remained in exile until it was safe for him to return to California.

grants, whose progress we cannot arrest." As the last Mexican governor, he had witnessed the military seizure of his country by the
United States. Soldiers had invaded his land. His brother, Andrés,
had rallied the native Californians in a final effort to halt American
forces marching north from San Diego. Resistance had been futile.
The Californians capitulated. Now Pio Pico was an old man. Most of
his companions during the angry years of the 1840's were gone. So
was Pico's wealth. The Pico House, a fashionable hotel he had once
owned in the city's plaza, had passed into the hands of his creditors.
Yet Pico was a proud grandee of the old tradition. He never forgot his
heritage, nor the fact that the tricolored flag of Mexico once flew over
the governor's house in Los Angeles. He had been reluctant to learn
the language of his conquerors. It is understandable.

27

A VOICE FOR THE INDIANS

In the 1880's, the Indians of California were slowly but inexorably being driven from the few lands they had been allocated by the government. In many sections, such as the fertile San Luis Rey Valley near San Diego, they had occupied small tracts owing to the benevolence of some of the Mexican ranchers. With the division of these large ranchos following the American acquisition of California, land titles became clouded in litigations that were to prevail for decades to come. It became possible during the 1880's for enterprising newcomers to secure patents from the federal government on large blocs of fertile land, many of which had numerous Indian families living upon them, where they had cultivated small farms for generations. They were promptly dispossessed, and little provision was made for their future welfare. It was during this period that the greatest defender of the California Indians arrived in California—Helen Hunt Jackson. After viewing their living conditions, and learning of the unfair treatment to which they had been subjected, she became their advocate. Her active pen touched off a controversy that for a brief time stirred the nation.

Helen Hunt Jackson reached Los Angeles some time late in 1881. She had been assigned to write a series of articles for *The Century Magazine,* after having achieved a reputation as a talented author and poet. Here she made the acquaintance of one of the early Mexican colonists, Don Antonio Coronel, who was highly esteemed throughout California. For a writer wishing to learn about the region, she had found the best informant, for Don Antonio was familiar with California's past, and related anecdotes he had learned as a boy that dated back to the coming of the Spaniards. He had been appointed Inspector of Southern Missions in 1844 by Governor Micheltorena, and had long understood the problems of the Indians. It was through the arrangements of the Coronel family that Miss Jackson visited the Mission San Luis Rey and the rancho Camulos in Ventura County. Both were to provide the setting for *Ramona,* the novel that dramatized the plight of the California Indians, bringing the author lasting fame. Before leaving the state, she had visited every mission from San Diego to San Francisco—or what was left of them, for many of the buildings were in ruins. Helen Hunt Jackson had a highly retentive memory and was able to record what she saw in the most minute detail. Nothing escaped her eye, and when she saw Indians in want, or learned of them being victimized, she was outspoken. This earned her a few enemies among the ranch owners. She was undaunted, and her articles were read by thousands of incensed readers throughout the United States. It was as a result of correspondence with Secretary Teller of the Department of Interior that Miss Jackson finally attracted the attention of the government. In 1883, she was appointed a Commissioner of Indian Affairs, and assigned to visit the Mission Indians of California, reporting on their conditions. She had a friend, Abbot Kinney, owner of a large ranch near Los Angeles, assigned to aid her in compiling the report. This study, augmented by additional comments, was presented to the public in *A Century of Dishonor—A Sketch of the United States Government's Dealings with some of the Indian Tribes*. In this book, Helen Hunt Jackson reported that there were 48,000 Indians living in California. Her description of the treatment they had received was an indictment of the white man's way of dealing with his Indian neighbors:

¶ The poorer, the more insignificant, the more helpless the band, the more certain the cruelty and outrage to which they have been subjected. This is especially true of the bands on the Pacific slope. These Indians found themselves of a sudden surrounded by and caught up in the great influx of gold-seeking settlers, as helpless creatures on a shore are caught up in a tidal wave. There was not time for the Government to make treaties; not even time for communities to make laws. The tale of the wrongs, the oppressions, the murders of the Pacific slope Indians in the last thirty years would be a volume by itself, and is too monstrous to be believed. . . .[1]

Miss Jackson stated in her report that she found the Indians living for the most part in small isolated villages, some on reservations set apart for them by governmental order, and some upon lands included within the boundaries of confirmed Mexican grants:

¶ Considerable numbers of these Indians are also to be found on the outskirts of white settlements, as at Riverside, San Bernardino, or in the colonies in the San Gabriel Valley, where they live like gypsies in brush huts, here to-day, gone tomorrow, eking out a miserable existence by days' works, the wages of which are too often spent for whiskey in the village saloons. Travellers in Southern California, who have formed their impressions of the Mission Indians from these wretched wayside creatures, would be greatly surprised at the sight of some of the Indian villages in the mountain valleys, where, freer from the contaminating influence of the white race, are industrious, peaceable communities, cultivating ground, keeping stock, carrying on their own simple manufactures of pottery, mats, baskets, &c., and making their living,—a very poor living, it is true; but they are independent and self-respecting in it, and ask nothing at the hands of the United States Government now, except that it will protect them in the ownership of their lands,—lands which, in many instances, have been in continuous occupation and cultivation by their ancestors for over one hundred years.

From tract after tract of such lands they have been driven out, year by year, by the white settlers of the country, until they can retreat no farther, some of their villages being literally in the last tillable spot on the desert's

[1] Helen Hunt Jackson, *A Century of Dishonor—A Sketch of the United States Government's Dealings with Some of the Indian Tribes* (Boston: Roberts Brothers, 1885).

edge or in mountain fastnesses. Yet there are in Southern California today many fertile valleys, which only thirty years ago were these same Indians' wheat-fields, orchards, and vineyards. Now, there is left in these valleys no trace of the Indians' occupation, except the ruins of their adobe houses; in some instances these houses, still standing, are occupied by the robber whites who drove them out. The responsibility for this wrong rests, perhaps, equally divided between the United States Government, which permitted lands thus occupied by peaceful agricultural communities to be put "in market," and the white men who were not restrained either by humanity or by a sense of justice, from "filing" homestead claims on lands which had been fenced, irrigated, tilled, and lived on by Indians for many generations. The Government cannot justify this neglect on the plea of ignorance. Repeatedly, in the course of the last thirty years, both the regular agents in charge of the Mission Indians and special agents sent out to investigate their condition have made to the Indian Bureau full reports setting forth these facts. . . .

Under the regulations of the Secularization Act, the Indians were to be given land to farm; cattle from the holdings of the Franciscan order were to be divided in an equitable manner. Farming implements and seeds were to be distributed. But, as Miss Jackson writes:

¶ These provisions were in no case faithfully carried out. The administration of the Missions' vast estates and property was too great a temptation for human nature, especially in a time of revolution and misrule. The history of the thirteen years between the passing of the Secularization Act and the conquest of California is a record of shameful fraud and pillage, of which the Indians were the most hapless victims. Instead of being permitted each one to work, maintain, and govern himself without dependence on any one, as they had been promised, their rights to their plots of land were in the majority of cases ignored; they were forced to labor on the mission lands like slaves; in many instances they were hired out in gangs to cruel masters. From these cruelties and oppressions they fled by hundreds, returning to their old wilderness homes. Those who remained in the neighborhood of the pueblos became constantly more and more demoralized, and were subjected to every form of outrage. By a decree of the Los Angeles *acumiento,* about the time of our taking possession of California, all Indians found without passes, either from the alcalde of the pueblos in which they lived, or from their "master" (significant phrase), were to be treated as horse-thieves and enemies. At this time there were . . . whole streets in Los Angeles where every other house was a grog-shop for Indians; and every Saturday night the town was filled with Indians in every stage of intoxication. Those who were helpless and insensible were carried to the jail, locked up, and on Monday morning bound out to the highest bidders at the jail gates. . . .[2]

The unjust treatment of the California Indians did not improve under American occupation and subsequent statehood. By the time Miss Jackson commenced her survey, disease and neglect had taken its toll among the tribes. The population was declining, and

¶ . . . with every year of our neglect the difficulties have increased and the wrongs have been multiplied, until now it is, humanly speaking, impossible to render to them full measure of justice. All that is left in our power is to make them some atonement. Fortunately for them, their numbers have greatly diminished. Suffering hunger, disease, and vice have cut down more than half of their numbers in the last thirty years; but the remnant is worth saving. Setting aside all question of their claim as a matter of atonement for injustice done, they are deserving of help on their own merits. No one can visit their settlements, such as Aqua Caliente, Saboba, Cahuilla Valley, Santa Ysabel, without having a sentiment of respect and profound sympathy for men who, friendless, poor, without protection from the law, have still continued to work, planting, fencing, irrigating, building houses on lands from which long experience has taught them that the white man can drive them off any day he chooses. That drunkenness, gambling, and other immoralities are sadly prevalent among them, cannot be denied; but the only wonder is that so many remain honest and virtuous under conditions which make practically null and void for them most of the motives which keep white men honest and virtuous. . . .

Helen Hunt Jackson is quoted as saying, "I am going to write a novel, in which will be set forth some Indian experiences in a way to move people's hearts. People will read a novel when they will not read serious books. I hope very much that I can succeed in writing a story to increase the interest so much aroused in the East over the Indian question." *Ramona* achieved her objective, far more than her official

[2] This was common practice. The Indians were fined for their drunkenness. The ranchers paid these fines, for which the hapless native was obligated to work through the following week to pay back his debt. The system provided a cheap source of labor, for the rancher encouraged his workers to return to Los Angeles each Saturday night, paying them just enough in wages to buy enough *mescal* to repeat the cycle of the previous week.

report, *A Century of Dishonor*. The novel took its place as the most popular book of the day. It failed, however, to institute progressive legislation and a realistic approach to the Indian problem. This did not occur during Miss Jackson's lifetime. Two years after her death in 1885, the Dawes Act was passed, which under its terms accepted responsibility for the care of all Indians. Prior to that time, they had been treated as "nations," and treaties had been negotiated with them. The public had finally become aware of its moral obligations toward the native races it had dispossessed.

Miss Jackson's novel had one immediate effect. It stimulated the tourist business in southern California. The rancho Camulos became a popular attraction for visitors. As John Steven McGroarty wrote, "Transcontinental trains catered to winter visitors and brought them by the thousands during the bleak wintry months that beset the outlands. A tremendous propaganda of publicity advertising in national publications was set in motion, by the railways, the chambers of commerce and civic organizations. The romance and fascination of the Old Missions was particularly stressed with good effect." [3]

Those who had read the sad account of Ramona and her husband Alessandro being displaced from their small farm by a greedy American landowner were the first to respond. A visit to the various missions was on every traveler's itinerary. Most of them were falling apart from neglect. Their walls had crumbled. Weeds and underbrush covered fields that had once been neatly subdivided into gardens, vineyards, and orchards. A movement was inaugurated to restore the entire mission chain. It would require many years, but today this is a reality. The Indians did not disappear from California, as Helen Hunt Jackson feared they would. Her efforts in their behalf must have had some effect, even though it is difficult to point to any specific accomplishments that occurred as a direct result of her writing. The evolution of social reform has always been a slow process. It is motivated by myriad ideas—of individual and collective action. Violence often acts as a catalyst. In some measure, the California Indians have survived their passage. Today, more than 40,000 of them live throughout the state.

[3] John Steven McGroarty, *California of the South—A History* (Chicago: S. J. Clarke Publishing Co., Inc., 1933) Vol. 1, p. 166.

28

BOOSTERS, BOOM AND BUST

An extensive advertising campaign in the East, sponsored in a large measure by the Southern Pacific Company, was responsible for a sizable increase in California's tourism business during the early 1880's, but it failed to bring an influx of new residents. For those with low incomes, the cost of a railroad ticket for a cross-country journey was still prohibitive. Among the wealthier classes, it became fashionable to travel west on the luxurious Pullman cars during the winter months to escape the colder climate of the Midwest and the eastern seaboard. Relatively few bought property on the West Coast. They patronized the hotels and returned to their homes in the spring. A change was noted around 1885. The Easterners were beginning to invest in California land, and an estimated 50,000 visited the state in search of homesites.

The Southern Pacific had long held a monopoly on railroad transportation to the West, until a competitor entered the field. The Atchison, Topeka & Santa Fe Railroad had been a long time coming west, but in 1885 the company completed a transcontinental line when it reached San Diego by way of San Bernardino. In 1887, Santa Fe purchased a branch line running from that city to Los Angeles. Meanwhile, Santa Fe officials attempted to negotiate with the Southern Pacific for an equitable share of freight and passenger traffic. What they proposed was that the two railroads should divide present and future business. The plan was unacceptable to Southern Pacific. The two companies began a rate war that reached its height during 1886–1887. Fares fell at an astonishing rate. For $15, one could buy a one-way ticket from the Missouri River to the Pacific coast, and for a brief time the price was as low as one dollar. Those who had longed to travel west, but had hesitated because of the cost, now packed their bags. Thousands of these eager people were farmers from Iowa, Kansas, Indiana, Illinois, Wisconsin, and other agricultural regions. They had read the handbills and literature distributed by the railroads. Visions of orange groves and a land with an abundant harvest uprooted entire midwestern communities, as hundreds boarded the coaches for the uncomfortable journey west. The emigrant cars were devoid of the more modern facilities reserved for the discriminating travelers who could afford first-class accommodations. But the less pretentious came by the tens of thousands to be welcomed by the real-estate agents, who were often unscrupulous purveyors of the land.

Speculation in homesites and farming property rivaled the excitement caused by the discovery of Nevada's Comstock Lode. In the stampede for real estate, San Francisco and the northern half of the state was neglected. The area was confined to southern California. For the first time, Los Angeles emerged as an important city, destined to become a great metropolis. San Diego, long overshadowed as a port by San Francisco, was another city destined to grow into a major metropolis. New communities began to appear through the southern section of the state. Some would survive, while others would become ghost towns within a few years. Promoters subdivided large parcels of real estate in isolated desert localities that lacked enough water to sustain animal life. Other lots were sold on inaccessible mountaintops to purchasers who often resold them at a profit without having ever taken the time to look at the property.

T. S. Van Dyke was a writer who witnessed the beginning of the great land boom. Suddenly, to the surprise of many residents, the transient vacation population did not disappear when the winter season ended. They remained and the cities began to grow. He describes the era in *Millionaires of a Day, An Inside History of the Great Southern California Boom:*

¶ . . . the travel in the spring of 1885, instead of falling off, remained about the same as in the winter, and continued so all summer. It had long been noticed that though the majority of the settlers were people who had been captured by the fine weather of the winter, a much larger proportion had always been ensnared by the summer. Thousands had spent a winter here and gone away, never to return. But of the hundreds who dallied with the long, bright summer, with its dry air, cool nights, and unfailing sea-breeze, few ever went away to stay long.

This difference was now more striking than ever, and before summer was half over the rate of settlement was much more rapid than formerly, and prices were already rising a little. New houses were dotting the landscapes far and near; new settlements like Redlands were springing up here and there; Los Angeles, Pasadena, and San Bernardino were growing rapidly; on the north Santa Barbara and San Buenaventura were beginning to feel the effect; and even San Diego began to rub its eyes after the long sleep that followed the collapse of the Texas Pacific Railroad some twelve years back. . . .

Professional tourists, hearing that there were now some good hotels in California and good eating-houses along the way, and Pullman cars to ride in, concluded to add Southern California to their stock of subjects to talk about. People who had been here before and were pleased with everything but the prospects of making anything out of the soil, hearing now of its great advance, came back to see if there were sufficient inducement to stay. Along with these came invalids and other climate-seekers, and people whose relatives here had been advising them to come out, and farmers by the hundred, tired of vibrating for seven months in the year between the fireplace and the woodpile, dodging cyclones and taking quinine. And with these came schemers and promoters of all kinds, with a little money which they were anxious to increase at the expense of some one else and without risking any of their own; and capitalists of high and low degree, who had heard that the country was prosperous, for prosperity makes friends for a country as well as for persons.

The winter of 1885-6 was well adapted to capture any one, for the rains had come early and by the middle of January the whole land was a rolling sheet of green. He who stood on any of the higher hills around Los Angeles with a good glass could see an area of country immediately around the city that when worked to its full capacity under the improved methods of the time would make almost a State in itself. Below him, surrounded by a wealth of green reaching away from the center in long lines of ten, twenty, and forty acre tracts, lay a rapidly growing city of some twenty thousand people, scattered amid groves of oranges in which the golden gleam of the ripening fruit and the snowy bloom of the crop to come contrasted brightly with the dark sheen of the evergreen leaves. Miles away into the southeast until lost in the hazy green of the great San Joaquin rancho reached a vast plain sloping gently up to the foot of the Santa Ana mountains, and as gently down on the south to the edge of the great shining ocean. From there to where the verdant carpet of the land curled up into the highlands above San Pedro and on the west rolled away to where Santa Monica slept beside the sea, villages, hamlets, and farms dotted the land on every side. . . . The man of means who at this time could spend an hour on any hill from which a good view of Los Angeles County could be had without calling on a real-estate agent before sundown was the exception, and not the rule.

But perhaps the stranger concluded to look about a little more, and went down to San Diego. There he saw from the heights above the town the whole surroundings of the bay with a single sweep of the eye. From the long promontory of Point Loma, which miles away on the west forms one barrier of the harbor, to the tablelands of Tia Juana fifteen miles in the southeast, from the water's edge to the highest point of the slope, the whole lay undulating in a hundred shades of green under the soft sunlight that streamed from the clear sky. From every direction in the city below him came the sound of the saw and the hammer; and at National City, the terminus of the Santa Fe Railroad, four miles up the bay, new houses not yet ready for the paint were glimmering in all the freshness of new lumber. Miles away on either hand shone the bright water of the bay, unbroken save by the dark hulls of the shipping or the splash of the fishhawk and pelican. Coronado Beach, the outer guard of the harbor, had then no settlers except the coyote, the hare, and the quail; but its green chapparal and thousands of springing flowers and its happy location on the bay plainly foretold its future. . . .[1]

[1] T. S. Van Dyke, *Millionaires of a Day, An Inside History of the Great Southern California Boom* (New York: Fords, Howard & Hulbert, 1890).

Land was not the only factor contributing to the population rise. The climate was proclaimed as being beneficial for those suffering from a variety of ailments. Thousands of health seekers arrived in southern California from more intemperate climates in the East. For them, the fact that the annual rainfall was often light was not a deterrent, as it was to prospective purchasers of farm property. These newcomers were searching for a land of eternal sunshine. An editorial published in the Los Angeles *Times* for September 18, 1887, points out ecstatically the advantages of the region for either health or agriculture:

> ¶ All the world is interested in California. As of old, search was instituted for the fountain of eternal youth, and men dreamed of drinking its waters and living forever, so men today turn their steps in the direction of the Golden State, looking for the springs of health which are hidden in its atmosphere. Better than the Utopia of the ancients is this modern Utopia of the Pacific. Better than the Gardens of Hesperides, with their golden fruits, the gardens of this sunset land, where "all that is pleasant to the sight and good for food," may be found growing in fruitful abundance. . . .
>
> The absence of rain for six or eight months of the year, when the skies are filled with the warmth of effulgent sunshine, and the heat is tempered and the air kept pure by the fresh sea breeze, is what fits it for the world's sanitarium. The character of its soils with their wonderful capacity for retaining moisture makes all the year a growing time, and each month a harvest month. . . .[2]

It was inevitable that with the widespread speculation in southern California real estate, there would be some unscrupulous land sharks who would bilk the public with spurious advertisements. Tracts proclaimed as being fertile acreage where harvests would be bountiful often turned out to be desert wastelands, or in some cases simply nonexistent. Land changed hands many times, rising in price with each successive transaction, with both seller and buyer unaware that the property deed was a bogus one issued initially by a dishonest real-estate promoter. The *Times* reported these distressing conditions on the editorial page of its November 19, 1887, edition:

[2] The *Times* editorial writer, carried away by his theme, failed to mention that since the rainfall was sparse, crops had to be irrigated to ensure an abundant harvest.

¶ MORE SWINDLES—THE FAKIRS INCREASING

The first number of the Providencia Times—a new paper not a week old—contains a stereotyped advertisement of the second edition, or addition, of the Manchester free-gift townsite swindle. Of course the Providencia Times is no exclusive offender in this regard. Doubtless the same advertisement appears in dozens of papers, or wherever the enterprising Manchester fakir can get in his work.

The ad refers all who desire to share in the wonderful advantages offered to the same Newman of whom the Times has already had something to say in connection with the Manchester scheme.

The first fraud having been fully exposed, the astute Newman has located another townsite(?) on the same bald mountain a few hundred yards from the same Manchester, and he dubs his new venture "Border City." This is the new addition which Newman now advertises.

The fact that Newman has stereotyped his ad, looks as though he had adopted the plan of keeping it in the columns of new-born prints, or prints located in isolated districts—a deep and cunning move. Newman raised the price of the lots from $2 to $3.

"Border City" is situated high up on the Sierra Madre Mountains, and, as its name indicated, is just barely within Los Angeles county, being where the mountains corner at the junction of Los Angeles and San Bernardino counties.

None but crows and eagles can ever make a settlement there. And even they will have to carry well-filled haversacks with them as they fly over that inhospitable waste.

Cannot this nefarious scoundrelism be stopped? Is there no power whereby recording such townsites can be prevented? If the County Recorder should refuse to record the maps of such townsites, or the deeds their swindling projectors issue, would it not stop the swindle or lay the swindlers liable to an action for obtaining money under false pretenses?

The townsite fake and free-gift lot swindle is rapidly seeking its low-down level. . . . Drifting still lower, the town-fake business has reached the barn-storming strollers who infest Lunar California. The *Times* is in possession of a cheap dodger of a cheap playhouse in San Francisco which guarantees each of its patrons a "grand gift" order for a lot in the town of "Newberry," San Bernardino County. Of course, the inevitable $2 is specified as an A1 condition.

"Newberry" is the name, which the fakirs have given to a stretch of the

Mojave Desert. It is a stretch of white glistening sand, where nothing of earth, air or water ever lived or can live. Even the scorpions and tarantulas have fled the place.

The railroad rate war, which was responsible for bringing thousands to California, also brought about a traffic snarl causing freight revenues to come to a standstill. With so many passenger trains being pressed into use to carry people to the West Coast, there were not enough locomotives left for use in hauling freight. This created a hopeless tangle across the continent, with freight cars left sitting on sidings waiting to be moved to California. Foodstuffs spoiled and other shipments went astray for months before they were located. Articles appearing in the Los Angeles *Times* reported the freight-car fiasco. This story is from the November 16, 1887, edition:

¶ THE RAILROADS

THE FREIGHT BLOCKADE ON THE SANTA FE

SIX HUNDRED CARS OF FREIGHT SIDETRACKED

BETWEEN HERE AND ALBUQUERQUE—HOPES FOR RELIEF

The most important matter just now in railroad circles . . . is the blockade on the Santa Fe system. As is well known, by far the greatest number of passengers are coming in from the East over that route; and the crowds come in such overwhelming multitudes as to tax every resource of the great corporation. The company is still feeding and lodging hundreds of passengers in Kansas City, and its trains are still coming in here in sections with fifteen to thirty crowded coaches daily. It is understood that tickets sold for California in Kansas City now cannot be used till three days after date—it being impossible to get a ticket to be used on the day it is bought.

A Times man talked yesterday with Judge Anson Brunson, solicitor and highest official of the Santa Fe system in California, about the blockade. Said the Judge: "I have been telegraphing some cold-blooded facts to Boston, and hope we may get some relief. We are completely overwhelmed. The passenger travel alone is too big for us, to say nothing of freight. We have 200 cars of freight at San Diego for this city. Along the line of the Atlantic and Pacific there are between 600 and 700 loaded freight cars lying sidetracked and deserted. We haven't power to haul them, as we need all our locomotives and more, too, for our passenger business. . . ."

The Central Pacific, or Southern Pacific, which was the parent company, was also in difficulty, as this article published in the *Times* on December 22nd of the same year attests:

¶ TREMENDOUS FREIGHT BLOCKADE ON THE C.P.

Such a mammoth stoppage of freight as has oppressed the coast for the past two months was never known in the history of the West. The enormous blockade on the Atlantic and Pacific has, luckily, passed its worst, and freight is now coming in over that line in comparatively good shape, though there is still a good deal of trouble. Now the seat of difficulty lies in another quarter. This time it is the Central Pacific which is in a state of siege. The fact has been adverted in these columns, and though denials have been made the facts remain. The Chicago Times of December 15th says:

"The freight blockade of the Central Pacific is now the worse in the history of the company. Twelve hundred loaded cars are crowded on the side-tracks between Ogden and San Francisco, and more than 800 of these are on the Salt Lake division. The cause of this blockade is the inability of the company to secure enough locomotives to handle the freight trains. Unless something can be done by the Central Pacific to secure motive power soon, eastern agents will be forced to refuse freight."

The following day the *Times* was able to report that there had been some improvement in conditions on the Santa Fe, which certainly must have pleased Los Angeles merchants. At long last they would have goods to sell:

¶ The obstruction of the freight movement on the transcontinental roads is still—and probably will remain for a good while—the most important matter in railroad lines. The northern freight blockade shows no signs of amelioration. The trouble with every important railroad in the United States is the lack of motive power. . . . The new factories which turn out good locomotives are all buried under an avalanche of orders. Some of them can turn out one or two locomotives a day, but that doesn't go far among so many scores of hungry roads—the Santa Fe alone having an order for 200 locomotives. . . . The last car of 700 which were side-tracked and deserted along the line of the Atlantic and Pacific for so many weary weeks will arrive here this forenoon, leaving the company freehanded to wrestle with the enormous traffic. . . .

Local traffic over the lines of the Southern Pacific is simply enormous, and the road is now doing the heaviest business in its history. Said a well-known local official to a Times reporter last evening:

"Our business over our local lines has increased to such an extent that it is all we can do to handle it, and our resources are taxed to their utmost capacity. We are doing everything in our power to handle the business, and are adding to our facilities as rapidly as possible. The bulk of the travel is eastern tourists traveling over our local lines. There is not much eastbound travel at present. Everybody is going this way, and when they get here they seem determined to see everything in this section of the country, judging from the way they go up and down our Southern California branches. . . .

People continued to come to southern California by the thousands during the fall of 1887. As the weather grew colder in the East, the traffic increased. Many were merely visitors intent on wintering in California, but the tourists were in the minority. They were outnumbered by those who brought their life savings to invest in land bargains. There was a far greater number lacking sufficient funds to buy property. They carried little luggage, for they had few possessions. They came in search of employment, and for them, even at bargain rates, a one-way ticket west was all they could afford. The Los Angeles *Times* headlined a story published on November 17, 1887:

¶ IN DROVES, AND STILL THEY COME,
  AND STILL THE WONDER GROWED—
  243 TOURISTS IN ONE PARTY YESTERDAY—
  MOST OF WHOM HAVE COME TO STAY.

The newspaper's account of the arrival carried the entire passenger list, together with the various localities where the newcomers planned to settle. The following day, the head over a lead story announced:

¶ STILL STAMPEDING—175 MORE TOURISTS
  FLEE FROM THE WRATH OF AN EASTERN WINTER
  AND SEEK ETERNAL SUMMER AND BLOOMING FLOWERS
  IN SOUTHERN CALIFORNIA.

On December 6th, the *Times* published this news item:

¶ The Santa Fe Company estimates that it brought 10,000 passengers to

California during November last. The Southern Pacific is selling from 700 to 1000 acres per day. . . .

Times reporters were kept busy covering the arrival of each crowded train. Another headline appeared:

¶ FOUR EXCURSIONS—A REGULAR TOURIST
ARMY ARRIVES YESTERDAY.
TRAIN-LOAD AFTER TRAIN-LOAD COMES IN OVER
THE SOUTHERN PACIFIC—THE LIST OF SEEKERS FOR
A WINTERLESS CLIME.

Every man, woman, and child on those trains could see their names printed the next day in the newspaper. It was shrewd thinking upon the part of management. The *Times'* circulation was showing substantial gains.

*   *   *

There is always a day of reckoning when any era of prosperity is the result of a highly inflated economy. The rate war between the railroads was settled, and on December 21, 1887, the *Times* carried an announcement that the Southern Pacific Railroad Company, "in compliance with the Interstate Commerce Act, will give notice of an advance on the 1st. of January of $10 in first class rates to points beyond the Missouri River, St. Louis, Cairo, Memphis or New Orleans . . . the old emigrant third class ticket will now be known as second class. First class rates to Chicago will be $72.50; St. Louis $67.50, New York $91.00; Boston; $93.00."

The spring of 1888 brought a decline in the number of visitors and new residents. The market for real estate suddenly vanished, and those holding large tracts of land dumped them on the market for whatever prices could be obtained, and in most cases these were substantially lower than the previous year. Some communities simply disappeared from the map, as the townsites were deserted—particularly those which had been built in arid regions. Other towns managed to survive, and today are among the largest cities in southern California. During the decade between 1880–1890, approximately 700,-

ooo people moved into the state, and the majority had no intention of leaving, despite the financial outlook. Money became scarce, and banks were reluctant to make loans. Unemployment increased. Those with capital did little investing, and new construction came to a standstill. However, no widespread depression followed in the wake of the boom. Conditions merely reverted to what they had been before the excitement began. There were plenty of newcomers who were determined to stay and make a go of it. By 1890, Los Angeles had 50,000 residents, and cities such as San Diego and Santa Barbara also showed marked population increases. As some of the newcomers reasoned, they might not have much money, but there was one benefit that had been enthusiastically advertised, and despite many other false promises, it was available in abundance in southern California. They called it sunshine.

29

WAR WITH THE RAILROAD

C alifornia was having its own problems during a decade when
there was a public outcry for reform and a demand that the
federal government exercise controls against the great monopolies.
The chief target within the state was the Southern Pacific Company,
which the public charged had become so powerful that the corporation ruled California.

In 1894, a pamphlet aroused popular indignation, and undoubtedly
provided novelist Frank Norris with the title as well as the theme for
his novel that attacked the power of the Southern Pacific. The booklet
was published in San Francisco and entitled *The Octopus—A History
of the Construction, Conspiracies, Extortions, Robberies and Villain-
ous Acts of the Central Pacific, Southern Pacific of Kentucky, Union
Pacific and Other Subsidized Railroads*. The author was John Robinson, and in his denunciation of the railroads he writes:

¶ They have always opposed competition, and no device however mean
and contemptible, or criminal but what they have adopted to obtain their

base ends. Huntington testified, "that competition is killing, and that there ought to be only one railroad for the whole country." All classes, especially the whole western country, have been compelled to contribute by extortionate rates to the payment of interest and dividends on watered stock and fictitiously created capital. [The railroads] have constituted themselves as arbiters of trade and directors of the channels it should follow. They have expended millions in encroachments upon territory and enterprises claimed by others. They have increased the cost of living.

They discriminate between and favor individuals, localities and articles. They destroy competition and build up particular localities to the injury of others, till it has come to such a pass that no man dares to engage in any enterprise where transportation is largely required, without first asking and obtaining permission of a railroad manager. They exert a terrorism over merchants and communities and the lawful pursuits of the people; they interfere with and dictate elections; they menace business; paralyze capital and retard investment and development. From 1864 to 1869 they claimed that their roads were fully equipped, obtained bonds from the government, declared dividends, but when the United States demanded the percentage, as agreed in the original contract, they refused to make any payments, stating that their roads were not fully completed until 1874!!

And now comes the impudence and bareface assurance of Huntington in his last resort by asking the Government to assume the indebtedness of his railroads and satisfying its creditors if possible, or compelling them to exchange their investments and securities by new bonds bearing 2½ per cent interest for 125 years; saddling the next four succeeding generations with taxes amounting to $3,350,000 annually, aggregating in 125 years the enormous sum of $438,750,000 for interest; the principal, $134,000,000 added by [sic] making a total of $572,750,000.

Are we to tamely submit to this additional extortion and imposition and allow this monstrous monopoly to dominate the politics, industries and progress of California and the Pacific Coast for the next century and a quarter? Or will the people rise in their majesty and power and shake off this grasping and crushing octopus, and by the investment and execution of just and equitable law, subject it and all similar organizations and trusts to honest and fair dealing . . . ?

Stuart Daggett, in his monumental and creditable study [1] of the

---

[1] Stuart Daggett, *Chapters on the History of the Southern Pacific* (New York: The Ronald Press Company, 1922), pp. 214–215. Daggett states that Bassett's letters appeared in the San Francisco Daily Report after November, 1892. They were subsequently pub-

railroad, cites the charges made by another writer of the period, J. M. Bassett:

¶ Mr. Bassett was one of the early pioneers. He came to California in 1851, and was at various times miner, printer, newspaper man, railroad employee and member of the Oakland city council. At one time he was Leland Stanford's secretary. After Mr. Stanford had been forced out of the presidency of the Southern Pacific, Bassett began to publish a series of open letters to Collis P. Huntington, and continued them weekly, with occasional intervals, for several years. The sustained vivacity and pungency of this polemic, and the systematic virulence with which Bassett reviewed and criticised the Huntington policies make the series a noteworthy journalistic achievement. Mr. Bassett denounced Mr. Huntington for overcapitalization of the Southern Pacific system, for its failure to pay taxes, for its carelessness of the lives of its employees and of the public, for its attempt to evade repayment of the debt which it owed to the United States government, and for the general mismanagement which, he asserted, had taken place under Huntington's control. With respect to the interference of the Southern Pacific in politics, Bassett wrote Huntington in 1895:

"What chief executive of the State, before the present incumbent, has there been who did not owe his nomination and election to the Southern Pacific Company and in acknowledgment of his debt hasten to obey its slightest command? Has there ever been a Board of Railroad Commissioners before last November in which you did not own at least two members? Have you not named every Harbor Commissioner appointed during the past twelve years?

"Have you not hitherto chosen San Francisco's Police Commissions and do you not now exercise a dictatorial power over the city's police, especially the Harbor Police? Were not the judges of the two United States Courts in San Francisco appointed at the instance of Leland Stanford? How many Superior Courts are there in the State in which a citizen may bring an action against you in full confidence that he will be fairly and impartially dealt with? Doubtless there are such, but the difficulty is to find them. Before the recent elections, how long did you control the government of San Francisco? Have you not dictated the government of Oakland for the past twenty-five years? Until last election had you not continuous control of Alameda County's government . . . ?"

lished at various times after his death in 1903, and were credited with a considerable share in preventing the refunding of the Central Pacific indebtedness to the United States government on terms favorable to the railroad.

Daggett had the following comments of his own in summing up the influence the railroad exerted within the state, and its flagrant disregard for the welfare of the people:

¶ One rises from the study of the political activities of the owners of the Central Pacific with a feeling of indignation at the selfishness of these men, their indifference to all save the considerations of private gain, and their readiness to use any and all methods which would advance their financial interests. The associates met the proposal of government regulation as a threat to rob them of their property and resisted it as they would have opposed any other attack. They never conceded that any question of public interest was involved which it was necessary for them to respect. They frankly defended the use of money as a method of persuading men to do what was right—which inevitably meant, of course, what in their judgement was right. They fell out among themselves, not because any one of them questioned the philosophy which inspired their opposition to public control, but because one of them was suspected of using power, developed in the course of the defense of the railroad interests, to advance personal ambition which ran counter to the views of his associates. . . .[2]

Robert Glass Cleland, one of the most distinguished of all California historians, was even more caustic in his assessment of the evils committed by Collis Huntington and his associates, when he wrote:

¶ It is difficult to make an accurate and objective estimate of the pioneer railroad-builders of California. They were, beyond question, one of the most constructive of the forces of a highly creative generation, and aided incalculably in the development and enrichment of the state. It is equally obvious, on the other hand, that they looked upon the railroads as their private, personal possessions and used them, both directly and indirectly, within the law or without the law as occasion demanded, to build up huge fortunes for themselves and to acquire tremendous economic and political power.

"The Big Four" clearly had no conception of a public utility as a public trust, and brushed aside the quixotic idea that the welfare of a community,

[2] *Ibid.*, p. 220. The author refers here to Huntington's growing dissatisfaction with the small amount of time Leland Stanford devoted to railroad affairs, preferring to remain in the public eye. The election of Stanford to the U.S. Senate in 1883 in place of A. A. Sargent, a close friend of Collis Huntington, deepened the rift. Huntington finally ousted Stanford as president of the Southern Pacific in 1890, and had himself elected to fill the vacancy.

or of a great commonwealth, was vastly more important than the ambitions and fortunes of four private citizens. Public opinion charged them with corrupting the fountainheads of government, setting up puppet legislatures and city councils, and making lackeys and henchmen out of public officials. To all such charges Huntington angrily replied: "We have served California better than any other set of men have ever served any other state in the Union."

In all fairness the practices of the California railroad-builders must be judged by the standards of the society to which they belonged and not by the ethics of a more socially-minded generation. But whether we condemn or excuse, the facts and their consequences remain the same. Long after the men who complacently accepted the title of the "Big Four" had been gathered to their fathers, the Southern Pacific machine still remained an arrogant and hateful reality to the people of California—the personification of all that was dictatorial and corrupt in state politics. And the builders of great enterprises, the initiators of a revolution in industry and transportation, were cast, by popular tradition, in the role of economic buccaneers.[3]

Strikes and labor violence plagued the period, and unrest among the working classes was widespread throughout the United States. The strike at the Homestead plant of the Carnegie Steel Company in Pittsburgh was a particularly bitter one. Workers protested a reduction in wages being paid for piecework. The company imported Pinkerton guards to maintain order, and a bloody fight ensued in July, 1892, when workers attacked a boat carrying the Pinkerton men up the river to the steel mills. The state militia had to be called out to maintain order.

Unemployment continued to grow. Many jobless Californians joined Jacob S. Coxey's army in the spring of 1894, when they made an abortive march on the nation's capital. The supplicants were asking for jobs on public works. Coxey was jailed for walking on the lawn of the Capitol building, and the great march collapsed.

A violent strike erupted in Chicago during the summer of 1894, when workers protesting wage cuts walked out of the Pullman Company yards. The American Railway Union ordered its members to boycott any railway using the Pullman sleeping cars on its lines. When the strike threatened to paralyze the railroads, President Cleve-

[3] Robert Glass Cleland, *From Wilderness to Empire, A History of California* (New York: Alfred A. Knopf, 1959), pp. 174–175.

land ordered federal troops to intervene. It served only to deepen public hostility against the large corporations.

The presidential election of 1896 was closely watched in the West. The chief issue in the campaign between the Democratic candidate, William Jennings Bryan, and the Republicans' choice, William McKinley, was the argument of maintaining the gold standard against the philosophy of free and unlimited coinage of silver. The latter would be an inflationary measure, but its supporters, many of whom were farmers, believed it would increase the money supply. Silver from western mines was in far greater abundance than gold. Bryan campaigned for the free and unlimited coinage of silver at a ratio of sixteen to one on a whirlwind tour of the nation, which brought him to California. Thousands filled parks and auditoriums to listen to his eloquent oratory.

An equal use of both silver and gold, as endorsed by the Democrats, had a strong appeal in California and the West, but the opposition to this policy was strong in the more populous manufacturing states of the East and Midwest. McKinley in his plea for "sound money," as gold-standard currency was known, hammered at his listeners that if free coinage of silver was permitted, the mints would have to pay the miners, or banks holding silver bullion, a dollar for every fifty-three cents worth of silver. The public would still have to accept the dollar at its face value as legal tender. The hard-money thesis won out. McKinley received 60.63 percent of the electoral vote when the public went to the polls on November 3, 1896, while Bryan was accorded 39.37 percent. McKinley's plurality over his Democratic opponent was nearly 380,000 votes. When the complete tally was in, he had received 7,104,779 votes. Bryan counted 6,502,925 from his own party, and an additional 222,583 votes from the Populist, or People's, Party, which had endorsed him.

Hopes for an uptrend in business conditions were prevalent, and there was a flurry of mining excitement that year with the news that gold had been discovered along the Yukon River and its tributaries in Alaska. Thousands of prospectors jammed the ships leaving San Francisco and other California ports for the Klondike, as the strike developed into a full-scale rush to the gold fields in 1897.

The following year was a momentous one in American history, for it marked the inauguration of an era of expansion and the emergence of the United States as a major power in international affairs. The Philippines became an American colony. Hawaii was annexed, and the island of Guam was acquired. All of these events came as a result of the Spanish-American War.

The war, declared on April 23, 1898, created considerable excitement in California. There was a rush for the recruiting offices in Los Angeles, San Francisco, and other cities. The battleship *Oregon* left her berth at Mare Island and sailed through San Francisco's Golden Gate, bound for Havana. The voyage around Cape Horn was 14,000 miles, and the vessel reached Key West on May 26. The distance the ship had to travel to reinforce the Atlantic Fleet renewed interest in the proposal for digging a canal across Panama.

The war ended August 12, 1898. Spain relinquished its claim to Cuba and Puerto Rico. On December 10, in a formal treaty, the Spanish government ceded the Philippines to the United States, receiving a payment of $20,000,000 for the islands. Peace was short-lived in the Philippines, where the rebel leader Emilio Aguinaldo, who had supported the American invasion, rallied his people in a bloody insurrection on the grounds that their colonial status had been continued.

In 1900 William McKinley was reelected President. His Vice-President was Theodore Roosevelt. On September 6, 1901, McKinley was shot and mortally wounded in Buffalo, New York, by a fanatic named Leon Czolgosz. He died September 14. Theodore Roosevelt took his oath as President on that day. He was not quite forty-three years old, but he was a veteran of close to twenty years in political life, and was at the height of his popularity.

The business outlook was encouraging, but all was not in perfect harmony to promote an upward trend in the national economy. There were more strikes, and the rift between labor and capital widened. In San Francisco, conditions were in a violent foment, as the waterfront unions, known as the City Front Federation, engaged in a ruthless struggle with the Employers' Association, a combine of manufacturers and business concerns pledged to destroy organized labor. Five men were killed and hundreds beaten and injured during three chaotic months in 1901. The unions utilized their voting power by electing

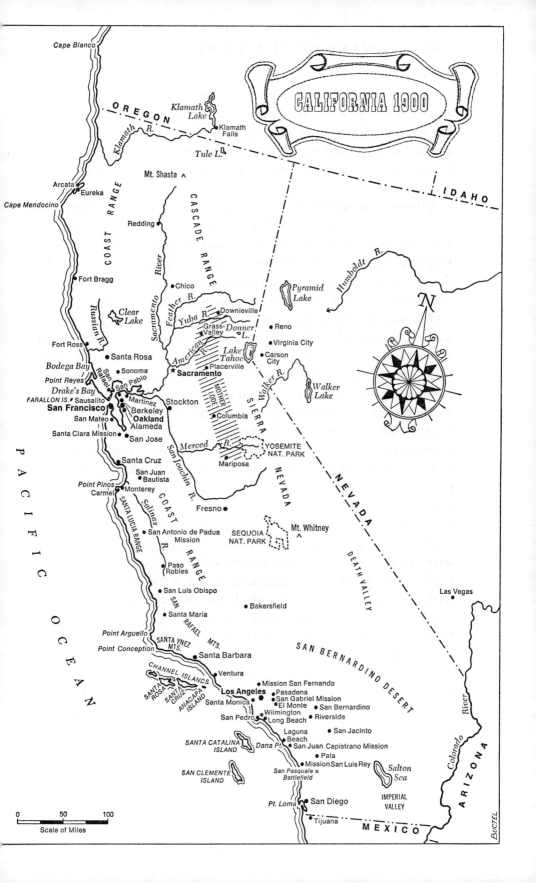

Eugene E. Schmitz as the city's mayor. The man who pulled the strings in San Francisco government was a corrupt political boss named Abraham Ruef. The Schmitz-Ruef machine was entrenched in the body politic between 1901–1907, in which time they looted the city treasury, extorted money from businessmen, and grew wealthy on the profits they accrued from vice, gambling, and other forms of graft.

Although the unions had made progress in San Francisco, Los Angeles remained the last bastion against organized labor in the state. Here an organization, the Merchants and Manufacturers Association, waged a continuous campaign to counter the inroads being made by the unions. The employers refused to arbitrate, and when it was necessary, strikebreakers were imported to maintain the open shop.

One issue that had caused such bitterness for so long at last seemed near settlement. The political power of the Southern Pacific was on the decline. Before the turn of the century, Collis Huntington had his lobby introduce a funding bill in Washington. While the railroad had been under construction, the federal government loaned the Southern Pacific $27,500,000. Payment had at last fallen due, and with accrued interest, the debt was in the neighborhood of $60,000,000. What Huntington proposed was to retire the 36-year bonds that the railroad had put up to obtain government subsidies, and which carried a 6 percent interest rate; replacing them with new 99-year bonds. The new interest rate would be one half of 1 percent. The plan backfired, when the publisher of the San Francisco *Examiner,* William Randolph Hearst, joined other prominent dissidents against the bill in seeing to its defeat. Hearst sent his best writer to Washington to aid in crushing the proposed legislation. This was Ambrose Bierce, whose scathing pen wrote the final epitaph for the Funding Bill. His first dispatch, printed in the *Examiner* during February, 1896, proclaimed "Huntington Lying in His Last Ditch." The tenor of Bierce's articles was that the Southern Pacific was attempting to evade payment of its obligations to the government. Bierce's stories created a furor. An interesting anecdote of an encounter in Washington between the two adversaries is described in Carey McWilliams' excellent biography of Bierce:

¶ One day, coming out of a committee session, Bierce and some other men met Collis P. Huntington on the steps of the Capitol. Previously Bierce had declined Huntington's hand in a committee session. But on this occasion Huntington approached and began to inquire as to how much Bierce wanted to withdraw from the fight. Meeting with a stony rejection of every bid, Huntington finally shouted: "Well, name your price; every man has his price." It was then that Bierce made the famous statement that his price was the amount that Huntington owed the government, and that he might pay it to the Secretary of the Treasury.[4]

The Funding Bill was defeated in January, 1897. Californians were elated. Huntington suffered another defeat in Los Angeles. Here for many years business leaders had wished to establish a navigable harbor at San Pedro. It would require financial aid from the federal government to make this possible, for the project required a great amount of dredging, and breakwaters had to be constructed. Huntington wanted the port established at Santa Monica, where he owned most of the shoreline, and Southern Pacific would have another rail monopoly on the freight traffic from there to Los Angeles and other points. The Los Angeles *Times* led the fight for a harbor at San Pedro. The bill was finally passed in the Senate in May, 1896, with San Pedro being selected as the site for the port. In August, 1900, as work was in progress on the new harbor for the city of Los Angeles, Collis P. Huntington died. With his passing, others within his organization sought to maintain the railroad's political control over the state. It was only after the formation of the Lincoln-Roosevelt League in California, during 1907, that Southern Pacific's tight grip was at last broken. The new political action group was pledged to clean up the state legislature, and curtail the power of the railroad. It backed Hiram Johnson, a San Francisco attorney, for governor in 1910, and with his election in the following year after a turbulent campaign in which his principal slogan was "Kick the Southern Pacific out of politics," California entered a new era. At last it had a governor who was a champion of governmental and social reform. But first, almost as a prelude to this era of progress that would instill new vitality into

[4] Carey McWilliams, *Ambrose Bierce, A Biography* (New York: Albert & Charles Boni, 1929), p. 240.

a society growing increasingly moribund from the wanton pillaging of financial vandals, a great holocaust had to scorch the earth, leaving a city in ruins—the land torn asunder and littered with the ashes of hundreds of her people and the charred, skeleton-like fragments of scores of buildings.

In the early morning hours of April 18, 1906, the worst catastrophe ever to strike California occurred. San Francisco was rocked by a massive earthquake. A great conflagration was ignited by a succession of underground shocks. The city became an inferno.

30

THE SAN FRANCISCO EARTHQUAKE

The jolt shook the sleepy city of San Francisco at 5:12 A.M. Buildings tumbled into the streets as though they had been constructed of matchsticks and papier-mâché. The fire that followed the earthquake completed the destruction. Thousands were left homeless. Property damage ran into millions of dollars, and an estimated 452 persons perished. There were probably many more, but their bodies were never found. San Francisco newspapers were forced to suspend operations. Reporters working for the Associated Press finally reached Oakland, across the bay, from whence the first telegraphed reports of the disaster were flashed to a shocked nation. There was no direct telegraph communication with San Francisco. The lines were down. This was the Associated Press account as it appeared on the front page of the Los Angeles *Times* on April 19th:

¶ SAN FRANCISCO—It looks now as if the entire city would be burned, following the great quake of yesterday. The government is furnishing tugs to convey news to Oakland, but the confusion is so great that they cannot be relied upon. It will be impossible to send full details for several days. The latest reports from Leland Stanford University indicate that the magnificent stone buildings of that institution have sustained severe damage. Many of the buildings were ruined by cracks, which split them from cornice to foundation. . . . Only a few structures collapsed in Berkeley, the earthquake shock being slight there. At 10 o'clock at night, the fire was unabated, and thousands of people are fleeing to the hills and clamoring for places on the ferry boats. The damage is now believed to have reached $200,000,000 and 50,000 people are thought to be homeless. Under the fierce heat of the sun today, 29 bodies lay in Washington Square, where they were taken at the order of the Mayor when the morgues and Hall of Justice basement held all that could be cared for.

The *Times* ran the AP's first report, date-lined April 18th, which had been delayed in transit:

¶ During six hours of mortal dread and nameless terror San Francisco was today tossed upon the seismic wave of the most disastrous earthquake known to the history or the traditions of America's west coast. In the mad confusion and helpless horror of this night uncounted bodies of dead men and women are lying in morgues and under unuplifted walls. It is believed that nearly 1000 lives have been lost. The number cannot fall far short of that, and it may prove to be much greater. Fire and flame have added to the destruction, the ruination and despair. The material losses are beyond computation. Wounded and hurt inexpressibly, the chief city of the West lies at this hour humbled to the dust, blackened, battered and charred, her glory of yesterday but a hideous dream, and the moans from her stricken heart filling the pitying world.

The first shock came while still the mighty city lay deep in slumber, weary with the revelries and pleasures of the night before. In the quiet homes, in the crowded hotels, men had not yet awakened to the strifes and endeavors of the new-dawned day. The stars had but waned, and the morn was just breaking through the mists and fogs that hung in gray curtains across the waters of the placid bay and over the waiting hills. In through the Golden Gate were blowing the first piping winds with the greeting of the sea to the green-clad heights and flower-strewn fields that skirted the shores and stretched away into the dim distances beyond. The sailors still slept in their hammocks in the harbored ships. A few wan-eyed wanderers of the night were stealing through the street, a few early toilers were astir. But that was all.

Then came the rumble of deep thunder from the mighty bowels of the startled earth. The city shook like an aspen leaf, and her gray highways suddenly cracked and split as though the batteries of Satan and his upper hell had been opened against them from underneath. Along shore the wharves warped and creaked, and the rakish shacks of the water front fell like stacks of cards. The hills of Sausalito and Piedmont, the Oakland heights and the dim bluffs of San Jose rocked like forests in the wind. The waters of the bay were whipped into lashes of white foam against the Barbary Coast. The clock in the tall tower of the Ferry Building stopped as though the spirit of a demi-god were passing. The majestic structures of steel and stone that reared their domes against the sky along Market street, and up and down Montgomery and the other splendid thoroughfares that line and intersect the mart-crowded town, swayed and swung like pendulums. Then the batteries from below broke forth again and still again. Shock followed shock, as though the enemy that lay masked beneath the buttresses of the earth were determined to annihilate the city by storm. . . .

Death and sorrow have leveled all differences, social or otherwise. Saint and sinner are huddled alike in the gloom of this sad night, the same grief tugging at the heart of each. The holy men of the tabernacles and the ungodly denizens of the shadows walk side by side, the same livid fear blanching their lips. Lady of quality and woman of the slums, the vestal virgin and the painted haridan are weeping their tears together. . . .

The journalist of today shudders at the flowery prose employed by the above unknown writer, but one must remember that it was a literary style employed by most of the nation's press during this era, and the readers did not find it objectionable. They liked it. Besides, the AP reporter was obviously short of facts when he filed his initial story. No one had really had time to assess the extent of damage to the city. Following the earthquake, he hurried by boat to Oakland in search of a telegraph office. Being a resourceful newspaperman, what he lacked in the way of notes in his pocket he used his imagination to supply, and padded out the dispatch. Later, as additional knowledge was obtained and a clearer picture emerged, the stories became tighter and more readable. Another "take" reached the telegraph desk in the Los Angeles *Times* newsroom and was hurried to the editor:

¶ . . . The first shock, apparently, was not the severest, but it sufficed to arouse sleepers and thus warn them of the impending danger. To this fact, perhaps, is due the saving of unnumbered lives, as shock followed shock until the whole north end of the city was wrecked.

Following the first shock, almost immediately came a heavier one, and then, swaying and prostrating great buildings came the third shock, which was the cause of the chief destruction. It seemed that the city was practically destroyed. From the ruins of the buildings shaken down by the five quakes that followed in such close succession arose great bursts of flames which swept inward from the bay.

Water mains had been destroyed by the quakes, rendering the fire department engines, such as could be dragged from fallen walls, almost useless, and a report went out, subsequently denied, that Fire Chief Sullivan had perished.

The police department was put to work early and with the assistance of Federal troops sent from the Presidio military reservation on the outskirts of the city by Gen. Funston, succeeded in enforcing some measure of order in the panic which followed the disaster. From lodging-houses that had fallen, and from other quarters, poured streams of naked or half-clothed people, dazed, hysterical or frenzied, not knowing which way to turn in the great horror of devastation and still further impending peril which had seized the city.

Husbands were separated from wives and mothers from children. Business men trembled with the thoughts of the losses which had befallen them and over all palled the overmastering sense that the danger might not be ended. The firemen, with the assistance of the volunteers permitted to do work by the troops and the police, vigorously endeavored to discover human beings buried under the masses of stone, brick, mortar and wood, and to snatch the corpses, and such persons as might be living, from the rapidly increasing volume of flame.

At 9:45 A.M. the city was a mass of fire from Montgomery street to the water's edge. The fire fighters, in their efforts to stay the progress of the flames, used dynamite freely in destroying structures which might leave material for the pitiless element to fasten upon. South of Market Street was a sea of roaring red destruction from which came reports of exploding gas tanks.

The city morgue was early filled and Mechanics' Pavilion, across from the City Hall, which was early reported in ruinous condition, was turned into a mammoth receptacle for the bodies of the dead and as a resting place for the injured.

Before 10 A.M. three hundred dead had been taken out and this number grew and grew until the space reserved could hold no more. All the physicians, surgeons and nurses in the city, who had escaped alive from the terrible cataclysm, hastened to offer their assistance in the service of those who were in great need of help. . . .

There were many eye-witness accounts, a number of which were later published in book form. One of these was by Jerome B. Clark, a resident of Berkeley, who took the ferry to San Francisco on the morning of the quake, en route to his business. This is what he found:

¶ In every direction from the ferry building flames were seething, and as I stood there, a five-story building half a block away fell with a crash, and the flames swept clear across Market Street and caught a new fireproof building recently erected. The streets in places had sunk three or four feet, in others great humps had appeared four or five feet high. The street car tracks were bent and twisted out of shape. Electric wires lay in every direction. Streets on all sides were filled with brick and mortar, buildings either completely collapsed or brick fronts had just dropped completely off. Wagons with horses hitched to them, drivers and all, lying on the streets, all dead, struck and killed by the falling bricks, these mostly the wagons of the produce dealers, who do the greater part of their work at that hour of the morning. Warehouses and large wholesale houses of all descriptions either down, or walls bulging, or else twisted, buildings moved bodily two or three feet out of a line and still standing with the walls all cracked.

The *Call* building, a twelve-story skyscraper, stood, and looked all right at first glance, but had moved at the base two feet at one end out into the sidewalk, and the elevators refused to work, all the interior being just twisted out of shape. It afterward burned as I watched it. I worked my way in from the ferry, climbing over piles of brick and mortar and keeping to the centre of the street and avoiding live wires that lay around on every side, trying to get to my office. I got within two blocks of it and was stopped by the police on account of falling walls. I saw that the block which I was located in was on fire, and seemed doomed, so turned back and went up into the city.

Not knowing San Francisco, you would not know the various buildings, but fires were blazing in all directions, and all the finest and best of the office and business buildings were either burning or surrounded. They pumped water from the bay, but the fire was soon too far away from the water front to make any efforts in this direction of much avail. The water mains had been broken by the earthquake, and so there was no supply for the fire engines and they were helpless. The only way out of it was to dynamite, and I saw some of the finest and most beautiful buildings in the city, new modern palaces, blown to atoms. First they blew up one or two buildings at a time. Finding that of no avail, they took half a block; that was no use; then they took a block; but in spite of them all the fire kept on spreading. . . .

When I finally left the city, it was all in flames as far as Eighth Street, which is about a mile and a quarter or half from the water front. I had to walk at least two miles around in order to get to the ferry building, and when I got there you could see no buildings standing in any direction. Nearly all the docks caved in or sheds were knocked down, and all the streets along the water front were a mass of seams, upheavals and depressions, car tracks twisted in all shapes. Cars that had stood on sidings were all in ashes and still burning.[1]

Not all of the residents of San Francisco were asleep when the earthquake occurred. P. Barrett, an editor of the *Examiner,* relates his experience on that fateful morning:

¶ I stood with two other members of the *Examiner* staff on the corner of Market Street, waiting for a car. Newspaper duties had kept us working until five o'clock in the morning. Sunlight was coming out of the early morning mist. It spread its brightness on the roofs of the skyscrapers, on the domes and spires of churches, and blazed along up the wide street with its countless banks and stores, its restaurants and cafes. In the early morning the city was almost noiseless. Occasionally a newspaper wagon clattered up the street or a milk wagon rumbled along. One of my companions had told a funny story. We were laughing at it. We stopped—the laugh unfinished on our lips.

Of a sudden we had found ourselves staggering and reeling. It was as if the earth was slipping gently from under our feet. Then came a sickening swaying of the earth that threw us flat upon our faces. We struggled in the street. We could not get on our feet.

I looked in a dazed fashion around me. I saw for an instant the big buildings in what looked like a crazy dance. Then it seemed as though my head were split with the roar that crashed into my ears. Big buildings were crumbling as one might crush a biscuit in one's hand. Great gray clouds of

[1] Charles Morris, ed., *The San Francisco Calamity by Earthquake and Fire* (San Francisco: W. E. Scull, 1906).

dust shot up with flying timbers, and storms of masonry rained into the street. Wild, high jangles of smashing glass cut a sharp note into the frightful roaring. Ahead of me a great cornice crushed a man as if he were a maggot—a laborer in overalls on his way to the Union Iron Works, with a dinner pail on his arm.

Everywhere men were on all fours in the street, like crawling bugs. Still the sickening, dreadful swaying of the earth continued. It seemed a quarter of an hour before it stopped. As a matter of fact, it lasted about three minutes. Footing grew firm again, but hardly were we on our feet before we were sent reeling again by repeated shocks, but they were milder. Clinging to something, one could stand.

The dust clouds were gone. It was quite dark, like twilight. But I saw trolley tracks uprooted, twisted fantastically. I saw wide wounds in the street. Water flooded out of one. A deadly odor of gas from a broken main swept out of the other. Telegraph poles were rocked like matches. A wild tangle of wires was in the street. Some of the wires wriggled and shot blue sparks.

From the south of us, faint, but all too clear, came a horrible chorus of human cries of agony. Down there in a ramshackle section of the city the wretched houses had fallen in upon the sleeping families. Down there throughout the day a fire burned the great part of whose fuel it is too gruesome a thing to contemplate.

That was what came next—the fire. It shot up everywhere. The fierce wave of destruction had carried a flaming torch with it—the agony, death and a flaming torch. It was just as if some fire demon was rushing from place to place with such a torch.

Another eyewitness was D'Arcy Weatherbee, whose article was published in the San Francisco *Mining and Scientific Press* following the earthquake and fire. He wrote:

¶ Many instances of plundering the dead, wilful incendiarism, persistent selling of liquor, and violence to women were summarily punished by shooting on the spot, and in most instances the punishment was well deserved at such a crisis, though the example to some of the youths in soldier's clothes was bad, particularly as many of these were under the influence of liquor. . . .

The streets of Chinatown, which we passed through, were thronged by fully 3,000 Mongolians of all casts and ages. Some of the older men and some women looked more like leprous animals than human beings, and many have probably not been out of their over-crowded dens for years. Their squalid effects, piled in every conceivable shape, impeded progress through the narrow streets, and passing through their district toward dusk we hastened our steps ferryward, traversing that disreputable locality known as the Barbary Coast. Here beasts in human shape in every stage of drunkenness, and delirious from stolen liquor taken from the wrecked saloons, shouted or sang in a perfect pandemonium. Within a few blocks the roar of the flames, the noises of constantly falling walls, and the dynamiting supplied a sufficiently hellish accompaniment to that orgy.

Refugees from the densely populated Mission district fled along Mission road toward San Mateo, and the sights on this highway on Friday, the 20th, are never to be forgotten. An endless procession had left the city on Wednesday and Thursday with carts, buggies, motor cars, and vehicles of every possible description, including hand carts and wheel barrows. Part of the throng camped wearily in the fields on the outskirts of the city, while others kept on toward the southern towns. On the fire burning itself out in this direction some of the refugees returned, and the scene on Friday morning was pitiful in the extreme.

Under a blazing sky, the heat of the sun being intensified by the pall of smoke that hung over the city to the east, were seen old men and women helplessly and aimlessly carrying bundles hither and thither. Children with fevered faces and women with babes in arms, trudged through the dust, which lay nearly a foot deep on the road, and was raised in blinding clouds by the passing wagons; this intensified a thirst already strong by reason of the unnatural conditions. . . .[2]

Hunger and thirst added to the misery of the homeless victims of the quake and fire. The Associated Press reported on April 19th:

¶ There is no drinking water to be had except at the Presidio and in a few private wells. It is being carted to Black Point, where a majority of the residents are. In several instances buildings were dynamited that still had people inside. They were killed when the buildings collapsed. Over 150,000 people were without homes last night. Many are suffering untold tortures from hunger and thirst. Thousands of special police have been sworn in by Schmitz, many of whom are crazy drunk and are driving people like cattle. Clubs were used promiscuously even on women. . . .

[2] *After Earthquake and Fire: A Reprint of the Articles and Editorial Comment Appearing in the* Mining and Scientific Press, *San Francisco, April 18, 1906* (San Francisco: Mining and Scientific Press, 1906).

The evacuation of Chinatown commenced early this morning. Many Chinese are crazy from fright and are running wildly about. Others loaded down with belongings are making for Ocean Beach. Many have been killed and injured in trying to escape. The wounded are left lying in the streets, it being impossible for hospital corps to render aid. Many wounded will burn to death. Hundreds of Chinese reached the ferry in a roundabout way and are leaving for interior towns. Express wagons rent at $50 an hour, but when the soldiers catch teamsters charging this rate, the teams are confiscated.

.   .   .

SAN FRANCISCO, April 20 (By the Associated Press)—Bread lines were established at Fillmore and Turk streets, at Golden Gate Park, and at the Presidio, and every person who stood in line was given a whole loaf. The line at Fillmore and Turk was four blocks long all afternoon, and those at the parks were even longer.

A large supply of milk came over from Oakland this morning, and this was distributed to women and children wherever they were found in need. A great deal of this milk was used for the exhausted women who arrived at the ferry throughout the day, and proved a great boon to them. The bread lines at the parks furnished striking instances of the absolute patience and fortitude that has marked the behaviour of the people throughout their trying experience. There was no disorder when the hungry thousands were told to form a line and received their bread and canned goods. All were content to wait their turn. Silk-hatted men of affairs followed good-naturedly behind Chinese and took their loaves from the same hand. Soup kitchens were established in the streets of the unburned section, no fires whatever being allowed indoors and many hungry persons were fed by these individual efforts. Bread and such other foodstuffs as may be at hand will be distributed at the various stations twice a day.

Unfortunately, not everyone lined up patiently to receive the food that was being dispatched by the trainload from Los Angeles and other cities throughout the nation. There were cases of looting, and when the offenders were captured, justice was swift and violent. This account appeared in the Los Angeles *Times* on April 21st. It was filed by one of its reporters on the scene:

¶ Fiends incarnate made a hell broth of the center of the ruined district last night. Rapine and vice, assault, robbery, and desecration of the dead were included in the unspeakable horrors. There was a short shrift for at least a score of these bestial wretches. This morning they lie stinking in the streets with bullet holes or bayonet thrusts through their vitals. Sixteen men were shot down by soldiers, as they were caught robbing the dead or attempting to assault unprotected women and helpless girls.

Near Washington Park a wretch was caught in the very act of severing a dead woman's wrist from her body, in order to secure a diamond set bracelet. Soldiers rushed toward him and he started on a run, firing a revolver at them several times. As he attempted to pass through the line he was thrust through by three bayonets. The body of the wretch was cast aside into an alley like refuse on a dunghill.

On Market street a man was found cutting a finger from a corpse to get possession of a diamond ring. He was promptly lynched. He was strung up to a standard with wire and his neck broken. No mercy is shown looters by the soldiers. They are shot or bayonetted without parley.

People on the water front and in the North Beach district are becoming frantic for food. At 10 o'clock this morning, several large warehouses were thrown open to them, and there was a riot among refugees while attempting to get canned goods and flour. Soldiers finally had to force the mob back with their bayonets.

In Charles Morris's previously cited book, Willis Ames, a Salt Lake City resident who was in San Francisco, describes the kind of justice administered to thieves that he witnessed:

¶ I saw man after man shot down by the troops. Most of these were ghouls. One man made the trooper believe that one of the dead bodies lying on a pile of rocks was his mother, and he was permitted to go up to the body. Apparently overcome by grief, he threw himself across the corpse. In another instant the soldiers discovered that he was chewing the diamond earrings from the ears of the dead woman. "Here is where you get what is coming to you," said one of the soldiers, and with that he put a bullet through the ghoul. The diamonds were found in the man's mouth afterward.[3]

Max Fast, a garment worker, later related to Morris how several men were shot to save them from the horror of being burned alive:

[3] Charles Morris, ed., *The San Francisco Calamity by Earthquake and Fire.*

¶ When the fire caught the Windson Hotel at Fifth and Market Streets there were three men on the roof, and it was impossible to get them down. Rather than see the crazed men fall in with the roof and be roasted alive, the military officer directed his men to shoot them, which they did in the presence of 5,000 people. . . .

Relief for the destitute citizens of San Francisco came from throughout the United States. Hundreds of thousands of dollars were contributed. The wealthy gave large sums, but much of the money raised came from those who could spare but a few dollars. As the ashes cooled, civic leaders probed in the rubble, wondering where to begin the task of reconstruction. There were people across the nation who doubted that the city would ever be rebuilt. An editorial in the Los Angeles *Times* on April 19, 1906, commented:

¶ San Francisco will rise from its ruins and its ashes, grander, more beautiful, more influential than before. The resources which she has to draw upon are undiminished. Her site upon the coast of the world-beating ocean is unexcelled for commanding the world's commerce. . . .

The men who have made the Pacific Coast what it is are not the men to be disheartened by the disaster. . . . They will continue to go forward in the magnificent work to which they have set their hands.

In San Francisco, a number of business leaders assembled. They were determined to rebuild the city. There had been reports that people would refuse to live by the bay, fearing a recurrence. In the history of San Francisco, the city had been leveled by flames on several occasions. Engineers now planned a water system that would protect against future conflagrations. The industrialists had their architects draw up plans for a new city that would surpass the one that had been destroyed. One business leader declared:

¶ In one quick sweep, we have eradicated all the slums which were a blight and a disgrace. We shall build a new metropolis that will rival any city in the nation as a desirable place to live and to work. Each year it will attract thousands of visitors, who will enjoy its charm and its beauty. And when they leave, they will always want to return, and many will settle here. This is what we shall do.[4]

The work began at once.

[4] Quoted in a letter by Michael Ferris, San Francisco resident, in the authors' collection.

EPILOGUE

So we end at another beginning. That is the way of history, a merging and continuous pattern of openings and terminations. Sometimes these do not conform to the neat configurations of chronology. We might have selected 1900 as a terminal date, for by the turn of the century the nature of the California experience had changed qualitatively and quantitatively. A certain thrust remained: the California dream, West of the West, born of distance and flight, of second chances and the vision of opportunity, still collides with California reality. People come in their thousands and tens of thousands for reasons not much different from those that motivated earlier migrants: wealth, climate, openness, a promise. For many it works; for others, illusions turn to ashes, as in the Watts Riots.

And yet the very numbers, the very acceleration of the process bear within them orders of magnitude that produce the differences between nineteenth-century and twentieth-century California. In certain ways, the new patterns suggest a recapitulation of the earlier ones. Oil was the gold of the first half of the twentieth century; motion pictures were another sort of Cibola, of El Dorado. Water-seekers like William Mulholland combined the vision and harshness in the Owens Valley war,[1] which surely is an echo of how the land was wrested from the Indians. The great metropolis of the south needed the waters of that remote mountain valley and would stick at nothing to get it from the ranchers. This equation of ends and means shaped the nature of California politics, culture, economics, and religion. As before, the state was an arena that could contain cruelty and compassion, prejudice and tolerance, assaults on the face of the lands along with the great conserving impulse of the Sierra Club, ticky-tack tracts of houses near individual homes, unique and aspiring in their architecture, great wealth and frustrating poverty, an aspiration toward culture and excellence with cheap *kitsch*, a humanistic higher education existing side by side with the most narrow of extremisms, the intellectual and the anti-intellectual, experimentation and reaction, piety and the proliferation of sects and occult groups. All of these are mixed together in an unlikely ferment, a microcosm of America itself and perhaps the ultimate meaning of the California experience. California's literature, music, and art reflect these polarities: a welcome reception for the avant garde accompanied paradoxically by the strong impulse to censor and suppress; rising taste and philistine crudity; great themes of such poets as Jeffers and Rexroth along with the celluloid factories of Hollywood.

We may ask, as we did in the prologue, where does this new California begin? Where does the old California end? One turning point, imbued with symbolism, certainly is that covered in the final chapter. The mindless upward thrust of the young earth along a formation named for a saint, the San Andreas Fault, in a few moments produced the great earthquake and fire of San Francisco on a quiet April morning in 1906. Hundreds died and a great city was laid waste, and men have told and retold the story countless times.

[1] In 1904, the City of Los Angeles acquired land in the Owens Valley, diverted the water of the Owens River, and built a 238-mile aqueduct to carry it south to the San Fernando Reservoir. The project was completed in 1913. Owens Valley ranchers, embittered by the loss of their water supply, resorted to dynamiting spillways, and in 1923 armed themselves with rifles to prevent the use of river water. Los Angeles proceeded even more vigorously to force its opponents from the Owens Valley.

Yet another story involving a single man—whose real name we do not even know—in its way symbolizes an end equally significant. This Indian, the last survivor of his Stone Age people, allowed us to call him *Ishi,* which in the language of his people, the Yahi, means, simply, Man. A war of attrition carried out by the settlers of northern California harried and destroyed his tribe. It was a fate as total for them as a hydrogen-bomb holocaust might be for us. Ishi wandered from the slopes of his mountains in hunger, terror, and exhaustion. (A survey party for an electrical company had taken his weapons and artifacts for souvenirs, leaving him without the means of survival.) On the morning of August 29, 1911, he was found, barely alive and resigned to his death, in the corral of a slaughterhouse near Oroville, California.

If San Francisco of 1906 turned toward the future, Ishi in 1911 reminded us of a past. For San Francisco represented one aspect of California's determination to shape the land to the will and vision of men, while Ishi symbolized the other side of man's nature, the willingness to blend and harmonize with the demands of terrain and landscape. He came from the wilds of the Lassen Foothills, the country of the Cascade Range, to what Theodora Kroeber, the wife of the anthropologist who rescued and befriended Ishi, called "the wilds of civilization." By 1911, San Francisco had been rebuilt much as we know it now. Ishi had walked from the dawn age of man into the trolley culture of the twentieth century.

He fully expected to be killed, as he had witnessed the rest of his tribe being killed. Instead, he found that the world of his enemies had changed enough to make him unique, a curiosity, an anachronism. Men like Kroeber and his colleague Waterman, of the same people who had destroyed Ishi's world, now came forward to take him from Oroville to San Francisco. They showed Ishi their bridges and buildings, their cars and clothes, their motion pictures and their food. For him these could not have been more remote than his wildest imaginings. He in turn showed them the ways of his people, how bows and arrows were made, how game was tracked, how his language was spoken. In that confrontation of past and present, something characteristically human and characteristically Californian emerged.

Yet no one, not even the physician and the scientists who respected him and grew to value his friendship, knew precisely what to do with him. So he became the janitor of the Hearst museum, lived out his days as a living museum piece. He loved children and they him, as though in their purity and candor he recognized a survival in part of his own lost life. In a confused and neurotic world, he responded with poise and dignity, a gentleness and wholeness that suggested that another kind of wisdom could come from the California experience.

Of his regrets we know little, for his last years were crowded with small ironies. Kroeber and Waterman and Dr. S. T. Pope, the physician who had become Ishi's closest friend, took him on a final journey to the land that had been his. They had to get special permission from the Fish and Game Commission "to take for scientific purposes one male deer at any time and in such manner as the gentleman mentioned above may select." In those familiar hills, Ishi killed his last deer. At first they had difficulty finding their quarry. Ishi believed it was because the men were smoking tobacco. He persuaded the hardheaded, rational scientists to stop using tobacco. Then they took a deer.

And tuberculosis took Ishi. His small circle of friends felt the numbing sense of loss. Dr. Pope wrote:

¶ And so, stoic and unafraid, departed the last wild Indian of America. He closes a chapter in history. He looked upon us as sophisticated children—smart but not wise. We knew many things, and much that is false. His were the qualities that last forever. He was kind; he had courage and self-restraint, and though all had been taken from him, there was no bitterness in his heart. His soul was that of a child, his mind that of a philosopher.[2]

With Ishi's death in 1916, perhaps a small matter really in the bookkeeping of time, the cycle that began centuries before, closed for California.

For reasons of his own, he was loath to use the Yahi words of farewell. Instead he fashioned from English his final good-bye: "You stay, I go."

[2] Theodora Kroeber, *Ishi in Two Worlds. A Biography of the Last Wild Indian in North America* (Berkeley and Los Angeles: University of California Press, 1961).

BIBLIOGRAPHY

In preparing this book, the authors have consulted hundreds of volumes. From these, titles have been selected which the reader will find readily available—either currently in print, or in the collections of most public libraries—or which are the sources of extracts from contemporary writings quoted in this book. Most of the rarer volumes are in the collection of the Henry E. Huntington Library and Art Gallery, San Marino, California. A number of them may also be found in the Library of Congress, British Museum, and other larger libraries.

United States History

Craven, Avery, and Johnson, Walter. *The United States—Experiment in Democracy.* New York: Ginn and Co., 1947.

Hicks, John D., Mowry, George E., and Burke, Robert E. *A History of American Democracy.* New York: Houghton Mifflin, 1966.

Morison, Samuel Eliot. *The Oxford History of the American People.* New York: Oxford University Press, 1965.

Nevins, Allan. *The Emergence of Modern America, 1865–1878.* New York: The Macmillan Company, 1927.

——, and Commager, Henry Steele. *America, The Story of a Free People.* New York: Little, Brown, 1942.

Nichols, Jeannette P., and Roy F. *The Republic of the United States—A History.* 2 vols. New York: D. Appleton-Century, 1942.

Perkins, Dexter. *Hands Off, A History of the Monroe Doctrine.* New York: Little, Brown, 1941.

Perkins, D., and Van Deusen, G. G. *The United States of America—A History*. 2 vols. New York: The Macmillan Company, 1962.

Stephenson, Nathaniel Wright. *A History of the American People*. New York: Charles Scribner's Sons, 1934.

Wellborn, Fred W. *The Growth of American Nationality, 1492–1865*. New York: The Macmillan Company, 1943.

The Following Two Volumes Deal with Spanish Involvement During the American Revolution

Bemis, Samuel Flagg. *The Hussey-Cumberland Mission and American Independence— An Essay in the Diplomacy of the American Revolution*. Princeton, N.J.: Princeton University Press: 1931.

———. *Pinckney's Treaty—A Study of America's Advantage From Europe's Distress— 1783–1800*. Baltimore: The Johns Hopkins Press, 1926.

Europe and the Philippines

Dewe, J. A. *Medieval and Modern History*. New York: Hinds, Noble & Eldredge, 1907.

Heawood, Edward. *Geographical Explorations in the Seventeenth and Eighteenth Centuries*. London: Cambridge at the University Press, 1912.

McCarthy, Rev. Edward J. *Spanish Beginnings in the Philippines 1564–1572*. Washington: The Catholic University of America Press, 1943.

Morga, Antonio de. *The Philippine Islands at the Close of the Sixteenth Century*. Translated by the Hon. Henry E. J. Stanley. London: Printed for the Hakluyt Society, 1868.

Thatcher, Oliver J., and Schwill, Ferdinand. *A General History of Europe 350–1900*. London: John Murray, 1901.

Wakeman, Henry Offley. *European History 1598–1715*. London: Percival & Co., 1894.

Lower California

Baegert, Johann Jakob, S.J. *Observations in Lower California*. Translated from the German by M. M. Brandenburg and Carl L. Baumann. Berkeley: University of California Press, 1952.

Bolton, Herbert E. *Essay on Black Robes—Wider Horizons of American History*. New York: D. Appleton-Century Co., 1939.

Clavigero, Don Francisco Javier, S.J. *The History of Lower California*. Translated from the Italian by Sara E. Lake and A. A. Gray. Palo Alto, Calif.: Stanford University Press, 1937.

Clinch, Bryan J. *Lower California and Its Missions*. Vol. I. San Francisco: The Whitaker & Ray Co., 1904.

Dunne, Peter Masten, S.J. *Black Robes in Lower California*. Berkeley: University of California Press, 1952.

Harney, Martin P., S.J., M.A. *The Jesuits in History*. New York: The America Press, 1941.

Meigs, Peveril, III. *The Dominican Mission Frontier of Lower California*. Berkeley: University of California Press, 1935.

Nelson, Edward W. *Lower California and Its Natural Resources*. Washington: Government Printing Office, 1921.

Nordhoff, Charles. *Peninsula California*. New York: Harper & Brothers, 1888.

Ridley, F. A. *The Jesuits*. London: Secker and Warburg, 1938.

Venegas, Miguel. *Spain in the West—Juan Maria De Salvatierra*. Cleveland: Arthur H. Clark Co., 1929.

The Frontier and the Pacific Northwest

Bannon, John Francis (ed.). *Bolton and the Spanish Borderlands*. Norman, Okla.: University of Oklahoma Press, 1964.

Billington, Ray Allen. *The Far Western Frontier—1830–1860*. New York: Harper, 1956.

Clark, Dan Elbert. *The West in American History*. New York: Thomas Y. Crowell, 1937.

Lyman, William Denison. *The Columbia River—Its History, Its Myths*. New York: G. P. Putnam's Sons, 1917.

Pomeroy, Earl. *The Pacific Slope: A History of California, Oregon, Washington, Idaho, Utah, and Nevada*. New York: Alfred A. Knopf, 1965.

Schafer, Joseph. *A History of the Pacific Northwest*. New York: The Macmillian Company, 1926.

The Land

Farquhar, Francis P. *History of the Sierra Nevada*. Berkeley: University of California Press, 1965.

King, Clarence. *Mountaineering in the Sierra Nevada*. Philadelphia: J. B. Lippincott Company, 1963.

Leadabrand, Russ. *A Guidebook to the Sunset Ranges of Southern California*. Los Angeles: The Ward Ritchie Press, 1965.

Lee, W. Storrs. *The Great California Deserts*. New York: G. P. Putnam's Sons, 1963.

Muir John. *The Mountains of California*. New York: Doubleday & Co., Inc., 1961.

———. *The Yosemite*. New York: Doubleday & Co., Inc., 1962.

Stoer, Tracey I., and Usinger, Robert L. *Sierra Nevada Natural History*. Berkeley and Los Angeles: University of California Press, 1963

The Indians of California

Caughey, John Walton (ed.). *The Indians of Southern California in 1852*. San Marino, Calif.: The Huntington Library, 1952.

Driver, Harold E. *Indians of North America*. Chicago: University of Chicago Press, 1961.

Eggan, Fred (ed.). *Social Anthropology of North American Tribes*. Chicago: University of Chicago Press, 1955.

Jackson, Helen Hunt. *A Century of Dishonor—A Sketch of the United States Government's Dealings with Some of the Indian Tribes*. Boston: Roberts Brothers, 1885.

Kroeber, Theodora. *Ishi in Two Worlds. A Biography of the Last Wild Indian in North America*. Berkeley: University of California Press, 1961.

Merriam, C. Hart. *Studies of California Indians*. Berkeley: University of California Press, 1955.

Ray, Verne F. *Primitive Pragmatists: The Modoc Indians of Northern California*. Seattle: University of Washington Press, 1963.

Robinson, W. W., and Powell, Lawrence Clark. *The Malibu*. Los Angeles: Dawson's Book Shop, 1958.

Webb, Edith Buckland. *Indian Life at the Old Missions.* Los Angeles: Warren F. Lewis, 1952.

General Reference Works on California History

Bancroft, Hubert Howe. *Works.* 23 vols. San Francisco: A. L. Bancroft Co., 1882–1890.
Caughey, John Walton. *California.* New York: Prentice-Hall, Inc., 1940.
Cleland, Robert Glass. *From Wilderness to Empire—A History of California.* New York: Alfred A. Knopf, 1959.
Forbes, Alexander. *A History of Upper and Lower California.* London: Smith, Elder & Co., Cornhill, 1839.
Hittel, Theodore H. *History of California.* 4 vols. San Francisco: N. J. Slone & Co., 1898.
McWilliams, Carey. *California: The Great Exception.* New York: A. A. Wyn, 1949.
Murphy, Bill. *A Pictorial History of California.* San Francisco: Fearon Publishers, 1958.
Rolle, Andrew F. *California: A History.* New York: Thomas Y. Crowell Co., 1963.
Venegas, Miguel. *A Natural History of California, Translated from the Original Spanish of Miguel Venegas, published at Madrid, 1758.* London: Printed for James Rivington and James Fletcher, at the Oxford Theatre, in Pater-Noster-Row, 1759.

Los Angeles and Southern California

McGroarty, John Steven. *California of the South.* Chicago: S. J. Clarke Publishing Co., 1933.
Murphy, Bill. *The Dolphin Guide to Los Angeles and Southern California.* New York: Doubleday & Co., Inc., 1962.
Newmark, Harris. *Sixty Years in Southern California—1853–1913.* Boston and New York: Houghton Mifflin Co., 1930.
Robinson, W. W. *Los Angeles from the Days of the Pueblo.* San Francisco: California Historical Society, 1959.
Van Dyke, T. S. *Millionaires of a Day, An Inside History of the Great Southern California Boom.* New York: Fords, Howard & Hulbert, 1890.
Workman, Boyle. *The City That Grew—1840–1936.* Los Angeles: The Southland Publishing Co., 1936.

San Francisco

Atherton, Gertrude. *Golden Gate Country.* New York: Duell, Sloan & Pearce, 1945.
Bolton, Herbert Eugene. *Outpost of Empire—The Story of the Founding of San Francisco.* New York: Alfred A. Knopf, 1931.
Eldgredge, Zoeth Skinner. *The Beginnings of San Francisco.* San Francisco: published by the author, 1912.
Mining and Scientific Press. *After Earthquake and Fire: A Reprint of the Articles and Editorial Comment Appearing in the* Mining and Scientific Press, *San Francisco, April 18, 1906.* San Francisco: *Mining and Scientific Press,* 1906.
Morris, Charles (ed.). *The San Francisco Calamity by Earthquake and Fire.* San Francisco: W. E. Scull, 1906.
Riesenberg, Felix, Jr. *Golden Gate—The Story of San Francisco Harbor.* New York: Alfred A. Knopf, 1940.

Spain, Mexico, and the Early California Explorations

Beechey, Captain Frederick W. *Narrative of a Voyage to the Pacific and Beering's Strait.* 2 vols. London, 1831.

Benítez, Fernando. *The Century After Cortés.* Translated by Joan MacLean. Chicago: The University of Illinois Press, 1965.

Bernal, Ignacio. *Mexico Before Cortéz: Art, History, Legend.* Translated by Willis Barnstone. New York: Doubleday & Co., Inc., 1963.

Bolton, Herbert Eugene. *Anza's California Expeditions.* 5 vols. Berkeley: University of California Press, 1930.

———. *Fray Juan Crespí—Missionary Explorer on the Pacific Coast, 1769–1774.* Berkeley: University of California Press, 1927.

Carter, Hodding and Betty W. *Doomed Road of Empire: The Spanish Trail of Conquest.* New York: McGraw-Hill Book Co., 1963.

Chapman, Charles E. *The Founding of Spanish California.* New York: The Macmillan Company, 1916.

———. *A History of California—The Spanish Period.* New York: The Macmillan Company, 1921.

Dalrymple, Alexander. *An Historical Journal of the Expeditions by Sea and Land to the North of California; In 1768, 1769, and 1770.* London: Published by Dalrymple, 1790. Contains a translation of Miguel Costansó's journal relating to the Serra expedition.

Del Castillo, Bernal Diaz. *The True History of the Conquest of Mexico.* 2 vols. New York: Robert M. McBride & Company, 1927.

Denis, Alberta Johnston. *Spanish Alta California.* New York: The Macmillan Company, 1927.

Drake, Sir Francis. *The World Encompassed carefully collected out of the notes by Master Francis Fletcher, preacher.* London: Printed by E. P. for Nicholas Bourne, 1635.

Durán, Fray Diego. *The Aztecs: The History of the Indies of New Spain.* Translated by Doris Heyden and Fernando Horcasitas. New York: The Orion Press, 1964.

Englebert, Omer. *The Last of the Conquistadors, Junípero Serra—1713–1784.* New York: Harcourt, Brace & Co., 1956.

"Francis Drake," *California Historical Society Quarterly,* Vol. 16, March, 1937. Articles by Herbert E. Bolton and others; Bibliography of 100 works relating to Drake.

Fuentes, Patricia de (ed.). *The Conquistadors.* New York: The Orion Press, 1963.

Gómara, Francisco López de. *Cortés: The Life of the Conqueror.* Ed. and trans. by Lesley Byrd Simpson. Berkeley and Los Angeles: University of California Press, 1964.

Guillermard, F. H. H. *Ferdinand Magellan and the First Circumnavigation of the Globe.* New York: Dodd, Mead & Co., 1890.

Hakluyt, Richard. *The Principal Navigators, Voyages, Traffiques & Discoveries of the English Nation.* Glasgow: James MacLehose & Co., 1904. Contains accounts on Thomas Cavendish and Woodes Rogers.

Hume, Martin A. S. *Spain, Its Greatness and Decay—1479–1788.* London: Cambridge at the University Press, 1931.

Kotzebue, Otto von. *Voyage of Discovery in the South Sea and to Behring's Straits in Search of a North-East Passage: Undertaken in the Years 1815, 16, 17, and 18* London: Printed for Sir Richard Phillips & Co., 1821.

MacNutt, Francis Augustus. *Bartholomew de las Casas.* Cleveland: Arthur H. Clark Co., 1909.

Means, Philip Ainsworth. *The Spanish Main—Focus of Envy 1492–1700.* New York: Charles Scribner's Sons, 1935.

Moses, Bernard. *Spain Overseas.* New York: Hispanic Society, 1929.

Picón-Salas, Mariano. *A Cultural History of Spanish America.* Translated by Irving A. Leonard. Berkeley and Los Angeles: University of California Press, 1963.

Priestley, Herbert Ingram. *The Mexican Nation, A History*. New York: The Macmillan Company, 1930.

Richman, Irving Berdine. *California Under Spain and Mexico, 1535–1847*. New York: Houghton Mifflin Co., 1911.

Rogers, Cameron. *Drake's Quest*. New York: Doubleday, Page & Co., 1927.

Sanchez, Nellie Van de Grift. *Spanish Arcadia*. San Francisco: Powell Publishing Co., 1929.

Simpson, Lesley Byrd. *Many Mexicos*. New York: G. P. Putnam's Sons, 1941.

Teggart, Frederick J. (ed.). *The Anza Expedition of 1775–1776—Diary of Pedro Font*. Berkeley: University of California, March, 1913—Academy of Pacific Coast History Publications, Vol. III, 1913–14.

Thomas, A. B. (ed. and trans.). *After Coronado: Spanish Exploration Northeast of New Mexico, 1696–1727*. Norman, Okla.: University of Oklahoma Press, 1935.

Tibesar, Antonine, O.F.M. (ed.). *Writings of Junípero Serra*. Washington: Academy of American Franciscan History, 1955.

Vancouver, George. *A Voyage of Discovery to the North Pacific Ocean and Round the World*. London, 1798.

Wagner, Henry R. *Juan Rodríguez Cabrillo: Discoverer of the Coast of California*. San Francisco: California Historical Society, 1941.

――――. *Sir Francis Drake's Voyage Around the World—Its Aims and Achievements*. San Francisco: John Howell, 1926.

Walpole, Fred. *Four Years in the Pacific in her Majesty's Ship Collingwood from 1844 to 1848*. 2 vols. London: Richard Bentley, 1850.

Wilkes, Charles. *Narrative of the United States Exploring Expedition During the Years 1838, 1839, 1840, 1841, 1842*. 5 vols, and atlas. Philadelphia: Lea & Blanchard, 1845.

The California Missions

Berger, John A. *The Franciscan Missions of California*. New York: Doubleday & Co., Inc., 1948.

Clinch, Bryan J. *California and Its Missions*. 2 vols. San Francisco: Whitaker & Ray Co., 1904.

Geary, Rev. Gerald J., A.M. *The Secularization of the California Missions (1810–1846)*. Washington: The Catholic University of America, 1934.

Hall, Trowbridge. *California Trails, Intimate Guide to the Old Missions*. New York: The Macmillan Company, 1920.

Hawthorne, Hildegarde. *California's Missions—Their Romance and Beauty*. New York: D. Appleton-Century Co., 1942.

James, George Wharton. *The Old Franciscan Missions of California*. Boston: Little, Brown and Co., 1913.

Lockwood, Frank C. *Story of the Spanish Missions of the Middle Southwest*. Santa Ana, Calif.: Fine Arts Press, 1934.

Older, Mrs. Fremont. *California Missions and Their Romances*. New York: Coward McCann, Inc., 1938.

Early California Visitors

Bean, John Lowell, and Mason, William Marvin (eds.). *Diaries & Accounts of the Romero Expeditions in Arizona and California 1823–1826*. Los Angeles: The Ward Ritchie Press, 1962.

Cleveland, Richard J. *Voyages and Commercial Enterprises of the Sons of New England*. New York: Leavitt & Allen, 1842.

Coblentz, Stanton A. *The Swallowing Wilderness.* New York: Thomas Yoseloff, 1961.

Corney, Peter. *Voyage in the Northern Pacific.* Honolulu: Thom. G. Thrum, publisher, 1896.

Dana, Richard Henry, Jr. *Two Years Before the Mast: A Personal Narrative of Life at Sea.* Los Angeles: The Ward Ritchie Press, 1964.

Dillon, Richard. *The Legend of Grizzly Adams: California's Greatest Mountain Man.* New York: Coward-McCann, Inc., 1966.

Leonard, Zenas. *Narrative of the Adventure of Zenas Leonard a Native of Clearfield, Pa. who spent five years in Trapping for Furs, Trading with the Indians &c., of the Rocky Mountains.* Clearfield, Pa.: Printed by D. W. Moore, 1839.

MacKay, Douglas. *The Honourable Company.* New York: Bobbs-Merrill, 1936.

Morgan, Dale. *Jedediah Smith and the Opening of the West.* New York: Bobbs-Merrill, 1953.

Nichols, Roy F. *Advance Agents of American Destiny.* Philadelphia: University of Pennsylvania Press, 1956.

Pinkerton, Robert E. *Hudson's Bay Company.* New York: Henry Holt & Co., 1931.

Schooling, Sir William, K.B.E. *The Hudson's Bay Company, 1670-1920.* London: The Hudson's Bay Company, 1920.

Shaler, William. *Journal of a Voyage Between China and the North-Western Coast of America Made in 1804.* Appeared in Vol. 3 (1808) of the *American Register or General Repository of History.*

Shapiro, Samuel. *Richard Henry Dana, Jr., 1815-1882.* East Lansing: Michigan State University Press, 1961.

Simpson, Sir George. *Narrative of a Journey Round the World.* 2 vols. London: Henry Colburn, 1847.

Underhill, Reuben L. *From Cowhides to Golden Fleece—A Narrative of California, 1832-1858—Based Upon Unpublished Correspondence of Thomas Oliver Larkin, Trader, Developer, Promoter, and Only American Consul.* Palo Alto, Calif.: Stanford University Press, 1939.

Willson, Beckles. *Hudson's Bay—The Great Company, 1667-1871.* 2 vols. London: Smith Elder & Co., 1900.

The Mexican War Period

Athern, Robert G. *William Tecumseh Sherman and the Settlement of the West.* Norman, Okla.: University of Oklahoma Press, 1956.

Bill, Alfred Hoyt. *Rehearsal for Conflict.* New York: Alfred A. Knopf, 1947.

Clarke, Dwight L. *Stephen Watts Kearny—Soldier of the West.* Norman, Okla.: University of Oklahoma Press, 1961.

Downey, Joseph T. *The Cruise of the Portsmouth, 1845-1847.* New Haven: Yale University Press, 1958.

Duvall, Marius. *A Navy Surgeon in California, 1846-1847—The Journal of Marius Duvall.* San Francisco: John Howell Books, 1957.

Frémont, Jessie Benton. "The Origin of the Frémont Expedition," *The Century Magazine,* March, 1891.

Frémont, John Charles. "The Conquest of California," *The Century Magazine,* April, 1891.

———. *Geographical Memoir Upon Upper California.* Addressed to the Senate of the United States, 30th Congress, 2nd Session. Washington: printed by Tippen & Streeper, 1849.

Grivas, Theodore. *Military Governments in California, 1846-1850.* Glendale, Calif.: The Arthur H. Clark Company, 1963.

Hawgood, John A. (ed.). *First and Last Consul—Thomas Oliver Larkin and the Americanization of California—A Selection of Letters.* San Marino, Calif.: The Huntington Library, 1962.

Heffernan, William Joseph. *Edward M. Kern—The Travels of an Artist Explorer.* Bakersfield, Calif.: Kern County Historical Society, 1953.

Henry, Robert Selph. *The Story of the Mexican War.* New York: Bobbs-Merrill, 1950.

Hine, Robert V. *Edward Kern and American Expansion.* New Haven and London: Yale University Press, 1962.

Kemble, Edward C. *A History of California Newspapers, 1846–1858.* Los Gatos, Calif.: The Talisman Press, 1962.

McCoy, Charles A. *Polk and the Presidency.* Austin: University of Texas Press, 1960.

Marti, Werner H. *Archibald Gillespie, Messenger of Destiny.* San Francisco: John Howell Books, 1960.

Nevins, Allan. *Frémont, Pathmarker of the West.* New York: D. Appleton-Century Co., 1939.

Phillips, Catherine Coffin. *Jessie Benton Frémont—A Woman Who Made History.* San Francisco: John Henry Nash Printers, 1935.

Pitt, Leonard. *The Decline of the Californios: A Social History of the Spanish-Speaking Californians, 1846–1890.* Berkeley and Los Angeles: University of California Press, 1966.

Polk, James Knox. *Polk: The Diary of a President,* ed. Allan Nevins. New York: Longmans, Green, 1929.

Richardson, James D. *A Compilation of the Messages and Papers of the Presidents, 1789–1897.* Vol. IV, 1841–1849. Washington, D.C.: Published by Authority of Congress, 1899.

Rogers, Fred Blackburn. *William Brown Ide—Bear Flagger.* San Francisco: John Howell Books, 1960.

Royce, Josiah. *California—From the Conquest in 1846 to the Second Vigilance Committee in San Francisco.* New York: Alfred A. Knopf, 1948.

Sherman, William T. *Memoirs of General William T. Sherman by Himself.* Vol. I. New York: D. Appleton and Co., 1875.

Singletary, Otis A. *The Mexican War.* Chicago: University of Chicago Press, 1960.

Wilbur, Marguerite Eyer. *John Sutter, Rascal and Adventurer.* New York: Liveright Publishing Corporation, 1949.

Wilcox, General Cadmus M. *The History of the Mexican War.* Washington: The Church News Publishing Co., 1892.

Zollinger, James Peter. *Sutter—The Man and His Empire.* New York: Oxford University Press, 1939.

Early Migration and the Gold Rush Era

Bidwell, John. *A Journal to California with Observations About the Country, Climate and the Route to This Country.* St. Louis, 1842.

Cain, Ella M. *The Story of Early Mono County: Its Settlers—Gold Rushes—Indians—Ghost Towns.* San Francisco: Fearon Publishers, 1961.

Greever, William S. *The Bonanza West: The Story of the Western Mining Rushes, 1848–1900.* Norman, Okla.: University of Oklahoma Press, 1963.

Hunt, Rockwell. *John Bidwell—Prince of California Pioneers.* Caldwell, Idaho: The Caxton Printers, Ltd., 1942.

Jackson Joseph Henry. *Anybody's Gold—The Story of California's Mining Towns.* New York: D. Appleton-Century Company, 1941.

Johnson, Overton, and Winter, Wm. H. *Route Across the Rocky Mountains with a Description of Oregon and California.* Lafayette, Ind.: John B. Semans, Printer, 1846.

Lewis, Oscar. *Sea Routes to the Gold Fields—The Migration by Water to California in 1849–1852.* New York: Alfred A. Knopf, 1949.

Nadeau, Remi. *Ghost Towns and Mining Camps of California.* Los Angeles: The Ward Ritchie Press, 1965.

Pattie, James Ohio. *The Personal Narrative of James Ohio Pattie.* ed. Timothy Flint. Cincinnati, 1833.

Paul, Rodman Wilson. *Mining Frontiers of the Far West, 1848–1880.* New York: Holt, Rinehart and Winston, 1963.

Pigney, Joseph. *For Fear We Shall Perish: The Story of the Donner Party Disaster.* New York: E. P. Dutton & Co., Inc., 1961.

Root, Riley. *Journals of Travels from St. Joseph to Oregon Together with Some Description of the Gold Mines.* Galesburg, Ill., 1850.

Scamehorn, Howard L. (ed.). *The Buckeye Rovers in the Gold Rush.* Athens, Ohio: Ohio University Press, 1965.

Stewart, George R. *The California Trail: An Epic with Many Heroes.* New York: McGraw-Hill Book Company, Inc., 1962.

Taylor, Bayard. *Eldorado, or Adventures in the Path of Empire; comprising a voyage to California via Panama; Life in San Francisco and Monterey; Pictures of the Gold Region, and Experiences of Mexican Travel.* New York: George P. Putnam; London: Richard Bentley, 1850.

Wells, Evelyn, and Peterson, Harry C. *The '49ers.* New York: Doubleday & Co., 1949.

Statehood, and the 1850's

Bloss, Roy S. *Pony Express—The Great Gamble.* Berkeley: Howell-North, 1959.

Bradley, Glenn D. *The Story of the Pony Express.* Chicago: A. C. McClurg & Co., 1913.

Buchanan, A. Russell. *David S. Terry—Dueling Judge.* San Marino, Calif.: The Huntington Library, 1956.

Chapman, Arthur. *The Pony Express.* New York: G. P. Putnam's Sons, 1932.

Dillon, Richard H. (ed.). *California Trail Herd: The 1850 Missouri-to-California Journal of Cyrus C. Loveland.* Los Gatos, Calif.: The Talisman Press, 1961.

Hafen, Le Roy R. *The Overland Mail, 1849–1869.* Cleveland: The Arthur H. Clark Co., 1926.

Neville, Amelia Ransome. *The Fantastic City—Memoirs of the Social and Romantic Life of Old San Francisco.* New York: Houghton Mifflin, 1932.

Ormsby, Waterman L. *The Butterfield Overland Mail,* ed. Lyle H. Wright and Josephine Bynum. San Marino, Calif.: The Huntington Library, 1960.

Reinhart, Herman Francis. *The Golden Frontier: The Recollections of Herman Francis Reinhart, 1851–1869.* Austin: University of Texas Press, 1962.

Scherer, James A. B. *The Lion of the Vigilantes.* New York: Bobbs-Merrill, 1939.

Stewart, George R. *Committee of Vigilance—Revolution in San Francisco, 1851.* Boston: Houghton Mifflin Co., 1964.

Valentine, Alan. *Vigilante Justice.* New York: Reynal & Co., 1956.

Winther, Oscar Osburn. *Express and Stagecoach Days in California from the Gold Rush to the Civil War.* Palo Alto, Calif.: Stanford University Press, 1946.

The Civil War Period

Hunt, Aurora. *The Army of the Pacific.* Glendale, Calif.: The Arthur H. Clark Company, 1951.
———. *James H. Carleton—Frontier Dragoon.* Glendale, Calif.: The Arthur H. Clark Company, 1958.
Record of California Men in the War of the Rebellion. Compiled by the State Adjutant General. Sacramento: State Printing Office, 1890.
Simonds, William Day. *Starr King in California.* San Francisco: Paul Elder & Co., 1917.
Union Army Operations in the Southwest—From the Official Records. Albuquerque, N.M.: Horn & Wallace, 1961.

The Building of the Western Railroads

Beebe, Lucius. *The Central Pacific & The Southern Pacific Railroads.* Berkeley: Howell-North, 1963.
Bradley, Glenn Danford. *The Story of the Santa Fe.* Boston: Richard G. Badger—The Gorham Press, 1920.
Daggett, Stuart. *Chapters on the History of the Southern Pacific.* New York: The Ronald Press Company, 1922.
Holbrook, Stewart H. *The Story of American Railroads.* New York: Crown Publishers, 1947.
Lewis, Oscar. *The Big Four—The Story of Huntington, Stanford, Hopkins, and Crocker and of the Building of the Central Pacific.* New York: Alfred A. Knopf, 1938.
Wilson, Neill C., and Taylor, Frank J. *Southern Pacific—The Roaring Story of a Fighting Railroad.* New York: McGraw-Hill, 1952.

The Modoc War

Brown, William S. *Annals of Modoc—California Northeast, the Bloody Ground.* Oakland, Calif.: Biobooks, 1951.
Murray, Keith A. *The Modoc and Their War.* Norman, Okla.: University of Oklahoma Press, 1959.
Payne, Doris Palmer. *Captain Jack, Modoc Renegade.* Portland, Ore.: Binford & Mort, 1958.
War Department, Adjutant General's Office. *Official Copies of Correspondence Relative to the War with Modoc Indians in 1872-73.* Washington, D.C., Government Printing Office, January 7, 1874.

Additional Books Covering Events from the Close of the Civil War to 1906

Asbury, Herbert. *The Barbary Coast—An Informal History of the San Francisco Underworld.* New York: Alfred A. Knopf, 1933.
Baur, John E. *The Health Seekers of Southern California, 1870–1900.* San Marino, Calif.: The Huntington Library, 1959.
Beebe, Lucius, and Clegg, Charles M. *San Francisco's Golden Era—A Picture Story of San Francisco Before the Fire.* Berkeley: Howell-North, 1960.
Beers, George, *Vazquez or the Hunted Bandits of the Joaquin—Containing Thrilling Scenes and Incidents Among the Outlaws and Desperadoes of Southern California.* New York: Robert M. DeWitt Publishers, 1875.
Bishop, William Henry. *Old Mexico and Her Lost Provinces—A Journey in Mexico,*

Southern California, and Arizona by Way of Cuba. New York: Harper & Brothers, 1883.

Bronson, William. *The Earth Shook, The Sky Burned.* New York: Doubleday & Co., 1959.

Cleland, Robert Glass. *California in Our Time, 1900 to 1940.* New York: Alfred A. Knopf, 1947.

Dillon, Richard H. *The Hatchet Men—The Story of the Tong Wars in San Francisco's Chinatown.* New York: Coward-McCann, 1962.

Dumke, Glenn S. *The Boom of the Eighties in Southern California.* San Marino, Calif.: The Huntington Library, 1944.

Jury, John G. *A History of the Bench and Bar of California,* ed. Oscar T. Shuck. San Francisco: The Occident Printing House, 1888.

Kennedy, John C. *The Great Earthquake and Fire, San Francisco, 1906.* New York: William Morrow and Co., 1963.

Lawson, Andrew C. *The California Earthquake of April 18, 1906.* 3 vols. Washington, D.C.: The Carnegie Institution, 1908.

Lyman, George D. *Ralston's Ring—California Plunders the Comstock Lode.* New York: Charles Scribner's Sons, 1937.

McWilliams, Carey. *Ambrose Bierce, A Biography.* New York: Albert & Charles Boni, 1929.

Nordhoff, Charles. *California: For Health, Pleasure and Residence.* New York: Harper & Brothers, 1872.

Odell, Ruth. *Helen Hunt Jackson.* New York: D. Appleton-Century Company, 1939.

Willard, Charles Dwight. *The Herald's History of Los Angeles City.* Los Angeles: Kingsley-Barnes & Neuner Co., 1901.

Wright, William. *History of the Big Bonanza: An Authentic Account of the Discovery, History, and Working of the World Renowned Comstock Silver Lode of Nevada.* San Francisco: Hartford Publishing Co., A. L. Bancroft Publishing Co., 1876.

INDEX